THE CONSTITUTION OF THE UNITED STATES

THE
CONSTITUTION
OF THE
UNITED STATES

BY EDWARD DUMBAULD

UNIVERSITY OF OKLAHOMA PRESS : NORMAN

BY EDWARD DUMBAULD

Interim Measures of Protection in International Controversies
(The Hague, 1932)

Thomas Jefferson, American Tourist (Norman, 1946)

The Declaration of Independence and What It Means Today
(Norman, 1950)

The Political Writings of Thomas Jefferson
(New York, 1955)

The Bill of Rights and What It Means Today
(Norman, 1957)

The Constitution of the United States
(Norman, 1964)

The publication of this book has been aided
by a grant from the FORD FOUNDATION.

Library of Congress Catalog Card Number: 64–11324

Copyright 1964 by the University of Oklahoma Press, Publishing Division of the University. Composed and printed at Norman, Oklahoma, U.S.A., by the University of Oklahoma Press. First edition, June, 1964; second printing, February, 1965.

TO THE MEMORY OF

EDWARD S. CORWIN (1878–1963)

AND JOHN DICKINSON (1894–1952)

HONORED MENTORS

IN THE REALM OF FUNDAMENTAL LAW

ρ

PREFACE

MY earlier volumes *The Declaration of Independence and What It Means Today* and *The Bill of Rights and What It Means Today* were written because they were needed to fill a gap in scholarly literature. Amazing as it seems, it is a fact that until I wrote those books there was no convenient source to which a reader might turn for a well-documented commentary on the historical background and current significance of those important landmarks in the history of American political philosophy and constitutional law.

The present work, however, owes its origin to the stimulus of a suggestion from my publisher. It will complement my earlier books by covering the chronological gap between 1776, when independence was declared, and 1789, when the Bill of Rights was formulated.

There are already in existence a number of excellent works on the Constitution, as a glance at the Bibliography in this volume will disclose. By consulting a half-dozen or so of these, a reader could indeed familiarize himself with a wide range of pertinent data. The situation is quite different from that with respect to the Declaration of Independence and the Bill of Rights. Instead of a scarcity and lack of literature on the subject there is an *embarras de richesses*.

But perhaps for that very reason my book will serve a useful purpose in guiding the reader to what he is looking for, without the necessity of seeking a needle in a haystack.

My method of treatment is to give, in the sequence established by the Constitution itself, the text of each clause (from the photographic reproduction in *Charters of Freedom*, National Archives Publication No. 53–14), followed by an account of the origin and evolution of the clause in the Convention of 1787 (based mainly on Max Farrand's extremely useful compilation of the *Records of the Federal Convention of 1787*), and by an analysis of the meaning of the clause as interpreted by the decisions of the United States Supreme Court.

The opinions of that august tribunal (now filling over 375 volumes) of course constitute the raw material for such analysis, and must ultimately be evaluated by each student for himself.

In any event, it has been pleasurable as well as beneficial to me (and will, I trust, be equally so to the reader) to traverse this familiar ground. It is good for every citizen to undertake such a patriotic pilgrimage for himself, among the venerable landmarks of our national life.

Of the American constitutional heritage, it may be said in Goethe's words: "He only deserves freedom and life who daily conquers them anew."

Such assimilation of the achievements of the past was exemplified in the inspiring spectacle at Independence Hall on September 17, 1962, when a throng of citizens trudged through the rain to ceremonies commemorating the 175th anniversary of the signing of the Constitution. They saw and heard a jovial and spirited former President (who lived in a town called Independence) describe with earnestness and sincerity the emotions twice experienced by him upon taking the inaugural oath to "preserve, protect and defend the Constitution of the United States." But that task cannot be performed by a President alone, or by the courts, or by Congress. The Constitution can be effectively preserved, protected, and defended only by "the People of the United States," by whom it was ordained and established.

EDWARD DUMBAULD

Pittsburgh, Pennsylvania
January 4, 1964

CONTENTS

ix

Contents

ILLUSTRATIONS

THE CONSTITUTION OF THE UNITED STATES

INTRODUCTION

The Constitution as Fundamental Law

IN one sense, every state has a constitution. By scrutiny and analysis of human conduct and behavior within a politically organized society, legal scientists can ascertain what rules of law are in force within the community, and can identify a portion of that body of law as being fundamental or "constitutional" in its nature. Such constitutional or organic law comprises those legal rules which prescribe the process by which law is created. Constitutional law is that which constitutes or establishes a form of government for the state. It confers lawmaking authority upon certain individuals or groups when they act in accordance with specified procedures. Ultimately the legal validity of all official action rests upon the basic or fundamental law which may properly be called the constitution of the particular society under consideration.[1] From this analytical standpoint it does not matter whether the constitution establishes a free government or one that is despotic, a democracy or a monarchy, an oligarchy or a tyranny. The constitution may be good or bad, wise or foolish, just or unjust. Whatever sort it may be, every state has its fundamental law.

But in another sense it is proper to speak of "constitutional government" in a narrower connotation. Constitutional government is essentially limited government.[2]

The notion of constitutional limitations upon the power of govern-

[1] Edward Dumbauld, "The Place of Philosophy in International Law," *University of Pennsylvania Law Review*, Vol. LXXXIII, No. 5 (March, 1935), 590, 593; Dumbauld, "Judicial Review and Popular Sovereignty," *University of Pennsylvania Law Review*, Vol. XCIX, No. 2 (November, 1950), 197, 198–99.

[2] Charles H. McIlwain, *Constitutionalism and the Changing World*, 248.

ment was first clearly formulated in Magna Charta. In that historic document, signed by King John in 1215 in the presence of the barons of England at Runnymede, the monarch recognized his duty to rule in accordance with law.[3] Before that time, since the Norman Conquest in 1066, the English kings had governed with as great a degree of absolutism as any Byzantine despot ever displayed.[4] Their royal power was curbed, however, by two characteristic features of medieval thought. The first of these was a consequence of feudalism. Public law and the law of private property in land were not distinguished under the feudal system,[5] and the rule that all land is ultimately held of the king did not prevent the recognition of specific rights in subordinate landlords and tenants. The second restraining influence upon the omnipotence of the crown was the notion that the function of the king was not to create law by legislation but simply to enforce rules of natural law which existed independently and were not the product of his will, or indeed of human volition at all.[6]

The basic importance of Magna Charta in the history of constitutional law does not depend so much upon the specific terms of that instrument, which for the most part deal with obsolete features of the feudal system, as upon the fact that it established clearly the existence of known rules of law which the king was bound (and could be com-

[3] George B. Adams, *An Outline Sketch of English Constitutional History*, 43–46.

[4] *Ibid.*, 16, 38, 42. The absolutism of the Eastern Roman Empire was based theoretically upon the power of the people, which had been transferred to the Emperor by a mythical *lex regia*. Justinian's codification contains the well-known statement of the jurist Ulpian: "*Quod principi placuit, legis habet vigorem: utpote cum lege regia, quae de imperio eius lata est, populus ei et in eum omne suum imperium et potestatem conferat.*" ("The prince's pleasure has the force of law, since by the *lex regia* which was enacted concerning his sovereignty the people has conferred upon him all its sovereignty and power.") Dig. 1, 4, 1, pr. See also Inst. 1, 2, 6, and John N. Figgis, *Studies of Political Thought from Gerson to Grotius*, 8, 197–98. Bracton acknowledges of the English king that it is the law which is the source of all his royal powers: "*Ipse autem rex non debet esse sub homine sed sub deo et sub lege, quia lex facit regem.*" ("For the king ought not be under any man, but under God and the law, since the law makes him king.") Bracton, *De Legibus et Consuetudinibus Angliae*, II, 33.

[5] Frederic W. Maitland, *Constitutional History of England*, 38; Theodore F. T. Plucknett, "Bonham's Case and Judicial Review," *Harvard Law Review*, Vol. XL, No. 1 (November, 1926), 30, 52.

[6] Edward Jenks, *Law and Politics in the Middle Ages*, 8–10; William S. Holdsworth, *Sources and Literature of English Law*, 40; John Dickinson, *Administrative Justice and the Supremacy of Law in the United States*, 84–85.

pelled) to obey, and the existence of definite legal rights in the people which the king was obliged to recognize and respect.[7] Moreover, some of the specific provisions of Magna Charta became important topics in constitutional history. Thus the germ of the principle that taxation without representation is illegal was found in Magna Charta,[8] as well as the "due process of law" clause and the guarantee of jury trial.[9]

The famous Chapter 39 of Magna Charta reads:

> No free man shall be seized or imprisoned or disseized or outlawed or exiled or destroyed in any manner, nor will we go upon him, nor will we send upon him, unless by the lawful judgment of his peers, or by the law of the land. To no one will we sell, to no one deny or delay right or justice.[10]

Much of the significance of Magna Charta in the development of constitutional law was due to its interpretation and the glosses placed upon it by Sir Edward Coke in his commentary contained in his *Second Institute*. Perhaps Lord Coke may have expounded the Great Charter with some inaccuracies from the historical standpoint, but his doctrines were influential for the growth of English public law.

The acknowledged pre-eminence of Lord Coke as an oracle of the law and a doughty champion of constitutional rights does not rest

[7] George B. Adams, *The Origin of the English Constitution*, 157, 167, 179, 184, 250.

[8] In Chapter 12, which requires consent to new impositions not based upon the feudal relation itself. *Ibid.*, 217. The king, like other property owners, was expected to defray from the revenues of his own land the expenses of maintaining his servants, not only those who served his personal comfort but also those who attended to the administration of his governmental functions. It was lack of money in special situations such as expensive foreign wars which necessitated the calling of parliaments to provide additional funds.

[9] Chapter 39. *Ibid.*, 242–44, 262–74. The right to habeas corpus was also by lawyers of a later time regarded as a deduction from this clause. Faith Thompson, *Magna Carta*, 87; William S. Holdsworth, *History of English Law*, IX, 104–25; William S. McKechnie, *Magna Carta*, 133.

[10] "*Nullus liber homo [decetero] capiatur vel imprisonetur aut disseisiatur [de aliquo libero tenemento suo vel libertatibus vel liberis consuetudinibus suis], aut utlagetur, aut exuletur aut aliquo [alio] modo destruatur, nec super eum ibimus, nec super eum mittemus, nisi per legale judicium parium suorum, vel per legem terrae. Nulli vendemus, nulli negabimus aut differemus rectum vel justiciam.*"

The above wording constitutes Chapter 29 in the standard form of Magna Charta as confirmed in 1225. The bracketed words did not appear in what was Chapter 39 in John's Charter. The last sentence was Chapter 40 of John's Charter. The text as given above is from Thompson, *Magna Carta*, 380.

solely upon his fame as a legal writer. His *Institutes* were but part of his contribution to the law. His career as judge and member of Parliament afforded additional opportunities to advance the cause of constitutional rights and the imposition of limits upon the royal power.

Coke repeatedly declared that a statute contrary to Magna Charta was void.[11] He held that the law of nature was part of the law of England,[12] and that a statute contrary to natural law or equity was void.[13] These precedents furnished important authority to American lawyers such as James Otis and John Adams,[14] though in England the movement was toward recognition of the omnipotence of Parliament and reliance upon that body to represent the people in their struggle with the crown.

The independence of the judiciary also owes much to Coke's example. He was removed from his office as chief justice of the Court of King's Bench in mid-November, 1616, after a Sunday-morning conference where he alone of all the judges refused to promise to delay justice (in violation of Magna Charta) in order to await consultation with the king concerning certain types of litigation. Coke said that if such a case should arise he would do that which befits a judge.[15] In the same conference he declared that the king himself should not

[11] Co. Litt. 81 a; 2 Inst. proeme; 3 Inst. 111.

[12] Calvin's case, 7 Rep. 1a, at 4b and 12b (1609).

[13] Dr. Bonham's case, 8 Rep. 114a (1610). For a discussion of this case and its predecessors and progeny, see the articles by Theodore F. T. Plucknett and Samuel E. Thorne listed in the Bibliography; see also Brinton Coxe, *An Essay on Judicial Power and Unconstitutional Legislation*, 172.

[14] Otis proclaimed in his famous argument against writs of assistance in 1761 that an act of Parliament contrary to natural right was unconstitutional and void. He cited Coke's language in Dr. Bonham's case, and also relied on the authority of Vattel. Edward Dumbauld, *The Declaration of Independence and What It Means Today*, 3, 41.

[15] Case of Commendams, 12 Rep. 63 (1616). A comparable instance of judicial courage was the refusal of Judge Charles C. Bradley to promise a mob of Iowa farmers during the depression that he would not sign mortgage foreclosure decrees in fifteen pending cases. He told them that he "would render decisions as each case came up according to its own particular merit and the specific legal points involved." For an account of this incident see Frank D. DiLeva, "Attempt to Hang an Iowa Judge," *Annals of Iowa* (3rd series), Vol. XXXII, No. 5 (July, 1954), 340–41, and the *Des Moines Register* for April 28 and 29, 1933. For another notable statement of the standards which should govern judicial behavior, see Justice Robert H. Jackson's address of April 13, 1945, in *Proceedings* of the Washington Meeting of the American Society of International Law (1945), 18.

6

participate in the decision of cases in court.[16] Coke was also responsible[17] for establishment of the rule that the king could not suspend or alter the standing law of the land by means of a royal proclamation.[18]

After his removal by James I as judge, Coke continued in another forum the struggle for English liberties. He was a leading spirit in the Parliament which on December 18, 1621, adopted a memorable Protestation declaring the freedom of the House of Commons to discuss all matters of state without imprisonment or molestation in any other place by reason of things done or said in Parliament. Shortly after Christmas, James I, in the presence of the Privy Council and of all the judges then in London, sent for the journal of the Commons and solemnly tore out with his own hands the page containing this offensive Protestation.[19] For his part in the affair Coke was sent to the Tower of London for eight months, and eight other members were likewise punished.

Coke also took a prominent part in the proceedings of a later Parliament which culminated in the Petition of Right, to which Charles I gave assent on June 7, 1628.[20] This instrument ranks with Magna Charta and the Bill of Rights of 1689 among the most significant English "liberty documents."

The Petition of Right prohibited four grievances: the exaction of taxes or forced loans not consented to by Parliament; arbitrary imprisonment by command of the king; the billeting or quartering of soldiers and sailors in houses without the consent of the owners; and the trial of criminal offenses by martial law in time of peace.

The first of these grievances related to a constitutional principle of

[16] Holdsworth, *History of English Law*, V, 340.

[17] Case of Proclamations, 12 Rep. 74 (1611).

[18] The dispensing power was later prohibited in the English Bill of Rights of 1689. Edward Dumbauld, *The Bill of Rights and What It Means Today*, 167. An attempted exercise of such power by James II led to his abdication, although a subservient court held for the king in Godden v. Hales, 2 Shower *475, Comberbach 21, in Thomas B. Howell, *State Trials* (hereinafter cited as *State Trials*), XI, 1165–1199 (1686). See Holdsworth, *History of English Law*, VI, 203, 217–25.

[19] Joseph R. Tanner, *Constitutional Documents of the Reign of James I*, 275, 288–89; Thomas P. Taswell-Langmead, *English Constitutional History*, 508–509; Zechariah Chafee, Jr., *Three Human Rights*, 57–59.

[20] Taswell-Langmead, *English Constitutional History*, 517–26; Thompson, *Magna Carta*, 342; Frances H. Relf, *The Petition of Right*, 46–50, 63–67; Proceedings in Parliament Relating to the Liberty of the Subject, *State Trials*, III, 59–234; Harold Hulme, *Sir John Eliot*, 226–56.

great antiquity[21] that assumed decisive importance at the time of the American Revolution.[22] Likewise, in England, Charles I did not abandon his efforts to collect revenue illegally after his assent to the Petition of Right. The great controversy over ship-money, which made the name of John Hampden immortal, came before the king's judges in 1637. Seven judges voted in favor of the king and five in favor of Hampden;[23] but public opinion did not permit the ultimate determination of the legality of such unauthorized taxation to be pronounced in that fashion. In 1641 the Long Parliament declared the proceedings against Hampden void, and annulled the judgment that the court had rendered against him.[24] Subsequently the Bill of Rights in 1689 declared generally "That levying money for or to the use of the crown, by pretence of prerogative, without grant of parliament, for longer time, or in other manner than the same is or shall be granted, is illegal."[25]

The second grievance dealt with in the Petition of Right was the matter of arbitrary imprisonment. Many persons of high rank who refused to contribute in accordance with the scheme of forced loans devised by Charles I were imprisoned. Sir Thomas Darnel and four other knights sought release upon a writ of habeas corpus. The return to the writ made by the warden of the Fleet prison stated that the prisoners were detained by virtue of a warrant signed by two members of the Privy Council and declaring that they were "committed by special command of his majesty" ("*per mandatum speciale domini regis*"). After elaborate argument the Court of King's Bench held that no other specific cause of detention need be set forth, and the prisoners were remanded to jail.[26] They were later released by order of

---

[21] See note 8 above.

[22] For example, see the answer of the Massachusetts Council on January 25, 1773, to the speech of Governor Hutchinson. *Massachusetts State Papers*, 345.

[23] The Case of Ship-Money, *State Trials*, III, 826–1316 (1637).

[24] Act of August 7, 1641, 16 Car. I c. 14. George B. Adams and H. Morse Stephens, *Select Documents*, 369–71. Likewise the Long Parliament by the Act of 16 Car. I c. 8 overthrew the decision in the Case of Impositions, *State Trials*, II, 371–534 (1606), which had upheld the king's right to impose duties on foreign commerce without legislation. See Tanner, *Constitutional Documents*, 243–65.

[25] 1 Wm. & Mary, 2nd sess., c. 2. Printed in Dumbauld, *The Bill of Rights and What It Means Today*, 168.

[26] The Case of the Five Knights, *State Trials*, III, 1–234 (1627). See also Holdsworth, *History of English Law*, VI, 32–40; Zechariah Chafee, Jr., *How Human Rights*

the Privy Council. The case aroused earnest debate in Parliament, and led to the provision in the Petition of Right prohibiting imprisonment without a definite charge to which the defendant "might make answer according to the law."

The other two grievances prohibited by the Petition of Right (quartering of troops without the householder's consent and martial law in time of peace) have also left their impress on the Constitution of the United States.[27]

But the Petition of Right did not end the abuses perpetrated by the crown. On March 2, 1629, a boisterous scene occurred in the House of Commons in defiance of the authority of the king to adjourn Parliament. When the Speaker, Sir John Finch, declared the king's pleasure that the house should adjourn and attempted to leave the chair, shouts of "No! No!" resounded on every hand. Two members, Denzil Holles and Benjamin Valentine, pushed the speaker back into his chair. "God's wounds," exclaimed Holles, "you shall sit till we please to rise." The door of the chamber was locked and the king's messenger, the Usher of the Black Rod, excluded. Sir John Eliot had prepared resolutions condemning innovation in religion and the levying of certain taxes (known as tonnage and poundage) without their having been granted by Parliament. The Speaker refused to put the question, and Eliot threw his resolutions into the fire. However, Holles reformulated the resolutions from memory and put them to a vote. They were adopted by acclamation, and the house adjourned.[28]

The next day Eliot, Holles, Valentine, and six other members were summoned before the Privy Council and committed to prison. When they sought habeas corpus, having been committed "by special mandate of the king," contrary to the Petition of Right, new charges of conspiracy and sedition were substituted; the king's attorneys convinced the king's subservient judges that these were distinguishable from actions protected by the parliamentary privileges of members of the house. Fearing that the judges might admit the prisoners to bail for those offenses, the king refused to produce them before the court, upon the pretext that their behavior was wanting in appropriate "mod-

Got into the Constitution, 64–72; Thompson, *Magna Carta,* 326–35; Relf, *The Petition of Right,* 2–9.

[27] Amendments III and V.

[28] Taswell-Langmead, *English Constitutional History,* 530–31; Chafee, *Three Human Rights,* 64–69; Hulme, *Sir John Eliot,* 307–15.

esty and civility."[29] Later the prisoners were offered release on bail upon giving surety for their good behavior. "Security for future good behavior was hardly ever asked by English courts except from turbulent disturbers of the peace, profligate women, or keepers of disorderly houses. So Eliot and his companions in the Tower regarded this offer as a deadly insult, to be indignantly repelled."[30]

In the course of time all the prisoners but three made their peace with the crown. Eliot died in the Tower on November 27, 1632, "universally regarded as a martyr in the cause of liberty";[31] Strode and Valentine were not liberated from prison until the Short Parliament met in 1640.[32] Parliament on July 8, 1641,[33] and again on December 11, 1667,[34] declared that the judgment of condemnation was illegal, and on April 15, 1668, the judgment was reversed by the House of Lords, of which Holles was then a member.[35]

Holles and Strode were involved in another eventful episode which contributed substantially to the downfall of Charles I. Soon after Parliament had adopted the Grand Remonstrance against that monarch's misgovernment, he undertook to "impeach" five members of the House of Commons[36] and one member of the House of Lords[37] for high treason.[38] In an attempt to arrest the five members, Charles I entered the House of Commons on January 4, 1641/2,[39] accompanied by a band of several hundred armed men, who stood outside the chamber but forcibly kept the door open. Being forewarned, the five members had been directed to withdraw.[40] From Westminster Steps

---

[29] The Case of the Nine Members, *State Trials*, III, 235–336 (1629); Chafee, *Three Human Rights*, 67; Holdsworth, *History of English Law*, VI, 38–39, 97–98.

[30] Chafee, *Three Human Rights*, 67.

[31] Taswell-Langmead, *English Constitutional History*, 531–33; Hulme, *Sir John Eliot*, 391.

[32] Holdsworth, *History of English Law*, VI, 39.

[33] *State Trials*, III, 310–14.

[34] *Ibid.*, III, 319.

[35] *Ibid.*, III, 332–33.

[36] Besides Holles and Strode, the victims were John Pym, John Hampden, and Sir Arthur Haslerig.

[37] Lord Kimbolton.

[38] Proceedings against Lord Kimbolton and the Five Members, *State Trials*, IV, 82–112 (1641/2); Chafee, *Three Human Rights*, 74–78; Taswell-Langmead, *English Constitutional History*, 572–80; John Forster, *Arrest of the Five Members*, 188–95.

[39] Never before or since has the king set foot in the House of Commons.

[40] Forster, *Arrest of the Five Members*, 179.

they were rowed to a place of safety in the City of London.[41] Six days later the king fled to Hampton Court.[42] Upon the following day, the five members were triumphantly escorted from the City to their places in Parliament.[43]

The climax of English constitutional development (the enactment of the Bill of Rights) came after Charles I had been executed, after Cromwell and the Commonwealth had disappeared, after Charles II had ended his travels and revels, and after James II had abdicated by fleeing to France. The last-named king, for the benefit of his Roman Catholic coreligionists, had issued a Declaration of Indulgence on April 4, 1687, in which he announced the suspension of all penal laws relating to ecclesiastical matters.[44] He reaffirmed the same policy in a declaration on April 27, 1688, which was ordered to be read in all churches. The bishops were directed to distribute the declaration throughout their dioceses for that purpose.[45]

The Archbishop of Canterbury and six bishops presented to the king on May 18, 1688, a petition stating that their unwillingness to make themselves parties to the dissemination of the king's declaration was "because that declaration is founded upon such a dispensing power, as hath been often declared illegal."[46] For this they were committed to the Tower and prosecuted for seditious libel ("as though it were a libel to petition the king").[47] On June 30, 1688, the defendants were acquitted, amid great public rejoicing and jubilation.[48] On the same day Prince William of Orange was invited to come to England.[49] The

[41] Sir Winston Churchill recounts an interesting custom which commemorates the saga of the five members: "To this day the Members for the City take their place on the Treasury bench at the opening of a session, in perpetual acknowledgment of the services rendered by the City in protecting the five." Churchill, *The New World*, 230.

[42] Forster, *Arrest of the Five Members*, 356. He never returned to the capital except to face trial and execution. The Trial of Charles Stuart, King of England, *State Trials*, IV, 989–1154 (1649). The king went to the scaffold on January 30, 1649.

[43] *State Trials*, IV, 100; Forster, *Arrest of the Five Members*, 348, 369.

[44] Regarding dispensation from the laws of the land, see note 18 above, and Holdsworth, *History of English Law*, VI, 217–30.

[45] *State Trials*, XII, 233–38.　　　　[46] *Ibid.*, XII, 239.

[47] As their counsel, Sergeant Pemberton, observed. *Ibid.*, XII, 240. The right to petition the king was recognized in the Bill of Rights, doubtless by reason of the fact that the Seven Bishops' case was still in the public mind. The First Amendment to the United States Constitution recognizes the right of petition.

[48] The Trial of the Seven Bishops, *State Trials*, XII, 183–524 (1688).

[49] Taswell-Langmead, *English Constitutional History*, 617; Chafee, *Three Human Rights*, 15–20.

11

terms upon which William and Mary accepted the throne included the enactment as law of the Bill of Rights.[50]

The English Bill of Rights, formulated one hundred years before the American Bill of Rights,[51] established thirteen propositions, all of which were addressed to the abolition of grievances suffered by the English people during Tudor and Stuart times (particularly, as the preamble recites, during the reign of James II):

1. That the pretended power of suspending of laws, or the execution of laws, by regal authority, without consent of parliament, is illegal.

2. That the pretended power of dispensing with laws, or the execution of laws, by regal authority, as it hath been assumed and exercised of late, is illegal.

3. That the commission for erecting the late court of commissioners for ecclesiastical causes, and all other commissions and courts of like nature are illegal and pernicious.

4. That levying money for or to the use of the crown, by pretence of prerogative, without grant of parliament, for longer time, or in other manner than the same is or shall be granted, is illegal.

5. That it is the right of the subjects to petition the King, and all committments [sic] and prosecutions for such petitioning are illegal.

6. That the raising or keeping a standing army within the kingdom in time of peace, unless it be with consent of parliament, is against law.

7. That the subjects which are protestants, may have arms for their defence suitable to their conditions, and as allowed by law.

8. That election of members of parliament ought to be free.

9. That the freedom of speech, and debates or proceedings in parliament, ought not to be impeached or questioned in any court or place out of parliament.

10. That excessive bail ought not to be required, nor excessive fines imposed, nor cruel and unusual punishments inflicted.

11. That jurors ought to be duly impanelled and returned, and jurors which pass upon men in trials for high treason ought to be freeholders.

[50] Act of December 16, 1689, 1 Wm. and Mary, 2nd sess. c. 2. In the following year a duly summoned Parliament confirmed all legislation of the Convention Parliament. 2 Wm. & Mary c. 1.

[51] The first ten Amendments to the Constitution of the United States, commonly called the Bill of Rights, were adopted by Congress on September 25, 1789. They went into force on December 15, 1791, when Virginia furnished the last necessary ratification. Dumbauld, *The Bill of Rights and What It Means Today*, 48–50, 159.

12. That all grants and promises of fines and forfeitures of particular persons before conviction, are illegal and void.

13. And that for redress of all grievances, and for the amending, strengthening, and preserving of the laws, parliaments ought to be held frequently.[52]

The "Glorious Revolution" which placed William and Mary upon the English throne effectively established the principle that government must be conducted according to law. The duty of the king to respect constitutional limitations was thereafter unchallenged. Transfer of the crown by action of Parliament likewise made plain that government must be based upon the consent of the governed, and not upon theories of "divine right" to rule by hereditary succession.[53] That the royal power was an authority conferred by law and measured by law[54] was now indisputable.[55]

A systematic justification of the Glorious Revolution from the standpoint of political theory was provided by the English philosopher John Locke, who in 1690 published his celebrated *Two Treatises of Government*.[56] Locke's basic thesis was that politically organized society arose by virtue of a "social contract" entered into by individuals originally in a "state of nature," governed by the law of nature.[57] Thereby

[52] *Ibid.*, 167–68. The influence of some of these propositions can be traced in provisions of the United States Constitution.

[53] Holdsworth, *History of English Law*, VI, 230. For the theory of divine right, see *ibid.*, VI, 276–81. For Locke's doctrines, see *ibid.*, VI, 283–90. Regarding succession to the crown, see Taswell-Langmead, *English Constitutional History*, 180–81, 202. Acts of 28 Hen. VIII c. 7 and 35 Hen. VIII c. 1 authorized that monarch to transfer the crown by his last will and testament in writing.

[54] See note 4 above.

[55] Regarding royalist contentions that certain prerogatives were inherent in the crown, Selden aptly remarked: "A king that claims privileges in his own country because they have them in another is just as a cook that claims fees in one lord's house because they are allowed in another. If the master of the house will allow them, well and good. . . . To know what obedience is due to the prince, you must look into the contract betwixt him and the people; as if you would know what rent is due from the tenant to the landlord, you must look into the lease." *The Table Talk of John Selden*, 90, 191.

[56] Holdsworth, *History of English Law*, VI, 283–90. Locke was also the philosopher of the American Revolution. Many traces of language and ideas from his treatise are discernible in the Declaration of Independence. Dumbauld, *The Declaration of Independence and What It Means Today*, 30, 42, 57, 63–66, 69–70, 75–78, 82, 85, 104, 139, 142.

[57] *Two Treatises of Government*, 119–20, 164–66, 168.

was created a more effective mechanism for enforcing the natural rights of the individuals.[58]

From this view of the nature and purpose of political society, it follows that "the power of the society or legislative constituted by them can never be supposed to extend farther than the common good" or to have any "other end but the peace, safety, and public good of the people."[59]

Locke declared that "the first and fundamental law of all commonwealths" is that which establishes "the legislative power."[60] This power he defined as "that which has a right to direct how the force of the commonwealth shall be employed for preserving the community and the members of it."[61]

The legislative power, "though it be the supreme power in every commonwealth," is nevertheless itself subject to certain restrictions. It cannot be "absolutely arbitrary over the lives and fortunes of the people." For the individuals establishing a political society cannot confer upon it any power which they did not possess while they were still in a state of nature.[62] Since "the law of Nature stands as an eternal rule to all men, legislators as well as others," it follows that legislation must be "conformable to the law of Nature—*i.e.*, to the will of God."[63]

Moreover, since subjection to absolute arbitrary authority would be "a worse condition than the State of nature," the ruling power ought

[58] *Ibid.*, 159–60, 180–81. Locke recognized a natural property right over things that a person has "mixed his labour with." *Ibid.*, 130. Jefferson regarded property as a right derived from the state rather than as a natural right. Dumbauld, *The Declaration of Independence and What It Means Today*, 61.

[59] Locke, *Two Treatises of Government*, 182.

[60] *Ibid.*, 183. "The constitution of the legislative is the first and fundamental act of society." *Ibid.*, 225. "This legislative is not only the supreme power of the commonwealth, but sacred and unalterable in the hands where the community have once placed it." *Ibid.*, 183–84. This may cause inconvenience when change of conditions requires modification of the basis of representation (as by abolishing rotten boroughs), "because the constitution of the legislative being the original and supreme act of the society, antecedent to all positive laws in it, and depending wholly on the people, no inferior power can alter it." *Ibid.*, 197. In the Philadelphia convention of 1787, Madison was always opposed in principle to any proposals which permitted Congress to affect the basis of representation, or prescribe their own qualifications, privileges, or compensation. Max Farrand, ed., *Records*, II, 203, 249–50. See note 152, page 93, and page 454, below.

[61] *Two Treatises of Government*, 190.

[62] *Ibid.*, 184–85, 205.

[63] *Ibid.*, 185.

to govern by declared and promulgated standing laws, not by arbitrary or extemporized decrees.[64]

It also follows that "the supreme power cannot take from any man any part of his property without his own consent."[65] Hence no taxes can be imposed without the consent of the people. "For what property have I in that which another may by right take when he pleases to himself?"[66]

Finally, since only the people can prescribe how and by whom the legislative power shall be exercised, it cannot be delegated.[67] Locke plainly declares that attempted exercise of legislative power otherwise than in accordance with the terms prescribed in the constitution is void. "When any one, or more, shall take upon them to make laws whom the people have not appointed so to do, they make laws without authority, which the people are not therefore bound to obey."[68] In the language of the Declaration of Independence, such unconstitutional exercise of authority could produce nothing but "acts of pretended legislation."[69]

The same doctrine was forcefully voiced in 1786 by James Iredell, a North Carolinian who later served as a justice of the United States Supreme Court: "The people have chosen to be governed under such and such principles. They have not chosen to be governed, or promised to submit upon any other; and the Assembly have no more right to

[64] *Ibid.*, 185–87.

[65] *Ibid.*, 187. "For the preservation of property being the end of government, and that for which men enter into society, it necessarily supposes and requires that the people should have property, without which they must be supposed to lose that by entering into society which was the end for which they entered into it; too gross an absurdity for any man to own. Men, therefore, in society having property, they have such a right to the goods, which by the law of the community are theirs, that nobody hath a right to take them, or any part of them, from them without their own consent; without this they have no property at all. For I have truly no property in that which another can by right take from me when he pleases against my consent." *Ibid.*, 187–88. At the time of the American Revolution the colonists emphasized that "we can call nothing our own, which others assume a Right to take from us without our consent." John Dickinson, *Writings*, 451; see also *Massachusetts State Papers*, 126, 346.

[66] Locke, *Two Treatises of Government*, 189. See note 65 above.

[67] *Ibid.*, 189. Any alteration in the legislative power amounts to dissolution or subversion of the existing government. *Ibid.*, 225–26.

[68] Locke, *Two Treatises of Government*, 225. Legislation not enacted in the manner prescribed by the people would lack "that which is absolutely necessary to its being a law, the consent of the society." *Ibid.*, 184.

[69] Dumbauld, *The Declaration of Independence and What It Means Today*, 76, 119.

obedience on other terms, than any different power on earth has a right to govern us; for we have as much agreed to be governed by the Turkish Divan as by our own General Assembly,[70] otherwise than on the express terms prescribed."[71]

Iredell was speaking of the North Carolina constitution, by virtue of which in 1787 a statute was held unconstitutional which would have deprived a litigant of jury trial with respect to real estate which had been confiscated from a British subject. The court said:

"That by the constitution every citizen had undoubtedly a right to a decision of his property by a trial by jury. For that if the legislature could take away this right, and require him to stand condemned in his property without a trial, it might with as much authority require his life to be taken away without a trial by jury, and that he should stand condemned to die, without the formality of any trial at all: that if the members of the General Assembly could do this, they might, with equal authority, not only render themselves the legislators of the state for life, without any further election by the people, from thence transmit the dignity and authority of legislation down to their heirs male forever.

"But that it was clear, that no act they could pass, could by any means repeal or alter the constitution, because if they could do this, they would at the same instant of time, destroy their own existence as a legislature, and dissolve the government thereby established."[72]

The court here was following, without mentioning, the frequently quoted maxim of Emmerich de Vattel that "it is from the constitution that the legislators derive their power; how, then, could they change it without destroying the source of their authority?"[73]

[70] James Otis had similarly asserted in 1762 that "it would be of little consequence to the people whether they were subject to George or Lewis, the King of Great Britain or the French King, if both were arbitrary, as both would be if both could levy Taxes without the Parliament. . . . It is of little importance what a King's christian name is." Charles F. Mullett, *Some Political Writings of James Otis*, 21, 25.

[71] Griffith J. McRee, *Life and Correspondence of James Iredell*, II, 146. See also Coxe, *Judicial Power and Unconstitutional Legislation*, 255.

[72] Bayard v. Singleton, Martin 42, 47 (1787); as quoted in Coxe, *Judicial Power and Unconstitutional Legislation*, 250–51. See also Charles G. Haines, *The American Doctrine of Judicial Supremacy*, 112–20.

[73] Vattel, *The Law of Nations*, III, 19 (Book I, c. iii, § 34). Vattel defines the constitution of a state as "the fundamental law which determines the manner in which the public authority shall be exercised." He goes on to say that those public laws "which relate to . . . the very nature of the society, to the form of government and the manner in which the public authority is to be exercised—those laws, in a word, which together

16

The Massachusetts legislature in their famous circular letter of February 11, 1768, to the other colonies, voiced the view "that in all free states the constitution is fixed,[74] and as the supreme legislative derives its power and authority from the constitution, it cannot overleap the bounds of it, without destroying its own foundation."[75] The House of Representatives in the course of controversy with Governor Thomas Hutchinson in 1773 likewise referred to the same passage from Vattel.[76]

Again in 1786 the familiar language of Vattel was cited by counsel during argument to a Rhode Island court.[77] The case involved prosecution of a butcher for refusal to accept paper money. Legislation had been enacted authorizing trial of such offenders "without any jury, by a majority of the Judges present, according to the laws of the land."[78]

The court held that the information was not cognizable before it.[79] It did not expressly declare the act unconstitutional and void. The judges were summoned to appear before the legislature to explain their action. They were not removed from office, but when their terms expired they were not re-elected by the legislature.[80]

The decision, even if it be taken as showing that the court regarded the act as unconstitutional and void, goes no further than the English precedents applicable to a statute which is self-contradictory and hence

form the constitution of the State, are the *fundamental laws*." *Ibid.*, III, 17 (Book I, c. iii, §§ 27, 29.

[74] Oliver Cromwell in an address to Parliament on September 12, 1654, declared: "Some things are fundamentals. . . . In every government there must be somewhat fundamental, somewhat like a *Magna Charta*, that should be standing and be unalterable." Wilbur C. Abbott, ed., *Writings and Speeches of Oliver Cromwell*, III, 458–59.

[75] *Massachusetts State Papers*, 134.

[76] Statements of January 26, 1773, and March 2, 1773. *Ibid.*, 362, 395. The governor had first invoked the authority of Vattel by quoting a passage about colonies. *Ibid.*, 337; Vattel, *The Law of Nations*, III, 86 (Book I, c. xviii, § 210).

[77] James M. Varnum, *The Case, Trevett against Weeden*, 23–26; Coxe, *Judicial Power and Unconstitutional Legislation*, 119–20, 240. Regarding this case, see also Haines, *The American Doctrine of Judicial Supremacy*, 105–12. At that time Rhode Island did not have a written constitution, but its colonial charter was still in force.

[78] Varnum, *The Case, Trevett against Weeden*, 2, 59; Coxe, *Judicial Power and Unconstitutional Legislation*, 235.

[79] Varnum, *The Case, Trevett against Weeden*, 1, 38; Coxe, *Judicial Review and Unconstitutional Legislation*, 245. This may have meant merely that the court was without jurisdiction, and that only the specially convened courts authorized by the statute could try such offenses.

[80] Varnum, *The Case, Trevett against Weeden*, 37–53; Coxe, *Judicial Review and Unconstitutional Legislation*, 246–47. One judge was retained in office.

"impertinent to be observed" or "impossible of performance."[81] How could trial without a jury be trial according to the law of the land?

Akin to the doctrines of Locke and Vattel were the views of Thomas Jefferson regarding a constitution as fundamental law. In his *Notes on the State of Virginia* and elsewhere Jefferson made clear his belief that nothing deserves to be called a constitution except a fundamental law, emanating directly from the authority of the people, which defines and limits the powers of the ordinary legislature and which cannot be altered or affected by ordinary legislation. Hence, a true constitution, that is to say, a law binding upon the ordinary organs of government and unchangeable by them, must be established by the people itself, acting through special agents appointed for that particular purpose, as in a constitutional convention.[82] The Virginia Constitution of 1776 he regarded as an enactment by the ordinary legislature rather than by a convention to which the people had delegated power to adopt a constitution.[83] He spoke in later life of the British constitution, which can be changed by any act passed by Parliament, as "no constitution at all."[84]

Jefferson desired a fixed constitution,[85] which would "bind up the several branches of government by certain laws, which when they transgress their acts shall become nullities."[86] An essential feature of "a real constitution"[87] was that it "be rendered permanent by a power superior to that of the ordinary legislature,"[88] and that it should proclaim and

---

[81] Varnum, *The Case, Trevett against Weeden*, 31; Coxe, *Judicial Power and Unconstitutional Legislation*, 154–55, 243–44.

[82] Jefferson, *Notes on the State of Virginia*, 204. On Locke and Vattel, see notes 60 and 73 above.

[83] Jefferson, *Notes on the State of Virginia*, 197–205; answers to queries of Jean Nicolas Démeunier, *circa* January 24, 1786, in Jefferson, *Papers of Thomas Jefferson*, X, 28–29; letter to John H. Pleasants, April 19, 1824, in Jefferson, *Works of Thomas Jefferson*, XII, 252. This view was not accepted by the Virginia courts. Dumbauld, "Thomas Jefferson and American Constitutional Law," *Journal of Public Law*, Vol. II, No. 2 (Fall, 1953), 373. Throughout his life Jefferson was desirous of replacing the Constitution of 1776 by a true fundamental law that would give the government of Virginia a genuinely democratic character.

[84] Letter to A. Coray, October 31, 1823, in Jefferson, *Writings of Thomas Jefferson*, XV, 488.

[85] Answers to Démeunier, *circa* January 24, 1786, in Jefferson, *Papers*, X, 29.

[86] Jefferson, *Notes on the State of Virginia*, 213.

[87] Answers to Démeunier, January 24, 1786, in Jefferson, *Papers*, X, 18.

[88] Jefferson, *Notes on the State of Virginia*, 357.

"declare those fundamentals to which all our laws present and future shall be subordinate."[89]

Where such a "real constitution" is in force, Jefferson declared, "the judges would consider any law as void, which was contrary to the constitution."[90] In 1798 he informed a prospective immigrant to Virginia that "should you chuse [*sic*] it for your asylum, the laws of the land, administered by upright judges, would protect you from any exercise of power unauthorized by the Constitution of the United States."[91] One of the important consequences of incorporating a Bill of Rights in the Constitution, Jefferson pointed out to Madison, is "the legal check which it puts into the hands of the judiciary."[92] The author of the Declaration of Independence may therefore be numbered among those who at an early date accepted the principle of judicial review,[93]

[89] *Ibid.*, 358. A draft of a proposed constitution for Virginia, prepared by Jefferson in 1783, expressly provided that "The general assembly shall not have power to infringe this constitution." *Ibid.*, 363.

[90] Answers to Démeunier, January 24, 1786, in Jefferson, *Papers*, X, 18. Among the reasons why Jefferson had "long wished to see a convention called" in Virginia was "the making our constitution paramount the powers of the ordinary legislature so that all acts contradictory to it may be adjudged null." Jefferson to Edmund Pendleton, May 25, 1784, in *ibid.*, VII, 293.

[91] Jefferson to A. H. Rowan, September 26, 1798, in Jefferson, *Works*, VIII, 448. Jefferson regarded the Alien and Sedition laws as unconstitutional, and later as President pardoned all victims of this legislation. Dumbauld, "Thomas Jefferson and American Constitutional Law," *loc. cit.*, 374.

[92] Jefferson to Madison, March 15, 1789, in Jefferson, *Papers*, XIV, 659. He goes on to say: "This is a body, which if rendered independent, and kept strictly to their own department merits great confidence for their learning and integrity. In fact what degree of confidence would be too much for a body composed of such men as Wythe, Blair and Pendleton?" A dictum by Jefferson's law teacher, George Wythe, in Commonwealth v. Caton, 4 Call 5, 8 (1782), was one of the earliest statements in America of the doctrine of judicial review. Chancellor Wythe said that "if the whole legislature, an event to be deprecated, should attempt to overleap the bounds, prescribed to them by the people, I, in administering the public justice of the country, will meet the united powers, at my seat in this tribunal; and, pointing to the constitution, will say to them, here is the limit of your authority; and hither shall you go, but no further." Colonial experience with the practice of testing in judicial proceedings before the Privy Council upon appeal the validity of acts passed by American legislatures may also have contributed to the development of judicial review. Joseph H. Smith, *Appeals to the Privy Council from the American Plantations*, 523–652.

[93] Caleb P. Patterson, *The Constitutional Principles of Thomas Jefferson*, 73–77. Madison and Hamilton took the same position. Madison, *Writings of James Madison*, V, 385; *Federalist* (No. 78), 484–85. For the views of members of the Philadelphia convention, see Haines, *The American Doctrine of Judicial Supremacy*, 132–35.

that is to say, the principle that courts may declare legislation unconstitutional and void. That principle was not an innovation[94] originated by Chief Justice John Marshall when in 1803[95] he established it as a distinctive feature of American constitutional practice.

The Constitution itself simply declares that "This Constitution . . . shall be the supreme Law of the Land"[96] and that the federal judicial power "shall extend to all Cases . . . arising under this Constitution."[97]

---

[94] Charles G. Haines, *The Role of the Supreme Court in American Government and Politics, 1789–1835*, 253. As counsel in Ware v. Hylton, 3 Dall. 199, 211 (1796), Marshall had denied the existence of such power in courts unless expressly conferred by the constitution.

[95] In the famous case of Marbury v. Madison, 1 Cr. 137 (1803). Marshall's opinion in this case was "a political coup of the first magnitude." Edward S. Corwin, *John Marshall and the Constitution*, 66. A forceful expression of the theory of Vattel and Jefferson was given by Justice Paterson in Vanhorne's Lessee v. Dorrance, 2 Dall. 304, 308 (1795). See also Hayburn's Case, 2 Dall. 409 (1792); Hylton v. U.S., 3 Dall. 171, 175 (1796); and Calder v. Bull, 3 Dall. 386, 398–99 (1798).

[96] Art. VI, cl. 2. Laws "made in Pursuance" of the Constitution are accorded the same status. Is this a "negative pregnant" indicating that federal legislation violating the Constitution (i.e., not "in Pursuance thereof") is not entitled to such recognition as "Law of the Land"?

[97] Art. III, sec. 2, cl. 1. A case involving determination of the question whether the Constitution prohibits or permits the enactment of a particular statute is obviously one "arising" under the Constitution. According to Chief Justice Marshall, a case arises under the Constitution "whenever its correct decision depends on the construction" of the Constitution. Cohens v. Virginia, 6 Wheat. 264, 379 (1821).

The Essentials Constituting Free Government

Having discussed the nature of constitutional law as fundamental law, binding upon the organs of government, limiting their powers, and prescribing the methods by which ordinary law may be validly created, we turn now to the content of the constitutional law which must prevail in a state if it is to be regarded as having free government.

Jefferson considered "freedom of religion, freedom of the press, trial by jury, habeas corpus, and a representative legislature" as "the essentials constituting free government."[1] He regarded government as republican only to the extent that popular participation in the political process was provided for. He considered it desirable that the people have a share in the enforcement of the laws (through the jury system), as well as in their enactment by a representative legislature and in the election of the executive magistrate.[2]

So too Alexander Hamilton declared: "That country is free where the people have a representation in the government, so that no law can pass without their consent; and where they are secured in the administration of justice by trial by jury."[3]

Samuel Adams had expressed a similar sentiment: "The two main provisions by which a certain share in the government is secured to the people are their Parliaments and their juries; by the former of which no laws can be made without their consent, and by the latter none can be executed without their judgment."[4]

[1] Jefferson to P. S. Dupont de Nemours, February 28, 1815, in Jefferson, *Writings*, XIV, 255. On another occasion he spoke of "the vital elements of free government," and went on to specify "trial by jury, habeas corpus, freedom of the press, freedom of opinion, and representative government." Jefferson to John Adams, November 25, 1816, in Lester J. Cappon, *The Adams-Jefferson Letters*, II, 497.

[2] Dumbauld, *The Declaration of Independence and What It Means Today*, 73. Trial by jury was considered by Jefferson as "the only anchor ever yet imagined by man, by which a government can be held to the principles of its constitution." Jefferson to Thomas Paine, July 11, 1789, in Jefferson, *Writings*, VII, 408.

[3] Richard B. Morris, *Alexander Hamilton and the Founding of the Nation*, 484.

[4] William V. Wells, *The Life and Public Services of Samuel Adams*, I, 21. The chief grievance of which the Stamp Act Congress in 1765 complained was the British government's encroachment upon these two basic features of constitutional liberty. Dumbauld, *The Declaration of Independence and What It Means Today*, 74.

John Adams wrote in his diary in 1771 that "There is nothing to distinguish the government of Great Britain from that of France or of Spain, but the part which the people are, by the constitution, appointed to take in the passing and execution of laws. Of the legislature, the people constitute one essential branch; and, while they hold this power unlimited, and exercise it frequently, as they ought, no law can be made, and continue long in force, that is inconvenient, hurtful, or disagreeable to the mass of the society. . . . In the administration of justice, too, the people have an important share. Juries are taken, by lot or by suffrage, from the mass of the people, and no man can be condemned of life, or limb, or property, or reputation, without the concurrence of the voice of the people."[5] In 1774, Adams asserted that "The very definition of a freeman is one who is bound by no law to which he has not consented."[6]

In similar terms William Penn said: "Any government is free . . . where the laws rule, and the people are a party to those laws."[7]

John Dickinson declared in 1774 that "the freedom of a people consists in being governed by laws, in which no alteration can be made, without their consent."[8] In 1768, in his famous *Letters from a Farmer*, he had written: "For who are a free people? Not those over whom government is reasonably and equitably exercised, but those who live under a government so constitutionally checked and controlled that proper provision is made against its ever being otherwise exercised."[9]

Accordingly, it may safely be concluded that the right to popular representation in the legislature and the right to jury trial are indispensable ingredients of a free government. Such participation of a representative cross section of the public in the political and judicial process ensures fairness to all interested parties and minimizes the likelihood of arbitrary or oppressive action in either the enactment or the enforcement of laws.

[5] *The Works of John Adams*, II, 252–53. Adams notes that attacks upon the rights of juries and of free elections have always been made simultaneously.

[6] *Ibid.*, IV, 28.

[7] Frame of Government of Pennsylvania, 1682. Francis N. Thorpe, *The Federal and State Constitutions*, V, 3054.

[8] *The Political Writings of John Dickinson*, I, 403.

[9] Charles J. Stillé, *The Life and Times of John Dickinson*, 89. See also Ford, ed., *The Writings of John Dickinson*, 356 (Letter VII). As Blackstone says: "surely the true liberty of the subject consists not so much in the gracious behavior as in the limited power of the sovereign." Blackstone, *Commentaries*, IV, *433.

However excellent the substantive law of a state may be, in point of justice and wisdom, nevertheless if the enforcement procedures are inadequate, dilatory, arbitrary, or unjust, the excellence of the substantive law is of little value to the citizens. In the words of Justice Robert H. Jackson, "The right to fair trial is the right that stands guardian over all other rights."[10]

So is habeas corpus a powerful weapon for enforcing other legal rights.[11] "This one human right is the safeguard of most other human rights."[12] In states where the remedy of habeas corpus is available,[13] it ensures that in practice a person in custody receives those benefits which the law in theory accords him.[14] Habeas corpus is a practical and workable mechanism by means of which the humblest citizen can call upon the courts to give effect to the limitations placed by the constitution and laws upon the power of the government.[15]

Habeas corpus procedure enables every person who is deprived of liberty in a criminal case[16] to test in court the validity of the reason

[10] Dennis v. U.S., 339 U.S. 162, 173 (1950). As Justice Jackson said on another occasion: "Paper 'rights' are worth, when they are threatened, just what some lawyer makes them worth. Civil liberties are those which some lawyer, respected by his neighbors, will stand up to defend." 349 U.S. L.

[11] "When imprisonment is possible without explanation or redress, every form of liberty is impaired. A man in jail cannot go to church or discuss or publish or assemble or enjoy property or go to the polls." Chafee, *How Human Rights Got into the Constitution*, 51.

[12] *Ibid.*, 53.

[13] Compare the ease with which Frenchmen could be imprisoned by *lettres de cachet* before the French Revolution. While Jefferson was American envoy at Paris, a frequent guest at his house was De la Tude, who had spent thirty-five years in prison for writing a poem critical of the beauty of Mme de Pompadour, the king's mistress. Jefferson to Maria Cosway, October 12, 1786, in Jefferson, *Works*, V, 216; Jefferson, *Papers*, X, 453.

[14] Dr. Samuel Johnson regarded habeas corpus as "the single advantage our government has over that of other countries." James Boswell, *The Life of Samuel Johnson*, I, 358.

[15] Regarding the history and functioning of habeas corpus, see Chafee, *How Human Rights Got into the Constitution*, 51–74.

[16] In the case of injuries to property, as distinguished from imprisonment, the citizen does not have so efficacious a remedy against the government. The rule still persists that "the king can do no wrong," that the government is immune from suit except where specific legislation grants consent. With respect to the federal government, suits based on contracts can be brought in the Court of Claims, established in 1887. Tucker Act of March 3, 1887, 24 St. 505, 28 U.S.C. 1491. Since 1946 suit in certain negligence cases can be brought against the government, but jury trial is not granted. Federal Tort Claims Act of August 2, 1946, 60 St. 843–44, 28 U.S.C. 1346 (b), 2674,

for his detention. If the cause set forth by his jailer is insufficient in law, the prisoner must be released. Ever since the Petition of Right in 1628 it has been settled that the mere command of the executive government is not a sufficient reason to justify the imprisonment of a citizen.[17] The sovereign's pleasure is not enough. There must be proof of a violation of law, sufficient to satisfy a jury.[18] Habeas corpus thus serves to guarantee the principle, accepted since Magna Charta, that a citizen cannot be imprisoned or punished or made to suffer in body, land, or goods except after trial by jury under due process of law for a definite violation of the law of the land.[19]

However, habeas corpus is an effective remedy only against unlawful imprisonment. "But it is useless against a lawful imprisonment, however unwise or unjust. Much consequently depends on the location of the line between lawful and unlawful imprisonments. If the area of lawful imprisonments is made large, the value of habeas corpus is correspondingly lessened. The existence of the writ enables a prisoner to find out from judges where the line lies, but the writ does not fix the line. That is done by other parts of the law."[20]

Freedom of speech and the press may also be deemed essential features of a free government. In a democracy, where the people have a

---

2680. When land is taken, "just compensation" must be paid. Often officials can be sued as individuals on the theory that their illegal acts were *ultra vires* and unauthorized; and hence that such a suit is not one against the government. See pages 329 and 345 below.

[17] See note 26, pages 8–9, above.

[18] If the prisoner is in custody awaiting trial, he is entitled to a "speedy trial." If the offense is bailable, he is entitled to release on bail (and "excessive" bail shall not be required). Until recent years, the sentence of a court of competent jurisdiction, after a conviction by a jury's verdict of guilty, was always deemed a sufficient cause for detention.

[19] In his dissent in Shaughnessy v. U.S., 345 U.S. 206, 218 (1953), Justice Robert H. Jackson said: "Fortunately it is still startling, in this country, to find a person held indefinitely in executive custody without accusation of crime or judicial trial. Executive imprisonment has been considered offensive and lawless since John, at Runnymede, pledged that no free man should be imprisoned, dispossessed, outlawed, or exiled save by the judgment of his peers or by the law of the land."

[20] Chafee, *How Human Rights Got into the Constitution*, 72. Thus it has been by expanding the area of federally protected constitutional rights that the Supreme Court has correspondingly enlarged the scope of federal habeas corpus under 22 U.S.C. 2242, and encouraged a flood of unmeritorious applications for habeas corpus by inmates of penal institutions who are in prison by virtue of the sentence of a court after conviction by a jury. This "trivializes the great writ." Brown v. Allen, 344 U.S. 443, 532–36 (1953). See page 364 below.

voice in the law-making function, both freedom of discussion and a comprehensive system of public education are necessary for the successful operation of the system.[21] The value to society of free inquiry and unrestricted search for truth has been recognized and proclaimed by thinkers throughout the ages.[22]

The kindred right of freedom of religion is prized not so much as a necessary prerequisite to the effective functioning of democratic institutions but as an end in itself. For centuries martyrs have faced persecution and death rather than forsake their innermost convictions and the sacred tenets of their faith. Indeed, it was because men struggled valiantly for religious freedom that they won political liberty.[23]

[21] Dumbauld, *The Political Writings of Thomas Jefferson*, 93.

[22] Forceful utterances proclaiming the importance of freedom to think and to speak have been made from time to time by Hebrew prophets and Greek philosophers, by John Milton, by Thomas Jefferson, by John Stuart Mill, by Justices Holmes and Brandeis, and by Professor Zechariah Chafee. Dumbauld, *The Bill of Rights and What It Means Today*, 147–52.

[23] "Political liberty is the residuary legatee of ecclesiastical animosities." Figgis, *Studies of Political Thought from Gerson to Grotius*, 118.

Constitutional Rights before Independence

LONG before the venerable document entitled the Constitution of the United States was drawn up in 1787 at Philadelphia, there existed in America a constitution. This was true both in the sense that there was in force a fundamental law and in the sense that there had been established a form of polity which comprehended certain essential features of free government.

Many instances of use of the word "constitution" before that date can be found.[1] Statesmen of the pre-Revolutionary period often claimed constitutional rights derived from principles of the unwritten British constitution. The Declaration of Independence itself spoke of "our Constitution."[2] The report of the Annapolis convention, where delegates of five states met in 1786 to discuss regulation of trade and commerce, proposed calling a convention of all the states "to devise such further provisions as shall appear to them necessary to render the constitution of the Foederal [sic] Government adequate to the exigencies of the Union."[3]

Earlier in the same year Jefferson, when explaining certain peculiar provisions of the Articles of Confederation to a French writer, said: "Perhaps it might have been better when they were forming the federal constitution, to have assimilated it as much as possible to the particular constitutions of the states. All of these have distributed the Legislative, executive and judiciary powers into different departments. In the federal constitution the judiciary powers are separated from the others; but the legislative and executive are both exercised by Congress."[4]

[1] For earlier use of the term "constitutio" in Roman law as meaning a statutory enactment as distinguished from custom, see Charles H. McIlwain, Constitutionalism: Ancient and Modern, 23–25; and Jefferson, Notes on the State of Virginia, 201–202.

[2] Dumbauld, The Declaration of Independence and What It Means Today, 119–24. In Jefferson's Summary View of the Rights of British America in 1774 he referred to the British Parliament as "a body of men, foreign to our constitutions, and unacknowledged by our laws." Ibid., 120.

[3] Charles C. Tansill, ed., Documents, 43.

[4] Answers to Démeunier, circa January 24, 1786, in Jefferson, Papers, X, 22–23. See also pages 33 and 110 below. Regarding tribunals set up by the old Congress, see J. C. Bancroft Davis, "Federal Courts Prior to the Adoption of the Constitution," 131 U.S. xix (1889) [Appendix].

And Richard Henry Lee hoped for beneficial alterations "in our federal constitution" as a result of the Philadelphia convention.[5]

A notable instance where rights under the British constitution were claimed by Americans occurred when the cabinet of George Grenville procured the enactment by Parliament of the Stamp Act of March 22, 1765, for the purpose of raising revenue from America in order to relieve the burdens of English taxpayers. This legislation provoked a storm of opposition. Nine colonies sent delegates to a congress which met at New York. That body on October 19, 1765, adopted fourteen resolutions protesting the tax as unconstitutional and petitioning for its repeal. Similar sentiments had been voiced by the Virginia House of Burgesses as a result of the eloquent oratory of Patrick Henry.[6]

Taxation without consent and denial of jury trial were the principal violations of their constitutional rights which were enumerated in the Stamp Act resolutions. After claiming that American subjects of the king were entitled to all the "inherent rights and privileges" of subjects born in Great Britain,[7] the resolutions declared "that it is inseparably essential to the freedom of a people, and the undoubted right of Englishmen, that no taxes should be imposed on them, but with their own consent, given personally or by their representatives,"[8] and "that the only representatives of the people of these colonies, are persons chosen therein, by themselves; and that no taxes ever have been, or can be constitutionally imposed on them, but by their respective legislatures."[9] It was further stated "that all supplies to the crown, being free gifts of the people, it is unreasonable and inconsistent with the principles and spirit of the British constitution, for the people of Great Britain to grant to his majesty the property of the colonists."[10]

It was next proclaimed "that trial by jury is the inherent and invaluable right of every British subject in these colonies."[11]

The Stamp Act, the resolutions then pointed out, both imposed taxes on the colonists without representation and deprived them of

[5] Lee to George Mason, May 15, 1787, in Lee, *Letters of Richard Henry Lee*, II, 419.

[6] Dumbauld, *The Declaration of Independence and What It Means Today*, 4.

[7] Second resolution.   [8] Third resolution.

[9] Fifth resolution. The fourth resolution pointed out "that the people of the colonies are not, and from their local circumstances cannot be, represented in the house of commons in Great Britain."

[10] Sixth resolution.   [11] Seventh resolution.

trial by jury ("by extending the jurisdiction of the courts of admiralty beyond its ancient limits," no jury trial being available in those courts.)[12] Hence it was doubly violative of the constitutional rights of Americans.

Even more significant than the constitutional claims urged against the validity of the Stamp Act were the propositions enunciated by the First Continental Congress, which met at Carpenters' Hall in Philadelphia on September 5, 1774. It sat until October 26, 1774, and may well be regarded as the first federal government in the United States. On October 14, 1774, the Congress adopted a set of ten resolutions embodying a declaration of constitutional rights claimed by the colonies and alleged to have been infringed by legislation of Parliament enacted since the end of the Seven Years' War in 1763.[13]

Invoking "the principles of the English Constitution," the Americans declared that they were "entitled to life, liberty, & property" and that these could not be disposed of "without their consent."[14]

Then was proclaimed the fundamental principle "that the foundation of English liberty, and of all free government, is a right in the people to participate in their legislative council."[15]

The Congress went on to claim for the colonies the benefit of the common law, especially "the great and inestimable privilege" of being tried by a jury "of the vicinage."[16]

It was also declared to be illegal to interfere with the right of the people peaceably to assemble and petition for redress of grievances,[17] or to keep a standing army in time of peace.[18]

---

[12] Eighth resolution. Other resolutions attacked the expediency of the legislation, pointing out its burdensome nature and the harm it would cause to British merchants.

[13] Dumbauld, *The Declaration of Independence and What It Means Today*, 7–9; *Journals of the Continental Congress*, I, 63–73.

[14] First resolution. The next two resolutions declared that "our ancestors" when they emigrated were entitled to all the rights of "free and natural-born subjects within the realm of England" and did not lose any of such rights by emigration.

[15] Fourth resolution. Exclusive legislation "in all cases of taxation and internal polity" was claimed for the local legislatures, although "we cheerfully consent" to regulation of external commerce by Parliament, "excluding every idea of taxation, internal or external, for raising a revenue on the subjects in America, without their consent."

[16] Fifth resolution. The benefit of English statutes applicable to local circumstances was also claimed (Sixth resolution), as were the immunities and privileges granted by royal charters or the codes of provincial laws (Seventh resolution).

[17] Eighth resolution.   [18] Ninth resolution.

In conclusion, the resolutions asserted the principle of separation of powers: "It is indispensably necessary to good government, and rendered essential by the English constitution, that the constituent branches of the legislature be independent of each other; that, therefore, the exercise of legislative power in several colonies, by a council appointed, during pleasure, by the crown, is unconstitutional, dangerous, and destructive to the freedom of American legislation."[19]

The Declaration of Independence, adopted on July 4, 1776, was patterned in part upon the British Bill of Rights, and may be regarded as a vindication of constitutional privileges which had been infringed by the British government in "a long train of Abuses and Usurpations."[20] The American Revolution may properly be considered as a constitutional conflict.[21]

[19] Tenth resolution. The Congress went on to enumerate violations of the foregoing rights since 1763 and to adopt "peaceable measures" for obtaining redress by curtailing trade with Great Britain and appealing to the British king and people.

[20] Dumbauld, *The Declaration of Independence and What It Means Today*, 21–22.

[21] Charles H. McIlwain, *The American Revolution: A Constitutional Interpretation*, 5, 16–17, 187, 193, 196. The legal controversy soon became a military contest. Neither side recognized the possibilities of federalism as a solution of their difficulties, although American political thinkers had long contended that constitutionally the colonies were connected with the central government and with each other only through the crown. Dumbauld, *The Declaration of Independence and What It Means Today*, 31–32, 120–22.

The American Constitution after Independence

F ROM the Declaration of Independence to the adoption of the Articles of Confederation on March 1, 1781, there was no written constitution fixing the powers of Congress. From the fact that these powers were indefinite it does not follow, however, that they were unlimited.[1]

The task of Congress was largely one of providing political solidarity and unified leadership. It could accomplish whatever its sovereign constituent states were willing to co-operate in achieving, just as an international organization today can take effective action of almost any character when it is genuinely supported by a united public opinion directing the policies of its component governments.

Operating under such a flexible unwritten constitution, based upon popular acquiescence and political expediency, Congress was bolder in its exercise of authority during the early days of the Revolution than it became after the Articles of Confederation finally took effect.[2] "Prior to that event, the power of Congress was measured by the exigencies of the war, and derived its sanction from the acquiescence of the States."[3]

It is a difficult question to determine whether the adoption of the Articles made any change in the location of sovereignty or whether the situation prevailing under the prior unwritten constitution continued without modification. It seems most probable that no change was effected.

It was quite clear, however, that under the Articles of Confederation each state was free, sovereign, and independent. The language of the instrument expressly described the Confederation as a "league"[4]

---

[1] Dumbauld, *The Declaration of Independence and What It Means Today*, 32.

[2] The Articles of Confederation did not go into force until Maryland ratified them, after that state was satisfied with the cession of western lands to the national government by the larger states.

[3] Madison to Andrew Stevenson, November 27, 1830, in Madison, *Writings*, IX, 419. Madison went on to say: "After that event, habit and a continued expediency, amounting often to a real or apparent necessity, prolonged the exercise of an undefined authority; which was the more readily overlooked, as . . . its acts . . . depended for their efficacy on the will of the States."

30

and declared that "Every State retains its sovereignty, freedom and independence, and every power, jurisdiction and right, which is not by this confederation expressly delegated to the United States, in Congress assembled."[5]

[4] Article III. In the terminology of German political theorists, the Confederation was a *Staatenbund*, not a *Bundesstaat*. Josef Kunz, *Die Staatenverbindungen*, 595–713. See page 41 below.

[5] Article II. This wording resulted from an amendment sponsored by Thomas Burke of North Carolina, which modified an earlier provision drafted by John Dickinson, a conservative who favored a strong central government vested with sovereign power. Merrill Jensen, *The Articles of Confederation*, 130, 167–69, 174–76.

Defects of the Articles of Confederation

THERE were serious defects in the form of government established by the Articles of Confederation. To be sure, conditions under the Confederation were not so desperate as is often asserted. As testy Senator William Maclay of Pennsylvania wrote in 1791: "It has been usual with declamatory gentlemen, in their praises of the present Government, by way of contrast, to paint the state of the country under the old Congress as if neither wood grew nor water ran in America before the happy adoption of the new Constitution."[1] Jefferson, while abroad in the diplomatic service, observed that in spite of all the defects of federal and state constitutions, a comparison of American governments with those of Europe is "like a comparison of heaven and hell."[2]

But no one was more acutely aware of certain weaknesses in the Confederation than Jefferson at his post in Paris. He had personally experienced the harmful effect of conflicting state policies upon the conduct of foreign affairs, and knew how detrimental it was to American interests and prestige abroad. His attempts to negotiate commercial treaties in Europe had been paralyzed because foreign nations lacked confidence in the ability of the American government to fulfill its obligations. Much of his time was spent in persuading European bankers to advance money in order to provide for payment of his own salary and other obligations of the government. On occasion his diplomatic duties required him to answer complaints of treaty violation by states. It was painfully clear to Jefferson that the federal government lacked adequate power to regulate commerce and to raise revenue by taxation.[3]

Moreover, having been a member of Congress, he was quite familiar with its exasperating procedural shortcomings. Voting was by states, and on many questions the vote of nine states was necessary in order

---

[1] *Journal of William Maclay*, 411. See also *ibid.*, 321. George Washington and Benjamin Franklin also spoke optimistically of conditions in America under the old constitution. Merrill Jensen, *The New Nation*, 248–55.

[2] Jefferson to Joseph Jones, August 14, 1787, in Jefferson, *Papers*, XII, 34. See also Jefferson to Edward Carrington, August 4, 1787, in *ibid.*, XI, 678; and Jefferson to George Washington, August 14, 1787, in *ibid.*, XII, 36.

[3] Dumbauld, "Thomas Jefferson and American Constitutional Law," *loc. cit.*, 385–86.

to take action; but many states failed to maintain their representatives at the seat of government. There was no separation of powers, and the attention of Congress was often dissipated upon trifles while important matters were neglected.[4]

Accordingly, Jefferson hoped for three "ameliorations . . . in our federal constitution." He wished to "make our states one" as to "whatever may concern another state, or any foreign nation," while keeping them separate "in whatever concerns themselves alone." He also desired "to give to the federal head some peaceable mode of enforcing their just authority" and "to organize that head" into separate legislative, executive, and judicial departments.[5]

Of these, the power over commerce was the most important. The supposed lack of coercive power to compel delinquent states to comply with their obligations he believed was conferred "by the law of nature, which authorizes one party to an agreement to compel the other to performance."[6] With respect to the need for separate legislative, executive, and judicial departments, it is noteworthy that throughout the Philadelphia convention of 1787 many members emphasized the impropriety of vesting extensive powers in a body so defectively organized as the old Congress.[7]

Alexander Hamilton, who was later to become Jefferson's political adversary when the new Constitution had been adopted, voiced similar views regarding the modifications needed in the Articles of Confederation:

"The confederation in my opinion should give Congress complete sovereignty; except as to that part of internal police, which relates to the rights of property and life among individuals and to raising money

[4] Answers to Démeunier, January 24, 1786, in Jefferson, *Papers*, X, 14–16, 21–23; Jefferson to Edward Carrington, August 4, 1787, in *ibid.*, XI, 679. For separation of powers, see page 26 above.

[5] Jefferson to George Washington, August 14, 1787, and to George Wythe, September 16, 1787, in *ibid.*, XII, 36, 128–29. See also Jefferson to John Blair, August 13, 1787, and to Francis dal Verme, August 15, 1787, in *ibid.*, 28, 42–43.

[6] Jefferson to Edmund Randolph, August 3, 1787, and to Edward Carrington, August 4, 1787, in *ibid.*, XI, 672, 678. See also Answers to Démeunier, January 24, 1786, in *ibid.*, X, 19.

[7] Farrand, *Records*, I, 34 (Butler, May 30); I, 253 (Wilson, June 16); I, 287 (Hamilton, June 18); I, 339 (Mason, June 20); II, 666 (letter to Congress, September 17). John Jay wrote in similar vein to John Adams on May 12, 1787. Charles Warren, *The Making of the Constitution*, 815.

by internal taxes. It is necessary, that every thing, belonging to this, should be regulated by the state legislatures. Congress should have complete sovereignty in all that relates to war, peace, trade, finance, and to the management of foreign affairs, the right of declaring war of raising armies, officering, paying them, directing their motions in every respect, of equipping fleets and doing the same with them, of building fortifications arsenals magazines &c. &c., of making peace on such conditions as they think proper, of regulating trade, determining with what countries it shall be carried on, granting indulgencies laying prohibitions on all the articles of export or import, imposing duties granting bounties & premiums for raising exporting importing and applying to their own use the product of these duties, only giving credit to the states on whom they are raised in the general account of revenues and expences, instituting Admiralty Courts &c., of coining money, establishing banks on such terms, and with such privileges as they think proper, appropriating funds and doing whatever else relates to the operations of finance, transacting every thing with foreign nations, making alliances offensive and defensive, treaties of commerce, &c. &c."[8]

In Congress itself the need of amendments conferring additional powers had been recognized. Madison was a member of a committee which reported on May 2, 1781, regarding this subject.[9] Another committee on August 22, 1781, presented a long list of twenty-one needed reforms.[10] On August 7, 1786, a set of seven proposed amendments designed to "render the federal government adequate to the ends for which it was instituted" was offered by a committee on which Charles Pinckney of South Carolina served.[11] All these efforts proved fruitless.

Perhaps the most thorough and detailed analysis of the "vices" of the system of government established under the Articles of Confederation was that prepared by Madison early in 1787.[12] He enumerated the following evils: (1) failure of the states to comply with the

[8] Hamilton to James Duane, September 3, 1780, in *Papers of Alexander Hamilton*, I, 407–408.

[9] Duane and Varnum were his colleagues. *Journals of the Continental Congress*, XX, 469–71.

[10] *Ibid.*, XXI, 894–96. This committee was composed of Varnum, Ellsworth, and Randolph. See also Irving Brant, *James Madison*, II, 118–19.

[11] *Journals of the Continental Congress*, XXXI, 494–98.

[12] In April, 1787, Madison outlined in a memorandum entitled "Vices of the Political system of the U. States" eleven principal shortcomings experienced under the Articles of Confederation. *Writings of James Madison*, II, 361–69.

constitutional requisitions; (2) encroachments by the states on the federal authority; (3) violations by the states of the law of nations and of treaties; (4) trespasses by the states on the rights of each other; (5) want of concert in matters where common interest requires it; (6) want of guaranty to the states of their constitutions and laws against internal violence; (7) want of sanction to the laws, and of coercion in the government of the Confederacy; (8) want of ratification by the people of the Articles of Confederation; (9) multiplicity; (10) mutability; and (11) injustice in the laws of the states.

It will be noted that Madison included in his list of defects the lack of protection for creditors against paper money and other legislation permitting withdrawal of legal remedies, or permitting installment payments, or tender of property in payment of debts. Madison, Mason, Richard Henry Lee, and many other leaders keenly felt the injustice of state legislation impairing property and contract rights.[13] The excesses of state legislatures with respect to measures of this sort were extremely influential in causing certain groups to support the proposal for a new constitution.[14] Contrary views on the part of those favorable to debtors were regarded by Madison as the true motive of opposition to the Constitution of 1787 by its adversaries. "The articles [of the Constitution] relating to Treaties, to paper money, and to contracts, created more enemies than all the errors in the System, positive & negative put together."[15]

Believing that Virginia would be expected to take the initiative in furnishing proposals for discussion at the Philadelphia convention, Madison elaborated in a "systematic" plan his ideas regarding the constitutional reforms which he considered necessary.[16] His scheme was outlined in a tactful letter to Governor Randolph.[17]

Fundamental propositions advanced by Madison were: (1) that the new system be founded upon ratification by the people rather than

[13] Brant, *James Madison*, II, 362–63; Warren, *The Making of the Constitution*, 165–66, 301. Farrand, *Records*, I, 134 (June 6); I, 154 (June 7); II, 110 (July 25).

[14] Edward S. Corwin, "The Progress of Constitutional Theory between the Declaration of Independence and the Meeting of the Philadelphia Convention," *American Historical Review*, Vol. XXX, No. 3 (April, 1925), 513, 533.

[15] Madison to Jefferson, October 17, 1788, in Madison, *Writings*, V, 271.

[16] Madison to Edmund Randolph, April 8, 1787, in *ibid.*, II, 337.

[17] *Ibid.*, II, 338–40. The plan was also set forth in letters to Jefferson, March 19, 1787, and to Washington, April 16, 1787, in *ibid.*, II, 326–27, 344–49.

by the legislatures of the states; (2) a federal negative upon state legislation in all cases whatsoever; (3) representation in proportion to population; (4) separation of powers, including a national executive in some form (and perhaps including a Council of Revision).[18]

The plan also provided: (5) that the federal government should have all the existing powers conferred upon it under the Articles of Confederation, and should in addition have positive and complete authority "in all cases which require uniformity," such as regulation of trade, taxation, and naturalization; (6) that the federal judiciary should have jurisdiction in admiralty and of appeals in all cases involving foreigners or diversity of citizenship, and that state judges should be bound by their oaths to support the federal constitution; (7) a guarantee of the states against internal as well as external dangers;[19] (8) that state executive departments should be appointed by the federal government, and that the militia should be under federal control; and (9) that the right of coercion should be expressly declared.[20]

The immediate occasion for the calling of the Philadelphia convention was the failure of an earlier meeting at Annapolis. The necessity of concerted action among the states with reference to regulation of trade led to the appointment by Virginia of a commission to meet with representatives of other states "to consider how far a uniform system in their commercial regulations may be necessary to their common interest and their permanent harmony; and to report to the several States, such an act relative to this great object, as, when unanimously ratified by them, will enable the United States in Congress, effectually to provide for the same."[21] Twelve commissioners from five states met

[18] These four propositions were contained in all three of the letters mentioned in note 17 above. The national executive and Council of Revision were mentioned in the letters to Randolph and Washington. The Council of Revision was a feature of the New York constitution which appealed to Jefferson. Edward Dumbauld, *The Political Writings of Thomas Jefferson*, 46. See page 41 below. Concerning Madison's pet idea of a federal negative, see pages 39 and 50 below.

[19] The three preceding propositions were mentioned only in the letters to Randolph and Washington.

[20] The last two propositions were mentioned only in the letter to Washington. These variations in the three statements of the plan show how it was becoming more detailed in Madison's mind as time went on. For coercion, see notes 5 and 6 above, and page 41 below.

[21] Tansill, *Documents*, 38; Brant, *James Madison*, II, 381; and Douglas S. Freeman, *George Washington*, VI, 66.

at Annapolis in September, 1786. In view of the fact that so few states were represented, they decided not to proceed with the business of their mission. Instead they proposed that all the states appoint commissioners to meet in Philadelphia on the second Monday of May, 1787, "to devise such further provisions as shall appear to them necessary to render the constitution of the Foederal Government adequate to the exigencies of the Union; and to report such an Act for that purpose to the United States in Congress assembled, as when agreed to, by them, and afterwards confirmed by the Legislatures of every State, will effectually provide for the same."[22]

After some wrangling, Congress approved the proposal on February 21, 1787, in the following terms: "Resolved that in the opinion of Congress it is expedient that on the second Monday in May next a Convention of delegates who shall have been appointed by the several states be held at Philadelphia for the sole and express purpose of revising the Articles of Confederation and reporting to Congress and the several legislatures such alterations and provisions therein as shall when agreed to in Congress and confirmed by the states render the federal constitution adequate to the exigencies of Government & the preservation of the Union."[23]

---

[22] Tansill, *Documents*, 40–43. See also Brant, *James Madison*, II, 387. Only New York, New Jersey, Pennsylvania, Delaware, and Virginia were represented at Annapolis. "The entire purpose for which the delegates assembled at Annapolis, was to devise means for the uniform regulation of trade. They found no means but in a general government; and they recommended a convention to accomplish that purpose. Over whatever other interests of the country this government may diffuse its benefits, and its blessings, it will always be true, as matter of historical fact, that it had its immediate origin in the necessities of commerce." Daniel Webster's argument in Gibbons v. Ogden, 9 Wheat. 1, 12–13 (1824). See also Brown v. Maryland, 12 Wheat. 419, 446 (1827).

[23] Tansill, *Documents*, 46. See Madison to Edmund Pendleton, February 24, 1787, in Madison, *Writings*, II, 317–18.

The Work of the Constitutional Convention

FIFTY-FIVE delegates from twelve states assembled in Philadelphia during the summer of 1787 and formulated the Constitution by which the United States has been governed for more than a century and a half.[1] The members of the convention were statesmen of high ability. Jefferson described the gathering as "really an assembly of demigods."[2] The fruitfulness of their deliberations was doubtless furthered by the rule adopted preserving secrecy.[3] This enabled members to change their minds without embarrassment.

On Monday, May 14, 1787, the date appointed for the convening of the body, Virginia and Pennsylvania were the only states represented. While awaiting the arrival of a quorum, the Virginia delegates, knowing that specific proposals would be expected from them because of their state's initiative in promoting the convention, formulated what is commonly known as the "Virginia Plan."[4] Not until May 25 were the necessary seven states represented. On that day George Washington was chosen as president of the convention and Major William Jackson

[1] Farrand, *Records*, III, 555–90, lists the names of the delegates, reproduces their credentials, and shows the dates of their attendance. Rhode Island sent no delegates. Those from New Hampshire did not arrive until July 23, 1787. There were never more than eleven states represented at any one time. Warren, *The Making of the Constitution*, 124.

[2] Jefferson to John Adams, August 30, 1787, in Jefferson, *Papers*, XII, 69. There was one delegate whose presence, though he only once spoke from the floor, was indispensable to the adoption of the Constitution. That was George Washington. Benjamin Franklin's benignant urbanity was also influential. If the influence of members is to be measured by the frequency with which they spoke, the leading figures in the convention were Gouverneur Morris, who made 173 speeches; James Wilson, 168; James Madison, 161; Roger Sherman of Connecticut, 138; George Mason, 136; Elbridge Gerry, 119. Warren, *The Making of the Constitution*, 125. For sketches of the principal delegates, see *ibid.*, 56–61; Farrand, *Records*, III, 87–97; and Brant, *James Madison*, III, 156–69.

[3] The rules were adopted on May 28. Farrand, *Records*, I, 7–9. Several additional rules, including those relating to secrecy and reconsideration of matters determined by a majority, were adopted the following day. *Ibid.*, I, 15–16. Jefferson disapproved of the secrecy rule. Jefferson to Adams, August 30, 1787, in Jefferson, *Papers*, XII, 69.

[4] Warren, *The Making of the Constitution*, 101, 111–12. It will be noted how closely the plan corresponded to Madison's program of needed reforms. See pages 35–36 above.

as secretary. A committee to prepare rules was named, and doorkeepers were appointed.[5] On May 29, ten states being represented, the Virginia Plan was presented to the convention by Governor Edmund Randolph.[6] Charles Pinckney of South Carolina, one of the youngest of the delegates, also submitted a plan embodying his ideas. The two drafts were referred to the Committee of the Whole.[7]

The Virginia Plan contemplated a "National Legislature" of two branches, the first elected by the people of the several states, the other elected by the first branch from persons nominated by state legislatures. The states were not to be represented equally in the Legislature, but representation was to be "proportioned to the Quotas of contribution, or to the number of free inhabitants." The Legislature was to be empowered to enjoy the existing "Legislative Rights vested in Congress by the Confederation & moreover to legislate in all cases to which the separate States are incompetent, or in which the harmony of the United States may be interrupted by the exercise of individual Legislation; to negative all laws passed by the several States, contravening in the opinion of the National Legislature the articles of Union; and to call forth the force of the Union agst. any member of the Union failing to fulfil its duty under the articles thereof."

Provision was made for establishment of a "National Executive" (to be chosen by the National Legislature), entrusted with "general authority to execute the National laws," in addition to the existing executive powers "vested in Congress by the Confederation." A "National Judiciary" to consist of "one or more supreme tribunals, and of inferior tribunals to be chosen by the National Legislature" was to have jurisdiction of "piracies & felonies on the high seas, captures from an enemy; cases in which foreigners or citizens of other States . . . may be interested, or which respect the collection of the National revenue; impeachments of any National officers, and questions which may involve

[5] Farrand, *Records*, I, 2–4. The rules committee was composed of George Wythe of Virginia, Alexander Hamilton of New York, and Charles Pinckney of South Carolina. Its report was adopted on May 28. *Ibid.*, I, 7–9.

[6] *Ibid.*, I, 16. For the text of the fifteen resolutions making up the Virginia Plan, see *ibid.*, I, 20–22. Concerning the sources of the text, see *ibid.*, III, 593–94, and Warren, *The Making of the Constitution*, 140. The text is also given in Jonathan Elliot, *Debates*, IV, 41–43; William M. Meigs, *The Growth of the Constitution*, 325–27; and Tansill, *Documents*, 116–19.

[7] Farrand, *Records*, I, 16. Regarding the contents of Pinckney's plan, see the articles by John Franklin Jameson listed in the Bibliography.

39

the national peace and harmony." A "council of revision" composed of "the Executive and a convenient number of the National Judiciary" was to be authorized to exercise a suspensive veto over acts of the National Legislature and over the exercise by the National Legislature of the federal negative upon state legislation.

Other resolutions in the Virginia Plan called for admission of new states by less than unanimous vote, guarantee of "a Republican Government & the territory of each State," provision for amendment of the Constitution without assent of the National Legislature, and for requiring "the Legislative Executive & Judiciary powers within the several States" to be bound "by oath to support the articles of Union." Transitional provisions called for continuance of the old Congress until the new government took effect and "for the completion of all their engagements," as well as for adoption of the new constitution by assemblies "expressly chosen by the people" for that purpose.

The Randolph resolutions were debated and revised in Committee of the Whole[8] from May 30 until June 13, when the Committee of the Whole rose and reported to the convention a set of nineteen resolutions.[9] When the Virginia Plan had been thus perfected, the convention adjourned on the following day, upon motion of William Paterson of New Jersey, in order that the plan as reported might be studied, and opportunity given for the preparation of "one purely federal."[10] Such a "federal" plan, limited strictly to amendments to the old Articles of Confederation, was submitted by Paterson on July 15. It is commonly called the "New Jersey Plan." It contained nine resolutions.[11] It was referred to the Committee of the Whole, together with the previous report, which was recommitted.[12]

---

[8] Nathaniel Gorham of Massachusetts, who had presided over the old Congress, replaced George Washington in the chair while the Committee of the Whole was deliberating.

[9] Farrand, *Records*, I, 224–32, 234–37. The text is also printed in Meigs, *The Growth of the Constitution*, 328–30; Elliot, *Debates*, V, 76–78; Tansill, *Documents*, 201–203.

[10] Farrand, *Records*, I, 240.

[11] *Ibid.*, I, 242–45. See also *ibid.*, III, 611–16, and Warren, *The Making of the Constitution*, 221, regarding texts of the New Jersey Plan. It is also printed in Meigs, *The Growth of the Constitution*, 330–33; Elliot, *Debates*, V, 70–72; Tansill, *Documents*, 204–209.

[12] Farrand, *Records*, I, 241–42.

On May 30, when debate on Randolph's proposals began, he proposed, as a substitute for the first of his fifteen resolutions, a declaration that "an union of the States, merely foederal, will not accomplish the objects proposed" by the Articles of Confederation, namely, "common defence, security of liberty, and general welfare."[13] A second substitute, which he then offered, was adopted, declaring "that a national government ought to be established consisting of a supreme legislative, judiciary and executive."[14]

The term "federal," as used by Randolph, Paterson, and other members of the convention, is descriptive of the nature of a mere league or federation of independent sovereignties (*Staatenbund*), as distinguished from a government operating directly upon individuals (*Bundesstaat*).[15] It is altogether unlikely that any of the proponents of the Virginia Plan favored the complete "consolidation" of political power in a unitary national government, with the consequent abolition of the states.[16] Indeed, Madison had pointed out before the convention met that such complete consolidation "into one simple republic would be as inexpedient as it is unattainable."[17]

Madison favored direct operation of the central government upon individual citizens, and abandoned as impracticable the notion of coercing delinquent states by the use of force.[18] The Council of Revision was another provision of the Virginia Plan which was scrapped. In place of it a proposal by Elbridge Gerry of Massachusetts to give the execu-

---

[13] The first resolution was simply a general statement that the Articles of Confederation should be "so corrected & enlarged" as to accomplish their objects. Farrand, *Records*, I, 20.

[14] *Ibid.*, I, 30.

[15] Not until later did "Federalist" come to mean a supporter of the new Constitution. For an explanation of the terms by Madison, see Farrand, *Records*, II, 93 (July 23).

[16] *Ibid.*, I, 137 (June 6), 153 (June 7), 322–23 (June 19). However, Alexander Hamilton would have been willing to abolish the states. *Ibid.*, I, 287, 323 (June 18 and 19). So would Read of Delaware. *Ibid.*, I, 463 (June 29). Henry Knox, outside the convention, was equally desirous of that measure. Warren, *The Making of the Constitution*, 308. Paterson argued that as a precedent to establishment of a national government, state lines should be done away with and all territory divided equally into new districts. Farrand, *Records*, I, 178, 251 (June 9 and 16). Wilson and Madison regarded this as impracticable. *Ibid.*, I, 180, 321 (June 9 and 19).

[17] *Writings*, II, 344. See note 17, page 35, above.

[18] Farrand, *Records*, I, 54 (May 31); I, 165 (June 8); II, 4 (July 4). See also comments of Wilson and Randolph, *ibid.*, I, 252, 256 (June 16).

tive a veto on legislation, unless overruled by a two-thirds vote in each branch of the Legislature, was adopted.[19]

With respect to the judiciary, a compromise was reached empowering, but not requiring, the Legislature to establish inferior federal courts. John Rutledge of South Carolina had opposed the creation of "any national tribunal except a single supreme one." He preferred decision of all cases by state courts in the first instance.[20] Consideration of the scope of federal jurisdiction and the method of appointing judges was postponed for the time being. Benjamin Franklin in that connection gave an entertaining account of a method of selection used in Scotland, where the lawyers always chose the ablest of the profession in order to get rid of him and share his practice among themselves.[21]

There was extensive debate regarding the method of electing representatives and of choosing the executive. Election of one branch of the Legislature by the people, the mode strongly favored by Madison and George Mason of Virginia as well as by James Wilson of Pennsylvania, was finally accepted, over the opposition of Roger Sherman of Connecticut and Elbridge Gerry of Massachusetts.[22] Wilson also advocated election of the executive by the people, through a system of electors, though he feared that this plan might be thought "chimerical."[23] But election by the Legislature, for a seven-year term, was the method decided upon.[24] Wilson's proposal that the executive "consist of a single person" was accepted.[25]

[19] *Ibid.*, I, 104 (June 4). Two later attempts by Wilson to revive the Council of Revision were unsuccessful. *Ibid.*, I, 138–40 (June 6); II, 73–80 (July 21). So was an attempt by Madison. *Ibid.*, II, 298 (August 15). See note 18, page 36, above. It was in speaking against the Council of Revision, in which judges would have passed upon the wisdom of legislation, that Gerry first mentioned the power of the judiciary to declare legislation unconstitutional. *Ibid.*, I, 97–98 (June 4). Rufus King of Massachusetts supported Gerry's position. See page 104 below.

[20] *Ibid.*, I, 119, 124–25 (June 5). Elimination of federal courts of first instance except for admiralty matters was one of the proposed amendments to the Constitution desired by Virginia and several other states. Dumbauld, *The Bill of Rights and What It Means Today*, 25.

[21] Farrand, *Records*, I, 120 (June 5).

[22] *Ibid.*, I, 48–50 (May 31).

[23] *Ibid.*, 68, 80 (June 1 and 2). Ultimately, of course, this plan (see Constitution, Art. II, sec. 1, cl. 2 through cl. 4) was adopted. *Ibid.*, II, 528–29 (September 6).

[24] *Ibid.*, I, 69, 81 (June 1 and 2).

[25] *Ibid.*, I, 65, 97 (June 1 and 4). Randolph and Mason were strongly opposed to the proposal for a single executive.

Sherman had favored leaving the organization of the executive department to the Legislature. Since he "considered the Executive magistracy as nothing more than an institution for carrying the will of the Legislature into effect," he concluded "that the person or persons ought to be appointed by and accountable to the Legislature only, which was the despository [*sic*] of the supreme will of the Society. As they were the best judges of the business which ought to be done by the Executive department, and consequently of the number necessary from time to time for doing it, he wished the number might not be fixed, but that the legislature should be at liberty to appoint one or more as experience might dictate." Executive independence of the legislature was in his opinion "the very essence of tyranny."[26]

To the state legislatures was given the task of electing the members of the Senate.[27] Heated debate[28] arose over the method of representation in the two branches of the Legislature. It was finally voted that representation in the more numerous branch should be in proportion to population, counting slaves as three-fifths; and that states should not have equal voting power in the Senate, but that the same rule should apply there as had been adopted for the other branch of the Legislature.[29]

Supporters of the New Jersey Plan rejected the elaborate structure thus fashioned by the Committee of the Whole in its report on the revised Virginia Plan. The New Jersey Plan simply proposed to retain the old Congress, but to give it several additional powers,[30] and to

---

[26] *Ibid.*, I, 65, 68 (June 1).

[27] This proposal was made by John Dickinson. *Ibid.*, I, 149, 156 (June 7). For convenience the term "Senate" is used rather than "second branch of the National Legislature," although the former appellation (as well as "House of Representatives") did not officially appear in the proceedings of the convention until the report of the Committee of Detail on August 6. Before that time, however, Wilson and Madison had spoken of the "Senate." *Ibid.*, I, 151, 233 (June 7 and 13).

[28] In which Paterson and Wilson clashed. *Ibid.*, I, 176–80, 183 (June 9).

[29] *Ibid.*, I, 193, 201–202 (June 11). On June 11, Roger Sherman proposed for the first time what was later called the "Connecticut Compromise," that the states should have equal voting power in the Senate, but not in the House. *Ibid.*, I, 196.

[30] The new powers were (1) to raise a revenue by import duties, stamp tax, and postage; (2) to regulate trade and commerce "as well with foreign nations as with each other," provided that all judicial proceedings against violators of federal enactments must be commenced in state courts, with federal appellate review as to both law and fact. *Ibid.*, I, 243 (June 15).

authorize it to elect "a federal Executive" to consist of an unspecified number of persons.[31] The executive, in turn, was to be empowered to appoint "a supreme Tribunal" with original jurisdiction of "all impeachments of federal officers," but only appellate jurisdiction in other matters of federal concern.[32] It was also proclaimed that Acts of Congress made in pursuance of delegated powers and treaties made under the authority of the United States "shall be the supreme law of the respective States . . . and that the Judiciary of the several States shall be bound thereby in their decisions, any thing in the respective laws of the Individual States to the contrary notwithstanding"; and that in case of any opposition to execution of such acts or treaties, "the federal Executive shall be authorized to call forth ye power of the Confederated States, or so much thereof as may be necessary" to compel obedience thereto.[33]

Except with respect to import duties, stamp taxes, and postage charges, the old method of raising revenue by requisitions was to be continued, except that such requisitions might be made in proportion to the whole number of free citizens and three-fifths of the slaves. It was further declared that in the absence of timely compliance with such requisitions, Congress was to be authorized "to direct the collection thereof" in the non-complying states, provided that these powers should not be exercised without the assent of a certain number of states.[34] Other provisions related to admission of new states into the Union, uniform rules for naturalization, and equal treatment of citizens of other states committing offenses against the laws of a particular state.[35]

The principal argument in favor of the New Jersey Plan was made by Paterson on June 16.[36] Wilson, in reply, analyzed and compared the distinctive features of the Virginia and New Jersey Plans.[37] On the following day Alexander Hamilton in a notable address declared that in his opinion neither plan went far enough toward establishing a

[31] *Ibid.*, I, 244.
[32] *Ibid.*, I, 244.
[33] *Ibid.*, I, 245.
[34] *Ibid.*, I, 243–44. Patrick Henry and other opponents of ratification of the Constitution desired to preserve the system of requisitions upon states rather than taxes imposed upon taxpayers themselves, and many states desired amendments to the Constitution restricting the taxing powers of Congress. Dumbauld, *The Bill of Rights and What It Means Today*, 16, 26, 33, 43, 48, 163.
[35] Farrand, *Records*, I, 245.   [36] *Ibid.*, I, 250–52, 258–60.
[37] *Ibid.*, I, 252–55, 260–61, 276–78. Thirteen contrasts were enumerated.

powerful national government. He asserted that the British government was the best in the world, and that "he doubted whether anything short of it would do in America." He proposed a plan of government in which the Senate and the chief executive should hold office for life during good behavior, and in which the governor of each state should be appointed by the central government and have a power to veto state laws.[38] This brilliant speech, between five and six hours in length, was doubtless helpful in shocking the convention into a full realization of the perilous situation confronting the nation.

On June 19, following an important speech by Madison, the Committee of the Whole rose and re-reported the Virginia Plan.[39] The convention in plenary session then proceeded to consider the report of the Committee of the Whole, item by item.

During debate on the composition of the Senate, Charles Pinckney of South Carolina delivered a significant speech, emphasizing the uniqueness of conditions in America. Hence he regarded precedents derived from antiquity, from the countries of Europe, and especially from the British constitution, as not being particularly helpful. Lacking the distinctions of fortune and rank which characterize the respective classes of society in England, the American population is entirely similar to the commons in England. It would therefore be foolish to establish in America two superfluous features of the British government, a hereditary executive and a hereditary Senate (as Hamilton had urged), merely "because the King & Lords of England are so." In America the principal classes are professional, commercial, and landed interests, composing "one great & equal body of citizens . . . among whom there are no distinctions of rank, and very few or none of fortune." The government to be framed for America must be one suited to the people. It should extend "to its citizens all the blessings of civil & religious liberty" and be "capable of making them happy at home." This is the true end of republican government. "Conquest or superiority among other powers is not or ought not ever to be the object of republican systems."[40]

---

[38] *Ibid.*, I, 282–93. In the course of his address Hamilton remarked: "Our Situation . . . leaves us room to dream." Joseph R. Strayer, *The Delegate from New York*, 64. Dr. William Samuel Johnson of Connecticut said of Hamilton: "Though he has been praised by every body, he has been supported by none." Farrand, *Records*, I, 363.

[39] Farrand, *Records*, I, 314–22.

[40] *Ibid.*, I, 397–404 (June 25).

When the subject of representation in the lower house was taken up, Luther Martin of Maryland delivered a tiresome two-day speech in favor of an equal vote for each state.[41] After lengthy debate the recommendation of the Committee of the Whole was approved, providing for the substitution of an equitable ratio in place of the system of state equality observed in the old Congress.[42]

On June 29 the subject of representation in the Senate was considered, and Ellsworth moved that every state have an equal vote in that body.[43] From that moment until adoption of the "Connecticut Compromise" on July 16, acrimonious debate raged in the convention, revealing such a divergence of views that the possibility of national union on any terms whatever seemed to be doomed.

Madison and Wilson spoke strongly in favor of proportional representation of the people in both branches of the Legislature. Wilson exclaimed: "Can we forget for whom we are forming a Government? Is it for *men*, or for the imaginary beings called *States?*"[44] Gunning Bedford of Delaware in an impassioned speech on behalf of the small states threatened that "The Large States dare not dissolve the confederation. If they do the small ones will find some foreign ally of more honor and good faith, who will take them by the hand and do them justice."[45]

When a vote was taken on Ellsworth's motion, it resulted in a tie. This was technically a victory for the nationalists and a defeat for the small states claiming equal representation in the Senate, since the proposition reported by the Committee of the Whole stood when Ellsworth's amendment failed to pass. But politically there was an impasse which threatened to frustrate completely the work of the convention, with disastrous consequences to the public interest. To avert the impending calamity, General Pinckney proposed that a committee be appointed "to devise & report some compromise."[46]

[41] *Ibid.*, I, 437–38, 444–45 (June 27 and 28).   [42] *Ibid.*, I, 460, 468 (June 29).
[43] *Ibid.*, 468 (June 29).
[44] *Ibid.*, I, 482–84, 485–87 (June 30).
[45] *Ibid.*, I, 492, 501. For this intemperate outburst he was rebuked by King. *Ibid.*, I, 493, 502. Bedford later apologized. *Ibid.*, I, 531 (July 5).
[46] *Ibid.*, I, 509, 510 (July 2). The committee consisted of Gerry, Ellsworth, Yates, Paterson, Franklin, Bedford, Martin, Mason, Davy, Rutledge, and Baldwin. *Ibid.*, I, 516. Being composed of a member from every state, it was called a "grand committee." Gouverneur Morris added fuel to the flames by proposing appointment of the Senate for life by the executive. *Ibid.*, I, 511–14.

On July 5, Gerry presented the committee's report. It proposed a "package" compromise, originally suggested by Franklin, giving each state an equal vote in the Senate, but providing that in the lower house each state be allowed one member for every forty thousand inhabitants (and in any event at least one member), and also providing that all money bills must originate in the lower house (without being subject to amendment in the Senate).[47]

Madison did not regard the exclusive privilege of originating money bills as any concession on the part of the small states. That provision had previously been rejected when considered on its own merits.[48] Gouverneur Morris also opposed the plan in a spirited speech, in the course of which he offended the smaller states by saying: "This Country must be united. If persuasion does not unite it, the sword will."[49] Bedford, Gerry, and Mason urged harmony.

The first part of the "Connecticut Compromise" to be debated was that relating to representation in the lower house. Gouverneur Morris objected to a method based entirely upon population and excluding property as a factor in determining representation.[50] As a result of his motion to refer the matter to a committee, the compromise plan was amended so as to specify the original number of representatives to be allotted to each state, and to require a periodical census to facilitate future adjustments in accordance with wealth and population.[51]

[47] *Ibid.*, I, 522–24.

[48] *Ibid.*, I, 527 (July 5). Wilson, Pinckney, and General Pinckney agreed. *Ibid.*, I, 544–46 (July 6). The earlier rejection had been on June 13. *Ibid.*, I, 224. Mason, Gerry, and Randolph attached value to the money bill provision. *Ibid.*, II, 273–75 (August 13).

[49] *Ibid.*, I, 530 (July 5). For Paterson's comment, see *ibid.*, I, 532.

[50] *Ibid.*, I, 533 (July 5). Morris wittily observed: "Life and liberty were generally said to be of more value, than property. An accurate view of the matter would nevertheless prove that property was the main object of Society. The savage State was more favorable to liberty than the Civilized; and sufficiently so to life. It was preferred by all men who had not acquired a taste for property; it was only renounced for the sake of property which could only be secured by the restraints of regular government." The volatile Morris later argued, when he thought the South was getting more than a fair share of representation: "Property ought to have its weight; but not all the weight." *Ibid.*, I, 567 (July 10).

[51] *Ibid.*, I, 540–42 (July 6); I, 557–62 (July 9). Randolph first suggested a census. I, 564, 570 (July 10); I, 567, 578–79 (July 10 and 11); I, 594, 597 (July 12). Williamson of North Carolina proposed that three-fifths of the slave population should be included in determining the number of a state's inhabitants. *Ibid.*, I, 579 (July 11). This was the traditional ratio adopted by the old Congress in its resolution of April 18,

The fertile mind of Gouverneur Morris was also responsible for a proviso that representation be in proportion to direct taxation.[52] This facilitated acceptance of the traditional three-fifths ratio for counting slaves when computing the population of a state. Southern members wished to include the entire number of slaves,[53] while Northern members wished to exclude them entirely. Paterson of New Jersey declared that he could regard slaves "in no light but as property." If they are not represented in the states to which they belong, he inquired, why should they be represented in the general government? "What is the true principle of Representation? It is an expedient by which an assembly of certain individls. chosen by the people is substituted in place of the inconvenient meeting of the people themselves. If such a meeting of the people was actually to take place, would the slaves vote? they would not. Why then shd. they be represented."[54] In reply Madison twitted him by agreeing that the sound doctrine of representation which Paterson was now advancing "must for ever silence the pretensions of the small States to an equality of votes with the large ones."[55] Wilson, too, could not understand "on what principle the admission of blacks in the proportion of three-fifths could be explained. Are they admitted as Citizens? Then why are they not admitted on an equality with White Citizens? Are they admitted as property? Then why is not other property admitted into the computation?"[56] Gouverneur Morris likewise made it plain that the people of Pennsylvania "would revolt at the idea of being put on a footing with slaves. They would reject any plan that was to have such an effect."[57]

The sprightly eloquence and volatile candor of Morris contributed many interesting facets to the debate during this critical period of the convention's labors. He deplored the extent to which "the great objects of the nation had been sacrificed constantly to local views," and "the dignity and splendor of the American Empire" had been neglected.

1783, to amend Art. VIII. *Journals of the Continental Congress*, XXIV, 260–61. That amendment was accepted by eleven states. Brant, *James Madison*, II, 241; Farrand, *Records*, III, 160. See note 25, page 190, below.

[52] Farrand, *Records*, I, 592 (July 12).

[53] *Ibid.*, I, 542 (July 6); I, 580–81 (July 11); I, 596 (July 12).

[54] *Ibid.*, I, 561 (July 9). [55] *Ibid.*, I, 562 (July 9). [56] *Ibid.*, I, 587 (July 11).

[57] *Ibid.*, I, 583 (July 11). He emphasized that "it is in vain for the Eastern States to insist on what the Southern States will never agree to. It is equally vain for the latter to require what the other States can never admit." *Ibid.*, I, 593 (July 12). See also *ibid.*, I, 603 (July 13).

During the Revolution, he declared, the small states took advantage of the exigencies of the times and "extorted from the large ones an equality of votes. Standing now on that ground, they demand under the new system greater rights as men, than their fellow Citizens of the large States. The proper answer to them is that the same necessity of which they formerly took advantage does not now exist, and that the large States are at liberty now to consider what is right, rather than what may be expedient." Of what consequence would it be "to the happiness of America," he exclaimed, "if all the Charters & Constitutions of the States were thrown into the fire, and all their demagogues into the ocean?"[58]

Morris frankly avowed his belief that control of the government should remain in the states along the Atlantic seaboard. He feared the growth of the West. "The Busy haunts of men not the remote wilderness, was the proper School of political Talents."[59]

Wilson's skill in devious draftsmanship made acceptance of the three-fifths ratio more palatable to opponents of slavery. He proposed that slaves should not be included as a direct factor in determining representation, but only in determining the quantum of taxation; representation was then based upon taxation. Wilson "observed that less umbrage would perhaps be taken agst. an admission of the slaves into the Rule of representation, if it should be so expressed as to make them indirectly only an ingredient in the rule, by saying that they should enter into the rule of taxation; and as representation was to be according to taxation, the end would be equally attained."[60] This formulation was adopted.

The Connecticut Compromise, as amended, was finally adopted in its entirety on July 16.[61] On the following day Gouverneur Morris made a motion (which was not seconded) to reconsider it, as he wished the convention to consider "in the abstract" and on its own merits the question of what powers it was necessary to entrust to the federal gov-

[58] *Ibid.*, I, 552–53 (July 7). Rutledge after adoption of the Connecticut Compromise remarked that all that the large states had to do "was to decide whether they would yield or not." He felt that "altho' we could not do what we thought best in itself, we ought to do something." *Ibid.*, II, 19 (July 16).

[59] *Ibid.*, I, 583 (July 11). See also I, 571 (July 10). Gerry shared the views of Morris. *Ibid.*, II, 3 (July 14). Mason, Madison, Wilson, and Sherman favored equal treatment for the West without "degrading discriminations." *Ibid.*, I, 578–79, 584–85 (July 11); I, 605 (July 13); II, 3 (July 14); II, 454 (August 29).

[60] *Ibid.*, I, 595 (July 12).   [61] *Ibid.*, II, 13–14, 15–16 (July 16).

ernment. He feared that such consideration might be frustrated by reason of the decision to permit equality of voting in the Senate; that actions of the convention would be governed by members' opinions concerning what powers can properly be given to a government so constituted, rather than what powers must be given to the federal government in order to serve the best interests of the nation.[62]

Having settled the thorny question of representation, the convention proceeded to consider the scope of the powers to be vested in the National Legislature. It now appeared that, having won the battle for equality of representation in the new government, the smaller states were quite willing to increase the powers vested in it.[63]

A provision was promptly accepted authorizing Congress "to legislate in all cases for the general interests of the Union, and also in those to which the States are separately incompetent, or in which the harmony of the United States may be interrupted by the exercise of individual legislation."[64]

At the suggestion of Gouverneur Morris, the federal negative on state laws was eliminated. Morris pointed out that this veto power was unnecessary and would be unpalatable to the states. Sherman "thought it unnecessary, as the Courts of the States would not consider as valid any law contravening the Authority of the Union, and which the legislature would wish to be negatived." Luther Martin drew attention to a practical difficulty: "Shall all the laws of the States be sent up to the Genl. Legislature before they shall be permitted to operate?" In lieu of the federal negative, Martin offered a provision taken from the New Jersey Plan, which grew into the "supremacy clause" in Article VI, section 2, of the Constitution.[65]

[62] *Ibid.*, II, 25 (July 17). See note 7, page 33, above. Madison had said "that it wd. be impossible to say what powers could be safely & properly vested in the Govt. before it was known, in what manner the States were to be represented in it." *Ibid.*, I, 551 (July 7).

[63] On June 16, Charles Pinckney had said: "Give N. Jersey an equal vote, and she will dismiss her scruples, and concur in the Natil. system." *Ibid.*, I, 255.

[64] *Ibid.*, II, 21, 27 (July 17).

[65] *Ibid.*, II, 27–29 (July 17). Madison, supported by Pinckney, fought hard for his pet notion. *Ibid.*, I, 164–68 (June 8); II, 390–91 (August 23); II, 589 (September 12). Jefferson had disliked the notion from the beginning, and had recommended leaving the determination of unconstitutionality of state laws to the federal judiciary. Dumbauld, "Thomas Jefferson and American Constitutional Law," *loc. cit.*, 387. Disallowance of Colonial laws, and the requirement of a suspending clause, accompanied by delay in acting on legislation forwarded to England for consideration by the Board of

The convention then turned to problems relating to the executive. This subject proved more troublesome to the convention than any other topic discussed during its deliberations.[66] Many different plans were adopted from time to time, and the one finally agreed upon was not formulated until the closing days of the convention.[67] When discussion of other features of the report of the Committee of the Whole had been completed, the convention voted on July 23 "that the proceedings of the Convention for the establishment of a national government, except what respects the Supreme Executive, be referred to a Committee for the purpose of reporting a Constitution conformably to the proceedings aforesaid."[68] Commonly known as the Committee of Detail, it was composed of five members (Rutledge, Randolph, Gorham, Ellsworth, and Wilson).[69] On July 26 the convention adjourned until August 6 in order that the committee might have time "to prepare & report the Constitution."[70]

On August 6, John Rutledge of South Carolina[71] submitted the report of the Committee of Detail, printed copies of which were distributed to the members. It contained a preamble and twenty-three

Trade and Privy Council were grievances enumerated in the Declaration of Independence. Dumbauld, *The Declaration of Independence and What It Means Today*, 87–93.

[66] This was Wilson's opinion. Farrand, *Records*, II, 501 (September 4).

[67] The final plan was substantially completed on September 6. *Ibid.*, II, 528–29. See pages 261–63 below.

[68] *Ibid.*, II, 85, 95. A document found in the papers of James Wilson, a member of the Committee of Detail, which evidently embodies the proceedings here referred to, is printed in Farrand, *Records*, II, 129–33. Twenty-three numbered resolutions (as compiled by the editor of the printed *Journal* published in 1819) are printed in Meigs, *The Growth of the Constitution*, 333–36; Elliot, *Debates*, V, 112–15; Tansill, *Documents*, 465–71.

[69] The members were chosen by ballot on July 24. *Ibid.*, II, 97.

[70] *Ibid.*, II, 128. On July 26 the convention reinstated the recommendation of the Committee of the Whole regarding election of the executive (by the Legislature, for a seven-year term, with ineligibility for a second term). *Ibid.*, II, 116. This decision was transmitted to the Committee of Detail. Previously it had been decided to eliminate ineligibility, and this necessitated election otherwise than by the Legislature. An electoral system had been contrived, and a six-year term prescribed. *Ibid.*, II, 51–52, 57–59 (July 19).

[71] Work papers that have been preserved show that Rutledge, Randolph, and Wilson took an active part in the work of the Committee of Detail. *Ibid.*, II, 129–75. Oliver Ellsworth of Connecticut is reported to have said late in life to his son that he was "one of the five men who drew up that Constitution." William G. Brown, *Life of Oliver Ellsworth*, 169. Gorham doubtless also shared in the work.

articles, divided into forty-one sections.[72] It was printed by John Dunlap, the Philadelphian who had printed the Declaration of Independence on the night of July 4, 1776.[73]

Besides developing and organizing into a coherent fabric the twenty-three propositions referred to it by the convention, the Committee of Detail wove into their appropriate place those provisions of the Articles of Confederation which were of continued applicability. Suitable features from state constitutions were likewise borrowed, particularly those relating to details of the legislative process.[74]

The term "Congress" was adopted by the Committee of Detail to designate the body in which the legislative power was vested. The Congress was to be composed of two branches designated respectively as a "House of Representatives" and a "Senate."[75] The title "President" was given to the officer in whom the executive power was vested.[76] The judicial power was vested in "one Supreme Court." Restrictions on the exercise of judicial power included the requirement of jury trial of criminal offenses (except impeachments) in the state where committed, and the limitation of the punishment in cases of impeachment to removal from office and disqualification to hold office.[77]

The scope of the legislative power was set forth in a detailed enumeration (quite similar to that in Article I, section 8, of the Constitution) containing eighteen specific items, rather than in the vague and general language of the convention's resolution on that subject.[78] The article

[72] Farrand, *Records*, II, 177–89. The text of the report is also printed in Meigs, *The Growth of the Constitution*, 337–47; Elliot, *Debates*, V, 116–24; Tansill, *Documents*, 471–82. For comment on the report, see Warren, *The Making of the Constitution*, 384–91.

[73] Dumbauld, *The Declaration of Independence and What It Means Today*, 16.

[74] The convention had accepted the suggestion contained in the Virginia Plan that the National Legislature should possess, *inter alia*, all legislative powers vested in the old Congress by the Articles of Confederation. *Ibid.*, I, 21; II, 131. Regarding the influence of state constitutions, see Sydney G. Fisher, *The Evolution of the Constitution of the United States*, 114–214, 267–309.

[75] Art. III. Art. I adopted the name "United States of America," and Art. II provided for separation of legislative, executive, and judicial powers. Arts. IV, V, and VI contained detailed provisions regarding the House, Senate, and legislative procedure. Art. IX, on powers of the Senate, outlined a complex procedure for settling territorial disputes between states.

[76] Art. X.   [77] Art. XI.

[78] Art. VII. See page 50 above. It should be noted that in Dunlap's print two articles were numbered VI, so that Art. VII and subsequent articles were misnumbered. The correct numbers are used herein.

granting these legislative powers also contained six restrictions upon their exercise.[79] Ten prohibitions were likewise imposed upon state action.[80] A "supremacy clause" made federal enactments the supreme law of the states, and state as well as federal officials were required to take oaths to support the Constitution.[81] Provision was made for the admission of new states, and for guaranteeing to every state a republican form of government as well as protection against foreign invasion or domestic violence.[82]

Relations between the states were regulated by articles dealing with privileges and immunities of citizens, interstate rendition of fugitives from justice, and full faith and credit to the legislation and judicial proceedings of other states.[83]

Other articles provided for amendment of the Constitution when a convention for that purpose was requested by the legislatures of two-thirds of the states; and prescribed the number of ratifications by state conventions which would be required in order to establish the new government.[84] Transitional procedures were recommended concerning the manner of obtaining ratifications and "commencing proceedings under this Constitution."[85]

With respect to three topics it will be noted that the Committee of Detail introduced innovations on the strength of its own ipse dixit, without any prior authorization in the resolutions of the convention. In two instances these were gratuitous concessions to Southern interests, and it may be suspected that Randolph and Rutledge took advantage of their position as draftsmen to insert provisions favorable to the South. One of these was that "No tax or duty shall be laid . . . on articles exported from any State; nor on the migration or importation

[79] These related to the definition of treason; regulation of direct taxation in accordance with population under the three-fifths rule (see page 49 above); prohibition of taxation of exports or taxation or prohibition of importation of slaves; prohibition of capitation tax except in accordance with census; requirement of two-thirds vote to pass a navigation act; prohibition of titles of nobility.

[80] States were absolutely forbidden by Art. XII to coin money; grant letters of marque and reprisal; enter into any treaty, alliance, or confederation; or grant any title of nobility. Without the consent of Congress, states were forbidden by Art. XIII to emit bills of credit; make anything but specie legal tender; tax imports; keep troops or ships of war in time of peace; enter into any agreement or compact with another state or with any foreign power; or engage in war unless in case of actual or imminent invasion.

[81] Arts. VIII and XX.   [82] Arts. XVII and XVIII.
[83] Arts. XIV, XV, and XVI.   [84] Arts. XIX and XXI.   [85] Arts. XXII and XXIII.

of such persons as the several States shall think proper to admit; nor shall such migration or importation be prohibited."[86] The other was that "No navigation act shall be passed without the assent of two thirds of the members present in each House."[87] A draft in Randolph's handwriting among the work papers of the Committee of Detail, with emendations in the handwriting of Rutledge, shows the possible origin of both these provisions desired by the South.[88] There was vehement debate in the convention on these proposals of the Committee of Detail.[89] In another of the noteworthy compromises which made acceptance of the Constitution possible, the navigation act provision was given up in exchange for retention of the provisions regarding exports and slaves.[90]

The third instance of innovation by the Committee of Detail upon its own authority was its proposal that the salaries of members of the House and Senate should be paid by the states.[91] Doubtless other members of the convention besides Carroll of Maryland were surprised to see this clause in the report.[92] The Committee of the Whole had twice rejected the same proposal when offered by Ellsworth.[93] Hence in this instance we may suspect that it was Ellsworth who was the culprit who dealt with the subject in the report of the Committee of Detail, in accordance with his own views rather than the earlier decisions of the convention. This suspicion is corroborated by the circumstance that

[86] Art. VII, sec. 4, of the draft. Farrand, *Records*, II, 183. The committee may have sought to forestall further outbursts by General Charles Cotesworth Pinckney on the subject. *Ibid.*, I, 592 (July 12); II, 95 (July 23). He mentioned the matter just at the time when the Committee of Detail was being established on July 23.

[87] Art. VIII, sec. 6, of the draft. *Ibid.*, II, 183.

[88] Under exceptions to the taxing power, Randolph notes: "No Taxes on exports." Under exceptions to the commerce power, he notes: "no Duty on exports." Randolph's draft also listed as an exception to the commerce power the prohibition against forbidding or taxing the importation of slaves, and included the navigation act provision as a restriction on the exercise of that power. Drafting changes in Rutledge's handwriting occur with respect to the two last-named subjects. *Ibid.*, II, 142–43.

[89] *Ibid.*, II, 396, 400 (August 24); II, 408–409, 416–17 (August 25); II, 446, 449–53 (August 29). See pages 185–88, and 205–206, below.

[90] *Ibid.*, II, 359–75 (August 21 and 22). The matter was referred to a grand committee which reported on August 24. *Ibid.*, II, 396, 400.

[91] Art. VI, sec. 10, of the draft. *Ibid.*, II, 180.

[92] *Ibid.*, II, 292 (August 14).

[93] *Ibid.*, I, 371, 374 (June 22); I, 427, 428 (June 26). On June 12 it had been decided that payment should be out of the national treasury. *Ibid.*, I, 216.

when this portion of the report of the Committee of Detail was taken up in convention it was Ellsworth, acknowledging that "in reflecting on this subject he had been satisfied" that payment by the states was undesirable, who made the motion to substitute payment from the national treasury.[94]

On August 18, Madison and Pinckney submitted a long list of additional powers to be vested in the Congress. These proposals were referred to the Committee of Detail, along with other proposals of Pinckney and Gouverneur Morris.[95] On August 25 the Maryland delegates offered certain proposals designed to protect the ports of that state against preferential regulations of commerce. These were referred to a committee.[96]

Various committee reports dealing with particular matters[97] were received from time to time, and amendments were made in the provisions reported by the Committee of Detail. By August 31 the convention had completed its consideration of the draft Constitution, except for items that had been postponed. On that date a grand committee, known as the Committee on Postponed Parts, was appointed to deal with "such parts of the Constitution as have been postponed, and such parts of reports as have not been acted on."[98] Among the matters reported upon by that committee was the troublesome problem of choos-

[94] *Ibid.*, II, 290 (August 14). The motion was carried. *Ibid.*, II, 282, 292.

[95] *Ibid.*, II, 324–26 (August 18); II, 340–44 (August 20). One of Pinckney's proposals would have authorized the President and each branch of Congress to call for opinions of the Supreme Court "upon important questions of law, and upon solemn occasions." See Manley O. Hudson, "Advisory Opinions of National and International Courts," *Harvard Law Review*, Vol. XXXVII, No. 8 (June, 1924), 975–76. Others of Pinckney's proposals were of the nature of a Bill of Rights. See Dumbauld, *The Bill of Rights and What It Means Today*, 5–6. Morris proposed to establish a Council of State, from whom the President might require written opinions. This was a favorite idea with Mason. Farrand, *Records*, II, 541–42 (September 7). See note 119, page 85, below.

[96] Farrand, *Records*, II, 410, 417–18 (August 25). The grand committee reported on August 28. *Ibid.*, II, 434, 437. The report was approved on August 31. *Ibid.*, II, 473, 480–81.

[97] Such as the important report of a grand committee on August 21 regarding payment of debts incurred during the Revolutionary War by the United States and by the states "for the common defence and general welfare." *Ibid.*, II, 355–56.

[98] Farrand, *Records*, II, 473, 481 (August 31). The committee made reports on September 1, 4, and 5. *Ibid.*, II, 483–85, 493–95, 497–99, 505, 508–509. Judge David Brearley of New Jersey presented the reports.

ing the executive.[99] By September 8 work had progressed to such a point that the convention was able to appoint a committee, known as the Committee of Style, "to revise the style of and arrange the articles agreed to" by the convention.[100] This committee was composed of Dr. William Samuel Johnson, Alexander Hamilton, Gouverneur Morris, James Madison, and Rufus King.

On September 12 the Committee of Style made its report, which was ordered to be printed for use of members of the convention.[101] The work of arrangement and stylistic revision was performed with great distinction. Much of the literary felicity of the Constitution is attributable to Gouverneur Morris.[102]

The Committee of Style produced the Preamble as it now stands.[103] It organized the forty-three articles referred to it into the seven articles which make up the Constitution as adopted. Articles I, II, and III deal with the legislative, executive, and judicial branches of the government, respectively; Articles IV and VI deal with interstate and federal-state relations; Article V deals with the amending process; and Article VII provides for establishment of the new government upon ratification by the conventions of nine states.

Numerous minor changes were made during the three days devoted to consideration of the draft of the Committee of Style.[104] Having completed the task of perfecting the text of the Constitution, the con-

[99] See note 66, page 51, above, and pages 261–63 below.

[100] *Ibid.*, II, 547, 553. The articles referred to the Committee of Style, as compiled from the proceedings by Farrand, comprise slightly more than fifteen printed pages. *Ibid.*, II, 565–80. On September 10 the article relating to amendments was revised in convention. *Ibid.*, II, 555, 559. Other subjects were considered on September 12. *Ibid.*, II, 582, 587, 588–89, 605, 607.

[101] *Ibid.*, II, 582, 585. For the text see *ibid.*, II, 590–603; Elliot, *Debates*, IV, 186–94; Meigs, *Growth of the Constitution*, 347–58; Tansill, *Documents*, 702–12.

[102] Farrand, *Records*, III, 420, 499. Ezra Stiles noted in his diary that Wilson also took part in the task. *Ibid.*, III, 170.

[103] The word "to" before "establish justice" was deleted in convention on September 13. *Ibid.*, II, 605. How effectively the revisers worked is made clear by glancing at the original preamble submitted by the Committee of Detail: "We the people of the States of New Hampshire, Massachusetts, Rhode-Island and Providence Plantations, Connecticut, New-York, New-Jersey, Pennsylvania, Delaware, Maryland, Virginia, North-Carolina, South-Carolina, and Georgia do ordain, declare, and establish the following Constitution for the Government of Ourselves and our Posterity." *Ibid.*, II, 177.

[104] *Ibid.*, II, 605–31 (September 13, 14, 15).

vention on September 15 unanimously voted to agree to the instrument as amended. "The Constitution was then ordered to be engrossed."[105]

On Monday, September 17, 1787, the final day of the convention, Benjamin Franklin rose with a speech, which Wilson read to the delegates. He urged unanimity in accepting the completed work, and proposed a form of attestation prepared by Gouverneur Morris: "Done in Convention, by the *unanimous* consent of the *States* present." This would enable dissenting members to signify by their signatures to the document merely that all the states had voted for it, though individual members had not endorsed its contents.[106]

One alteration was made, even after the parchment had been engrossed. A proposal by Gorham to allow one representative in the House for each thirty thousand people (rather than forty thousand) was agreed to, after George Washington had made his first speech in the convention in support of the change.[107] The erasure is still plainly visible on the document.

All the states then agreed to the Constitution "enrolled in order to be signed." Randolph and Gerry repeated their unwillingness to sign. It was resolved to place the journal and other papers of the convention in the hands of the presiding officer, George Washington, who was to retain them "subject to the order of Congress, if ever formed under the Constitution." The members then proceeded to sign the instrument.[108]

While the last signatures were being affixed, Doctor Franklin, looking toward the chair of the presiding officer, at the back of which a rising sun happened to be painted, observed to a few members near him that artists had often found it difficult to distinguish in their paintings a rising from a setting sun. "I have often and often," he said, "in the

[105] *Ibid.*, II, 633 (September 15). The session continued until 6:00 P.M. *Ibid.*, III, 81. On September 15, Randolph, Mason, and Gerry set forth the reasons that impelled them to withhold their signatures. *Ibid.*, II, 631–33. Five hundred copies were ordered to be printed. *Ibid.*, II, 634. Concerning these copies, see Denys P. Myers, ed., *The Constitution of the United States of America*, 18, 21–22.

[106] Farrand, *Records*, II, 641–43 (September 17). The signature of Blount of North Carolina, at least, was gained by this form of wording. *Ibid.*, II, 646. General Pinckney and Butler disliked the subterfuge. *Ibid.*, II, 647.

[107] *Ibid.*, II, 644. For other accounts of this speech, see Warren, *The Making of the Constitution*, 712–13.

[108] Farrand, *Records*, II, 644–48.

THE CONSTITUTION OF THE UNITED STATES

course of the Session, and the vicissitudes of my hopes and fears as to its issue, looked at that behind the President without being able to tell whether it was rising or setting: But now at length I have the happiness to know that it is a rising and not a setting Sun."[109]

In his diary for that day George Washington recorded: "The business being thus closed, the Members adjourned to the City Tavern, dined together and took a cordial leave of each other." After the farewell feast was over, the delegates dispersed. Washington returned to his lodgings. There he "did some business with, and received the papers from the secretary of the Convention, and retired to meditate" on the momentous work which had been brought to completion.[110]

[109] *Ibid.*, II, 648 (September 17).

[110] *Ibid.*, III, 81. Major William Jackson, the secretary of the convention, left Philadelphia by stage at 10:00 A.M. on September 18 and arrived in New York at 2:00 P.M. the next day. On September 20 he delivered the engrossed Constitution to Arthur St. Clair, president of the old Congress. Myers, *The Constitution of the United States of America*, 19, 22. Pursuant to the resolution of Congress of September 28, 1787, copies were forwarded to the states by a circular letter of that date, for ratification. *Ibid.*, 24.

TEXT, HISTORY, AND INTERPRETATION
OF THE CONSTITUTION OF THE UNITED STATES

PREAMBLE

*We the People of the United States, in Order to form a more perfect
Union, establish Justice, insure domestic Tranquility, provide for the
common defence, promote the general Welfare, and secure the Blessings of Liberty to ourselves and our Posterity, do ordain and establish
this Constitution for the United States of America.*

HISTORY

THE Preamble is noteworthy for its literary felicity. It represents a
revision by the Committee of Style of the Preamble drafted by the
Committee of Detail. The original version was little more than a list
of states.[1] This list was necessarily omitted after the decision of August
31 that upon ratification by nine states the Constitution would go into
force "between the States so ratifying the Same." It could not be known
in advance which nine states would be the first to ratify.

The purposes set forth in the Preamble include those expressed in
the Articles of Confederation,[2] with the addition of three phrases
thought to characterize the improvements aimed at in the new Constitution: "to form a more perfect Union, establish Justice, insure domestic Tranquility." Since the Articles of Confederation proclaimed (in

---

[1] See note 103, page 56, above.

[2] Art. III: "for their common defence, the security of their liberties, and their
mutual and general welfare."

Article XIII) that "the Union shall be perpetual," it seems that in its new form it would be properly describable as "more perfect."[3]

The word "to" before "establish justice" was deleted in convention on September 13.[4]

INTERPRETATION

PATRICK HENRY, in the Virginia ratifying convention, was sharply critical of the use of the expression "We the people." He asked "Who authorized them to speak the language of, *We, the People*, instead of *We, the States?* States are the characteristics, and the soul of a confederation. If the states be not the agents of this compact, it must be one great consolidated national government, of the people of all the states."

The reply came quickly from the venerable Edmund Pendleton: "Permit me to ask the gentleman . . . who but the people can delegate powers? Who but the people have a right to form government? The expression is a common one, and a favorite one with me."[5]

Similar debate took place in the Pennsylvania ratifying convention. John Smilie of Fayette County contended that the phrase "We the people" was "a proof of a consolidated government."[6] James Wilson argued, as Pendleton did, that "The power of the people . . . is the great foundation of the proposed system."[7]

However, complete consolidation was not sought or effected by the adoption of the Constitution. James Madison had declared before the Philadelphia convention met that such a result was as inexpedient as it was unattainable.[8]

In Madison's opinion the government of the United States under the Constitution was neither a mere confederation or league of states

---

[3] In Texas v. White, 7 Wall. 700, 725 (1868), the Supreme Court said: "What can be indissoluble if a perpetual Union, made more perfect, is not? . . . The Constitution, in all its provisions, looks to an indissoluble Union, composed of indestructible States."

[4] Farrand, *Records*, II, 605.

[5] Elliot, *Debates*, II, 47, 57 (June 4 and 5, 1788); David J. Mays, *Edmund Pendleton*, II, 232–36.

[6] John B. McMaster and Frederick D. Stone, *Pennsylvania and the Federal Constitution*, 268. He described the issue before the convention as "whether this system proposes a consolidation or a confederation." *Ibid.*, 267. William Findley of Westmoreland County made the same point. *Ibid.*, 301.

[7] *Ibid.*, 265. See also *ibid.*, 229–31, 249, 315–16, 341, 384.

[8] See page 41 above.

nor a completely consolidated unitary state. It was not "created by the people of the U.S. as one community, and as such acting by a numerical majority of the whole." It was a unique experiment, and *sui generis*. Madison declared that "the Constitution was created by the people, but by the people as composing distinct States, and acting by a majority in each."[9]

Madison definitely asserted that the Preamble was not a separate source of substantive power, distinct from the particular powers subsequently specified. It enumerates purposes, not powers.[10] The Supreme Court has accepted this view.[11]

[9] Madison to M. L. Hulbert, May, 1830, in Madison, *Writings*, IX, 371. See also *ibid.*, 347, 384–85, 568–69, 599–600.

[10] *Ibid.*, VI, 334, 382. The same is true of the "general welfare" clause appended to the taxing power in Art. I, sec. 8, cl. 1. *Ibid.*, IX, 411. A recent unorthodox writer asserts that the government is empowered to do anything which contributes toward accomplishment of the purposes set forth in the Preamble. William W. Crosskey, *Politics and the Constitution in the History of the United States*, I, 374–79, 391. He also accepts the substantive view of the general welfare clause in Art. I, sec. 8, par. 1. *Ibid.*, I, 393–408.

[11] Jacobson v. Massachusetts, 197 U.S. 11, 22 (1905).

Article I—The Legislative Branch

Organization and Powers of Congress

All legislative Powers herein granted shall be vested in a Congress of the United States, which shall consist of a Senate and House of Representatives.

HISTORY

THE names "Congress," "House of Representatives," and "Senate" first appeared in the draft of the Committee of Detail.[1] These were familiar, the first being the title of the old Congress, in which there was no separation of powers into separate legislative, executive, and judicial branches. Such separation was one of the most widely desired reforms leading to the constitutional convention. The names of the two branches of the national legislature were in common use to designate similar branches of the legislative assemblies of many states.[2]

That there should be a bicameral legislature had been agreed since the presentation of the Virginia Plan.[3]

INTERPRETATION

ARTICLE III of the draft of the Committee of Detail had said that "the legislative power" shall be vested in Congress, just as its Article X had provided for similar vesting of "the executive power" in the President.

The concept of a general and undefined executive power was retained in the Constitution, but the Committee of Style by confining the authority of Congress to "all legislative powers herein granted" doubtless meant to imply that the government of the United States was one of delegated and limited powers. This change anticipated the theory embodied in the Tenth Amendment.

A lengthy enumeration of specific legislative powers expressly granted to Congress appears in Article I, section 8.

That law can be made otherwise than by the exercise of "the legisla-

[1] See page 52 above.   [2] Warren, *The Making of the Constitution*, 388.
[3] See page 39 above.

tive power" is shown by the fact that Article VI, clause 2, includes "This Constitution . . . and all Treaties made, or which shall be made, under the Authority of the United States" as parts of "the supreme Law of the Land." The Constitution is amendable by three-fourths of the states (Article V); and treaties are made by the President, "by and with the Advice and Consent of the Senate . . . provided two-thirds of the Senators present concur" (Article II, section 2, paragraph 2).

ART. I, SEC. 2, CL. 1

The House of Representatives shall be composed of Members chosen every second Year by the People of the several States, and the Electors in each State shall have the Qualifications requisite for Electors of the most numerous Branch of the State Legislature.

HISTORY

POPULAR election of members of the House of Representatives was not won without struggle in the convention. There was vigorous debate on several occasions. Madison, Mason, Wilson, and Dickinson were champions of the people. Gerry, Sherman, the two Pinckneys, and Butler led the opposition.

Madison considered election of at least one branch of the national legislature by the people as an indispensable and essential feature of any system established in conformity with principles of free government.[4] Mason made the same point, declaring that the lower House "was, so to speak, to be our House of Commons."[5] Wilson "was for raising the federal pyramid to a considerable altitude, and for that reason wished to give it as broad a basis as possible. No government could long subsist without the confidence of the people. In a republican Government this confidence was peculiarly essential. He also thought it wrong to increase the weight of the State Legislatures by making them the electors of the national Legislature."[6] He believed that "The Legislature ought to be the most exact transcript of the whole Society," for representation was simply a convenient substitute for direct action by the people.[7] Wilson considered popular election not only as the

[4] Farrand, *Records*, I, 49 (May 31); I, 134 (June 6).   [5] *Ibid.*, I, 48 (May 31).
[6] *Ibid.*, I, 49 (May 31).   [7] *Ibid.*, I, 132 (June 6). See page 48 above.

cornerstone but as the foundation of the new plan of government.[8]

Opponents of popular choice either distrusted the people or desired to increase the influence of the states in the new government to the maximum possible degree. Gerry exclaimed: "The evils we experience flow from the excess of democracy."[9] The advocates of election by the people prevailed on May 31, and again on June 6 when the subject was reconsidered upon motion of Charles Pinckney, and again on June 21 when General Charles Cotesworth Pinckney offered a motion that Representatives be elected "in such manner as the Legislature of each State should direct." Even Hamilton opposed this effort "to transfer the election from the people to the State Legislatures, which would essentially vitiate the plan." It would increase state influence, which was something that could not be too watchfully guarded against.[10]

Hamilton openly avowed his dislike of republican government, and his admiration of the British system.[11] But like Mason, he recognized that even in England one branch of the legislature, the House of Commons, was designed to represent the people. John Adams, in his then recent and influential book *A Defence of the Constitutions of Government of the United States of America*, had emphasized the need for separation and balance of powers. But he recognized the need for one branch of government to represent the people. He declared, as Madison did in the convention, that "There can be no free government without a democratical branch in the constitution."[12]

The term of two years is a compromise between those who favored annual elections as a matter of principle (including Gerry and Wilson)[13] and those who preferred a longer term, either for reasons of

[8] *Ibid.*, I, 359 (June 21). He believed that "The majority of people wherever found ought in all questions to govern the minority." *Ibid.*, I, 605 (July 13).

[9] *Ibid.*, I, 48 (May 31). Butler "thought an election by the people an impracticable mode." *Ibid.*, I, 50.

[10] *Ibid.*, I, 358 (June 21).

[11] *Ibid.*, I, 288 (June 18); I, 424 (June 26). Dickinson, while considering it "essential that one branch of the Legislature shd. be drawn immediately from the people," likewise expressed "warm eulogiums on the British Constitution." *Ibid.*, I, 136 (June 6).

[12] *Works of John Adams*, IV, 289. The first volume of this work was published in London in 1787, and was immediately reprinted in Boston, New York, and Philadelphia.

[13] Farrand, *Records*, I, 214 (June 12); I, 361 (June 21).

convenience[14] or of policy.[15] On June 12 a term of three years had been accepted, but on June 21 this was changed to two years.[16]

The Committee of Detail proposed the provision prescribing the same qualifications for electors as those prescribed by the state for electors of the most numerous branch of the state legislature.[17] An attempt by Gouverneur Morris to insert a property qualification was defeated, after Ellsworth, Mason, and Rutledge had remarked that it would not promote adoption of the Constitution to disfranchise in federal elections voters who could participate in elections for state offices. Moreover the restriction proposed by Morris would have been unfavorable to New England mercantile interests. Franklin had also emphasized the desirability of not doing anything which would "depress the virtue & public spirit of our common people; of which they displayed a great deal during the war, and which contributed principally to the favorable issue of it."[18]

INTERPRETATION

THE qualifications entitling citizens to vote for representatives in Congress, as well as the qualifications entitling candidates for that office to be voted for by the people, are fundamental features in a republican form of government and should be regulated in its Constitution (as Madison emphasized in connection with Article I, section 5, clause 1).

With regard to eligibility to serve as a member of Congress, definite requirements with respect to age, citizenship, and residence are set forth in Article I, section 2, clause 2. But with regard to the qualifications of voters, the Constitution simply accepts as federal electors those persons

[14] Madison emphasized the time necessary to be spent in traveling and in becoming familiar with the business to be done. *Ibid.*, I, 214 (June 12); I, 361 (June 21).

[15] Hamilton desired to discourage "democratic spirit" and too great dependence on popular sentiment. *Ibid.*, I, 362 (June 21). Jennifer thought a better class of candidates would be available if the term of office were longer. *Ibid.*, I, 214 (June 12).

[16] *Ibid.*, I, 209, 215, 354, 362.

[17] Art. IV, sec. 1, of the draft. *Ibid.*, I, 178. The provision originated in Randolph's draft. *Ibid.*, I, 139–40.

[18] *Ibid.*, II, 201–206 (August 7). Contrasting the patriotism of American captured seamen, who refused to fight against their own countrymen, with that of British seamen who gladly served on American ships for a share in prizes captured from the British, he attributed this difference to "the different manner in which the common people were treated" in America and in Great Britain.

65

who are qualified as state electors to vote for the most numerous branch of the state legislature.

This was doubtless done as a matter of convenience, in order to avoid cumbersome duplication of state regulations prescribing in detail the mechanics of election procedures. Inasmuch as it seemed improbable that any state would ever seek to hamstring the operation of its own governmental institutions, there was no fear in this connection (as there was in the case of federal control of elections, dealt with in Article I, section 4, clause 1) that states might by inaction paralyze completely the functioning of the federal government.

Just as a national citizenship was originally a derivative status, dependent upon enjoyment of state citizenship (see Article I, section 8, clause 4), so it seemed practicable in the case of determining the eligibility of voters for the federal government to adopt the regulations established by the states.

The state's discretion with respect to qualifications for suffrage is restricted, of course, by the anti-discrimination provisions of the Fourteenth, Fifteenth, Nineteenth, and Twenty-fourth Amendments.

ART. I, SEC. 2, CL. 2

No Person shall be a Representative who shall not have attained to the Age of twenty five Years, and been seven Years a Citizen of the United States, and who shall not, when elected, be an Inhabitant of that State in which he shall be chosen.

HISTORY

THE age requirement was adopted on June 22, upon motion of Mason.[19] The seven-year citizenship requirement was also substituted at Mason's suggestion, on August 8, for the three-year requirement recommended by the Committee of Detail.[20] The requirement of residence in the state was introduced by the Committee of Detail.[21]

[19] *Ibid.*, I, 375 (June 22). Mason confessed that his own political opinions at the age of twenty-one were "too crude & erroneous to merit an influence on public measures." Wilson opposed the motion.

[20] Mason did not choose "to let foreigners and adventurers make laws for us & govern us." *Ibid.*, II, 216 (August 8). No change was made when the subject was reconsidered on August 13. *Ibid.*, II, 268–72.

[21] *Ibid.*, II, 178 (August 6). On motion of Sherman the word "inhabitant" was inserted in place of "resident." *Ibid.*, II, 216, 218 (August 8).

INTERPRETATION

IT should be noted that there is no legal requirement that a member of Congress be a resident of the particular congressional district which he represents. The political preferences of the electorate may be relied upon, however, to enforce such a requirement in practice.

ART. I, SEC. 2, CL. 3

Representatives and direct Taxes shall be apportioned among the several States which may be included within this Union, according to their respective Numbers, which shall be determined by adding to the whole Number of free Persons, including those bound to Service for a Term of Years, and excluding Indians not taxed, three fifths of all other Persons. The actual Enumeration shall be made within three Years after the first Meeting of the Congress of the United States, and within every subsequent Term of ten Years, in such Manner as they shall by Law direct. The Number of Representatives shall not exceed one for every thirty Thousand, but each State shall have at Least one Representative; and until such enumeration shall be made, the State of New Hampshire shall be entitled to chuse three, Massachusetts eight, Rhode-Island and Providence Plantations one, Connecticut five, New-York six, New Jersey four, Pennsylvania eight, Delaware one, Maryland six, Virginia ten, North Carolina five, South Carolina five, and Georgia three.

HISTORY

THE question of representation in the House of Representatives and Senate gave rise to the bitterest of the controversies that beset the deliberations of the convention. At first the advocates of the Virginia Plan won a sweeping success, and representation in both branches in proportion to population was agreed to. Then the small states threatened to disrupt the Union unless they were at least given an equal vote in the Senate. Such equality was at length accorded by the "great compromise" which was finally accepted on July 16.[22]

The original Virginia Plan in Randolph's second resolution provided, with respect to *both* branches of the national legislature, that

[22] See pages 46–49 above. Regarding the demands of the small states, Hamilton commented: "The truth is it is a contest for power, not for liberty." *Ibid.*, I, 466 (June 29).

representation "ought to be proportioned to the Quotas of contribution, or to the number of free inhabitants, as the one or the other rule may seem best in different cases."[23] When this resolution was discussed in Committee of the Whole, a substitute would have been adopted stating "that the equality of suffrage established by the articles of Confederation ought not to prevail in the national Legislature, and that an equitable ratio of representation ought to be substituted,"[24] but the subject was postponed when the Delaware delegates called attention to the restrictions contained in their instructions.[25] When the topic was again considered, Brearley of New Jersey admitted the fairness of the proposal, but only upon condition "that all the existing boundaries be erased, and that a new partition of the whole" territory embraced in the Union be made into thirteen equal parts.[26] Paterson repeated the same thought, and likewise asserted warmly that New Jersey would never confederate on the plan under consideration. "He had rather submit to a monarch, to a despot, than to such a fate."[27] Wilson replied that for New Jersey to have the same vote and influence in the councils of the nation as Pennsylvania was unjust. "I never will confederate on this plan. . . . If no state will part with any of its sovereignty, it is in vain to talk of a national government."[28]

On June 11, Sherman of Connecticut first mentioned the ultimately successful "Connecticut Compromise" of proportional representation in the lower house with equality in the Senate. Franklin also sought to pour oil on the troubled waters by a temporizing proposal. The provision for "some equitable ratio" was then agreed to.[29] Upon motion of Wilson, seconded by Pinckney, language was added adopting the rule that three-fifths of the slave population should be included when computing the number of a state's inhabitants.[30] A vote was taken on the

[23] *Ibid.*, I, 20 (May 29).   [24] *Ibid.*, I, 36–38 (May 30).

[25] These instructions had been so formulated at the request of the delegates themselves in order to relieve them of pressure. *Ibid.*, III, 575–76.

[26] *Ibid.*, I, 177 (June 9).

[27] *Ibid.*, I, 178–79. Wilson at once decried this proposal as impracticable. *Ibid.*, I, 180. It was renewed by Paterson on June 16. *Ibid.*, I, 251. Read also advanced it on June 29. *Ibid.*, I, 463. Madison repeated on June 19 that it was not practicable. *Ibid.*, I, 321. See note 16, page 41, above.

[28] *Ibid.*, I, 180, 183.   [29] *Ibid.*, I, 196–200 (June 11).

[30] *Ibid.*, I, 201 (June 11). Gerry "thought property not the rule of representation," and inquired why "the blacks, who were property in the South," should be counted "in the rule of representation more than the cattle & horses of the North." See note 51, page 47, above.

question whether each state should have an equal vote in the Senate, and that proposal was defeated. On motion of Wilson seconded by Hamilton, it was then decided that the same rule of representation should apply in the Senate as in the House.[31]

When on June 27 the topic of representation in the lower house was taken up, during debate on the report of the Committee of the Whole, heated controversy arose and continued until acceptance of the "great compromise."

Luther Martin began the discussion by his wearisome two-day speech in favor of equality of voting. In reply Madison contended that the rule of equality was neither just nor necessary for the safety of the small states. He pointed out that the interests of the large states were so diverse that no concert of action among them could be anticipated. He stated that "the two extremes before us" were "a perfect independence & a perfect incorporation" of the thirteen states. In the first case they would be independent nations, subject to no law but the law of nations. In that event the smaller states would have everything to fear from the larger. "In the last they would have nothing to fear. The true policy of the small States therefore lies in promoting those principles & that form of Govt. which will most approximate the States to the condition of Counties."[32] Before adjournment on the day of Madison's important speech, Benjamin Franklin made his proposal that sessions of the convention be opened with prayer, observing that "the longer I live, the more convincing proofs I see of this truth—*that God governs in the affairs of men.* And if a sparrow cannot fall to the ground without his notice, is it probable than an empire can rise without his aid?"[33]

The next day Gorham emphasized that the small states, rather than the large ones, had most to fear in the unhappy event of a rupture of the Union.[34] Madison impressively conjectured that if the Union were destroyed, military forces would have to be maintained which would be destructive of liberty.[35] After several other speeches, the convention on June 29 voted in favor of the proposition that representation ought not to be according to the rule established by the Articles of Confedera-

[31] *Ibid.*, I, 201–202 (June 11). In this form the seventh and eighth resolutions of the Committee of the Whole were reported. *Ibid.*, I, 236 (June 13). For later discussion of representation in the Senate, see commentary on Art. I, sec. 3, cl. 1, below.

[32] *Ibid.*, I, 446–49 (June 28). [33] *Ibid.*, I, 451.

[34] *Ibid.*, I, 462 (June 29). [35] *Ibid.*, I, 464–65 (June 29).

tion "but according to some equitable ratio of representation."[36] The rest of the seventh resolution of the Committee of the Whole was then postponed, and debate on voting in the Senate began, continuing until acceptance of the "great compromise." Part of that compromise, reported by the grand committee on July 5, was that each state be allowed one member in the lower house for every forty thousand inhabitants.[37]

The next day, on motion of Gouverneur Morris, this provision was recommitted to a committee of five, with the thought that the original number of Representatives might be fixed, and provision made for future changes in accordance with wealth and population.[38] The committee reported on July 9, but the allocation of Representatives was regarded as unsatisfactory, although the provision for future changes was accepted.[39] The first part of the report was recommitted to a grand committee,[40] which reported a new allocation the next day. This was accepted.[41] Thereupon Randolph moved to add a provision requiring Congress to cause a census to be taken within one year after its first meeting, and at regular periods thereafter.[42]

This proposal led to heated debate, in the course of which numerous conflicting amendments were advanced. Williamson of North Carolina moved that in taking the census, three-fifths of the slave population should be counted.[43] South Carolina delegates contended that slaves should be included in the census on the same basis as free citizens.[44] Gouverneur Morris replied that the people of Pennsylvania "would

---

[36] *Ibid.*, I, 460, 468 (June 29).   [37] *Ibid.*, I, 524, 526 (July 5).
[38] *Ibid.*, I, 540–42 (July 6).   [39] *Ibid.*, I, 557–60 (July 9).
[40] *Ibid.*, I, 558, 562 (July 9).
[41] *Ibid.*, I, 563–64, 570 (July 10). General Charles Cotesworth Pinckney felt that the South was insufficiently represented: "If they are to form so considerable a minority, and the regulation of trade is to be given to the Genl. Government, they will be nothing more than overseers for the Northern States." *Ibid.*, I, 567 (July 10). During debate on the allocation of representatives, King of Massachusetts mentioned that the real conflict of interest was not between the large and small states, as had been assumed in previous discussion, but "between the Southern & Eastern." *Ibid.*, I, 566 (July 10). Madison had previously emphasized this point. *Ibid.*, I, 476 (June 29); I, 486 (June 30); I, 601 (July 13); II, 10 (July 14).
[42] *Ibid.*, I, 570–71 (July 10).   [43] *Ibid.*, I, 579 (July 11).
[44] *Ibid.*, I, 580 (July 11). General Pinckney later renewed this proposal without success. *Ibid.*, I, 596 (July 12). Only South Carolina and Georgia supported the proposal the second time. Delaware had also voted for it when it was first considered. *Ibid.*, I, 581 (July 11).

revolt at the idea of being put on a footing with slaves."[45] King of Massachusetts thought that inclusion of slaves at all "would incite great discontents among the States having no slaves."[46] The convention voted against the three-fifths rule, but then rejected the whole resolution as amended.[47]

On July 12, Gouverneur Morris successfully proposed as a compromise that "direct taxation ought to be proportioned to representation."[48] This suggestion was elaborated by Randolph and reworded by Wilson. The latter believed "that less umbrage would perhaps be taken" against counting the slaves in computing representation if it were done indirectly by making them an ingredient in the rule of taxation; and since representation was to be measured in accordance with taxation, the end in view would be attained with less dissatisfaction.[49] As adopted by the convention, Wilson's plan required a census within six years, and every ten years thereafter.[50] Upon motion of Gerry there was added a provision making direct taxation proportional to representation even before a census was taken.[51] An amendment offered by Randolph eliminated reference to "wealth" in the resolution, since population under the three-fifths rule had been accepted as the sole criterion.[52]

The resolution was finally adopted as an integral part of the "great compromise" on July 16.[53]

The Committee of Detail dealt with the subject in three sections of its draft. The first of these established the arbitrary allocation of representatives to go into force at the outset of the new government; the second provided for future regulation "by the number of inhabitants, according to the provisions herein after made"; the third regulated direct taxation in accordance with the three-fifths rule and provided for a census within six years and every ten years afterward.[54]

When these provisions were debated in convention, few changes

[45] *Ibid.*, I, 583 (July 11). See also *ibid.*, I, 593 (July 12).
[46] *Ibid.*, I, 586 (July 11).   [47] *Ibid.*, I, 576, 588 (July 11).
[48] *Ibid.*, I, 589, 592–93 (July 12).   [49] *Ibid.*, I, 595 (July 12).
[50] *Ibid.*, I, 590–91, 597 (July 12).   [51] *Ibid.*, I, 598, 603 (July 13).
[52] *Ibid.*, I, 599, 603, 606 (July 13).   [53] *Ibid.*, II, 13–16 (July 16).
[54] Art. IV, sec. 3; Art. IV, sec. 4; Art. VII, sec. 3. *Ibid.*, II, 178, 182–83 (August 6). In accordance with Wilson's scheme (see note 49 just above), there was no reference to slaves in Art. IV dealing with representation. The three-fifths rule appeared, at a discreet distance farther on, in the provisions of Art. VII regarding the taxing power. The Committee of Style ignored this artifice by combining the two topics as

were made. Upon motion of Williamson of North Carolina, the words "according to the provisions hereinafter made" were replaced by "according to the rule hereafter to be provided for direct taxation."[55] This was merely a verbal clarification, without any change of meaning, but it sufficed to set off anew the controversy over inclusion of slaves. King of Massachusetts did not wish to preclude opposition to the three-fifths rule when the provisions regarding taxation were reached.[56]

Gouverneur Morris was inspired by the occasion to deliver another vigorous philippic against slavery, in support of an amendment which he offered apportioning representatives according to the number of "free" inhabitants.[57] In spirited language he proclaimed that "He never would concur in upholding domestic slavery. It was a nefarious institution—It was the curse of heaven on the States where it prevailed." Morris asked: "Upon what principle is it that the slaves shall be computed in the representation? Are they men? Then make them citizens & let them vote? Are they property? Why then is no other property included?" The houses in the city of Philadelphia, he asserted, "are worth more than all the wretched slaves which cover the rice swamps of South Carolina," and the "tea used by a Northern freeman, will pay more tax than the whole consumption of the miserable slave."

Sherman spoke in favor of conciliation and compromise. He interpreted the language used as providing only for representation of freemen in the South; they were to be represented according to the criterion of taxation; the slaves were included only in the formula by which taxes were to be measured. At all events, he and Wilson remarked, the debate on this topic was premature. Acceptance of the

---

they now appear in Art. I, sec. 2, cl. 3: "Representatives and direct taxes shall be apportioned" according to the three-fifths rule. *Ibid.*, II, 590 (September 12); II, 607–608 (September 13).

[55] *Ibid.*, II, 219 (August 8).

[56] Besides Art. VII, sec. 3, incorporating the three-fifths rule, Art. VII, sec. 4, of the draft of the Committee of Detail had granted an additional twofold advantage to the South: "The importation of slaves could not be prohibited—exports could not be taxed. Is this reasonable? . . . He never could agree to let them be imported without limitation & then be represented in the Natl. Legislature. . . . At all events, either slaves should not be represented, or exports [produced by their labor] should be taxable." *Ibid.*, II, 220 (August 8). For the compromise on this subject, see page 54 above.

[57] *Ibid.*, II, 221–23 (August 8). For earlier comments by Morris on this subject, see pages 70–71 above.

representation provision under discussion would not foreclose any desired amendments when the provisions regarding taxation were taken under consideration.[58] Accordingly, the motion made by Morris was defeated, and the recommendation of the Committee of Detail was accepted, with an amendment inserting the words "not exceeding" before "one for every forty thousand" inhabitants. Madison feared that increase in population would render the number of Representatives excessive in the future.[59] At Dickinson's suggestion it was provided that each state should have at least one Representative.[60]

Subsequently an amendment was adopted requiring the first census to be taken within three years, rather than six, from the first meeting of Congress.[61]

The Committee of Style rearranged the material dealing with representation in substantially the form in which it now stands as Article I, section 2, clause 3, of the Constitution.[62] One final change was made on the last day of the convention, following George Washington's first speech: in order to increase the number of Representatives, "thirty thousand" was substituted for "forty thousand."[63]

INTERPRETATION

THE provisions regarding inclusion of slaves under the three-fifths rule in determining the basis of representation have been replaced by section 2 of Amendment XIV, which provides that "Representatives shall be apportioned among the several States according to their respective numbers, counting the whole number of persons in each State, excluding Indians not taxed," and have also been rendered inapplicable by reason of section 1 of Amendment XIII, abolishing slavery.

[58] *Ibid.*, II, 221, 223 (August 8).

[59] *Ibid.*, II, 221. Gorham pessimistically replied: "It is not to be supposed that the Govt will last so long as to produce this effect. Can it be supposed that this vast Country including the Western territory will 150 years hence remain one nation?"

[60] *Ibid.*, II, 223 (August 8).

[61] *Ibid.*, II, 339, 350 (August 20). Art. VII, sec. 3, of the draft was then under consideration. Another verbal change was made: the words "white and other" were deleted as superfluous. No one answered when King asked "what was the precise meaning of direct taxation?" As amended, the section was agreed to without further changes on August 21. *Ibid.*, II, 351, 357.

[62] *Ibid.*, II, 590–91 (September 12). On motion of Randolph, "service" was substituted for "servitude." *Ibid.*, II, 607 (September 13).

[63] *Ibid.*, II, 643–44 (September 17). See page 57 above.

The requirement of apportionment of direct taxes contained in Article I, section 2, clause 3, and in Article I, section 9, clause 4, has made resort to "direct" taxes impracticable and obsolete. Amendment XVI relieves Congress from the requirement of apportionment insofar as "taxes on incomes, from whatever source derived," are concerned.

In the convention, no one answered when King inquired just what was meant by direct taxes. This silence was symptomatic of future uncertainty on the subject.

In 1796 the Supreme Court decided that a tax[64] on carriages kept for the conveyance of persons was not unconstitutional.[65] Alexander Hamilton was one of the attorneys arguing in support of the tax. James Madison, in Congress, had contended that it was unconstitutional. President Washington had not vetoed the measure, thus evincing his opinion that there was no violation of the Constitution in imposing such a tax without apportioning it. James Wilson and William Paterson, likewise former members of the Philadelphia convention, were then justices of the Supreme Court. Having sat on the court below, in the circuit court of Virginia, Wilson did not express his views other than to indicate that his prior opinion in favor of the constitutionality of the tax had not been changed. Justice William Cushing did not take part in the decision, since on account of illness he had not heard the argument. Justices Samuel Chase and James Iredell agreed with Paterson that the tax was valid.

Chase concluded that the carriage tax was a "duty" or "excise," and could be imposed without apportionment. "It seems to me, that a tax on expense is an indirect tax; and I think, an annual tax on a carriage for the conveyance of persons, is of that kind; because a carriage is a consumable commodity; and such annual tax on it, is on the expense of the owner."[66] In other words, he construed the tax as laid upon the *use* of the carriage rather than upon *ownership* of it.

Chase went on to say by way of obiter dictum[67] "that the direct taxes

---

[64] Imposed by the Act of June 5, 1794, "upon all carriages for the conveyance of persons, which shall be kept by or for any person, for his or her own use, or to be let out for hire, or for the conveying of passengers." 1 Stat. 373–74.

[65] Hylton v. U.S., 3 Dall. 171 (1796). Hamilton's argument was not reported by Dallas but appears in Hamilton's published writings. *The Works of Alexander Hamilton*, VII, 332.

[66] 3 Dall. at 175. The rule of uniformity, prescribed by Art. I, sec. 8, par. 1, was therefore applicable, rather than the rule requiring apportionment.

contemplated by the constitution, are only two, to wit, a capitation or poll tax . . . and a tax on land. I doubt, whether a tax, by a general assessment of personal property, within the United States, is included within the term direct tax."[68]

A further argument advanced by Chase in support of his conclusion appears to be unsound. This is the argument *ab inconvenienti*, that no tax was contemplated by the Constitution as being a direct tax if it could not be apportioned without creating "great inequality and injustice."[69] To show the impossibility of equitably apportioning the carriage tax, he put the hypothetical case of two states, equal in population, required to pay $80,000 each; in one state there are 100 carriages, in the other 1,000. Taxpayer A in the one state would pay $80 for use of his carriage, while taxpayer B in the other state would pay only $8. This tax therefore could not be apportioned without great inequality and injustice.

It would seem that the impracticability of equitably apportioning a tax is not a proof that the tax is not a direct tax. The requirement of apportionment was doubtless intended to discourage resort to direct taxes by the federal government except in case of extraordinary emergencies.[70] In fact direct taxes were seldom imposed, and (except for the income tax, specifically exempted by Amendment XVI from the requirement of apportionment) are now practically obsolete.

Paterson declared that it was unnecessary to decide "whether a tax on the product of land be a direct or indirect tax." In his opinion it was questionable whether direct taxes, within the meaning of the Constitution, included any other tax than "a capitation tax, and tax on land."

[67] Dictum is judicial utterance not strictly necessary for the decision of the issues involved in the particular case before the court, and is therefore not considered as a binding precedent in future cases under the rule of *stare decisis.*

[68] Since he held the tax to be valid, he found it unnecessary to consider whether the Court had power to declare an Act of Congress void for unconstitutionality, but declared that if the Court had such power he would never exercise it except "in a very clear case." *Ibid.,* 175.

[69] *Ibid.,* 174. This is reasoning in a circle. Paterson pointed out that the advocates on both sides of the case were guilty of circular reasoning. *Ibid.,* 176. Iredell also expressed the view that perhaps a direct tax "can mean nothing but a tax on something inseparably annexed to the soil: something capable of apportionment, under all such circumstances. A land or a poll tax may be considered of this description." He remarked that it was not necessary to give a complete definition of direct taxes; it was sufficient to find that the carriage tax was not a direct tax. *Ibid.,* 183.

[70] See statement of Attorney General Richard Olney at 158 U.S. 606.

He pointed out that the constitutional provision requiring apportionment of direct taxes was made for the benefit of the Southern states, which "possessed a large number of slaves" and "had extensive tracts of territory thinly settled, and not very productive." Without the requirement of apportionment, those states would have been at the mercy of the other states. Congress could have taxed slaves at so much a head and land at so much an acre, to the disadvantage of the South.[71] Paterson concluded by quoting with approval from Adam Smith's *Wealth of Nations* the characterization of an indirect tax as one falling upon expense or consumption. Hence, in Paterson's opinion, "All taxes on expenses or consumption are indirect taxes; a tax on carriages is of this kind, and of course, is not a direct tax."[72]

The dictum in the carriage tax case was accepted as law by legal writers and by the Supreme Court in subsequent opinions. However, in 1895 the Court was invited by eminent counsel to correct "a century of error" by holding that a tax on income from land or personalty was a direct tax, and that the statute imposing such a tax[73] was void for want of apportionment. The Court, perhaps frightened by the specter of socialism,[74] did make such a holding.[75]

[71] 3 Dall. at 177. Paterson held that the rule of apportionment should not be extended any further than necessary. It was the product of compromise; "it is radically wrong; it cannot be supported by any solid reasoning. Why should slaves, who are a species of property, be represented more than any other property? The rule, therefore, ought not to be extended by construction." *Ibid.*, 178.

[72] *Ibid.*, 180. "In many cases of this nature, the individual may be said to tax himself." In other words, he need not use his property in such a way as to incur the tax. The tax is not an obligation inseparable from ownership of the property. (See 157 U.S. at 627.) Accepting this definition of the tax from the economists, was not Madison right in believing that the tax was unconstitutional? Did it not fall upon the *ownership* of carriages as such, rather than upon their *use* for conveying persons? On numerous occasions the Court repeated the notion that land and poll taxes were the only form of direct tax.

[73] Section 27 of the Act sent to the President on August 15, 1894, which became law without his approval, imposed a tax of 2 per cent on income (over $4,000 a year) "derived from any kind of property, rents, interest, dividends, or salaries, or from any profession, trade, employment, or vocation carried on in the United States or elsewhere, or from any other source whatever." 28 Stat. 553.

[74] At the outset of his argument Joseph H. Choate asserted that the legislation was "communistic in its purposes and tendencies," and was defended (by eminently respectable James C. Carter and Attorney General Richard Olney) "upon principles as communistic, socialistic—what shall I call them—populistic as ever have been addressed to any political assembly in the world." 157 U.S. 532.

[75] Pollock v. Farmers' Loan and Trust Co., 157 U.S. 429; 158 U.S. 601 (1895).

In its first opinion, the Court decided that a tax on income from real estate was a direct tax.[76] The Court also concluded unanimously that interest from state or municipal bonds could not be taxed (either directly or indirectly). But the Court was equally divided and could not reach a decision on the taxability of income from other personal property.[77] After rehearing, the Court reaffirmed its former rulings and further held that a tax on income from personal property was also direct.[78]

The Court also held that, although the tax imposed on earned income from professions, trades, employment, or vocations was valid as an excise, the entire scheme of income taxation must fall since Congress would not have wished the entire burden of the levy to be borne by this one group of taxpayers after income from real estate and personal property had been excluded.[79]

As pointed out by Justice Edward Douglass White (later Chief Justice) in a dissenting opinion, the Court's decision discriminated against taxpayers whose income was not derived from rents, dividends, or interest. Earned income, based upon the exercise of a trade, profession, or business, could be subjected to an *excise* tax, based not upon ownership of property but upon the gainful activity engaged in by the taxpayer. This discrimination was unfair and unjust.[80] Consequently, in 1913, after strenuous political efforts by William Jennings Bryan

[76] 157 U.S. at 583. This ruling was made by a five-to-four vote.

[77] *Ibid.*, 586.

[78] 158 U.S. at 618, 628. This ruling was made by a five-to-four vote. One Justice must have changed his mind, since Justice Jackson, who did not participate in the first hearing, dissented in the second decision.

[79] *Ibid.*, 637.

[80] 158 U.S. at 712. Justice Harlan made the same point in his dissent. *Ibid.*, 661. In measuring the extent of an excise tax the Court did not apply the familiar aphorism of Justice Holmes that "Upon this point a page of history is worth a volume of logic." N.Y. Trust Co. v. Eisner, 256 U.S. 345, 349 (1921). Justice Field's vigorous condemnation of the overruling of prior decisions (157 U.S. at 638) was comparable to the similar caustic complaint of Justice Roberts in Smith v. Allwright, 321 U.S. 649, 669 (1944), against bringing "adjudications of this tribunal into the same class as a restricted railroad ticket, good for this day and train only." It should be noted that in Springer v. U.S., 102 U.S. 586, 602 (1881), the precise point decided was that an income tax was not a direct tax. The opinion did not state what type of income was there involved, but examination of the original record showed that it was interest on United States bonds and professional fees as an attorney at law. Hence the Pollock court did not consider the Springer case as authoritative with respect to income derived from real or personal property. 157 U.S. at 579.

and others to empower Congress to meet the nation's revenue needs by an income tax applicable to the vested interests as well as to the working classes, the Sixteenth Amendment was ratified. Its provisions authorized Congress "to lay and collect taxes on incomes, from whatever source derived, without apportionment among the several States, and without regard to any census or enumeration."[81]

ART. I, SEC. 2, CL. 4

When vacancies happen in the Representation from any State, the Executive Authority thereof shall issue Writs of Election to fill such Vacancies.

HISTORY

THIS provision originated in the Committee of Detail.[82] Accepted without debate on August 9,[83] it was improved in its wording by the Committee of Style.[84] Randolph's draft used by the Committee of Detail shows that at first he had written: "Vacancies shall be supplied by a writ from the speaker or any other person, appointed by the house." This was changed to read: ". . . governor of the state, wherein they shall happen."[85] The idea may have been taken from the Virginia constitution of 1776, which empowered the lower house to "direct writs of election, for the supplying of intermediate vacancies."[86]

---

[81] In spite of the inclusiveness of the phrase "from whatever source derived," income from salaries paid by the state or to federal judges, or from interest on federal, state, or municipal bonds, was long exempt from federal income tax. The exemption of state salaries accorded in Collector v. Day, 11 Wall. 113, 127 (1871), was nullified by Graves v. New York, ex rel. O'Keefe, 306 U.S. 466, 480 (1939). The exemption of federal judges granted in Evans v. Gore, 253 U.S. 245, 259 (1920), was withdrawn in O'Malley v. Woodrough, 307 U.S. 277, 282 (1939). Federal government bonds issued since March 1, 1941, are taxable, the prior exemption having been merely statutory. State and municipal bonds are still exempt.

[82] Art. IV, sec. 7. "Vacancies in the House of Representatives shall be supplied by writs of election from the executive authority of the State, in the representation from which it shall happen." Farrand, *Records*, II, 179 (August 6).

[83] *Ibid.*, II, 227, 231.   [84] *Ibid.*, II, 591 (September 12).   [85] *Ibid.*, II, 140.

[86] Thorpe, *Federal and State Constitutions*, VII, 3816. Other state constitutions contained similar provisions. *Ibid.*, I, 563 (Delaware); II, 779 (Georgia); V, 2791 (North Carolina). See also Fisher, *The Evolution of the Constitution of the United States*, 313.

INTERPRETATION

SINCE the House of Representatives, in Mason's words, is "the grand depository of the democratic principle" of the government,[87] a vacancy can be filled only by popular election. Compare the provisions for filling vacancies in the Senate. Under Article I, section 3, clause 2, a temporary appointment to the Senate could be made by the state executive until the next meeting of the legislature. Under Amendment XVII, section 2, temporary appointments may be made by the executive if the state law so provides.

ART. I, SEC. 2, CL. 5

The House of Representatives shall chuse their Speaker and other Officers; and shall have the sole Power of Impeachment.

HISTORY

THIS provision also originated in the Committee of Detail.[88] One of the resolutions referred to that committee had provided that the executive should be impeachable.[89] That the House of Representatives should be the impeaching body was in accordance with English practice, and with the provisions of several state constitutions.[90] One of the ill-starred acts of Charles I preceding the loss of his throne was an attempt to impeach in the House of Lords a peer and five members of the House of Commons.[91]

INTERPRETATION

THE power of impeachment was a weapon often used by the Commons during their struggle with the crown in Stuart times as a means of removing royal favorites from high office.[92] Impeachment differed

[87] Farrand, *Records*, I, 48 (May 31).

[88] Art. IV, sec. 6. *Ibid.*, II, 178–79 (August 6). It was adopted without debate on August 9, and slight verbal changes were made by the Committee of Style and the convention. *Ibid.*, II, 227, 231 (August 9); II, 591 (September 12); II, 610 (September 14).

[89] *Ibid.*, II, 132, 134.

[90] See Chafee, *Three Human Rights in the Constitution*, 105–44; Taswell-Langmead, *English Constitutional History*, 631–43; Fisher, *The Evolution of the Constitution of the United States*, 78; Thorpe, *Federal and State Constitutions*, III, 1897.

[91] Chafee, *Three Human Rights in the Constitution*, 74. See page 10 above.

[92] Chafee, *Three Human Rights in the Constitution*, 98–144.

from a bill of attainder in that the latter required the royal assent, like any other legislation by Parliament, whereas an impeachment was tried before the House of Lords, sitting as a court.[93] Ordinarily, in those days, the fall of a detested royal favorite, whether by impeachment or attainder, meant condemnation to death as a traitor.[94] Not until the nineteenth-century doctrine of responsibility of the king's ministers to Parliament had been developed was it possible for Parliament to remove a minister from office by a mere vote of no confidence. The United States Constitution anticipated the merciful mildness of later English practice by providing that impeachment should be attended by no harsher consequences than exclusion from public office.[95] Neither by impeachment nor by attainder could Congress get rid of an unwanted official by condemning him to death.

The two most prominent instances where impeachment has been resorted to by Congress are those of Supreme Court Justice Samuel Chase in 1804[96] and of President Andrew Johnson in 1868.[97] Both cases resulted in acquittal.

ART. I, SEC. 3, CL. 1

The Senate of the United States shall be composed of two Senators from each State, chosen by the Legislature thereof, for six Years; and each Senator shall have one Vote.

[93] *Ibid.*, 104. See comment on Art. I, sec. 9, cl. 3, and Art. I, sec. 10, regarding bills of attainder.

[94] *Ibid.*, 103.

[95] *Ibid.*, 144. See commentary on Art. I, sec. 3, cl. 6 and cl. 7, and on Art. II, sec. 4.

[96] The articles of impeachment were delivered to the Senate on December 7, 1804. On January 2, 1805, Chase appeared and requested time to prepare his answer. On the following day the trial was postponed until February 4, 1805. On March 1, 1805, the vote of acquittal was taken. Charles Evans, *Report of the Trial of the Hon. Samuel Chase*, 3–11, 268. See also Henry Adams, *History of the United States*, II, 218–44; and Albert J. Beveridge, *Life of John Marshall*, III, 157–222.

[97] On March 4, 1868, the articles of impeachment were delivered to the Senate. Trial began on March 13, 1868, and the votes of acquittal were taken on May 16 and May 26, 1868. *Proceedings in the Trial of Andrew Johnson*, 3, 8, 853–54, 860–61. See also Lloyd P. Stryker, *Andrew Johnson*, 581–731; H. H. Walker Lewis, "The Impeachment of Andrew Johnson," *American Bar Association Journal*, Vol. XL, No. 1 (January, 1954), 15–18, 80–87.

HISTORY

THE struggle over representation in the Senate was the most violent of the controversies which marked the deliberations of the convention. At first the proponents of the Virginia Plan prevailed in establishing the principle that proportional representation of the population of the several states should be the rule in the Senate, as well as in the House of Representatives.[98] As late as July 2, when the defeat by a tie vote of a proposal for equal voting by states in the Senate was a technical victory for the proponents of the Virginia Plan, they were still ruling the convention.[99] But the unshakable insistence of the small states upon equality, at least in one branch of the Congress, could not be denied. Without concession on this point they would have refused to continue in the Union.[100] After the "great compromise" on this issue, sponsored by Connecticut, the small states were in the forefront of those who proposed to grant increased powers to the national government.

Ellsworth of Connecticut proposed equality in the Senate as soon as the vote accepting representation proportioned to population had been accepted for the House of Representatives. "He was not sorry on the whole he said that the vote just passed, had determined against this rule in the first branch. He hoped it would become a ground of compromise with regard to the 2d. branch. We were partly national; partly federal. The proportional representation in the first branch was conformable to the national principle & would secure the large States agst. the small. An equality of voices was conformable to the federal principle and was necessary to secure the Small States agst. the large. He trusted that on this middle ground a compromise would take place. He did not see that it could on any other. And if no compromise should take place, our meeting would not only be in vain, but worse than in vain."[101]

[98] See commentary on Art. I, sec. 2, cl. 3, above.

[99] Farrand, *Records*, I, 509, 510 (July 2).

[100] A grand committee was appointed to endeavor to effect a compromise. *Ibid.*, I, 509, 511, 516 (July 2). The committee reported on July 5. *Ibid.*, I, 524, 526. This "great compromise" was finally adopted on July 16. *Ibid.*, II, 13–16. The part relating to equality of voting had been tentatively accepted on July 7. *Ibid.*, II, 549, 551.

[101] *Ibid.*, I, 468–69 (June 29). Dr. Johnson, of Connecticut, had outlined the same proposal earlier on that day. *Ibid.*, I, 462. On June 11, Sherman had unsuccessfully made the same proposal. *Ibid.*, I, 196, 201.

In arguing against the position of the small states, Madison empha-sized that there was no danger of a combination of the large states against the small; the real conflict of interests was between the North-ern and Southern states.[102] He also argued that if there were separa-tion, it was not the large states that would suffer most. He foreshadowed Lincoln's question: can enemies make treaties more easily than friends can make laws? Gunning Bedford's threat that the small states might find foreign powers "who will take them by the hand and do them justice" was made on the same day.[103] King of Massachusetts spoke firmly for the large-state view.

Wilson had consistently favored election of Senators by the people rather than by state legislatures.[104] The latter mode was accepted, how-ever, upon Dickinson's motion.[105]

A seven-year term was agreed to on June 12; this was later reduced to six.[106]

Voting per capita in the Senate was suggested by Gerry, in order to avoid the inconveniences of voting by states as had been the practice under the Articles of Confederation.[107] On July 23 it was decided that there should be two Senators from each state, voting per capita.[108]

INTERPRETATION

IN 1913 the provision that Senators should be "chosen by the Legisla-ture" of the state which they were to represent was changed by the Seventeenth Amendment to read "elected by the people." The same

---

[102] Ibid., I, 486 (June 30). General recognition of the truth of this observation, first enunciated by Madison, caused further deadlock on the issues of slave trade and regulation of commerce, necessitating another of the important compromises adopted by the convention. See note 41, page 70, above.

[103] Ibid., I, 492 (June 30). See page 46 above.

[104] Ibid., I, 52 (May 31); I, 151, 154, 155 (June 7).

[105] Ibid., I, 148–49, 156 (June 7).

[106] Ibid., I, 211, 219 (June 12); I, 418, 426 (June 26). The change was made in conjunction with adoption of triennial rotation. Williamson of North Carolina was the first to propose six years. His motion was defeated. Ibid., I, 409 (June 25). After five years and nine had been rejected, Gorham successfully renewed the six-year proposal.

[107] Ibid., II, 5 (July 14). It was adopted on July 23. Ibid., II, 85, 94–95. Martin opposed it "as departing from the idea of the States being represented" in the Senate.

[108] Ibid., II, 85, 94–95 (July 23). The decisions of the convention were embodied in Art. V, sec. 1, of the draft of the Committee of Detail. Ibid., II, 179 (August 6). The wording was improved by the Committee of Style. Ibid., II, 591 (September 12).

qualifications for electors were prescribed as were in force with respect to the election of Representatives by virtue of Article I, section 2.

ART. I, SEC. 3, CL. 2

Immediately after they shall be assembled in Consequence of the first Election, they shall be divided as equally as may be into three Classes. The Seats of the Senators of the first Class shall be vacated at the Expiration of the second Year, of the second Class at the Expiration of the fourth Year, and of the third Class at the Expiration of the sixth Year, so that one third may be chosen every second Year; and if Vacancies happen by Resignation, or otherwise, during the Recess of the Legislature of any State, the Executive thereof may make temporary Appointments until the next Meeting of the Legislature, which shall then fill such Vacancies.

HISTORY

THE idea of rotation in the Senate in order to ensure continuity and stability was suggested by Gorham and supported by Randolph.[109] The principle was immediately accepted, although the length of the term had not yet been fixed at six years.[110]

The provision permitting temporary appointment of Senators to fill vacancies originated with the Committee of Detail.[111] To this was added, at Madison's suggestion, language recognizing the right of a Senator to resign, or to refuse to serve. Otherwise, Madison feared, a state legislature could render one of its citizens ineligible to civil office under the federal government by designating him as a Senator.[112] The

[109] *Ibid.*, I, 408 (June 25).

[110] See commentary on Art. I, sec. 3, cl. 1, above. For preliminary versions in the Committee of Detail, see Farrand, *Records*, II, 141, 154–55. The proposal became Art. V, sec. 2, of that committee's draft, which was later reworded by the Committee of Style. *Ibid.*, II, 179 (August 6); II, 591 (September 12). The words "by lot," which had been omitted by the Committee of Style, were restored but then deleted upon motion of Madison in order to ensure that no state would lose both of its Senators at the same time. *Ibid.*, II, 612 (September 14).

[111] In Art. V, sec. 1, of the draft, the third sentence reads: "Vacancies may be supplied by the Executive until the next meeting of the Legislature." *Ibid.*, II, 179 (August 6).

[112] *Ibid.*, II, 232 (August 9).

Committee of Style appended these provisions to those relating to rotation, and improved the wording.[113]

INTERPRETATION

THE method of filling vacancies is now regulated by Amendment XVII, paragraph 2, which provides that the executive authority of the state "shall issue writs of election to fill such vacancies: *Provided*, That the legislature of any State may empower the executive thereof to make temporary appointments until the people fill the vacancies by election as the legislature may direct."

ART. I, SEC. 3, CL. 3

No Person shall be a Senator who shall not have attained to the Age of thirty Years, and been nine Years a Citizen of the United States, and who shall not, when elected, be an Inhabitant of that State for which he shall be chosen.

HISTORY

THE original Virginia Plan had proposed an age requirement, but had left blank the number of years to be required. On June 12 in Committee of the Whole thirty years was accepted as the requisite age.[114]

The Committee of Detail proposed a requirement of four years' citizenship for Senators.[115] Since the requirement for Representatives had been increased to seven years, it seemed proper that the requirement for Senators be proportionately increased. Gouverneur Morris proposed fourteen. After considerable debate, the nine-year requirement was adopted.[116] During the course of this debate Wilson remarked that he would find it embarrassing to be excluded from office "under the very Constitution which he had shared in the trust of making."[117]

[113] *Ibid.*, II, 591 (September 12). The words "which shall then fill such vacancies" were then added in convention. *Ibid.*, II, 610 (September 14).

[114] *Ibid.*, I, 20 (May 29); I, 211, 217 (June 12).

[115] Art. V, sec. 3. *Ibid.*, II, 179 (August 6). It proposed three years for members of the lower house. Art. IV, sec. 2. *Ibid.*, II, 178. That had been increased to seven years at the suggestion of Mason. *Ibid.*, II, 213, 216 (August 8). The Committee of Detail proposed the requirement of residence within the state at the time of election for both Representatives and Senators.

[116] *Ibid.*, II, 228, 239 (August 9). "Inhabitant" was substituted for "resident" to conform to a similar amendment previously made in Art. I, sec. 2, cl. 2. *Ibid.*, II, 213, 216–18 (August 8).

His subsequent attempt to reduce the nine-year requirement to seven was unsuccessful.[118]

INTERPRETATION

IT was decided in the case of Henry Clay, and more recently in the case of Rush D. Holt of West Virginia, that a Senator could be elected before reaching the age of thirty; it is sufficient that he is qualified when he assumes his duties. The residence requirement, however, is applicable as of the date of election.

ART. I, SEC. 3, CL. 4

The Vice President of the United States shall be President of the Senate, but shall have no Vote, unless they be equally divided.

HISTORY

"IF the vice-President were not to be President of the Senate, he would be without employment," said Sherman, in answer to opponents of this intrusion of an executive officer into the midst of legislative affairs. Further explanation of the reason for creating the office was given by Williamson of North Carolina, who "observed that such an officer as vice-President was not wanted. He was introduced only for the sake of a valuable mode of election which required two to be chosen at the same time."[119]

The method of choosing the executive was among the matters referred to the Committee of Postponed Parts, which on September 4 reported a system requiring electors in each state to vote for two persons, one of whom had to be an inhabitant of some other state.[120] The Vice-Presidency was a sort of consolation prize to the person getting the second highest number of votes in the balloting for President.

[117] *Ibid.*, II, 237 (August 9).

[118] *Ibid.*, II, 266, 272 (August 13). At the same time he had unsuccessfully sought to reduce from seven to four years the citizenship requirement for Representatives. *Ibid.*, II, 265, 268–69 (August 13).

[119] *Ibid.*, II, 537 (September 7). Gerry, Randolph, and Mason opposed this provision. Mason renewed the proposal for a Privy Council. See note 95, page 55, above, and note 9, page 280, and note 17, page 282, below.

[120] *Ibid.*, II, 493–95, 497–98 (September 4). The words "ex officio" before "President of the Senate" were deleted as superfluous. *Ibid.*, II, 610, 612 (September 14). For fuller discussion of this method of election, see commentary on Art. II, sec. 1, below.

INTERPRETATION

THE right of the Vice-President to break a tie in the Senate by his "casting vote" was frequently exercised by John Adams, the first Vice-President of the United States. On March 9, 1925, there was an equal division in the Senate with respect to confirmation of Charles Beecher Warren as attorney general. Vice-President Charles G. Dawes scurried to the Capitol in a taxicab, but before he reached the Senate chamber the nomination was defeated when one of the Senators who had supported it changed his vote.

ART. I, SEC. 3, CL. 5

The Senate shall chuse their other Officers, and also a President pro tempore, in the Absence of the Vice President, or when he shall exercise the Office of President of the United States.

HISTORY

THE Committee of Detail had proposed that "The Senate shall chuse its own President and other officers."[121] The wording was subsequently revised by the Committee of Style in order to conform to the plan of choosing the executive reported by the Committee on Postponed Parts on September 4.[122]

INTERPRETATION

ARTICLE II, section 1, clause 5, specifies the circumstances under which the Vice-President "shall exercise the Office of President."

ART. I, SEC. 3, CL. 6

The Senate shall have the sole Power to try all Impeachments. When sitting for that Purpose, they shall be on Oath or Affirmation. When the President of the United States is tried, the Chief Justice shall preside: And no Person shall be convicted without the Concurrence of two thirds of the Members present.

[121] Art. V, sec. 4. *Ibid.*, II, 179 (August 6).
[122] *Ibid.*, II, 495, 498 (September 4); II, 592 (September 12).

THE Committee of Detail in a supplemental report on August 22 proposed that "Judges of the Supreme Court shall be triable by the Senate, on impeachment by the House" of Representatives.[123] The Committee on Postponed Parts extended this procedure to all impeachments.[124]

The provision that the Chief Justice shall preside in case of impeachment of the President was derived from the proposal regarding the functions of the Vice-President reported on September 4 by the Committee on Postponed Parts.[125]

The procedure for impeachment by the House and trial by the Senate was derived from the practice of the English Parliament, except that in England judges were not impeached in that manner.[126]

INTERPRETATION

POWER to impeach is given to the House of Representatives by Article I, section 2, clause 5.

Article II, section 4, provides that the President, Vice-President, and all civil officers of the United States are impeachable for treason, bribery, and other high crimes and misdemeanors, and shall be removed from office on conviction thereof.[127]

[123] *Ibid.*, II, 367 (August 22). Gerry had proposed that this subject be referred to the committee. *Ibid.*, II, 344 (August 20). The committee's original draft had provided that the jurisdiction of the Supreme Court should extend "to the trial of impeachments of Officers of the United States." Art. XI, sec. 3. *Ibid.*, II, 186 (August 6). This provision was derived from the ninth resolution of the Virginia Plan. *Ibid.*, I, 22 (May 29); II, 39, 42, 46 (July 18). Obviously this method was inappropriate for impeachments of the judges themselves.

[124] *Ibid.*, II, 493, 497 (September 4). The provision reported was approved after addition, at the suggestion of Gouverneur Morris, of the words "and every member shall be on oath." *Ibid.*, II, 547, 552 (September 8). The words "or affirmation" were added later. *Ibid.*, II, 610, 612 (September 14).

[125] *Ibid.*, II, 495, 498 (September 4). This provision constituted an exception to the rule established in Art. I, sec. 3, cl. 4, that the vice-President was to be the presiding officer of the Senate.

[126] See pages 79–80 above. By the Act of Settlement of June 12, 1701, 12 & 13 Wm. III, c. 2, sec. 3, judges were removable upon the address of both houses of Parliament. Guy C. Lee, *Source-Book of English History*, 435; Taswell-Langmead, *English Constitutional History*, 656.

[127] See page 315 below. Members of Congress are not included in the category of civil officers. They are amenable to punishment by the house of which they are members. Art. I, sec. 5, cl. 2.

Article I, section 3, clause 7, provides that the penalty imposed under impeachment proceedings shall not extend further than to removal from office and disqualification to hold office. Impeachment does not preclude additional punishment according to the course of the common law if the same offenses constitute indictable crimes.

ART. I, SEC. 3, CL. 7

Judgment in Cases of Impeachment shall not extend further than to removal from Office, and disqualification to hold and enjoy any Office of honor, Trust or Profit under the United States: but the Party convicted shall nevertheless be liable and subject to Indictment, Trial, Judgment and Punishment, according to Law.

HISTORY

THIS provision, derived from the New York constitution, was proposed in its present wording by the Committee of Detail.[128]

INTERPRETATION

IN England impeachment ordinarily resulted in the death penalty.[129] Jefferson regarded impeachment as an ineffective "scarecrow" after the acquittal of Justice Chase on March 1, 1805.[130]

ART. I, SEC. 4, CL. 1

The Times, Places and Manner of holding Elections for Senators and Representatives, shall be prescribed in each State by the Legislature thereof; but the Congress may at any time by Law make or alter such Regulations, except as to the Places of chusing Senators.

[128] Art. XI, sec. 5. *Ibid.*, II, 187 (August 6). It first appeared in Rutledge's handwriting as an insertion in a working draft in the Wilson papers. *Ibid.*, II, 173. Only typographical changes were made in the committee draft during the course of subsequent consideration. *Ibid.*, II, 435, 438 (August 28); II, 592 (September 12). For the New York precedent, see Thorpe, *Federal and State Constitutions*, VI, 2635.

[129] See page 80 above.

[130] Henry Adams, *History of the United States*, II, 218–44. For the earlier impeachment and removal of Judge Pickering, see *ibid.*, II, 143–59.

HISTORY

THIS provision originated in the Committee of Detail, substantially in its present form except for two additions.[131] Fearful that the states might prevent the functioning of the federal government by completely failing to make any regulations at all, the convention amended the clause to ensure that if necessary Congress might "make" as well as "alter" the applicable regulations.[132] Likewise the proviso regarding the places of choosing Senators was inserted lest the state legislatures be compelled to meet for that purpose "in a different place from that of their usual sessions," which would cause unnecessary inconvenience.[133]

INTERPRETATION

FEDERAL control of elections was a controversial issue not only in the Philadelphia convention but afterwards. All of the eight states which during debate on ratification proposed amendments to the Constitution desired modifications of this provision.[134] They feared that Congress might require elections to be held at inconvenient times or places, as that the election for choosing Pennsylvania's Representatives in Congress might be held at Pittsburgh.[135] Proponents of the new government, on the other hand, regarded this federal authority over elections as indispensable, lest otherwise the entire structure collapse by reason of deliberate or inadvertent failure on the part of the states to elect members of Congress.

The term "Legislature" in this clause means the lawmaking power of the state. Hence, if the state constitution so requires, the assent of the Governor is necessary in order to enact a valid redistricting statute.[136]

[131] Art. VI, sec. 1. Farrand, *Records*, II, 179 (August 6).

[132] *Ibid.*, II, 229, 242 (August 9). The wording was improved, without any change of meaning, by the Committee of Style. *Ibid.*, II, 592 (September 12).

[133] *Ibid.*, II, 613 (September 14); III, 311.

[134] Dumbauld, *The Bill of Rights and What It Means Today*, 32–33. Madison rejected in formulating the amendments which became the Bill of Rights all proposals which merely renewed controversies that had been settled by the convention at Philadelphia. *Ibid.*, 26.

[135] Warren, *The Making of the Constitution*, 763.

[136] Smiley v. Holm, 285 U.S. 355, 366–68 (1932). Similarly a popular referendum is required if made a part of the state's lawmaking power by the state constitution. Davis v. Ohio, 241 U.S. 565, 567 (1916). On the other hand, it has been held that the word "Legislatures" in Article V with respect to amending the Constitution does not have the same extensive meaning. Ratification of an amendment, the Supreme

In 1842, Congress first undertook to prescribe regulations regarding elections. In that year a statute was enacted requiring that Representatives be elected by district. Nevertheless four states (Alabama, Georgia, Mississippi, and Missouri) refused to heed this legislation and continued to elect Representatives by the general ticket system, and they were seated, there being a Democratic majority in the Twenty-eighth Congress. Similar statutes, with additional requirements, were subsequently enacted. A provision that districts be "composed of contiguous and compact territory, and containing as nearly as practicable an equal number of inhabitants" was established in 1901 and repeated in 1911, but eliminated in 1929 legislation.[137] The determination of the boundaries of electoral districts being left to the states, the Supreme Court ordinarily regards flagrant inequality among such districts as presenting a "political question" rather than a judicial question.[138]

Congress may act to such extent as it deems necessary, regulating the subject of elections either in whole or in part, and need not occupy the field entirely, to the exclusion of state action.[139] But federal power extends to every stage of the process by which members of Congress are chosen.[140]

ART. I, SEC. 4, CL. 2

The Congress shall assemble at least once in every Year, and such

Court says, is not an act of legislation but is an "expression of the assent of the State" to the amendment proposed by Congress. Hawke v. Smith (No. 1), 253 U.S. 221, 229 (1920); National Prohibition Cases, 253 U.S. 350, 386 (1920).

[137] See the articles by Emanuel Celler and Joel F. Paschal listed in the Bibliography, and the cases of Wood v. Broom, 287 U.S. 1, 5–7 (1932); and Colegrove v. Green, 328 U.S. 549, 555 (1946).

[138] Colegrove v. Green, 328 U.S. 549, 555 (1946). But see the new trend typified by Gomillion v. Lightfoot, 364 U.S. 339, 346–47 (1960); and Baker v. Carr, 369 U.S. 186, 209–10 (1962). The latter case was one dealing under the equal protection clause with state regulation of state legislative districts. If congressional districts had been involved, the question would perhaps still have been regarded as political because under Art. I, sec. 4, the matter is subject to the supervision of Congress.

[139] Ex parte Siebold, 100 U.S. 371, 383 (1880). Congress can enforce by penalties the duties it prescribes with regard to federal elections, and may do this by adding federal sanction to state election laws, insofar as federal offices are concerned, rather than by enacting entirely independent regulations. *Ibid.*, 387–88. See also Ex parte Yarbrough, 110 U.S. 651, 660–63 (1884).

[140] Newberry v. U.S., 256 U.S. 232, 250, 256 (1921); U.S. v. Classic, 313 U.S. 299, 317 (1941); Smith v. Allwright, 321 U.S. 649, 664 (1944).

Meeting shall be on the first Monday in December, unless they shall by Law appoint a different Day.

HISTORY

THIS provision originated with the Committee of Detail,[141] which patterned many details regarding the organization and functioning of Congress after similar provisions in state constitutions, especially that of Massachusetts.[142]

On August 7, during debate, Madison questioned the wisdom of fixing the date for the meeting of Congress, suggesting "that it be required only that one meeting at least should be held every year leaving the time to be fixed or varied by law."[143] Gouverneur Morris wished to eliminate the entire provision. After debate, an amendment by Randolph was accepted, adding the words "unless a different day shall be appointed by law." Morris then proposed to substitute May for December, because "It might frequently happen that our measures ought to be influenced by those in Europe, which were generally planned during the Winter and of which intelligence would arrive in the Spring." Madison supported the proposal because in May the season of the year would be better for traveling. Wilson observed that "The Winter is the most convenient season for business," and Ellsworth remarked that a summer session would interfere with farming operations. Randolph concluded that December would be more harmonious with the dates fixed in state constitutions for holding elections, and pointed out that it would be desirable "to render our innovations as little incommodious as possible." The change proposed by Morris was voted down.[144]

INTERPRETATION

THE "lame duck" amendment sponsored by Senator George Norris of Nebraska, which took effect in 1933 (Amendment XX), provided that the yearly session should "begin at noon on the 3d day of January" rather than on the first Monday in December.

[141] Art. III, last sentence. Farrand, *Records*, II, 177 (August 6).

[142] The December date of meeting had a precedent in Art. XI of the South Carolina constitution of 1776. Thorpe, *Federal and State Constitutions*, VI, 3245.

[143] Farrand, *Records*, II, 197 (August 7).

[144] *Ibid.*, II, 198–200. No change was made by the Committee of Style. *Ibid.*, II, 592 (September 12).

ART. I, SEC. 5, CL. I

Each House shall be the Judge of the Elections, Returns and Quali-
fications of its own Members, and a Majority of each shall constitute
a Quorum to do Business; but a smaller Number may adjourn from
day to day, and may be authorized to compel the Attendance of
absent Members, in such Manner, and under such Penalties as each
House may provide.

HISTORY

THIS clause originated in the Committee of Detail, being derived from the provisions of various state constitutions.[145] During debate, Gorham contended that it should be possible to do business with less than a majority present; otherwise great delay and inconvenience might result. Mercer pointed out that the requirement of a majority would "put it in the power of a few by seceding at a critical moment" to paralyze the government. "He was for leaving it to the Legislature to fix the Quorum, as in Great Britain." Mason replied that it would be dangerous to the distant states to permit a small number of members to make laws, as the centrally located states could always be more fully represented at all times. He also argued on principle that "If the Legislature should be able to reduce the number at all, it might reduce it as low as it pleased" and the government would be transformed into an oligarchy.[146] At Randolph's suggestion, in order to meet Mercer's objection, language was added authorizing the attendance of absent members to be compelled.[147]

[145] Art. VI, sec. 3 and sec. 4. *Ibid.*, II, 180 (August 6). The most similar provision regarding membership is found in the Massachusetts constitution. Thorpe, *Federal and State Constitutions*, III, 1897, 1899. For less extensive provisions in Delaware, Maryland, New Jersey, New York, and North Carolina, see *ibid.*, I, 563; III, 1692; V, 2595; V, 2631; V, 2790. The New Hampshire constitution of 1784 and the Vermont constitution of 1786 provided that a majority of the members should constitute a quorum. *Ibid.*, IV, 2462.

[146] Jefferson in his *Notes on Virginia* had enumerated as one of the defects of the Virginia constitution of 1776 the fact that the assembly exercised the power to fix a quorum, "and if they may fix it at one number, they may at another till it loses its fundamental character of being a representative body." Dumbauld, *The Political Writings of Thomas Jefferson*, 105.

[147] Farrand, *Records*, II, 251–54 (August 10). The Committee of Style merely

INTERPRETATION

ALTHOUGH in practice the power of a legislative assembly to decide election cases is often influenced by political considerations, the proceeding is theoretically a judicial inquiry.[148] The Congress cannot add to the qualifications prescribed by the Constitution; its task is merely to determine whether the particular candidate for admission possesses the necessary qualifications.[149] In practice members have been excluded for polygamy and upon other grounds, but in principle it is the right of the people in a republican form of government to choose their own representatives,[150] subject only to the requirements of the Constitution, which neither Congress nor the states may add to or modify.[151]

Madison in the convention indicated that provisions regarding the choice of representatives were fundamental matters that required regulation by the Constitution. To allow Congress to determine qualifications would vest "an improper & dangerous power in the Legislature. The qualifications of electors and elected were fundamental articles in a Republican Govt. and ought to be fixed by the Constitution. If the Legislature could regulate those of either, it can by degrees subvert the Constitution. A Republic may be converted into an aristocracy or oligarchy as well by limiting the number capable of being elected, as the number authorised to elect."[152] If Congress can go beyond the Constitution and substitute its own preferences for those of the voters in determining who shall exercise the lawmaking power, it is changing

reversed the order of sec. 3 and sec. 4 of Art. VI of the draft of the Committee of Detail as amended. *Ibid.*, II, 592 (September 12). For an illustration of the importance of the power to compel the attendance of absent members, see Fisher, *Evolution of the Constitution*, 136. Such authority had been proposed in Randolph's preliminary draft in the Committee of Detail. Farrand, *Records*, II, 140, 141.

[148] Accordingly the testimony of witnesses can be compelled. Barry v. U.S. 279 U.S. 597, 613, 616 (1929).

[149] See Art. I, sec. 2, cl. 2, and Art. I, sec. 3, cl. 3.

[150] The case of John Wilkes, whose exclusion from Parliament in 1769 was in 1782 declared to be "subversive of the rights of the whole body of electors of this kingdom," is a notable precedent. Zechariah Chafee, Jr., *Freedom of Speech*, 311–54.

[151] Joseph Story held that the qualifications prescribed by the Constitution could not be modified. *Commentaries on the Constitution*, I, § 625. For Jefferson's view, see Dumbauld, *The Political Writings of Thomas Jefferson*, 150.

[152] Farrand, *Records*, II, 249–50 (August 10). The same principle was recognized in discussion of the fixing of a quorum. See note 146, page 92, above. Madison thought it applicable to salaries. See note 2, page 97, below.

the form of government.[153] If Congress can replace the representative government established by the Constitution by adding new qualifications, there would be no limit to the autocratic power which it could exercise. It could limit membership of the Senate to persons who had served three terms in the House; it could "turn our democracy into an oligarchy by imposing high property qualifications, or into a dictatorship of the proletariat by declaring ineligible all persons deriving income from rents and invested capital."[154]

ART. I, SEC. 5, CL. 2

Each House may determine the Rules of its Proceedings, punish its Members for disorderly Behaviour, and, with the Concurrence of two thirds, expel a Member.

HISTORY

THIS clause likewise originated with the Committee of Detail, and was patterned after state constitutions.[155] On motion of Madison, who observed that the right of expulsion was "too important to be exercised by a bare majority of a quorum," it was decided that a two-thirds vote should be required for that purpose.[156]

INTERPRETATION

WHERE rules affect private rights, judicial questions arise, which courts will decide.[157]

[153] See the maxims of Locke and Vattel, pages 15, 16, and note 60, page 14, above.

[154] Chafee, *Freedom of Speech*, 348.

[155] Art. VI, sec. 6. Farrand, *Records*, II, 180 (August 6). Randolph's preliminary draft provided that each house "shall have power to make rules for its own government." *Ibid.*, II, 140, 142. Rule-making power was specified in the constitutions of Delaware, Georgia, Maryland, Massachusetts, and New Hampshire. Thorpe, *Federal and State Constitutions*, I, 563; II, 779; III, 1695; III, 1899; IV, 2460, 2462. Expulsion was authorized by Delaware, Maryland, Pennsylvania, and Vermont. *Ibid.*, I, 563; III, 1692; V, 3085; VI, 3742, 3755.

[156] Farrand, *Records*, II, 254 (August 10). The Committee of Style made no change except verbal condensation. *Ibid.*, II, 592 (September 12).

[157] U.S. v. Smith, 286 U.S. 6, 33 (1932); Christoffel v. U.S., 338 U.S. 84, 89 (1949). Cf. U.S. v. Bryan, 339 U.S. 323, 344–45 (1950).

ART. I, SEC. 5, CL. 3

Each House shall keep a Journal of its Proceedings, and from time to time publish the same, excepting such Parts as may in their Judgment require Secrecy; and the Yeas and Nays of the Members of either House on any question shall, at the Desire of one fifth of those Present, be entered on the Journal.

HISTORY

THE Committee of Detail was also responsible for this clause, doubtless derived from Article IX of the Articles of Confederation.[158] The exception of parts requiring secrecy was inserted in convention.[159]

INTERPRETATION

THE purpose of this clause is of course to ensure publicity of the proceedings in order to enable the people to keep an eye on the conduct of their representatives.[160]

The journals cannot be used in court to impeach the accuracy of an enactment signed by the presiding officers of each house and by the President, and deposited with the Department of State as a law.[161]

ART. I, SEC. 5, CL. 4

Neither House, during the Session of Congress, shall, without the Consent of the other, adjourn for more than three days, nor to any other Place than that in which the two Houses shall be sitting.

[158] Art. VI, sec. 7. Farrand, *Records*, II, 180 (August 6). Six states also had such provisions. The most similar was that of New York. Thorpe, *Federal and State Constitutions*, V, 2632. New Hampshire, North Carolina, and Vermont had substantially the same type of provision. *Ibid.*, IV, 2462; V, 2794; VI, 3744, 3757. In Delaware, Pennsylvania, and Vermont the council was required to keep records (so that individual councilors might record their dissent). *Ibid.*, I, 564; V, 3088; VI, 3745, 3756.

[159] The wording accepted was apparently a revision of defeated proposals suggested by Madison and Gerry. *Ibid.*, II, 257, 259–60 (August 11). Only verbal changes were made by the Committee of Style. *Ibid.*, II, 592–93 (September 12). A later attempt by Mason and Gerry to amend the clause so as to require complete publication by the House of Representatives was defeated. *Ibid.*, II, 613 (September 14).

[160] Field v. Clark, 143 U.S. 649, 670 (1892).   [161] *Ibid.*, 672–73.

HISTORY

THIS provision also originated with the Committee of Detail.[162] A proposal by Gouverneur Morris led to insertion of the words "during the session."[163]

INTERPRETATION

THE old Congress sat in eight capitals.[164]

Under English rule, the king claimed the right to fix both the time and place of meeting of legislative assemblies. In the Declaration of Independence this was charged as a grievance, which had been experienced in Massachusetts and Virginia.[165]

---

[162] Art. VI, sec. 8. Farrand, *Records*, II, 180 (August 6). This may have been derived from Art. XVII of the South Carolina constitution. Thorpe, *Federal and State Constitutions*, VI, 3252. See also Farrand, *Records*, II, 140, 142.

[163] Farrand, *Records*, II, 261–62 (August 11). The amendment was designed to prevent the practice followed by the old Congress of moving about from place to place. The subject was complicated by the troublesome rivalry regarding the location of the seat of government. *Ibid.*, II, 261. The Committee of Style made only verbal changes. *Ibid.*, II, 593 (September 12).

[164] Robert Fortenbaugh, *The Nine Capitals of the United States*, 9.

[165] Dumbauld, *The Declaration of Independence and What It Means Today*, 100–102.

Privileges of Members

ART. I, SEC. 6, CL. I

The Senators and Representatives shall receive a Compensation for their Services, to be ascertained by Law, and paid out of the Treasury of the United States. They shall in all Cases, except Treason, Felony and Breach of the Peace, be privileged from Arrest during their Attendance at the Session of their respective Houses, and in going to and returning from the same; and for any Speech or Debate in either House, they shall not be questioned in any other Place.

HISTORY

THE Virginia Plan contemplated that members of each house would "receive liberal stipends by which they may be compensated for the devotion of their time to public service."[1] In Committee of the Whole, upon Franklin's objection, the word "liberal" was omitted, and "fixed" inserted upon Madison's suggestion. On motion of Pierce it was added, in the case of Representatives, "that the wages should be paid out of the National Treasury."[2] In the case of Senators, the Committee of the Whole rejected a proposal by Butler that no salaries be paid.[3] A subsequent proposal to the same effect, sponsored by Charles Cotesworth Pinckney and Franklin, was likewise defeated by a close vote. Pinckney thought that the Senate was meant to represent property and "ought to be composed of persons of wealth." Franklin argued that many members of the convention would likely be candidates for Senate

[1] Resolutions 4 and 5. Farrand, *Records*, I, 20 (May 29).

[2] *Ibid.*, I, 215–16 (June 12). Madison felt that it was "indecent" as well as possibly "dangerous" to "leave them to regulate their own wages." He suggested that salaries be fixed by the Constitution in terms of so many bushels of wheat, or some other staple article. See also *ibid.*, II, 45 (July 18). Randolph in a draft preserved among the work papers of the Committee of Detail attempted to formulate a provision for payment in wheat. *Ibid.*, II, 142. A motion to delete the provision for payment out of the national treasury was defeated, and it was agreed to substitute "adequate compensation" for "fixed stipends." *Ibid.*, I, 369, 374 (June 22). However, when a vote was later taken on language combining both points ("adequate compensation to be paid out of the Natl. Treasury") it was also defeated. *Ibid.*, I, 383, 385 (June 23).

[3] *Ibid.*, I, 211, 219 (June 12).

97

seats, and "If lucrative appointments should be recommended we might be chargeable with having carved out places for ourselves."[4] By the same margin Ellsworth's proposal to substitute payment by the states was defeated.[5]

However, the report of the Committee of Detail surprisingly contained a recommendation that members of both houses should be paid by the states.[6] After debate the convention in place of this provision restored the method of payment "out of the Treasury of the United States."[7] Instead of attempting to fix the scale of pay, it was decided that compensation was "to be ascertained by law."[8] Only verbal changes were made by the Committee of Style.[9]

The privilege from arrest and the protection of freedom of speech during debate were proposed by the Committee of Detail.[10]

INTERPRETATION

THE privilege from arrest is no longer of much practical importance. Following English precedent, the exception of "treason, felony, and breach of the peace" has been construed as including all criminal prosecutions; and arrest in civil cases is rare[11] since the abolition of imprisonment for debt.[12]

[4] *Ibid.*, I, 418, 426–27 (June 26). The vote was six states to five. The word "fixed" was eliminated in the interest of flexibility. *Ibid.*, I, 418, 427.

[5] *Ibid.*, I, 418, 427–28 (June 26).

[6] Art. VI, sec. 10. *Ibid.*, II, 180 (August 6). See page 54 above.

[7] *Ibid.*, II, 282, 292 (August 14).

[8] *Ibid.*, II, 283, 293 (August 14). See note 2, page 97, above.

[9] *Ibid.*, II, 593 (September 12).

[10] Article VI, sec. 5. *Ibid.*, II, 140, 141, 180 (August 6). This section was agreed to without debate on August 10. *Ibid.*, II, 254. The Committee of Style merely reversed the order of the topics, and improved the language. *Ibid.*, II, 593 (September 12). Art. V of the Articles of Confederation, as well as the Massachusetts and New Hampshire constitutions, furnished precedent. Thorpe, *Federal and State Constitutions*, III, 1899; IV, 2462.

[11] Williamson v. U.S., 207 U.S. 425, 438 (1908); Long v. Ansell, 293 U.S. 76, 83 (1934). In the latter case Justice Louis D. Brandeis said: "When the Constitution was adopted, arrests in civil suits were still common in America. It is only to such arrests that the provision applies." Mere service of summons, as distinguished from arrest, is permissible in both civil and criminal cases.

[12] Robert Morris and James Wilson, prominent members of the Philadelphia convention, subsequently suffered considerable vexation as the result of arrest for debt following financial reverses. Charles P. Smith, *James Wilson*, 384–86.

Freedom from being questioned in any other place for any speech or utterance on the floor of Congress is a right that embodies the fruits of long and strenuous struggles in Parliament against the power of the crown during the reign of the Tudors and Stuarts.[13] Peter Wentworth died in the Tower of London in 1597 for discussing matters which Queen Elizabeth I did not wish to be debated in Parliament; King James I tore out of the Commons' journal with his own hands the page on which the protest of December 18, 1621, claiming freedom of debate had been recorded; Sir John Eliot died in the Tower in 1632 after he and eight other members had been committed in violation of the Petition of Right for their part in the exciting events of March 2, 1629, when the door was locked and the speaker held in his chair to prevent adjournment by royal command before the passage of resolutions distasteful to Charles I asserting rights of the people; the same sovereign invaded the precincts of Parliament on January 4, 1642, vainly seeking to arrest five members, who had been spirited down the Thames to safety within the confines of the City of London.[14] With these and other colorful struggles in mind, the founding fathers cherished the important privilege of freedom of debates in Congress.

The privilege is equally important now, although it is sometimes abused as a means of "smearing" individuals without responsibility for libel.

Immunity from question "in any other Place" does not prevent punishment of members by Congress itself for "disorderly Behavior."[15] No instances of such discipline by Congress in fact occurred, however, prior to December 2, 1954, when the Senate censured Joseph McCarthy of Wisconsin "for insulting language about fellow-members. The carefully chosen bipartisan committee which considered the charges also recommended that the same Senator be censured for grossly insulting a distinguished general. The Senate did not bother to take a vote on this question of protecting an outsider. Thus the practice of the Senate allows a Senator to utter any falsehoods and insults he pleases, so long as he does not aim them at other Senators."[16]

[13] See Chafee, *Three Human Rights in the Constitution*, 4–89; Tenney v. Brandhove, 341 U.S. 367, 372 (1951).

[14] See pages 10–11 and 79, above.

[15] Art. I, sec. 5, cl. 2; Kilbourn v. Thompson, 103 U.S. 168, 190 (1881).

[16] Chafee, *Three Human Rights in the Constitution*, 88–89.

ART. I, SEC. 6, CL. 2

*No Senator or Representative shall, during the Time for which he
was elected, be appointed to any civil Office under the Authority of
the United States, which shall have been created, or the Emoluments
whereof shall have been encreased during such time; and no Person
holding any Office under the United States, shall be a Member of
either House during his Continuance in Office.*

HISTORY

THE Virginia Plan proposed a restriction making members of Congress "ineligible to any office established by a particular State, or under
the authority of the United States, except those peculiarly belonging
to the functions" of the legislature, during their term of service and
for one year thereafter.[17] Upon motion of Charles Cotesworth Pinckney
the ineligibility to state offices was deleted on June 23.[18] Madison then
moved that the prohibition against holding federal offices be limited
"to such offices only as should be established, or the emoluments thereof,
augmented," during the legislator's term of service. This proposal was
defeated.[19] In the case of Representatives, the period of ineligibility was
reduced to the term of service, the provision regarding one year thereafter being eliminated.[20] The Committee of Detail reported accordingly.[21] After considerable debate on August 14, the matter was postponed,[22] and was dealt with by the Committee on Postponed Parts in
its report of September 1.[23] Two days later, through the efforts of

[17] Resolutions 4 and 5. Farrand, *Records*, I, 20–21 (May 29). The period of ineligibility after expiration of the term, left blank in the original resolutions, was set
at one year for Representatives. *Ibid.*, I, 210, 217 (June 12). The same provision was
adopted for Senators. *Ibid.*, I, 211, 219 (June 12). See also *ibid.*, I, 419, 429 (June 26).
A motion by Gorham to delete the ineligibility provision in the case of Representatives
was defeated by a tie vote on June 22. *Ibid.*, I, 370, 375–77.

[18] *Ibid.*, I, 383, 386. The same deletion was made in the case of Senators on June
26 upon motion of Butler. *Ibid.*, I, 419, 429.

[19] *Ibid.*, I, 386–90 (June 23). On Sherman's motion the words "and incapable of
holding" were inserted after "ineligible to." *Ibid.*, I, 384, 390.

[20] *Ibid.*, I, 384, 390 (June 23).

[21] Art. VI, sec. 9. *Ibid.*, II, 180 (August 6).

[22] *Ibid.*, II, 283–90 (August 14).

[23] *Ibid.*, II, 483, 484 (September 1). The committee's proposal deleted the one-year

King and Williamson, language was adopted limiting the ineligibility to offices which were created or the emoluments whereof were increased during the term of service.[24] The Committee of Style made only verbal changes in this clause.[25]

INTERPRETATION

THE precedent inspiring this provision was doubtless the English Act of Settlement.[26] The king's influence in Parliament was obtained through corruption of the members by executive patronage. Hamilton, however, voicing the views of the English historian David Hume, considered "all that influence on the side of the crown, which went under the name of corruption, an essential part of the weight which maintained the equilibrium of the Constitution."[27]

Justice Hugo L. Black was appointed to the Supreme Court in 1937, when he was still a Senator. Legislation for the benefit of Justices had been passed during his term in the Senate as an aftermath of President Franklin D. Roosevelt's Supreme Court reorganization plan. An astute lawyer tried to raise the question of Senator Black's eligibility to the judicial office to which he had been appointed. The Supreme Court held, however, that the petitioner did not have the standing to raise that question.[28]

period of ineligibility after expiration of the term of service in the case of Senators. See note 20, page 100, above. The converse proposition was added that no officeholder may be a member of Congress during the term of his office.

[24] *Ibid.*, II, 487, 492 (September 3). This revived Madison's suggestion of June 23. See note 19, page 100, above.

[25] *Ibid.*, II, 593 (September 12). A loophole pointed out by Baldwin was not plugged: that members of the first Congress could hold offices created by the Constitution. *Ibid.*, II, 613 (September 14). The only such office created is that of Chief Justice. Art. I, sec. 3, cl. 6.

[26] Act of June 12, 1701, 12 & 13 Wm. III, c. 2, sec. III: "That no person who has an office or place of profit under the King, or receives a pension from the Crown, shall be capable of serving as a Member of the House of Commons." Lee, *Source-Book of English History*, 435; Taswell-Langmead, *English Constitutional History*, 656.

[27] Farrand, *Records*, I, 376 (June 22). Jefferson later made much of Hamilton's attachment to the British constitution, even including its corruption. *Writings of Thomas Jefferson*, I, 179–80. For Jefferson's opinion of the Tory historian Hume, see Dumbauld, *The Political Writings of Thomas Jefferson*, 191.

[28] Ex parte Albert Levitt, 302 U.S. 633 (1937). Apparently there is no permissible procedure by which the question could be raised. See the article by Ernest E. Clulow, Jr., listed in the Bibliography.

Article I—The Legislative Branch
Legislative Procedure

ART. I, SEC. 7, CL. I

All Bills for raising Revenue shall originate in the House of Representatives; but the Senate may propose or concur with Amendments as on other Bills.

HISTORY

WHEN originally proposed by Gerry, the provision requiring money bills to originate in the House of Representatives was defeated.[1] But it was incorporated in the "great compromise" of July 5 regarding representation in the Senate.[2] As there formulated, alteration or amendment of such bills by the Senate was prohibited. The Committee of Detail reported it in the same form.[3] On August 8, the whole clause was deleted on motion of Pinckney.[4] This vote was criticized by Randolph as disrupting the compromise of which the money bill provision had been a part,[5] and after considerable debate[6] the Committee on Postponed Parts reinstated it, modified so as to permit amendments and alterations by the Senate.[7] Gouverneur Morris moved to postpone the provision until other parts of the compromise arrangement had been accepted.[8] When satisfaction in these respects had been given, the money bill provision was accepted, with an amendment inserting the words of the Massachusetts constitution "but the Senate may propose or concur with amendments as on other bills."[9] The Committee of Style made no change.[10]

[1] Farrand, *Records*, I, 224, 233–34 (June 13).

[2] *Ibid.*, I, 524, 526–27 (July 5); I, 538–39, 543–47 (July 6).

[3] Art. IV, sec. 5. *Ibid.*, II, 178 (August 6). Art. VI, sec. 12, provided that: "Each House shall possess the right of originating bills, except in the cases before mentioned." *Ibid.*, II, 181 (August 6).

[4] *Ibid.*, II, 214, 224–25 (August 8).   [5] *Ibid.*, II, 262–63 (August 11).

[6] *Ibid.*, II, 273–80 (August 13); II, 297–98 (August 15); II, 357–58 (August 21).

[7] *Ibid.*, II, 505, 508–509 (September 5).   [8] *Ibid.*, II, 509–10 (September 5).

[9] *Ibid.*, II, 545, 552 (September 8); Thorpe, *Federal and State Constitutions*, III, 1899.

[10] Farrand, *Records*, II, 593 (September 12).

INTERPRETATION

THIS section has little practical importance, since the Senate's amending power is broad enough to permit any action desired. Thus the Senate may substitute one type of tax for another in a revenue measure originating in the House.[11]

ART. I, SEC. 7, CL. 2

Every Bill which shall have passed the House of Representatives and the Senate, shall, before it become a Law, be presented to the President of the United States; If he approve he shall sign it, but if not he shall return it, with his Objections to that House in which it shall have originated, who shall enter the Objections at large on their Journal, and proceed to reconsider it. If after such Reconsideration two thirds of that House shall agree to pass the Bill, it shall be sent, together with the Objections, to the other House, by which it shall likewise be reconsidered, and if approved by two thirds of that House, it shall become a Law. But in all such Cases the Votes of both Houses shall be determined by yeas and Nays, and the Names of the Persons voting for and against the Bill shall be entered on the Journal of each House respectively. If any Bill shall not be returned by the President within ten Days (Sundays excepted) after it shall have been presented to him, the Same shall be a Law, in like Manner as if he had signed it, unless the Congress by their Adjournment prevent its Return, in which Case it shall not be a Law.

HISTORY

THE Virginia Plan contained a proposal, modeled on the New York constitution, establishing a Council of Revision composed of the executive together with "a convenient number of the National Judiciary." The disapproval of legislation by this council would amount to rejection thereof, unless the acts thus vetoed were repassed by a certain majority.[12]

In Committee of the Whole, Gerry questioned whether the judi-

[11] Flint v. Stone Tracy Co., 220 U.S. 107, 143 (1911).

[12] Resolution 8. Farrand, *Records*, I, 21 (May 29). See Art. III of the New York constitution. Thorpe, *Federal and State Constitutions*, V, 2628–29. In his 1783 draft for revision of the Virginia constitution Jefferson favored including judges in a council of revision. Jefferson, *Papers*, VI, 282, 302–303.

ciary ought to form a part of such a council, "as they will have a sufficient check agst. encroachments on their own department by their exposition of the laws, which involved a power of deciding on their Constitutionality." It was quite foreign from the nature of their office "to make them judges of the policy of public measures." He proposed to substitute a provision giving the National Executive power to negative any legislative act which was not later re-enacted by a certain majority of each house. Rufus King seconded this proposal, "observing that the Judges ought to be able to expound the law as it should come before them, free from the bias of having participated in its formation."[13] After considerable debate Gerry's substitute was adopted,[14] with the majority necessary to override a veto being fixed at two-thirds.[15] The convention approved this provision on July 21.[16] It was amplified by the Committee of Detail,[17] which took from the Massachusetts and New York constitutions the procedure now set forth in Article I, section 7, clause 2.[18] Only slight changes of wording were made by the Committee of Style.[19]

INTERPRETATION

THE President has four alternatives, under this provision, when a bill is presented to him: (1) If he approves it, he signs it within ten days after presentation of the bill to him.[20] (2) He may allow ten days to pass without signing it; the bill will then become law without his signature, if Congress is in session. (3) He may allow ten days to pass without signing it, and if Congress adjourns in the meantime, the bill will not become law; this result is known as a "pocket veto."[21] (4) If he

[13] Farrand, *Records*, I, 97–98 (June 4).

[14] *Ibid.*, I, 94, 104 (June 4). Wilson and Madison repeatedly, but unsuccessfully, endeavored to associate the judiciary in the exercise of veto power. *Ibid.*, I, 131, 138–40 (June 6); II, 71, 73–80 (July 21); II, 294–95, 298–301 (August 15).

[15] This was later changed to three-fourths, and then restored to two-thirds. *Ibid.*, II, 295, 301 (August 15); II, 582, 585–87 (September 12).

[16] *Ibid.*, II, 41 (July 18); II, 71, 80 (July 21).

[17] Art. VI, sec. 13. *Ibid.*, II, 181 (August 6). The period within which the President had to return a bill with his objections was seven days. This was later changed to ten days (Sundays excepted). *Ibid.*, II, 295, 302 (August 15).

[18] Thorpe, *Federal and State Constitutions*, III, 1893–94; V, 2628–29.

[19] Farrand, *Records*, II, 593–94 (September 12).

[20] He may sign during a recess or after the adjournment of Congress. La Abra Silver Mining Co. v. U.S., 175 U.S. 423, 453–55 (1899); Edwards v. U.S., 286 U.S. 482, 492 (1932).

[21] The Pocket Veto Case, 279 U.S. 655, 682–83 (1929).

disapproves the bill and returns it within ten days, with a veto message stating his objections, to the house in which it originated,[22] the bill will not become law unless it is again passed in each house by a two-thirds vote.[23]

ART. I, SEC. 7, CL. 3

Every Order, Resolution, or Vote to which the Concurrence of the Senate and House of Representatives may be necessary (except on a Question of Adjournment) shall be presented to the President of the United States; and before the Same shall take Effect, shall be approved by him, or being disapproved by him, shall be repassed by two thirds of the Senate and House of Representatives, according to the Rules and Limitations prescribed in the Case of a Bill.

HISTORY

THIS provision originated in a suggestion by Madison, subsequently expanded by Randolph. It was feared that the President's veto might be evaded if it was limited to matters presented in the form of a bill.[24]

INTERPRETATION

IT has long been settled that proposed amendments to the Constitution do not require presentation to the President for his approval before they are referred to the states for ratification.[25]

---

[22] The veto is effective, even though the house where the bill originated is in recess (for not more than three days, in accordance with Art. I, sec. 5, cl. 4) when the veto message is delivered, if Congress as a whole has not adjourned. Wright v. U.S., 302 U.S. 583, 587 (1938).

[23] This means a two-thirds vote of members present, a quorum being present. Mo. Pac. Ry. Co. v. Kansas, 248 U.S. 276, 280 (1919).

[24] Farrand, *Records*, II, 295, 301–302 (August 15); II, 303, 304–305 (August 16).

[25] Hollingsworth v. Virginia, 3 Dall. 378, 381–82 (1798); Hawke v. Smith (No. 1), 253 U.S. 221, 229 (1920).

ART. I, SEC. 8, CL. I

The Congress shall have Power To lay and collect Taxes, Duties, Imposts and Excises, to pay the Debts and provide for the common Defence and general Welfare of the United States; but all Duties, Imposts and Excises shall be uniform throughout the United States;

HISTORY

SECTION 8 of Article I is one of the most important portions of the Constitution. It delineates the scope of the legislative powers delegated to the federal government. It specifies what Congress can do. Section 9 of this Article, by way of contrast, specifies what Congress cannot do. It enumerates the subject matter with regard to which the exercise of federal legislative power is prohibited. Section 10 contains prohibitions upon state action.

The manner in which the undefined legislative power originally proposed in the Virginia Plan was transformed by the Committee of Detail into a specific enumeration of particular powers has previously been described.[1]

Because the lack of a taxing power had been most severely felt under the Confederation, it was appropriately enough the first to be mentioned in the enumeration of powers to be granted to Congress.

As reported by the Committee of Detail, this provision simply read: "The Legislature of the United States shall have the power to lay and collect taxes, duties, imposts and excises."[2]

In convention there was prefixed to the clause relating to the taxing power a provision regarding payment of debts incurred under the Confederation.[3] The clause then read: "The Legislature shall fulfil the

---

[1] See pages 50, 52, above.

[2] Art. VII, sec. 1. Farrand, *Records*, II, 181 (August 6). Randolph's draft in the Committee of Detail read: "To raise money by taxation, unlimited as to sum, for the past & future debts and necessities of the union and to establish rules for collection." *Ibid.*, II, 142.

[3] Concerning this subject, see commentary on Art. VI, cl. 1. On August 21 a grand committee had reported a proposal that "The Legislature . . . shall have power to fulfil the engagements which have been entered into by Congress, and to discharge as

engagements and discharge the debts of the United-States, and shall have the power to lay and collect taxes, duties, imposts, and excises."[4] Subsequently Sherman "thought it necessary to connect with the clause for laying taxes . . . an express provision for the object of the old debts." He proposed to add the words "for the payment of said debts and for the defraying the expences that shall be incurred for the common defence and general welfare." His proposal was rejected as unnecessary,[5] but was later revived by its inclusion in the report of the Committee on Postponed Parts.[6] The Committee of Style made no change except to insert a semicolon instead of a comma before the words "to pay the debts."[7] The comma was restored in the engrossed parchment.

On September 14 was added the final clause providing for uniformity of duties, imposts, and excises throughout the United States.[8]

INTERPRETATION

AS indicated by its genesis, the true interpretation of the "general welfare" clause is that it designates the purpose for which taxes may be imposed;[9] however, it does not constitute a separate substantive power

well the debts of the United States, as the debts incurred by the several States during the late war, for the common defence and general welfare." *Ibid.*, II, 352, 355–56. This was the first reference to "common defence and general welfare" in the convention. (The phrase was doubtless derived from the Articles of Confederation.) On motion of Gouverneur Morris this language was amended to read: "The Legislature shall fulfil the engagements and discharge the debts of the United States." *Ibid.*, II, 368, 377 (August 22). This mandatory requirement was later modified. *Ibid.*, II, 408, 414 (August 25).

[4] *Ibid.*, II, 382, 392 (August 23).   [5] *Ibid.*, II, 408, 414 (August 25).
[6] *Ibid.*, II, 493, 495, 497, 499 (September 4).
[7] *Ibid.*, II, 594 (September 12). Insertion of the semicolon may have been a piece of sharp practice on the part of Gouverneur Morris, which was detected by Sherman. Max Farrand, *The Framing of the Constitition*, 178, 182–83; Farrand, *Records*, III, 379.
[8] *Ibid.*, II, 614 (September 14). This provision had been accepted previously, but was omitted by apparent inadvertence in the report of the Committee of Style. *Ibid.*, II, 473, 481 (August 13); II, 594 (September 12). According to Meigs, *Growth of the Constitution*, 133, the motion to reinsert it was made by Gouverneur Morris. For its origin, see commentary on Art. I, sec. 9, cl. 6, below.
[9] Madison believed that the power to tax and spend could be exercised only to execute other granted powers. *Writings of James Madison*, IX, 411–29; Edward M. Burns, *James Madison*, 111–12. Charles Warren regards Madison's views as truly representing the intentions of the framers of the Constitution. Warren, *The Making of the Constitution*, 475–79. The broader view of Hamilton and Story, that the taxing power was a distinct grant, limited only by the restriction that it must be used to promote the

to provide for the general welfare by measures other than taxation.[10]

The "general welfare" clause originated in an attempt to make sure that payment of old debts incurred under the Confederation, as well as current expenses, was a legitimate occasion for exercise of the taxing power of the new government. Regardless of punctuation, the words "to provide for . . . the general welfare" do not constitute a substantive power but merely specify the purposes for which taxes may be imposed. The words were first used, in this connection, when speaking of assumption of state debts, and amounted to a declaration that these debts incurred for prosecution of the Revolutionary War were indeed incurred for the general welfare of the United States, and not merely for the local benefit or individual welfare of the particular debtor state. If the words were interpreted as a substantive power to legislate for the general welfare of the nation and people, the subsequent enumeration of specific powers granted in Article I, section 8, of the Constitution as adopted would be superfluous. Moreover, the federal government would then for all practical purposes be one of unlimited general legislative power, contrary to the general understanding of the time that it was one of enumerated and limited powers.[11]

The requirement of uniformity applies to the "indirect" taxes specified in this provision. In the case of "direct" taxes the rule of apportionment applies.[12] By Article I, section 9, clause 5, taxation of exports is prohibited. In all other respects, the taxing power of Congress is plenary. A tax may be imposed as a means of conveniently enforcing regulations established by virtue of some other power possessed by Congress.[13] Nor is a tax invalid because it has a collateral regulatory purpose.[14]

"general welfare" (as distinguished from local welfare), was accepted by the Supreme Court in U.S. v. Butler, 297 U.S. 1, 65–67 (1936). The Court pointed out, however, that "The view that the clause grants power to provide for the general welfare, independently of the taxing power, has never been authoritatively accepted." *Ibid.*, 64.

[10] In 1798, Albert Gallatin claimed that Gouverneur Morris had sought, while revising the style of the Constitution, to make the "general welfare" clause "into a distinct paragraph, so as to create not a limitation, but a distinct power. The trick, however, was discovered" in time by Roger Sherman. Farrand, *Records*, III, 379. See note 7, page 107, above.

[11] Story, *Commentaries on the Constitution*, I, 662–82, §§ 907–30. See note 9, page 107, above.

[12] See Art. I, sec. 2, cl. 3, page 67, above.

[13] Sunshine Anthracite Coal Co. v. Adkins, 310 U.S. 381, 392 (1940).

[14] Sonzinsky v. U.S., 300 U.S. 506, 513 (1937); Cincinnati Soap Co. v. U.S., 301 U.S. 308, 320 (1937).

ARTICLE I—THE LEGISLATIVE BRANCH

Legislative Powers of Congress, *Finance*

ART. I, SEC. 8, CL. 2
To borrow Money on the credit of the United States;

HISTORY

THIS provision originated in the Committee of Detail. The Committee's draft read: "To borrow money, and emit bills on the credit of the United States."[15] The words "and emit bills" were deleted, on motion of Gouverneur Morris, after strenuous debate.[16] Madison accepted this amendment, in the belief that it would discourage paper money but would not prevent issuance of bills by the government if there were a real necessity to do so.

INTERPRETATION

MADISON'S ambiguous view was later accepted by the Supreme Court, after President Ulysses S. Grant had "packed" it, when emission of paper money as legal tender during the war of 1861–65 was upheld as valid.[17]

ARTICLE I—THE LEGISLATIVE BRANCH

Legislative Powers of Congress, *Commerce*

ART. I, SEC. 8, CL. 3
To regulate Commerce with foreign Nations, and among the several States, and with the Indian Tribes;

[15] Art. VII, sec. 1, cl. 8. Farrand, *Records*, II, 182 (August 6). In the committee Rutledge apparently called attention to the subject, since the words "Power to borrow Money" appear in his handwriting on Randolph's working draft. *Ibid.*, II, 144. The provision was derived from Art. IX of the Articles of Confederation.

[16] *Ibid.*, II, 303, 308–10 (August 16). The Committee of Style made no change. *Ibid.*, II, 594 (September 12).

[17] Legal Tender Cases, 12 Wall. 457, 553 (1871); overruling Hepburn v. Griswold, 8 Wall. 603, 625 (1870).

HISTORY

OF the defects felt to exist in the government under the Articles of Confederation, lack of adequate authority in Congress to regulate commerce with foreign nations was one of the principal shortcomings stressed by critics.[18] Under the wording of the Articles, federal power could be exercised only by means of a treaty.[19] As Jefferson explained to Monroe in 1785:

> Congress, by the Confederation have no original and inherent power over the commerce of the states. But by the 9th. article they are authorized to enter into treaties of commerce. The moment those treaties are concluded the jurisdiction of Congress over the commerce of the states springs into existence, and that of the particular states is superseded so far as the articles of the treaty may have taken up the subject. There are two restrictions only on the exercise of the power of treaty by Congress. 1st. that they shall not by such treaty restrain the legislatures of the states from imposing such duties on foreigners as their own people are subject to. 2dly. nor from prohibiting the exportation of any particular species of goods. Leaving these two points free, Congress may by treaty establish any system of commerce they please. But, as I before observed, it is by treaty only they can do it. Though they may exercise their other powers by resolution or ordinance, those over commerce can only be exercised by forming a treaty, and this probably by an accidental wording of our Confederation. If therefore it is better for the states that Congress should regulate their commerce, it is proper that they should form treaties with all nations with whom we may possibly treat. You see that my primary object in the formation of treaties is to take the commerce of the states out of the hands of the states, and to place it under the superintendence of Congress, so far as the imperfect provisions of our constitution will admit, and until the states shall by new compact make them more perfect. I would say then to every nation on

[18] See pages 32–33 above.

[19] Art. IX gave Congress "the sole and exclusive right and power of . . . entering into treaties and alliances, provided that no treaty of commerce shall be made whereby the legislative power of the respective States shall be restrained from imposing such imposts and duties on foreigners, as their own people are subjected to, or from prohibiting the exportation of any species of goods or commodities whatsoever." Art. VI provided that "No State shall lay any imposts or duties, which may interfere with any stipulations in treaties, entered into by the United States." In fact, however, the states disregarded their legal obligations and interfered with foreign commerce in spite of treaty provisions. In the absence of federal courts, there was no remedy for such usurpation of power by the states.

earth, *by treaty*, your people shall trade freely with us, & ours with you, paying no more than the most favoured nation, in order to put an end to the right of individual states acting by fits and starts to interrupt our commerce or to embroil us with any nation.[20]

Equally urgent was the need of a system of regulating interstate trade which would make it impossible for one state to oppress its neighbor or exploit the monopolistic advantages of its geographical situation.[21] In Madison's familiar example, New Jersey, located between the commercial cities of Philadelphia and New York, "was likened to a cask tapped at both ends," or North Carolina, between Virginia and South Carolina, "to a patient bleeding at both Arms."[22] Connecticut taxed imports from Massachusetts higher than those from England.[23] Many other instances of the evil consequences of economic localism and selfish rivalry were experienced.

Accordingly, the Virginia Plan dealt with commerce in its proposal to vest in Congress the general power "to legislate in all cases to which the separate States are incompetent, or in which the harmony of the United States may be interrupted by the exercise of individual Legislation."[24] The Committee of Detail in its more specific elaboration of the powers to be conferred upon Congress included one "To regulate commerce with foreign nations, and among the several States."[25]

A subsequent proposal to require a two-thirds majority for passage of a navigation act was defeated, after extensive debate, in accordance with a compromise reached between North and South on this topic and on the importation of slaves.[26]

An amendment relating to Indian affairs was proposed by Madison[27] and reported by the Committee of Detail.[28] Not having been acted upon, however, it was subsequently resubmitted by the Committee on Postponed Parts in a simpler form, which merely added to the commerce clause the words "and with the Indian tribes."[29]

[20] Jefferson to James Monroe, Paris, June 17, 1785. Jefferson, *Works*, IV, 420–21.

[21] See page 35 above.   [22] *Writings of James Madison*, II, 395.

[23] *Ibid.*, II, 405.   [24] Resolution 6. Farrand, *Records*, I, 21 (May 29).

[25] *Ibid.*, II, 181 (August 6). This was agreed to by the convention without debate on August 16. *Ibid.*, II, 304, 308.

[26] *Ibid.*, II, 446, 449–53 (August 29). See page 54 above, and commentary on Art. I, sec. 9, cl. 1 and cl. 5, below.

[27] *Ibid.*, II, 321, 324 (August 18).   [28] *Ibid.*, II, 367 (August 22).

[29] *Ibid.*, II, 493, 497 (September 4). This was agreed to without debate. *Ibid.*, II, 495, 499. No change was made by the Committee of Style, except that the word "and"

INTERPRETATION

THE evils which the commerce clause was meant to end were foremost among the causes which led to the Annapolis convention of 1786[30] and the subsequent convention at Philadelphia in 1787 which framed a new form of government to replace the inadequate Articles of Confederation. In the new Constitution the commerce clause was naturally a central feature.[31] It has retained its importance in the American scheme of government ever since. With the possible exception of the post office, the income tax, and the agencies directing national defense and foreign affairs, there is no branch of federal power which so directly affects the daily life of the average citizen as does that which flows from the commerce clause. Likewise with respect to the number and importance of cases brought to the Supreme Court for decision, no provision of the Constitution (except the due process clause) outranks the commerce clause.

The clause is so comprehensive and flexible that its application expands and contracts in accordance with national needs and changing circumstances. It embodies a principle which permits adequate governmental control of matters which genuinely concern more states than one without resort to the cumbersome and undesirable process of amending the Constitution. As it was capable of dealing with the transition from sailing vessels to steamboats,[32] so it is capable of coping with the problems arising from aviation and spacecraft in the atomic age. It gives expression to the distinctive feature of American federalism. In the apt words of Chief Justice John Marshall: "The genius and character of the

---

after "nations" was eliminated. *Ibid.*, II, 595 (September 12). Apparently it was restored on September 13 or 14. *Ibid.*, II, 610.

[30] See page 36 above.

[31] *Federalist* (No. 62), Lodge ed., 262–63. The persistence (in spite of the commerce clause) of narrowly parochial policies and selfish attempts to secure local advantages at the expense of outsiders is not surprising. It is simply a normal and irrepressible aspect of human nature. As Justice Oliver Wendell Holmes, Jr., said, "one in my place sees how often a local policy prevails with those who are not trained to national views and how often action is taken that embodies what the Commerce Clause was meant to end." Holmes, *Collected Legal Papers*, 296. See also Minnesota v. Barber, 136 U.S. 313, 321–22 (1890); Allen Bradley Co. v. Electrical Workers, 325 U.S. 797, 799–800 (1945); Freeman v. Hewit, 329 U.S. 249, 252, 254 (1946); H. P. Hood & Sons v. DuMond, 336 U.S. 525, 533–35, 539 (1949); Dean Milk Co. v. Madison, 340 U.S. 349, 354 (1951); Memphis Steam Laundry v. Stone, 342 U.S. 389, 395 (1952).

[32] Gibbons v. Ogden, 9 Wheat. 1, 219–21 (1824).

whole government seem to be, that its action is to be applied to all the external concerns of the nation, and to those internal concerns which affect the states generally; but not to those which are completely within a particular state, which do not affect other states, and with which it is not necessary to interfere, for the purpose of executing some of the general powers of the government."[33]

In two significant respects the interpretation placed upon the commerce clause by the Supreme Court might come as a surprise to one who looked merely at the words of the clause. In the first place, the Constitution simply confers upon Congress the power to regulate interstate and foreign commerce; it says nothing with respect to state power. Yet in a multitude of cases the Supreme Court has held that the mere existence of the clause by itself, without any exercise by Congress of the power conferred, operates by its own force as a limitation and denial of state power over subject matter included in the grant to Congress.[34] Indeed, before the enactment of the Interstate Commerce Act in 1887,[35] there was little attempt by Congress to regulate economic enterprise, and the chief significance of the commerce clause was its effect as a barrier to regulation by the states.[36]

In the second place, the Constitution says nothing in the commerce clause with respect to the exercise by Congress of power over intrastate commerce. Yet many decisions of the Supreme Court have made it

[33] *Ibid.*, 195. Jefferson expressed the same view concerning the scope of federal and state activities: "The capital and leading object of the Constitution was to leave with the States all authorities which respected their own citizens only, and to transfer to the United States those which respected citizens of foreign or other States: to make us several as to ourselves, but one as to all others. . . . And indeed, between citizens and citizens of the same State, and under their own laws, I know but a single case in which a jurisdiction is given to the General Government. That is, where anything but gold or silver is made a lawful tender, or the obligation of contracts is any otherwise impaired. The separate legislatures had so often abused that power, that the citizens themselves chose to trust it to the general government, rather than to their own special authorities." To William Johnson, June 12, 1823, in Jefferson, *Writings*, XV, 448–49.

[34] As a recent instance, see Freeman v. Hewit, 329 U.S. 249, 252 (1946).

[35] Act of February 4, 1887, 24 St. 379, 49 U.S.C.A. 1.

[36] Wickard v. Filburn, 317 U.S. 111, 121 (1924). Thus it has been said that Chief Justice Taney favored "States' rights" because the federal government had not yet undertaken affirmative regulation of commerce on an extensive scale; and advocates of exclusive federal control merely sought to block state regulation, thereby freeing business from all regulation. Charles G. Haines and Foster H. Sherwood, *The Role of the Supreme Court in American Government and Politics, 1835–1864*, 140–41, 509–10.

plain that Congress may regulate intrastate activities when such regulation is a necessary incident to the effective exercise of federal power over interstate commerce.[37]

Any discussion of judicial interpretation of the commerce clause must begin with Marshall's notable decision in the New York steamboat monopoly case.[38] That state's legislation undertook to give an exclusive right to use steamboats in New York waters to Robert R. Livingston and Robert Fulton, who licensed one Aaron Ogden to operate ferryboats between New York and certain points in New Jersey. In competition with Ogden, one Thomas Gibbons began to operate boats between the two states in reliance upon a coasting license issued by the federal government.[39] In a notable opinion, Chief Justice Marshall held that the New York legislation was unconstitutional because of conflict with the license issued in exercise of the power of Congress to regulate commerce between the states.[40] In the presence of such a collision, the federal law must prevail, by virtue of the supremacy clause (Article VI, clause 2).[41] Hence it was not necessary for the Court to determine the validity of the proposition advanced in Daniel Webster's eloquent argument[42] that the power of Congress over commerce was

[37] Chief Justice Stone said in U.S. v. Wrightwood Dairy Co., 315 U.S. 110, 119 (1942): "The commerce power is not confined in its exercise to the regulation of commerce among the states." Federal regulation of intrastate railroad rates was sustained in Houston, E. & W. Texas Ry. Co. v. U.S. [Shreveport case], 234 U.S. 342, 351–52 (1914); and Wisconsin R.R. Co. v. C. B. & Q. R.R. Co., 257 U.S. 563, 588 (1921). In Wickard v. Filburn, 317 U.S. 111, 128–29 (1942), it was held that Congress could prohibit a farmer from raising wheat for his own consumption. Congressional control of labor relations has also been approved in a number of extreme cases where the connection with interstate commerce is quite tenuous and remote, as in the case of maintenance employees in a building some of whose tenants do interstate business. U.S. v. Darby, 312 U.S. 100, 118–21 (1941); Kirschbaum Co. v. Walling, 316 U.S. 517, 524–26 (1942); Schulte Co. v. Gangi, 328 U.S. 108, 116–21 (1946).

[38] Gibbons v. Ogden, 9 Wheat. 1 (1824). Regarding this case, see Beveridge, *Life of John Marshall*, IV, 397–450; and Charles Warren, *The Supreme Court in United States History*, II, 57–80.

[39] Under the Act of February 18, 1793, 1 St. 305.

[40] 9 Wheat. at 221.   [41] *Ibid.*, 210–11.

[42] *Ibid.*, 9–14. Webster's threefold classification of exclusive powers was based upon Hamilton's analysis in *Federalist* (No. 32), Lodge ed., 186. Some powers are expressly conferred in exclusive terms (as the power to govern the District of Columbia). Others are exclusive because they are expressly denied to the states (as the power to tax imports). The third class of exclusive powers arises when an authority is granted to the Union "to which a similar authority in the States would be absolutely and totally *contradictory* and *repugnant*" (as the power to establish a uniform rule of naturalization;

exclusive, and hence that the state legislation was void whether or not there was actual conflict between it and an act of Congress.[43]

In response to the contention that the term "commerce" did not include navigation but was limited to traffic, or buying and selling commodities, Marshall formulated a comprehensive definition: "Commerce, undoubtedly, is traffic, but it is something more; it is intercourse. It describes the commercial intercourse between nations, and parts of nations, in all its branches, and is regulated by prescribing rules for carrying on that intercourse."[44] The power to "regulate," he went on to say, is the power "to prescribe the rule by which commerce is to be governed."[45] Commerce "among the several States" was defined by Marshall as "that commerce which concerns more states than one."[46]

Although Marshall spoke favorably regarding Webster's argument that the power of Congress was exclusive,[47] a later case decided by the Chief Justice seems to concede that a concurrent power of regulating commerce remains with the states, and can be exercised in the absence of conflicting action by Congress.[48]

The controversy between advocates of exclusive and concurrent power over commerce continued after Marshall's era, and was discussed at length in several cases.[49] There was great diversity of opinion among

for if each state had power to prescribe a different rule, there could not be a uniform rule).

[43] 9 Wheat. at 200, 209. Marshall said, "There is great force in this argument, and the court is not satisfied that it has been refuted." *Ibid.*, 209.

[44] *Ibid.*, 189–90. Hence it includes transportation of passengers. *Ibid.*, 215.

[45] *Ibid.*, 196. "This power, like all others vested in Congress, is complete in itself, may be exercised to its utmost extent, and acknowledges no limitations, other than are prescribed in the constitution." The power "is vested in Congress as absolutely as it would be in a single government, having in its constitution the same restrictions on the exercise of the power as are found in the constitution of the United States." *Ibid.*, 196–97.

[46] *Ibid.*, 194.

[47] Marshall pointed out that when "each government exercises the power of taxation, neither is exercising the power of the other. But, when a state proceeds to regulate commerce with foreign nations, or among the several states, it is exercising the very power that is granted to Congress, and is doing the very thing which Congress is authorized to do." *Ibid.*, 199–200. See also note 43 just above.

[48] Willson v. Blackbird Creek Marsh Co., 2 Pet. 245, 252 (1829). State legislation authorizing a dam across a navigable creek was held not to be "repugnant to the power to regulate commerce in its dormant state." Perhaps the police power was involved. Marshall mentioned that the dam, by excluding water from the marshland, would probably improve the health of the inhabitants. *Ibid.*, 251.

[49] City of New York v. Miln, 11 Pet. 102, 131–32 (1837). Here a requirement that a ship furnish a list of persons landed was held valid under the police power, and the

the members of the Court in Chief Justice Roger Brooke Taney's time, although he himself strongly espoused the concurrent power theory.[50]

At length a compromise was reached, distinguishing between subjects which imperatively require a uniform rule and those which call for diversity of treatment in accordance with local conditions. With respect to the first type of subjects the power of Congress is exclusive, and the failure of Congress to act is an implied assertion of the will of Congress that there shall be no restraints imposed. With respect to the second type, the states are free to regulate in the absence of contrary legislation by Congress.[51] With some wavering and uncertainty concerning the appropriate classification of particular cases, this rule is still followed today.[52]

In recent years the increased legislative activity of Congress has often given rise to the question whether federal statutes have preempted or "occupied the field" to the exclusion of state regulation, or whether state laws may stand unless there is an actual conflict between their provisions and those enacted by Congress.[53] This is chiefly a ques-

Court did not reach the question whether the power to regulate commerce was exclusive or concurrent. Story regarded the law as a commercial regulation, and void by reason of the exclusive power of Congress. *Ibid.*, 157–58. He stated that Marshall agreed with his view. *Ibid.*, 161. The liquor laws involved in the License Cases, 5 How. 504, 577, 595, 627, 631–32 (1847), were also upheld as an exertion of police power. But in the Passenger Cases, 7 How. 283, 572–73 (1849), the state laws requiring payment of a certain sum for each passenger landed were held void as being a revenue measure, or a regulation of commerce, and not a police measure as in the Miln case. *Ibid.*, 404, 412–14, 447–48, 457–58.

[50] See the License Cases, 5 How. 504, 578–79 (1847). According to Justice James M. Wayne in the Passenger Cases, 7 How. 283, 430–31 (1849), four Justices in the Miln case thought the power of Congress exclusive, while three did not. Two thought transportation of persons was not commerce; four disagreed. See 11 Pet. at 136, and Taney's comments at 7 How. 477, 488–89. The issue of slavery was beginning to color interpretation of the commerce clause, and Taney feared that if a state could not expel or exclude persons whom Congress saw fit to introduce, the state's control over the South's "peculiar institution" would be annihilated. 7 How. at 457, 465–66, 493, 542. See commentary on Art. IV, sec. 2, cl. 1, below.

[51] Cooley v. Board of Wardens of the Port of Philadelphia, 12 How. 299, 319 (1851). Pilotage was a subject matter of the second type, where the states were free to act in accordance with local conditions.

[52] Leisy v. Hardin, 135 U.S. 100, 109–10 (1890); Minnesota Rate Cases, 230 U.S. 352, 396–417 (1913); S.C. Hwy. Dept. v. Barnwell Bros., 303 U.S. 177, 184–85, 188 (1938); Southern Pacific Co. v. Arizona, 325 U.S. 761, 766–69 (1945). See also Noel T. Dowling, "Interstate Commerce and State Power," *Virginia Law Review*, Vol. XXVII, No. 1 (November, 1940), 1–4, 20.

[53] See page 447 below.

tion of statutory interpretation. The expressed or implied intention of Congress governs. For although it has often been said, ever since Marshall's day, that from a theoretical standpoint Congress cannot change the Constitution and confer upon the states a legislative authority which is otherwise forbidden to them,[54] nevertheless in practice it is now well established that by the consent of Congress state regulation of matters falling within the sphere of interstate commerce can be sanctioned.[55]

The Commerce Clause as a Curb on State Power

In determining the impact of the commerce clause upon state legislation, it is helpful to distinguish the type of power which the state is exerting. If a state undertakes directly to regulate commerce, it is exerting the very function that has been confided by the Constitution to other hands,[56] and this type of state legislation is least likely to receive sympathetic appraisal by the Supreme Court. It is sometimes difficult to determine whether a law requiring the payment of money is a regulation of commerce, a tax, or a police or inspection measure. Yet it is often possible to distinguish between these types of legislation with adequate certainty. The distinction between regulation of commerce and taxation is much the same as that drawn by American colonists before the Revolution when attempting to define the power of Parliament.[57] A law intended to encourage or discourage the flow of trade, or to promote the economic advantage of a particular group or locality, is a regulation of commerce; while a law intended primarily to raise

[54] Gibbons v. Ogden, 9 Wheat. 1, 207 (1824); License Cases, 5 How. 504, 580 (1847); Cooley v. Board of Wardens, 12 How. 299, 318 (1851).

[55] Bowman v. C. & N.W. Ry. Co., 125 U.S. 465, 485 (1888); Leisy v. Hardin, 135 U.S. 100, 119 (1890); *In re* Rahrer, 140 U.S. 545, 562 (1891); Clark Distilling Co. v. Western Md. Ry. Co., 242 U.S. 311, 326–31 (1917); Southern Pacific Co. v. Arizona, 325 U.S. 761, 769 (1945); International Shoe Co. v. Washington, 326 U.S. 310, 315 (1945); Prudential Ins. Co. v. Benjamin, 328 U.S. 408, 424–25 (1946); California v. Zook, 336 U.S. 725, 728 (1949).

[56] As Marshall pointed out long ago. Gibbons v. Ogden, 9 Wheat. 1, 199–200 (1824). See note 47, page 115, above.

[57] Dumbauld, *The Declaration of Independence and What It Means Today*, 6, 8, 132. The difference is likewise much the same as that between a "protective" tariff and a tariff "for revenue only." A bounty or subsidy, while the opposite of a protective tariff in its intended result, is equally a regulation of trade. It was Madison's view that the power to regulate commerce (Art. I, sec. 8, cl. 3) included the power to tax it by a protective tariff, without invoking Art. I, sec. 8, cl. 1. Madison to Joseph C. Cabell, September 18, 1828, in *Writings of James Madison*, IX, 317–18, 326.

revenue to support the expenses of government is a tax. The Supreme Court is likely to strike down a state law which attempts to control the flow of trade for the benefit of local interests at the expense of outsiders.[58] It is to Congress that the Constitution has granted the authority to determine economic policy, and to determine whether commerce shall be free or restrained or subjected to price-fixing or rate regulation.

The mounting revenue needs of the states in recent years, as the volume of public services demanded by citizens of the "welfare state" increases, have led the Court to sustain tax laws where there is no direct burden or regulation imposed upon interstate commerce,[59] and where there is no discrimination against interstate commerce as compared with intrastate commerce,[60] and no likelihood of multiple taxation.[61]

The earliest case where the Supreme Court struck down an exercise

[58] See cases cited in note 31, page 112, above; also the "drummer" cases condemning laws designed to protect local merchants by burdening itinerant sellers. Robbins v. Shelby County Taxing District, 120 U.S. 489, 492–97 (1887); Brennan v. Titusville, 153 U.S. 289, 302 (1894); Best & Co. v. Maxwell, 311 U.S. 454, 455–56 (1940); Nippert v. Richmond, 327 U.S. 416, 425 (1946).

[59] The "direct burden" test formerly in vogue [Minnesota Rate Cases, 230 U.S. 352, 396–97 (1913)] is sometimes thought to be too verbalistic or artificial a criterion to be useful. Freeman v. Hewit, 329 U.S. 249, 269–70 (1946). But the importance of direct regulation, designed to control the course of trade for the purpose of effectuating an economic policy, or procuring economic advantage for a particular group or locality as a criterion for distinguishing such legislation from that enacted under police power, is shown by comparing H. P. Hood & Sons v. DuMond, 336 U.S. 525, 531, 533, 570 (1949), with Milk Control Bd. v. Eisenberg Farm Products, 306 U.S. 346, 352 (1939). Compare also Passenger Cases, 7 How. 283 (1849), with City of New York v. Miln, 11 Pet. 102 (1837); see note 49, page 115, above. Compare Schollenberger v. Pennsylvania, 171 U.S. 1, 12 (1898), with Powell v. Pennsylvania, 127 U.S. 678, 684 (1888), and Plumley v. Massachusetts, 155 U.S. 462, 467–78 (1894). See also Breard v. Alexandria, 341 U.S. 622, 640 (1951).

[60] Discrimination against interstate commerce as such, or singling it out for a special burden not borne by intrastate commerce, is of course always fatal. Memphis Steam Laundry v. Stone, 342 U.S. 389, 394 (1952); Nippert v. Richmond, 327 U.S. 416, 425 (1946); Best & Co. v. Maxwell, 311 U.S. 454, 455 (1940); McGoldrick v. Berwind-White Co., 309 U.S. 33, 45, 56 (1940); Welton v. Missouri, 91 U.S. 275, 281–82 (1876).

[61] Justices Stone and Rutledge seemed to regard the possibility of multiple taxation as the chief test of the validity of a state tax. Western Live Stock v. Bureau of Revenue, 303 U.S. 250, 255–56 (1938); Gwin, White, & Prince, Inc. v. Henneford, 305 U.S. 434, 439 (1939); Freeman v. Hewit, 329 U.S. 249, 260 (1946). But this criterion was rejected by the Court in the last-named case. Ibid., 256–57. Perhaps the possibility of multiple taxation (to which intrastate commerce, of course, would not be subjected) is to be regarded as merely one species of discrimination against interstate commerce.

of state taxing power because of its effect upon commerce was one decided in Chief Justice Marshall's time.[62] A Maryland law requiring importers of foreign goods to obtain a state license, costing $50, was held unconstitutional, both as violating the provision of Article I, section 10, clause 2, prohibiting states from laying "any Imposts or Duties on Imports,"[63] and as being repugnant to the commerce clause.[64] The right to sell, in the original package, articles brought into the state is an integral part of commerce, and an inseparable incident of the importation authorized by Congress. The states' taxing power, although admitted by Marshall to be "sacred," cannot be used "so as to obstruct or defeat the power to regulate commerce. It has been observed, that the powers remaining with the States may be so exercised as to come in conflict with those vested in Congress. When this happens, that which is not supreme must yield to that which is supreme."[65] Hence the state cannot tax imported property until it has become mingled with the general mass of property in the state. As a useful rule of thumb, Marshall enunciated the "original package" doctrine, stating that "when the importer has so acted upon the thing imported that it has become incorporated and mixed up with the mass of property in the country, it has, perhaps, lost its distinctive character as an import, and has become subject to the taxing power of the State; but while remaining the property of the importer, in his warehouse, in the original form or package in which it was imported, a tax upon it is too plainly a duty on imports to escape the prohibition in the constitution."[66]

Marshall in a dictum indicated that the original package doctrine would apply to interstate commerce as well as to foreign commerce.[67] However, it was rejected in a later case where the Supreme Court held that a nondiscriminatory tax on all sales at auction could constitutionally be applied to the sale of goods from another state in their original packages.[68] Subsequent decisions utilized the original package doctrine

[62] Brown v. Maryland, 12 Wheat. 419 (1827).

[63] *Ibid.*, 439.   [64] *Ibid.*, 447–48.   [65] *Ibid.*, 448.

[66] *Ibid.*, 441–42. Concerning qualifications of the original package rule as applied to imports in foreign commerce, see note 69, page 120, below.

[67] *Ibid.*, 449: ". . . we suppose the principles laid down in this case to apply equally to importations from a sister State."

[68] Woodruff v. Parham, 8 Wall. 123, 139–40 (1869). See note 121, page 243, below.

to prevent state control of the liquor traffic.[69] More recently, the rule has been criticized[70] as artificial.

Property which is part of the general mass of property within the state is of course subject to taxation, whether before[71] or after[72] its movement in interstate commerce.[73] A state may impose not only an ordinary ad valorem property tax[74] but also a use tax[75] upon property

[69] Leisy v. Hardin, 135 U.S. 100, 124 (1890). See note 55, page 117, above. The rule was also applied to legislation against cigarettes and oleomargarine. Austin v. Tennessee, 179 U.S. 343, 349 (1900); Schollenberger v. Pennsylvania, 171 U.S. 1, 23–24 (1898). Cf. Plumley v. Massachusetts, 155 U.S. 461, 467–68, 474 (1894), where a law forbidding sale of oleomargarine deceptively colored to look like butter was upheld. The Court apparently was distinguishing between police power exercised to prevent fraud and that used to regulate trade on grounds of economic policy, insisting that only Congress can exercise the latter power with respect to interstate commerce. See note 59, page 118, above. In Brown v. Maryland, 12 Wheat. 419, 443–44 (1827), the original package rule was apparently not considered applicable as a restriction upon the police power of the states.

[70] By Justices William Howard Taft, George Sutherland, Benjamin N. Cardozo, and Harlan F. Stone. Sonneborn Bros. v. Cureton, 262 U.S. 506, 508 (1923); Whitfield v. Ohio, 297 U.S. 431, 440 (1936); Baldwin v. Seelig, 294 U.S. 511, 526 (1935); McGoldrick v. Berwind-White Co., 309 U.S. 33, 51–53 (1940).

[71] Coe v. Errol, 116 U.S. 517, 525–28 (1886); Heisler v. Thomas Colliery Co., 260 U.S. 245, 259 (1922). See pages 207–209 below.

[72] Brown v. Houston, 114 U.S. 622, 632–33 (1885); General Oil Co., v. Crain, 209 U.S. 211, 229–31 (1908); Minnesota v. Blasius, 290 U.S. 1, 9–10 (1933); Southern Pacific Co. v. Gallagher, 306 U.S. 167, 177 (1939). In the last-named case the tax was a use tax on storage of oil brought into the state for use as fuel by locomotives operating interstate trains.

[73] The general rule is that interstate commerce begins when property is delivered to a common carrier for shipment, and ends when it has come to rest and become a part of the general mass of property within the state of destination.

[74] Property within the state may be taxed not merely on its intrinsic value when separately considered but on its "going concern value," as a proportionate share of the total enterprise, even if such value arises from doing a purely interstate business. Adams Express Co. v. Ohio, 165 U.S. 194, 220–21, 227 (1897); Galveston, Harrisburg & San Antonio Ry. Co. v. Texas, 210 U.S. 217, 227 (1908); Ry. Express Agency v. Virginia, 347 U.S. 359, 366–67 (1954). Likewise a tax on railroad cars, where a substantial number are constantly present in the state, may be measured by the value of the company's capital stock, apportioned in accordance with the ratio of the length of routes within the state to total mileage operated. Pullman's Palace Car Co. v. Pennsylvania, 141 U.S. 18, 25–26 (1891). The same rule was applied to barges on inland waterways in Ott v. Mississippi Valley Barge Line, 336 U.S. 169, 174 (1949); Standard Oil Co. v. Peck, 342 U.S. 382, 383–84 (1952). A carrier's state of domicile may tax all its vehicles which do not have a permanent situs elsewhere. Northwest Airlines v. Minnesota, 322 U.S. 292, 294–97 (1944); C. R.R. of Pa. v. Pa., 372 U.S. 607, 611–12 (1962). Cf. Braniff Airways v. Nebraska Board, 347 U.S. 590, 597–98 (1954).

[75] Henneford v. Silas Mason Co., 300 U.S. 577, 582 (1937); Nelson v. Sears Roe-

considered to be part of the general mass of property within its territorial jurisdiction. Similarly an occupation[76] or privilege[77] tax may be laid upon local activities within the state, without obstructing or burdening interstate commerce. The Supreme Court in recent years has gone very far in finding that some local incident, rather than the interstate commerce to which it is appurtenant, is the "taxable event" upon which the tax "impinges." Thus in one dubious decision it upheld a New York City sales tax upon interstate sales of coal shipped from Pennsylvania pursuant to contracts made in the city, where the vendor maintained a sales office. The term "sale" was defined as transfer of title or possession, and the Court held that delivery of the coal in New York was a sufficient local incident or taxable event to sustain the tax.[78]

However, as Justice Wiley Blount Rutledge has pointed out,[79] it is

buck & Co., 312 U.S. 359, 363–64 (1941); General Trading Co. v. Tax Commission, 322 U.S. 327, 338 (1944). Justice Jackson, dissenting in the last-named case, said: "So we are holding that a state has power to make a tax collector of one whom it has no power to tax." 322 U.S. at 339. See also Norton Co. v. Dept. of Revenue of Illinois, 340 U.S. 534, 537 (1951). Cf. Miller Bros. v. Maryland, 347 U.S. 340, 345 (1954).

[76] Such a tax may be imposed even if the occupation is manufacturing or mining products for immediate shipment in interstate commerce. Oliver Iron Mining Co. v. Lord, 262 U.S. 172, 178–79 (1923); Hope Natural Gas Co. v. Hall, 274 U.S. 284, 288 (1927). The same rule applies to generation of electric current transmitted interstate, even though generation and transmission are simultaneous. Utah Power & Light Co. v. Pfost, 286 U.S. 165, 181–82 (1932). Likewise it is a local business to maintain an international bridge or to furnish labor for loading interstate vessels. Detroit Int. Bridge Co. v. Tax Board, 294 U.S. 83, 86 (1935); Puget Sound Stevedoring Co. v. Tax Commission, 302 U.S. 90, 94 (1937).

[77] See note 72, page 120, above. Independent Warehouses v. Scheele, 331 U.S. 70, 75, 83–85 (1947), sustained a license tax on the privilege of storing coal in transit. In Toomer v. Witsell, 334 U.S. 385, 394–95 (1948), the state imposed a tax of ⅛¢ a pound on shrimp caught in its coastal waters. The Court said: "the taxable event, the taking of shrimp, occurs before the shrimp can be said to have entered the flow of interstate commerce."

[78] McGoldrick v. Berwind-White Co., 309 U.S. 33, 43–44, 58 (1940). The Court considered this tax as little different from a use tax. *Ibid.*, 49. It declined to distinguish between interstate shipment to fill an order already contracted for, and local peddling of goods brought into the state in advance of sales efforts. *Ibid.*, 54. Such "peddler" activities had previously been considered as a taxable local business, as contrasted with the activities of "drummers" who solicited orders for subsequent shipment. Wagner v. City of Covington, 251 U.S. 95, 100–103 (1919). See note 58, page 118, above. The Court undertook to distinguish the drummer cases as based upon discrimination in favor of local merchants. 309 U.S. at 56.

[79] Nippert v. Richmond, 327 U.S. 416, 423 (1946). The line of "drummers" cases was followed here, rather than the Berwind-White case. *Ibid.*, 420.

always possible, by the exercise of sufficiently resourceful mental gymnastics, to find some "incident" of the transactions and events "forming an unbroken process of interstate commerce"[80] which can be separately identified and localized for the purpose of serving as a peg upon which to hang the "impingement" of the tax.[81]

It has long been recognized that commerce includes both buying and selling;[82] and therefore a sales tax on transactions in interstate commerce is a direct burden on such commerce and is accordingly invalid,[83] just as is a tax on interstate transportation.[84] Likewise a tax on the gross receipts from interstate commerce is unconstitutional,[85] just as is a privilege or license tax upon the privilege of engaging in interstate commerce.[86]

[80] This expression is used by Justice Felix Frankfurter in McLeod v. Dilworth Co., 322 U.S. 327, 331 (1944). See also Justice Jackson's comments in Ry. Express Co. v. Virginia, 347 U.S. 359, 367–68 (1954), regarding the insufficiency of local incidents (such as the origination, transportation, and delivery of shipments) which constitute an integral part of the interstate movement. In the McLeod case the circumstances were such that Arkansas might validly have enacted a use tax, but the tax actually levied was a sales tax on interstate commerce. The Berwind-White case was distinguished by reason of the fact that there something was done in New York to complete the sale, whereas in the McLeod case Arkansas had no contacts with the transaction at all. *Ibid.*, 330. To the same effect, see Freeman v. Hewit, 329 U.S. 249, 257–58 (1946); Ry. Express Agency v. Va., 347 U.S. 359, 363–64 (1954). The result is, as Justice Tom C. Clark plaintively notes, that "If the label makes the tax invalid, the label is accepted; if the label validates the tax, the Court will pierce the label." This is proper, because it is the legislature which has the task of choosing the type of tax to impose, but the Court should not be deceived by a state's self-serving verbiage. See Hale v. Bimco Trading Co., 306 U.S. 375, 380 (1939). Cf. Wisconsin v. J. C. Penney Co., 311 U.S. 435, 443–44 (1940); Wisconsin v. M.M. & M. Co., 311 U.S. 452, 453 (1940).

[81] See 322 U.S. at 356.

[82] Dahnke-Walker Co. v. Bondurant, 257 U.S. 282, 290 (1921); Lemke v. Farmers Grain Co., 258 U.S. 50, 54–55 (1922); Currin v. Wallace, 315 U.S. 1, 10 (1939). See also the "drummers" cases, note 58, page 118, above.

[83] McLeod v. Dilworth Co., 322 U.S. 327, 330–31 (1944); Crew Levick Co. v. Pennsylvania, 245 U.S. 292, 295 (1917).

[84] State Freight Tax Case, 15 Wall. 232, 279 (1873); Gloucester Ferry Co. v. Pennsylvania, 114 U.S. 196, 211 (1885); Joseph v. Carter & Weekes Co., 330 U.S. 422, 433 (1947).

[85] Philadelphia & Southern Steamship Co. v. Pennsylvania, 122 U.S. 326, 336 (1887); Leloup v. Port of Mobile, 127 U.S. 640, 645–47 (1888); Crew Levick Co. v. Pennsylvania, 245 U.S. 292, 295 (1917); Minnesota v. Blasius, 290 U.S. 1, 9 (1933); Fisher's Blend Station v. State Tax Commission, 297 U.S. 650, 655–56 (1936); Puget Sound Stevedoring Co. v. Tax Commission, 302 U.S. 90, 92, 94 (1937); Joseph v. Carter & Weekes Co., 330 U.S. 422, 433 (1947).

[86] Spector Motor Service v. O'Connor, 340 U.S. 602, 607–609 (1951); Gwin,

If, however, what is being taxed is not the privilege of engaging in interstate commerce but some other activity which is a legitimate subject of state taxation, then the tax is not affected by the operation of the commerce clause. Thus if a company doing an interstate business also does an intrastate business, the latter activity is one that can be taxed by the state. Indeed, were it not for the "doctrine of unconstitutional conditions,"[87] the state could exact whatever price it chose in exchange for the grant of the privilege to engage in such local business. If the state can exclude a foreign corporation from doing a local business, it can admit it subject to such conditions as it may see fit to prescribe.[88] Yet the Supreme Court will interfere and strike down a tax ostensibly laid upon a local activity if in fact the state is using the grant of a local privilege as a means for extorting an exaction which in substance is a burden upon interstate business.[89]

The general rule for determining the propriety of a tax on the intrastate business of a company doing both local and interstate business has been formulated as follows by the Supreme Court: "Where the tax is exacted from one doing both an interstate and intrastate business, it must appear that it is imposed solely on account of the latter; that

White & Prince v. Henneford, 305 U.S. 434, 441 (1939); Helson & Randolph v. Kentucky, 279 U.S. 245, 249 (1929). See also Crutcher v. Kentucky, 141 U.S. 47, 58 (1891); International Textbook Co. v. Pigg, 217 U.S. 91, 111 (1910).

[87] Gerard C. Henderson, *The Position of Foreign Corporations in American Constitutional Law*, 127–47.

[88] *Ibid.*, 141. As Justice Holmes said, dissenting in Western Union Telegraph Co. v. Kansas, 216 U.S. 1, 53 (1910), "Even in the law, the whole generally includes its parts."

[89] Western Union Telegraph Co. v. Kansas, 216 U.S. 1, 35–37 (1910). Commenting on this decision, Gerard C. Henderson argues that "if, as a matter of business experience, an interstate railroad cannot be properly conducted without deriving some revenue from local business, to cut off that revenue does in fact interfere with economical railroading. It is not the bare power to carry on interstate commerce that the Constitution guarantees. It is the power to carry it on in a normal, business-like way. . . . To say that these corporations cannot be expelled, as to their local business, for a bad reason, is to beg the whole question, for if the power of expulsion exists, the power exists to exact any pecuniary compensation as a condition of admission, and the refusal of the corporation to pay that compensation is *not* a bad reason. It can be termed a bad reason, only if the interstate business is by virtue of the Commerce Clause deemed entitled to a reasonable contribution on the part of the local business, toward the payment of the fixed charges; or, on the other hand, if the local business is entitled on its own account to constitutional protection against arbitrary exactions." Henderson, *The Position of Foreign Corporations in American Constitutional Law*, 130–31. See also Anglo-Chilean Nitrate Sales Corp. v. Alabama, 288 U.S. 218, 228 (1933).

the amount exacted is not increased because of the interstate business; that one engaged exclusively in interstate commerce would not be subject to the tax; and that the one who is taxed could discontinue the intrastate business without also withdrawing from the interstate business."[90] When, as in the case of a railroad or telephone company, the two types of business are in practice "inextricably intertwined," so that the possibility of actually withdrawing from the intrastate business is academic or theoretical, a tax is nevertheless valid if the intrastate business is profitable, or potentially so, and the company desires to continue it, even though it is temporarily being conducted at a slight loss.[91]

Where a tax is imposed on a proper subject (such as the privilege of doing an intrastate business, or upon property, including corporate franchises, within the state), and where the tax is not excessive in amount and where it bears a reasonable relationship to the benefit or protection accorded by the state, the tax is valid, under some circumstances, even if it refers to gross receipts as the measure of the amount of the tax.[92] A tax on net income, as distinguished from gross receipts, is valid if it is fairly apportioned so as to apply only to income attributable to business done within the state (whether such business be interstate or intrastate or both).[93] As formulated in a recent Supreme Court decision,

[90] Cooney v. Mountain States Tel. Co., 294 U.S. 384, 393 (1935); Sprout v. South Bend, 277 U.S. 163, 171 (1928). "In the instant case, the tax, being indivisible and indiscriminate in its application, necessarily burdens interstate commerce." 294 U.S. at 394.

[91] Pacific Tel. & Tel. Co. v. Tax Commission, 297 U.S. 403, 411–14 (1936); Postal Telegraph-Cable Co. v. Fremont, 255 U.S. 124, 127 (1921); Postal Telegraph-Cable Co. v. Richmond, 249 U.S. 252, 257–58 (1919). Of course if the intrastate business were definitely unprofitable but compulsory, there would be a burden on interstate commerce.

[92] In his concurring opinion in Freeman v. Hewit, 329 U.S. 249, 265 (1946), Justice Rutledge enumerated as types of gross receipts taxes which have been upheld— (a) those that were fairly apportioned and (b) those that were held to impinge upon a local incident. A tax on the exercise of corporate franchise (i.e., the privilege of doing a local business), measured by gross receipts, apportioned in accordance with the ratio of mileage within the state to total mileage operated, was sustained in Maine v. Grand Trunk Line Ry. Co., 142 U.S. 217, 228–29 (1891). See also Sonneborn Bros. v. Cureton, 262 U.S. 506, 508 (1923); Hope Gas Co. v. Hall, 274 U.S. 284, 288 (1927).

[93] U. S. Glue Co. v. Oak Creek, 247 U.S. 321, 326–29 (1918); Matson Navigation Co. v. State Board, 297 U.S. 441, 444 (1936). In the last-named case a tax on exercise of corporate franchise was measured by net income attributable to all business done within the state. See also Memphis Gas Co. v. Beeler, 315 U.S. 649, 656 (1942); International Harvester Co. v. Dept. of Treasury, 322 U.S. 340, 349 (1944); Northwestern Cement Co. v. Minnesota, 358 U.S. 450, 452 (1959). In Illinois Central R.R.

"net income from the interstate operations of a foreign corporation may be subjected to state taxation provided the levy is not discriminatory and is properly apportioned to local activities within the taxing State forming sufficient nexus to support the same."[94]

In general, as Justice Rutledge has remarked, "The trend of recent decisions has been toward sustaining state taxes formerly regarded as outlawed by the commerce clause."[95]

Taxation is not the only exertion of state power which affects interstate commerce and gives rise to adjudications under the commerce clause. As previously stated, it is often difficult to determine whether legislation constitutes an outright regulation of commerce, or is a tax, or is a measure enacted in the exercise of a state's police power or as an inspection law.[96]

The Supreme Court in applying the commerce clause is more favorable toward measures enacted in the exercise of a state's police power than toward state taxes. There are many sources of revenue which a state may tap, and there are usually numerous alternatives available to the state whereby it may replenish its treasury without burdening interstate commerce; whereas police measures are ordinarily directed against a specific evil or some particular type of harmful practice, and the importance to the public interest of enforcing the legislation outweighs the indirect and remote effects which such enforcement might have on interstate commerce.[97]

Thus quarantine[98] and health[99] regulations have long been recog-

Co. v. Minnesota, 309 U.S. 157, 164 (1940), a tax on railroads (in lieu of all other taxes), measured by gross earnings from operations within the state, apportioned in accordance with the ratio of mileage within the state to total mileage, was upheld as having a fair relation to the company's property used within the state.

[94] 358 U.S. at 452.   [95] 329 U.S. at 282.

[96] Inspection laws, designed to maintain the quality of products, especially articles of food, are themselves police measures, but require special treatment because they constitute an exception to the constitutional provision prohibiting states from laying any "Imposts or Duties on Imports or Exports." See commentary on Art. I, sec. 10, cl. 2.

[97] Freeman v. Hewitt, 329 U.S. at 249, 253 (1946). See also note 49, pages 115–16, above.

[98] Minnesota Rate Cases, 230 U.S. 352, 406 (1913); Compagnie Française v. Board of Health, 186 U.S. 380, 387 (1902). Such legislation is sometimes upheld even where there is ground for a strong suspicion that it is in fact being used for the advantage of local interests. Louisiana v. Texas, 176 U.S. 1, 21–22 (1900). Cf. Minnesota v. Barber, 136 U.S. 313, 321–22 (1890); Dean Milk Co. v. Madison, 340 U.S. 349, 354 (1951).

[99] Fertilizing Co. v. Hyde Park, 97 U.S. 659, 667 (1878); Clason v. Indiana, 306 U.S. 439, 443 (1939).

nized as proper subjects for state legislation. Safety,[100] good order[101] and public morals,[102] and protection against fraud and deception[103] are likewise well-established fields for the legitimate exercise of a state's police power.

According to Chief Justice Taney, a state's police power is unlimited in its nature; it is simply the sovereign power to govern men and things within the jurisdiction of a state.[104] Insofar as the constitutional prohibition forbidding deprivation of liberty or property without due process of law is concerned, the police power is indeed extensive and indefinite in its scope. In particular, it may be exercised to promote the economic welfare of the public (or of a particular group in need of relief from hardship or distress).[105] Thus minimum wage laws[106] and price-fixing legislation[107] are now recognized as valid from the standpoint of due process.

[100] South Carolina Highway Dept. v. Barnwell Bros., 303 U.S. 177, 189 (1938); Maurer v. Hamilton, 309 U.S. 598, 603–605 (1940). Ostensible considerations of safety urged in support of an excessive inspection fee which Florida sought to apply to cement imported into the state did not deceive the Court in Hale v. Bimco Trading Co., 306 U.S. 375, 380 (1939).

[101] Thus zoning regulation restricting the uses of property in certain areas is permissible as an exercise of police power. Euclid v. Ambler Realty Co., 272 U.S. 365, 395 (1926).

[102] Thus prohibition of intoxicating liquors and of lotteries is within the scope of the police power. Kidd v. Pearson, 128 U.S. 1, 26 (1888); Beer Co. v. Massachusetts, 97 U.S. 25, 32–33 (1878); Stone v. Mississippi, 101 U.S. 814, 817–18 (1880).

[103] Plumley v. Massachusetts, 155 U.S. 462, 467–68, 472 (1894); Milk Control Board v. Eisenberg Farm Products, 306 U.S. 346, 350 (1939), as explained in H. P. Hood & Sons v. DuMond, 336 U.S. 525, 531 (1949).

[104] License Cases, 5 How. 504, 583 (1847).

[105] Sligh v. Kirkwood, 237 U.S. 52, 59 (1915); Nebbia v. New York, 291 U.S. 502, 538 (1934); Parker v. Brown, 317 U.S. 341, 367 (1943).

[106] West Coast Hotel Co. v. Parrish, 300 U.S. 379, 398 (1937).

[107] Nebbia v. New York, 291 U.S. 502, 538 (1934). Price-fixing restrains trade (and hence violates the antitrust laws enacted by Congress to forbid restraints of trade). U.S. v. Socony-Vacuum Oil Co., 310 U.S. 150, 221–24 (1940). A restraint of trade is one form of a regulation of trade. Hence a state price-fixing law affecting sales in interstate commerce is obviously an exercise of the power to regulate commerce and is unconstitutional unless warranted by the implied permission of Congress, or upheld by a "mechanical" test as applying to a "local activity" preceding or following the interstate movement. Hope Gas Co. v. Hall, 274 U.S. 284, 288 (1927); Champlin Refining Co. v. Corp. Comm. of Oklahoma, 286 U.S. 210, 234–35 (1932); Natural Gas Pipeline Co. v. Panoma Corp., 349 U.S. 44 (1955); Parker v. Brown, 317 U.S. 341, 360–62, 367 (1943). Of course Congress may itself prescribe price-fixing for interstate commerce, just as a state may for intrastate commerce. Sunshine Anthracite Coal Co. v. Adkins, 310 U.S. 381, 394–96 (1940).

But a sharp distinction must be drawn when the validity of measures enacted by virtue of the police power is being considered under the commerce clause. For purposes of the commerce clause, genuine health, safety, or other scientifically justifiable regulations are legitimate, and the Court will regard their effect upon interstate commerce as remote or incidental.[108] But measures that are only ostensibly related to such objectives, and that really are designed to promote the economic welfare or financial advantage of particular groups or individuals, will be held unconstitutional.[109] This is because such economic legislation in fact amounts to a regulation of commerce, and with respect to interstate commerce the Constitution has conferred upon the federal government, and not the states, the power to make decisions and determine policy with regard to such matters.

The Commerce Clause as a Source of Federal Power

Notwithstanding the historical significance of the commerce clause as a limitation upon state power, the clause in recent years has attained major importance as a source of federal power.[110] Utilization of the commerce clause has enabled governmental regulation in the public interest to keep pace with the development of the national economy. This has been accomplished without disrupting the political federalism which has been a distinctive characteristic of the traditional structure of American government.[111]

The power of Congress to protect and promote interstate commerce can be exerted against any obstacle or obstruction to such commerce, or to remove any burden upon it, from whatever source. The hindrance to commerce may arise from an activity which otherwise would be purely local or intrastate and not subject to federal regulation apart from its effect upon interstate commerce. As epitomized in the colorful language of Justice Robert H. Jackson, "If it is interstate commerce

---

[108] See cases cited in notes 98–103, pages 125–26, above.

[109] Buck v. Kuykendall, 267 U.S. 307, 315–16 (1925); H. P. Hood & Sons v. DuMond, 336 U.S. 525, 531, 570 (1949); Fry Roofing Co. v. Wood, 344 U.S. 157, 161 (1952); Chicago v. A., T. & S. F. Ry. Co., 357 U.S. 77, 85 (1958). See also notes 59 and 69, pages 118 and 120, above.

[110] See note 36, page 113, above.

[111] On the fundamental importance of federalism, see Dumbauld, *The Political Writings of Thomas Jefferson*, 95–101.

that feels the pinch, it does not matter how local the operation which applies the squeeze."[112]

A good illustration of this principle is the power vested by Congress in the Interstate Commerce Commission to regulate intrastate railroad rates when necessary to remove discrimination against interstate traffic[113] or to prevent interstate traffic from bearing an undue proportion of the burden of overhead costs attributable to both interstate and intrastate business.[114] Safety regulations for the protection of persons and property transported in interstate commerce and of employees of carriers engaged in such transportation are likewise valid, since the federal over interstate commerce is plenary and capable of safeguarding such commerce in every respect, "no matter what may be the source of the dangers which threaten it."[115]

Federal legislation limiting the hours of work of railroad employees was also upheld as a safety measure.[116] Regulation of the legal principles governing liability to employees for personal injuries occurring in the course of their employment was likewise sustained as a constitutional exertion of the commerce power.[117] The Supreme Court in 1917 even permitted Congress to direct that railroad employees be granted a temporary wage increase in order to prevent a strike which would have constituted a national emergency and interrupted the movement of interstate commerce.[118] A further step was taken in 1930, when the

[112] U.S. v. Women's Sportswear Assn., 336 U.S. 460, 464 (1949). See also Wickard v. Filburn, 317 U.S. 111, 122–25 (1942).

[113] Minnesota Rate Cases, 230 U.S. 352, 399, 431–32 (1913); Shreveport Case, 234 U.S. 342, 351–54 (1914).

[114] Wisconsin R.R. Comm. v. C. B. & Q. R.R. Co., 257 U.S. 563, 584, 588 (1921); C., M., St. P. & P. R.R. Co. v. Illinois, 355 U.S. 300, 305–308 (1958).

[115] Southern Ry. Co. v. U.S., 222 U.S. 20, 27 (1911). The Court went on to explain that "it is no objection to such an exertion of this power that the dangers intended to be avoided arise, in whole or in part, out of matters connected with intrastate commerce." Hence federal safety standards were applicable to all equipment used on any railway engaged in interstate commerce and to all equipment used in connection therewith.

[116] Act of March 4, 1907, 34 Stat. 1415, upheld in B. & O. R.R. Co. v. Interstate Commerce Commission, 221 U.S. 612, 618–19 (1911).

[117] Second Employers Liability Cases, 223 U.S. 1, 48–51 (1912). This decision sustained the constitutionality of the Act of April 22, 1908, 35 Stat. 65. The earlier Act of June 11, 1906, 34 Stat. 232, had been held void in The Employers' Liability Cases, 207 U.S. 463, 495, 498–99 (1908).

[118] Wilson v. New, 243 U.S. 332, 345–48 (1917). The intricate verbosity of Chief Justice White seems to give weight to several factors in sustaining the law (Act

Court held that "Congress may facilitate the amicable settlement of disputes which threaten the service of necessary agencies of interstate transportation."[119]

It was not until the "New Deal" era, however, that the Court recognized the validity of federal legislation regulating the relations between management and labor generally in industries where labor trouble would have an adverse effect upon interstate commerce.[120] Subsequently it was held that Congress could prescribe minimum wages and maximum hours of labor for workers engaged in the production of goods for interstate commerce.[121]

of September 3, 5, 1916, 39 Stat. 721): (1) that railroading is a business affected with a public interest; (2) that the "entire interruption of interstate commerce" was threatened, with "infinite injury to the public"; (3) that although fixing wages is a matter "primarily private" and not subject to control by public authority, the parties had failed to "establish by private agreement" the essential standard of wages; (4) that the law was temporary, and merely required payment for eight hours' work of the previous wage for a ten-hour day during a reasonable period permitting a commission to report and affording "an opportunity for the meeting of the minds of employers and employees on the subject of wages." The Wilson case was regarded as without authority as a precedent in R.R. Retirement Board v. Alton R.R. Co., 259 U.S. 330, 369 (1935), holding that a pension system for railroad employees, established by the Act of August 29, 1935, 49 Stat. 967, to promote morale and efficiency, had no relation to regulation of commerce. *Ibid.*, 365–68. Cf. R.R. Retirement Bd. v. Duquesne Warehouse Co., 326 U.S. 446 (1946), dealing with the extent of coverage of a similar statutory scheme (Act of June 24, 1937, 50 Stat. 307), with no discussion of constitutionality.

[119] T. & N. O. R.R. Co. v. Ry. Clerks, 281 U.S. 548, 570 (1930). That case upheld provisions of the Railway Labor Act of May 20, 1926, 44 Stat. 577, forbidding interference, influence, or coercion upon the choice of representatives for collective bargaining. In Virginian Ry. v. Federation, 300 U.S. 515, 553 (1937), the Court said: "The power of Congress over interstate commerce extends to such regulations of the relations of rail carriers to their employees as are reasonably calculated to prevent the interruption of interstate commerce by strikes and their attendant disorders," citing Wilson v. New as authority for the proposition. In Adair v. U.S., 208 U.S. 161, 178 (1908), the Court had held void a law prohibiting discharge of a railroad employee because of union membership.

[120] The Wagner Act of July 5, 1935, 49 Stat. 449, was upheld in an epoch-making opinion rendered on April 12, 1937, by Chief Justice Hughes in National Labor Relations Board v. Jones & Laughlin Steel Corp., 301 U.S. 1, 31, 36–40 (1937). On May 18, 1936, similar labor provisions in the Guffey-Snyder Bituminous Coal Conservation Act of August 30, 1935, 49 Stat. 991, had been held unconstitutional in an opinion by Justice Sutherland which asserted that "The relation of employer and employee is a local relation" over which the federal government has no legislative control. Carter v. Carter Coal Co., 298 U.S. 238, 308 (1936).

[121] Fair Labor Standards Act of June 25, 1938, 52 Stat. 1060, upheld in U.S. v. Darby, 312 U.S. 100, 118 (1941). This case overruled Hammer v. Dagenhart, 247

It is now clearly established that the power to regulate interstate commerce not only includes the power to promote such commerce and to protect it against dangers from whatever sort, but also includes the power to curtail or prohibit such commerce.[122] The power to regulate being, as Chief Justice Marshall declared, the power to prescribe the rule by which commerce is to be governed, the content of the rule may vary from time to time in accordance with shifting tides of public opinion. The public policy to be effectuated in regulating commerce depends upon the views which prevail in Congress with regard to the most expedient methods of promoting the national welfare.

Thus in one era Congress may authorize lotteries,[123] and at another era prohibit traffic in lottery tickets.[124] Congress may permit or prohibit the transportation of intoxicating beverages.[125] Congress may prescribe a regime of free competition (as embodied in the antitrust laws)[126] or of price-fixing[127] (as in the case of milk and other agricultural products) in accordance with what it judges most desirable for the public welfare.

With respect to foreign commerce, it has been well understood ever since the Embargo Law of Jefferson's administration that Congress can prohibit commerce as well as encourage it.[128] With respect to interstate commerce, however, there prevailed at one time the indefensible view that the power of Congress over interstate commerce, though conferred

U.S. 251 (1918), where it had been held (over a notable dissent by Justice Holmes) that Congress could not exclude from interstate commerce the products of child labor. The Darby case also overruled Carter v. Carter Coal Co., 298 U.S. 238 (1936).

[122] U.S. v. Darby, 312 U.S. 100, 113 (1941); Mulford v. Smith, 307 U.S. 38, 48 (1939); U.S. v. Carolene Products Co., 304 U.S. 144, 147–48 (1938).

[123] Cohens v. Virginia, 6 Wheat. 264, 441 (1821).

[124] Champion v. Ames, 188 U.S. 321, 356 (1903).

[125] U.S. v. Hill, 248 U.S. 420, 424–27 (1919).

[126] See note 107, page 126, above.

[127] U.S. v. Rock Royal Cooperative, 307 U.S. 533, 569–71 (1939); U.S. v. Wrightwood Dairy Co., 315 U.S. 110, 121 (1942); Wickard v. Filburn, 317 U.S. 111, 128 (1942). Price-fixing in the coal industry was held constitutional in Sunshine Anthracite Coal Co. v. Adkins, 310 U.S. 381, 394–96 (1940). Cf. Carter v. Carter Coal Co., 298 U.S. 238, 316 (1936). See notes 120 and 121, page 129, above. Congress may also relax the antitrust laws in order to permit state price-fixing laws to apply to sales in interstate commerce. Schwegmann Bros. v. Calvert Distillers Corp., 341 U.S. 384, 386 (1951).

[128] U.S. v. The William, Fed. Cas. No. 16,700 (D. Mass. 1808); Gibbons v. Ogden, 9 Wheat. 1, 191–93 (1824); U.S. v. Marigold, 9 How. 560, 566–67 (1850); Buttfield v. Stranahan, 192 U.S. 470, 492–93 (1904); The Abby Dodge, 223 U.S. 166, 176 (1912); Weber v. Freed, 239 U.S. 325, 329 (1915); Univ. of Illinois v. U.S., 289 U.S. 48, 57 (1933).

by the same clause of the Constitution, was less extensive than its power over foreign commerce;[129] and that interstate commerce could be prohibited only in the case of noxious, fraudulent, or otherwise harmful articles, and that a legitimate article of commerce could not be excluded from the channels of trade.[130] The first breach in this concept came when it was held that lottery tickets could be excluded.[131] Intoxicating liquor,[132] stolen automobiles, [133] victims of kidnapping,[134] prison-made goods,[135] and the transportation of women for immoral purposes[136] were later added to the category of items which Congress might constitutionally forbid. Goods manufactured by child labor, however, the Supreme Court held, could not be excluded from interstate commerce.[137] Here, the Court reasoned, the evil at which Congress was striking took place before commerce commenced. The situation was unlike the instances where "the use of interstate transportation was necessary to the accomplishment of harmful results."[138] In the case of products manufactured by child labor, "The goods shipped are of themselves harmless."[139]

Justice Oliver Wendell Holmes was eloquent in dissent: "It does not matter whether the supposed evil precedes or follows the transportation. It is enough that in the opinion of Congress the transportation encourages the evil. . . . It is not for this Court to pronounce when prohibition is necessary to regulation if it ever may be necessary—to say that it is permissible as against strong drink but not as against the product of ruined lives."[140]

Replying to the argument that what the statute really sought to

[129] Brolan v. U.S., 236 U.S. 216, 222 (1915); dissenters in Champion v. Ames, 188 U.S. 321, 373 (1903). Marshall and Taney agreed that the power of Congress was the same over both foreign and interstate commerce. Gibbons v. Ogden, 9 Wheat. 1, 194 (1824); License Cases, 5 How., 504, 578 (1847).

[130] Hammer v. Dagenhart, 247 U.S. 251, 270–71 (1918); Wilson v. New, 243 U.S. 332, 347 (1917).

[131] Champion v. Ames, 188 U.S. 321, 355 (1903).

[132] Clark Distilling Co. v. Western Maryland Ry. Co., 242 U.S. 311, 326 (1917).

[133] Brooks v. U.S., 267 U.S. 432, 436 (1925).

[134] Gooch v. U.S., 297 U.S. 124, 128 (1936).

[135] Kentucky Whip & Collar Co. v. Ill. Central R.R. Co., 299 U.S. 334, 346–48 (1937).

[136] Hoke v. U.S., 227 U.S. 308, 320–23 (1913); Caminetti v. U.S., 242 U.S. 470, 491 (1917); Cleveland v. U.S., 329 U.S. 14, 19 (1946).

[137] Hammer v. Dagenhart, 247 U.S. 251, 270 (1918).

[138] *Ibid.*, 271.   [139] *Ibid.*, 272.   [140] *Ibid.*, 279–80.

regulate was a local matter related to production rather than commerce,[141] Holmes said: "The act does not meddle with anything belonging to the States. They may regulate their internal affairs and their domestic commerce as they like. But when they seek to send their products across the state line they are no longer within their rights. If there were no Constitution and no Congress their power to cross the line would depend upon their neighbors. Under the Constitution such commerce belongs not to the States but to Congress to regulate. . . . Instead of being encountered by a prohibitive tariff at her boundaries the State encounters the public policy of the United States which it is for Congress to express."[142]

Not until 1941, however, did the views of Holmes prevail.[143]

Congress first exercised its commerce power by regulating navigation. It was in connection with a statute licensing vessels to engage in the coasting trade that Chief Justice John Marshall made his earliest notable pronouncements regarding the scope of the commerce clause.[144] Water transportation over navigable rivers likewise received the attention of Congress at an early date.[145] The Supreme Court has enunciated the doctrine that navigable waters in the United States "are the public property of the nation, and subject to all the requisite legislation by Congress."[146] From this it follows, according to the Court, that "al-

141 See note 120, page 129, above. 142 247 U.S. at 281.
143 See note 121, page 129, above. The stolen automobile case in 1925 virtually undermined the reasoning of the child-labor case. See note 133, page 131, above.
144 Gibbons v. Ogden, 9 Wheat. 1, 189–90, 196 (1824). It was in this famous case that Marshall defined commerce as intercourse (including navigation) and regulation as the power to prescribe the rule by which commerce is to be governed. The New York steamboat monopoly was held invalid because of conflict with the Act of February 18, 1793, 1 Stat. 305.
145 Pennsylvania v. Wheeling & Belmont Bridge Co., 13 How. 518, 561, 565 (1852). The Court there held that a bridge which was too low to permit steamboats to pass was an obstruction to navigation of the Ohio River. Congress by the Act of August 31, 1852, 10 Stat. 112, declared that the bridge was a lawful structure and that vessels must be so navigated as not to interfere with the bridge. In Pennsylvania v. Wheeling & Belmont Bridge Co., 18 How. 421, 430–31 (1856), the Court upheld the constitutionality of that law, stating that "The regulation of commerce includes intercourse and navigation, and, of course, the power to determine what shall or shall not be deemed in judgment of law an obstruction to navigation." To the same effect, see Gilman v. Philadelphia, 3 Wall. 713, 724–25 (1866); The Daniel Ball, 10 Wall. 557, 564 (1871). Of course Congress may also direct that bridges of insufficient height shall be removed. Union Bridge Co. v. U.S., 204 U.S. 364, 386 (1907).
146 3 Wall. at 725.

though the title to the shore and submerged soil is in the various States and individual owners under them, it is always subject to the servitude in respect of navigation created in favor of the Federal government by the Constitution."[147]

Hence the construction by the government of a dike obstructing access by boat to a truck farm and diminishing the value of the land was held not to constitute a taking of property for which compensation must be paid by virtue of the Fifth Amendment. The Court said that "riparian ownership is subject to the obligation to suffer the consequences of the improvement of navigation in the exercise of the dominant right of the Government in that regard." Construction of the dike "was an assertion of a right belonging to the Government, to which riparian property was subject, and not of a right to appropriate private property not burdened with such servitude, to public purposes."[148]

Similarly, Congress may decide that, in the interest of navigation, structures built by the landowner must be removed from the bed of a navigable river.[149] "The dominant power of the federal Government, as has been repeatedly held, extends to the entire bed of a stream, which includes the lands below ordinary high-water mark. The exercise of the power within these limits is not an invasion of any private property right in such lands for which the United States must make compensation. The damage sustained results not from a taking of the riparian owner's property in the stream bed, but from the lawful exercise of a power to which that property has always been subject."[150]

While "the riparian owner has no right as against improvements of navigation to maintenance of a level below high-water mark," it is a taking of property when damage is inflicted to lands above that level. "High-water mark bounds the bed of the river. Lands above it are fast lands and to flood them is a taking for which compensation must be paid."[151] Compensation is also due when improvements on a navigable

---

[147] Gibson v. U.S., 166 U.S. 269, 272 (1897).

[148] *Ibid.*, 276. To the same effect, see Union Bridge Co. v. U.S., 204 U.S. 364, 388–89, 399–401 (1907); Philadelphia Co. v. Stimson, 223 U.S. 605, 634–38 (1912).

[149] U.S. v. Chandler-Dunbar Co., 229 U.S. 53, 70–72 (1913). Hence, in depriving an electric company of power-plant facilities constructed in the river, Congress did not take any private property for which compensation is required.

[150] U.S. v. C., M., St. P. & P. R.R. Co., 312 U.S. 592, 596–97 (1941).

[151] U.S. v. Willow River Co., 324 U.S. 499, 509 (1945).

stream result in damage to land located on a tributary nonnavigable stream.[152]

The "improvement" which Congress has power to make on a navigable stream may consist of rendering it nonnavigable.[153] If the improvement is "not unrelated to the control of navigation" it may be undertaken, even if the real motive for the project is irrigation or the incidental production of electric power.[154]

With regard to land transportation Congress expressed its concern during the administration of Thomas Jefferson, when legislation was enacted looking toward construction of the National Pike, to connect the newly formed state of Ohio with the Atlantic seaboard.[155] As westward expansion progressed, the federal government participated in the establishment of transcontinental railroads.[156] When the outcry of farmers oppressed by monopolistic practices led to the growth of the Granger movement, public opinion called for regulation of rail rates. After it became clear that state regulation was insufficient,[157] Congress

[152] Ibid., 506–507; U.S. v. Cress, 243 U.S. 316, 326–27 (1917); U.S. v. Kansas City Life Ins. Co., 339 U.S. 799, 808–809 (1950). However, compensation is denied for that part of the market value of the land which is due to the flow of the navigable stream. U.S. v. Twin City Power Co., 350 U.S. 222, 225–26 (1956).

[153] U.S. v. Commodore Park, 324 U.S. 386, 392–93 (1945). "There is power to block navigation at one place to foster it at another." Ibid., 393. See also South Carolina v. Georgia, 93 U.S. 4, 10–12 (1876). On the other hand Congress could prevent diversion of the waters of a nonnavigable stream where such diminution of flow from the stream might destroy the navigability of a navigable stream. U.S. v. Rio Grande Irrigation Co., 174 U.S. 690, 709 (1899).

[154] Arizona v. California, 283 U.S. 423, 455–56 (1931); Ashwander v. Tennessee Valley Authority, 297 U.S. 288, 328–30 (1936); U.S. v. Twin City Power Co., 350 U.S. 222, 224 (1956). In determining the navigability of a river, it is proper to consider not only its natural state but its availability for navigation after reasonable improvements which might be made. U.S. v. Appalachian Power Co., 311 U.S. 377, 407–409 (1940).

[155] Act of March 29, 1806, 2 Stat. 357; Edward Dumbauld, Thomas Jefferson, American Tourist, 134–35; Searight v. Stokes, 3 How. 151 (1845). President Monroe had constitutional scruples regarding the power of the federal government to build roads. James D. Richardson, Messages of the Presidents, II, 142–83.

[156] Union Pacific R.R. Co. v. U.S., 99 U.S. 402 (1879).

[157] Wabash, St. Louis & Pacific Ry. Co. v. Illinois, 118 U.S. 557, 572–77 (1886), held void, as applied to interstate traffic, an Illinois law prohibiting a lower rate for a longer haul than for a shorter haul within the state. It was held that regulation of interstate rates was a matter requiring uniformity and which only Congress could effectuate. The earlier case of Peik v. C. & N. W. Ry. Co., 94 U.S. 164, 177–78 (1877), was repudiated. See page 116 above.

in 1887 created the Interstate Commerce Commission.[158] This pioneering legislation served as the model when federal administrative agencies designed to exercise the function of economic regulation were multiplied, particularly during the "New Deal" era, in order to meet the needs of a modern industrial economy.

In addition to regulating the reasonableness of rates and transportation practices, Congress has also legislated extensively regarding safety measures and labor relations in connection with the operations of interstate railroads.[159]

The monopolistic activities of the Standard Oil Company[160] led to legislation giving the Interstate Commerce Commission authority over transportation of oil by means of pipelines.[161] Later statutes gave the Federal Power Commission jurisdiction over the transportation of natural gas in interstate commerce and the sale in interstate commerce of natural gas for resale.[162] The same agency deals with transmission of

[158] The Interstate Commerce Act of February 4, 1887, 24 Stat. 379, related solely to railroads. The Motor Carrier Act of August 9, 1935, 49 Stat. 543, which became Part II of the Interstate Commerce Act, conferred upon the Commission regulatory jurisdiction over interstate motor carriers. Part III, dealing with water carriers, was added by the Act of September 18, 1940, 54 Stat. 929. Part IV, dealing with freight forwarders, was added by the Act of May 16, 1942, 56 Stat. 284.

[159] See notes 115–19, pages 128–29, above.

[160] On this topic, see Standard Oil Co. v. U.S., 221 U.S. 1 (1911).

[161] The Hepburn Act of June 29, 1906, 34 Stat. 584, amended the Interstate Commerce Act by adding "That the provisions of this Act shall apply to any corporation . . . engaged in the transportation of oil or other commodity, except water and except natural or artificial gas, by means of pipe lines . . . who shall be considered and held to be common carriers." For the interpretation of this provision, see The Pipe Line Cases, 234 U.S. 548, 559–61 (1914); Valvoline Oil Co. v. U.S., 308 U.S. 141, 145–46 (1939); Champlin Refining Co. v. U.S., 329 U.S. 29, 33–35 (1946); U.S. v. Champlin Refining Co., 341 U.S. 280, 295–96 (1951).

[162] The Natural Gas Act of June 21, 1938, 52 Stat. 821, 15 U.S.C.A. 717, was enacted to fill a regulatory gap existing under earlier decisions of the Supreme Court. The Court had held that retail distribution of gas to consumers at the burner tip, although technically interstate commerce, was "essentially local" and subject to state regulation. P.U.C. v. Landon, 249 U.S. 236, 245 (1919); Pa. Gas Co. v. P.S.C. of N.Y., 252 U.S. 18, 28, 31 (1920). But sale at the state line to such a local distributing company was not subject to regulation by the producer's state. P.U.C. of R. I. v. Attleboro Co., 273 U.S. 83, 89 (1927). The Natural Gas Act reflected this division of regulatory authority. Panhandle Pipe Line Co. v. P.S.C. of Indiana, 332 U.S. 507, 514–20 (1947); F.P.C. v. E. Ohio Gas Co., 338 U.S. 464, 472–73 (1950).

Besides the peculiar situation regarding local distribution of gas or electricity, there are other "sports" or unusual decisions where commerce admittedly interstate or foreign is regarded as "essentially local" or "not very foreign." Buck v. California,

electric energy in interstate commerce and the sale of such energy at wholesale in interstate commerce.[163] Regulation of interstate or foreign communication by means of telephone, telegraph, radio, and television is entrusted to the Federal Communications Commission.[164] Air commerce is subject to the authority of the Civil Aeronautics Board and the Federal Aviation Agency.[165]

Among the innovations introduced by "New Deal" legislation were the provisions of the laws establishing the Securities and Exchange Commission,[166] and authorizing it to simplify the structure of public utility holding companies.[167]

343 U.S. 99, 102 (1952); Bob-Lo Excursion Co. v. Michigan, 333 U.S. 28, 44 (1948).

See also Central Greyhound Lines v. Mealey, 334 U.S. 653, 663 (1948); Port Richmond Ferry v. Hudson County, 234 U.S. 317, 326–27 (1914); Clason v. Indiana, 306 U.S. 439, 443 (1939); Parker v. Brown, 317 U.S. 341, 358–62 (1943); McCready v. Virginia, 94 U.S. 391, 396 (1877); Geer v. Connecticut, 161 U.S. 519, 528 (1896); Silz v. Hesterberg, 211 U.S. 31, 38–41 (1908).

Mention may be made here also of the rule that organized professional baseball is not regarded as interstate commerce, while other sports are. Federal Baseball Club v. National League, 259 U.S. 200, 208–209 (1922); Toolson v. New York Yankees, 346 U.S. 356, 357 (1953); U.S. v. International Boxing Club, 348 U.S. 236, 241–43 (1955); Radovich v. National Football League, 352 U.S. 445, 450–52 (1957).

[163] Federal Power Act of August 26, 1935, 49 Stat. 847, 16 U.S.C.A. 824, interpreted in Connecticut Light & Power Co. v. F.P.C., 324 U.S. 515, 525–31 (1945); U.S. v. P.U.C. of California, 345 U.S. 295, 307–11 (1953).

[164] Communications Act of June 19, 1934, 48 Stat. 1064, 47 U.S.C.A. 151. Telephone and telegraph companies are common carriers; broadcasting stations are not. F.C.C. v. Sanders Bros. Radio Station, 309 U.S. 470, 474 (1940). But federal power over broadcasting is exclusive. "No state lines divide the radio waves, and national regulation is not only appropriate but essential." Federal Radio Commission v. Nelson Bros. Co., 289 U.S. 266, 279 (1933).

[165] The Agency was created by the Federal Aviation Act of August 23, 1958, 72 Stat. 737, which continued the Board, created by the Civil Aeronautics Act of June 23, 1938, 52 Stat. 977. Generally speaking, the Board exercises functions of economic regulation and conducts quasi-judicial proceedings, including accident investigations. The Agency, headed by an administrator, handles airport construction matters and prescribes safety regulations, operational standards, and traffic rules.

[166] Securities Exchange Act of June 6, 1934, 48 Stat. 881, which established the Commission and transferred to it functions previously delegated to the Federal Trade Commission by the earlier Securities Act of May 27, 1933, 48 Stat. 74. The purpose of these statutes was to protect the investing public by prohibiting interstate traffic in securities without disclosure of certain information necessary to intelligent appraisal of the value of the securities, and by preventing other fraudulent manipulative practices. Apparently the constitutional validity of these statutes as an exertion of the commerce power was never challenged with sufficient earnestness to elicit a ruling by the Supreme Court. See Jones v. S.E.C., 298 U.S. 1, 28 (1936). See note 172, page 137, below.

[167] Public Utility Holding Company Act of August 26, 1935, 49 Stat. 803. The

The Federal Trade Commission is an agency dating from the "New Freedom" of the Woodrow Wilson administration.[168] Its function is to prevent the use of "unfair methods of competition in commerce and unfair or deceptive acts or practices in commerce," by issuing orders "to cease and desist" therefrom. It was expected by the framers of the law establishing the Federal Trade Commission that it would determine what constituted unfair competition in particular cases just as the Interstate Commerce Commission had been in the habit of determining what were "unjust and unreasonable" rates or what constituted "undue preference" or "undue prejudice" to particular shippers or localities. This expectation was frustrated by the Supreme Court's narrow interpretation of the Federal Trade Commission's powers.[169] Accordingly, the effectiveness of the Commission in achieving its intended purposes has proved somewhat disappointing.[170]

Besides establishing independent administrative agencies with quasi-judicial functions, Congress has confided similar powers directly to executive departments. The Secretary of Agriculture has been authorized to make orders regulating rates and practices in connection with the handling and sale of cattle at the stockyards located at the great marketing centers of the nation.[171] As the Supreme Court stated, in upholding this legislation: "The stockyards are not a place of rest or final destination. Thousands of head of livestock arrive daily by carload and trainload lots, and must be promptly sold and disposed of and moved out to give place to the constantly flowing traffic that presses behind. The stockyards are but a throat through which the current flows, and the transactions which occur therein are only incident to this current from the West to the East, and from one State to another. . . . The sales are not . . . merely local transactions. They create a local change of title, it is true, but they do not stop the flow."[172]

---

constitutionality of this act was upheld in North American Co. v. S.E.C., 327 U.S. 686, 694, 700–707 (1946); Electric Bond & Share Co. v. S.E.C., 303 U.S. 419, 440–41 (1938).

[168] The Federal Trade Commission was created by the Act of September 26, 1914, 38 Stat. 717.

[169] Federal Trade Commission v. Gratz, 253 U.S. 421, 427, 431, 437 (1920).

[170] It has often functioned as a "fifth wheel" duplicating judicial enforcement of the antitrust laws. Federal Trade Commission v. Cement Institute, 333 U.S. 683, 692 (1948).

[171] Packers and Stockyards Act of August 15, 1921, 42 Stat. 159.

[172] Stafford v. Wallace, 258 U.S. 495, 515–16 (1922). Doubtless the constitution-

THE CONSTITUTION OF THE UNITED STATES

The same doctrine was soon applied to dealings in grain.[173] Likewise warehousemen were forbidden to charge unreasonable or exorbitant rates for the storage of grain.[174]

In addition to his regulatory function of keeping rates down on services used by farmers, the Secretary of Agriculture also administers programs designed to keep the prices of farm products up.[175]

Moreover, in addition to regulation of commerce by administrative agencies or executive departments, Congress may establish self-executing rules governing commerce which are to be enforced by the courts when appropriate legal proceedings are instituted. Thus the antitrust laws prohibit monopolies and restraints of trade.[176] Enforcement of these mandates is effectuated by criminal or civil proceedings in federal courts.[177] In addition to litigation instituted by the federal Department of Justice, private parties aggrieved by monopolistic practices may bring suit for triple damages.[178] Trade-mark legislation[179] is another example of direct action by Congress rather than authorization empowering an

ality of securities exchange regulation was established by this concept. See note 166, page 136, above. The "flow" or "current of commerce" doctrine originated with the opinion of Justice Holmes in Swift & Co. v. U.S., 196 U.S. 375, 398–99 (1905), where he said that "commerce among the States is not a technical legal conception, but a practical one, drawn from the course of business." The doctrine was a transitional device to escape the effect of the "mechanical" test with regard to the point where commerce begins and ends. *Ibid.*, 397. Holmes distinguished U.S. v. E. C. Knight Co., 156 U.S. 1, 12 (1895), and Hopkins v. U.S., 171 U.S. 578, 596–97 (1898). Cf. Wickard v. Filburn, 317 U.S. 111, 122–25 (1942).

[173] Grain Futures Act of September 21, 1922, 42 Stat. 998, upheld in Chicago Board of Trade v. Olsen, 262 U.S. 1, 33–36 (1923). See also Rice v. Chicago Board of Trade, 331 U.S. 247, 249–53 (1947).

[174] The United States Warehouse Act of August 11, 1916, 39 Stat. 486, 7 U.S.C.A. 241; Rice v. Sante Fe Elevator Corp., 331 U.S. 218, 224–33 (1947). Ever since the Granger era, abuses by warehousemen and grain elevators have been a grievance to farmers. Munn v. Illinois, 94 U.S. 113, 130–32, 135 (1877).

[175] See note 127, page 130, above.

[176] The Sherman Act of July 2, 1890, 26 Stat. 209, 15 U.S.C.A. 1, is the basic statute. It is supplemented by the Clayton Act of October 15, 1914, 38 Stat. 730, 15 U.S.C.A. 12.

[177] According to Justice Holmes, criminal "indictments . . . logically ought to follow" the Supreme Court's decision that stock control of two competing transcontinental railroads by means of a holding company was a violation of the Sherman Act which could be restrained by an injunction. Northern Securities Co. v. U.S., 193 U.S. 197, 405 (1907).

[178] Section 4 of the Clayton Act, 15 U.S.C.A. 15, authorizes such suits.

[179] The Lanham Act of July 5, 1946, 60 Stat. 427, 15 U.S.C.A. 1051, consolidated and revised previous legislation on the subject.

administrative agency to apply appropriate standards in particular cases. In other recent enactments Congress has required automobile manufacturers "to act in good faith in performing or complying with" the terms and provisions of their franchise contracts with their dealers, "or in terminating, canceling, or not renewing the franchise,"[180] and to affix to new cars a label identifying the make and model, together with certain price information.[181] Congress has also prohibited distribution in interstate commerce of switchblade knives[182] (a weapon widely used by juvenile delinquents), and of household refrigerators not equipped with a device enabling the door to be opened from the inside.[183]

ARTICLE I—THE LEGISLATIVE BRANCH
Legislative Powers of Congress, *Naturalization and Bankruptcy*

ART. I, SEC. 8, CL. 4
To establish an uniform Rule of Naturalization, and uniform Laws on the subject of Bankruptcies throughout the United States;

HISTORY

UNDER the Articles of Confederation "the free inhabitants" of one state (except paupers, vagabonds, and fugitives from justice) were "entitled to all privileges and immunities of free citizens in the several States";[184] but it was left to each state individually to prescribe the terms upon which it would admit foreigners to citizenship. A policy of easy naturalization in one state could thus frustrate the stricter policies of other states. Hence the purpose of giving the federal government power over naturalization, Roger Sherman said in 1790, was "to prevent particular States receiving citizens, and forcing them upon others who would not have received them."[185]

[180] Act of August 8, 1956, 70 Stat. 1125, 15 U.S.C.A. 1222.
[181] Act of July 7, 1958, 72 Stat. 325, 15 U.S.C.A. 1232.
[182] Act of August 12, 1958, 72 Stat. 562, 15 U.S.C.A. 1242.
[183] Act of August 2, 1956, 70 Stat. 953, 15 U.S.C.A. 1211.
[184] Art. IV. Cf. Art. IV, sec. 2, cl. 1, of the Constitution.
[185] Farrand, *Records*, III, 359. This grievance had been discussed in the Old Congress. Madison to Edmund Randolph, August 27, 1782. Edmund C. Burnett, ed., *Letters of Members of the Continental Congress*, VI, 455.

The New Jersey Plan proposed that "the rule for naturalization ought to be the same in every State."[186] The Committee on Detail reported a proposed power "To establish an uniform rule of naturalization throughout the United States."[187] This was agreed to on August 16.[188]

During debate on August 29, Charles Pinckney offered a proposition "To establish uniform laws upon the subject of bankruptcies and respecting the damages arising on the protest of foreign bills of exchange."[189] On September 1, Rutledge reported favorably on behalf of the committee to which the proposal had been referred, insofar as the provision regarding bankruptcy laws was concerned.[190] This was agreed to, Connecticut casting the only dissenting vote. Sherman had "observed that Bankruptcies were in some cases punishable with death by the laws of England—& He did not chuse to grant a power by which that might be done here." Gouverneur Morris remarked that "this was an extensive & delicate subject" but that he would accept the proposal since he saw no danger of abuse of the power by the federal legislature.[191]

The Committee of Style combined the topics of naturalization and bankruptcy in a single clause.[192]

INTERPRETATION

UNDER international law, in order to be a member of the family of nations, a state must possess people, territory, and government. A nation with no citizens would be as imperfect and incomplete as if it had no land or form of government. Yet the original Constitution of 1787 contained no provisions specifying who were to be citizens of the United States. Apparently national citizenship was a derivative status, dependent upon enjoyment of state citizenship.[193] The right to vote for Representatives in Congress is given by Article I, section 2, clause 1, to "Electors" qualified as such under state law. Article II, section 1, clause 5, speaks of "a natural born Citizen," thus contemplating that some

[186] Farrand, *Records*, I, 245 (June 15).

[187] Art. VII, sec. 1, cl. 3. *Ibid.*, II, 182 (August 6). Randolph's draft had included a power "To regulate naturalization." *Ibid.*, II, 144.

[188] *Ibid.*, II, 304 (August 16).   [189] *Ibid.*, II, 445, 447 (August 29).

[190] *Ibid.*, II, 483, 484 (September 1).   [191] *Ibid.*, II, 486, 489 (September 3).

[192] *Ibid.*, II, 595 (September 12).

[193] The status of state citizenship is recognized in Art. III, sec. 2, cl. 1, and Art. IV, sec. 2. In Dred Scott v. Sandford, 19 How. 393, 405–407, 576–78 (1857), both Taney and Curtis agreed that United States citizenship was derivative and depended upon state citizenship.

persons acquire national citizenship (derivatively) at birth.[194] Article IV, section 2, gives to the citizens of each state "all Privileges and Immunities of Citizens in the several States." Besides obtaining such privileges in every state upon becoming a citizen of one state, the citizen of one state also acquired the status of national citizenship in the same way. Similarly, a person excluded by state law from the privileges of state citizenship (as a slave) was apparently thereby deprived of national citizenship.

By the Fourteenth Amendment, which took effect in 1868, national citizenship was conferred upon persons born in the United States, and state citizenship was made an automatic consequence of national citizenship, rather than vice versa as theretofore. "All persons born or naturalized in the United States, and subject to the jurisdiction thereof, are citizens of the United States and of the State wherein they reside."[195]

But from the beginning Congress had power to establish a uniform rule of naturalization, that is to say, a rule regarding the mode of acquisition of national citizenship by persons not acquiring that status at birth.

Besides citizenship *jure soli*, by reason of birth in the United States as contemplated by the Fourteenth Amendment, Congress has in practice undertaken to legislate regarding acquisition (and loss) of nationality by various means. For example, a person born abroad whose parents are citizens (if one of them has resided in the United States) becomes a citizen at birth *jure sanguinis*.[196] Possibly any method of acquiring citizenship other than by virtue of the Fourteenth Amendment (by birth in the United States) may be regarded as a form of naturalization. Thus there can be collective naturalization of the inhabitants of territory annexed to the United States, without any formalities on the part of the individuals concerned.[197]

Ordinarily, however, naturalization is a privilege accorded only to

[194] The status of national citizenship is recognized also in Art. I, sec. 2, cl. 2, and Art. I, sec. 3, cl. 3, specifying the qualifications of Representatives and Senators.

[195] In Gassies v. Ballon, 6 Pet. 761, 762 (1832), Chief Justice Marshall said: "A citizen of the United States, residing in any state of the Union, is a citizen of that state."

[196] 8 U.S.C.A. 1401. Nationality Act of 1940, revised June 27, 1952, 66 Stat. 163, 235. This is considered as naturalization in U.S. v. Wong Kim Ark, 169 U.S. 649, 672, 688 (1898). For a recent decision narrowly construing the rule of *jus sanguinis* in American legislation, see Montana v. Kennedy, 366 U.S. 308, 309–12 (1961).

[197] Boyd v. Nebraska, 143 U.S. 135, 162 (1892); U.S. v. Wong Kim Ark, 169 U.S. 649, 702–703 (1898); Contzen v. U.S., 179 U.S. 191, 193 (1900).

particular categories of qualified persons[198] after they have undergone a careful screening procedure and taken the oath of allegiance[199] in solemn judicial ceremonies. Naturalization can be and ordinarily is effected in state courts as well as in federal courts.[200]

Naturalized citizens in the eyes of the law have the same rights and privileges as native-born citizens. There are no second-class citizens in the United States.[201] Nevertheless, naturalized citizens upon displaying certain disloyal attitudes are subject to having their naturalization canceled for fraud.[202] Also, if they resume residence in their native land, there is a presumption that their naturalization was a subterfuge, perhaps undertaken for economic gain, and they are subject to denaturalization.[203]

Congress has also undertaken to provide that natural-born citizens may lose their nationality by reason of certain acts, indicative of unwillingness to sustain the obligations of citizenship, such as taking the oath of allegiance to a foreign state.[204] However, the Supreme Court has recently held that, while voting in a foreign political election may be a proper ground of denaturalization,[205] desertion from the armed forces in time of war is not.[206]

Congress can also exclude aliens from the United States, and regulate the terms of their admission, by virtue of the commerce power and the inherent attributes of sovereignty.[207]

Whether Congress can deprive natural-born citizens of their status,

[198] For a list of disqualifications, see 8 U.S.C.A. 1423–27, 1429.

[199] The oath is set forth in 8 U.S.C.A. 1448 (a). Since Girouard v. United States, 328 U.S. 61, 64 (1946), willingness to bear arms has not been required. Cf. U.S. v. Schwimmer, 279 U.S. 644 (1929), and U.S. v. Macintosh, 283 U.S. 605 (1931).

[200] 8 U.S.C.A. 1421 (a); Holmgren v. U. S., 217 U.S. 509, 517 (1910).

[201] Knauer v. U.S., 328 U.S. 654, 658 (1946).

[202] *Ibid.*, 673; 8 U.S.C.A. 1451.

[203] 8 U.S.C.A. 1484; 8 U.S.C.A. 1451 (d); Perkins v. Elg, 307 U.S. 325 (1939).

[204] 8 U.S.C.A. 1481. Marriage of an American woman to a foreigner was formerly regarded as a voluntary action which might involve the United States in international complications and to which Congress could attach the consequence of loss of citizenship during the continuance of the marriage relationship. Mackenzie v. Hare, 239 U.S. 299, 312 (1915).

[205] Perez v. Brownell, 356 U.S. 44, 59–60 (1958).

[206] Trop v. Dulles, 356 U.S. 86, 101, 107 (1958). Cf. Kennedy v. Mendoza-Martinez, 372 U.S. 144, 164–67 (1963).

[207] Chinese Exclusion Case, 130 U.S. 581, 603, 609 (1889); Fong Yue Ting v. U.S., 149 U.S. 698, 707 (1893).

and if so under what limitations, is less certain. The Supreme Court has said that "The power of naturalization, vested in Congress by the Constitution, is a power to confer citizenship, not a power to take it away."[208] But later cases indicate that as an incident of its power over foreign relations Congress can deprive a citizen of nationality without his consent.

Naturalization and bankruptcy have nothing in common except that they are to be regulated by Congress in a "uniform" manner. In the case of naturalization a "uniform Rule" is to be established; in the case of bankruptcy "uniform Laws" on the subject are to be established "throughout the United States."

The requisite uniformity is not lacking if the bankruptcy legislation incorporates provisions of state law with respect to exemptions. The uniformity required is geographical, not personal.[209]

The "subject" of bankruptcy embraces everything relating to the administration and distribution of a debtor's property for the benefit of his creditors, and his discharge from the obligation of his debts.[210] It extends to the entire area of readjustment of the relationship between a nonpaying debtor and his creditors, for his or their benefit.[211] It is not limited to the powers exercised in England before our Constitution was adopted.[212] In modern legislation the relief of the debtor is an aspect of bankruptcy which is just as important as the distribution to creditors.[213] Readjustment of debts of municipalities and political subdivis-

---

[208] U.S. v. Wong Kim Ark, 169 U.S. 649, 703 (1898). Chief Justice Marshall used similar language in Osborn v. U.S. Bank, 9 Wheat. 738, 827 (1824). The question was avoided in Mackenzie v. Hare, 239 U.S. 299, 311 (1915). In Perkins v. Elg, 307 U.S. 325, 329 (1939), the court said that citizenship must be deemed to continue until it is cut off "through the operation of a treaty or congressional enactment or by [the citizen's] voluntary action in conformity with applicable legal principles." Regarding the constitutionality of certain provisions for loss of nationality contained in the Nationality Acts of 1940 and 1952, see notes 205 and 206, page 142, above.

[209] Hanover Nat. Bank v. Moyses, 186 U.S. 181, 188–89 (1902).

[210] *Ibid.*, 188. Congress can discharge the debtor from the obligation of his contracts, as Congress is not subject to the restriction imposed on the states by Art. I, sec. 10, cl. 1; but Congress is subject to the due process clause of the Fifth Amendment in exercising the bankruptcy power. Louisville Joint Stock Bank v. Radford, 295 U.S. 555, 589 (1935).

[211] Wright v. Union Central Life Ins. Co., 304 U.S. 502, 513–14 (1938). See also 294 U.S. 648, at 673, quoting 186 U.S. 181, 186.

[212] Contl. Ill. Nat. Bank v. C., R. I. & P. Ry. Co., 294 U.S. 648, 668 (1935).

[213] U.S. v. Bekins, 304 U.S. 27, 33, 47 (1938). See also 295 U.S. at 588.

ions of a state may be accomplished through exercise of the federal bankruptcy power.[214]

A bankruptcy proceeding supersedes an incompleted foreclosure under state law.[215] State insolvency laws are permitted, in the absence of conflicting federal legislation, provided there is no violation of the obligation of contracts clause and no action affecting the rights of citizens of other states.[216]

ARTICLE I—THE LEGISLATIVE BRANCH
Legislative Powers of Congress, *Money, Weights, and Measures*

ART. I, SEC. 8, CL. 5
To coin Money, regulate the Value thereof, and of foreign Coin, and fix the Standard of Weights and Measures;

HISTORY

THE Committee of Detail reported as three separate powers those of coining money, regulating the value of foreign coin, and fixing the standard of weights and measures.[217] These were agreed to without debate.[218] The Committee of Style added the provision for regulation of the value of the United States money, and worded the entire clause in its present form.[219]

INTERPRETATION

THE power to "establish a standard of value by which all other values may be measured, or, in other words, to determine what shall be lawful

[214] U.S. v. Bekins, 304 U.S. 27, 51 (1938). Cf. Ashton v. Cameron Co. District, 298 U.S. 513, 528 (1936).

[215] Kalb v. Feuerstein, 308 U.S. 433, 439 (1940); Wright v. Union Central Life Ins. Co., 304 U.S. 502, 514–16 (1938). Wright v. Vinton Branch, 300 U.S. 440, 470 (1937), permits reasonable modifications of mortgagee's rights. Cf. Radford case.

[216] Sturges v. Crowninshield, 4 Wheat. 122, 208 (1819); Ogden v. Saunders, 12 Wheat. 213, 368 (1827).

[217] Farrand, *Records*, II, 182 (August 6). Charles Pinckney may have proposed this topic. *Ibid.*, II, 136. It was derived from similar provisions in Art. IX of the Articles of Confederation. Rutledge noted it on Randolph's draft. *Ibid.*, II, 143, 144.

[218] *Ibid.*, II, 304, 308 (August 16).   [219] *Ibid.*, II, 595 (September 12).

money and a legal tender" is an attribute of sovereignty exercised by the government of every country.[220]

Under the Articles of Confederation, the Congress had power to borrow money, and in pursuance of this authority, emitted bills of credit to a large amount, but "did not, perhaps could not, make them a legal tender."[221] This power then resided in the states, and they did enact legislation giving the quality of legal tender to the bills issued by Congress.[222]

In the clause giving Congress power to coin money and regulate the value thereof, the Constitution clearly gave the federal government power to establish a standard of value and issue metallic currency with the quality of legal tender. The power thus conferred obviously embraced the power "to mould the metallic substances into forms convenient for circulation and to stamp them with the impress of the government authority indicating their value with reference to the unit of value established by law."[223]

But can the quality of legal tender be attached by Congress to paper money as well as to metallic coins? The first law attempting to do this was enacted on February 25, 1862, during the exigencies of wartime need for revenue and credit.[224] But after the re-establishment of peace the Supreme Court held that Congress did not have power to require acceptance of paper money in payment of debts contracted before the date of the legislation.[225] The majority opinion was written by Chief Justice Salmon P. Chase, who as secretary of the treasury had sponsored the legal tender measure because of its necessity but had upon further reflection become convinced of its unconstitutionality.[226]

Within less than a year and a half, this decision was overruled after

---

[220] Hepburn v. Griswold, 8 Wall. 603, 615 (1870). See argument of Attorney General Cummings in Norman v. B. & O. R.R. Co., 294 U.S. 240, 271 (1935).

[221] Chief Justice Marshall spoke thus guardedly regarding the question of legal tender in Craig v. Missouri, 4 Pet. 410, 435 (1830).

[222] 12 Wall. at 645. Congress had under the Articles of Confederation "the sole and exclusive right and power of regulating the alloy and value of coin struck by their own authority, or by that of the respective States." Congress also had the similar right of "fixing the standard of weights and measures throughout the United States." Art. IX.

[223] Legal Tender Case, 110 U.S. 421, 462 (1884). (Field, J., dissenting).

[224] 12 Stat. 345. See Legal Tender Cases, 12 Wall. 457, 540–41 (1871).

[225] Hepburn v. Griswold, 8 Wall. 603, 616 (1870). Miller, Swayne, and Davis dissented.

[226] Chase, C. J., diss., 12 Wall. at 576.

two new Justices, whose views were known to be favorable to the legal tender legislation, had been appointed.[227]

The power of Congress thus sustained was not derived directly from the power to coin money.[228] Rather the decision is based on the "necessary and proper" clause. The challenged power is regarded as an appropriate means (not expressly prohibited by the Constitution) for carrying into execution expressly granted powers, namely the power to wage war, borrow money, and preserve the existence of the Union itself.[229] Weight was also given to the fact that under previous decisions relating to the provision of a national currency, it had been held that Congress could provide (besides coin) national bank notes[230] and its own notes, and could tax competing forms of currency out of existence.[231]

The dissent of Chief Justice Chase emphasized that the quality of legal tender was not necessary to make the federal paper acceptable as an aid to the war power and borrowing power. Receivability to pay taxes and debts due to the government was enough to sustain the issue of notes.[232] Justice Stephen J. Field's dissent emphasized that constitutionality was not proved by the mere fact that the notes would be made more desirable if they were legal tender. For the same effect might be produced by giving the holder of notes the right of admission to places of amusement or to use transportation agencies, but that fact would not justify such interference with the rights of third parties or warrant the insertion of such terms in a debtor-creditor transaction between the government and a lender.[233]

In Justice Nathan Clifford's dissent he remarked that the Constitution itself seems to recognize the "dollar" as the standard of value,[234]

[227] Legal Tender Cases, 12 Wall. 457 (1871).

[228] 12 Wall. at 553. This is also made clear in the concurring opinion of Justice Bradley, who regarded it as incidental to the power to borrow money. 12 Wall. at 560. See also note 237, page 147, below.

[229] 12 Wall. at 541, 544. The existence of an implied power can be deduced as an appropriate means of enforcing a combination of several expressly granted powers. *Ibid.*, at 534.

[230] McCulloch v. Maryland, 4 Wheat. 316, 422 (1819).

[231] Veazie Bank v. Fenno, 8 Wall. 533, 549 (1869).

[232] 12 Wall. at 577. This seems to be a question of expediency, properly determinable by the legislative branch of the government. He also argued due process. *Ibid.*, 580. That is really an indirect consequence of granted power.

[233] 12 Wall. at 638, 643.

[234] 12 Wall. at 590, 598, 601. See Art. I, sec. 9, cl. 1.

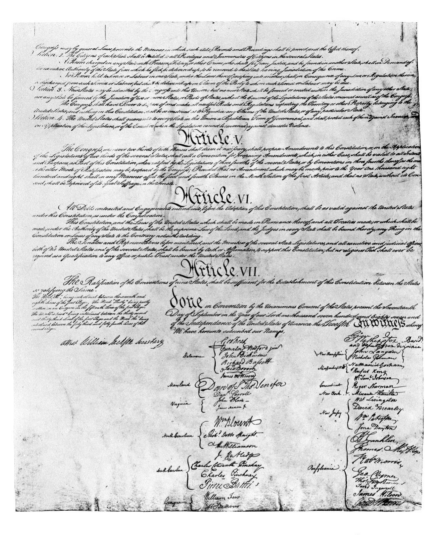

Fourth page of the Constitution, showing signatures and errata.

Courtesy National Archives

State House (Independence Hall),
where the Supreme Court first sat in Philadelphia (1791).

From an engraving by Thomas Birch
Courtesy Library of Congress

and argued that credit currency could not serve as a standard of value.[235]

Just as the Court held that there was no significant distinction between debts contracted before and after the legal tender act,[236] so in a later case reaffirming the validity of the legal tender provision it held that it made no difference whether such legislation applied only in time of war or also in time of peace.[237]

In the twentieth century, five days after the inauguration of Franklin D. Roosevelt in the midst of an unprecedented economic crisis, paper money became virtually the sole legal tender and circulating medium. Gold coin, gold bullion, and gold certificates were required to be turned over to the government, and exportation, possession, or trading in gold was prohibited except under special licenses and for settlement of international balances. Other legislation outlawed clauses in past or future obligations requiring payment in gold coin or a particular type of money, or in the value so measured. In a notable opinion by Chief Justice Charles Evans Hughes, after argument by Attorney General Homer S. Cummings and other distinguished lawyers, the Supreme Court by a vote of five to four upheld the government's contention that these clauses "obstructed" the power of Congress to regulate the value of money.

The Court recognized however that this power did not come solely from the clause empowering Congress to coin money but from the aggregate of granted powers constituting authority "to establish a monetary system."[238]

In companion cases involving gold certificates and United States bonds containing a gold clause, the Court held that payment of these obligations in paper money did not cause any substantial damage to the holders, because even if they had been paid in gold the holders would have had to turn the metal back to the government and could not have benefited by its value in the world market, since they had no lawful access to that market.[239]

[235] *Ibid.*, at 601.

[236] 12 Wall. at 530. The Court emphasized the injustice of requiring payment in gold for debts contracted since the prevalence of paper money.

[237] Legal Tender Case, 110 U.S. 421, 448, 450 (1884). This case emphasized that the power was a prerogative of sovereignty enjoyed by other foreign governments. 110 U.S. at 447, 450.

[238] Norman v. B. & O. R.R. Co., 294 U.S. 240, 302–303 (1935). For similar reasoning regarding "the war power," see page 165 and note 312, page 162, below.

[239] Nortz v. U.S., 294 U.S. 317, 329 (1935); Perry v. U.S., 294 U.S. 330, 357

Undoubtedly these decisions were in large part dictated by inexorable economic conditions. There simply was not enough gold in the world to provide adequate currency for the needs of commerce; and it would have been a gross injustice to allow one particular group of creditors an undue benefit. But the results reached by the Court were likewise a logical sequel to its earlier pronouncements evoked by the aftermath of the Civil War.[240]

ARTICLE I—THE LEGISLATIVE BRANCH
Legislative Powers of Congress, *Counterfeiting*

ART. I, SEC. 8, CL. 6

To provide for the Punishment of counterfeiting the Securities and current Coin of the United States;

HISTORY

RANDOLPH'S draft in the Committee of Detail contained a clause "To declare the law of piracy, felonies and captures on the high seas, and captures on land."[241] The Committee of Detail in its report had modified this to read: "To declare the law and punishment of piracies and felonies committed on the high seas, and the punishment of counterfeiting the coin of the United States, and of offences against the law

---

(1935). In the Perry case, the Court insisted that the sovereign power to borrow money could not be defeated by repudiation and that theoretically the holders were entitled to payment as stipulated, although in practice no loss was suffered because there was no access to the benefit of the world market. 249 U.S. at 353. Justice Stone regarded this hypocritical sophistry distinguishing between the validity of the gold clause in government and private obligations as undesirable and inexpedient. *Ibid.*, 359. The legality of the prohibition on exports of gold was sustained by a precedent dating from the Taft administration. Ling Su Fan v. U.S., 218 U.S. 302, 311 (1910).

240 Justice Field had foreseen the possibility of repudiation by the government. 12 Wall. at 673–74. Justice McReynolds was extremely vehement in his dissent when the gold cases were decided on February 18, 1935. Drew Pearson and Robert S. Allen, *The Nine Old Men*, 234–35.

241 Farrand, *Records*, II, 143. Another clause read "To provide tribunals and punishment for mere offences against the law of nations."

of nations."[242] After amendments offered by Madison, Morris, and Ellsworth the clause read: "[T]o define and punish piracies and felonies committed on the high seas, counterfeiting the securities and current coin of the U. States, and offences agst. the law of Nations."[243] The Committee of Style separated this into two parts, the first of which was: "To provide for the punishment of counterfeiting the securities and current coin of the United States."[244]

INTERPRETATION

THIS clause, together with Article I, section 8, clause 10, giving power "to define and punish Piracies and Felonies committed on the high Seas, and Offences against the Law of Nations," and Article III, section 3, clause 2, empowering Congress to punish (but not to define) treason, constitutes the only express mention of criminal jurisdiction in the Constitution.

These provisions are in practice superfluous. The entire structure of federal criminal law (and its incidental enforcement agencies, such as the Secret Service and the Federal Bureau of Investigation) rests upon the "necessary and proper" clause as its legal basis.

Notwithstanding the fact that this clause permits only punishment of "counterfeiting," the Supreme Court has held that Congress has power to punish the act of passing or circulating counterfeited coin.[245]

The distinction between "securities" and "coin" of the United States in this clause was relied upon by the Justices who believed that the power to coin money did not authorize giving the quality of legal tender to notes issued by the United States.[246]

---

[242] *Ibid.*, II, 182 (August 6).

[243] *Ibid.*, II, 312, 315–16, 570 (August 17).

[244] *Ibid.*, II, 595 (September 12).

[245] U.S. v. Marigold, 9 How. 560, 567–68 (1850). While the term "counterfeiting" refers to fabrication rather than passing or uttering of spurious coin, Congress has power to prevent substitution of spurious coin for the constitutional currency it is empowered to create by virtue of the power to coin money. If the circulating medium created and established by Congress could be replaced by currency which it had not authorized, "then the power conferred by the Constitution would be useless." Importation of counterfeit money can be prohibited under the commerce power. Likewise "the power to coin money includes the power to prevent its outflow from the country of origin, as well as to punish its defacement and mutilation." Ling Su Fan v. U.S., 218 U.S. 302, 311 (1910).

[246] 12 Wall. at 650.

ARTICLE I—THE LEGISLATIVE BRANCH
Legislative Powers of Congress, *Postal Service*

ART. I, SEC. 8, CL. 7
To establish Post Offices and post Roads;

HISTORY

THE Articles of Confederation entrusted to Congress the sole and exclusive right and power of "establishing and regulating post-offices from one State to another, throughout all the United States, and exacting such postage on the papers passing thro' the same as may be requisite to defray the expenses of the said office."[247] The Randolph draft in the Committee of Detail contained a clause "To establish post-offices."[248] On motion of Gerry in the convention the words "and post-roads" were added.[249] A proposal by Charles Pinckney "To regulate Stages on the post-roads" was referred to the Committee of Detail on August 18.[250] Nothing came of this proposal. The Committee of Style reported the clause without change in its present form.[251]

INTERPRETATION

DURING the long controversy over the power of Congress to engage in "internal improvements," strict constructionists contended that the power to "establish" post roads did not include the power of constructing such roads, but merely that of designating which of existing highways constructed by the states should be used for transportation of mail.[252]

Later, however, the Supreme Court recognized that "the power possessed by Congress embraces the regulation of the whole postal system of the country." More than mere designation of the routes and of the places where mail is to be received and delivered is included.

[247] Art. IX.

[248] Farrand, *Records*, II, 144. The Committee of Detail reported the clause without change. *Ibid.*, II, 182 (August 6).

[249] *Ibid.*, II, 303, 308 (August 16).   [250] *Ibid.*, II, 322, 326, 328 (August 18).

[251] *Ibid.*, II, 595 (September 12).

[252] Searight v. Stokes, 3 How. 150, 160, 180–81 (1845). See also Jefferson to Madison, March 6, 1796, in Jefferson, *Works*, VIII, 226.

There is also included carriage of the mail and all measures necessary for its speedy transit and prompt delivery. Congress may specify what may be carried in the mails and what shall be excluded.[253] Congress may also protect its monopoly by prohibiting transportation of mailable matter otherwise than by mail.[254] The power to exclude from the mails may be used in order to prevent use of the postal facilities for fraudulent or immoral purposes.[255]

The federal government may exercise, without the consent of the states affected, the power of eminent domain in order to condemn land required for the construction of post offices.[256] The entire executive power may be exerted to remove obstructions to the carriage of the mails, and the judicial power may also be invoked in order to enjoin interference with the functioning of the postal service.[257]

Use of the mails may also be denied as a means of enforcing other valid regulations enacted by Congress, such as the registration requirements imposed upon public utility holding companies.[258]

Denial of second-class rates (which are in effect a subsidy to newspapers and other publications disseminating "information of a public character, or devoted to literature, the sciences, arts, or some special industry") may have a disastrous financial effect on a publication to which such rates are refused. Arbitrary withholding by the postmaster general of the second-class privilege would in effect make him a censor of the reading matter available to the American people.

Hence in a case where that official had endeavored to revoke the

[253] Ex parte Jackson, 96 U.S. 727, 732 (1878); *In re* Rapier, 143 U.S. 110, 133 (1892); Public Clearing House v. Coyne, 194 U.S. 497, 506–507 (1904). Congress is now acknowledged to possess "practically plenary power over the mails." U.S. *ex rel.* Milwaukee Social Dem. Pub. Co. v. Burleson, 255 U.S. 407, 411 (1921). Administrative details, such as designation of the places where mail shall be received or delivered, may be delegated by Congress to the postmaster general. Ware v. U.S., 4 Wall. 617, 632 (1867).

[254] 96 U.S. at 735. Since Congress cannot prohibit (at least by virtue of the postal power) the transportation of unmailable matter as merchandise by means other than the mails, the exclusion of any matter from the mails does not constitute an interference with freedom of speech or of the press. *Ibid.*, at 735–36. Cf. the views of Justice Holmes discussed in note 261, page 152, below.

[255] 194 U.S. at 507–508. Since mail addressed to a person against whom a fraud order is outstanding is returned to the sender, and not opened by the postal authorities, there is no violation of the Fourth Amendment. 96 U.S. at 735.

[256] Kohl v. U.S., 91 U.S. 367, 371, 374 (1876).

[257] *In re* Debs, 158 U.S. 564, 599 (1895).

[258] Electric Bond & Share Co. v. S.E.C., 303 U.S. 419, 442 (1938).

second-class permit of *Esquire* magazine, on the ground that its spicy items, though not unmailable as obscene, did not constitute "information of a public character" or "literature," the Supreme Court held that in the United States no public officer had authority to determine what constitutes good literature.[259] In the absence of more explicit statutory language the Court could not believe that Congress had "made such a radical departure from our traditions" and undertaken to "clothe the Postmaster General with the power to supervise the tastes of the reading public of the country."[260] To interpret the statute as giving the postmaster general the power claimed would enable him to visit publishers with financial ruin on account of the economic or political views disseminated in their publications, and would be of dubious constitutionality. The Court stated that "grave constitutional questions are immediately raised once it is said that the use of the mails is a privilege which may be extended or withheld on any ground whatever."[261]

ARTICLE I—THE LEGISLATIVE BRANCH

Legislative Powers of Congress, *Patents and Copyrights*

ART. I, SEC. 8, CL. 8

To promote the Progress of Science and useful Arts, by securing for limited Times to Authors and Inventors the exclusive Right to their respective Writings and Discoveries;

HISTORY

PROVISIONS dealing with copyright and patents were offered by Madison and Pinckney,[262] and were reported by the Committee on

---

[259] Hannegan v. Esquire, Inc., 327 U.S. 146, 149, 157 (1946).

[260] *Ibid.*, at 156.

[261] *Ibid.*, at 156. The Court referred to the constitutional questions raised by Justice Brandeis in his dissenting opinion in U.S. *ex rel.* Milwaukee Social Democratic Publishing Co. v. Burleson, 255 U.S. 407, 430 (1921). These points were later brushed aside lightly in a fraud case. Donaldson v. Read Magazine, Inc., 333 U.S., 178, 189–91 (1948). Justice Holmes had likewise urged that "the use of the mails is almost as much a part of freedom of speech as the right to use our tongues." 255 U.S. at 437; Leach v. Carlisle, 258 U.S. 138, 140–41 (1922).

[262] Farrand, *Records*, II, 321, 322, 325 (August 18).

152

Postponed Parts[263] in language which was adopted without change.[264]

INTERPRETATION

THE primary purpose of the American patent and copyright laws, enacted in pursuance of this clause, is to promote the progress of science and useful arts. The economic reward and private gain accruing to authors and inventors by reason of the exclusive rights granted to them by those laws is merely the means by which the public good is promoted, the incentive by which gifted individuals are induced to persevere in their labors and to make the fruits thereof available to mankind at large. The economic philosophy underlying this system is "the conviction that encouragement of individual effort by personal gain is the best way to advance public welfare through the talents of authors and inventors."[265]

Hence the element of novelty has always been regarded as essential; a patent cannot be obtained unless the invention covers something not previously known or used by the public; it must mark an advance over the pre-existing state of the art. Accordingly, if an inventor permits public use of his invention without applying for a patent, he cannot thereafter patent it; for it has entered the public domain, and his delay in seeking a patent might otherwise permit him to prolong the period of the patent monopoly specified in the patent laws.[266] In England the exclusive right of inventors was recognized as an exception in the statute prohibiting monopolies.[267] In the United States an attempt by the holder of a patent to extend his monopoly beyond the terms of the grant contained in the patent may constitute a violation of the antitrust laws.[268]

[263] *Ibid.*, II, 505, 509 (September 5).

[264] *Ibid.*, II, 595 (September 12).

[265] Mazer v. Stein, 347 U.S. 201, 219 (1954); Sinclair & Carroll Co. v. Interchemical Corp., 325 U.S. 327, 330–31 (1945).

[266] Pennock v. Dialogue, 2 Pet. 1, 19, 23–24 (1829).

[267] *Ibid.*, 20. The statute was 21 Jac. I, c. 3, sec. 6. The inventor's rights were granted by letters patent; hence the origin of the term "patent." This is as if in the United States the patent laws were an exception to the antitrust laws, which is perhaps true analytically though not historically. U.S. v. Line Material Co., 333 U.S. 287, 310 (1948). The first patent law was enacted in 1790 (Act of April 30, 1790, 1 St. 109); the Sherman Act became law a century later in 1890 (Act of July 2, 1890, 26 Stat. 209).

[268] U.S. v. Line Material Co., 333 U.S. 287, 308 (1948). A valid patent "does not give the patentee any exemption from the provisions of the Sherman Act beyond

It follows from the language used in the Constitution, limiting patentability to inventions which in fact contribute to the "progress" of science, that every case involving the validity of a patent presents a constitutional question. Hence the Supreme Court of the United States is often required to devote its time and effort to determinations involving minute questions of fact with respect to the patentability of trivial gadgets.[269] Mere combination of previously known and used features does not constitute "invention," unless there is a new function or operation in which they are used. For "the function of a patent is to add to the sum of human knowledge. Patents cannot be sustained when, on the contrary, their effect is to subtract from former resources freely available to skilled artisans." The union of old elements with no change in function would merely withdraw what is already known into the field of monopoly.[270] Commercial success alone, without invention and novelty, will not assure patentability.[271]

Similarly, a patent was held invalid which expedited the printing of magazines on glossy paper by adding to the ink an ingredient which caused it to evaporate quickly when heated, though not evaporating at ordinary room temperature. The claimant of the patent on this commercially valuable process had simply selected several suitable substances from the catalogue of a chemical company, which listed their respective evaporation temperatures. The Supreme Court said: "Reading a list and selecting a known compound to meet known requirements is no more ingenious than selecting the last piece to put into the last opening of a jig-saw puzzle. It is not invention."[272]

In the field of copyright law English precedent has likewise been influential. The effect of English statutes and judicial decisions on that subject was considered by the Supreme Court of the United States in an interesting and important case between two reporters of that Court's

---

the limits of the patent monopoly." The economic reward derived from reasonable and proper exploitation of the patent, however, is permissible. *Ibid.*, 314.

[269] Great A. & P. Tea Co. v. Supermarket Equipment Corp., 340 U.S. 147, 154 (1950). For a list of gadget patents litigated, see ibid., 157–58. Concerning the desirability of freeing the members of the Supreme Court for the performance of their more important duties, see Ex parte Peru, 318 U.S. 578, 602–603 (1943).

[270] 340 U.S. at 152.

[271] *Ibid.*, 153. The device involved in that case was a rack, widely used in supermarkets, to draw merchandise along the counter toward the cashier. The Court held that this was a mere combination of previously used elements, and was not patentable.

[272] Sinclair & Carroll Co. v. Interchemical Corp., 325 U.S. 327, 335 (1945).

decisions. When Henry Wheaton resigned as reporter in 1827 in order
to accept a diplomatic post offered to him by President John Quincy
Adams, Richard Peters was named to succeed him. Peters proceeded to
publish a series of *Condensed Reports*, reproducing the decisions of the
Court appearing in the reports previously published by his predecessors
(the four volumes of Alexander J. Dallas, the nine volumes of Judge
William Cranch, and the twelve volumes of Wheaton). Peters at first
professed that his books contained only the text of the opinions of the
Court, which were a matter of public record and not copyrightable,
and did not include any of the valuable notes and appendices which
were the work of Wheaton. Later Peters claimed that there was no
valid copyright at all to Wheaton's reports, as the publisher had failed
to comply with the requirements of the copyright statutes. Wheaton's
suit for an accounting and an injunction against Peters was decided by
the Supreme Court in 1834.[273]

The Court being "unanimously of opinion, that no reporter has or
can have any copyright in the written opinions delivered by this court;
and that the judges thereof cannot confer on any reporter any such
right,"[274] Wheaton was as a practical matter the losing party in the
litigation, although the actual decision of the majority of the Court was
that the case be remanded to the court below for determination by a
jury of the questions of fact regarding compliance with the requirements of the copyright law, with respect to advertising in a newspaper
and depositing a copy in the office of the Secretary of State. Compliance
with those requirements was held to be mandatory and not directory;
they were essential steps for the protection of the general public in
enabling the work which was copyrighted to be identified adequately.
They were therefore necessary conditions precedent to acquisition of a
valid copyright.[275]

The Court held that if Wheaton had a copyright at all, it was by
virtue of the protection extended by the Act of Congress;[276] that the
author's right was *created* by the statute, and was not a pre-existing
common law right which the legislation merely "secured."[277] Wheat-

---

[273] Wheaton v. Peters, 8 Pet. 591 (1834). See Frederick C. Hicks, *Men and Books
Famous in the Law*, 198–211. Daniel Webster was counsel for Wheaton. Thomas
Sergeant and Jared R. Ingersoll, prominent Philadelphia lawyers, appeared for Peters,
a fellow Pennsylvanian.

[274] 8 Pet. at 668.   [275] *Ibid.*, 664, 667–68.   [276] *Ibid.*, 662.

[277] *Ibid.*, 661. Regarding the meaning of the word "secure" in other contexts, see

on's claim that common law copyright continued to exist even after publication of a literary work was rejected.[278] The Court declared that there was no federal common law in the United States,[279] and that there was no evidence that the courts of Pennsylvania had ever recognized a common law copyright of the sort claimed by Wheaton.[280] Emphasizing that only such portions of the law of England as were suitable to conditions in the colonies were received there, the Court asserted that the law of literary property (not established by court decisions in England until 1769 and 1774) was not brought "into the wilds of Pennsylvania by its first adventurers" who settled there in 1682.[281]

Later legislation and decisions have extended copyright protection to photographs,[282] posters,[283] maps, charts, etchings, engravings, music, motion pictures, sculpture,[284] and to various other means by which

---

Dumbauld, *The Declaration of Independence and What It Means Today*, 63; Hague v. C.I.O., 307 U.S. 496, 527 (1939).

[278] 8 Pet. at 658. The Court interpreted the English cases of Millar v. Taylor, 4 Burr. 2303 (1769), and Donaldson v. Beckett, 4 Burr. 2408 (1774), as holding that perpetual copyright existed at common law before the Act of 8 Anne c. 9 (1710) but was taken away by that statute, and that thereafter the duration of copyright was limited to the period specified in that Act, of "twenty one years and no longer." 8 Pet. at 656. Justices Smith Thompson and Henry Baldwin dissented, emphasizing that the Act of Congress did not contain the words "and no longer" and that the statute of 8 Anne was never in force in Pennsylvania, which was settled in 1682. *Ibid.*, 678, 680, 687–88.

[279] 8 Pet. at 658.   [280] *Ibid.*, 659.

[281] *Ibid.*, 660. The federal Supreme Court was here asserting greater liberty to declare the law of Pennsylvania in the absence of state court pronouncements than would now be permissible under Erie R.R. Co. v. Tompkins, 304 U.S. 64 (1938).

[282] In Burrow-Giles Lithographic Co. v. Sarony, 111 U.S. 53, 56, 58 (1884), the Court, although conceding that "the constitutional question is not free from difficulty," concluded that copyright of photographs, "so far as they are representative of original intellectual conceptions of the author," and not a mere mechanical or chemical process, was permissible.

[283] A picture used to advertise a circus was held copyrightable in Bleistein v. Donaldson Lithographing Co., 188 U.S. 239, 251 (1903). Justice Holmes declared that it was dangerous for lawyers to judge the value of works of art, and that "the taste of any public is not to be treated with contempt." *Ibid.*, 251–52. Two dissenting Justices argued that these posters were like labels, with no value apart from the article to which they were attached.

[284] Statuettes, to be used as the base of table lamps, were held copyrightable in Mazer v. Stein, 347 U.S. 201, 218 (1954). The Court emphasized that it was only the specific work of art that was protected; other artists were free to make their own statuettes of human figures and to use them in the manufacture of lamps, provided that they did not copy plaintiff's work.

"intellectual conceptions" of an artist are given expression. However, there is some doubt how far the category of "writings" may be extended by the inclusion of such media of expression.[285]

Trade-marks, which are distinctive names or devices by which manufacturers designate and identify their products, ordinarily are neither patentable nor copyrightable.[286] Priority in use of such a mark is protected by the courts in order to prevent misleading the public with respect to the origin of products.[287] It is perversion of the function of trade-marks, however, to permit them to be used, as is allowed by present custom laws,[288] for the purpose of preventing the importation of genuine articles in order to maintain a higher price for the same articles in the domestic market when imported and sold by the owner of the trade-mark.[289]

[285] Justices Hugo L. Black and William O. Douglas desired reargument of the case, to deal with the constitutional question. "Is a sculptor an 'author' and is his statue a 'writing' within the meaning of the Constitution? . . . The Copyright Office has supplied us with a long list of such articles which have been copyrighted—statuettes, book ends, clocks, lamps, door knockers, candlesticks, inkstands, chandeliers, piggy banks, sundials, salt and pepper shakers, fish bowls, casseroles, and ash trays. Perhaps these are all 'writings' in the constitutional sense. But to me, at least, they are not obviously so. It is time that we came to the problem full face. I would accordingly put the case down for reargument." *Ibid.*, 220–21.

[286] Trade-Mark Cases, 100 U.S. 82, 94 (1879). That case held unconstitutional a federal trade-mark registration statute not limited to interstate or foreign commerce. Federal registration of trade-marks is now governed by the Lanham Act of July 5, 1946, 60 St. 427, 15 USCA 1051 *et seq.*

[287] "Passing off" one manufacturer's products as another's is a form of what is correctly described as "unfair competition" or "unfair trade." In recent years, since the NRA codes, the term "fair trade" has been improperly used to describe "price-fixing" when it has been permitted by legislation. Price-fixing is ordinarily a violation per se of the antitrust laws. U.S. v. Trenton Potteries Co., 273 U.S. 392 (1927); U.S. v. Socony-Vacuum Oil Co., 310 U.S. 150 (1940). Courts now tend to hold unconstitutional legislation which purports to make price-fixing agreements binding on non-signers.

[288] Act of June 17, 1930, 46 St. 741, 19 U.S.C.A. 1526.

[289] For example, in Sturges v. Clark D. Pease, Inc., 48 F. (2d) 1035 (C.C.A. 2, 1931), plaintiff bought a Hispano Suiza automobile abroad and brought it to the United States. At the port it was detained by the collector of customs, to be destroyed as contraband, at the request of defendant, a dealer in that make of cars and holder of the trade-mark in the United States. On rehearing, the owner of the car was permitted to bring it in if it was possible to delete the name Hispano Suiza wherever it appeared on the car. French perfume dealers have been able to maintain high prices in the United States by the same device. However, it was held in U.S. v. Guerlain, Inc., 155 F. Supp. 77 (E.D. N.Y. 1957), an antitrust case, that if the holder of the American trade-mark and the foreign trade-mark are combined in a single "international enterprise," the power to exclude competitive imports under 19 U.S.C.A. 1526 cannot be exercised,

ARTICLE I—THE LEGISLATIVE BRANCH
Legislative Powers of Congress, *Courts*

ART. I, SEC. 8, CL. 9
To constitute Tribunals inferior to the Supreme Court;

HISTORY

THE Virginia Plan contemplated "that a National Judiciary be established to consist of one or more supreme tribunals, and of inferior tribunals to be chosen by the National Legislature, to hold their offices during good behaviour. . . . that the jurisdiction of the inferior tribunals shall be to hear & determine in the first instance, and of the supreme tribunal to hear and determine in the dernier resort, all piracies & felonies on the high seas, captures from an enemy; cases in which foreigners or citizens of other States applying to such jurisdictions may be interested, or which respect the collection of the National revenue; impeachments of any National officers, and questions which may involve the national peace and harmony."[290]

In Committee of the Whole, the first clause of this proposal was accepted, amended to read "that a National Judiciary be established, to consist of one supreme tribunal, and of one or more inferior tribunals."[291] On reconsideration at the request of Rutledge, the entire provision for establishing inferior tribunals was expunged, over the opposition of Madison and Wilson, who then successfully moved to add a provision authorizing, but not requiring, the national legislature to institute inferior tribunals. "They observed that there was a distinction between establishing such tribunals absolutely, and giving a discretion to the Legislature to establish or not establish them."[292]

---

that privilege being intended only for the benefit of an independent importer, not an affiliate of the foreign manufacturer.

[290] Resolution 9. Farrand, *Records*, I, 21–22 (May 29).

[291] *Ibid.*, I, 95, 104–105 (June 4). The words "one or more" were then deleted. *Ibid.*, I, 116, 119 (June 5).

[292] *Ibid.*, I, 118, 124–25 (June 5). Rutledge and Sherman favored channeling all litigation into state courts in the first instance, "the right of appeal to the supreme national tribunal being sufficient" to secure the national rights and uniformity of judgments. Madison argued that it would be burdensome for appeals to be heard at a distant

This compromise was confirmed in convention after debate.[293] The Committee of Detail included in the enumeration of legislative powers one "To constitute tribunals inferior to the Supreme Court."[294]

THE inferior "Tribunals" authorized by this clause are apparently identical with the "inferior Courts" authorized by Article III, section 1. They are thus "constitutional" courts, exercising "the judicial Power of the United States," and enjoying tenure during good behavior.

Under its power to legislate for the District of Columbia and to make rules and regulations respecting the territory belonging to the United States, Congress can also establish "legislative" courts, which are not "constitutional" courts and which can therefore be vested with powers not strictly judicial.[295]

In view of the history of this clause, which clearly shows that it was intended to make it optional with Congress whether or not inferior federal courts should be established, it seems clear that Justice Joseph Story was wrong in arguing that it was the mandatory duty of Congress to establish such courts.[296] It is now well understood that Congress may withhold from federal courts such portions as it chooses of the constitutionally defined "judicial Power of the United States." Indeed,

capital. Wilson said that "the admiralty jurisdiction ought to be given wholly to the national Government."

[293] *Ibid.*, II, 38–39, 45–46 (July 18). Butler and Martin favored deletion of the power; Gorham, Randolph, Gouverneur Morris, and Mason supported its retention. Sherman accepted the compromise; he "was willing to give the power to the Legislature but wished them to make use of the State Tribunals whenever it could be done" with safety to the general interest.

[294] Art. VII, sec. 1. *Ibid.*, II, 182 (August 6). Randolph's draft read: "To appoint tribunals, inferior to the supreme judiciary." *Ibid.*, II, 144. No change was made in convention or by the Committee of Style. *Ibid.*, II, 315 (August 17), 595 (September 12).

[295] Art. I, sec. 8, cl. 17; Art. IV, sec. 3, cl. 2. Ex parte Bakelite Corp., 279 U.S. 438, 450 (1929).

[296] Martin v. Hunter's Lessee, 1 Wheat. 304, 330 (1816). Story reasoned that Congress must "vest the whole judicial power" in some federal court or courts, and that since the Supreme Court has original jurisdiction in only a limited class of cases, and the state courts might have no original jurisdiction in a particular class of cases falling within the federal judicial power, there might be a lack of jurisdiction if no inferior federal courts were created. It must be remembered that Madison's *Notes* of the Philadelphia convention were not published until 1840. See page 42 above, and pages 320–21 and 360–61, below.

in one notable instance Congress took away from the Supreme Court jurisdiction of a pending case, the decision in which might have proved politically embarrassing to Reconstructionists after the war of 1861–65.[297]

ARTICLE I—THE LEGISLATIVE BRANCH

Legislative Powers of Congress, *Piracy and International Law*

ART. I, SEC. 8, CL. 10

To define and punish Piracies and Felonies committed on the high Seas, and Offences against the Law of Nations;

HISTORY

IN pursuance of the general resolution of the Committee of the Whole that the national legislature ought to be empowered "to enjoy the legislative rights" vested in Congress by the Articles of Confederation,[298] the Committee of Detail framed a provision to carry forward the power conferred by that instrument of "appointing courts for the trial of piracies and felonies committed on the high seas."[299] In Randolph's draft this provision read: "To declare the law of piracy, felonies and captures on the high seas, and captures on land."[300] The report of the Committee of Detail elaborated this language: "To declare the law and punishment of piracies and felonies committed on the high seas, and the punishment of counterfeiting the coin of the United States, and of offences against the law of nations."[301]

After several amendments in convention at the instance of Gouverneur Morris and Madison, the wording adopted was "To define and punish" the three types of offenses covered by the clause.[302] The Com-

---

[297] Act of March 27, 1868, 15 St. 44; Ex parte McCardle, 7 Wall. 506, 514 (1869). See also Durousseau v. Tyler, 6 Cr. 307, 314 (1810).

[298] Farrand, *Records*, I, 229, 236 (June 13); II, 131.

[299] Art. IX of the Articles of Confederation. The same article provided for establishment of rules and tribunals for dealing with captures on land and water.

[300] Farrand, *Records*, II, 143. The preceding paragraph read "To provide tribunals and punishment for mere offences against the law of nations." (Presumably this refers to offenses merely injuring a foreign state and not directly affecting the interests of the United States.)

[301] Art. VII, sec. 1. *Ibid.*, II, 182 (August 6).

[302] *Ibid.*, II, 312, 315–16 (August 17). Ellsworth added an amendment enlarging the scope of the provision on counterfeiting.

mittee of Style eliminated counterfeiting, treating it in a separate clause.[303] The Committee's version apparently read: "To define and punish piracies and felonies committed on the high seas, and punish offences against the law of nations."[304] On motion of Gouverneur Morris the word "punish" before "offences against the law of nations" was stricken out, "so as to let these be *definable* as well as punishable, by virtue of the preceding member of the sentence."[305]

INTERPRETATION

PIRACY flourished extensively in the early decades of the nineteenth century, and gave rise to much litigation. In an important opinion by Chief Justice Marshall, the Supreme Court held that Congress could sufficiently "define" piracy by including in that offense several other crimes as defined by the common law.[306] It was also held to be an adequate exercise of the power of Congress to "define" piracy when the definition of that crime as given by the law of nations was adopted by Congress, without specifically enumerating the acts forbidden.[307]

Congress has power under this clause to punish foreigners as pirates,[308] but will not be presumed to have intended to punish an act by a foreigner against a foreigner upon a foreign ship, where such offenses would be punishable, in the exercise of its ordinary criminal jurisdiction,[309] by the government whose flag the vessel flies.

[303] See Art. I, sec. 7, cl. 6, above.   [304] Farrand, *Records*, II, 595 (September 12).

[305] *Ibid.*, II, 614–15 (September 14). Wilson opposed the amendment, thinking that it would be ridiculous arrogance for one nation to pretend to define the law of nations "which depended on the authority of all the Civilized Nations of the World." Morris replied that this law of nations was "often too vague and deficient to be a rule" enforceable in a criminal court without statutory definition.

[306] U.S. v. Palmer, 3 Wheat. 610, 630 (1818). In the Act of April 30, 1790, Congress enacted "That if any person or persons shall commit upon the high seas . . . murder, robbery, or any other offence which if committed within the body of a county, would by the laws of the United States be punishable with death . . . every such offender shall be deemed, taken and adjudged to be a pirate and felon, and being thereof convicted, shall suffer death." 1 St. 112, 113–14. The Court held that robbery, though not punishable with death, was made piracy by the statute. Otherwise robbery on the high seas would be unpunished. 3 Wheat. at 628–29.

[307] U.S. v. Smith, 5 Wheat. 153, 159–61 (1820). This statute provided "That if any person or persons whatsoever, shall, on the high seas, commit the crime of piracy as defined by the law of nations . . . every such offender or offenders shall . . . be punished with death." Act of March 3, 1819, 3 St. 510, 513–14.

[308] 3 Wheat. at 630.

[309] *Ibid.*, 631–34. See also U.S. v. Rogers, 150 U.S. 249, 264–65 (1893); U.S. v. Flores, 289 U.S. 137, 155 (1933).

The Supreme Court has also had occasion to decide that this clause is not a restriction (under the maxim *expressio unius exclusio alterius*) of the general criminal jurisdiction exercisable under the admiralty power given by Article III, section 2, of the Constitution.[310] If such a restrictive interpretation were accepted, it would mean that minor crimes not amounting to felony could not be punished when committed on the high seas, and crimes of every grade would not be punishable when committed on board an American ship in the territorial waters of a foreign state.[311]

Under its power to punish offenses against the law of nations (aided by the "necessary and proper" clause) Congress can punish the counterfeiting in the United States of bank notes issued by a foreign financial institution, especially when they circulate as currency in the state of origin.[312] The crime here involved is not within the provision empowering Congress to punish "counterfeiting the Securities and current Coin *of the United States*."[313] But the responsibility of the federal government to foreign nations for violations of international law serves as the basis of its power to prevent and punish such violations in the exercise of its criminal jurisdiction.

One of the most important parts of the law of nations is the law of war. In exercising its power to punish violations of the law of nations, Congress can therefore provide for punishment of violations of the law of war. Traditionally such offenses by belligerent agents, such as espionage, are punished by military commissions and not by civilian courts of justice. Saboteurs who landed in the United States from German submarines, and did not remain in military uniform, were

[310] U.S. v. Flores, 289 U.S. 137, 149 (1933). The Court pointed out that Art. I, sec. 8, cl. 10, transfers to the federal government the powers formerly granted by Art. IX of the Articles of Confederation; while Art. III, sec. 2, vests in the federal government the admiralty powers theretofore remaining with the states. *Ibid.*, 147.

[311] *Ibid.*, 149–50.

[312] U.S. v. Arjona, 120 U.S. 479, 483 (1887). The Court lumps together various powers relating to international relations which are exclusively vested in the federal government, as if they formed a sort of composite "foreign affairs power." So also it has come to speak of the "war power" as an aggregate which goes beyond the specific terms of the particular powers relating to warfare which are enumerated in the Constitution. See Art. I, sec. 8, cl. 11 through cl. 16, below. See also note 238, page 147, above.

[313] Italics supplied. Art. I, sec. 8, cl. 6, above. In the Philadelphia Convention, Gouverneur Morris and another member desired to add a provision to permit punishment of counterfeiting foreign bills. Farrand, *Records*, II, 315 (August 15).

properly triable by a military commission and subject to the death penalty as spies for a common law offense under international law.[314]

After the close of World War II, a Japanese general who had surrendered was tried in the same manner for "permitting" acts of cruelty by troops under his command during the war. The Supreme Court held that the offense charged constituted a violation of the laws of war, and hence was punishable as an offense against the law of nations.[315]

ARTICLE I—THE LEGISLATIVE BRANCH
Legislative Powers of Congress, *War Powers*

ART. I, SEC. 8, CL. 11

To declare War, grant Letters of Marque and Reprisal, and make Rules concerning Captures on Land and Water;

HISTORY

THIS clause originated in the Committee of Detail, in pursuance of the direction given by the Committee of the Whole to grant to the national legislature every power possessed by the old Congress under the Articles of Confederation.[316] Randolph's draft, as amended by Rutledge, contained a power "To make war, raise armies & equip Fleets."[317] The Committee of Detail reported as a separate power: "To make war."[318] On motion of Madison, "declare" was substituted for

[314] Ex parte Quirin, 317 U.S. 1, 28 (1942). The Court also considered whether any constitutional rights had been violated by the procedures used in dealing with these saboteurs, and found no violations. *Ibid.*, 39, 45. The Court pointed out that the law of nations adequately defined the offense committed here, just as in the piracy case, U.S. v. Smith, 5 Wheat, 153, 159–61 (1820), discussed in note 307, page 161, above.

[315] *In re* Yamashita, 327 U.S. 1, 7, 14 (1946). Dissenting Justices denied the existence of such an offense under international law, in the absence of personal culpability in connection with the atrocities perpetrated. *Ibid.*, 28. They also believed that an enemy belligerent should have been accorded constitutional rights under American law. *Ibid.*, 43–44, 61, 79.

[316] See page 52 above; and note 298, page 160, above.

[317] Farrand, *Records*, II, 143.

[318] Art. VII, sec. 1. *Ibid.*, II, 182 (August 6). "To raise armies" and "To build and equip fleets" were likewise reported as separate powers at the same time. See Art. I, sec. 8, cl. 12 and cl. 13, below. "To make rules concerning captures on land and water" was reported at the same time. See notes 299 and 300, page 160, above.

"make" in order to meet Pinckney's criticism that the legislature would act too slowly to be the proper depositary of this power, which he favored vesting in the Senate. Butler wished to give the power to the President, to which Gerry replied that he "never expected to hear in a republic a motion to empower the Executive alone to declare war."[319]

Power to grant letters of marque and reprisal was included among a number of proposals by Pinckney which were referred to the Committee of Detail.[320] That committee not having disposed of the matter, it was favorably reported by the Committee on Postponed Parts and accepted as an addition to the power to declare war.[321]

The Committee of Style combined with this proposed clause a separate provision on the subject of captures.[322] The clause then read as it now stands in the Constitution.

INTERPRETATION

THE power to declare war, which in England belonged to the king, was given by the Philadelphia convention to the representatives of the people.[323] Thomas Jefferson during his Presidency scrupulously respected the constitutional function of Congress by ordering the armed forces to confine their operations to defensive rather than offensive measures when attacks by foreign powers occurred while Congress was not in session.[324] As a practical matter, the President's powers as commander in chief and over the conduct of foreign affairs enable him to confront Congress with a situation where it has little real choice between

[319] *Ibid.*, II, 313, 318 (August 17). Under Madison's wording the executive would be "able to repel and not to commence war." Mason also opposed giving the power to the executive or to the Senate. *Ibid.*, 319.

[320] *Ibid.*, II, 322, 326 (August 18).

[321] *Ibid.*, II, 505, 508–509 (September 5).

[322] *Ibid.*, II, 182 (August 6); II, 315 (August 17); II, 595 (September 12). See notes 299 and 300, page 160, and note 318, page 163, above. This provision on captures came from the Articles of Confederation.

[323] The word "declare" was substituted for "make" in the convention, so that the executive might be able to repel sudden attacks but not commence war. It was recognized that to "conduct" war is an executive function. Farrand, *Records*, II, 313, 318–19 (August 17). Art. II, sec. 2, makes the President "Commander in Chief of the Army and Navy."

[324] To Madison, September 6, 1789, in Jefferson, *Papers*, XV, 397; draft of message on Southern Indians, in Jefferson, *Works*, VII, 192–93; to Madison, March, 1793, in *ibid.*, 250; message of December 8, 1801, in *ibid.*, IX, 332; to W. H. Cabell, June 29, 1807, in *ibid.*, VIII, 433.

war or peace. In recent wars, Congress has worded its declarations of war so as to indicate that the United States was not acting aggressively but was merely recognizing and declaring the existence of a state of war brought about by the action of other states.[325]

That the purpose of the clause now under consideration was merely to ascribe this power to Congress instead of to the executive, rather than to create the power, is indicated by a questionable decision of the Supreme Court which asserts that powers of external sovereignty exercisable by the federal government do not depend upon the affirmative grants contained in the Constitution, but that "the powers to declare and wage war, to conclude peace, to make treaties, to maintain diplomatic relations with other sovereignties, if they had never been mentioned in the Constitution, would have vested in the federal government as necessary concomitants of nationality."[326]

The declaration of war enables the federal government to exercise vast powers which would not be open to it in peacetime.[327] The Supreme Court has created this expanded area of federal jurisdiction by lumping together this clause with other clauses of the Constitution relating to martial activities[328] and treating them as forming a single concept designated "the war power." This power is then defined as one which permits the government to do whatever is deemed necessary in order to wage war successfully.[329]

[325] Resolutions of April 25, 1898, 30 St. 364; April 6, 1917, 40 St. 1; December 8, 1941, 55 St. 795. The last-named reads: "That the state of war between the United States and the Imperial Government of Japan which has thus been thrust upon the United States is hereby formally declared."

[326] U.S. v. Curtiss-Wright Export Corp., 299 U.S. 304, 318 (1936). Justice Sutherland may have been trying to distinguish sharply between domestic and foreign affairs in order to avoid weakening his anti-New Deal decision in Carter v. Carter Coal Co., 298 U.S. 238, 295, 311 (1936). This case was overruled in U.S. v. Darby, 312 U.S. 100, 123 (1941). Besides many previous statements that all power must be derived from the Constitution, a statement to that effect subsequent to the Curtiss-Wright case is found in Ex parte Quirin, 317 U.S. 1, 25 (1942). The notion that in every government "the powers of war" appertained to the sovereign was voiced in Penhallow v. Doane's Admrs., 3 Dall. 54, 80, 111 (1795).

[327] U.S. v. Macintosh, 283 U.S. 589, 622 (1931); Korematsu v. U.S., 323 U.S. 214, 224 (1944).

[328] Art. I, sec. 8, cl. 12 through cl. 16, plus the "Commander in Chief" clause of Art. II, sec. 2, and the "necessary and proper" clause (Art. I, sec. 8, cl. 18) are ingredients in the composite "war power." Ex parte Quirin, 317 U.S. 1, 26, 29 (1942).

[329] Supreme Court decisions on the "war power" constitute a striking illustration of the technique condemned by Justice Holmes of substituting other words for those

Thus the Court proclaimed, in sweeping language formulated by Chief Justice Hughes:

> While emergency does not create power, emergency may furnish the occasion for the exercise of power. . . . Thus, the war power of the Federal Government is not created by the emergency of war, but it is a power given to meet that emergency. It is a power to wage war successfully, and thus it permits the harnessing of the entire energies of the people in a supreme coöperative effort to preserve the nation. But even the war power does not remove constitutional limitations safeguarding essential liberties.[330]

The Hughes language was relied on by the Court when upholding drastic curfew orders applicable to American citizens of Japanese ancestry and orders directing their compulsory relocation in concentration centers:

> The war power of the national government is the power to wage war successfully. . . . It extends to every matter and activity so related to war as substantially to affect its conduct and progress. The power is not restricted to the winning of victories in the field and the repulse of enemy forces. It embraces every phase of the national defense, including the protection of war materials and the members of the armed forces from injury and from the dangers which attend the rise, prosecution and progress of war.[331]

By the same token, action is authorized which is necessary to remedy the evils produced by military operations.[332] Thus the trial by court-

---

being construed, and basing the construction on the language thus surreptitiously inserted. Northern Securities Co. v. U.S., 193 U.S. 197, 403 (1903).

The phrase "war power" appears as early as Hamilton v. Dillin, 21 Wall. 73, 87 (1875). It had been used in a nontechnical sense by President Abraham Lincoln in a message to Congress on July 4, 1861: "no choice was left but to call out the war power for its destruction by force for its preservation. . . . It was with the deepest regret that the executive found the duty of employing the war power in defence of the government forced upon him." Arthur B. Lapsley, *The Writings of Abraham Lincoln*, VI, 323, 339 (1906).

[330] Home Bldg. & Loan Assn. v. Blaisdell, 290 U.S. 398, 426 (1934). Chief Justice White in N. Pac. Ry. Co. v. North Dakota, 250 U.S. 135, 149 (1919), had already spoken of "the complete and undivided character of the war power."

[331] Hirabayashi v. U.S., 320 U.S. 81, 93 (1943). See also Korematsu v. U.S., 323 U.S. 214, 219 (1944). Legislation suspending operation of the statute of limitations during the course of a conflict was sustained as an exertion of the power "to remedy the evils which have arisen from its rise and progress." Stewart v. Kahn, 11 Wall. 493, 507 (1871).

[332] *In re* Yamashita, 327 U.S. 1, 12 (1946).

martial of enemy officers for permitting barbarities violating the laws of war is permissible.

The same reasoning sanctions legislation designed to remedy the inflationary consequences of wartime economic conditions. Price-fixing,[333] rent control,[334] renegotiation of contracts in order to eliminate excess profits,[335] and vesting in a designated official of property belonging to aliens[336] constitute legitimate exercise of the "war power."

Compulsory service in the armed forces is another obligation which can be imposed by virtue of the same composite "war power." (Here the particularly pertinent clause of the Constitution is Article I, section 8, clause 12: "To raise and support Armies.") Chief Justice White flatly declared: "As the mind cannot conceive an army without the men to compose it, on the face of the Constitution the objection that it does not give power to provide for such men would seem to be too frivolous for further notice."[337] The argument that this clause refers to armies composed of volunteers was brushed aside as being a contention that the power was not truly a power, for a power that could be exercised only by the consent of the citizen would not be a genuine compulsory power at all.[338]

Yet if there were any validity in the often-asserted rule that the Constitution is to be given perpetually the very same meaning which

[333] Yakus v. U.S., 321 U.S. 414, 422 (1944). This case held that Congress could deprive all courts but one special tribunal of jurisdiction to consider the constitutionality of orders made by the price-control administration. *Ibid.*, 443–44.

[334] Bowles v. Willingham, 321 U.S. 503, 519 (1944).

[335] Lichter v. U.S., 334 U.S. 742, 756 (1948).

[336] Clark v. Allen, 331 U.S. 503, 511 (1947); Silesian-American Corp. v. Clark, 332 U.S. 469, 475–77 (1947). Congress can prohibit trading with the enemy, but can also permit it on such terms as it sees fit, including payment of charges prescribed by administrative order; and such regulation will not be considered as an unauthorized exercise of the taxing power but as an exercise of belligerent rights "incident to the power to declare war and to carry it on to a successful termination." Hamilton v. Dillin, 21 Wall. 73, 97 (1875).

[337] Selective Draft Law Cases, 245 U.S. 366, 377 (1918). The power to compel military service is coterminous with the constitutional grant to declare war and raise armies; it is not limited to the type of service which can be exacted of the militia when it is called into federal service. Cox v. Wood, 247 U.S. 3, 6 (1918). Historically the militia cannot be compelled to serve abroad, or outside the state. Frederick B. Wiener, "The Militia Clause of the Constitution," *Harvard Law Review*, Vol. LIV, No. 2 (1940), 187. The National Guard is now organized under the power to raise armies, rather than under the clause for calling forth the militia, in order to permit foreign service. *Ibid.*, 209.

[338] 245 U.S. at 378.

it had at the time of its adoption,[339] the argument against conscription would have to be treated more seriously. Historically, the only army then known was an army of volunteers. The only type of compulsory service known was in the "militia," a force then under state control.[340] Opponents of the Constitution feared a standing army as dangerous to liberty.[341] Under the English Bill of Rights a standing army was forbidden, "unless it be with consent of parliament."[342] Under the Articles of Confederation, Congress could only determine the number of troops to be raised; they were actually raised by the states. The Constitution permitted Congress to act directly.

Power to draft men for war service implies an equal power to compel industry to support the war effort by mobilizing its productive capacity. The Supreme Court has said: "Under this authority [power to raise and support armies, to provide and maintain a navy, the "necessary and proper" clause] Congress can draft men for battle service. . . . Its power to draft business organizations to support the fighting men who risk their lives can be no less."[343]

Besides the ability to "support" armies by compelling industry to furnish the necessary weapons and supplies for effective prosecution of hostilities, the army clause permits the government "to guard and promote the health and efficiency of the men composing the army" in numerous ways.[344] To "enhance the morale of the serviceman" insurance protection for designated beneficiaries is a legitimate means of promoting national defense.[345] Hospitalization, pensions, educational opportunities, re-employment privileges, and many other veterans' bene-

[339] Dred Scott v. Sandford, 19 How. 393, 426 (1857); South Carolina v. U.S., 199 U.S. 437, 448 (1905); Home Bldg. & Loan Assn. v. Blaisdell, 290 U.S. 398, 449-51 (1934).

[340] 245 U.S. at 380. See Art. I, sec. 8, cl. 15 and cl. 16, below, empowering federal use of the militia under certain circumstances. See also the Third Amendment, prohibiting infringement by the federal government of the right of the people to bear arms and compose a militia.

[341] See commentary on Art. I, sec. 8, cl. 12, below. Six states sought an amendment to the Constitution forbidding a standing army. Dumbauld, *The Bill of Rights and What It Means Today*, 163.

[342] *Ibid.*, 168. See also the Virginia Bill of Rights of 1776. *Ibid.*, 172.

[343] U.S. v. Bethlehem Steel Corp., 315 U.S. 289, 305 (1942). See also Lichter v. U.S., 334 U.S. 742, 756 (1948).

[344] Thus legislation to suppress brothels in proximity to army installations is valid. McKinley v. U.S., 249 U.S. 397, 399 (1919).

[345] Wissner v. Wissner, 338 U.S. 655, 660 (1950).

fits which could be justified upon the same principle might be enumerated here.

The Supreme Court has expressly recognized that "the war power does not necessarily end with the cessation of hostilities."[346] If it did, the result "would be paralyzing. It would render Congress powerless to remedy conditions the creation of which necessarily followed from the mobilization of men and materials for successful prosecution of the war. So to read the Constitution would be to make it self-defeating."[347]

At the same time, the Court acknowledged that reliance on the war power might be carried to excess. "We recognize the force of the argument that the effects of war under modern conditions might be felt in the economy for years and years, and that if the war power can be used in days of peace to treat all the wounds which war inflicts on our society, it might not only swallow up all the other powers of Congress but largely obliterate the Ninth and Tenth Amendments as well. There are no such implications in today's decision."[348]

In similar vein Justice Robert H. Jackson, concurring in the decision, emphasized that "No one will question that this power is the most dangerous one to free government in the whole catalogue of powers. It usually is invoked in haste and excitement when calm legislative consideration of constitutional limitation is difficult. It is executed in a time of patriotic fervor when moderation is unpopular. Particularly when the war power is invoked to do things to the liberties of the people, or to their property or economy that only indirectly affect conduct of the war and do not relate to the management of the war itself, the constitutional basis should be scrutinized with care."[349]

Without such circumspection, there would be no limit to the expansion of power. "I would not be willing to hold that war powers may be indefinitely prolonged merely by keeping legally alive a state of war that had in fact ended. I cannot accept the argument that war powers last as long as the effects and consequences of war, for if so they are permanent—as permanent as the war debts." Nevertheless it was clear that as far as the case in hand was concerned, the existing state of war was more than a technicality.[350]

[346] Woods v. Miller Co., 333 U.S. 138, 141 (1948). This case dealt with rent control. [347] *Ibid.*, 143.

[348] *Ibid.*, 143–44. The Court pointed out that it would be a question for the courts whether the war power was being abused.

[349] *Ibid.*, 146. [350] *Ibid.*, 147.

Letters of marque, which Congress is authorized to issue, permit private ships to make captures at sea of enemy vessels as prize. Letters of marque and reprisal permit similar retaliation in time of peace against a nation which has wronged the nation issuing the commission. During the eighteenth and early nineteenth centuries privateering was a very profitable occupation for seafaring men. It was also a practice beneficial to small nations, as it enabled a government very cheaply to establish the equivalent of a navy by permitting its merchant fleets to operate as armed vessels preying upon enemy trade. The practice is now obsolete, having been condemned by international law since the Declaration of Paris in 1856.[351]

The power to make rules concerning captures on land and water had been vested in the Old Congress by the Articles of Confederation.[352] Where land warfare is concerned, this power is similar to that of defining and punishing offenses against the law of nations.[353] Where captures on water are concerned, the subject matter falls within admiralty jurisdiction under Article III, section 2, of the Constitution.

ARTICLE I—THE LEGISLATIVE BRANCH
Legislative Powers of Congress, *Armies*

ART. I, SEC. 8, CL. 12
To raise and support Armies, but no Appropriation of Money to that Use shall be for a longer Term than two Years;

HISTORY

THIS clause originated in the Committee of Detail, probably as an outgrowth of the decision that Congress should be given all the powers conferred under the Articles of Confederation. The Old Congress, however, had merely the power to agree upon the number of troops to be raised; the men were actually to be raised by the states, though

---

[351] Charles G. Fenwick, *International Law*, 493.   [352] Art. IX.

[353] See Art. I, sec. 8, cl. 10, above. It enables Congress to speak for the United States as a participant in the development of international law. See Robert H. Jackson, *The Nürnberg Case*, 85. In other respects the executive and the treaty power would so speak.

at Continental expense.[354] Randolph's working draft contained a power to "raise armies."[355] The Committee of Detail reported the clause in the same form.[356] During debate the words "and support" were added, at the suggestion of Gorham.[357]

Subsequently Pinckney submitted for consideration by the Committee of Detail a number of provisions in the nature of a Bill of Rights, including a provision that no troops be kept in time of peace except by consent of Congress, that the military should be subordinate to the civil power, and that no grants of money for the support of land forces should be made for more than one year at a time.[358] No action having been taken by the Committee of Detail on these proposals, they were referred to the Committee on Postponed Parts, which proposed adding to the clause on the support of armies the proviso "But no appropriation of money to that use shall be for a longer term than two years."[359]

INTERPRETATION

THE extensive interpretation which has been given to this clause by the Supreme Court as part of the so-called war power has been discussed in connection with the power to declare war.[360]

For some reason, less jealousy was felt with regard to naval forces than in the case of land forces,[361] and the two-year limitation was not made applicable to appropriations to "provide and maintain a Navy."[362]

[354] Art. IX.

[355] Farrand, *Records, II*, 143.

[356] Art. VII, sec. 1. *Ibid.*, II, 182 (August 6).

[357] *Ibid.*, II, 323, 329 (August 18). On the same date was passed a motion by Mason that a clause be prepared for preventing a perpetual revenue. *Ibid.*, II, 327. With this restriction in view, a motion by Martin and Gerry to limit the number of troops to be maintained as a standing army in time of peace was rejected as impracticable. *Ibid.*, II, 330.

[358] *Ibid.*, II, 334, 341 (August 20).

[359] *Ibid.*, II, 505, 508–509 (September 5). The Committee of Style made no change. *Ibid.*, II, 595 (September 12). A later attempt by Mason to add language condemning standing armies was unsuccessful. *Ibid.*, II, 617 (September 14).

[360] Art. I, sec. 8, cl. 11, above.

[361] The prevailing sentiment may have been that voiced by Jefferson: "Every rational citizen must wish to see an effective instrument of coercion, & should fear to see it on any other element but the water. A naval force can never endanger our liberties, nor occasion bloodshed: a land force would do both." To James Monroe, August 11, 1786, in Jefferson, *Works*, V, 150.

[362] Art. I, sec. 8, cl. 13, below.

ARTICLE I—THE LEGISLATIVE BRANCH
Legislative Powers of Congress, *Navy*

ART. I, SEC. 8, CL. 13
To provide and maintain a Navy;

HISTORY

UNDER the Articles of Confederation the Old Congress had power "to build and equip a navy."[363] Rutledge inserted in the working draft of the Committee of Detail, after the provisions relating to declaration of war and raising armies, the words "& equip fleets."[364] The Committee's report amplified this language in the form of a separate power "To build and equip fleets."[365] During debate this was rephrased: "To provide and maintain a navy."[366]

INTERPRETATION

APPROPRIATIONS for a navy, as has been noted above, are not subject to the two-year limitation applicable to appropriations for land forces.[367]

Apparently the Constitution authorizes only one "Navy," whereas any number of "Armies" may be raised.

ARTICLE I—THE LEGISLATIVE BRANCH
Legislative Powers of Congress, *Rules for Armed Forces*

ART. I, SEC. 8, CL. 14
To make Rules for the Government and Regulation of the land and naval Forces;

[363] Art. IX.   [364] Farrand, *Records*, II, 143.

[365] *Ibid.*, II, 182 (August 6).

[366] *Ibid.*, II, 323, 330, 333 (August 18). There was no change by the Committee of Style. *Ibid.*, II, 595 (September 12).

[367] Art. I, sec. 8, cl. 12, above.

HISTORY

DURING debate on the preceding clause, this clause was added. It was taken from the Articles of Confederation.[368]

INTERPRETATION

BY virtue of this clause, Congress has enacted Articles of War and Articles for the Government of the Navy. These have now been re-placed by the Uniform Code of Military Justice.[369] Recent legislation, in keeping with the change in the character of the armed services in which under present-day conditions practically the entire population of the country may have occasion to serve, exhibits a trend toward according to persons subject to military discipline the same types of privileges which are guaranteed to civilians by provisions of the Bill of Rights.[370]

Article I—The Legislative Branch
Legislative Powers of Congress, *Use of Militia*

ART. I, SEC. 8, CL. 15

To provide for calling forth the Militia to execute the Laws of the Union, suppress Insurrections and repel Invasions;

HISTORY

IN Randolph's working draft in the Committee of Detail, he enu-merated among the legislative powers of Congress one "To draw forth the militia, or any part, or to authorize the Executive to embody

[368] Farrand, *Records*, II, 323, 330 (August 18). There was no change by the Committee of Style. *Ibid.*, II, 595 (September 12). Under Art. IX the Old Congress had the sole and exclusive right and power of "making rules for the government and regulation of the said land and naval forces, and directing their operations." Power to direct operations is given by the Constitution to the President as "Commander in Chief." Art. II, sec. 2.

[369] 50 U.S.C.A. 551, *et seq.* Under this clause Congress can provide courts-martial for the trial of military and naval offenses, quite independently of the judicial power under Art. III of the Constitution. Dynes v. Hoover, 20 How. 65, 79 (1858).

[370] Frederick B. Wiener, "Courts-Martial and the Bill of Rights: The Original Practice," *Harvard Law Review*, Vol. LXXII, No. 2 (December, 1958), 301.

them."[371] In lieu of this Rutledge substituted language which, with slight modifications, was reported by the Committee of Detail: "To call forth the aid of the militia, in order to execute the Laws of the Union, enforce treaties, suppress insurrections, and repel invasions."[372] When this clause was under consideration by the convention, its wording was improved by amendments offered by Gouverneur Morris.[373]

INTERPRETATION

THE Shays' Rebellion in Massachusetts in 1786 may have influenced members of the convention to provide for federal authority to use force for the purpose of suppressing insurrections and enforcing the laws, as well as to repel foreign foes.[374]

ARTICLE I—THE LEGISLATIVE BRANCH
Legislative Powers of Congress, *Regulation of Militia*

ART. I, SEC. 8, CL. 16

To provide for organizing, arming, and disciplining, the Militia, and for governing such Part of them as may be employed in the Service of the United States, reserving to the States respectively, the Appointment of the Officers, and the Authority of training the Militia according to the discipline prescribed by Congress;

HISTORY

MASON proposed, to be referred to the Committee of Detail, "a power to regulate the militia." He thought it necessary to give the

[371] Farrand, *Records*, II, 144.   [372] *Ibid.*, II, 182 (August 6).

[373] *Ibid.*, II, 382, 390 (August 23). To "enforce treaties" was superfluous, since treaties were to be "laws." In place of "call forth the aid of the militia" Morris substituted "provide for calling forth the militia." No change was made by the Committee of Style. *Ibid.*, II, 595 (September 12). This clause had been postponed until agreement was reached regarding Art. I, sec. 8, cl. 16, below, on control of the militia. *Ibid.*, II, 337, 344 (August 20).

[374] Farrand, *Records*, II, 332. Resolutions of October 20, 1786, to raise troops under the pretext of protection against Indians in the West were really motivated by fear of the Massachusetts rebels. Burnett, *Letters of Members of the Continental Congress*, VIII, 517. For an account of the Shays' affair, see George R. Minot, *The History of the Insurrections*, 61, 99, 134.

general government such a power, as he hoped that there would be no large standing army in time of peace. "The Militia ought therefore to be the more effectually prepared for the public defence." He felt certain that the states would never concur in any one system if the matter were left in their hands. "If they will not give up the power over the whole, they probably will over a part as a select militia."[375]

Apparently recurring to the subject on the same day, Mason moved to empower Congress "to make laws for the regulation and discipline of the Militia of the several States reserving to the States the appointment of the Officers."[376] Ellsworth and Sherman thought that this went too far, and proposed to empower Congress to prescribe "uniformity of exercise and arms for the militia" and rules for their government when actually called into service under the authority of the United States, as well as to "establish and regulate a militia in any State" where the local legislature neglected to do so.[377]

Dickinson expressed the opinion "that the States never would nor ought to give up all authority over the Militia. He proposed to restrain the general power to one fourth part at a time, which by rotation would discipline the whole Militia." Mason then withdrew his original motion, substituting one limited to a select militia "not exceeding one tenth part in any one year." Mason's original motion was renewed by General Charles Cotesworth Pinckney, who thought divided authority would be "an incurable evil."[378] Madison thought that regulation of the militia naturally should be placed in the hands of the authority charged with the public defense. If the states would trust the general government with a power over the public treasure, they would likewise grant it the direction of the public force. Ellsworth replied that the states would "never submit to the same militia laws," remarking that a penalty of four shillings would "enforce obedience better in New England, than forty lashes in some other places."[379] After further debate Mason's original motion and his substitute version were referred to a committee having a member from every state.[380]

---

[375] Farrand, *Records*, II, 326 (August 18). [376] *Ibid.*, II, 323, 330.

[377] *Ibid.*, II, 323, 331. [378] *Ibid.*, II, 331.

[379] *Ibid.*, II, 332. Sherman, in reply to Madison, pointed out that the states retained a concurrent taxing power when the general government was given that power; and that they could not surrender complete authority over the militia because they would themselves need to use it for defense against invasions and insurrections and for enforcing obedience to their laws. [380] *Ibid.*, II, 333.

The committee three days later reported a clause virtually in the same form as it now stands in the Constitution.[381] There was long and acrimonious debate, during which numerous amendments were offered and were rejected, before the clause was finally adopted piecemeal, after a separate vote on each of its three parts.[382]

During this discussion King explained "that by *organizing* the committee meant, proportioning the officers & men—by *arming*, specifying the kind size and caliber of arms—& by *disciplining* prescribing the manual exercise evolutions &c." Gerry angrily exclaimed that this would make the states mere drill sergeants. Madison observed that "arming" as explained did not include furnishing arms, nor did "disciplining" include "penalties & Courts martial for enforcing them." Thereupon King added to his former explanation "that *arming* meant not only to provide for uniformity of arms, but included authority to regulate the modes of furnishing" them, and that "*laws* for disciplining, must involve penalties and every thing necessary for enforcing penalties."[383]

INTERPRETATION

THE debates in the convention clearly disclose that the dangers of a standing army were much in the minds of members. Reliance for the common defense was placed in a corps of part-time citizen-soldiers, who after averting the danger to their country would return to their daily occupations as did Cincinnatus to his plow, rather than in a permanent professional army.

This preference for "raw recruits and green generals" rather than a well-trained fighting force has persisted to the present day.[384] The confusion resulting from state participation in military affairs still makes for inefficiency, even though the militia, or National Guard in each state, is now organized under the "army clause" of the Constitution, rather than the "militia clause," in order to enable it to be used

[381] *Ibid.*, II, 352, 356 (August 21). The beginning of the clause as reported read "To make laws" rather than "To provide," and the last words were "the United States" instead of "Congress." These changes were made by the Committee of Style. *Ibid.*, II, 595 (September 12). An amendment subsequently proposed by Mason was defeated. *Ibid.*, II, 617 (September 14).

[382] *Ibid.*, II, 368, 377 (August 22); 380–81, 384–88 (August 23).

[383] *Ibid.*, II, 385.

[384] Wiener, "The Militia Clause of the Constitution," *loc. cit.*, 182.

in wars on foreign soil.[385] Moreover, it is debatable whether the present system of universal conscription of part-time citizen-soldiers, drafting multitudes of young men for a short period of service, is as effective as it would be if a smaller number of persons were encouraged, by adequate pay and advancement, to make a career in the armed forces and remain in the service long enough to acquire the specialized technical skills necessary to enable them to be genuinely useful participants in an efficient program of national defense.

Although the framers of the Constitution contemplated the use of militia by the states for dealing with local emergencies, it is clear that they likewise intended the national government to organize and use this type of force, composed of citizen-soldiers, as a federal instrumentality. Thus there would be less occasion for establishing a standing army.[386] The prohibition in existing federal law against the maintenance of troops by the states, except in accordance with the provisions of federal law, is of doubtful constitutionality if it is interpreted as prohibiting employment of militia by the states.[387]

ARTICLE I—THE LEGISLATIVE BRANCH
Legislative Powers of Congress, *District of Columbia*

ART. I, SEC. 8, CL. 17

To exercise exclusive Legislation in all Cases whatsoever, over such District (not exceeding ten Miles square) as may, by Cession of particular States, and the Acceptance of Congress, become the Seat of the Government of the United States, and to exercise like Authority over all Places purchased by the Consent of the Legislature of the State in which the Same shall be, for the Erection of Forts, Magazines, Arsenals, dock-Yards, and other needful Buildings;—And

[385] *Ibid.*, 209. See note 337, page 167, above.

[386] Farrand, *Records*, II, 330–32, 386–87.

[387] Act of June 3, 1916, 39 St. 198, 32 U.S.C.A. 194; Wiener, "The Militia Clause of the Constitution," *loc. cit.*, 216–17. If the word "Troops" in Art. I, sec. 10, cl. 3, refers only to a permanent professional army and does not include a militia of part-time citizen-soldiers, there would appear to be no warrant for federal interference with the state's right to use militia for proper state purposes as contemplated by the framers. See note 379, page 175, above.

AMONG the additional proposals referred to the Committee of Detail on August 18 at the suggestion of Madison and Pinckney were provisions relating to the seat of government and the acquisition of land for forts, magazines, and other necessary buildings.[388]

The Committee of Detail having taken no action, the topic was dealt with by the Committee on Postponed Parts, which reported a clause substantially the same as that now standing in the Constitution.[389] An amendment requiring consent of the state legislature to purchases of land for federal buildings was adopted in response to Gerry's objection to the second part of the clause on the ground "that this power might be made use of to enslave any particular State by buying up its territory, and that the strongholds proposed would be a means of awing the State" into an undue obedience to the general government.[390]

CHOICE of the site where the seat of the national government was to be located was the occasion of much controversy inspired by local jealousies and interests, both before and after adoption of the Constitution.[391] The final decision fixing the permanent capital at Washington was not reached until 1790. At that time a "deal" was made selecting the site favored by Southern interests, in exchange for enactment of legislation for assumption of state debts by the federal government, a measure favored by financiers in the Northern states.[392]

Cessions of territory were made by Maryland in 1788 and by

[388] Farrand, *Records*, II, 321–22, 325 (August 18). A previous proposal by Mason to prevent location of the seat of the national government at a state capital had been withdrawn. *Ibid.*, II, 127–28 (July 26).

[389] *Ibid.*, II, 505, 509 (September 5). The Committee of Style substituted "Congress" for "the Legislature." *Ibid.*, II, 596 (September 12). The words "by the Consent of the Legislature of the State" were inserted following "purchased" on motion of King. *Ibid.*, II, 506, 510 (September 5). The Committee of Style added the clarifying phrase "in which the same shall be." *Ibid.*, II, 596.

[390] *Ibid.*, II, 510 (September 5).

[391] Fortenbaugh, *The Nine Capitals of the United States*, 9, 60, 77, 81–85; Saul K. Padover, *Thomas Jefferson and the National Capital*, 1–10.

[392] Dumas Malone, *Jefferson and the Rights of Man*, 297–305; Padover, *Thomas Jefferson and the National Capital*, 11–27; Maclay, *Journal of William Maclay*, 134–69, 231, 244, 249, 267–342.

James Madison, "Father of the Constitution" (1751–1836)

From a painting by Gilbert Stuart
Courtesy Independence National Historical Park

Gouverneur Morris (1752–1816)

From a painting by Thomas Sully
Courtesy Library of Congress

Virginia in 1789. After acceptance by Congress in 1790, President Washington fixed the boundaries of the District of Columbia by his proclamation of March 30, 1791. Proprietors of land at the site chosen for the seat of government, in view of the anticipated increase in value of their property on account of the location of the federal city there, deeded their property to trustees under an arrangement whereby approximately half of the lots would be sold for the benefit of the former owners and half for account of the public.[393]

By virtue of this clause, Congress is empowered to exercise over the District of Columbia all the plenary legislative power which a state would possess, as well as the federal powers which Congress can exercise within a state.[394]

But in exercising its local legislative power, Congress is acting in its capacity as legislature of the Union. Hence, according to a dictum of Chief Justice Marshall, if a felon escapes from the District, he may be apprehended anywhere in the United States. A criminal escaping from one state to another could be reclaimed only by demand upon the executive of the state of refuge. "The reason is, that congress is not a local legislature, but exercises this particular power, like all its other powers, as the legislature of the Union."[395]

Under this clause, Congress can empower courts of the District of Columbia to exercise judicial or administrative authority which is not part of "the judicial power of the United States" as defined in Article III of the Constitution.[396] Nevertheless courts of the District, which as

[393] Morris v. U.S., 174 U.S. 196 (1899). In 1846, Congress authorized retrocession of Alexandria County to Virginia if desired by a vote of the inhabitants. Act of July 9, 1846, 9 Stat. 35. After a favorable vote, Virginia assumed authority over the county, without any further action by Congress. The Supreme Court recognized this *de facto* government by Virginia as valid in Phillips v. Payne, 92 U.S. 130 (1876).

[394] Mattingly v. D.C., 97 U.S. 687, 690 (1878); Capital Traction Co. v. Hof, 174 U.S. 1, 5 (1899); Keller v. Potomac Electric Power Co., 261 U.S. 428, 443–44 (1923); O'Donoghue v. U.S., 289 U.S. 516, 539 (1899); D.C. v. Thompson Co., 346 U.S. 100, 108 (1953). The fact that inhabitants of the District have no vote does not limit the power of Congress to impose a tax in the District, the proceeds of which go into the general treasury of the United States. Heald v. D.C., 259 U.S. 114, 124 (1922).

[395] Cohens v. Va., 6 Wheat. 264, 424, 428–29 (1821). The actual decision in this case was that in authorizing the District government to establish a lottery, Congress was not sanctioning sale of the lottery tickets throughout the nation in violation of state prohibitory legislation. *Ibid.*, 442–43.

[396] Keller v. Potomac Electric Power Co., 261 U.S. 428, 443–44 (1923). But the Supreme Court cannot review decisions of the District courts on such matters outside "the judicial power of the United States." *Ibid.*, 444. See note 295, page 159, above.

capital of the nation enjoys a permanent position different from the transitory status of territories before their admission as states of the Union, are capable of receiving and exercising judicial power under Article III.[397]

Before cession, the Constitution had been in force in the territory which became the District of Columbia, and the cession did not withdraw the protection of that document.[398] Hence constitutional rights such as trial by jury are available in the District.[399]

The District of Columbia is not a "state" within the meaning of the provisions authorizing diversity of citizenship jurisdiction of federal courts.[400] For the sake of reciprocity in international dealings, where the government is viewed as a unit, a treaty provision that "In all the States of the Union . . . Frenchmen shall enjoy the right of possessing real and personal property" was held applicable in the District of Columbia.[401]

The exclusive authority conferred by the latter portion of this clause does not, of course, come into force over territory acquired by the United States without the consent of the state where it is situated. It is settled that the United States may acquire land for public purposes by condemnation.[402] In that event the federal government does

[397] O'Donoghue v. U.S., 289 U.S. 516, 538–40, 544–46 (1933). Hence salaries of judges in the District courts are protected by Art. III, sec. 1, against diminution. But it was decided in Williams v. U.S., 289 U.S. 553, 565 (1933), that the Court of Claims, being purely a legislative court, enjoys no such protection. However, that case was overruled by Glidden Co. v. Zdanok, 370 U.S. 530, 584 (1962), after Congress had declared in the Act of July 28, 1953, 67 Stat. 226, 28 U.S.C.A. 171, that the Court of Claims was created under Art. III.

[398] Downes v. Bidwell, 182 U.S. 244, 259 (1901). Nevertheless by the Act of February 21, 1871, 16 St. 419, 426, Congress expressly extended the Constitution to the District of Columbia. Ibid., 263.

[399] Capital Traction Co. v. Hof, 174 U.S. 1, 5 (1899); U.S. v. Moreland, 258 U.S. 433, 439 (1922).

[400] Hepburn v. Ellzey, 2 Cr. 445, 451 (1805). In National Mutual Ins. Co. v. Tidewater Transfer Co., 337 U.S. 582, 588–89 (1949), an extremely divided Court upheld the Act of April 20, 1940, 54 St. 143, which opened federal courts in the states to suits by citizens of the District of Columbia. The question of the Supreme Court's appellate jurisdiction in this type of case had not been raised. Ibid., 600. Three Justices followed the Hepburn case but upheld the Act under Art. I, sec. 8, cl. 17, and the "necessary and proper" clause. Two others would have overruled Marshall's decision, contending, contrary to the O'Donoghue case, that an Art. III court cannot be given non–Art. III jurisdiction. Ibid., 604, 607. Four Justices dissented. Ibid., 626, 646.

[401] Geofroy v. Riggs, 133 U.S. 258, 268, 271 (1890).

[402] Kohl v. U.S., 91 U.S. 367, 371, 374 (1876). In the District of Columbia, if not

not obtain "exclusive" legislative power, but only such powers as are necessary to carry out the public purpose for which the land was condemned.[403]

Where the property in question was not "purchased" with state consent but was already public domain owned by the federal government when the state was admitted to the Union, the state may nevertheless cede exclusive jurisdiction to the federal government.[404] Such a transaction does not fall within the scope of Article I, section 8, clause 17, and the state and federal government may apportion jurisdiction between themselves upon such terms as they may agree upon.[405]

The terms of the cession as made and accepted govern.[406] Mere ownership and use of property by the United States does not necessarily confer the "exclusive" jurisdiction.[407] But unrestricted transfer of government property as surplus to private hands terminates and operates as a "relinquishment" of the exclusive legislative power of the United States.[408]

Where exclusive federal jurisdiction exists over enclaves, state laws enacted after the cession do not apply, and, as in the case of the District of Columbia, "Congress has the combined powers of a general and a state government."[409]

The words "needful buildings" in this clause are not interpreted

elsewhere, the establishment of a park is a proper purpose to justify condemnation. Shoemaker v. U.S., 147 U.S. 282, 298 (1893).

[403] James v. Dravo Contracting Co., 302 U.S. 134, 147 (1937); Arlington Hotel Co. v. Fant, 278 U.S. 439, 451 (1929).

[404] Arlington Hotel Co. v. Fant, 278 U.S. 439, 447, 455 (1929); Benson v. U.S., 146 U.S. 325, 329–30 (1892). The scope of the cession is a political question. In the Benson case it was decided that the fact that the particular place where a murder was committed was used for farming rather than for military purposes did not oust federal jurisdiction. *Ibid.*, 331.

[405] Collins v. Yosemite Park Co., 304 U.S. 518, 528 (1938). The Court rejected the argument that Art. I, sec. 8, cl. 17, furnishes the only mode in which exclusive jurisdiction may be obtained by the federal government.

[406] James v. Dravo Contracting Co., 302 U.S. 134, 142 (1937).

[407] Surplus Trading Co. v. Cook, 281 U.S. 647, 650, 652 (1930); Silas Mason Co. v. Tax Comm. of Washington, 302 U.S. 186, 197 (1937).

[408] S.R.A. Inc. v. Minnesota, 327 U.S. 558, 564 (1946). The Court held that the state could tax property where the United States held title merely to secure payment of the purchase price, and where a tax sale under state law would not divest the federal title. *Ibid.*, 565–66.

[409] Pacific Coast Dairy, Inc. v. Dept. of Agriculture of California, 318 U.S. 285, 294 (1943); Paul v. U.S., 371 U.S. 245, 264–69 (1963).

under the rule of *ejusdem generis* as referring only to military installations, but embrace locks, dams, and "whatever structures are found to be necessary in the performance of the functions of the Federal Government."[410]

Since under applicable Supreme Court decisions[411] the federal government can condemn land without state consent, and the state may cede land under such qualifications as it may choose with respect to reservation of concurrent jurisdiction, it would appear that the latter part of Article I, section 8, clause 17, is now in reality superfluous.

Article I—The Legislative Branch

Legislative Powers of Congress, *Necessary and Proper Clause*

ART. I, SEC. 8, CL. 18

To make all Laws which shall be necessary and proper for carrying into Execution the foregoing Powers, and all other Powers vested by this Constitution in the Government of the United States, or in any Department or Officer thereof.

HISTORY

FOLLOWING the enumeration of legislative powers in the working draft of the Committee of Detail is an insertion in Rutledge's handwriting: "and a right to make all Laws necessary to carry the foregoing Powers into Execu[tion]."[412] In the Committee's report this was expanded to read: "And to make all laws that shall be necessary and proper for carrying into execution the foregoing powers, and all other powers vested, by this Constitution, in the government of the United States, or in any department or officer thereof."[413]

[410] James v. Dravo Contracting Co., 302 U.S. 134, 143 (1937).

[411] See Kohl, Collins, and James cases, notes 402, 405, and 406, pages 180–81, above.

[412] Farrand, *Records*, II, 144.

[413] *Ibid.*, II, 182 (August 6). The clause was agreed to without amendment on August 20. *Ibid.*, II, 337, 345. The Committee of Style substituted "which" for "that." *Ibid.*, II, 596 (September 12).

INTERPRETATION

THIS clause, commonly called the "necessary and proper" clause,[414] has been extremely important as a means of expanding the scope of federal power. It was relied on by Chief Justice John Marshall in one of his most noteworthy decisions extending the sphere of federal authority.[415] As has been noted,[416] the entire structure of federal criminal law rests on this clause. The clause is also an important ingredient in the monetary powers of Congress[417] and in the complex of powers known as the "war power."[418]

It should be observed that the "necessary and proper" clause not only aids in effectuating the other legislative powers specifically granted to Congress, but also may be invoked in support of powers vested in other branches, departments, or officers of the federal government.[419]

Thus, the "necessary and proper" clause, plus the provisions of Article III, section 2, regarding the judicial power, constitutes the sole basis for the federal government's authority in the field of admiralty and maritime law.[420] It likewise supports legislation for carrying the judicial power into execution in other respects.[421]

The "necessary and proper" clause also serves to validate the practice of gathering data on various subjects by use of inquisitorial methods.

[414] It was often also called the "sweeping" clause, and is sometimes referred to as the "coefficient" clause.

[415] McCulloch v. Maryland, 4 Wheat. 316, 420 (1819), where in holding that Congress has power to incorporate a bank, Marshall used the often-quoted words: "Let the end be legitimate, let it be within the scope of the Constitution, and all means which are appropriate, which are plainly adapted to that end, which are not prohibited, but consist with the letter and spirit of the Constitution, are constitutional." Congress can also protect the instrumentalities which it has constitutionally created. Thus it may exempt their operations from state taxation. Fed. Land Bank v. Bismarck Lumber Co., 314 U.S. 95, 102 (1941). See also note 344, page 168, above.

[416] See page 149 above.

[417] See pages 146 and 147 above.

[418] See page 165 above. See also note 312, page 162, above.

[419] Thus, though not relied upon by the Court, this clause may have served to support the conclusions reached in *In re* Debs, 158 U.S. 564 (1895), and *In re* Neagle, 135 U.S. 1 (1890). It may also have served to buttress the federal government's power to condemn land by eminent domain, which is not expressly granted in the Constitution, but was upheld in Kohl v. U.S., 91 U.S. 367 (1876).

[420] Swanson v. Marra Bros., 328 U.S. 1, 5 (1946).

[421] Wayman v. Southard, 10 Wheat. 1, 22 (1825); Rhode Island v. Massachusetts, 12 Pet. 657, 721 (1838).

Besides the privately employed public opinion pollster, testing the popularity of political candidates, commercial products, and entertainment programs, the census-taker operating by authority of the federal government has become a familiar figure.

The constitutional authorization for a census (Article I, section 2, clause 3) is limited to an enumeration of population in the states which have the right of representation in Congress. In practice the census inquiries have covered a wider range of subject matter, and have also extended to the District of Columbia and territories not represented in Congress.[422]

However, such wider inquiries are doubtless valid by virtue of the "necessary and proper" clause, if relevant to legitimate governmental functions. The investigative function of Congress in aid of intelligently framed legislation may surely be exercised through a census as well as by holding committee hearings.[423] But such inquiries are subject to other constitutional limitations, such as the Fifth Amendment and the provisions of the First Amendment guaranteeing freedom of religion.[424]

---

[422] Thus 13 U.S.C.A. 141 calls for a census of "population, agriculture, irrigation, drainage, and unemployment in each State, the District of Columbia, Alaska, Hawaii, and Puerto Rico." 13 U.S.C.A. 142 calls for a census of "housing." That territorial inquiries are valid is intimated in Legal Tender Cases, 12 Wall. 457, 536 (1871). Additional data on agriculture and local government finances are provided for by 13 U.S.C.A. 146 and 161.

[423] U.S. v. Moriarty, 106 Fed. 886, 891 (S.D. N.Y. 1901); Watkins v. U.S., 354 U.S. 178, 187–88 (1957).

[424] Penalties for refusal to answer questions are prescribed by 13 U.S.C.A. 221 and 224. The latter section is probably unconstitutional insofar as it applies to religious bodies, since the exception in 13 U.S.C.A. 240 (d) is not as extensive as the right of freedom of religion guaranteed by the First Amendment. Cf. Counselman v. Hitchcock, 142 U.S. 547, 564–65, 585 (1892).

Restrictions upon the Powers of Congress, *Importation of Slaves*

ART. I, SEC. 9, CL. 1

The Migration or Importation of such Persons as any of the States now existing shall think proper to admit, shall not be prohibited by the Congress prior to the Year one thousand eight hundred and eight, but a Tax or duty may be imposed on such Importation, not exceeding ten dollars for each Person.

HISTORY

IN the Committee of Detail, Randolph's draft, as amended in Rutledge's handwriting, qualified the grant of power to regulate commerce by specifying as an exception: "no prohibition on ye Importations of such inhabitants or People as the sevl. States think proper to admit." A further exception provided that "no duties by way of such prohibition" were to be collected.[1] In the Committee's report these provisions were expanded and combined to read: "No tax or duty shall be laid by the Legislature on articles exported from any State; nor on the migration or importation of such persons as the several States shall think proper to admit; nor shall such migration or importation be prohibited."[2]

Heated debate arose regarding the propriety of permitting the importation of slaves. Luther Martin of Maryland contended that "it was inconsistent with the principles of the revolution and dishonorable to the American character to have such a feature in the Constitution." He also argued that since slaves were to be counted under the three-fifths ratio in determining the representation of states in Congress, the slave trade would be encouraged by permitting unrestricted importations.[3] Dickinson likewise "considered it inadmissible on

[1] Farrand, *Records*, II, 143. Another exception was "No Duty on exports." There was also a restriction prohibiting passage of a navigation act without a two-thirds vote of the members present in each house.

[2] Art. VII, sec. 4. *Ibid.*, II, 183 (August 6).

[3] *Ibid.*, II, 364 (August 21). Charles Pinckney replied that South Carolina could never receive the Constitution "if it prohibits the slave trade."

every principle of honor & safety that the importation of slaves should be authorized to the States by the Constitution."[4] Mason joined in denouncing the slave trade as an "infernal" traffic which "originated in the avarice of British Merchants." Hence the British government had "constantly checked the attempts of Virginia to put a stop to it." He deplored the pernicious effect of slavery on manners. "Every master of slaves is born a petty tyrant." He lamented that "some of our Eastern brethren had from a lust of gain embarked in this nefarious traffic."[5]

Ellsworth of Connecticut with dry humor replied that "As he had never owned a slave [he] could not judge of the effects of slavery on character. He said however that if it was to be considered in a moral light we ought to go farther and free those already in the Country." He also pointed out that Virginia's position was not entirely altruistic, since in that climate slaves multiplied so fast that "it is cheaper to raise than import them, whilst in the sickly rice swamps [of South Carolina and Georgia] foreign supplies are necessary."[6] The South Carolina delegates strenuously sought to justify slavery in principle, as well as to insist that their state, as well as North Carolina and Georgia, would refuse to accept the Constitution if it permitted interference with the slave trade.

Pinckney asserted that "If slavery be wrong, it is justified by the example of all the world. . . . In all ages one half of mankind have been slaves." He stressed that interference with this institution would "produce serious objections to the Constitution, which he wished to see adopted."[7] Rutledge declared that "Religion & humanity had nothing to do with this question—Interest alone is the governing principle with Nations. . . . If the Northern States consult their interest, they will not oppose the increase of Slaves which will increase the commodities of which they will become the carriers." Ellsworth agreed that every state should "import what it pleases. The morality or wisdom of slavery are considerations belonging to the States themselves. . . . The old

[4] *Ibid.*, II, 372 (August 22). Randolph emphasized that the clause as reported "would revolt the Quakers, the Methodists, and many others in the States having no slaves." *Ibid.*, II, 374 (August 22).

[5] *Ibid.*, II, 370 (August 22).

[6] *Ibid.*, II, 370–71 (August 22). The same difference of policy between slave-breeding and slave-importing states had existed before the Revolution. Dumbauld, *The Declaration of Independence and What It Means Today,* 89.

[7] Farrand, *Records,* II, 371 (August 22).

confederation had not meddled with this point, and he did not see any greater necessity for bringing it within the policy of the new one."[8]

General Charles Cotesworth Pinckney conceded, however, that slaves should be "liable to an equal tax with other imports," and he moved to commit the provision in order that it might be amended to that effect.[9] Gouverneur Morris "wished the whole subject to be committed including the clauses relating to taxes on exports & to a navigation act. These things may form a bargain among the Northern & Southern States."[10]

The bargain which Morris anticipated was quickly made, in spite of Sherman's objection that to tax slaves would amount to "acknowledging men to be property."[11] The grand committee to whom the matter was referred promptly reported a clause providing that "The migration or importation of such persons as the several States now existing shall think proper to admit, shall not be prohibited by the Legislature prior to the year 1800, but a tax or duty may be imposed on such migration or importation at a rate not exceeding the average of the duties laid on imports."[12] This was later amended on motion of General Charles Cotesworth Pinckney, to extend until 1808 the period

---

[8] *Ibid.*, II, 364 (August 21). Gerry agreed that "we had nothing to do with the conduct of the States as to Slaves, but ought to be careful not to give any sanction to it." King "thought the subject should be considered in a political light only," but pointed out that if two states would not accept the Constitution if it curtailed the slave trade, "great & equal opposition" would be experienced from other states if it authorized it. *Ibid.*, II, 372, 373 (August 22).

[9] *Ibid.*, II, 373 (August 22). Wilson and King had pointed out that it was in fact a bounty on slaves to exempt them from duty "whilst every other import was subjected to it." *Ibid.*, II, 372, 373.

[10] *Ibid.*, II, 374 (August 22). Sherman was opposed to a tax on slaves imported "because it implied they were *property*." He observed also that the clause relating to taxes on exports had already been agreed to, and hence could not be committed. *Ibid.*, II, 354, 363 (August 21). However, the provisions regarding capitation tax and navigation acts were committed, in accordance with Morris' wish, in addition to those dealing with importation of slaves. *Ibid.*, II, 366, 374, 375 (August 22).

[11] *Ibid.*, II, 416 (August 24). According to Richard H. Barry, in *Mr. Rutledge of South Carolina*, 329, the bargain had in fact been made at a dinner given by Rutledge to Sherman in the taproom of the Indian Queen tavern on June 30, 1787.

[12] Farrand, *Records*, II, 396, 400 (August 24). The provision regarding capitation tax was accepted as reported by the Committee of Detail, but the provision regarding navigation acts was deleted. Abolition of the requirement of a two-thirds vote for a navigation act was the *quid pro quo* which the Northern commercial states received in exchange for accepting the provision permitting importation of slaves. Gouverneur

within which importation of slaves could not be prohibited.[13] Another amendment modified the latter part of the clause to read: "but a tax or duty may be imposed on such importation not exceeding ten dollars for each person."[14] A final amendment substituted "any of the States" for "the several States."[15]

INTERPRETATION

ARTICLE I, section 9, of the Constitution specifies the powers *denied* to Congress. It limits the legislative powers granted by Article I, section 8. Similarly, Article I, section 10, enumerates the powers denied to the states.

Under the granted power to regulate commerce (Article I, section 8, clause 3) Congress would have been able to prohibit the slave trade, as well as the immigration of free persons, in the absence of the provisions of Article I, section 9, clause 1.[16]

The temporary ban upon prohibition of the slave trade, which this clause contained, was the result of a compromise between Northern commercial states and the slave-importing states of the South (South Carolina, Georgia, North Carolina). As a *quid pro quo* for acceptance of this prohibition, the requirement of a two-thirds vote for the enactment of a navigation act was eliminated. Removal of this restriction upon the federal power to regulate commerce gratified the New England shipping interests.

In his message of December 2, 1806, President Jefferson, long a foe to slavery,[17] congratulated Congress upon "the approach of the period at which you may interpose your authority constitutionally to

---

Morris made, but later withdrew, a proposal expressly mentioning "slaves" and naming the three states for whose benefit the permission to import was given. *Ibid.*, II, 415–16 (August 25).

[13] *Ibid.*, II, 408, 415 (August 25).

[14] *Ibid.*, II, 409, 417 (August 25). The Committee of Style substituted "Congress" for "Legislature." *Ibid.*, II, 596 (September 12).

[15] *Ibid.*, II, 610 (September 14).

[16] Gibbons v. Ogden, 9 Wheat. 1, 216 (1824); Groves v. Slaughter, 15 Pet. 449, 514 (1841).

[17] British refusal to permit Virginia and other Colonies to enact laws curtailing the slave trade was one of the grievances enumerated by Jefferson in the Declaration of Independence. Dumbauld, *The Declaration of Independence and What It Means Today*, 89, 174. A specific denunciation of the slave trade was deleted in Congress. *Ibid.*, 146.

withdraw the citizens of the United States from all further participation in those violations of human rights which have been so long continued on the unoffending inhabitants of Africa, and which the morality, the reputation, and the best interests of our country have long been eager to proscribe. Although no law you may pass can take prohibitory effect till the first day of the year 1808, yet the intervening period is not too long to prevent by timely notice expeditions which can not be completed before that day."[18] In accordance with this recommendation, Congress promptly exercised its newly unshackled powers.[19]

It should be noted that this section distinguishes between migration and importation,[20] and empowers Congress to tax importation but not migration.[21] It is not clear whether the special power to tax here conferred expired in 1808 or is of continuing effect as a limitation to ten dollars of any tax imposed upon the "importation" of persons; but this question is of no practical importance since prohibition by Congress of the importation of slaves, and the subsequent abolition of slavery. In fact the whole section is obsolete and now of only historical interest.[22]

[18] Richardson, *Messages of the Presidents*, I, 408.

[19] Act of March 2, 1807, 2 St. 426. By the Act of February 28, 1803, 2 St. 205, Congress had banned bringing persons of color (other than Indians) into ports of the United States situated "in any state which by law has prohibited or shall prohibit the admission or importation of such . . . persons of colour."

[20] As explained by Chief Justice John Marshall: "Migration applies as appropriately to voluntary, as importation does to involuntary, arrivals." Gibbons v. Ogden, 9 Wheat. 1, 216 (1824). The same view is forcefully expressed in Justice William Johnson's concurring opinion. *Ibid.*, 230. Hence it is erroneous to suppose that the term "migration" applies exclusively to the entry of free black men, as said in People v. Compagnie Générale Transatlantique, 107 U.S. 56, 62, (1882), and as contended by Chief Justice Roger B. Taney and Justices Peter V. Daniel and Levi Woodbury in the Passenger Cases, 7 How. at 474–76, 511–13, 540–44. Justices James M. Wayne and John McKinley took the contrary view. *Ibid.*, 412, 453.

[21] This was Wilson's view. Farrand, *Records*, III, 161. Cf. *ibid.*, III, 210. Power to tax "migration" seems to have been eliminated at the suggestion of Gouverneur Morris, although Mason thought it necessary in order to prevent the introduction of convicts. *Ibid.*, II, 417 (August 25). Madison in 1819 commented that the term "migration" allowed those who opposed express acknowledgment of property in human beings "to view *imported* persons as a species of emigrants, whilst others might apply the term to foreign malefactors sent or coming into the country. It is possible, tho' not recollected, that some might have had an eye to the case of freed blacks, as well as malefactors." *Ibid.*, III, 437.

[22] In Dred Scott v. Sandford, 19 How. 393, 411 (1857), Chief Justice Taney

It is noteworthy also that while the purpose of this section was to impose a temporary ban on legislation prohibiting the importation of slaves, the word "slaves" nowhere appears in the language used.[23] For that matter, there is no express mention of slavery anywhere in the Constitution as adopted.[24] Wherever the Constitution refers to slavery, circumlocution is employed, and such euphemistic expressions as "other Persons"[25] or "Person held to Service or Labour" appear.[26]

It should be noted also that the language of Article I, section 9, clause 1, merely prevents Congress from prohibiting the entry of such persons as the states then existing choose to admit; it does not give Congress power to compel those states to receive persons whom they choose to exclude.[27] The ban on Congressional exclusion is applicable only with respect to states existing at the time the Constitution took effect. New states subsequently admitted into the Union would not be entitled to insist upon the entry of persons they desired to admit during the period ending in 1808, if Congress under other provisions (such as the commerce power) had authority to regulate immigration; a fortiori, new states could not interfere after 1808 with Congress' power to exclude.[28]

---

cited Art. I, sec. 9, cl. 1, in conjunction with Art. IV, sec. 2, cl. 3, to buttress his conclusion that slaves were not "citizens" entitled to sue in federal courts.

[23] Gouverneur Morris at one stage of the heated debate on the subject had proposed to speak openly of "importation of slaves." See note 12, page 188, above.

[24] As Luther Martin reported to the legislature of Maryland: "The design of this clause is to prevent the general government from prohibiting the importation of slaves; but the same reasons which caused them to strike out the word 'national,' and not admit the word 'stamps,' influenced them here to guard against the word 'slaves.' They anxiously sought to avoid the admission of expressions which might be odious to the ears of Americans, although they were willing to admit into their system those *things* which the *expressions* signified. And hence it is, that the clause is so worded, as really to authorize the general government to impose a duty of ten dollars on every foreigner who comes into a State to become a citizen, whether he comes *absolutely* free, or *qualifiedly* so, as a servant; although this is contrary to the design of the framers, and the duty was only meant to extend to the importation of *slaves*." Farrand, *Records*, III, 210. Martin is in error in what he says in the last sentence quoted. See note 20, page 189, above.

[25] Art. I, sec. 2, cl. 3. The formula here used was taken from the April 18, 1783, proposal to amend the Articles of Confederation, which eleven states accepted. See note 51, page 47, and page 70 above.

[26] Art. IV, sec. 2, cl. 3.

[27] Passenger Cases, 7 How. at 476.

[28] 7 How. at 454. Madison held the same view. Farrand, *Records*, III, 436.

ARTICLE I—THE LEGISLATIVE BRANCH

Restrictions upon the Powers of Congress, *Suspension of Habeas Corpus*

ART. I, SEC. 9, CL. 2

The Privilege of the Writ of Habeas Corpus shall not be suspended, unless when in Cases of Rebellion or Invasion the public Safety may require it.

HISTORY

ONE of the propositions offered by Charles Pinckney and referred to the Committee of Detail related to habeas corpus: "The privileges and benefit of the writ of habeas corpus shall be enjoyed in this government in the most expeditious and ample manner: and shall not be suspended by the Legislature except upon the most urgent and pressing occasions, and for a limited time not exceeding ———— months."[29] He renewed this proposal during debate. Rutledge was for "declaring the Habeas Corpus inviolable." He did not suppose that a suspension could ever be necessary at the same time through all the states. Wilson also doubted whether suspension could be necessary, as the courts would have discretionary power whether "to keep in Gaol or admit to Bail." The provision was adopted in language offered by Gouverneur Morris: "The privilege of the writ of Habeas Corpus shall not be suspended, unless where in cases of Rebellion or invasion the public safety may require it."[30]

INTERPRETATION

HABEAS CORPUS is a traditional safeguard of the liberty of citizens. It prevents arbitrary imprisonment at the pleasure of the government without legal ground. Indeed, according to the celebrated Dr. Samuel Johnson in conversation with Boswell in September, 1769, "The *habeas corpus* is the single advantage which our government has over that of

[29] *Ibid.*, II, 334, 341 (August 20).

[30] *Ibid.*, II, 435, 438 (August 28). The Committee of Style substituted "when" for "where." *Ibid.*, II, 596 (September 12).

other countries."[31] The writ directs the officer having custody of the prisoner to produce his body in court, together with the reasons for his detention. If the grounds are not sufficient in law,[32] the prisoner is released.

This clause does not explicitly specify by whom the privilege of habeas corpus may be "suspended." The better view seems to be that suspension must be authorized by Congress.

This view is supported by language used by Chief Justice Marshall in a case involving accomplices of Aaron Burr who were held on a charge of treason: "If at any time the public safety should require the suspension . . . it is for the legislature to say so. That question depends on political considerations on which the legislature is to decide."[33] During the war of 1861–65, President Lincoln claimed that the executive could exercise this power. In a celebrated case where a civilian resident of Maryland had been confined in Fort McHenry, near Baltimore, at the order of a military commander in Pennsylvania, Chief Justice Taney issued the writ and when the prisoner was not produced issued an attachment against the commander of the fort for contempt. The marshal could not get into the fort to serve this process, and Taney excused him from further efforts in view of the impossibility of overcoming the resistance of the military authorities by summoning a *posse comitatus* to enforce the court's orders. The Chief Justice directed that the clerk of the court forward a copy of the proceedings to the President, whose constitutional duty it was to take care that the laws be faithfully executed.[34]

[31] Boswell, *The Life of Samuel Johnson,* I, 358.

[32] The effectiveness of habeas corpus procedure as a safeguard of individual liberty would of course have been materially lessened if the mere command of the king (or chief executive) had been accepted by the courts as a valid ground for detention. In the Case of the Five Knights, 3 St. Tr. 1 (1627), a subservient court held that the king's special command was a sufficient warrant for imprisonment. This holding was set at naught by the Petition of Right of June 7, 1628. Since then it has been clear that the sovereign's pleasure is not enough; there must be a definite charge of a crime, consisting of some specific violation of law, in order to deprive a citizen of his liberty. See page 24 above. The habeas corpus act of 1679 (31 Car. II, c. 2) strengthened the procedure for obtaining release. See Chafee, *How Human Rights Got into the Constitution,* 51–74; Taswell-Langmead, *English Constitutional History,* 597–602.

[33] Ex parte Bollman, 4 Cr. 75, 101 (1807). A proposal to suspend habeas corpus was defeated in the Senate after passing the House. Henry Adams, *History of the United States,* III, 338, 340.

[34] Ex parte Merryman, Fed. Cas. No. 9487 (1861).

One of the convincing arguments relied on by Taney in his opinion to support the conclusion that only Congress can suspend the privilege of habeas corpus is the fact that this clause is found in Article I of the Constitution, among the restrictions upon the legislative powers of Congress, and not in Article II dealing with the executive power. Mention is also made of the custom in England, requiring suspension by Parliament.

In 1863, Congress enacted an ambiguous declaration "That, during the present rebellion, the President of the United States, whenever, in his opinion, the public safety may require it, is authorized to suspend the privilege of the writ of habeas corpus in any case throughout the United States, or any part thereof."[35] In Indiana, where the civil courts were open and no hostilities were in progress, a citizen was arrested by the army and condemned to death by a military tribunal. The Supreme Court held, after peace was restored, that he was entitled to be discharged on habeas corpus.

The Court conceded that "It is essential to the safety of every government that, in a great crisis, like the one we have just passed through, there should be a power somewhere of suspending the writ of *habeas corpus*." But "the Constitution goes no further. It does not say after a writ of *habeas corpus* is denied a citizen, that he shall be tried otherwise than by the course of the common law." Civilians cannot be subjected to martial rule when the civil courts are open for business.[36]

The Court emphasized that "The suspension of the privilege of the writ of *habeas corpus* does not suspend the writ itself. The writ issues as a matter of course; and on the return made to it the court decides whether the party applying is denied the right of proceeding further with it."[37]

---

[35] Act of March 3, 1863, 12 St. 755. When so suspended, no military or other officer was required to produce the body of the prisoner, but could certify that he was detained "under authority of the President." Thereupon, "further proceedings under the writ of habeas corpus shall be suspended by the judge or court."

[36] Ex parte Milligan, 4 How. 2, 125, 126, 127 (1866).

[37] *Ibid.*, 130–31. In Milligan's case he was entitled to be discharged, notwithstanding the suspension, because the terms of the suspending act had not been complied with. Section 2 of the Act required that a list of "state or political prisoners" held in confinement under authority of the President be furnished to the court, and if they were not indicted by the next grand jury, they were entitled to be discharged.

ARTICLE I—THE LEGISLATIVE BRANCH

Restrictions upon the Powers of Congress, *Bills of Attainder and Ex Post Facto Laws*

ART. I, SEC. 9, CL. 3
No Bill of Attainder or ex post facto Law shall be passed.

HISTORY

TWO days after the convention had accepted the definition of treason[38] and empowered Congress to punish that crime, but subject to a restriction that "No attainder of treason shall work corruption of blood nor forfeiture, except during the life of the person attainted,"[39] Gerry proposed to add a further provision that "The legislature shall pass no bill of attainder, nor any ex post facto laws."[40] This was accepted, after discussion.[41]

A week later, in connection with a similar prohibition upon state action,[42] Dickinson "mentioned to the House that on examining Blackstone's Commentaries, he found that the terms 'ex post facto' related to criminal cases only; that they would not consequently restrain the States from retrospective laws in civil cases, and that some further provision for this purpose would be requisite."[43]

The Committee of Style modified the wording to read: "No bill of attainder shall be passed, nor any ex post facto law."[44] This was trans-

[38] Now found in Art. III, sec. 3.

[39] Farrand, *Records*, II, 182, 339, 350 (August 20).

[40] *Ibid.*, II, 368, 375–76 (August 22).

[41] Morris, Ellsworth, and Wilson thought that ex post facto laws were void of themselves, and that it would be superfluous and inelegant to prohibit them. Carroll and Williamson pointed out that experience showed the need of such a clause, which "the Judges can take hold of." *Ibid.*, II, 376 (August 22). Mason subsequently renewed the point, but without success. "He thought it not sufficiently clear that the prohibition meant by this phrase was limited to cases of a criminal nature—and no Legislature ever did or can altogether avoid them in Civil cases." *Ibid.*, II, 617 (September 14).

[42] Now Art. I, sec. 10, cl. 1.

[43] *Ibid.*, II, 448–49 (August 29). Accordingly a provision prohibiting state legislation impairing the obligation of contracts was added by the Committee of Style. *Ibid.*, II, 597 (September 12). No such additional curb on action by Congress was adopted, though Gerry favored it. *Ibid.*, II, 617 (September 10).

[44] *Ibid.*, II, 596 (September 12).

posed by the convention into the form found in Article I, section 9, clause 3: "No Bill of Attainder or ex post facto Law shall be passed."[45]

INTERPRETATION

A BILL of attainder is a legislative act which inflicts punishment without a judicial trial. If the punishment be less than death, the act is termed a bill of pains and penalties. Within the meaning of the Constitution, bills of attainder include bills of pains and penalties.[46]

Under English law, attainder was the immediate consequence of a death sentence. It resulted in forfeiture of property to the crown, and in "corruption of blood." This meant that neither could the attainted person inherit from his ancestors nor could his heirs inherit from him.[47] The Constitution limits the power of Congress to declare the punishment of treason by providing that "no Attainder of Treason shall work Corruption of Blood, or Forfeiture except during the Life of the Person attainted."[48]

Bills of attainder were usually passed in times of public excitement and political struggle, in order to punish alleged treasons.[49] They violated customary concepts of fairness and justice by depriving the condemned person of a judicial trial and of the procedural safeguards incident thereto. They also involved punishment for indeterminate offenses not defined by previously fixed and known rules of law.[50]

[45] *Ibid.*, II, 610 (September 14).

[46] Cummings v. Missouri, 4 Wall. 277, 323 (1867).

[47] Ex parte Garland, 4 Wall. 333, 387 (1867). Blackstone, *Commentaries*, II, 254; IV, 380–81, 388. Hence in order to preserve their lands for their heirs by avoiding corruption of blood, defendants would sometimes stand mute upon arraignment, and undergo *peine forte et dure*. Blackstone describes this ordeal as follows: "that the prisoner be . . . laid on his back on the bare floor, naked . . . that there be placed upon his body as great a weight of iron as he could bear, and more; that he have no sustenance, save only, on the first day, three morsels of the worst bread; and on the second day, three draughts of standing water that should be nearest to the prison door; and in this situation this should be alternately his daily diet *till he died*, or (as anciently the judgment ran) *till he answered*." Blackstone, *Commentaries*, IV, 325, 327, 329.

[48] Art. III, sec. 3, cl. 2.

[49] See page 80 above. They would sometimes declare to be treason acts which could not properly be so denominated; or would modify the rules of evidence by accepting the testimony of one witness as sufficient when two were required; or otherwise deviate from ordinary standards of fairness and justice. Calder v. Bull, 3 Dall. 386, 389 (1798). These abuses were also corrected by the Constitution. Art. III, sec. 3, cl. 1.

[50] Ex parte Garland, 4 Wall. 333, 388 (1867); Blackstone, *Commentaries*, IV,

Legislative declaration of guilt and imposition of punishment are the basic features of bills of attainder, as known historically.[51] A broader interpretation, however, has been accepted by the Supreme Court as a means of striking down legislation enacted as the result of wartime passion and hysteria.

A Missouri statute forbade a Roman Catholic priest from exercising his calling "to teach, or preach, or solemnize marriages" unless he took a lengthy oath that he had never been a Confederate sympathizer.

The Court noted the scope of the oath, covering past thoughts as well as overt acts, and its irrelevance to the issue of professional fitness. The legislature had not thought that the actions mentioned in the oath showed unfitness to be a priest, but merely that they were unpatriotic and deserved punishment.[52]

But the legislative infliction of punishment without a judicial trial constitutes a bill of attainder and is forbidden by the Constitution, the Court held. "The deprivation of any rights, civil or political, previously enjoyed, may be punishment."[53] So deprivation of the right to exercise a profession is conditional punishment, even though an avenue of escape is offered by way of the expurgatory oath. "To make the enjoyment of a right depend upon an impossible condition is equivalent to an absolute denial of the right under any condition, and such denial, enforced for a past act, is nothing less than punishment imposed for that act."[54]

In like manner the Missouri legislation was found to violate the prohibition against ex post facto laws. "By an *ex post facto* law is meant one which imposes a punishment for an act which was not punishable at the time it was committed; or imposes additional punishment to that

---

259. Often the offense punished was an act not unlawful when done. "This is the historic explanation for writing the two mischiefs [bills of attainder and ex post facto laws] in one clause" of the Constitution. U.S. v. Lovett, 328 U.S. 303, 323 (1946).

51 U.S. v. Lovett, 328 U.S. 303, 323 (1946).

52 Cummings v. Missouri, 4 Wall. 277, 317–20 (1867). Interference with religious freedom was discussed in the arguments of counsel but was not controlling, as the First Amendment was not construed until long afterwards as applicable to state as well as to federal action. 4 Wall. at 397–98; Dumbauld, *The Bill of Rights and What It Means Today*, 132–34.

53 4 Wall. at 320. The Court pointed out that disqualification from office can be a punishment as in case of impeachment. See Art. I, sec. 3, cl. 7; Art. II, sec. 4.

54 4 Wall. at 327.

then prescribed; or changes the rules of evidence by which less or different testimony is sufficient to convict than was then required."[55]

On the same day that it struck down the Missouri anti-Confederate oath, the Supreme Court held unconstitutional a similar oath which Congress had required of lawyers seeking to practice in federal courts.[56]

The Court reaffirmed its conviction that "exclusion from any of the professions or any of the ordinary avocations of life for past conduct can be regarded in no other light than as punishment for such conduct."[57] Hence the oath act was condemned both as a bill of attainder and as an ex post facto law.

A strong dissent in both cases was written by Justice Miller for four members of the Court. He regarded fidelity to the government as a reasonable and appropriate qualification to be required of a lawyer. "I maintain that the purpose of the act of Congress was to require loyalty as a qualification of all who practice law in the national courts. The majority say that the purpose was to impose a punishment for past acts of disloyalty." Is it punishment, he inquired, when persons other than native-born citizens are excluded from being President or Vice-President, or when judges reaching the age of retirement are forced to quit the bench?[58] He found no declaration of guilt or imposition of punishment in the act of Congress.[59] Hence the essential features of a bill of attainder were lacking. Pointing out that an ex post facto law must deal with retroactivity in a criminal, not a civil, matter,[60] he commented that "this is the first time in the history of jurisprudence that taking an oath of office has been called a criminal proceeding."[61]

After World War II the Supreme Court went even further in conjuring up a bill of attainder. After hearings regarding "un-American

[55] 4 Wall. at 325–26. In Calder v. Bull, 3 Dall. 386, 390 (1798), Justice Chase mentioned a fourth kind of ex post facto law: one "that aggravates a crime, or makes it greater than it was, when committed."

[56] The Act of January 24, 1865, 13 St. 424, required of attorneys the anti-Confederate oath previously prescribed for certain other offices by the Act of July 2, 1862, 12 St. 502.

[57] Ex parte Garland, 4 Wall. 333, 377 (1867). It is an interesting circumstance that in this case the Supreme Court was obliged to hold its own action unconstitutional. It had amended its rules in conformity with the Act of Congress of January 24, 1865, to require the oath.

[58] 4 Wall. at 395.   [59] 4 Wall. at 390.

[60] This rule was established in Calder v. Bull, 3 Dall. 386, 390, 395, 399 (1798). See page 194 above, and note 72, page 201, below.

[61] 4 Wall. at 392.

activities," Congress concluded that three particular government employees were "subversive," and in an attempt to "purge" them from the payroll inserted in an appropriation bill a provision that no money from that or future appropriations should be used to pay their salaries.[62]

In the light of this legislative history the Court construed the law as one directing the removal of these three employees from their posts and preventing them from ever holding a government job.[63] So construed, the statute was unconstitutional; it was a bill of attainder. It was a legislative act inflicting punishment without a judicial trial.[64]

A clearer case of violation of the ex post facto clause by increasing the punishment after commission of the crime is found in a law of the state of Washington which related to sentencing procedure. It made the previous maximum sentence mandatory, subject to parole procedures. Although it did not increase the term for which a defendant could be sentenced, it did eliminate the possibility that the court might impose a sentence *less* than the maximum. The Supreme Court pointed out that "The Constitution forbids the application of any new punitive measures to a crime already consummated, to the detriment or material disadvantage of the wrongdoer."[65]

[62] 57 St. 431, 450. The fact that this statute was directed specifically against certain named individuals was a significant circumstance in the Court's conclusion that it was punitive in nature. It did not establish generally applicable and prospectively operative standards prescribing appropriate qualifications for public employment. Garner v. Los Angeles Board, 341 U.S. 716, 722–23 (1951). The Lovett doctrine was rejected in DeVeau v. Braisted, 363 U.S. 144, 160 (1960), and Flemming v. Nestor, 363 U.S. 603, 613 (1960), on the ground that punitive intent, rather than mere deprivation of a benefit or other "unpleasant consequences," must be shown in order to condemn legislation as being either a bill of attainder or an ex post facto law.

[63] U.S. v. Lovett, 328 U.S. 303, 313 (1946). The law could have been construed as merely a stoppage of the normal disbursement procedure, without any effect upon their status as employees. They could then have collected their compensation by suit in the Court of Claims. In this situation the question concerning the desirability of making an appropriation or not would be a non-justiciable political question for determination by Congress. Justice Frankfurter, to avoid constitutional issues, would have accepted this interpretation of the statute as having "mere fiscal scope." *Ibid.*, 328–30. Even accepting the majority's "colloquial treatment of the statute," he found that none of the historical requisites of a bill of attainder (legislative declaration of guilt, imposition of punishment) were present. *Ibid.*, 320, 323. He emphasized that the specific purpose of Art. I, sec. 10, cl. 3, was "to take from the legislature a judicial function which the legislature once possessed." *Ibid.*, 322, 326.

[64] *Ibid.*, 315–16. The Court thus did not reach the question whether Congress was attempting to exercise the executive power of removal from office, or whether there was a denial of due process of law. *Ibid.*, 307.

It is often debatable whether the object of challenged legislation is to impose additional punishment for a past offense, or whether it is to exercise a legitimate regulatory function, in connection with which the past offense is a relevant circumstance which may properly be taken into account.

In the latter event, there is no violation of the constitutional prohibition of ex post facto laws. Thus, as Justice Samuel F. Miller contended, if loyalty to the government of the United States is a qualification reasonably necessary in a lawyer, it would be quite proper for Congress to exclude Confederate (or Communist) sympathizers from the practice of law, and to scrutinize their past conduct insofar as it is rationally relevant as evidence of their present fitness or unfitness for that profession.[66]

The relevance of past behavior to the issue of present professional fitness is clearly illustrated by a case involving the medical profession. A physician in New York was excluded from practice because he had been convicted twenty years previously for performing an abortion. The Supreme Court held that the state could properly require good character, as well as medical skill, as qualifications which must be possessed by those who wished to practice medicine. Moreover, it was not unreasonable to make conviction of crime a test of good character. "The State is not seeking to further punish a crime, but only to protect its citizens from physicians of bad character."[67] Nor does the hardship arising in individual cases by reason of the fact that some convicts may

[65] Lindsey v. Washington, 301 U.S. 401 (1937). Thus a mere change in the manner or circumstances of inflicting the death penalty is permissible. Holden v. Minnesota, 137 U.S. 483, 491 (1890); Rooney v. S.D., 196 U.S. 319, 326–27 (1905); Malloy v. S.C., 237 U.S. 180, 185 (1915). But additional punishment, such as solitary confinement, or suspense and uncertainty with respect to the date of execution, productive of mental anxiety, is forbidden. Medley, Petitioner, 134 U.S. 160, 171–72 (1890).

[66] Ex parte Garland, 4 Wall. 333, 395 (1867); Schware v. Board of Bar Examiners, 353 U.S. 232, 239, 246 (1957); Beilan v. Bd. of Education, 357 U.S. 399, 405–406 (1958); Lerner v. Casey, 357 U.S. 468, 476 (1958); Konigsberg v. State Bar, 366 U.S. 36, 44 (1961); *In re* Anastaplo, 366 U.S. 82, 88 (1961); Cohen v. Hurley, 366 U.S. 117, 127 (1961).

[67] Hawker v. N.Y., 170 U.S. 189, 191, 196 (1898). The Cummings and Garland cases were explained as condemning exclusion from an occupation upon the basis of criteria which had no rational connection with professional qualifications or fitness. *Ibid.*, 198. In this connection it may be suspected that the true purpose of many licensing requirements is not legitimate protection of the public but economic benefit to existing

be persons of good character make it arbitrary or unreasonable for the state to adopt a rule of general application excluding as unfit all persons convicted of crime.[68]

Similarly, a law disfranchising a "polygamist" as a voter will be interpreted as a legitimate regulation of the qualifications of electors, rather than as an additional punishment imposed upon violators of criminal provisions penalizing polygamy.[69] And legislation inflicting severer punishment upon previous offenders or recidivists does not violate the ex post facto clause, for "They are not punished the second time for the earlier offense, but the repetition of criminal conduct aggravates their guilt and justifies heavier penalties when they are again convicted."[70] The same principle prevails in other instances where the legislation does not really have a retrospective operation but applies (after its enactment) to a continuing situation which originated before the law took effect, such as a continuing conspiracy in restraint of trade which began before passage of an antitrust statute, or possession of liquor lawfully acquired before, but retained after, the establishment of prohibition.[71]

A fortiori, aliens may be deported by reason of past offenses without violation of the prohibition against ex post facto laws. That prohibition applies only to laws inflicting criminal penalties;[72] and deportation,

practitioners by restricting competition. Walter Gellhorn, *Individual Freedom and Governmental Restraints*, 105–51; Hertz Drivurself v. Siggins, 359 Pa. 25, 47–50 (1948); cf. Williamson v. Lee Optical Co., 348 U.S. 483, 486–88 (1955).

[68] 170 U.S. at 197. The rule laid down in the Hawker case was well summarized in Bauer v. Acheson, 106 F. Supp. 445, 450 (D.C. 1952), as holding that "a statute which makes the right to engage in some activity in the future depend upon past behavior, even behavior before the passage of the regulating act, is not invalid as a bill of attainder or ex post facto law if the statute is a bona fide regulation of an activity which the legislature has power to regulate and the past conduct indicates unfitness to participate in the activity." See also Garner v. Los Angeles Board, 341 U.S. 716, 720 (1951): "Past conduct may well relate to present fitness; past loyalty may have a reasonable relationship to present and future trust."

[69] Murphy v. Ramsey, 114 U.S. 15, 41–43 (1885).

[70] Graham v. W. Va., 224 U.S. 616, 623 (1912). The severer sentence may be imposed in a separate and subsequent proceeding, if the defendant was not identified as a "repeater" at his trial. *Ibid.*, 625. See also McDonald v. Massachusetts, 180 U.S. 311, 312–13 (1901); Gryger v. Burke, 334 U.S. 728, 732 (1948).

[71] Waters-Pierce Oil Co. v. Texas (No. 1), 212 U.S. 86, 108 (1909); Samuels v. McCurdy, 267 U.S. 188, 193 (1925). See also Reetz v. Michigan, 188 U.S. 505, 510 (1903); Chicago & Alton R.R. Co. v. Tranbarger, 238 U.S. 67, 73 (1915); Garner v. Los Angeles Board, 341 U.S. 716, 721, 723 (1951).

though often harsh and catastrophic in its effects upon worthy individuals, is not regarded in the eyes of the law as a criminal penalty or punishment at all.[73] Hence when it occurs as a consequence of past offenses, it cannot be regarded as *additional* punishment superadded to that which was prescribed by the laws in force at the time when those past offenses were committed.[74]

Congress cannot evade the ban of the ex post facto clause, however, by disguising what is in essence a criminal penalty in the form of a civil proceeding (such as a suit to collect a tax).[75]

Another type of ex post facto law is one changing the rules of evidence, to permit conviction upon less or different testimony than was required at the time the crime was committed. Generally speaking, a person charged with crime has no vested right in procedural rules governing the conduct of a criminal trial.[76] Thus where after com-

[72] This interpretation has been undeviatingly adhered to by the Supreme Court since Calder v. Bull, 3 Dall. 386, 390, 395 (1798). It was also accepted by the framers of the Constitution on the basis of language in Blackstone. Farrand, *Records*, II, 448–49 (August 29); II, 617 (September 14); III, 328; Blackstone, *Commentaries*, I, 46. See page 194 above. On this point there is the authority not only of a page of history but of a volume. Galvan v. Press, 347 U.S. 522, 531 (1954). A more extensive interpretation has sometimes been urged. Ogden v. Saunders, 12 Wheat. 213, 286 (1827); Satterlee v. Matthewson, 2 Pet. 380, 416 (1829); Marcello v. Bonds, 349 U.S. 302, 319–21 (1955); Crosskey, *Politics and the Constitution in the History of the United States*, I, 324–51.

[73] Deportation, as Justice Holmes points out, is simply the exercise of a nation's sovereign power to rid itself of aliens whom it does not choose to harbor. "The coincidence of the local penal laws with the policy of Congress is an accident." Bugajewitz v. Adams, 228 U.S. 585, 591 (1913). Congress can prescribe deportation for past crimes which were not grounds for deportation at the time when they were committed. Marcello v. Bonds, 349 U.S. 302, 314 (1955). It can also prescribe deportation for past conduct which was not criminal at all at the time when it occurred. Harisiades v. Shaughnessy, 342 U.S. 580, 594–95 (1952); Galvan v. Press, 347 U.S. 522, 531 (1954). Justice Black strongly repudiated this view.

[74] See pages 196–97 above.

[75] Burgess v. Salmon, 97 U.S. 381, 385 (1878); Harisiades v. Shaughnessy, 342 U.S. 580, 595 (1952). This statement from the Burgess case is really dictum. Earlier in the day on which the President signed the Act of March 3, 1875, 18 Stat. 339, increasing the tax on tobacco, the defendant withdrew tobacco from storage and paid tax at the lower rate then in force. The Court said that to penalize him for violation of a nonexistent law would subject him to the operation of an ex post facto law. 97 U.S. at 384. All this was academic, however, as the statute itself contained a proviso that the increase would not apply to "tobacco on which the tax under existing laws shall have been paid when the act takes effect." *Ibid.*, 381.

[76] Hopt v. Utah, 110 U.S. 574, 590 (1884). The same is true regarding rules gov-

mission of a crime but before trial a law was enacted permitting convicted felons to testify, there was no violation of the prohibition against
ex post facto laws. Merely to enlarge the class of persons entitled to be
heard as witness did not attach criminality to any act previously innocent, nor aggravate the offense, nor increase the punishment, nor alter
the degree or lessen the amount of proof required in order to convict.[77]
Similarly, a statute changing the place of trial by including within a
particular judicial district the territory where the offense occurred does
not violate the ex post facto clause.[78]

But where by subsequent legislation the situation of a party is materially changed to his disadvantage, as by depriving him of a defense
available at the time of commission of the crime, or otherwise impairing his substantive legal rights, the statute is an ex post facto law and
invalid.[79] Thus where at the time of the commission of the offense a
conviction or plea of second-degree murder, even if later set aside, was
operative as an acquittal of first-degree murder, a subsequent enactment
changing that rule was stricken down as an ex post facto law because it
took away a good defense to the charge of first-degree murder.[80]

Another example of what has been held to be an ex post facto law
materially impairing the right of a defendant "to have the question of
his guilt determined according to the law as it was when the offence was
committed" was a provision of the constitution of Utah permitting trial
and conviction by a jury of less than twelve persons. When the crime
was committed, Utah had not been admitted as a state, and under the
federal rule then applicable in the Territory of Utah a jury of twelve
was mandatory.[81]

---

erning the mode of execution of the death penalty. See note 65, page 199, above. It is
true also with respect to laws changing the qualifications of jurors, the place where the
court sits, or the number of judges composing it, or authorizing appeal by the prosecution, or requiring joint instead of separate trials. Gibson v. Mississippi, 162 U.S. 565,
590 (1896); Gut v. State, 9 Wall. 35, 38 (1870); Duncan v. Missouri, 152 U.S. 377,
382 (1894); Mallett v. North Carolina, 181 U.S. 589, 597 (1901); Beazell v. Ohio,
269 U.S. 167, 170–71 (1925).

[77] 110 U.S. at 588–89.

[78] Cook v. U.S., 138 U.S. 157, 183 (1891). The same rule is illustrated in cases
testing state legislation under Art. I, sec. 10, cl. 1. See note 65, page 199, above.

[79] Kring v. Missouri, 107 U.S. 221, 229 (1883). But there is no ex post facto law
where a new judicial interpretation is given to a statute existing at the time of the
offense. Ross v. Oregon, 227 U.S. 150, 161 (1913).

[80] 107 U.S. at 224, 229. Four Justices dissented, on the ground that the new rule
was in force at the time of defendant's original plea. *Ibid.*, 226.

A good illustration of a change detrimental to a defendant would be the repeal of a requirement that the testimony of two witnesses was necessary to convict of the particular crime (such as perjury),[82] so as to permit conviction upon the testimony of a single witness. Obviously, less or different evidence than was required at the time when the offense was committed would then be sufficient to convict. This would be a clear violation of the ex post facto clause.

ARTICLE I—THE LEGISLATIVE BRANCH

Restrictions upon the Powers of Congress, *Apportionment of Direct Taxes*

ART. I, SEC. 9, CL. 4

No Capitation, or other direct, Tax shall be laid, unless in Proportion to the Census or Enumeration herein before directed to be taken.

HISTORY

AMONG the restrictions upon the taxing power enumerated in Randolph's draft in the Committee of Detail were these: "direct taxation proportioned to representation" and "No (headpost) capitation-tax which does not apply to all inhabitants under the above limitation (& to be levied uniform)."[83]

It will be remembered that, in connection with the matter of representation (Article I, section 2, clause 3), strenuous conflict arose over the inclusion of slaves in the basis of representation. Ultimately, the three-fifths rule was accepted, with provision for a decennial census. In the course of the debate, Gouverneur Morris, in order to promote a spirit of compromise by linking the benefits and the burdens of the system to be established, proposed that direct taxation be proportioned to representation.[84] Wilson suggested, in order to allay the scruples of

---

[81] Thompson v. Utah, 170 U.S. 343, 349–51 (1898).

[82] See John H. Wigmore, "Required Numbers of Witnesses," *Harvard Law Review*, Vol. XV, No. 2 (June, 1901), 100–108; Weiler v. U.S., 323 U.S. 606, 608–609 (1945).

[83] Farrand, *Records*, II, 142–43.

[84] *Ibid.*, I, 592–93 (July 12). See page 71 above.

opponents of slavery, that the order of ideas be reversed: that representation be proportioned to direct taxation. Thereby only freemen would be entitled to representation; and the measure of representation of each state would be proportioned to that state's share in bearing the financial burden of the government. Only indirectly, in computing the state's share of taxation, would slaves be taken into consideration, under the three-fifths rule.[85]

Accordingly, the Committee of Detail reported that "The proportions of direct taxation shall be regulated by" the number of inhabitants, under the three-fifths rule, with provision for a decennial census,[86] and that "No capitation tax shall be laid, unless in proportion to the Census hereinbefore directed to be taken."[87] The Committee of Style made no change.[88] On motion of Read in convention the words "or other direct" tax were added.[89]

INTERPRETATION

A CAPITATION tax is a head or poll tax. Such a tax, as well as a tax on land, was generally understood as constituting a "direct" tax. As such, it fell within the requirement of apportionment prescribed by this clause and by Article I, section 2, clause 3. The latter clause directs the method of taking the census or enumeration in accordance with which direct taxation and representation are to be apportioned.[90]

[85] Ibid., II, 595 (July 12); II, 223 (August 8).

[86] Art. VII, sec. 3. Ibid., II, 182–83 (August 6). These provisions were later incorporated in Art. I, sec. 2, cl. 3, by the Committee of Style. Ibid., II, 590 (September 12).

[87] Art. VII, sec. 5. Ibid., II, 183 (August 6). This section was referred to a committee, and as part of the compromise on navigation acts and importation of slaves, was reported without modification. Ibid., II, 366, 374 (August 22); II, 396, 400 (August 24); II, 409, 417 (August 25).

[88] Ibid., II, 596 (September 12).

[89] Ibid., II, 610, 618 (September 14). The words "or enumeration" were added at the same time on motion of Mason. Ibid., II, 611, 618.

[90] See commentary on Art. I, sec. 2, cl. 3. The three-fifths rule set forth in that clause was superseded by section 2 of the Fourteenth Amendment, after slavery was abolished by the Thirteenth Amendment. The Sixteenth Amendment rendered the requirement of apportionment inapplicable to "taxes on incomes."

ARTICLE I—THE LEGISLATIVE BRANCH

Restrictions upon the Powers of Congress, *Tax on Exports*

ART. I, SEC. 9, CL. 5
No Tax or Duty shall be laid on Articles exported from any State.

HISTORY

WHEN Gouverneur Morris made the proposal that taxation should be in proportion to representation, he quickly limited it to direct taxes, recognizing that it would be impracticable to apply the rule to indirect taxes on exports and imports, and on consumption. Mention of the possibility of taxing exports produced an outburst from General Charles Cotesworth Pinckney. Declaring that in one year South Carolina has exported goods worth £600,000, "all which was the fruit of the labor of her blacks," he inquired: "Will she be represented in proportion to this amount? She will not. Neither ought she then to be subject to a tax on it. He hoped a clause would be inserted in the system restraining the Legislature from a taxing Exports."[91] He repeated the demand for "security to the Southern States" against an emancipation of slaves, "and taxes on exports" when the Committee of Detail was appointed.[92] Mindful of this threat, the Committee of Detail reported language providing that "No tax or duty shall be laid by the Legislature on articles exported from any State."[93]

Heated argument on this point broke out prematurely, in connection with discussion of the taxing power vested in Congress by Article I, section 8, clause 1.[94] When Article I, section 9, clause 5, was

[91] Farrand, *Records*, I, 592 (July 12). Logically, when the three-fifths ratio was adopted for representation, exports should have been made taxable to the same extent. The Southern states received a double advantage in the compromise accepted.

[92] *Ibid.*, II, 95 (July 23).

[93] Art. VII, sec. 4. *Ibid.*, II, 183 (August 6). Randolph's draft had read "No Taxes on exports." *Ibid.*, II, 142. The Committee's article also forbade taxation of importation of slaves, and prohibition of the slave trade. See commentary on Art. I, sec. 9, cl. 1, above. The Committee likewise gratuitously favored the South by originating a provision requiring a two-thirds vote of the members present in each house in order to pass a navigation act. See pages 53–54 above.

[94] *Ibid.*, II, 305–308 (August 16). Gouverneur Morris, Madison, and Wilson strongly contended for the advisability of power to tax exports.

reached in debate[95] Dickinson and FitzSimons called attention to the impolicy of forever precluding the possibility of taxing exports, even if such a tax were inadvisable at the present time.[96] Wilson regarded denial of the power as taking away "half the regulation of trade." He believed that "a power over exports might be more effectual than that over imports in obtaining beneficial treaties of commerce."[97] Ellsworth and Mason, on the other hand, emphasized that since all states imported similar articles, while exports were different, there would be greater opportunity for unfair discrimination if exports could be taxed.[98] Clymer "remarked that every State might reason with regard to its particular productions, in the same manner as the Southern States." He moved that the power to tax exports should be exercised only as a regulation of trade, but not for revenue. This proposal was defeated, as was a suggestion by Madison requiring a two-thirds vote in order to exercise the power. The prohibition was ultimately adopted by a vote of seven states to four.[99] The Committee of Style made no material change in the clause.[100]

INTERPRETATION

THIS clause, which prohibits Congress from laying any "Tax or Duty" on "Articles exported from any State," is substantially identical in scope with the prohibition in Article I, section 10, clause 2, which prevents a state (without the consent of Congress) from laying "any Imposts or Duties on . . . Exports" except in connection with its inspection laws.[101]

The word "exported" means exported to a foreign country.[102]

[95] *Ibid.*, II, 359–63 (August 21). [96] *Ibid.*, II, 361, 362.
[97] *Ibid.*, II, 362. [98] *Ibid.*, II, 360, 363.
[99] *Ibid.*, II, 363. Apparently this provision, having been adopted, was not referred to the committee which effected a compromise on the subjects of the slave trade and navigation acts. *Ibid.*, II, 374 (August 22). See note 10, page 187, above.
[100] It deleted the superfluous words "by the Legislature." *Ibid.*, II, 596 (September 12).
[101] Cornell v. Coyne, 192 U.S. 418, 427–28 (1904); Richfield Oil Corp. v. State Bd. of Equalization, 329 U.S. 69, 83 (1946); Empresa Siderurgica v. Merced County, 337 U.S. 154, 156 (1949).
[102] Dooley v. U.S., 183 U.S. 154 (1901). Hence shipments from New York to Puerto Rico are taxable under the general taxing power conferred by Art. I, sec. 8, cl. 1, since the prohibition in Art. I, sec. 9, cl. 5, is inapplicable because Puerto Rico was held in De Lima v. Bidwell, 182 U.S. 1, 200 (1901), not to be a foreign country.

It does not include shipments to another state. Regulation of interstate traffic is governed by the commerce clause (Article I, section 8, clause 3).

The prohibition has been construed as exempting from taxation the whole "process of exportation," as well as the articles themselves which are exported. The immunity extends to all "the transactions and documents embraced in the process,"[103] such as bills of lading,[104] charter parties,[105] marine insurance policies,[106] or other instrumentalities so closely and directly related to the process of exportation that for them to be subjected to the burden of taxation would in substance be an obstruction or hindrance to the process of exportation itself.[107]

On the other hand, a tax on the net income of persons engaged in the exporting business is valid.[108] Its effect on exportation is indirect and remote; it is laid on the proceeds remaining after the process of exportation has been concluded, when the money earned therefrom can be used for any purpose desired by the taxpayer.[109]

Similarly, a tax on manufacturing, or on property in general before exportation begins, is permissible.[110] In that connection the Supreme Court said: "The true construction of the constitutional provision is that no burden by way of tax or duty can be cast upon the exportation of articles," not that "articles exported are relieved from the prior ordinary burdens of taxation which rest upon all property similarly situated. The exemption attaches to the export and not to the article before its exportation."[111]

It therefore is often important to determine the precise point or moment at which exportation begins. Although recognizing that here, as often in the law, the line drawn may be arbitrary, the courts generally

[103] U.S. v. Hvoslef, 237 U.S. 1, 13 (1915); Willcutts v. Bunn, 282 U.S. 216, 228 (1931); Richfield Oil Corp. v. State Bd. of Equalization, 329 U.S. 69, 81–82 (1946); Empresa Siderurgica v. Merced County, 337 U.S. 154, 156 (1949).

[104] Fairbank v. U.S., 181 U.S. 283, 293 (1901).

[105] U.S. v. Hvoslef, 237 U.S. 1, 16 (1915).

[106] Thames & Mersey Marine Ins. Co. v. U.S., 237 U.S. 19, 25 (1915).

[107] Peck & Co. v. Lowe, 247 U.S. 165, 173 (1918).

[108] *Ibid.*, 174.

[109] *Ibid.*, 175.

[110] Cornell v. Coyne, 192 U.S. 418, 419 (1904). The tax here upheld was on the manufacturing of filled cheese, which was manufactured for export and was in fact exported. *Ibid.*, 426. See also Turpin v. Burgess, 117 U.S. 504, 507 (1886).

[111] *Ibid.*, 427. Only a burden by way of tax or duty is prohibited. The incidental effect of a legitimate exercise of regulatory power over a carrier's rates is not within that prohibition. Armour Packing Co. v. U.S., 209 U.S. 56, 79–80 (1908).

regard delivery of goods to a common carrier as the beginning of the process of exportation.[112] Pumping oil into a tanker belonging to the purchaser for transportation to a foreign port likewise suffices.[113] But in a later questionable ruling, where a cement plant had been sold to a South American corporation to be dismantled and exported, the Supreme Court held that only the part actually delivered to a carrier was to be regarded as exempt from tax. "It is the entrance of the articles into the export stream that marks the start of the process of exportation."[114]

When dealing with a tax not on the goods themselves but on the handling of them, the Supreme Court seems to adopt a narrower view, and to regard the process of loading the cargo on board a seagoing vessel as the beginning of exportation.[115] Hence it upheld a franchise tax, measured by gross receipts applied to the length of line within the state, in the case of a short-line railroad which switched cars between piers and connecting rail carriers, and also furnished storage, wharfage (*i.e.*, use of piers for transfer of lading), and a crane used for loading

[112] A. G. Spalding & Bros. v. Edwards, 262 U.S. 66, 69 (1923). The fact that the buyer might divert or reconsign the goods does not prevent regarding delivery to the carrier as the beginning of the exportation process. *Ibid.*, 70. But in later questionable decisions the Court insisted upon the certainty that there would be no diversion. "Nothing less will suffice." Empresa Siderurgica v. Merced County, 337 U.S. 154, 157 (1949); Joy Oil Co. v. Tax Commission, 337 U.S. 286, 288 (1949).

[113] Richfield Oil Corp. v. State Bd. of Equalization, 329 U.S. 69, 82–83 (1946). "The means of shipment are unimportant so long as the certainty of the foreign destination is plain."

[114] Empresa Siderurgica v. Merced County, 337 U.S. 154, 157 (1949). Ultimately the whole plant was exported; but on tax day 12 per cent had been delivered to the carrier (14 out of 123 carloads); 10 per cent was dismantled and crated for shipment; 34 per cent was dismantled but not crated; and 44 per cent had not yet been dismantled. *Ibid.*, 155, 158. Photographs of each machine or piece of equipment were to be taken before and after dismantling in order to facilitate reinstallation at destination. *Ibid.*, 159.

[115] Canton R.R. Co. v. Rogan, 340 U.S. 511, 514, 515 (1951). The Court said that since the connecting carrier here involved did not in fact perform the loading and unloading but merely rented its crane to stevedoring companies, the question whether loading was part of the process of exportation need not be decided. "We do conclude, however, that any activity more remote than that does not commence the movement of the commodities abroad nor end their arrival and therefore is not a part of the export or import process." See also Joy Oil Co. v. Tax Commission 337 U.S. 286, 288 (1949), where goods stored in transit for fifteen months because of unavailability of shipping were deemed not to be exports, although shipped by rail to the point of storage on export rates.

and unloading ships. Over half of the company's business was composed of shipments moving in foreign commerce.[116]

The rule that delivery to a carrier for transportation marks the beginning of the process of exportation was borrowed from a similar rule that such delivery is the beginning of interstate commerce, when shipments of goods are made to another state.[117] At the time when that rule originated with respect to interstate commerce, the Supreme Court was in the habit of drawing a sharp line between production and commerce, and of delineating accordingly a well-marked boundary between the respective powers of the state and federal governments.[118] Recent years have witnessed a tremendous expansion of the interstate commerce power of the federal government, and many aspects of production or manufacturing are now subject to federal regulation.[119] Hence it may be asked whether the rule regarding the precise point where the process of exportation begins has been weakened by the withering of the rule with respect to interstate commerce from which the export rule was derived. However, it is believed that the rule regarding exports has not been affected, since the effect of recognizing an earlier point as the beginning of the process of exportation would result in *curtailment*, rather than *expansion*, of the federal taxing power.[120] A corresponding curtailment of state taxing power would also result, under the analogous prohibition contained in Article I, section 10, clause 2.[121]

[116] Cf. Anglo-Chilean Nitrate Sales Corp. v. Alabama, 288 U.S. 218, 229 (1933), where a franchise tax on the amount of capital employed in the state was held invalid in the case of a company engaged solely in selling imported nitrate of soda in the original packages. See also State Freight Tax Case, 15 Wall. 232, 279 (1873); Puget Sound Stevedoring Co. v. Tax Commission of Washington, 302 U.S. 90, 92–94 (1937).

[117] Coe v. Errol, 116 U.S. 517, 527–28 (1886).

[118] The basic premise of these holdings was the proposition that "commerce succeeds to manufacture and is not a part of it." U.S. v. E. C. Knight Co., 156 U.S. 1, 12 (1895).

[119] U.S. v. Darby, 312 U.S. 100, 113–15 (1941); Wickard v. Filburn, 317 U.S. 111, 118–20 (1942).

[120] A dissenting opinion in Richfield Oil Corp. v. State Bd. of Equalization, 329 U.S. 69, 87 (1946), emphasizes the seriousness as a policy question of extending a constitutional immunity from taxation. In Hooven & Allison Co. v. Evatt, 324 U.S. 652, 668 (1945), the Court pointed out that under Art. I, sec. 10, cl. 2, Congress could consent to the exercise of state taxing power with respect to imports and exports, and hence that no reasons of policy militated against adherence by the Court to the settled rules derived from commerce clause decisions.

[121] Such curtailment of state taxing power would conflict with the trend of recent cases recognizing the importance of meeting the states' revenue needs. See Northwestern Cement Co. v. Minnesota, 358 U.S. 450, 452 (1959). See page 118 above.

ARTICLE I—THE LEGISLATIVE BRANCH

Restrictions upon the Powers of Congress, *Preference to Ports*

ART. I, SEC. 9, CL. 6

No Preference shall be given by any Regulation of Commerce or
Revenue to the Ports of one State over those of another: nor shall
Vessels bound to, or from, one State, be obliged to enter, clear, or
pay Duties in another.

HISTORY

THIS provision originated with the Maryland delegates.[122] They
feared that Congress might favor the ports of particular states; for
example, by requiring vessels to or from Baltimore to enter and clear
at Norfolk. Accordingly, Carroll and Luther Martin offered a proposal that "The Legislature of the United States shall not oblige
Vessels belonging to Citizens thereof, or to foreigners, to enter or pay
duties, or imposts in any other State than in that to which they may be
bound, or to clear out in any other than the State in which their cargoes
may be laden on board—Nor shall any privilege, or immunity, be
granted to any vessels on entering, clearing out, or paying duties or
imposts in one State in preference to another."

McHenry, seconded by General Charles Cotesworth Pinckney of
South Carolina, proposed two further provisions inspired by the same
fear of discrimination. One of these would have authorized the federal
government to determine only the *number* of new ports to be established in addition to those already established in the states, and would
have permitted the states to fix the places where those ports should be.
The other provided that: "all duties, imposts, and excises, prohibitions
or restraints laid or made by the Legislature of the U.S. shall be uniform and equal throughout the United States."[123]

[122] Farrand, *Records*, III, 213; II, 378.

[123] *Ibid.*, II, 410, 417–18 (August 25). See also *ibid.*, III, 213–14. These propositions were referred to a grand committee, which reported three days later. *Ibid.*, II, 434,
437 (August 28). McHenry's first proposition was eliminated in committee; the second
was later added at the end of Art. I, sec. 8, cl. 1. An attempt by the Maryland delegation
to bring the report up for consideration on August 30 was unsuccessful. *Ibid.*, II, 468,
470.

The grand committee to which these proposals were referred recommended the following language:

> Nor shall any regulation of commerce or revenue give preference to the ports of one State over those of another or oblige Vessels bound to or from any State to enter, clear, or pay duties in another,
> And all tonnage, duties, imposts, and excises, laid by the Legislature shall be uniform throughout the United States.[124]

The provision was duly adopted,[125] but seems to have been completely overlooked by the Committee of Style.[126] It was restored, apparently on motion of Gouverneur Morris,[127] the wording being modified by putting it in the passive voice to bring it into conformity with the other clauses limiting the powers of Congress: "No Preference shall be given by any Regulation of Commerce or Revenue."

INTERPRETATION

IT was natural that the Maryland delegates should fear the possibility of arbitrary or discriminatory exercise of the commerce power. In England it was a prerogative of the king to establish ports, that is to say, to prescribe places where goods could be brought into or taken out of the country. Traffic at places not so authorized was forbidden.[128] "No exportation or importation can be, but at the king's ports."[129] On the basis of his power over ports, which included the power of permitting or prohibiting trade to be carried on through the ports, King James I claimed the derivative right of permitting such trade conditionally, namely upon payment of taxes or impositions laid by the king without the assent of Parliament. The king's power to impose such

[124] *Ibid.*, II, 434, 437 (August 29). These paragraphs were to be added at the end of Art. VII, sec. 4, of the draft of the Committee of Detail, prohibiting taxation of imports or interference with the slave trade. *Ibid.*, II, 183, 571.

[125] *Ibid.*, II, 473, 480–81 (August 31). The word "tonnage" was struck out, as comprehended in "duties."

[126] *Ibid.*, II, 596; Warren, *The Making of the Constitution*, 588; Meigs, *The Growth of the Constitution*, 175.

[127] Farrand, *Records*, II, 610, 618 (September 14); Meigs, *The Growth of the Constitution*, 133. At this time the uniformity provision was transferred to Art. I, sec. 8, cl. 1, with a substitution of "but" for "and" at the beginning, and elimination of "laid by the Legislature."

[128] Blackstone, *Commentaries*, I, 264.

[129] The Case of Impositions, 2 St. Tr. 371, 389 (1606).

taxes, upheld by the Court of Exchequer, was strenuously contested by Parliament in 1610.[130]

Controversy over ports had also arisen in the New World. Geographical conditions in Virginia made ports unnecessary. A system of rivers, along which plantations had sprung up, facilitated direct access for maritime traffic. "Each planter dealt directly with the merchants, receiving English manufactured goods almost at his front door, and lading the ships with tobacco from his own warehouse." A Bill of Ports enacted in 1680 undertook to establish one town in each county as the exclusive place where all goods were to be landed and exports to be shipped, but this law proved ineffective. Another Bill of Ports in 1685 gave rise to controversy with the governor regarding his veto power.[131]

These conflicts regarding the location of ports might have been in the minds of the Maryland delegates. It would have been possible for Congress, under the broad terms of the commerce clause, to establish a single favored port through which all traffic for a large area (including adjacent states) might be required to pass. It will be remembered also that among the most pressing grievances of the government under the Articles of Confederation was the toll laid by certain commercial states upon the traffic of neighboring states.[132]

In practice this clause has not proved of importance. When Congress legalized a bridge at Wheeling, in what is now West Virginia, which was not high enough to permit the passage of vessels from Pittsburgh with masts of the usual height, the argument was advanced that this interruption of river traffic at Wheeling would give that port business to the detriment of Pittsburgh, in Pennsylvania. The Supreme Court held that many legitimate projects undertaken by Congress in one state (such as improvement of harbors or erection of lighthouses) may operate incidentally to the prejudice of ports in neighboring states. Such effects are not in violation of the constitutional prohibition against preference to the ports of one state over those of another. The Court construed this language narrowly. Preference to a state, not to an individual port therein, was held to be the forbidden evil. Otherwise Congress could not make one port a port of entry without extending the

[130] The Court of Exchequer, in the case cited in the preceding note, where John Bates, a merchant, refused to pay a royal impost on currants from Venice, upheld the king's power. See Joseph R. Tanner, *English Constitutional Conflicts of the Seventeenth Century*, 43–45.

[131] Thomas J. Wertenbaker, *Virginia under the Stuarts*, 246–48.

[132] See page 111 above.

same privilege to all ports in every state. "The truth seems to be, that what is forbidden is not discrimination between individual ports within the same or different States, but discrimination between States; and if so, in order to bring this case within the prohibition, it is necessary to show, not merely discrimination between Pittsburg and Wheeling, but discrimination between the ports of Virginia and those of Pennsylvania."[133]

In a later case it was held, in accordance with the same principle, that Congress might improve the southern channel of the Savannah River, benefiting the ports of Georgia, at the expense of the South Carolina ports on the northern channel of the river.[134]

Attempts to challenge, as violative of Article I, section 9, clause 6, rail rates established by the Interstate Commerce Commission have likewise proved unsuccessful.[135]

The clause is a limitation upon the powers of Congress, not upon those of the states.[136] Alaska (before its admission as a state) was not a state entitled to the benefits of this clause.[137]

The North Carolina ratifying convention proposed to amend the first part of this clause to read: "Nor shall vessels bound to a particular state be obliged to enter or pay duties in any other; nor when bound from any one of the States be obliged to clear in another."[138]

ARTICLE I—THE LEGISLATIVE BRANCH
Restrictions upon the Powers of Congress, *Control of Public Funds*

ART. I, SEC. 9, CL. 7
No Money shall be drawn from the Treasury, but in Consequence
of Appropriations made by Law; and a regular Statement and

[133] Pa. v. Wheeling & Belmont Bridge Co., 18 How. 421, 433, 435 (1856). This litigation was the aftermath of an earlier case, Pa. v. Wheeling Bridge Co., 13 How. 518 (1852).

[134] S.C. v. Ga., 93 U.S. 4, 11, 13 (1876).

[135] La. P.S.C. v. T. & N. O. R.R. Co., 284 U.S. 125, 131 (1931); Ala. Great So. R.R. Co. v. U.S., 340 U.S. 216, 229 (1951).

[136] Munn v. Illinois, 94 U.S. 113, 135 (1877); Morgan's Steamship Co. v. La., 118 U.S. 455, 467 (1886); Thompson v. Darden, 198 U.S. 310, 315 (1905).

[137] Alaska v. Troy, 258 U.S. 101, 111 (1922).

[138] Dumbauld, *The Bill of Rights and What It Means Today*, 31, 205. It is not clear how this amendment would change the meaning of the clause in any respect.

*Account of the Receipts and Expenditures of all public Money shall
be published from time to time.*

HISTORY

THIS clause originated as part of the provision that all money bills
must originate in the lower house.[139] As reported by the committee appointed to devise a compromise on the thorny subject of representation,
the clause read: "and that no money shall be drawn from the public
Treasury but in pursuance of appropriations to be originated by the
first Branch."[140] There was difference of opinion with regard to the
question whether the Senate should have power to amend money
bills,[141] and the Committee on Postponed Parts when reporting an
amendment granting such power amended the instant clause to read
"in consequence of appropriations made by law."[142] At the suggestion
of Mason, who desired annual publication of an account of public
expenditures, there were added, after debate, the words: "and a regular
statement and account of the receipts and expenditures of all publick
money shall be published from time to time."[143]

INTERPRETATION

LISTED (in section 9) among other limitations upon the powers of
Congress, this clause prohibits Congress from withdrawing money
from the treasury by any process less formal than the enactment of a
law.[144] However, this clause is also "a restriction upon the disbursing
authority of the Executive department."[145] Its effect is that no money

[139] That provision was part of the "great compromise" on representation, which
was finally accepted on July 16. See page 47 above.

[140] Farrand, *Records*, I, 524, 526 (July 5). This language was approved by the
convention. *Ibid.*, I, 538–39, 547 (July 6); II, 14, 16 (July 16). The Committee of
Detail after "appropriations" substituted "that shall originate in the House of Representatives." *Ibid.*, II, 178 (August 6).

[141] *Ibid.*, II, 266, 280 (August 13); II, 294, 297 (August 15); II, 353, 357
(August 21).

[142] *Ibid.*, II, 505, 509 (September 5). This was approved by the convention on
September 8. *Ibid.*, II, 545, 552. The Committee of Style made no change except to
separate the clause from the money bill provision which became Art. I, sec. 7, cl. 1.
Ibid., II, 596 (September 12).

[143] *Ibid.*, II, 610, 618–19 (September 14).

[144] This requirement puts it beyond the power of a single house to spend public
funds, and also requires the assent of the President, unless his veto is overridden. See
Art. I, sec. 7, cl. 2.

[145] Cincinnati Soap Co. v. U.S., 301 U.S. 308, 321 (1937).

can be paid out of the treasury unless it has been appropriated by an act of Congress.

This is true even where the judgment of a court has determined that a debt against the United States exists. "No officer, however high, not even the President, much less a Secretary of the Treasury or Treasurer, is empowered to pay debts of the United States generally, when presented to them. . . . The difficulty in the way is the want of any appropriation by Congress to pay this claim. It is a well-known constitutional provision, that no money can be taken or drawn from the Treasury except under an appropriation by Congress."[146]

On the other hand, when an act of Congress directs payment of a specific sum of money to a particular person, there remains no discretion in any official or court to inquire into the lawfulness or justice of the claimant's right to be paid.[147] Likewise effect must be given to any direction by Congress that certain classes of claims shall not be paid.[148]

Of course, if the law by which the appropriation was made is unconstitutional, payment could be refused. But judicial supervision over the actions of Congress in appropriating money is very limited.[149] The wisdom of such appropriations is a matter solely to be determined by Congress; and the legal powers of that body to spend money are subject to very few restrictions.[150]

[146] Reeside v. Walker, 11 How. 271, 291 (1851).

[147] U.S. v. Price, 116 U.S. 43, 44 (1885). The claimant in this case was said to have been a Confederate sympathizer, and not entitled to compensation for property taken from his father for use of the Union army. Moreover, the claimant was not in fact the sole heir of his father.

[148] Hart v. U.S., 118 U.S. 62, 67 (1886). In this case claimant was a Confederate sympathizer, but had received a pardon. However, Congress had provided (by joint resolution of March 2, 1867, 14 Stat. 571) that no claims accrued before April 13, 1861, in favor of such parties should be paid, irrespective of pardon, until modification of the joint resolution.

[149] U.S. v. Realty Co., 163 U.S. 427, 444 (1896). Here was upheld a payment which was made for the relief of domestic sugar producers affected by the repeal of a bounty established by an earlier law enacted to compensate them for a reduction in tariff protection. This payment was held to be an equitable debt of honor for which Congress could make an appropriation, whether the earlier act was constitutional or not. (The Court avoided deciding the constitutionality of the earlier act. *Ibid.*, 433.)

[150] See Charles Warren, *Congress as Santa Claus*, 28, 141–43. Theoretically Congress is empowered only to provide for the *general* welfare; and a particular appropriation could conceivably be stricken down as one for the benefit of *local* or *private* interests. But in practice Congress has a wide discretion to determine what constitutes general welfare. Helvering v. Davis, 301 U.S. 619, 640–41 (1937); U.S. *ex rel.* T.V.A. v.

Since this clause refers only to money "drawn from the Treasury," it does not apply to funds which have never been deposited in the treasury. A pardon for treason would be effective and enable the owner to recover confiscated property if it were still in the hands of the courts or executive officers; but where the confiscation procedure has been fully completed, and the property vested in the United States, it is impossible for the owner to reclaim it without authority from Congress. "Moneys once in the treasury can only be withdrawn by an appropriation by law."[151]

In like manner the effect of this clause may be escaped by handling public business through a government-owned corporation or trust fund, so that the moneys involved are never actually deposited in the treasury.[152] Thus it does not require an act of Congress for a purchaser to receive change when buying an article at an army PX or when having lunch at a government cafeteria.

ARTICLE I—THE LEGISLATIVE BRANCH

Restrictions upon the Powers of Congress, *Titles of Nobility and Gifts*

ART. I, SEC. 9, CL. 8

No Title of Nobility shall be granted by the United States: And no Person holding any Office of Profit or Trust under them, shall, without the Consent of the Congress, accept of any present, Emolument, Office, or Title, of any kind whatever, from any King, Prince, or foreign State.

Welch, 327 U.S. 546, 551–52 (1946). Relief of flood sufferers is a private benefit which is obviously in the public interest; so are veterans' and social security provisions; "redevelopment" of blighted areas has likewise been held a public purpose, even if land expropriated is ultimately resold for use by private enterprise. Berman v. Parker, 348 U.S. 26, 34 (1954). See Art. I, sec. 1, cl. 1, above.

[151] Knote v. U.S., 95 U.S. 149, 154 (1877).

[152] U.S. *ex rel.* Skinner & Eddy Corp. v. McCarl, 275 U.S. 1, 8 (1927); Varney v. Warehime, 147 F. 2d 238, 245 (C.C.A. 6, 1945); John McDiarmid, "Government Corporations and Federal Funds," *American Political Science Review*, Vol. XXXI, No. 6 (December, 1937), 1094, 1095.

HISTORY

THE first part of this clause was taken by the Committee of Detail[153] from a provision of the Articles of Confederation.[154] On motion of Charles Pinckney, the latter part was added, doubtless from the same source.[155] The framers had in mind, when imposing this restriction, the fact that a portrait of Louis XVI, adorned with 408 diamonds, had been given by that monarch to Benjamin Franklin when the venerable American envoy took leave of the French court.[156]

INTERPRETATION

THIS clause is of little practical importance. Apparently it has never been construed by the Supreme Court of the United States, as no litigation has arisen under it.

However, since the formation of the government, courtesy has required the President of the United States to accept gifts from heads of states in accordance with custom. In the course of a trip abroad in 1959, President Eisenhower was the recipient of, among other things, an Oriental rug. President Jefferson received a number of curious gifts.[157]

[153] Art. VII, sec. 7: "The United States shall not grant any title of Nobility." Farrand, *Records*, II, 183 (August 6).

[154] Art. VI.

[155] Farrand, *Records*, II, 381, 389 (August 23). Pinckney's proposal included the words "without the consent of the Legislature," which did not appear in Art. VI of the Articles of Confederation. The Committee of Style changed this to "Congress." *Ibid.*, II, 596 (September 12). Perhaps the scrivener of the engrossed Constitution (Jacob Shallus, assistant clerk of the Pennsylvania General Assembly) is responsible for changing the period to a colon between the two parts of the clause. One of the amendments to the Constitution proposed by Massachusetts and New York would have forbidden Congress to grant consent; Samuel Adams was said to have considered this proposal important. Dumbauld, *The Bill of Rights and What It Means Today*, 16, 29, 42, 44, 48, 177, 198.

[156] Farrand, *Records*, III, 327; Carl Van Doren, *Benjamin Franklin*, 722, 765; Van Doren, *Benjamin Franklin's Autobiographic Writings*, 690.

[157] Charles Warren, *Odd Byways in American History*, 3–29.

ART. I, SEC. 10, CL. 1

No State shall enter into any Treaty, Alliance, or Confederation; grant Letters of Marque and Reprisal; coin Money; emit Bills of Credit; make any Thing but gold and silver Coin a Tender in Payment of Debts; pass any Bill of Attainder, ex post facto Law, or Law impairing the Obligation of Contracts, or grant any Title of Nobility.

HISTORY

SECTION 10 enumerates the powers denied to the states, as section 9 does those denied to Congress. The instant clause specifies nine powers that are denied absolutely to the states; the two following clauses deal with eight powers which may not be exercised by states without the consent of Congress. Article VI of the Articles of Confederation served as a precedent for prohibitions upon state action; in that article practically all the prohibitions were of the conditional type, forbidding state action "without the consent of the United States in Congress assembled."

Of the nine powers referred to in Article I, section 10, clause 1, the first two and the last one (relating to treaties, letters of marque and reprisal, and titles of nobility) are based upon the Articles of Confederation.[1] The six other interpolated powers are innovations introduced

---

[1] Art. VI of the Articles of Confederation provided *inter alia:* "No State without the consent of the United States in Congress assembled, shall send any embassy to, or receive any embassy from, or enter into any conference, agreement, alliance or treaty with any king, prince or state; nor shall any person holding any office of profit or trust under the United States, or any of them, accept of any present, emolument, office or title of any kind whatever from any king, prince, or foreign state; nor shall the United States in Congress assembled, or any of them, grant any title of nobility.

"No two or more States shall enter into any treaty, confederation or alliance whatever between them, without the consent of the United States in Congress assembled, specifying accurately the purposes for which the same is to be entered into, and how long it shall continue."

Art. VI also forbade states (without consent of Congress) to keep up "vessels of

218

in order to remedy dissatisfaction experienced under the Articles of Confederation.

In connection with the provision of Randolph's draft in the Committee of Detail giving Congress exclusive power to coin money, an interlineation in Rutledge's hand reads: "no State to be perd. [permitted] in future to emit Paper Bills of Credit witht. [without] the App: [approval] of the Natl. Legisle [national legislature] nor to make any Thing but Specie a Tender in paymt. of debts."[2]

The Committee of Detail reported: "No State shall coin money; nor grant letters of marque and reprisals; nor enter into any treaty, alliance, or confederation; nor grant any title of Nobility."[3]

During debate, upon motion of Wilson seconded by Sherman, the words "nor emit bills of credit, nor make any thing but gold and silver coin a tender in payment of debts" were inserted.[4] King moved to add, in the words used in the Ordinance of 1787, "a prohibition on the States to interfere in private contracts."[5] After discussion a substitute offered by Rutledge for King's motion was adopted: "nor pass any bill of attainder or ex post facto laws."[6] The Committee of Style, apparently on its own initiative, added "nor laws altering or impairing the obliga-

war" or "any body of forces"; to engage in any war (except in case of imminent invasion); or to grant letters of marque or reprisal. Laying imposts or duties conflicting with treaties was also prohibited.

[2] Farrand, *Records*, II, 144. For a draft in Wilson's hand, lumping together all the prohibitions on state powers, see *ibid.*, II, 169.

[3] Art. XII. *Ibid.*, II, 187 (August 6). Art. XIII of the report specifies the powers not to be exercised by a state "without the consent of the Legislature of the United States." The first power so prohibited conditionally was to "emit bills of credit, or make any thing but specie a tender in payment of debts."

[4] *Ibid.*, II, 435, 439 (August 28). Those words were transferred from Art. XIII of the report of the Committee of Detail, which prohibited state action without the consent of Congress. Gorham opposed the transfer, fearing that "an absolute prohibition of paper money would rouse the most desperate opposition from its partizans." But Sherman "thought this a favorable crisis for crushing paper money. If the consent of the Legislature could authorize emissions of it, the friends of paper money would make every exertion to get into the Legislature in order to license it." *Ibid.*, II, 439.

[5] *Ibid.*, II, 439. Art. II of the Ordinance of 1787 declared "that no law ought ever to be made . . . that shall, in any manner whatever, interfere with or affect private contracts, or engagements, bona fide, and without fraud previously formed."

[6] *Ibid.*, II, 435, 440 (August 28). A prohibition in similar terms restricting the powers of Congress had been adopted six days before. *Ibid.*, II, 368, 375–76 (August 22). See Art. I, sec. 9, cl. 3, above. A motion by Madison to add "nor lay embargoes" was defeated. *Ibid.*, II, 435, 440 (August 28).

tion of contracts."[7] During discussion, the order and wording of the clause was changed to its present form.[8]

INTERPRETATION

FROM the threefold identity in the wording used, it would seem that the first portion of this clause is derived from the second paragraph of Article VI of the Articles of Confederation, providing that "No two or more States shall enter into any treaty, confederation or alliance whatever between them," rather than from the preceding paragraph providing that "No State . . . shall . . . enter into any conference, agreement, alliance or treaty with any king, prince or state."[9] This would indicate that it was meant to refer to political compacts between the states themselves rather than to international negotiations. However, the draft in Wilson's handwriting, with emendations by Rutledge, among the working papers of the Committee of Detail would indicate that it was intended to preclude such compacts with foreign powers as well. Wilson apparently wrote: "No State shall enter into any Treaty, Alliance or Confederation," and Rutledge added "with any foreign Power nor without consent of the United States into any agreement or compact with another State or Power."[10] As reported by the Committee of Detail, deleting the limiting words "with any foreign Power," the

[7] *Ibid.*, II, 587 (September 12). This may have been another instance in which Gouverneur Morris sought to embody his own views in the wording of the Constitution. *Ibid.*, III, 404, 419–20. See also note 10, page 108, above, and page 425, below. But see *ibid.*, II, 439, where Morris opposed King's motion. However, the new language may have been added in consequence of Dickinson's observation that on examining Blackstone's *Commentaries* he found that the term "ex post facto laws" referred only to criminal cases, and that this prohibition "would not consequently restrain the States from retrospective laws in civil cases, and that some further provision for this purpose would be requisite." *Ibid.*, II, 448–49 (August 29). See Meigs, *The Growth of the Constitution*, 186.

[8] Farrand, *Records*, II, 610, 619 (September 14).

[9] See note 1, page 218, above. For prior drafts of the Articles of Confederation, see Abraham C. Weinfeld, "What Did the Framers of the Federal Constitution Mean by 'Agreements or Compacts'?" *University of Chicago Law Review*, Vol. III, No. 3 (April, 1936), 453, 455–56.

[10] Farrand, *Records*, II, 169 [abbreviations expanded]. Worded in that fashion, the language prohibiting treaties, alliances, and confederations would apply *exclusively* to arrangements with foreign powers, while the conditionally permitted "agreement or compact" could be with another state or with a foreign power (as now provided in Art. I, sec. 10, cl. 3). See note 150, page 249, below.

language would seem to embrace arrangements both among the states themselves and with foreign powers.[11]

In either case, it is only alliances or confederations of distinctly political character, inconsistent with the federal government established by the Constitution, that are here prohibited; other types of stipulations, warranted by practical convenience, are permissible in the form of an "Agreement or Compact," when approved by Congress, under Article I, section 10, clause 3.[12]

Most of the remaining powers enumerated in this clause are in identical terms with grants to (or prohibitions upon) Congress set forth in previous clauses of sections 8 and 9.

To grant letters of marque and reprisal is to authorize armed depredations upon the shipping of foreign nations. This power to involve the United States in hostilities abroad is wisely denied to the states individually, but is conferred upon Congress by Article I, section 8, clause 11.[13]

To coin money is likewise a recognized prerogative of sovereignty which was given to Congress by Article I, section, 8, clause 5, in the interest of uniformity in the regulation of commerce.[14]

A power to emit bills on the credit of the United States was proposed by the Committee of Detail but deleted after strenuous debate.[15] Opponents of paper money believed that they had precluded Congress from resorting to that type of currency, which had been emitted freely by the Old Congress, as well as by the states, during the Revolution.[16] Similar sentiments dictated prohibiting the states from issuing paper currency.

The essential feature of bills of credit, within the meaning of the

[11] The prohibition was considered applicable to both types of arrangements by Chief Justice Marshall. Barron v. Baltimore, 7 Pet. 243, 249 (1833).

[12] See page 249 below. Felix Frankfurter and James M. Landis, "The Compact Clause of the Constitution," *Yale Law Journal*, Vol. XXXIV, No. 7 (May, 1925), 685, 695.

[13] See page 163 above. The states were limited by Art. VI of the Articles of Confederation in their power to issue letters of marque and reprisal.

[14] See page 144 above.

[15] See page 109 above. The effect of the deletion upon the power of Congress was ambiguous.

[16] Farrand, *Records*, II, 308–10 (August 16). But see commentary on Art. I, sec. 8, cl. 5, above.

constitutional prohibition in Article I, section 10, clause 1, is that they are intended to circulate as currency, and that they are issued by the state and rest upon its general credit, being unredeemable until a future date and supported by no specific fund.[17] It is not necessary that they be made legal tender.[18] However, the mere fact that the state promises to accept them in discharge of taxes and debts due to itself does not amount to circulation as money.[19] Nor does ownership by the state of all the stock of a bank make unlawful the bank notes issued by the bank. Such notes are issued by the bank, not by the state; and their circulation rests upon the credit of a particular fund in the hands of the bank, not upon the public faith of the state.[20]

Cognate with the prohibition of bills of credit as a means of eliminating the evils of paper money is the provision forbidding states to make anything but gold and silver coin a tender in payment of debts. During the Revolution, the states had passed laws giving the quality of legal tender to the paper issued by the Continental Congress. Other laws had permitted debtors to tender, in satisfaction of executions against them, property at an appraised valuation. Tobacco and other commodities had also served as a medium of exchange in some states.[21]

The prohibition against bills of attainder and ex post facto laws is identical with that laid upon Congress in Article I, section 9, clause 3.[22] Likewise the provision forbidding titles of nobility is equivalent to that in Article I, section 9, clause 8, which is operative upon the federal government.[23]

---

[17] Craig v. Missouri, 4 Pet. 410, 432 (1830); Briscoe v. Bank of Kentucky, 11 Pet. 257, 312–14 (1837); Poindexter v. Greenhow, 114 U.S. 270, 283–85 (1885); Houston & Texas C. R.R. Co. v. Texas, 177 U.S. 66, 85 (1900).

[18] 4 Pet. at 434.

[19] 114 U.S. at 285; 177 U.S. at 83.

[20] 11 Pet. at 322. This is true even if the state is ultimately liable as guarantor. Darrington v. Bank of Alabama, 13 How. 12, 16 (1851). However, if the state could withdraw the bank's assets, after its insolvency, in order to pay debts of the state contracted to borrow the money which became the bank's capital, there would doubtless be violation of the constitutional prohibition. Curran v. Arkansas, 15 How. 317, 318 (1853).

[21] Craig v. Missouri, 4 Pet. 410, 435 (1830); Farrand, *Records*, III, 215, 548; Charles Warren, *Bankruptcy in United States History*, 146–48; Mays, *Edmund Pendleton*, I, 110–11.

[22] See page 194 above.

[23] See page 216 above. States were also forbidden by Art. VI of the Articles of Confederation to grant titles of nobility.

The Contracts Clause

There remains in the instant clause one very important restriction against the states, which has no counterpart in the limitations upon federal legislative power. That is the provision that no state shall pass any law impairing the obligation of contracts.[24]

It should be noted that the language of this prohibition reads that no state shall "pass" any "Law" impairing the obligation of contracts. From this it is clear that the forbidden impairment must be one produced by the exercise, in some form, of the state's legislative authority.[25] Such exertion of state legislative authority need not take the form of a statute; it may be contained in a constitution (or amendment thereto),[26] or a municipal ordinance[27] or administrative regulation[28] enacted pursuant to delegated authority conferred by the state. But it does not include judicial decisions.[29]

This orthodox rule that a contract cannot be impaired, within the meaning of the Constitution, by state judicial decisions was in fact vio-

[24] A belated attempt to impose a like limitation upon Congress was unsuccessfully made by Gerry. Farrand, *Records*, II, 619 (September 14).

[25] In this respect the contracts clause is narrower than the Fourteenth Amendment, which provides that no state shall "deprive any person of life, liberty, or property, without due process of law; nor deny to any person within its jurisdiction the equal protection of the laws." Such deprivation or denial is forbidden, no matter by what agency or instrumentality of the state it is effected, whether legislative, executive, or judicial. Virginia v. Reeves, 100 U.S. 313, 318 (1880); Raymond v. Chicago Traction Co., 207 U.S. 20, 36 (1907); Home Tel. & Tel. Co. v. Los Angeles, 227 U.S. 278, 287 (1913); Shelley v. Kraemer, 334 U.S. 1, 14–18 (1948).

[26] Dodge v. Woolsey, 18 How. 331, 360 (1856); R.R. Co. v. McClure, 10 Wall. 511, 515 (1871); County of Clay v. Society for Savings, 104 U.S. 579, 590 (1882); New Orleans Gas Co. v. Louisiana Light Co., 115 U.S. 650, 672 (1885); Fisk v. Jefferson Police Jury, 116 U.S. 131, 135 (1885); Bier v. McGehee, 148 U.S. 137, 140 (1893); Houston & Texas Central Ry. Co. v. Texas, 170 U.S. 252, 261 (1898); Central of Georgia Ry. v. Wright, 248 U.S. 525, 527 (1919); Coombes v. Getz, 285 U.S. 434, 442 (1932).

[27] Murray v. Charleston, 96 U.S. 432, 444 (1878); Cuyahoga River Power Co. v. Akron, 240 U.S. 462, 464 (1916); Atlantic Coast Line R.R. Co. v. Goldsboro, 232 U.S. 548, 555 (1914).

[28] Appleby v. Delaney, 271 U.S. 403, 409 (1926); L. & N. R.R. Co. v. Garrett, 231 U.S. 298, 318 (1913); Grand Trunk Western Ry. Co. v. R.R. Commission, 221 U.S. 400, 403 (1911).

[29] The leading case is Tidal Oil Co. v. Flanagan, 263 U.S. 444, 451 (1924). See also Central Land Co. v. Laidley, 159 U.S. 103, 109 (1895); Ross v. Oregon, 227 U.S. 150, 161–62 (1913); Cleveland & Pgh. R.R. Co. v. Cleveland, 235 U.S. 50, 54 (1914); Stockholders v. Sterling, 300 U.S. 175, 182 (1937); Barrows v. Jackson, 346 U.S. 249, 260 (1953).

lated by the Supreme Court in several cases;[30] and "unguarded language"[31] in the opinions seemed to cast doubt on the rule. However, these cases were subsequently explained[32] as merely being instances of independent determination by the Supreme Court of issues arising under state law.[33] Since it is now settled that with respect to such questions of state law the Supreme Court must follow the decisions of the state courts,[34] it is clear that the long-standing rule that state court decisions cannot constitute an impairment of the obligation of a contract is now firmly established.

It is also obvious that a law cannot impair the obligation of a contract unless the law is one enacted *after* the contract was made. "Contracts made after the law was in force of course are made subject to it,

[30] The usual situation involved municipal bonds issued to aid the construction of railroads under legislation which had been upheld by the state courts when the bonds were issued but which was later pronounced unconstitutional as employing public credit for the benefit of private corporations. The leading case is Gelpcke v. Dubuque, 1 Wall. 175, 205–206 (1864). See also Great Southern Fireproof Hotel Co. v. Jones, 193 U.S. 532, 548 (1904).

[31] This expression was used by Chief Justice Taft in Tidal Oil Co. v. Flanagan, 263 U.S. 444, 454 (1924). He emphasized that the Gelpcke case and its congeners were not to be regarded as cases applying the contracts clause. In Twp. of Pine Grove v. Talcott, 19 Wall. 666, 678 (1874), it was said: "The National Constitution forbids a State to pass laws impairing the obligation of contracts. In cases properly brought before us that end can be accomplished unwarrantably no more by judicial decisions than by legislation." And in Douglass v. County of Pike, 101 U.S. 677, 687 (1880), it was said: "After a statute has been settled by judicial construction, the construction becomes, so far as contract rights acquired under it are concerned, as much a part of the statute as the text itself, and a change of decision is to all intents and purposes the same in its effect on contracts as an amendment of the law by means of a legislative enactment." In other words, the later court decision was regarded as the equivalent of a new statute which would have violated the contracts clause.

[32] 263 U.S. at 451–53. In Muhlker v. Harlem R.R. Co., 197 U.S. 544, 573 (1905), Justice Holmes said in his dissent: "we are asked to extend to the present case the principle of Gelpcke v. Dubuque. . . . That seems to me a great, unwarranted and undesirable extension of a doctrine which it took this court a long while to explain."

[33] Swift v. Tyson, 16 Pet. 1, 18–19 (1842); Burgess v. Seligman, 107 U.S. 20, 33–34 (1883). Hence it followed that if the case originated in a lower federal court, the Supreme Court followed the Gelpcke doctrine; but if it came up on writ of error from a state court, where the Supreme Court's jurisdiction existed only if a right under the federal Constitution (that is to say, the contracts clause) had been denied by the state court's decision, the case was dismissed for lack of jurisdiction. This is strikingly illustrated by Railroad Co. v. McClure, 10 Wall. 511, 515 (1871), where a case which involved the same bonds which were involved in Gelpcke v. Dubuque was dismissed for lack of jurisdiction. See 263 U.S. at 452.

[34] Erie R.R. Co. v. Tompkins, 304 U.S. 64, 78 (1938). See pages 352–53 below.

and impose only such obligations and create only such property as the law permits."[35] As early as the time of Chief Justice Marshall it was held that the laws in force at the time when a contract is made govern its validity and become part of its terms.[36] And according to a "New Deal" opinion by Chief Justice Hughes, "Not only are existing laws read into contracts in order to fix obligations as between the parties, but the reservation of essential attributes of sovereign power is also read into contracts as a postulate of the legal order."[37]

Similarly, after it had been held, in a famous decision by Chief Justice Marshall, that a charter of incorporation was a contract protected by the Constitution,[38] the practice of including in corporate charters a provision reserving to the state full power to amend or repeal them[39] had the effect of making the original contract conditional in character, so that it could later be modified without any impairment of its obligation. "No question can arise as to the impairment of the obligation of a contract, when the company accepted all of its corporate powers subject to the reserved power of the State to modify its charter and to impose additional burdens upon the enjoyment of its franchise."[40]

[35] Abilene National Bank v. Dolley, 228 U.S. 1, 5 (1913). See also Denny v. Bennett, 128 U.S. 489, 494–95, 498 (1888); Bacon v. Texas, 163 U.S. 207, 216 (1896); Cross Lake Shooting & Fishing Club v. Louisiana, 224 U.S. 632, 638–39 (1912); Munday v. Wisconsin, 252 U.S. 499, 503 (1920); Irving Trust Co. v. Day, 314 U.S. 556, 561–63 (1942).

[36] Ogden v. Saunders, 12 Wheat. 213, 259–60, 368–69 (1827). Hence a state law relieving insolvent debtors could validly be applied to debts subsequently created in that state. Marshall, who dissented in that case, believed that such an interpretation made the contracts clause of transitory value. *Ibid.*, 355. He did not deny that existing law determined whether a valid contract was created or not. *Ibid.*, 348, 354. His dissent was limited to laws relating to discharge of the contract which were in existence at the time of its formation. Here he feared that a general law might subject all subsequent contracts to legislative control, contrary to the intention of the contracts clause. *Ibid.*, 339. It had previously been held in Sturges v. Crowninshield, 4 Wheat. 122, 208 (1819), and McMillan v. McNeill, 4 Wheat. 209, 212 (1819), that a state insolvency law could not validly be applied to pre-existing debts or to debts contracted in another state. See 12 Wheat. at 254–55, 272–73, 333.

[37] Home Bldg. & Loan Assn. v. Blaisdell, 290 U.S. 398, 435 (1934). This case upheld a Minnesota mortgage moratorium statute. The same idea, in a context dealing with civil rights, recurs in Cox v. New Hampshire, 312 U.S. 569, 574 (1941).

[38] Dartmouth College v. Woodward, 4 Wheat. 517, 627, 650 (1819).

[39] Such reservation of power to amend could be contained in the charter itself, or in the state's constitution or general legislation. See Benjamin F. Wright, *The Contract Clause of the Constitution*, 58–59, 84–86, 168–78.

[40] Sioux City Street Ry. Co. v. Sioux City, 138 U.S. 98, 108 (1891). See also

Likewise, there is no impairment of the obligation of a contract when a law is passed which validates a void contract (that is to say, which gives legal effect to a transaction which previously, without the benefit of curative legislation, did not constitute a binding contract).[41]

Moreover, there is no violation of the contracts clause when state legislation, otherwise valid, has an indirect or incidental effect upon contracts, as by discouraging their continuance,[42] or creating a condition of affairs which renders contracts ineffective or regulating the physical objects concerning which parties have contracted.[43] Mere nonperformance or breach of contract by a state (where its liability continues unimpaired) must also be distinguished from impairment of the obligation.[44] So, too, there is no impairment when a contract right is condemned by eminent domain proceedings and just compensation is made.[45]

Plainly, too, there can be no impairment of obligation where such obligation does not exist, that is to say, if there is no contract at all between parties to such an alleged agreement.[46] Ordinarily the question whether a binding contract has been entered into is a question of state law; but in cases arising out of alleged violations of the contracts clause the Supreme Court has long held that, in order to prevent states from

Pennsylvania College Cases, 13 Wall. 190, 214 (1872); Noble State Bank v. Haskell, 219 U.S. 104, 110 (1911); Phillips Petroleum Co. v. Jenkins, 297 U.S. 629, 634–35 (1936).

[41] Satterlee v. Matthewson, 2 Pet. 380, 412 (1829); Ewell v. Daggs, 108 U.S. 143, 150–51 (1883); Gross v. U.S. Mortgage Co., 108 U.S. 477, 488 (1883); National Surety Co. v. Architectural Decorating Co., 226 U.S. 276, 282 (1912).

[42] Thus in Clement Natl. Bank v. Vermont, 231 U.S. 120, 143 (1913), the state taxed deposits in national banks, which had theretofore been untaxed, so that a national bank could offer depositors an advantageous differential in interest rates. The Court held that this did not impair the bank's contracts with depositors.

[43] See also Bridge Proprietors v. Hoboken County, 1 Wall. 116, 149–50 (1864); Knoxville Water Co. v. Knoxville, 200 U.S. 22, 36 (1906); Bayside Fish Co. v. Gentry, 297 U.S. 422, 427 (1936); Henderson Co. v. Thompson, 300 U.S. 258, 266 (1937). Cf. Home Bldg. & Loan Assn. v. Blaisdell, 290 U.S. 398, 438 (1934).

[44] Hays v. Port of Seattle, 251 U.S. 233, 237 (1920). Cf. Walla Walla v. Walla Walla Water Co., 172 U.S. 1, 8 (1898).

[45] Cincinnati v. L. & N. R.R. Co., 223 U.S. 390, 400 (1912); Penna. Hospital v. Philadelphia, 245 U.S. 20, 22 (1917).

[46] R. F. & P. R.R. Co. v. Louisa R.R. Co., 13 How. 71, 81 (1851); Bridge Proprietors v. Hoboken County, 1 Wall. 116, 147–48 (1864); Central Land Co. v. Laidley, 159 U.S. 103, 110 (1895); Ross v. Oregon, 227 U.S. 150, 160–62 (1913); Grand Trunk Western Ry. Co. v. R.R. Commission, 221 U.S. 400, 403–404 (1911).

nullifying their constitutional duty by simply determining that no contract exists, the federal tribunal will ascertain independently (1) whether a contract exists; (2) what its terms are (*i.e.*, what obligation arose from it); and (3) whether such obligation has been impaired by subsequent state legislation.[47]

"What is the obligation of a contract? and what will impair it?" Chief Justice John Marshall asked in the course of one of his well-known opinions dealing with the contracts clause. He went on to reply: "A contract is an agreement, in which a party undertakes to do, or not to do, a particular thing. The law binds him to perform his undertaking, and this is, of course, the obligation of his contract." Hence, "Any law which releases a part of this obligation, must, in the literal sense of the word, impair it." Accordingly it followed that a state law discharging an insolvent debtor from the obligation to pay a note which he had signed before the law went into force violated the contracts clause of the Constitution.[48]

The law which thus creates the obligation of a contract by compelling the parties to perform it is the positive law of a particular state or jurisdiction.[49] However, in an opinion written in 1827, Marshall toys with the notion that contracts are binding by virtue of the law of nature,[50] and that positive law cannot interfere with freedom of contract, a right retained and not surrendered by individuals upon entering into the "social compact" and establishing civil government.[51] A

[47] West Virginia *ex rel*. Dyer v. Sims, 341 U.S. 22, 29 (1951); Detroit United Ry. v. Michigan, 242 U.S. 238, 249 (1916). This rule goes back at least to Taney's opinion in Ohio Life Ins. Co. v. Debolt, 16 How. 416, 432–33 (1854).

[48] Sturges v. Crowninshield, 4 Wheat. 122, 197 (1819). A fortiori, if the law discharges the obligation entirely. *Ibid.*, 197–98. "The amount of the impairment of the obligation is immaterial." Farrington v. Tennessee, 95 U.S. 679, 683 (1878); Von Hoffman v. Quincy, 4 Wall. 535, 552–53 (1868); Planters' Bank v. Sharp, 5 How. 301, 327 (1848). See note 36, page 225, above.

[49] Ogden v. Saunders, 1 Wheat. 213, 259, 283, 300, 320–21 (1827). Marshall's dissent agrees that the Constitution is speaking of legal, not moral, obligation. *Ibid.*, 337–38.

[50] *Ibid.*, 346, 353–54. This was Marshall's first and only dissent during his thirty-four-year tenure as Chief Justice. Benjamin F. Wright, *The Contract Clause*, 50.

[51] Concerning the eighteenth-century ideas of the social compact, derived from John Locke and proclaimed in the Declaration of Independence, see Dumbauld, *The Declaration of Independence and What It Means Today*, 54–74; Dumbauld, *The Political Writings of Thomas Jefferson*, xxv–xxix.

similar intimation had been voiced years before in Marshall's first great case under the contracts clause.[52] In that litigation the purchaser of land sued the seller for breach of warranty of title, alleging that the seller's title, based upon a grant from the state of Georgia under an act passed in 1795, was void by reason of fraud and corruption in procuring passage of the act. The Yazoo scandal was notorious, and the Georgia legislature in 1796 passed legislation declaring that the act of 1795 was unconstitutional, fraudulent, null and void. Meanwhile the original grantees had disposed of the land to investors in other states, who claimed that they had bought it in good faith without knowledge of any fraud affecting the title.

Marshall held that when "a law is in its nature a contract, when absolute rights have vested under that contract, a repeal of the law cannot divest those rights." Indulging in speculation "whether the nature of society and of government does not prescribe some limits to the legislative power," he concluded that if any such implied limitations on the power of government exist, they would surely have the effect of preventing the seizure without compensation of "the property of an individual, fairly and honestly acquired." But Georgia, he went on to say, is limited by the express terms of the contracts clause in the federal Constitution.[53]

Marshall's major exploit and principal innovation was in construing an executed grant as a contract with continuing obligation. This was accomplished by asserting that the grant is accompanied by an implied contract that the grantor will not reassert his ownership over the property with which he has parted.[54] Having established that a grant is a contract, Marshall had little difficulty in concluding that the grants of the state itself, as well as those of individuals, were included within the protection afforded by the contracts clause.[55]

[52] Fletcher v. Peck, 6 Cr. 87, 135, 139 (1810). For a colorful account of the Yazoo speculations, see Beveridge, *Life of John Marshall*, III, 546–602.

[53] 6 Cr. at 135–36. The theory that there are limitations on governmental power "which grow out of the essential nature of all free governments" was again forcefully expressed in Loan Assn. v. Topeka, 20 Wall. 655, 663 (1875).

[54] "A contract executed, as well as one which is executory, contains obligations binding on the parties. A grant, in its own nature, amounts to an extinguishment of the right of the grantor, and implies a contract not to re-assert that right." 6 Cr. at 137.

[55] *Ibid.*, 137. Marshall went on to compare the prohibition against bills of attainder and ex post facto laws. Since Fletcher's estate in the land could not be forfeited for the

The result therefore was that, since the property had "passed into the hands of a purchaser for a valuable consideration without notice, the State of Georgia was restrained, either by general principles which are common to our free institutions, or by the particular provisions of the constitution of the United States, from passing a law whereby the estate of the plaintiff in the premises so purchased could be constitutionally and legally impaired and rendered null and void."[56]

Having thus held that an executed grant of land was a contract, it was not difficult for Marshall to take a further step, in his most influential contracts clause decision, and hold that the grant of a charter of incorporation to Dartmouth College by the crown in 1769 was also a contract.[57] Hence the act of June 27, 1816, by which the New Hampshire legislature sought to reorganize the college, was unconstitutional as impairing the obligation of a contract.[58]

The impact of this decision on regulation of corporate enterprise during the nineteenth century was tremendous. Except where reserved power to amend the charters of corporations was retained by the state at the time of granting the charter,[59] corporations were protected against any later action by the state inconsistent with the terms of the charter.

crimes of others by means of a bill of attainder or an ex post facto law, Marshall reasoned, why should it be taken from him by retroactive legislation annulling his title? *Ibid.*, 138–39. The doctrine established in Fletcher v. Peck is still applied by the Court. Wood v. Lovett, 313 U.S. 362, 369 (1941).

[56] *Ibid.*, 139. Marshall's reference to "general principles common to our free institutions" is quite akin to the present-day concept of "ordered liberty" which the Supreme Court uses in determining what portions of the federal Bill of Rights are applicable against the states by virtue of the Fourteenth Amendment. Dumbauld, *The Bill of Rights and What It Means Today*, 135–36.

[57] Dartmouth College v. Woodward, 4 Wheat. 517, 627 (1819). The donors, the trustees of the college, and the crown were said to be the parties to this contract. Marshall admitted that the framers of the Constitution might not have had such a transaction in mind when adopting the contracts clause. *Ibid.*, 643–44. The Dartmouth College case was decided on February 2, 1819. Fifteen days later came Sturges v. Crowninshield, for which see note 36, page 225, above.

[58] *Ibid.*, 626, 650, 652. Marshall did not go so far as to contend that the "social compact," establishing civil government, was protected by the contracts clause against change. He conceded that if Dartmouth College was a public institution or political body, it was subject to reorganization by the state. *Ibid.*, 629–30. But he found it to be a private eleemosynary institution. *Ibid.*, 640–41. Marshall also admitted that the contract of marriage was subject to impairment by the state's authority to grant divorces. *Ibid.*, 629.

[59] See note 39, page 225, above.

Monopolistic grants to public utilities, restrictions upon the taxing power, and other privileges which adroit lobbyists were able to include in charters were sacrosanct against amendment or repeal.[60]

The case which established the rule that a state may validly barter away its taxing power by contract[61] was also decided in Marshall's time.[62] However, in another opinion by Marshall it was declared that any relinquishment of the taxing power, or any other public grant, is to be construed strictly against the grantee and in favor of the public.[63] Since the ordinary function of a legislature is to legislate,[64] the courts whenever possible will construe a legislative enactment as a law, embodying public policy which can be altered when circumstances change,

[60] See Blair v. Chicago, 201 U.S. 400, 471 (1906).

[61] New Jersey v. Wilson, 7 Cr. 164, 166–67 (1812). There land purchased for Indians pursuant to an act of August 12, 1758, under a provision that it "shall not hereafter be subject to any tax," was sold, after the Indians moved away, under an act of December 3, 1801, saying nothing about taxation. A later act of December 1, 1804, repealing the act of 1758, was held unconstitutional, as violating the contracts clause. In Given v. Wright, 117 U.S. 648, 656 (1886), it was held that the exemption attaching to this particular land had been lost by nonuser.

[62] The rule, though often criticized, has never been abandoned. Typical cases include Piqua Branch v. Knoop, 16 How. 369, 389 (1854); Murray v. Charleston, 96 U.S. 432, 444 (1878); Erie R.R. v. Pennsylvania, 153 U.S. 628, 644 (1894); American Smelting Co. v. Colorado, 204 U.S. 103, 113–14 (1907); Central of Georgia R.R. Co. v. Wright, 248 U.S. 525, 527 (1919).

[63] Providence Bank v. Billings, 4 Pet. 514, 561 (1830). The same principle was reaffirmed by Chief Justice Taney in a famous case, Charles River Bridge v. Warren Bridge, 11 Pet. 420, 548 (1837). Typical later cases include R. F. & P. R.R. Co. v. Louisa R.R. Co., 13 How. 71, 81 (1851); Christ Church v. Philadelphia, 24 How. 300, 302 (1861); Delaware R.R. Tax, 18 Wall. 206, 225 (1874); R.R. Co. v. Ga., 98 U.S. 359, 363 (1878); R.R. Commission Cases, 116 U.S. 307, 325 (1886); Covington v. Kentucky, 173 U.S. 231, 239 (1899); Knoxville Water Co. v. Knoxville, 200 U.S. 22, 33–34 (1906); Blair v. Chicago, 201 U.S. 400, 471–72 (1906); Larson v. South Dakota, 278 U.S. 431, 435 (1929); Puget Sound Power & Light Co. v. Seattle, 291 U.S. 619, 627 (1934); N.Y. Rapid Transit Co. v. City of New York, 303 U.S. 573, 594 (1938); Keefe v. Clark, 322 U.S. 393, 396–97 (1944); Atlantic Coast Line v. Phillips, 332 U.S. 168, 172–73 (1947).

[64] "The principal function of a legislative body is not to make contracts but to make laws which declare the policy of the state and are subject to repeal when a subsequent legislature shall determine to alter that policy. Nevertheless, it is established that a legislative enactment may contain provisions which, when accepted as the basis of action by individuals, become contracts between them and the State or its subdivisions." Indiana ex rel. Anderson v. Brand, 303 U.S. 95, 100 (1938). See also West Chicago Street Railroad Co. v. Chicago, 201 U.S. 506, 521 (1906); Home Telephone Co. v. Los Angeles, 211 U.S. 265, 274 (1908); Texas & N.O. R.R. Co. v. Miller, 221 U.S. 408, 415 (1911).

rather than as a contract, which is protected by the contracts clause from subsequent modification or change.[65] The nuances involved in this distinction are strikingly illustrated by the varieties of legislation enacted with respect to the tenure of teachers in public schools.[66]

Unlike its power to tax, a state's power of eminent domain cannot be bartered away by contract. The power to condemn property for public use can always be exercised, provided just compensation be made. Where the taking violates a previous contract purporting to grant immunity from condemnation, additional compensation for the contract right which is confiscated must be made.[67]

Similarly, a state's police power is inalienable and cannot be bartered away by contract. This important principle was first clearly enunciated[68] when in 1869 Massachusetts enacted a prohibition law. This legislation was upheld when assailed under the contracts clause as impairing a beer company's charter granted in 1829. The Supreme Court declared: "Whatever differences of opinion may exist as to the extent and boundaries of the police power, and however difficult it may be to render a satisfactory definition of it, there seems to be no doubt that it does extend to the protection of the lives, health, and property of the citi-

[65] Christ Church v. Philadelphia, 24 How. 300, 302 (1861); Seton Hall College v. South Orange, 242 U.S. 100, 104–106 (1916); Troy Union R.R. Co. v. Mealy, 254 U.S. 47, 50 (1920). The question is one of legislative intent, and "a legislative enactment, in the ordinary form of a statute, may contain provisions which, when accepted as the basis of action by individuals or corporations, become contracts between them and the State." New Jersey v. Yard, 95 U.S. 104, 114 (1877). See note 64, page 230, above.

[66] In Dodge v. Board of Education of Chicago, 302 U.S. 74, 78–81 (1937), it was held that nothing more than statutory benefits or pensions had been created for retired teachers; and in Phelps v. Bd. of Education, 300 U.S. 319, 322–23 (1937), it was held that the tenure act there involved created only legislative, not contractual, status. But in Indiana *ex rel.* Anderson v. Brand, 303 U.S. 95, 105 (1938), the teachers' rights were found to be contractual.

[67] Cincinnati v. L. & N. R.R. Co., 223 U.S. 390, 400 (1912); Pennsylvania Hospital v. Philadelphia, 245 U.S. 20, 22–23 (1917). In the latter case legislation of 1854, in consideration of ground donated by the hospital for streets, forbade the opening of any street or alley through the hospital grounds. In 1913 the city, under later legislation, condemned "not only the land desired for the street, but the [hospital's] rights under the contract of 1854." *Ibid.*, 22.

[68] There had been earlier intimations of the principle in the statements of those Justices who dissented from the doctrine that the taxing power can be contracted away. Piqua Branch v. Knoop, 16 How. 369, 389, 398, 415 (1854); Ohio Life Ins. Co. v. Debolt, 16 How. 416, 442, 443, 444 (1854). See Benjamin F. Wright, *The Contract Clause*, 196–203.

zens, and to the preservation of good order and the public morals. The legislature cannot, by any contract, divest itself of the power to provide for these objects."[69]

Soon afterwards the same rule was applied to the charter of a corporation organized in 1867 for the purpose of "converting dead animals and other animal matter into an agricultural fertilizer" when the inhabitants of a growing Chicago suburb found "that the stench was intolerable," and an ordinance abating the nuisance was adopted under authority conferred by legislation enacted in 1869.[70] The charter of a lottery company met a similar fate when a Southern state's policy with respect to gambling changed after its Reconstruction government was replaced.[71] Likewise the rates fixed by a railroad pursuant to its charter powers were held to be subject to regulation by the state.[72]

While recognizing that the contracts clause does not restrict the police power of the state with respect to such matters as safety of a gas company's operations, the Court has held that such matters have no connection with the economic question of whether the franchise should be exercised by one monopolistic entrepreneur or by many competing concerns. Hence the protection of the contracts clause was accorded to the exclusive feature of a company's contract as against the contention that protection of the public from the evil effects of monopoly was an exercise of police power which could not be forestalled by contract.[73]

With respect to rate regulation of public utilities, the Court has held that it is a question of state law whether a municipality is authorized to bind itself by an irrevocable contract, for a reasonable period of time, not to exercise its power to regulate or otherwise modify the privileges granted to a company in its franchise. If such authority exists and is exercised, the contract rights thus created are protected by the federal Constitution against impairment.[74]

[69] Beer Co. v. Massachusetts, 97 U.S. 25, 32–33 (1878).

[70] Fertilizing Co. v. Hyde Park, 97 U.S. 659, 663–64, 667 (1878).

[71] Stone v. Mississippi, 101 U.S. 814, 817–18 (1880).

[72] R.R. Commission Cases, 116 U.S. 307, 329–30 (1886).

[73] New Orleans Gas Co. v. Louisiana Light Co., 115 U.S. 650, 671–72 (1885).

[74] Walla Walla v. Walla Walla Water Co., 172 U.S. 1, 13–15 (1898); Los Angeles v. Los Angeles City Water Co., 177 U.S. 558, 570, 577–78 (1900); Freeport Water Co. v. Freeport, 180 U.S. 587, 593 (1901); Vicksburg v. Vicksburg Waterworks Co., 206 U.S. 496, 508, 515–16 (1907); Home Telephone Co. v. Los Angeles, 211 U.S. 265, 273 (1908).

Numerous later cases have continued to emphasize the principle that contract rights are subject to the police power.[75]

Another important aspect of applying the contracts clause is the distinction between the obligation of a contract and the remedy provided for enforcement of the contract. This distinction dates from Chief Justice Marshall's early decisions involving the contracts clause. Marshall said: "The distinction between the obligation of a contract, and the remedy given by the legislature to enforce that obligation, has been taken at the bar, and exists in the nature of things. Without impairing the obligation of the contract, the remedy may certainly be modified as the wisdom of the nation may direct."[76]

But although the remedy may be changed, it cannot be totally eliminated, leaving the parties destitute of any remedy whatsoever.[77] "Nothing can be more material to the obligation than the means of enforcement."[78] When the remedy existing at the time of making the contract is altered, there must be left an adequate alternative remedy,

[75] For example, Pearsall v. G. N. Ry. Co., 161 U.S. 646, 666 (1896); Manigault v. Springs, 199 U.S. 473, 480–81 (1905); Noble State Bank v. Haskell, 219 U.S. 104, 110 (1911); Texas & N. O. R.R. Co. v. Miller, 221 U.S. 408, 414 (1911); Atlantic Coast Line R.R. Co. v. Goldsboro, 232 U.S. 548, 558 (1914); D. & R. G. R.R. Co. v. Denver, 250 U.S. 241, 244 (1919); Marcus Brown Co. v. Feldman, 256 U.S. 170, 198 (1921); Midland Realty Co. v. Kansas City Power & Light Co., 300 U.S. 109, 113 (1937); Home Bldg. & Loan Assn. v. Blaisdell, 290 U.S. 398, 436–37 (1934); Veix v. Sixth Ward B. & L. Assn., 310 U.S. 32, 38–40 (1940); East N.Y. Svgs. Bank v. Hahn, 326 U.S. 230, 232–34 (1945); Day-Brite Lighting, Inc. v. Missouri, 342 U.S. 421, 423–25 (1952).

[76] Sturges v. Crowninshield, 4 Wheat. 122, 200 (1819). Hence imprisonment for debt may be abolished. "Imprisonment is no part of the contract, and simply to release the prisoner does not impair its obligation." *Ibid.*, 201. See also Ogden v. Saunders, 12 Wheat. 213, 349–51 (1827).

[77] In Bronson v. Kinzie, 1 How. 311, 315–17 (1843), the Court said: "It is difficult, perhaps, to draw a line . . . between legitimate alterations of the remedy and provisions which, in the form of remedy, impair the right. But it is manifest that the obligation of the contract and the rights of a party under it, may, in effect be destroyed by denying a remedy altogether; or may be seriously impaired by burdening the proceedings with new conditions and restrictions." Illinois laws extending for twelve months the right to redeem after foreclosure, and prohibiting sale unless two-thirds of the value of the property sold, as determined by three householders, was bid therefor, were held to violate the contracts clause. *Ibid.*, 312, 319–20. However, the right to sue the state itself may be withdrawn without violation of the clause. Beers v. Arkansas, 20 How. 528, 529 (1858). Cf. R.R. Co. v. Tennessee, 101 U.S. 337, 339 (1879).

[78] Von Hoffman v. Quincy, 4 Wall. 535, 552–53 (1867); Walker v. Whitehead, 16 Wall. 314, 317 (1873); Edwards v. Kearzey, 96 U.S. 595, 600 (1878).

or a "substantial equivalent" must be provided.[79] If the remedy is materially abridged, there is a violation of the contracts clause.[80] The problem is most often presented in connection with legislation for exemptions from execution[81] or for the relief of mortgagors or banks[82] in times of financial stringency or depression.

A new era in interpretation of the contracts clause may be said to have begun with the notable decision of Chief Justice Hughes in 1934 upholding the constitutionality of a Minnesota mortgage moratorium statute enacted during a period of severe economic depression.[83] This decision relied not only upon the power of the state to modify the remedy but also upon the use of the police power to protect the public welfare in a time of emergency. If the police power is capable of affording temporary relief from the strict enforcement of contracts in the presence of disasters such as fire, flood, earthquake, or scarcity of housing, surely it is equally potent when the urgent public need for such relief arises from economic rather than physical causes.[84] The Court emphasized that "While emergency does not create power, emergency may furnish occasion for the exercise of power."[85]

The course of judicial decisions applying the contracts clause, says Chief Justice Hughes, makes it clear that "the prohibition is not an absolute one and is not to be read with literal exactness like a mathematical formula."[86] On the contrary, the contracts clause must be construed so as to effect a "rational compromise" or mutual accommoda-

[79] Mobile v. Watson, 116 U.S. 289, 305 (1886); Richmond Mtge. & Loan Corp. v. Wachovia Bank, 300 U.S. 124, 128–29 (1937); Oshkosh Waterworks Co. v. Oshkosh, 187 U.S. 437, 439 (1903).

[80] McGahey v. Virginia, 135 U.S. 662, 693 (1890); Oshkosh Waterworks Co. v. Oshkosh, 187 U.S. 437, 439 (1903).

[81] Edwards v. Kearzey, 96 U.S. 595, 598–99, 604, 607 (1878).

[82] Barnitz v. Beverly, 163 U.S. 118, 129 (1896); Hooker v. Burr, 194 U.S. 415, 419 (1904); Doty v. Love, 295 U.S. 64, 70 (1935); Veix v. Sixth Ward B. & L. Assn., 310 U.S. 32, 38–41 (1940).

[83] Home Bldg. & Loan Assn. v. Blaisdell, 290 U.S. 398, 447 (1934). Justice George Sutherland's dissent (in which Justices Willis Van Devanter, James C. McReynolds, and Pierce Butler joined) was a notable expression of his conservative philosophy. Ibid., 448–83.

[84] Ibid., 434, 439–40. This conclusion was reiterated in Veix v. Sixth Ward B. & L. Assn., 310 U.S. 32, 38–39 (1940).

[85] 290 U.S. at 426.

[86] Ibid., 428. This is true even though "the contract clause is associated in the same section with other and more specific prohibitions." Ibid., 427.

tion between it and the police power.[87] "This principle of harmonizing the constitutional prohibition with the necessary residuum of state power has had progressive recognition in the decisions of this Court."[88]

Applying these concepts to the Minnesota legislation, the Court found that it was justified by an emergency which furnished a proper occasion for exercise of the police power "to protect the vital interests of the community."[89] The Court emphasized that "the legislation was not for the mere advantage of particular individuals but for the protection of a basic interest of society." The interests of both mortgagors and mortgagees were taken into consideration in an effort "to prevent the impending ruin of both."[90]

In other post-depression litigation the Court continued to apply the same liberality of construction when dealing with the contracts clause. The modern trend is to appraise realistically the pecuniary value of a creditor's rights as measured in the market place, and to afford practical protection for his interests as thus defined, rather than for all his abstract legal rights as embodied in the terms of the contract. Hence the Court tends to uphold as a proper exertion of police power any modification of the remedy which does not diminish the actual value of a claim based upon contract, or which prevents a fortunately situated creditor from obtaining more than the amount to which he is justly entitled.

[87] "The reserved power cannot be construed so as to destroy the limitation, nor is the limitation to be construed to destroy the reserved power in its essential aspects. They must be construed in harmony with each other." *Ibid.*, 439. See also East N.Y. Bank v. Hahn, 326 U.S. 230, 232 (1945), where it is said that the Blaisdell case "put the Clause in its proper perspective in our constitutional framework."

[88] 290 U.S. at 435. "The economic interest of the State may justify the exercise of its continuing and dominant protective power notwithstanding interference with contracts. . . . It is manifest from this review of our decisions that there has been a growing appreciation of public needs and of the necessity of finding ground for a rational compromise between individual rights and public welfare." *Ibid.*, 442.

[89] *Ibid.*, 444. The temporary, emergency character of the legislation is stressed. *Ibid.*, 447.

[90] *Ibid.*, 445, 446. The Court noted the provisions in the statute for the protection of the mortgagee's interest, for example, the requirement that the mortgagor pay rent while remaining in possession. These features served to distinguish the case at bar from earlier decisions condemning mortgage moratorium legislation as a violation of the contracts clause. *Ibid.*, 434. It was also noted that the mortgagees involved were investors, concerned with the value of their investment, and not persons "seeking homes or the opportunity to engage in farming." *Ibid.*, 446.

Thus, there was no impairment of the obligation of contracts when an insurance company was reorganized under a plan which provided for the issuance of cancellable in place of noncancellable health policies, when dissenting policyholders were not obliged to accept the new policies, but had the option of receiving under the plan an amount equal to what they could have gotten as the result of a sale of the company's assets followed by a pro rata distribution of the proceeds.[91] Similarly, there was no violation of the contracts clause when a closed bank was reopened under a plan whereby stockholders who put up new capital were released from liability on their old shares. There were precautions in the plan which assured that all of the bank's assets would be applied to the payment of its debts, and that no profits could be made by the holders of new stock until all the debts had been paid. Hence the Court regarded the reopening of the bank as merely a different method of liquidating its assets, and pointed out that collection of items due the bank would be facilitated by its continued operation as a going concern. Creditors of the bank would therefore fare better than if liquidation were conducted by a receiver. Hence there was no impairment of their position; indeed, through the subscription of new capital, they received an advantage which they could not have obtained if there had been no legislative change in the method of liquidation.[92] Likewise the police power has been held to justify legislation curtailing a depositor's contractual right to withdraw his money from a financial institution.[93]

The modern tendency of looking to see whether the challenged legislation really harms the creditors in terms of dollars and cents is strikingly illustrated in a case involving municipal bonds. New Jersey legislation applied to insolvent municipalities the principles of equity receivership and provided that a plan of converting outstanding bonds

---

[91] Neblett v. Carpenter, 305 U.S. 297, 305 (1938).

[92] Doty v. Love, 295 U.S. 64, 68, 70–74 (1935).

[93] Veix v. Sixth Ward B. & L. Assn., 310 U.S. 32, 38 (1940). "Certainly the protection of building and loan associations against the catastrophe of excessive withdrawal is, today, within legislative power." *Ibid.*, 41. This case did not involve emergency legislation, but there was danger to the public interest. *Ibid.*, 37. Treigle v. Acme Homestead Assn., 297 U.S. 189, 194–96 (1936), was speciously distinguished. 310 U.S. at 41. Perhaps the Veix case illustrates the principle that "when a widely diffused public interest has become enmeshed in a network of multitudinous private arrangements" the authority of the state to safeguard the vital interests of its people cannot be defeated by treating a single contract as an isolated instance, constitutionally immune from impairment. East N.Y. Savings Bank v. Hahn, 326 U.S. 230, 232 (1945).

into new bonds at a lower interest rate should become binding, after court approval, upon all creditors. The validity of this procedure was upheld by the Supreme Court when it was challenged under the contracts clause.

The Court's opinion emphasized that "The principal asset of a municipality is its taxing power and that, unlike an asset of a private corporation, cannot be available for distribution. . . . A city cannot be taken over and operated for the benefit of its creditors, nor can its creditors take over the taxing power." The practical value of an unsecured claim against a city depends upon the effectiveness of its taxing power. The only remedy for the enforcement of such a claim is a mandamus or court order to compel the collection of taxes. But experience "shows that the right to enforce claims against the city through mandamus is the empty right to litigate." What is needed is "a temporary scheme of public receivership" assuring "impartial outside control over the finances of the city; concerted action by all the creditors to avoid destructive action by individuals; and rateable distribution." Such an arrangement offers the possibility of a workable and realistic plan of effectuating payment. "A policy of every man for himself is destructive." The best means of safeguarding the interests of creditors is by protecting the goose that lays the golden eggs, namely the revenue from taxes.[94]

Such methods do not violate the contracts clause. "The Constitution is 'intended to preserve practical and substantial rights, not to maintain theories.' " Whether the remedy has been impaired must be determined by considering what it was worth in practice. Nothing but confusion results "if we deal with empty abstract rights instead of worldly gains and losses."[95] The New Jersey legislation has the effect of resuscitating, rather than impairing, the value of the city's financial obligations. "To call a law so beneficent in its consequences on behalf of the creditor who, having had so much restored to him, now insists on the paper rights that were merely paper before this resuscitating scheme, an impairment of the obligation of contract is indeed to make of the Constitution a code of lifeless forms instead of an enduring framework of government for a dynamic society."[96]

[94] Faitoute Iron & Steel Co. v. Asbury Park, 316 U.S. 502, 509–12 (1942).
[95] *Ibid.*, 514, 515.
[96] *Ibid.*, 516. The Court points out that the new bonds had gone up in the market

THE CONSTITUTION OF THE UNITED STATES

Recent cases likewise establish that legislation is constitutional which merely prevents a creditor from profiting from a debtor's distress and collecting more than is rightfully due.[97] Hence when a mortgagee buys in the mortgaged property at a foreclosure sale, the legislature may properly direct that he shall not in addition obtain a deficiency judgment except for the excess of his debt over the fair and reasonable market value of the property acquired at the sale. "To hold that mortgagees are entitled under the contract clause to retain the advantages of a forced sale would be to dignify into a constitutionally protected property right their chance to get more than the amount of their contracts. . . . The contract clause does not protect such a strategical, procedural advantage."[98]

Another aspect of the application of the contracts clause which dates back to Marshall's time is the rule that it does not curtail the state's unfettered control over its own political institutions and governmental subdivisions.[99] The charter of a municipal corporation (unlike that of a private corporation) is not a contract protected by the federal Constitution against modification by subsequent legislation. Likewise subject to amendment or repeal at any time are laws conferring governmental powers upon a municipality, vesting it with public property, or exempting it from taxation. The state may at its discretion, with or without the consent of the residents of a municipality, or against their protest, reorganize or abolish the municipal corporation, or extend or curtail its geographical boundaries.[100] There is no implied contract, protected by

---

from 69 to 90. *Ibid.*, 513. Legislation which merely provides a more effectual remedy has uniformly been upheld under the contracts clause. Bernheimer v. Converse, 206 U.S. 516, 530 (1907).

[97] Richmond Mtge. & Loan Corp. v. Wachovia Bank, 300 U.S. 124, 130 (1937); Honeyman v. Jacobs, 306 U.S. 539, 542 (1939); Gelfert v. National City Bank, 313 U.S. 221, 223–24 (1941).

[98] Gelfert v. National City Bank, 313 U.S. 221, 234 (1941). Here, as in the Veix case, there was no reliance on the emergency character of the legislation, stressed in the Blaisdell opinion of Chief Justice Hughes. See notes 89 and 93, pages 235 and 236, above. Justice Douglas likewise discards more overtly the prior precedents distinguished in the Blaisdell case. "We cannot permit the broad language which those early decisions employed to force legislatures to be blind to the lessons which another century has taught." *Ibid.*, 235.

[99] Dartmouth College v. Woodward, 4 Wheat. 517, 629–30 (1819). See note 58, page 229, above.

[100] Hunter v. Pittsburgh, 207 U.S. 161, 178–79 (1907). This is true even where the city is asserting contractual rights as assignee of a private grantee. Trenton v. New

the Constitution, between a municipality and its citizens, that their taxes should be used only for the benefit of the area comprising the city at a particular time, and not for the benefit of a larger area into which the municipality may be merged by virtue of state legislation.[101]

During the heyday of the contracts clause, however, there was an exception to the principle that a state may alter or abolish municipal boundaries as it sees fit.[102] A law altering or abolishing a unit of local government would be held unconstitutional if it withdrew the municipality's taxing power in such a manner as to deprive creditors of an adequate remedy to enforce their contract with the municipality. Since the usual mode of obtaining funds to pay municipal debts is taxation, the taxing power possessed by the municipality at the time when a debt is contracted was regarded as an essential part of the creditor's remedy, which could not be taken away by subsequent legislation, unless an equivalent remedy was available. Federal courts frequently issued writs of mandamus to municipal officers to collect taxes levied under previously existing legislation for the purpose of paying debts.[103]

Public offices, as well as municipal corporations, are subject to a state's control. Hence laws creating a public office, or prescribing the salary to be paid to the incumbent thereof, do not constitute contracts.

Jersey, 262 U.S. 182, 184–86 (1923). Whether a state could, if it chose, confer upon a city the capacity to enter into private contracts with the state which would be protected by the federal Constitution is an open question. Boston v. Jackson, 260 U.S. 309, 316 (1922).

[101] 207 U.S. at 177. Private contracts implied in fact, as well as express contracts, have been protected by the contracts clause since Marshall's day. Fletcher v. Peck, 6 Cr. 87, 137 (1810); Ogden v. Saunders, 12 Wheat. 213, 341 (1817); Fisk v. Jefferson Police Jury, 116 U.S. 131, 134 (1885). See note 54, page 228, above. But the clause does not cover contracts implied by law, or obligations arising out of statutory liability. Louisiana v. Mayor of New Orleans, 109 U.S. 285, 287–88 (1833). So, too, a judgment not based on consent or agreement is not a contract within the meaning of the contracts clause. *Ibid.*, 288; Freeland v. Williams, 131 U.S. 411, 413 (1889); Garrison v. City of New York, 21 Wall. 196, 203 (1875).

[102] Another recent exception to the principle was enunciated in Gomillion v. Lightfoot, 364 U.S. 339, 342–45 (1960), where a rearrangement of municipal boundaries for the purpose of depriving residents of their right to vote, in violation of the Fifteenth Amendment, was held unconstitutional.

[103] Von Hoffman v. Quincy, 4 Wall. 535, 555, (1867); Butz v. Muscatine, 8 Wall. 575, 578 (1869); Meriwether v. Garrett, 102 U.S. 472, 501 (1880); Nelson v. St. Martin's Parish, 111 U.S. 716, 720 (1884); Mobile v. Watson, 116 U.S. 289, 305 (1886); Graham v. Folsom, 200 U.S. 248, 253 (1906). Cf. Faitoute Iron & Steel Co. v. Asbury Park, 316 U.S. 502, 510 (1942). See note 94, page 237, above.

The office may be abolished or the compensation reduced without violation of the contracts clause.[104] However, if the officer has in fact performed the prescribed service before the statute fixing his compensation therefor has been repealed or modified, "there arises an implied contract to pay for those services at that rate."[105] Moreover, a state may, if its legislation so provides, enter into contracts of employment, which are protected by the federal Constitution. The question sometimes arises whether certain employees (notably teachers in the public schools) enjoy contractual status or merely statutory status, subject to subsequent modification.[106]

The heyday of the contracts clause was the period from 1865 to 1890, during the tenures of Salmon P. Chase and of Morrison R. Waite as Chief Justice.[107] After 1890 the due process clause, rather than the contracts clause, was usually employed as the means of invalidating state legislation. A flurry of cases under the contracts clause arose as the aftermath of depression legislation enacted for the relief of widespread economic distress. Such measures received discriminating scrutiny at the hands of the Supreme Court.[108] In recent years the contracts clause has been of slight practical importance, being largely overshadowed by the due process clause.

[104] Butler v. Pennsylvania, 10 How. 402, 416–17 (1851); Higginbotham v. Baton Rouge, 306 U.S. 535, 538 (1939).

[105] Fisk v. Jefferson Police Jury, 116 U.S. 131, 134 (1885). The obligation of the implied contract is perfect, and confers a vested right to the compensation earned. Such right is protected by the contracts clause. To the same effect see Hall v. Wisconsin, 103 U.S. 5, 8 (1880).

[106] See note 66, page 231, above.

[107] Chase served from 1865 to 1873; Waite from 1873 to 1888. Under Chase, of fifty-two state statutes held unconstitutional, twenty were stricken down under the contracts clause. This was a mortality rate of almost 60 per cent of the total number of contracts clause cases considered. Under Waite, statutes were stricken down under the contracts clause in twenty-nine cases. Before 1889, state statutes were held unconstitutional under the contracts clause in seventy-five cases, almost 50 per cent of all the cases of unconstitutionality. The clause was invoked in almost 40 per cent of all cases involving validity of state legislation. Subsequently the percentage diminished. Benjamin F. Wright, *The Contract Clause of the Constitution*, 93–100.

[108] Minnesota's mortgage moratorium legislation was sustained in the Blaisdell case, but that case "did not sound the death knell of the contract clause." *Ibid.*, 100. In Worthen Co. v. Kavanaugh, 295 U.S. 59, 60 (1935), the Court struck down Arkansas legislation which, in the opinion of Justice Cardozo, "put restraint aside" and with "studied indifference to the interests of the mortgagee" took from the mortgage "the quality of an acceptable investment for a rational investor."

ARTICLE I—THE LEGISLATIVE BRANCH

Restrictions upon State Power, *Conditional Prohibitions*

ART. I, SEC. 10, CL. 2

No State shall, without the Consent of the Congress, lay any Imposts or Duties on Imports or Exports, except what may be absolutely necessary for executing it's inspection Laws: and the net Produce of all Duties and Imposts, laid by any State on Imports or Exports, shall be for the Use of the Treasury of the United States; and all such Laws shall be subject to the Revision and Controul of the Congress.

HISTORY

THE word "the" preceding "Congress" in this clause is twice interlined on the original parchment. The correction was apparently not made in the following clause, Article I, section 10, clause 3.

In Randolph's draft for the Committee of Detail, supplementing the power of Congress to regulate commerce, an interlineation in Rutledge's hand reads "no State to lay a duty on imports."[109] The Committee of Detail in its report provided that "No State, without the consent of the Legislature of the United States, shall . . . lay imposts or duties on imports."[110] The words "or exports" were added on motion of King.[111] On motion of Sherman a further addition was made: "nor with such consent but for the use of the treasury of the United States."[112]

Mason offered an additional proposal: "Provided nothing herein contained shall be construed to restrain any State from laying duties

[109] Farrand, *Records*, II, 143. A draft in Wilson's handwriting enumerates among powers denied to the states: "nor lay any Imposts or Duties on Imports." *Ibid.*, II, 169.

[110] Art. XIII. *Ibid.*, II, 187 (August 6). A motion by Madison to transfer this provision regarding imports from Art. XIII where the prohibition was conditional to Art. XII "which will make the prohibition on the States absolute" was defeated. *Ibid.*, II, 435, 441 (August 28). Such a transfer had just been made in the case of the prohibition of bills of credit and tender laws. *Ibid.*, II, 435, 439 (August 28).

[111] *Ibid.*, II, 435, 442 (August 28). Langdon had remarked, during the debate on prohibiting taxation of exports by Congress, that "the States are left at liberty to tax exports," and "suggested a prohibition on the States from taxing the produce of other States exported from their harbours." *Ibid.*, II, 359, 361 (August 21).

[112] *Ibid.*, II, 437, 442–43 (August 28). The Committee of Style made no change. *Ibid.*, II, 597 (September 12).

upon exports, for the sole purpose of defraying the charges of inspecting, packing, storing, and indemnifying the losses in keeping the Commodities, in the care of public Officers, before exportation."[113] This provision was inspired by the Virginia system of storing tobacco in public warehouses.[114] Madison and Morris supported the suggestion. Dayton, Gorham, and Langdon feared the possibility of oppression directed against states exporting through the ports of other states. "How was redress to be obtained in case duties should be laid beyond the purpose expressed?" Madison replied: "There will be the same security as in other cases—The jurisdiction of the supreme Court must be the source of redress. . . . His own opinion was that this was insufficient." But his favorite scheme of a negative on state laws had been overruled. Dickinson urged that nothing would save states in the situation of New Hampshire, New Jersey, Delaware, and others in the same position, from being oppressed by their neighbors, but requiring the assent of Congress to inspection duties.[115]

On the following day Mason offered a revision of his proposal, incorporating Dickinson's suggestion: "Provided that no State shall be restrained from imposing the usual Duties on produce exported from such State, for the sole purpose of defraying the charges of inspecting, packing, storing, and indemnifying the losses on such produce, while in the custody of public Officers: but all such regulations shall, in case of abuse, be subject to the revision and controul of Congress."[116] A substitute version, in the present form of the clause (Article I, section 10, clause 2), was then adopted, Virginia alone voting against it after an unsuccessful attempt to eliminate the requirement of supervision by Congress.[117]

INTERPRETATION

THE absolute prohibition forbidding Congress to tax exports provides (Article I, section 9, clause 5) that: "No Tax or Duty shall be laid on Articles exported from any State." The corresponding conditional ban on state taxation in the instant clause forbids "any Imposts or Duties,"

[113] *Ibid.*, II, 583, 588 (September 12).

[114] *Ibid.*, III, 268. See note 21, page 222, above. For numerous instances of inspection laws, see Turner v. Maryland, 107 U.S. 38, 51–54 (1883).

[115] Farrand, *Records*, II, 589.

[116] *Ibid.*, II, 605, 607 (September 13).

[117] *Ibid.*, II, 624 (September 15).

as contrasted with taxes or duties; and the exempted subjects include "Imports" as well as "Exports" (as contrasted with "Articles exported from any State").

An impost is evidently a tax or duty on imports, as distinguished from one on exports. A duty is a tax levied on either importation or exportation. There is no distinction recognized in judicial decisions between "exports" and "articles exported." Both the federal and state exemptions are construed as extending to the entire process of exportation, and including not only the articles exported but all instrumentalities of exportation.[118]

But what is included in the term "imports," which are exempt from state taxation, but subject to taxation by Congress?

Here, too, not just the articles imported but the process of importation is protected from state taxation. In one of the early cases under this clause, the Supreme Court struck down a Maryland law requiring all importers of foreign articles to take out a license, costing fifty dollars, before selling a bale or package of the imported goods.[119] The Court emphasized that in practice there was no difference between a power to prohibit the sale of an article and a power to prohibit its introduction into the country. "No goods would be imported if none could be sold."[120] The object of importation is sale; and fair dealing requires that an importer who has paid duties to the United States should be permitted to dispose of the articles imported by selling them in the original package without being subject to interference by state legislation. Undoubtedly "there must be a point of time when the prohibition ceases, and the power of the State to tax commences." Without attempting to lay down a rule of universal application, the Court said that "when the importer has so acted upon the thing imported, that it has become incorporated and mixed up with the mass of property in the country, it has, perhaps, lost its distinctive character as an import, and has become subject to the taxing power of the State."[121]

[118] The authorities establishing this principle have been considered in connection with Art. I, sec. 9, cl. 5. See page 207 above.

[119] Brown v. Maryland, 12 Wheat. 419, 437–38 (1827).   [120] *Ibid.*, 439.

[121] *Ibid.*, 441–42. The same criterion would apply to goods brought in for the importer's own use. *Ibid.*, 443. A dictum by Chief Justice Marshall intimating that the term "imports" includes goods brought from another state (*ibid.*, 448) was repudiated in Woodruff v. Parham, 8 Wall. 123, 139 (1869). It was there held that the term is to be interpreted as including only imports from a foreign country. *Ibid.*, 131, 132, 136.

Goods imported for the importer's own use do not lose their distinctive character as imports any sooner than those imported for sale.[122] But when imported raw materials enter the manufacturing process, or become part of the inventory required for current operational needs, they have lost their distinctive character as imports and become taxable by the states.[123]

Fish caught inside the three-mile limit cannot be considered as imports.[124]

The net revenue derived from all state taxes on imports or exports must go to the use of the United States. No such taxes may be imposed without the consent of Congress,[125] except in the case of "inspection laws." What type of legislation falls within this exception?

Originally the Virginia laws relating to the storage, inspection, and export of tobacco were in Mason's mind when he offered the proposal which led to the provision authorizing inspection laws. Many states had such laws relating to the form, size, weight, and marking of the packages in which their staple commodities were prepared for marketing.[126] Hence the Supreme Court rejected the contention that a Maryland enactment could not be an inspection law because it did not require

[122] Hooven & Allison Co. v. Evatt, 324 U.S. 652, 667 (1945). This case held that goods from the Philippines were imports. *Ibid.*, 679.

[123] Youngstown Sheet & Tube Co. v. Bowers, 358 U.S. 534, 546–49 (1959). In this case ore was placed in piles, mingled with other ore of the same sort, from which it was taken to bins containing a two-day supply. Bundles of imported veneers were broken open only at the time of use, and green lumber was piled in a manner that permitted it to dry. The Court emphasized that breaking the original package was only one way of so acting upon the imported articles as to terminate their distinctive character as imports; putting them to the use for which they were imported is another. In McGoldrick v. Gulf Oil Corp., 309 U.S. 414, 423, 429 (1940), the Court assumed, without deciding, that crude petroleum became part of the general mass of property when converted into fuel oil, but found the state tax inapplicable because of conflict with the policy of federal laws permitting import of oil in bond for use as ships' stores in foreign trade.

[124] Toomer v. Witsell, 334 U.S. 385, 394 (1948). On its face the state statute here involved did not impose tax on shrimp caught beyond the three-mile belt, and the Court had no occasion to rule upon the extent of the state's power in the abstract.

[125] No instances are known of a state tax imposed with consent of Congress on imports or exports. Conceivably a state might wish to promote consumption of its own products or to discourage consumption of luxurious imports by imposing a tax in addition to the duty imposed on such articles by Congress. Farrand, *Records*, II, 441; Woodruff v. Parham, 8 Wall. 123, 133 (1869).

[126] For a list of inspection laws, see Turner v. Maryland, 107 U.S. 38, 51–54 (1883).

the packages of tobacco to be opened and the quality tested.[127] However, a law prohibiting the transportation of liquor into Iowa from another state could not be justified as an inspection law.[128] To determine whether the article is merchantable and fit for its intended use would be a legitimate function of an inspection law, but to exclude it, regardless of its quality or condition, because its use is regarded as harmful or undesirable could not be sanctioned under this clause.[129]

If the charge made under an inspection law is exorbitant, the statute becomes a revenue measure and ceases to be permissible as an inspection law. If the receipts are excessive, it is presumed that the legislature will act to reduce them.[130] If the legislature takes no action, the courts will declare the exaction unconstitutional.[131]

ART. I, SEC. 10, CL. 3

No State shall, without the Consent of Congress, lay any Duty of Tonnage, keep Troops, or Ships of War in time of Peace, enter into any Agreement or Compact with another State, or with a foreign Power, or engage in War, unless actually invaded, or in such imminent Danger as will not admit of delay.

HISTORY

EXCEPT for the provision relating to tonnage, this clause had been a part of a lengthy article reported by the Committee of Detail.[132] It

[127] *Ibid.*, 49.

[128] Now, of course, a state can exclude intoxicants under the Twenty-first Amendment. See Duckworth v. Arkansas, 314 U.S. 390, 398 (1941).

[129] Bowman v. C. & N.W. Ry. Co., 125 U.S. 465, 488–89 (1888). "It has never been regarded as within the legitimate scope of inspection laws to forbid trade in respect to any known article of commerce, irrespective of its condition and quality, merely on account of its intrinsic nature and the injurious consequences of its use or abuse."

[130] Patapsco Guano Co. v. N.C., 171 U.S. 345, 354 (1898); Sprout v. South Bend, 277 U.S. 163, 169 (1928); Bourgeois, Inc. v. Chapman, 301 U.S. 183, 187–88 (1937); Hale v. Bimco Trading Co., 306 U.S. 375, 379, 381 (1939).

[131] Phipps v. Cleveland Refining Co., 261 U.S. 449, 450–51 (1923). It has been suggested that perhaps Congress is the only agency appropriate to determine whether a charge under an inspection law is excessive. Turner v. Maryland, 107 U.S. 38, 55 (1883). Congress has, of course, under the terms of this clause paramount power over inspection laws. Currin v. Wallace, 306 U.S. 1, 12 (1939). Compare the similar problem discussed in McCarroll v. Dixie Greyhound Lines, 309 U.S. 176, 188–89 (1940).

[132] Art. XIII, containing conditional prohibitions upon the states. Farrand,

was based on similar provisions in the Articles of Confederation.[133] Randolph's draft in the Committee of Detail contained language empowering Congress "To regulate the force permitted to be kept in each state."[134] The Committee version read: "No State, without the consent of the Legislature of the United States, shall . . . keep troops or ships of war in time of peace; nor enter into any agreement or compact with another State, or with any foreign power; nor engage in any war, unless it shall be actually invaded by enemies, or the danger of invasion be so imminent, as not to admit of delay, until the Legislature of the United States can be consulted."[135]

The provision on tonnage duties originated with the Maryland delegation. McHenry noted: "Upon looking over the constitution it does not appear that the national legislature can *erect light houses* or *clean out or preserve the navigation of harbours*—This expence ought to be borne by commerce—of course by the general treasury into which all the revenue of commerce must come."[136]

Accordingly, when the remainder of the prohibitions on state action recommended by the Committee of Style were under consideration, McHenry and Carroll moved that "no State shall be restrained from laying duties of tonnage for the purpose of clearing harbours and erecting lighthouses." Mason in support of this proposal explained "the situation of the Chesapeak which peculiarly required expences of this sort." Gouverneur Morris pointed out that "The States are not restrained from laying tonnage as the Constitution now stands." Madison doubted this conclusion, thinking that the state's power was precluded by the commerce clause. "He was more & more convinced that the regulation of Commerce was in its nature indivisible and ought to be wholly under one authority." Sherman saw no danger from a concurrent jurisdiction, since the federal power was supreme and could

---

Records, II, 187 (August 6). Bills of credit and legal tender had been transferred to the catalogue of absolute prohibitions which became Art. I, sec. 10, cl. 1. The language relating to imports and exports had been expanded to such an extent that it split off and became a separate clause, Art. I, sec. 10, cl. 2. The remaining part (concerning armaments, compacts, and war) became Art. I, sec. 10, cl. 3. The Committee of Style made only verbal changes ("nor" for "or"; "Congress" for "Legislature of the United States"). *Ibid.*, II, 597 (September 12).

[133] Art. VI. [134] Farrand, *Records*, II, 144.

[135] *Ibid.*, II, 187 (August 6). This language was approved without amendment on August 28. *Ibid.*, II, 437, 442–43. [136] *Ibid.*, II, 504 (September 4).

correct undesirable state regulations. Langdon insisted "that the regulation of tonnage was an essential part of the regulation of trade, and that the States ought to have nothing to do with it." A motion was agreed to "that no State shall lay any duty on tonnage without the Consent of Congress."[137] The whole paragraph was then remolded into its present form.[138]

INTERPRETATION

HISTORICALLY, "tonnage" was understood as a tax upon the privilege of access to the ports of a state, as distinguished from a charge for services or facilities provided by the state such as pilotage, towage, stevedoring, wharfage, storage, and the like. "Hence the prohibition against tonnage duties has been deemed to embrace all taxes and duties regardless of their name or form, and even though not measured by the tonnage of the vessel, which operate to impose a charge for the privilege of entering, trading in, or lying in a port. . . . But it does not extend to charges made by state authority, even though graduated according to tonnage, for services rendered to and enjoyed by the vessel, such as pilotage, or wharfage; or charges for the use of locks on a navigable river, or fees for medical inspection."[139]

The maintenance of a well-regulated militia by a state is not regarded as keeping "troops" in violation of this clause.[140] Madison cited as evils experienced under the Articles of Confederation the treaties and wars with Indians carried on by Georgia, the troops kept up without the consent of Congress by Massachusetts, and the compacts between Pennsylvania and New Jersey and between Virginia and Maryland entered into without the consent of Congress.[141]

---

[137] *Ibid.*, II, 625 (September 15). See also *ibid.*, 633–34.

[138] *Ibid.*, II, 626 (September 15).

[139] Clyde Mallory Lines v. Alabama, 296 U.S. 261, 265–66 (1935). A charge for policing and administration of the port of Mobile was upheld as valid, although imposed in the amount of $7.50 on all ships, since it was beneficial to them generally, and was not for a special service, such as pilotage, which might not be used by a particular vessel.

[140] Presser v. Illinois, 116 U.S. 252, 264 (1886). Nor is it "war" when a state resorts to armed force for the purpose of suppressing an internal insurrection. Luther v. Borden, 7 How. 1, 45 (1849). Indeed, it is the duty of the federal government to protect a state upon request against such "domestic violence." Art. IV, sec. 4.

[141] Farrand, *Records*, III, 548. From the legislative journals of Virginia it appears, Madison notes, that a vote to apply for the sanction of Congress was followed by a

Control of the army was a crucial point in dispute between the king and Parliament during the English civil war.[142] The English Bill of Rights of 1689 ordained "That the raising or keeping a standing army within the kingdom in time of peace, unless it be with consent of parliament, is against law."[143] The influence of this principle was strong in America. Charles Pinckney of South Carolina offered such a provision in the Philadelphia convention, but nothing came of it.[144] Six states desired an amendment to the Constitution covering that point,[145] but Madison refused to reopen any issues disposed of at the convention.[146] The prohibition of armed forces in Article I, section 10, clause 3, may be an echo of this widely accepted maxim derived from English experience and precedent.

It is more likely, however, that the instant clause is an attempt to deprive the individual states of all power over foreign relations.[147] Shorn of the physical power to wage war, as well as of the legal right to engage in hostilities except in emergencies, the states were likewise forbidden to conduct diplomatic negotiations and to conclude treaties. Article XIII as reported by the Committee of Detail covered the topics of that nature contained in Article VI of the Articles of Confederation which had not been incorporated in Article XII of the Committee's draft.[148]

Article VI contained two formulations of the forbidden treaty power: no state could "enter into any conference, agreement, alliance

vote against communication of the compact to Congress. These compacts are mentioned also in Wharton v. Wise, 153 U.S. 155, 170-71 (1894), where the Court draws the inference that the consent of Congress was not necessary from the circumstance that it was not sought.

[142] Churchill, *The New World*, 231, 262, 330-31.

[143] Dumbauld, *The Bill of Rights and What It Means Today*, 168.

[144] *Ibid.*, 5.

[145] *Ibid.*, 33, 163.

[146] *Ibid.*, 26.

[147] These powers were conferred exclusively upon the central government by Art. IX of the Articles of Confederation, as well as by the Constitution. Cf. Clark v. Allen, 331 U.S. 503, 516-17 (1947), and Holmes v. Jennison, 14 Pet. 540, 569, 572 (1840).

[148] Art. XII as reported by the Committee of Detail contained absolute prohibitions on the states. Here were placed issuance of letters of marque and reprisal and entering into "any treaty, alliance, or confederation" (both derived from Art. VI of the Articles of Confederation). The Articles of Confederation contained no such absolute prohibitions upon the states except with regard to titles of nobility; all the other forbidden practices specified in Art. VI could be authorized by the consent of Congress. See note 1, page 218, above.

or treaty with any king, prince or state";[149] nor could two or more States "enter into any treaty, confederation or alliance whatever between them," except under specified restrictions.[150] The latter wording seems to have been drawn upon to furnish the language of Article I, section 10, clause 1;[151] while from the former the term "agreement" was apparently borrowed by Rutledge to describe the type of compact permissible (with the consent of Congress) under Article I, section 10, clause 3.[152]

Since the framers of the Constitution were skilled in the use of language and every word in the instrument has meaning, it is clear that there is a distinction between a "treaty" and an "agreement."[153] It is less clear what the distinction is. One plausible view, suggested by Chief Justice Taney, is that the framers were adopting definitions derived from Vattel's celebrated treatise on the law of nations, according to which a "treaty" is executory over a long period of time or in perpetuity, whereas an "agreement" is concerned with transitory matters (such as a cession of territory) and is consummated by a single act of performance once for all.[154] Another view, advanced by Justice Story, regarded a "treaty" as a compact relating to political matters, whereas an "agreement" was one relating to "mere private rights of sovereignty," such as the establishment of boundaries and of regulations for the mutual comfort and convenience of bordering states.[155] Later

[149] Possibly this prohibition relates only to agreements with foreign nations; but the word "state" would presumably include one of the United States, since the following clause in Art. VI, dealing with acceptance of gifts by officers of the United States, speaks of "any king, prince or *foreign* state." (Italics supplied.)

[150] Hence it has been argued that under the Confederation "agreements" between states could be made without the consent of Congress; such an "agreement" being, as defined by Vattel, a compact having for its object a matter of temporary interest, fulfilled once for all by a single act (such as a cession of territory), whereas a "treaty" is executory in character over a long period of time or in perpetuity. Weinfeld, "What Did the Framers of the Federal Constitution Mean by 'Agreements or Compacts'?" *loc. cit.*, 453, 456, 460; Emmerich de Vattel, *Droit des Gens*, l.I, c. 12, § 153; Holmes v. Jennison, 14 Pet. 540, 572 (1840); Kansas v. Colorado, 185 U.S. 125, 140 (1902).

[151] The prohibition in Art. I, sec. 10, cl. 1, against "any Treaty, Alliance, or Confederation" forbids such an arrangement between two or more states of the United States, as well as with foreign nations. This clause, it would seem, relates only to combinations which present a potential danger politically. See pages 220–21 and note 10, page 220, above.

[152] Farrand, *Records*, II, 169.   [153] Holmes v. Jennison, 14 Pet. 540, 571 (1840).

[154] *Ibid.*, 572. See note 150 just above.

[155] Kansas v. Colorado, 185 U.S. 125, 140 (1902).

writers regard as hopeless the attempt to distinguish the two categories by means of any analytical test based upon subject-matter; in their opinion any compact to which Congress gives its consent should be deemed an "agreement" falling within the permitted class of transactions.[156]

Another troublesome problem is the question whether the term "agreement" should be given "its most extended signification," as Chief Justice Taney believed, to include unwritten and implied agreements of every character and description;[157] or whether later dicta should be accepted, according to which the term embraces only compacts of significant political importance involving the national interest, by reason of possible interference with the constitutional functions of the federal government or with the political balance of power among the states.[158]

The latter view, which would permit certain types of agreements between states to be made without the consent of Congress, appears to be unsound. The actual decisions upholding state action where approval by Congress was not secured can be explained as not actually amounting to agreements or compacts between states, but as being merely measures taken separately by two or more states in the exercise of their individual

[156] Frankfurter and Landis, "The Compact Clause of the Constitution," *loc. cit.*, 685, 695. The reasons for "leaving to Congress to circumscribe the area of agreement open to the States" are similar to those for leaving to Congress other political questions such as whether a state's form of government is "republican" within the meaning of Art. IV, sec. 4. See Pacific States T. & T. Co. v. Oregon, 223 U.S. 118, 133, 143 (1912); and note 131, page 245, above.

[157] Holmes v. Jennison, 14 Pet. 540, 572 (1840). In this case the question was whether the governor of Vermont could deliver to Canadian authorities a fugitive from justice. This question was not decided, as the case was dismissed for lack of jurisdiction. Justice John Catron accepted the finding of fact that no demand for delivery of Holmes had been made by Canada; therefore there was no "agreement," and hence no possible violation of the Constitution to be reviewed by the Court. *Ibid.*, 596–97. Though Catron's vote necessitated dismissal of the writ of error upon procedural grounds and left the question of substantive law undecided, the Vermont court released Holmes because it was satisfied that a majority of the Justices of the United States Supreme Court would have discharged him if the record had shown, as a supplemental return before the state court did, that in fact a request had been made by the governor general of Lower Canada. Ex parte Holmes, 12 Vt. 631, 641 (1840).

[158] Virginia v. Tennessee, 148 U.S. 503, 518–19 (1893). This language is repeated in Wharton v. Wise, 153 U.S. 155, 170 (1894); Louisiana v. Texas, 176 U.S. 1, 17 (1900); and Stearns v. Minnesota, 179 U.S. 223, 246–47 (1900).

powers. For example, if each of two bordering states recognizes a given line as the true boundary between them, there is no agreement or compact thereby created between them; but after such double recognition of the correct line any dispute theretofore existing with respect to the location of the boundary is eliminated by reason of each state's admission of the correctness of such line and the resulting disappearance of any divergence of views between the two states with respect thereto.[159] In like manner legislation applicable only if reciprocal provisions are effective in other states does not constitute a compact or agreement.[160] What a state has power to do of its own volition it can certainly do in co-ordination with harmonious action by another state.[161]

On the other hand, there is no reason why the rule of antitrust law that a contract, combination, or conspiracy in restraint of trade can result from conscious parallel action without specific agreement[162] should not apply in appropriate cases to interstate dealings. Indeed, it would seem that the Supreme Court has often been unduly astute to find the existence of a compact, and also to find consent to it by Congress.[163] Thus the admission of a state into the Union under a constitution containing contingent provisions for incorporating certain counties into the state was construed as consent to a compact so incorporating them.[164] Consent to a boundary settlement has likewise been implied from the subsequent action of Congress in establishing judicial districts

[159] Virginia v. Tennessee, 148 U.S. 503, 520 (1893); North Carolina v. Tennessee, 235 U.S. 1, 7 (1914).

[160] Clark v. Allen, 331 U.S. 503, 517 (1947); Bode v. Barrett, 344 U.S. 583, 586 (1953). Similarly in Holmes v. Jennison, 14 Pet. 540, 573, 596 (1840), the mere delivery of a fugitive by Vermont, without any request by Canada, was considered by the Justice whose vote was determinative of the disposition made of the case as not amounting to an "agreement" with a foreign state.

[161] The situation is somewhat analogous to the distinction between treaty and executive agreement in the international sphere. What the President has power to do by virtue of his executive power he can do in concert with another nation. See note 66, page 292, below.

[162] Interstate Circuit Inc., v. U.S., 306 U.S. 208, 226–27 (1939).

[163] Virginia v. West Virginia, 11 Wall. 39, 59 (1871).

[164] *Ibid.*, 60. See also Green v. Biddle, 8 Wheat. 1, 85–87 (1823), where admission of Kentucky under a constitution incorporating a compact with Virginia was construed as consent by Congress to the compact. The Court points out that the federal Constitution "makes no provision respecting the mode or form in which the consent of Congress is to be signified, very properly leaving that matter to the wisdom of that body." *Ibid.*, 85–86.

and election districts in accordance with the boundary as established by the states.[165]

As the Supreme Court said: "The Constitution does not state when the consent of Congress shall be given, whether it shall precede or may follow the compact made, or whether it shall be express or may be implied." In many cases it will be given in advance, but "where the agreement relates to a matter which could not well be considered until its nature is fully developed, it is not perceived why the consent may not be subsequently given," and given by implication.[166] Consent may also be given conditionally.[167]

In another instance of highly artificial and ingenious interpretation, the Court held that a state can make a compact with all the other states, represented by Congress, whose consent is evinced by its having proposed the terms of the compact and declared the state admitted on those terms.[168]

A compact between states is a contract the obligation of which cannot be impaired by state legislation.[169] It is a contract specific performance of which can be decreed by a court.[170] Congress can also provide remedies to ensure enforcement of a compact.[171] Although a compact is not "a law of the United States,"[172] its interpretation presents a federal

[165] Virginia v. Tennessee, 148 U.S. 503, 522 (1893).

[166] *Ibid.*, 521.

[167] Arizona v. California, 292 U.S. 341, 345 (1934); James v. Dravo Contracting Co., 302 U.S. 134, 148 (1937); Frankfurter and Landis, "The Compact Clause of the Constitution," *loc. cit.*, 685, 695.

[168] Stearns v. Minnesota, 179 U.S. 223, 248 (1900). The act of Congress admitting the state to the Union imposed a condition prohibiting taxation of federal property and interference with disposal by the federal government of public lands owned by it. *Ibid.*, 244. The Court doubtless wished to construe this as a compact in order to bring within the impairment of the obligation of contracts clause of the Constitution (Art. I, sec. 10, cl. 1) an act of state legislation changing the mode of taxing lands granted by the state to a railroad after they had been granted to the state by the United States. *Ibid.*, 225, 232, 253.

[169] Art. I, sec. 10, cl. 1; Green v. Biddle, 8 Wheat. 1, 92 (1823). See also note 167 just above.

[170] Kentucky v. Indiana, 281 U.S. 163, 178 (1930).

[171] Virginia v. West Virginia, 246 U.S. 565, 601 (1918): "The power of Congress to refuse or to assent to a contract between States carried with it the right, if the contract was assented to and hence became operative by the will of Congress, to see to its enforcement."

[172] Hinderlider v. La Plata Co., 304 U.S. 92, 109 (1938). Cf. Pennsylvania v. Wheeling Bridge Co., 13 How. 518, 566 (1852). Congress does not legislate when

question, ultimately determinable by the Supreme Court of the United States.[173] Such power in the Court is inescapable, since under Article III of the Constitution it has jurisdiction of all justiciable controversies between states,[174] and since such a controversy would arise if it were permissible for each state to pass independently upon the validity and construction of interstate compacts.

For a compact is a quasi-international treaty. As stated by Justice Brandeis, in rejecting a contention that a compact was invalid because it was the result of a compromise or trade rather than of a judicial decision of conflicting claims: "The compact—the legislative means—adapts to our Union of sovereign States the age-old treaty-making power of independent sovereign nations."[175] Before the Constitution, the states could enter into compacts as freely as sovereign nations into treaties.[176] After the adoption of the Constitution, they were restored to their original liberty to make compacts, if Congress consented.[177] Hence a compact entered into between states binds their citizens.[178] "The framers thus astutely created a mechanism of legal control over affairs that are projected beyond State lines and yet may not call for, nor be capable of, national treatment. They allowed interstate adjustments but duly safeguarded the national interest."[179]

it consents to a compact, any more than a state does when it ratifies an amendment to the Constitution. Hawke v. Smith, 253 U.S. 221, 229 (1920).

[173] 304 U.S. at 110; Del. River Commission v. Colburn, 310 U.S. 419, 427 (1940); Dyer v. Sims, 341 U.S. 22, 28 (1951); Petty v. Tenn.-Mo. Bridge Commission, 359 U.S. 275, 278 (1959).

[174] Kansas v. Colorado, 206 U.S. 4, 83–84, 97 (1907); Dyer v. Sims, 341 U.S. 22, 28 (1951). The United States may intervene in such suits, since otherwise the litigant states by collusion might evade the requirement of federal consent contained in the compact clause. Florida v. Georgia, 17 How. 478, 495 (1855).

[175] Hinderlider v. La Plata Co., 304 U.S. 92, 104 (1938).

[176] Compacts between states entered into before the Constitution remained in force after its adoption (except in case of actual conflict with its terms). The requirements of Art. I, sec. 10, cl. 3, are not applicable to such pre-existing compacts, but apply only *in futuro.* Wharton v. Wise, 153 U.S. 155, 171 (1894).

[177] Rhode Island v. Massachusetts, 12 Pet. 657, 752 (1838).

[178] Poole v. Fleeger, 11 Pet. 185, 209 (1837).

[179] Frankfurter and Landis, "The Compact Clause of the Constitution," *loc. cit.,* 685, 695. With respect to such matters Congress cannot legislate. Kansas v. Colorado, 206 U.S. 46, 97 (1907). War and diplomacy are banned to the states by the Constitution. Rhode Island v. Massachusetts, 12 Pet. 657, 726 (1838); Louisiana v. Texas, 176 U.S. 1, 17 (1900); Kansas v. Colorado, 185 U.S. 125, 143 (1902). But this does not mean that they must "submit to whatever might be done" by their neigh-

Early examples of interstate compacts related chiefly to boundaries, recognition of land titles, and regulation of interstate waters. Modern agreements cover a wide variety of public works, particularly the construction and operation of bridges, and the equitable distribution of water supply from interstate streams. The Port of New York Authority, created in 1921 by the states of New York and New Jersey, is a notable illustration of an important interstate enterprise established by means of compact.[180]

Another significant instance of interstate regulation of matters of general importance by means of compact is afforded by the compact of February 16, 1935, on conservation of oil and gas. This agreement, originally adopted by six states, is now in force among thirty states.[181]

An unusual form of compact, but one which may become more familiar as the need for improved educational facilities becomes increasingly urgent, is that between New Hampshire and Vermont, approved by Congress on November 13, 1963, establishing a joint interstate school district.[182]

---

bors: Georgia v. Tennessee Copper Co., 206 U.S. 230, 237 (1907). Compacts entered into with the consent of Congress, and the original jurisdiction of the Supreme Court over interstate controversies, furnish the appropriate remedy for the protection of state interests.

[180] Frankfurter and Landis, "The Compact Clause of the Constitution," loc. cit., 730–54.

[181] 49 Stat. 939; 77 Stat. 145

[182] Act of November 13, 1963, 77 Stat. 332. It will be noted that the actual agreement establishing the interstate district was between the school boards of the two localities concerned, but was authorized by identical legislation enacted by each state separately.

ARTICLE II—THE EXECUTIVE BRANCH
Mode of Election and Qualification

ART. II, SEC. 1, CL. 1 *through* CL. 4

The executive Power shall be vested in a President of the United States of America. He shall hold his Office during the Term of four Years, and, together with the Vice President, chosen for the same Term, be elected, as follows

Each State shall appoint, in such Manner as the Legislature thereof may direct, a Number of Electors, equal to the whole Number of Senators and Representatives to which the State may be entitled in the Congress: but no Senator or Representative, or Person holding an Office of Trust or Profit under the United States, shall be appointed an Elector.

The Electors shall meet in their respective States and vote by Ballot for two Persons, of whom one at least shall not be an Inhabitant of the same State with themselves. And they shall make a List of all the Persons voted for, and of the Number of Votes for each; which List they shall sign and certify, and transmit sealed to the Seat of the Government of the United States, directed to the President of the Senate. The President of the Senate shall, in the Presence of the Senate and House of Representatives, open all the Certificates, and the Votes shall then be counted. The Person having the greatest Number of Votes shall be the President, if such Number be a Majority of the whole Number of Electors appointed; and if there be more than one who have such Majority, and have an equal Number of Votes, then the House of Representatives shall immediately chuse by Ballot one of them for President; and if no Person have a Majority, then from the five highest on the List the said House shall in like Manner chuse the President. But in chusing the President, the Votes shall be taken by States, the Representation from each State having one Vote; A quorum for this Purpose shall consist of a Member or Members from two thirds of the States, and a Majority of all the States shall be necessary to a Choice. In every Case, after the Choice of the President, the Person having the greatest Number of Votes of the Electors shall be the Vice President. But if there should remain two or more who have equal Votes, the Senate shall chuse from them by Ballot the Vice President.

The Congress may determine the Time of chusing the Electors,
and the Day on which they shall give their Votes; which Day shall
be the same throughout the United States.

HISTORY

NO problem proved more troublesome to the framers of the Constitution than that of establishing the executive, particularly the mode of election and the length of term.[1] Many differences of opinion were voiced, and the convention frequently reversed itself in the course of its perplexed deliberations. The plan finally adopted was formulated in the closing days of the session, but proved to be almost the only important feature of the Constitution which escaped severe censure by opponents.[2] The objectives which members sought were to maintain the executive's independence of the legislature, and also to prevent the possibility of intrigue by foreign nations seeking to intermeddle in the election.[3]

The seventh resolution in the Virginia Plan proposed "that a National Executive be instituted; to be chosen by the National Legislature for the term of [seven][4] years, to receive punctually at stated times, a fixed compensation for the services rendered, in which no increase or diminution shall be made so as to effect the Magistracy, existing at the time of increase or diminution, and to be ineligible a second time; and that besides a general authority to execute the National laws, it ought to enjoy the Executive rights vested in Congress by the Confederation."[5] The Committee of the Whole, after the word "instituted," added "with power to carry into execution the national laws," and "to appoint to offices in cases not otherwise provided for."[6] Another addi-

---

[1] Farrand, *Records*, II, 118, 501; III, 132, 166, 394, 458. See page 51 above.

[2] Warren, *The Making of the Constitution*, 630, citing Hamilton in *The Federalist* (No. 78).

[3] Warren, *The Making of the Constitution*, 357–65, 623. See note 30, page 260, below.

[4] In Randolph's resolution the number of years was left blank. The blank was filled with "seven" in Committee of the Whole. Farrand, *Records*, I, 64, 69 (June 1).

[5] *Ibid.*, I, 21 (May 29).

[6] *Ibid.*, I, 63, 67 (June 1). This language, proposed by Madison and seconded by Wilson, replaced the wording in the resolution regarding the authority of the executive. A third clause proposed by them failed of adoption: "and to execute such powers, not legislative or judiciary in their nature, as may from time to time be delegated by the national legislature." This may have been derived from Jefferson's 1783 draft of a constitution for Virginia. Warren, *The Making of the Constitution*, 177.

256

tion made the executive subject "to be removable on impeachment and conviction of mal-practice or neglect of duty."[7] Not until after several days of intensive debate did Wilson's motion prevail that the executive was "to consist of a single person."[8]

When Wilson first brought forward this proposal, a considerable pause ensued. When the chairman asked if he should put the question, Dr. Franklin "observed that it was a point of great importance and wished that the gentlemen would deliver their sentiments on it before the question was put." Wilson and Rutledge spoke in favor of the motion, pointing out that there would be more energy, secrecy, dispatch, and responsibility with a single magistrate. Sherman and Randolph strenuously disagreed. The former "considered the Executive magistracy as nothing more than an institution for carrying the will of the Legislature into effect, that the person or persons ought to be appointed by and accountable to the Legislature only, which was the despositary [*sic*] of the supreme will of the Society." Hence as the legislature "were the best judges of the business which ought to be done by the Executive department, and consequently of the number necessary from time to time for doing it," he wished that the legislature should be left free to appoint one or more as experience might dictate.[9] He favored making the executive "absolutely dependent" on the legislature, as it was the will of the legislature that was to be executed. "An independence of the Executive on the supreme Legislative, was in his opinion the very essence of tyranny if there was any such thing."[10] Randolph regarded a single executive "as the foetus of monarchy."[11]

Considerable discussion likewise preceded acceptance of the provision in the original resolution that the executive was "to be chosen by

[7] Farrand, *Records*, I, 78, 88 (June 2).

[8] *Ibid.*, I, 63, 65–66 (June 1); I, 93, 97 (June 4). The language regarding salary was silently simplified to read "to receive a fixed stipend by which he may be compensated for the devotion of his time to public service to be paid out of the national Treasury." *Ibid.*, I, 230, 236. Apparently no vote was taken, in deference to Benjamin Franklin, who had proposed that no salary be paid. *Ibid.*, I, 81–85 (June 2); Meigs, *The Growth of the Constitution*, 195.

[9] Farrand, *Records*, I, 65.

[10] *Ibid.*, I, 68. See note 10, page 320, below.

[11] *Ibid.*, I, 66. Randolph continued his argument the next day. *Ibid.*, I, 88, 90 (June 2). He favored an executive of three persons, one from each of three regional groups of states. Wilson pointed out that "All the 13 States, tho' agreeing in scarce any other instance, agree in placing a single magistrate at the head of the Governmt." *Ibid.*, I, 96 (June 4).

the National Legislature."[12] Wilson proposed, with timidity at first, his plan of popular election through an electoral college which ultimately won acceptance. "Mr. Wilson said he was almost unwilling to declare the mode which he wished to take place, being apprehensive that it might appear chimerical. He would say however at least that in theory he was for an election by the people," a mode successfully practiced in New York and Massachusetts.[13] His first venture at establishing an electoral college, however, was rejected.[14] A subsequent proposition by Gerry that the national executive should be elected by the executives of the states met the same fate.[15]

Randolph's original proposal that the executive be chosen by the legislature, for a term of seven years, to be ineligible a second time, as amended during debate, was approved by the Committee of the Whole.[16] It went to the Committee of Detail in the same form,[17] but had meanwhile been replaced by several other proposals. At first it had been modified by deletion of the provision for ineligibility.[18] Upon reconsideration of this action two days later, an entirely different scheme was adopted. The executive was to be chosen by electors appointed by

[12] Ibid., I, 77, 81 (June 2).

[13] Ibid., I, 68 (June 1). He wished to derive not only both branches of the legislature from the people, without the intervention of the state legislatures, but the executive also, in order to make them as independent as possible of each other, as well as of the states. Ibid., I, 69. For the Massachusetts and New York provisions regarding election of the governor, see Thorpe, Federal and State Constitutions, III, 1900; V, 2632.

[14] Farrand, Records, I, 77, 80–81 (June 2). Strong opposition to popular election was voiced by Sherman, Pinckney, Mason, and Williamson. Ibid., II, 29–32 (July 17). Mason said that "it would be as unnatural to refer the choice of a proper character for chief Magistrate to the people, as it would, to refer a trial of colours to a blind man." Ibid., II, 31. Gerry declared "The people are uninformed, and would be misled by a few designing men." Ibid., II, 57 (July 19).

[15] Ibid., I, 174–76 (June 9). Gerry renewed this proposal later but without success. Ibid., II, 57 (July 19); II, 109 (July 25).

[16] Ibid., I, 230, 236 (June 13).

[17] Ibid., II, 116, 120–21 (July 26). Reinstatement of the article as reported by the Committee of the Whole was voted on the motion of Mason, after he had reviewed the various modes of election which had been proposed. Ibid., II, 118–20 (July 26). Madison had in the course of a similar review observed that "There are objections agst. every mode that has been, or perhaps can be proposed." Ibid., II, 109–11 (July 25).

[18] Ibid., II, 23, 33 (July 17). Election by the legislature and the seven-year term were retained. Ibid., II, 22, 23, 32, 36. A motion by Morris for election by the people, supported by Wilson, was defeated; so was a proposal by Luther Martin for election by electors appointed by state legislatures. Ibid., II, 22, 29, 32.

the state legislatures; the term was to be six years, without ineligibility.[19]

During the debate that led to this decision, Gouverneur Morris took the lead in opposing ineligibility. Such a ban, he declared, would "destroy the great incitement to merit public esteem by taking away the hope of being rewarded with reappointment. It may give a dangerous turn to one of the strongest passions in the human breast. The love of fame is the great spring to noble & illustrious actions. Shut the Civil road to Glory & he may be compelled to seek it by the sword." It would also tempt the executive to make the most of the short space of time allotted him to accumulate wealth and provide for his friends.[20] Morris "saw no alternative for making the Executive independent of the Legislature but either to give him his office for life, or make him eligible by the people."[21] Randolph favored election by the legislature with ineligibility to be chosen a second time.[22] King "did not like the ineligibility. He thought . . . that he who has proved himself to be the most fit for an Office, ought not to be excluded by the constitution from holding it. . . . On the whole he was of opinion that an appointment by electors chosen by the people for the purpose, would be liable to fewest objections."[23] Madison supported this suggestion; while Paterson and Ellsworth proposed electors chosen by the states, rather than by the people.[24] Wilson remarked that "It seems to be the unanimous sense that the Executive should not be appointed by the Legislature," unless rendered ineligible a second time. Wilson also "perceived with pleasure that the idea was gaining ground, of an election mediately or immediately by the people."[25]

[19] *Ibid.*, II, 50–51, 58–59 (July 19). Details of the plan were perfected on the two following days. *Ibid.*, II, 60–61, 63–64, 69 (July 20); II, 71, 73 (July 21). Proposals for electors chosen by state legislatures were defeated on July 17 and July 25. *Ibid.*, II, 22, 32; II, 107, 108.

[20] *Ibid.*, II, 53 (July 19). As Morris had earlier said: "It was saying to him, make hay while the sun shines." *Ibid.*, II, 33 (July 17).

[21] *Ibid.*, II, 54. The importance attached to executive independence is amusingly illustrated by the fact that for tactical reasons Madison had previously supported a proposal for life tenure when the executive was to be chosen by the legislature. *Ibid.*, II, 33–36 (July 17).

[22] *Ibid.*, II, 55 (July 19).

[23] *Ibid.*, II, 55–56. Gouverneur Morris also commented later that it was folly to give an executive "the benefit of experience, and then deprive ourselves of the use of it." *Ibid.*, II, 104 (July 24).

[24] *Ibid.*, II, 56–57. Gerry revived his proposal of election by electors chosen by the executives of the states. See note 15, page 258, above.

[25] *Ibid.*, II, 56.

But the new system survived only a week. Again reversing itself, the convention restored the original plan of election by the legislature, for a term of seven years, with ineligibility.[26] Houston, Spaight, and Williamson sponsored reinstatement of selection by the legislature.[27] Uncertainty and confusion marked the debate on ineligibility and the term of office. Gerry remarked: "We seem to be entirely at a loss on this head." He suggested that perhaps it would be best "to refer the clause relating to the Executive to the Committee of detail."[28] Several freakish expedients were proposed and rejected.[29] Meanwhile Madison, after reviewing the objections against "every mode that has been, or perhaps can be proposed," concluded in favor of "election by the people."[30] Replying to the objection that this method would favor the large states since voters would prefer a candidate from their own locality,[31] Williamson of North Carolina proposed "that each man should vote for 3 candidates." Gouverneur Morris "liked the idea, suggesting as an amendment that each man should vote for two persons one of whom at least should not be of his own State."[32] Dickinson believed that local partiality might be turned to a useful purpose: let the people of each state choose its best citizen, then from these thirteen names a choice could be made either by the national legislature or by

[26] See note 17, page 258, above.

[27] Farrand, *Records*, II, 97, 101 (July 24). Gouverneur Morris observed that: "Of all possible modes of appointment that by the Legislature is the worst. . . . He preferred a short period, a re-eligibility, but a different mode of election." *Ibid.*, II, 103, 105. Morris later said that: "He considered an election by the people as the best, by the Legislature as the worst, mode." *Ibid.*, II, 113 (July 25).

[28] *Ibid.*, II, 103 (July 24). Gerry and Butler agreed. *Ibid.*, II, 115 (July 25). It was the Committee on Postponed Parts that reported on September 4 the solution finally adopted.

[29] *Ibid.*, II, 97, 105 (July 24); II, 107, 108–109, 111, 112, 113, 115 (July 25). Though Wilson proposed one of these, "His opinion remained unshaken that we ought to resort to the people for the election." *Ibid.*, II, 106 (July 24). This was also Dickinson's view. *Ibid.*, II, 114 (July 25).

[30] *Ibid.*, II, 109–11 (July 25). See note 17, page 258, above. The two great evils of election by the legislature were summed up by Pierce Butler as "cabal at home, & influence from abroad." *Ibid.*, II, 112.

[31] This objection was mentioned by Madison and regarded by Ellsworth as "unanswerable." *Ibid.*, II, 111. It had previously been voiced by Sherman and Williamson. *Ibid.*, II, 29, 32 (July 17).

[32] *Ibid.*, II, 113 (July 25). Madison commented on the value of this suggestion. *Ibid.*, II, 114.

electors appointed by it.[33] These ideas later bore fruit, although for the time being, on Mason's motion, the perplexed delegates decided to restore the term of seven years, with ineligibility.

The Committee of Detail reported the provision as follows: "The Executive Power of the United States shall be vested in a single person. His stile shall be 'The President of the United States of America'; and his title shall be, 'His Excellency'. He shall be elected by ballot by the Legislature. He shall hold his office during the term of seven years; but shall not be elected a second time."[34]

When this article was under consideration in convention, amendments were adopted calling for a "joint" ballot and requiring a majority vote of the members present.[35] Gouverneur Morris again opposed election of the President by the legislature, and proposed the method of choice by electors "to be chosen by the people of the several States." His motion was defeated but by a narrow margin.[36] Further discussion was postponed, but never resumed, and the matter was considered by the Committee of Postponed Parts.

That committee presented an entirely new plan of election. Each state was to designate, in such manner as its legislature might direct, a number of electors equal to the number of its Senators and Representatives. Each elector was to vote for two persons, of whom one at least was to be an inhabitant of some other state. The person having the highest number of votes, if a majority, was to be President. In case of a tie among persons having a majority, the Senate was to choose one of them for President. If no one received a majority, the Senate was to choose the President from the five highest on the list. In every case, after the choice of the President, the person having the highest number of votes was to be Vice-President, the Senate choosing in case of a tie.

[33] *Ibid.*, II, 114–15. Cf. Wilson's earlier suggestion based on the Massachusetts constitution of 1780. *Ibid.*, II, 30 (July 17); Thorpe, *Federal and State Constitutions,* III, 1900.

[34] Art. X, sec. 1. Farrand, *Records,* II, 185 (August 6). For the development of this language in drafts in the handwriting of Randolph, Rutledge, and Wilson, see *ibid.*, II, 145, 158, 171.

[35] *Ibid.*, II, 397, 403 (August 24). A proposal to insert the words "each State having one vote" was defeated. A motion by Carroll, seconded by Wilson, to substitute election "by the people" for election "by the Legislature" had also been rejected. *Ibid.*, II, 402.

[36] *Ibid.*, II, 397, 404. The vote was six to five, Connecticut, New Jersey, Pennsylvania, Delaware, and Virginia supporting the proposal.

The President was to be elected for a four-year term, without being ineligible to re-election.[37]

This plan embodied features which had been favored by Madison, Wilson, Morris, King, Dickinson, and Williamson during earlier stages of debate. It is not known who was author of the plan, but presumably Gouverneur Morris had a large part in its preparation.[38] He was the spokesman who in convention enumerated the reasons why the committee had formulated a new method of electing the executive.[39]

The principal criticism urged was that the Senate was given too much power.[40] Morris replied that the Senate had been preferred over the whole legislature as the ultimate appointing body because fewer could then "say to the President, you owe your appointment to us."[41] Sherman reminded opponents of the new plan that if the small states had the advantage in deciding among the five highest candidates, the large states would have that of in fact making the nomination of these candidates.[42] Wilson moved to substitute "Legislature" for "Senate." This was opposed by Madison, lest it encourage the large states to emphasize the designation of candidates rather than their election in the first instance without resort to the ultimate electing body. If the Senate, in which small states predominate, were to make the final choice, the large states would make a more strenuous effort to effect election without recourse to that body. The motion was defeated.[43]

This problem was solved by Sherman's suggestion that the legisla-

[37] *Ibid.*, II, 493–94, 497–98 (September 4). The device of using electors was doubtless modeled on that employed in Maryland for the election of Senators. Thorpe, *Federal and State Constitutions*, III, 1693–94.

[38] The committee was composed of Gilman, King, Sherman, Brearley, Gouverneur Morris, Dickinson, Carroll, Madison, Williamson, Butler, and Baldwin. Farrand, *Records*, II, 473, 481 (August 31).

[39] *Ibid.*, II, 500 (September 4). He also defended the report against criticism by Wilson. *Ibid.*, II, 523 (September 6).

[40] *Ibid.*, II, 500–502, 511–13, 522 (September 4, 5, 6). There was also objection to the Vice-Presidency as an unnecessary office and as an intrusion by the executive into legislative proceedings. *Ibid.*, II, 536–37 (September 7). The office of Vice-President was found in the New Jersey and South Carolina constitutions of 1776. Thorpe, *Federal and State Constitutions*, V, 2596; VI, 3243.

[41] Farrand, *Records*, II, 502 (September 4).

[42] *Ibid.*, II, 512–13 (September 5). King also emphasized this point. *Ibid.*, II, 514. See also *ibid.*, III, 405, 461.

[43] *Ibid.*, II, 513 (September 5). An amendment proposed by Dickinson was adopted, adding the word "appointed" to make clear that a majority of all the electors,

ture vote by states.[44] He later formulated the proposal to require the House of Representatives to choose the President, the representation from each state having one vote. This proposal was accepted,[45] as was King's addition that a quorum be required consisting of a member or members from two-thirds of the states.[46]

Other additions to the plan were provisions prohibiting members of the Congress or officers under the United States from serving as electors,[47] requiring all electors to vote on the same day throughout the nation[48] and requiring for an election in the House the concurrence of a majority of all the states.[49]

Slight clarifications in wording were made by the Committee of Style,[50] and by the convention.[51]

INTERPRETATION

BY the opening words of Article II, "The executive Power" is vested in an official designated as the "President."[52] Similarly, by Article III, "The judicial Power of the United States" is vested in specified tribunals. However, Article I vests in Congress only "All legislative Powers herein granted." Probably none of these terms have any intrinsic meaning, or are themselves operative as grants of power, but simply serve to identify the grantee or recipient of the particular types of power mentioned,[53] the tripartite "separation of powers" being a

---

not merely of those voting, was necessary to elect. By another amendment, to the language empowering Congress to fix the time of choosing electors the words "and of their giving their votes" were added. *Ibid.*, II, 507, 515 (September 5).

[44] *Ibid.*, II, 522 (September 6).

[45] *Ibid.*, II, 519, 527 (September 6). Other propositions accepted were that the House was also to be present when the electoral votes were opened and counted, and to elect in case of a tie. *Ibid.*, II, 526, 527.

[46] *Ibid.*, II, 519, 527–28 (September 6). The purpose of this provision was to meet Madison's objection that it might be possible for a President to be elected by two states only, such as Virginia and Pennsylvania, if no other states were present, and the representation from those two large states would constitute a quorum in the House of Representatives. In the same vein was Gerry's amendment requiring the concurrence of a majority of all the states. See note 49 just below.

[47] *Ibid.*, II, 517, 521 (September 6).

[48] *Ibid.*, II, 518, 526 (September 6). See also note 50 just below.

[49] *Ibid.*, II, 532, 536 (September 7).   [50] *Ibid.*, II, 597–98 (September 12).

[51] *Ibid.*, II, 621, 628 (September 15).

[52] For an excellent discussion of executive power, see Edward S. Corwin, *The President: Office and Powers*, 2–10.

[53] Youngstown Sheet & Tube Co. v. Sawyer, 343 U.S. 579, 640–41 (1952). In

concept familiar to the framers of the Constitution, particularly by reason of the vogue of the French writer Montesquieu.[54]

"The executive Power" is therefore not a term which serves as a measure of the scope of the President's authority; the extent of such authority is prescribed, rather, by the subsequently enumerated provisions of Article II, particularly by the comprehensive general provision in Article II, section 3, clause 4, that "he shall take Care that the Laws be faithfully executed." These words define the essence of executive power as understood by the framers of the Constitution.[55] Taken together with the "necessary and proper" clause, they confer upon the President a vast but uncharted field of authority. There are practical advantages and grave dangers to the nation in such "comprehensive and undefined presidential powers."[56]

The method of selecting the President by means of electoral votes has operated in practice quite differently from what the framers anticipated. The electors are now merely "rubber stamps" registering the opinions of their political party, rather than thoughtful and well-informed individuals whose judgment with respect to the suitability of candidates is superior to that of the general public.[57]

Article II, section 1, clause 3, is now obsolete, having been superseded in 1804 by the Twelfth Amendment. It is now required that the electors distinctly specify the persons voted for as President and those voted for as Vice-President. If no candidate receives a majority, the House of Representatives shall choose a President from the three

---

that case the Solicitor General had argued, in defending President Truman's seizure of steel plants during the military action in Korea to resist international aggression, that Art. II, sec. 1, cl. 1, "constitutes a grant of all the executive powers of which the Government is capable." The Supreme Court did not accept this interpretation. Six opinions were written by the Justices forming the majority. The case was argued by John W. Davis for the steel companies.

[54] The draft of the Committee of Detail had spoken of "The legislative power," "The Executive Power of the United States," and "The Judicial Power of the United States." (Arts. III, X, and XI.) *Ibid.*, II, 177, 185, 186.

[55] See notes 6 and 9, pages 256 and 257, above. Cf. Hamilton, *Works*, IV, 438–39. In particular, the powers of the king in England are not to be taken as the proper measure of those of the President. Myers v. U.S., 272 U.S. 52, 68 (1926).

[56] Youngstown Sheet & Tube Co. v. Sawyer, 343 U.S. 579, 634 (1952).

[57] See note 14, page 258, above. See also Ray v. Blair, 343 U.S. 214, 232, 234 (1952), where Justice Jackson said: "As an institution the Electoral College suffered atrophy almost indistinguishable from *rigor mortis*. . . . The demise of the whole electoral system would not impress me as a disaster."

(rather than five) highest on the list. If no candidate for Vice-President receives a majority, the Senate shall choose from the two highest. This amendment was adopted as a result of the situation in 1800 when Thomas Jefferson and Aaron Burr received the same number of electoral votes and the election was thrown into the House of Representatives. Although it was clearly the intent of the people that Jefferson be President and Burr be Vice-President, the legal power to choose between them lay in the hands of the House of Representatives (practically speaking, in the hands of the opposite political party), and there was danger that the will of the people might be frustrated by means of intrigue between Burr and the Federalists. Jefferson's election (on the thirty-sixth ballot, on March 18, 1801) was effected by the efforts of his political adversary Alexander Hamilton, whom Burr thereafter slew in a duel at Weehawken.[58]

The Twentieth Amendment now provides that "The Congress may by law provide for the case of the death of any of the persons from whom the House of Representatives may choose a President whenever the right of choice shall have devolved upon them, and for the case of the death of any of the persons from whom the Senate may choose a Vice President whenever the right of choice shall have devolved upon them."

Complete discretion is granted to the state legislatures with respect to the method of choosing electors. Each state's electors are to be chosen in such manner "as the Legislature thereof may direct."[59] The legislature may select them itself, or prescribe popular election by districts, or at large by general ticket statewide. As a matter of history, many different methods have been used at various times and places.[60] Although electors perform a federal function, "they are no more officers or agents of the United States than are the members of the state legislatures when acting as electors of federal senators, or the people of the States when acting as electors of representatives in Congress."[61] But the federal government has the power to protect the purity of the im-

[58] Francis N. Thorpe, *The Constitutional History of the United States*, II, 301–28; Henry S. Randall, *The Life of Thomas Jefferson*, II, 583–600; Morris, *Alexander Hamilton and the Founding of the Nation*, 535–41, 602–41, 602–10; Harold C. Syrett and Jean G. Cook, *Interview in Weehawken*, 141.

[59] McPherson v. Blacker, 146 U.S. 1, 25, 27 (1892).   [60] *Ibid.*, 29–33.

[61] *Ibid.*, 35; *In re* Green, 134 U.S. 377, 379 (1890). In the Green case the Supreme Court upheld the right of a state to punish for election frauds in choosing electors.

portant national elections upon which its own existence depends against "the two great natural and historical enemies of all republics, open violence and insidious corruption."[62]

After the presiding officer of the Senate (in the presence of the Senate and House of Representatives) has opened all the sealed certificates transmitted by the electors, "the Votes shall then be counted." By whom? It is not stated that the computation shall be made by the Vice-President. Nor is it specified that the Congress shall make the count.[63]

This question became acute in the election of 1876 when Rutherford B. Hayes was the Republican candidate and Samuel J. Tilden the Democratic candidate.[64] The federal government's abnormal control over state governments in the South by reason of "Reconstruction" legislation enabled the Republican administration to procure the designation of Republican electors in several states, in addition to the Democratic electors who represented the actual sentiments of voters in those states.

To settle the resulting contest, Congress passed an act "to provide for and regulate the counting of votes for President and Vice-President, and the decision of questions arising thereon" for the particular election involved.[65] This statute was doubtless constitutional by virtue of the "necessary and proper" clause, in the absence of specific provisions in the Constitution itself regarding the manner of counting the votes or determining disputes with respect thereto.

The commission established under this legislation voted in strict accordance with party lines. The deciding vote was cast by a Republican

[62] Ex parte Yarbrough, 110 U.S. 651, 658 (1884); Burroughs v. U.S., 290 U.S. 534, 545 (1934). The former case related to elections of members of Congress; the latter case where Presidential electors were being chosen. The Court said that Congress possesses every power "essential to preserve the departments and institutions of the general government from impairment or destruction, whether threatened by force or corruption."

[63] Though the certificates are to be opened "in the Presence of the Senate and House of Representatives," no active function with respect to counting the votes is conferred on either branch of Congress. Nowhere in the Constitution is provision made for action by the two branches as a single collective body. Nor is there any implication that the task falls to the House of Representatives, to which specific duties are expressly confided in the event that the election is not decided by a count of the electoral votes.

[64] See Paul L. Haworth, *The Hayes-Tilden Disputed Presidential Election of 1876*, 177–86.

[65] Act of January 29, 1877, 19 Stat. 227.

member of the Supreme Court. Accordingly, Hayes emerged victorious.[66] Acquiescence in this result was obtained by a bargain pursuant to which federal control over the South was relinquished, and state governments in that region were permitted to function normally in the future.

ART. II, SEC. 1, CL. 5

No Person except a natural born Citizen, or a Citizen of the United States, at the time of the Adoption of this Constitution, shall be eligible to the Office of President; neither shall any Person be eligible to that Office who shall not have attained to the Age of thirty five Years, and been fourteen Years a Resident within the United States.

HISTORY

A MOTION by Mason[67] that property and citizenship qualifications be prescribed, applicable to all three branches of the government, was not heeded by the Committee of Detail insofar as the executive was concerned.[68] Accordingly, Gerry moved that the committee be instructed to report qualifications for the President.[69] The Committee of Detail thereupon recommended an insertion that "he shall be of the age of thirty five years, and a Citizen of the United States, and shall have been an Inhabitant thereof for Twenty one years."[70] Apparently no action was taken on this proposal by the convention, and it came before the Committee on Postponed Parts, which reported a clause reading: "No Person except a natural born Citizen, or a Citizen of the U.S. at the time of the adoption of this Constitution shall be eligible to the office of President: nor shall any Person be elected to that office, who shall be under the age of 35 years, and who has not been in the whole, at least 14 years a resident within the U.S."[71] Perhaps the liberalization

---

[66] For a detailed account of this contest, see Haworth, *The Hayes-Tilden Disputed Presidential Election of 1876*, 220–83.

[67] Farrand, *Records*, II, 116–17, 121 (July 26).

[68] See Art. VI, sec. 2, of the Committee's draft. *Ibid.*, II, 179 (August 6).

[69] *Ibid.*, II, 337, 344 (August 20).

[70] *Ibid.*, II, 367, 375 (August 22). This was to be added at the end of Art. X, sec. 1, of the draft of the Committee of Detail. *Ibid.*, II, 185.

[71] *Ibid.*, II, 494, 498 (September 4). This clause was approved by the convention

of the requirements concerning length of residence may have been due to Wilson's comment, while the qualifications for Senators were being discussed, that he might find himself "incapacitated from holding a place under the very Constitution which he had shared in the trust of making."[72]

INTERPRETATION

THE Supreme Court has said that "Under the Constitution, a natural-ized citizen stands on an equal footing with the native citizen in all re-spects, save that of eligibility to the Presidency."[73] In practice the naturalized citizen has the disadvantage that the legal transaction by which he became a citizen may be attacked and set aside upon grounds such as fraud,[74] whereas only in extremely unusual circumstances, if at all, can a native-born citizen be involuntarily expatriated or deprived of citizenship.[75]

The question has sometimes been asked whether a person born abroad (such as a Canadian-born son of President Franklin D. Roose-velt) could be President. Although the Supreme Court has never had occasion to pass upon this matter, it would seem that citizenship arising by operation of law and based upon the mere fact of birth, without any voluntary act establishing allegiance and without resort to natural-ization proceedings, would meet the requirements for eligibility as President. The words of the Constitution are "a natural born Citizen," rather than "born . . . in the United States."[76] A citizen *jure sanguinis*

without debate. *Ibid.*, II, 532, 536 (September 7). The Committee of Style made only verbal changes. *Ibid.*, II, 598 (September 12).

[72] *Ibid.*, II, 237 (August 9). See page 84 above. Gouverneur Morris, whose motion to require fourteen rather than four years' residence for Senators was being discussed by Wilson, was a member of the Committee on Postponed Parts, and may have preferred a fourteen-year period for the executive also. *Ibid.*, II, 238.

[73] Baumgartner v. U.S., 322 U.S. 665, 673 (1944).

[74] 8 U.S.C.A. 1451. The Baumgartner case was one where the government sought to set aside a naturalization order because the new citizen retained a liking for the methods of Hitler's Germany. A naturalized citizen may also lose nationality by non-residence. 8 U.S.C.A. 1484.

[75] See 8 U.S.C.A. 1481; Perez v. Brownell, 356 U.S. 44 (1958); Trop v. Dulles, 356 U.S. 86 (1958); and Nishikawa v. Dulles, 356 U.S. 129 (1958). See pages 142–43 above.

[76] As in the Fourteenth Amendment. George B. McClellan, Jr., mayor of New York and son of a prominent Civil War general, had Presidential ambitions, and did not regard his foreign birth as a disqualification. He distinguished between a "natural

as well as one *jure soli* would be "natural born." However, if United States nationality laws made the citizenship of a person born abroad of American parents conditional or inchoate, as by requiring performance of a further act, such as return to America or election to take an oath of allegiance, in order to perfect and render permanent the status of citizenship, the effect might be to disqualify such person for the presidency.[77]

Another ground for ineligibility as President has now been added by the Twenty-second Amendment, which prevents the election of a person who has served as President for more than six years.

ART. II, SEC. 1, CL. 6

In Case of the Removal of the President from Office, or of his Death, Resignation, or Inability to discharge the Powers and Duties of the said Office, the Same shall devolve on the Vice President, and the Congress may by Law provide for the Case of Removal, Death, Resignation or Inability, both of the President and Vice President, declaring what Officer shall then act as President, and such Officer shall act accordingly, until the Disability be removed, or a President shall be elected.

HISTORY

RANDOLPH'S draft in the Committee of Detail shows an addition in Rutledge's handwriting, at the end of the article on the executive, reading: "The Presid[en]t of ye Senate to succeed to the Executive in Case of Vacancy until the Meeting of the Legisl[atur]e."[78] A later draft in Wilson's handwriting reads: "In case of his Impeachment, Removal, Death, Resignation or Disability to discharge the Powers and Duties of his Office; the President of the Senate shall exercise those Powers and Duties, until another President of the United States be chosen, or until the President impeached or disabled be acquitted, or his Disability be removed."[79] The Committee of Detail reported: "In

born" and "native born" citizen. He reported a conversation with Justice David J. Brewer of the Supreme Court, who had been mentioned as a Presidential candidate, and had consulted his colleagues on the Court; they considered him eligible notwithstanding his birth in Syria. McClellan, *The Gentleman and the Tiger*, 197.

[77] See 8 U.S.C.A. 1401 (b), 1482.   [78] Farrand, *Records*, II, 146.
[79] *Ibid.*, II, 172.

case of his removal as aforesaid [upon impeachment], death, resignation, or disability to discharge the powers and duties of his office, the
President of the Senate shall exercise those powers and duties, until
another President of the United States be chosen, or until the disability
of the President be removed."[80]

When this provision was debated, Gouverneur Morris objected to
"the President of the Senate being provisional successor to the President,
and suggested a designation of the Chief Justice." Madison added "that
the Senate might retard the appointment of a President in order to
carry points whilst the revisionary power was in the President of their
own body." He suggested that the executive powers during a vacancy
"be administered by the persons composing the Council to the President." Williamson thought "that the Legislature ought to have power
to provide for occasional successors." He moved that consideration of
the subject be postponed. In seconding the postponement, Dickinson
remarked that the language was too vague, and asked a question which
remains unanswered to this day: "What is the extent of the term 'disability' & who is to be the judge of it?"[81]

The Committee on Postponed Parts reported the provision without
substantial change.[82] On motion of Randolph a provision was added
that "The Legislature may declare by law what officer of the United
States shall act as President in case of the death, resignation, or disability
of the President and Vice President; and such Officer shall act accordingly, until such disability be removed, or a President shall be
elected."[83] The Committee of Style inserted the ambiguous words "the
same shall devolve on the vice-president"; deleted "absence"; and
restored "until . . . the period of chusing another president arrive."[84]
The convention reinstated Madison's amendment.[85]

[80] Art. X, sec. 2. *Ibid.*, II, 186 (August 6).   [81] *Ibid.*, II, 427 (August 27).

[82] *Ibid.*, II, 495, 499 (September 4). The President's "absence" was added to the
grounds of superseding him, and "inability" substituted for "disability." The term
"Vice President" replaced "President of the Senate."

[83] *Ibid.*, II, 532, 535 (September 7). The motion at first read: "until the time of
electing a President shall arrive." Madison moved to amend it so as not to prevent
filling the vacancy "by an intermediate election of the President." Some members felt
that "according to the process established for chusing the Executive, there would be
difficulty in effecting it at other than the fixed periods." Others disliked the limitation
that only "officers" of the United States could be named when filling vacancies. *Ibid.*,
II, 535.

[84] *Ibid.*, II, 598–99 (September 12).

INTERPRETATION

IN providing that in case of the President's inability "to discharge the Powers and Duties of the said Office, the Same shall devolve on the Vice President," were the framers of the Constitution speaking of the *powers and duties* or of the *office* itself?

The ambiguity arose only after the Committee of Style modified the earlier wording of the clause. In prior versions it was clear that only the powers and duties were referred to.[86] Was the new wording another instance of an attempt by Gouverneur Morris to make a surreptitious change to favor his own opinions on a controversial point?[87] There is no evidence of such an intent.

However, in practice every Vice-President since John Tyler in 1841 upon the death of the President has assumed the *office* of President.[88] This practical construction of the clause, however, has extended only to cases of the *death* of the President. There has never been any interpretation of "inability" or "disability," or any official procedure for determination of its existence or effects. Presidents Garfield and Wilson continued to hold office until the death of the former and the end of the term of the latter. The problem was much discussed during the illnesses of President Eisenhower.[89] It is difficult to see why a constitutional amendment is needed to regulate the matter; legislation under the "necessary and proper" clause would doubtless be constitutional as a means of giving effect to this clause.

[85] *Ibid.*, II, 626 (September 15). See note 83, page 270, above.

[86] See notes 80 and 82, page 270, above.

[87] See note 7, page 107, above.

[88] Section 3 of the Twentieth Amendment makes it clear that "the Vice President elect *shall become President*" if the President-elect shall have died by the time his term begins. It is made equally clear that "the Vice President elect shall *act as President* until a President shall have qualified" where there has been failure to elect a President, or the President has failed to "qualify" by the time his term begins. When neither a President nor a Vice-President has qualified, Congress is given power by law to provide for selection of a person to act as President "until a President or Vice President shall have qualified."

[89] Herbert Brownell, "Presidential Disability: The Need for a Constitutional Amendment," *Yale Law Journal*, Vol. LXVIII, No. 2 (December, 1958), 189, 204, regards the Vice-President as judge of the existence of disability on the part of the President. This is based on the principle of law that a person who is to act upon a certain contingency, unless otherwise provided, must determine whether that contingency has occurred. This principle could be modified by statute without conflict with any constitutional provisions. The object of a constitutional amendment is to curtail the power of

It would seem that the portion of this clause empowering Congress to designate an acting President in case both the President and Vice-President are unable to serve is limited to that particular contingency, and that this power of Congress is exhausted when such designation is made. The language is susceptible of interpretation as granting a general power to "provide for the Case of . . . Inability . . . of the President," and to make similar provision in case of the "Inability . . . of the . . . Vice President." Such construction is somewhat farfetched, however, and requires disregard of the word "both." To regard the power as limited to the single contingency where *both* officers are unable to serve is more logical and natural.

The wording of the last part of the clause indicates that such an acting President shall serve only until the disability of either the President or the Vice-President be removed. Since the fourfold grounds necessitating the service of such an officer (removal, death, resignation, or inability) are the same as those necessitating devolution upon the Vice-President of the President's powers and duties, it would seem logical to conclude that the Constitution in the latter contingency likewise contemplates that if the President's temporary disability "be removed," he shall resume the exercise of the powers and duties of his office, and the Vice-President shall be relegated to his normal status and functions as Vice-President. Indeed, the history of the framing of the clause shows that the words "until the Disability be removed, or a President shall be elected" are applicable both to a Vice-President and to a successor designated by Congress.[90]

Does the alternative provision that the service of an acting President shall be terminated when "a President shall be elected" mean when a President normally would have been elected, or does it contemplate a special election to fill the vacancy?

The latter interpretation appears to be preferable, since Madison's amendment was adopted with that purpose in view, and was restored by the convention after the Committee of Style had reverted to the substance of Randolph's original wording, "until the time of electing a President shall arrive."[91] However, as was noted at the time of Madi-

---

the Vice-President in this regard and to ensure that the President will not be displaced permanently in case of inability. *Ibid.*, 195, 205.

[90] Until this clause was revised by the Committee of Style to eliminate repetition, the words appeared twice: once in connection with the Vice-President, and again in connection with a successor designated by Congress. See notes 80 and 83, page 270, above.

son's amendment, the cumbrous nature of the electoral process makes it inconvenient to hold an off-year election. Moreover, a special election would disrupt the synchrony of the system whereby a President is normally elected at the same time as the members of the House of Representatives and one-third of the Senators. In practice there has never been an intermediate election of a President, though it was authorized by the first Presidential succession act passed by Congress under this clause.[92]

That act also provided that the four-year term of the President should be computed from March 4, 1789, the date fixed by the Old Congress in its act of September 13, 1788, for the commencement of proceedings under the Constitution; in fact, however, President Washington did not take office until April 30, 1789. The chronological sequence of Presidential terms was disrupted by the Twentieth Amendment, which cut short the first term of President Franklin D. Roosevelt (as well as the terms of the Vice-President and the members of Congress), on January 20, 1937. That amendment specified that "the terms of their successors shall then begin." It also speaks of "the time fixed for the beginning of the term" of the President. In view of this policy of fixing specifically the time when terms begin and end, it would seem that in the event of a President's failure to qualify at the prescribed date, his term would not be extended beyond its normal expiration date by reason of his delay in qualifying, but would end four years after the date fixed for its beginning (see Article II, section 1, clause 1).

[91] See notes 83–85, pages 270–71, above.

[92] Act of March 1, 1792, 1 Stat. 239. The President pro tempore of the Senate was given priority by this law; then the Speaker of the House. This act was superseded by the Act of January 19, 1886, 24 Stat. 1, which first designated the Secretary of State, then other Cabinet members. The Act of July 18, 1947, 61 Stat. 380, 3 U.S.C.A. 19, gives priority to the Speaker, then the President pro tempore of the Senate, then the Secretary of State and other Cabinet members. This legislation was sponsored by President Truman. He considered it as undemocratic for a President, who had come into office upon the death of his predecessor, to be able to determine his successor by naming him as Secretary of State. Under the new law the Speaker of the House and the President pro tempore of the Senate are first in succession, ahead of appointive officers. However, as Madison pointed out in 1792, this arrangement violates the principle of separation of powers; and it is also not clear that either of these officials is an "officer" of the United States within the meaning of Art. II, sec. 1, cl. 6. Cf. Art. I, sec. 2, cl. 5; Art. I, sec. 3, cl. 5; Art. I, sec. 3, cl. 7; Art. I, sec. 6, cl. 2; Art. II, sec. 2, cl. 2. See Madison to Edmund Pendleton, February 21, 1792, in *Writings of James Madison*, VI, 95–96.

ART. II, SEC. I, CL. 7

The President shall, at stated Times, receive for his Services, a Compensation, which shall neither be encreased nor diminished during the Period for which he shall have been elected, and he shall not receive within that Period any other Emolument from the United States, or any of them.

HISTORY

RANDOLPH'S seventh resolution in the Virginia Plan contemplated a fixed compensation which could not be increased or diminished.[93] The Committee of the Whole recommended that the executive "receive a fixed stipend by which he may be compensated for the devotion of his time to public service to be paid out of the national Treasury."[94] The Committee of Detail reported: "He shall, at stated times, receive for his services, a compensation, which shall neither be increased nor diminished during his continuance in office."[95] On motion of Rutledge a provision was added in convention: "and he shall not receive, within that period, any other emolument from the U.S. or any of them."[96]

INTERPRETATION

IN view of current decisions overruling the earlier exemption of federal judicial salaries from income tax,[97] it would seem that the salary of the

[93] Farrand, *Records*, I, 21 (May 29). A proposal by Franklin that there be no salary was quietly put aside. *Ibid.*, I, 77–78, 81–85 (June 2). See notes 5 and 8, pages 256 and 257, above.

[94] *Ibid.*, I, 230, 236 (June 13). This was approved in convention, with "compensation" substituted for "stipend by which he may be compensated," and "public" substituted for "national." *Ibid.*, II, 61, 69 (July 20); II, 116, 121 (July 26). In the Committee of Detail an addition by Rutledge restored the provision for "no Increase or decrease during the Term of Service of the Executive." *Ibid.*, II, 146.

[95] Art. X, sec. 2. *Ibid.*, II, 185 (August 6). The identical provision appears in a draft in Wilson's handwriting. *Ibid.*, II, 172. The Committee of Style substituted "the President" for "he" and "the period for which he shall have been elected" for "his continuance in office." *Ibid.*, II, 599 (September 12).

[96] *Ibid.*, II, 626 (September 15). On the same day "receive for his services a compensation" was substituted for "receive a fixed compensation for his services." *Ibid.*, II, 621. This resembled an earlier proposal by Charles Pinckney to prohibit the President from "holding at the same time any other office of trust or emolument under the United States, or an individual State." *Ibid.*, II, 335, 341–42 (August 20).

[97] See note 81, page 78, above. Art. III, sec. 1, similarly provides that the compensation of federal judges "shall not be diminished during their Continuance in Office."

President is likewise taxable under nondiscriminatory legislation applicable to the public generally as one of the burdens of citizenship.[98]

ART. II, SEC. 1, CL. 8

Before he enter on the Execution of his Office, he shall take the following Oath or Affirmation:—"I do solemnly swear (or affirm) that I will faithfully execute the Office of President of the United States, and will to the best of my Ability, preserve, protect and defend the Constitution of the United States."

HISTORY

RANDOLPH'S working draft in the Committee of Detail provided that the executive "shall swear fidelity to the union, as the legislature shall direct." An emendation by Rutledge substituted for the last five words: "by taking an oath of office." This was elaborated in a draft in Wilson's handwriting to read: "Before he shall enter on the Duties of his Department, he shall take the following Oath or Affirmation, "I ———— solemnly swear,—or affirm,—that I will faithfully execute the Office of President of the United States of America."[99] The clause was reported without change by the Committee of Detail.[100] On motion of Mason, seconded by Madison, the convention added: "and will to the best of my judgment and power, preserve, protect and defend the Constitution of the United States."[101] The word "ability" seems to have been substituted during consideration by the convention.[102]

INTERPRETATION

THE oath of office is for the most part a ceremonial formality. The

[98] Justice Holmes often referred to taxes as the price paid for civilization. Compañía de Tabacos v. Collector, 275 U.S. 87, 100 (1927).

[99] Farrand, *Records*, II, 146, 172.

[100] Art. X, sec. 2. *Ibid.*, II, 185 (August 6). The Committee of Style substituted "Before he enter on the execution of his office" for "before he shall enter on the duties of his department." *Ibid.*, II, 599 (September 12).

[101] *Ibid.*, II, 422, 427 (August 27).

[102] *Ibid.*, II, 621 (September 15). The printed *Journal*, edited in 1819 by Secretary of State John Quincy Adams, in a list of amendments evidently compiled from interlineations in Brearley's copy of the printed report of the Committee of Style, contains the following: "In the oath to be taken by the president, strike out the word 'judgment', and insert 'abilities'."

inauguration of a President is an important social occasion, and political leaders from all over the land assemble in Washington to see their victorious candidate take over the reins of government. Legally the oath merely marks the moment when the President begins "the Execution of his Office." It has been customary for the oath to be administered to the President by the Chief Justice at noon in front of the Capitol.[103] It is now expressly provided by the Twentieth Amendment that the term of the incoming President shall begin at noon; theretofore it was uncertain precisely when the term of the outgoing President expired. In earlier years it was thought that midnight was the deadline, but no incoming President chose to take the oath at that hour,[104] and noon became the accepted time. This extension of the term of the outgoing President has been described as a striking instance of constitutional change effected by custom or political practice.[105]

The oath itself adds nothing to the President's powers, nor does it detract anything. Historically, the coronation oath of a monarch was a primitive type of constitutional limitation, and was intended to curtail royal power rather than augment it. The king swore that he would govern in accordance with law, or perhaps, more specifically, in accordance with the good old laws of King Edward I, or "the statutes in Parliament agreed on."[106]

It had also been the custom in England to require officeholders

[103] On account of his failing health, President Franklin D. Roosevelt took the oath at the beginning of his fourth term in 1945 at the White House, in a semiprivate ceremony. Of course a Vice-President who succeeds to the office of chief executive upon the death of the prior incumbent is sworn in wherever he happens to be, as was President Coolidge by his father in a New England farmhouse. See Corwin, *The President: Office and Powers*, 347–48. More recently, President Lyndon B. Johnson took the oath of office before United States District Judge Sarah T. Hughes (the first woman ever to administer the oath to a new President) in an airplane at Dallas, Texas, on November 22, 1963, little more than an hour after the assassination in that city of his predecessor, John F. Kennedy, whose body was making its final journey to the national capital on board the same plane.

[104] There is a legend that Jefferson put a stop to the appointment of "midnight judges" by John Adams at that hour. Sarah N. Randolph, *The Domestic Life of Thomas Jefferson*, 307–308; Beveridge, *The Life of John Marshall*, II, 561–62.

[105] Charles Warren, "Political Practice and the Constitution," *University of Pennsylvania Law Review*, Vol. LXXXIX, No. 8 (June, 1941), 1003.

[106] Lee, *Source-Book of English History*, 195, 335; Maitland, *The Constitutional History of England*, 99, 286–88; Percy E. Schramm, *A History of the English Coronation*, 179–227; John Wickham-Legg, *The Coronation Order of King James I*, 13–17; Leopold G. Wickham-Legg, *English Coronation Records*, xxxi, 326.

(and, indeed, at times the entire populace)[107] to take test oaths recognizing the supremacy of the monarch in spiritual as well as temporal matters.[108] But the United States Constitution (while requiring the above-mentioned oath to be taken by the President, and also that Senators, Representatives, members of state legislatures, and all executive and judicial officers, both of the United States and of the several states, "shall be bound by Oath or Affirmation, to support this Constitution") prohibits religious test oaths, of the type familiar in English practice, by providing: "but no religious Test shall ever be required as a Qualification to any Office or public Trust under the United States."[109]

Perhaps the prevalent "loyalty oaths"[110] do not constitute a religious test;[111] but they would be precluded in the case of the President,

[107] Act for administering the oath of allegiance, 7 & 8 Jac. I, c. 6 (1610), in Joseph R. Tanner, *Consitutional Documents of the Reign of James I*, 105.

[108] Act of Supremacy, 1 Eliz. c. I (1559), in George B. Adams and H. Morse Stephens, *Select Documents of English Constitutional History*, 299; Test Act of March 29, 1673, 25 Charles II, c. 2, *ibid.*, 436.

[109] Art. VI, cl. 3. South Carolina sought an amendment to the Constitution inserting the word "other" before "religious Test" in this clause. It is not clear what this amendment was expected to accomplish. No other state supported the proposal. Dumbauld, *The Bill of Rights and What It Means Today*, 20, 44, 48, 180. Religious tests are now forbidden by the Supreme Court as a qualification for state office. Torcaso v. Watkins, 367 U.S. 488, 489, 492 (1961).

[110] Besides many state laws requiring loyalty oaths, the federal Act of August 9, 1955, 69 Stat. 624–25, 5 U.S.C.A. 118p–118q, provides that "no person shall accept or hold office or employment in the Government of the United States" who advocates or knowingly is a member of an organization which "advocates the overthrow of our constitutional form of government in the United States"; and in section 2 that "every person who accepts office or employment in the Government of the United States after the date of enactment of this Act, shall, not later than sixty days after he accepts such office or employment, execute an affidavit that his acceptance and holding of such office or employment does not or . . . will not constitute a violation of the first section of this Act." Such affidavit is prima-facie evidence that there is no violation. By section 3 violation is punishable as a felony. This act repealed Section 9A of the Hatch Act of August 2, 1939, 53 Stat. 1147, 1148–49, which made unlawful the employment of such persons and required their removal from office and forbade their being paid from funds appropriated by Congress. Appropriation acts since 1941 often contained similar provisions, but this practice seems to have been abandoned since the Act of August 9, 1955. The Act of June 29, 1955, 69 Stat. 192, 197–98, appropriating money to pay the President's salary, contained such provisions in section 210. But the Act of June 13, 1956, 70 Stat. 276, for the same purpose, does not.

[111] In American Communications Assn. v. Douds, 339 U.S. 382, 414 (1950), where a loyalty oath applicable to union officials was upheld, the Court pointed out that the fact that the requirement was imposed in the form of an oath did not make it a religious test.

and of the other officials mentioned in Article VI, clause 3, if the rule *expressio unius exclusio alterius* applies.[112] But that conclusion would not prohibit resort to the old English practice of requiring an oath of all citizens indiscriminately.[113]

[112] A notable application of that maxim in construing the Constitution is found in Marbury v. Madison, 1 Cr. 137, 174 (1803).

[113] See note 108, page 277, above. Considerable opposition by Harvard, Princeton, and other leading universities to the loyalty oaths required by the Act of September 2, 1958, 72 Stat. 1602, led to repeal of that requirement by the Act of October 16, 1962, 76 Stat. 1070, 20 U.S.C.A. 581. The opposition was based upon the fact that this requirement singled out students for an invidious discrimination not applicable to the public generally, or even to all recipients of public bounty. For the same reason an attempt to require such an oath of members of the legal profession was resisted. Zechariah Chafee, Jr., "The Test Oath Proposal," *Pennsylvania Bar Association Quarterly*, Vol. XXII, No. 3 (April, 1951), 221–39; "The Proposed Anti-Communist Oath," *American Bar Association Journal*, Vol. XXXVII, No. 2 (February, 1951), 123–26.

ARTICLE II—THE EXECUTIVE BRANCH
Powers of the President

ART. II, SEC. 2, CL. I

The President shall be Commander in Chief of the Army and Navy of the United States, and of the Militia of the several States, when called into the actual Service of the United States; he may require the Opinion, in writing, of the principal Officer in each of the executive Departments, upon any Subject relating to the Duties of their respective Offices, and he shall have Power to grant Reprieves and Pardons for Offences against the United States, except in Cases of Impeachment.

HISTORY

RANDOLPH'S working draft in the Committee of Detail contained provisions empowering the Executive "to command and superintend the militia," and "to direct their discipline," as well as "to direct the executives of the states to call them or any part for the support of the national government." In Rutledge's handwriting a substitute version empowered him "to be Commander in Chief of the Land & Naval Forces of the Union & of the militia of the sevl. states."[1] Another addition by Rutledge provided that "The power of pardoning [shall be] vested in the Executive" but that "his pardon shall not however, be pleadable to an Impeachm[en]t."[2] A document in the handwriting of Wilson contains a provision "That the Executive direct all military Operations."[3] Another portion of the same paper, thought to embody a proposal originating with Charles Pinckney, declares of the Presi-

---

[1] Farrand, *Records*, II, 145. Several state constitutions designated the chief executive "commander-in-chief." Fisher, *Evolution of the Constitution*, 159–60.

[2] Farrand, *Records*, II, 146. This was based on the provision in section 3 of the Act of Settlement "That no pardon under the great seal of England be pleadable to an impeachment by the Commons in parliament." 12 & 13 Wm. III (1701), c. 2, George B. Adams and H. Morse Stephens, *Select Documents of English Constitutional History*, 479. See also Danby's Case, 11 *State Trials* 599, 763–69, 790 (1679); Holdsworth, *History of English Law*, I, 383; VI, 232. Blackstone, *Commentaries*, IV, 299.

[3] Farrand, *Records*, II, 157. This is thought to be an extract from the New Jersey Plan.

dent: "He shall, by Virtue of his Office, be Commander in chief of the Land Forces of the U.S. and Admiral of their Navy."[4]

The Committee of Detail reported: "He shall have power to grant reprieves and pardons; but his pardon shall not be pleadable in bar of an impeachment. He shall be commander in chief of the Army and Navy of the United States, and of the Militia of the Several States."[5] In convention "except in cases of impeachment" was substituted for the last part of the sentence dealing with that topic.[6] Upon motion of Sherman, there were added at the end of the provision about the command of state militia the words "when called into the actual service of the United States."[7] As proposed by the Brearley committee on the method of choosing the executive,[8] there was added by the convention at the end of the militia provision a further power: "and may require the opinion in writing of the principal officer in each of the executive departments, upon any subject relating to the duties of their respective offices."[9] The Committee of Style placed the military power first, then the power to call for opinions, and lastly the pardoning power.[10]

[4] *Ibid.*, II, 158. A plan proposed by Hamilton had provided that the executive was "to have the direction of war when authorized or begun; . . . to have the power of pardoning all offenses except Treason; which he shall not pardon without the approbation of the Senate." *Ibid.*, I, 292 (June 18). See also *ibid.*, III, 218.

[5] Art. X, sec. 2. *Ibid.*, II, 185.

[6] *Ibid.*, II, 411, 419 (August 25). A motion by Luther Martin to insert "after conviction" was withdrawn, upon Wilson's explanation "that pardon before conviction might be necessary in order to obtain the testimony of accomplices." *Ibid.*, II, 422, 426 (August 27).

[7] *Ibid.*, II, 422, 426 (August 27).

[8] *Ibid.*, II, 495, 499 (September 4). See note 38, page 262, above.

[9] *Ibid.*, II, 533, 541–43 (September 7). This action grieved Mason, who still favored an executive council for the President. *Ibid.*, II, 533, 537, 541–42. For previous efforts to establish a privy council (by Gerry, Sherman, Ellsworth, Gouverneur Morris, and Rutledge's Committee of Detail), see *ibid.*, I, 66 (June 1); I, 94, 97 (June 4); II, 328–29 (August 18); II, 335–37, 342–44 (August 20); II, 367, 375 (August 22). See also Warren, *The Making of the Constitution*, 643–50. John Adams likewise wished for a privy council. Cappon, *Adams-Jefferson Letters*, I, 213; Charles Page Smith, *John Adams*, II, 726.

[10] Farrand, *Records*, II, 599 (September 12). In the report of the Committee of Style the words "when called into the actual service of the United States" were misplaced. This was corrected in convention. *Ibid.*, II, 621 (September 15). A motion by Randolph to except cases of treason from the pardoning power was defeated. *Ibid.*, II, 626–27 (September 15). See note 4 just above.

INTERPRETATION

Commander in Chief

THIS clause simply vests in the President whatever authority the laws entrust to the person in supreme command of the armed forces. It prescribes *who* shall exercise such command but does not prescribe *what powers* such person shall possess. The clause recognizes military command as an executive function.

Undoubtedly the framers had in mind when adopting this clause the inconveniences experienced during the Revolution when the Continental Congress had, under the Articles of Confederation, "the sole and exclusive right and power" of "directing . . . operations" of the land and naval forces of the United States.[11] Perhaps they also meant to follow the practice in England after the Restoration under Charles II; conflicts between Parliament and Charles I over the power to control the army had been an immediate cause of the English civil war.[12]

A natural incident of the President's status as commander in chief is his power to use the armed forces at his discretion to resist enemy attack, even in advance of a declaration of war by Congress. He may exercise whatever prerogatives international law grants to the commander of a nation's armed forces during hostilities.[13] Another striking illustration of the President's power to direct movements of the armed forces was furnished by the sixteen-month cruise of the United States battle fleet around the world during the administration of Theodore Roosevelt. The thought of taking the fleet away from Atlantic waters filled wealthy Easterners with apprehension. "The great New York dailies issued frantic appeals to Congress to stop the fleet from going. The head of the Senate Committee on Naval Affairs announced that the fleet should not and could not go because Congress would refuse to appropriate the money—he being from an Eastern seaboard State. However, I announced in response that I had enough money to take

[11] Art. IX. See Douglas S. Freeman, *George Washington*, IV, 438–41, 455–57, 543–44, 561, 595, 609; V, 82, 91–94, 150, 158–59, 172, 487–88.

[12] Holdsworth, *History of English Law*, VI, 138–40, 167, 225; Taswell-Langmead, *English Constitutional History*, 644.

[13] Fleming v. Page, 9 How. 603, 615 (1850); Prize Cases, 2 Bl. 635, 668 (1863); Clarence A. Berdahl, *War Powers of the Executive in the United States*, 117.

the fleet around to the Pacific anyhow, that the fleet would certainly go, and that if Congress did not choose to appropriate enough money to get the fleet back, why, it would stay in the Pacific. There was no further difficulty about the money."[14]

In practice, Presidents Lincoln and Franklin D. Roosevelt undertook to exercise wide powers over various sorts of matters affecting the successful prosecution of the wars being waged during their administrations.[15] These executive actions constituted part of the complex concept designated as the "war power," and discussed above in connection with the powers of Congress (Article I, section 8, clause 11).

Opinions of Principal Officers

The President's power to call upon the heads of the departments for a written opinion upon subjects relating to the duties of their respective offices was frequently utilized by President Washington. It was his habit to obtain opinions from different members of his Cabinet upon the same subject,[16] although the constitutional provision does not seem to require an officer to give an opinion regarding a matter arising in some other department.

The opinions of Cabinet members are purely advisory; the authority and responsibility for executive action rest solely upon the President.[17] The chief value of the provision enabling him to call for opinions is apparently to make it impossible for Cabinet officers to evade stating their positions until after the success or failure of a particular policy has been demonstrated by subsequent events.

[14] Theodore Roosevelt, *An Autobiography*, 552–53.

[15] James G. Randall, *Constitutional Problems under Lincoln*, 513–17; Edward S. Corwin, *Total War and the Constitution*, 16–22, 47–70, 91–105.

[16] In these discussions Hamilton and Jefferson "were daily pitted in the cabinet like two cocks." Jefferson to Walter Jones, March 5, 1810, in Jefferson, *Works*, XI, 137–38. Secretary of War Knox supported Hamilton; Attorney General Randolph usually supported Jefferson, although somewhat waveringly: "The fact is that he has generally given his principles to the one party & his practice to the other; the oyster to one, the shell to the other." Jefferson to William Branch Giles, December 31, 1795, in *ibid.*, VIII, 202. See also *ibid.*, I, 268, on foreign-policy discussions.

[17] Attempts had been made, particularly by George Mason, to saddle the President with an executive council. See note 9, page 280, above. His position would then have been similar to that of a Governor of Virginia under the constitution of 1776. Thorpe, *Federal and State Constitutions*, VII, 3816–17.

The President's pardoning power is patterned after that of the English king.[18] In the words of Chief Justice Marshall: "The constitution gives to the president, in general terms, 'the power to grant reprieves and pardons for offences against the United States.' As this power had been exercised, from time immemorial, by the executive of that nation whose language is our language, and to whose judicial institutions ours bear a close resemblance; we adopt their principles respecting the operation and effect of a pardon, and look into their books for the rules prescribing the manner in which it is to be used by the person who would avail himself of it."[19]

Accordingly, Marshall defined a pardon in the following terms: "A pardon is an act of grace, proceeding from the power intrusted with the execution of the laws, which exempts the individual, on whom it is bestowed, from the punishment the law inflicts for a crime he has committed. It is the private, though official, act of the executive magistrate, delivered to the individual for whose benefit it is intended, and not communicated officially to the court."[20] Hence a party claiming the

---

[18] There was no objection in the convention to granting this power to the chief executive, except for Randolph's proposal to exclude cases of treason, where the President himself might be guilty and the traitors might be his own instruments. Farrand, *Records*, II, 626–27 (September 15). See also *ibid.*, III, 218. Apparently Jefferson's theoretical objection that a power to pardon was superfluous in a republican form of government was not raised. In 1786 he wrote to a French historian: "The principle of Beccaria is sound. Let the legislators be merciful but the executors of the law inexorable." Observations to Démeunier, June 22, 1786, in Jefferson, *Papers*, X, 47. This is a reference to the views of the noted Italian criminologist Cesare B. Beccaria, *Dei delitti e delle pene*, sec. 46, copied in Jefferson's legal commonplace book, item 830 (Library of Congress). In commenting on extracts from Charles Louis de Montesquieu, *Esprit des Lois*, l. 6, c. 16 and 21, Jefferson wrote: "quaere if in a republic, whose punishments should be mild & proportioned, he would not think with Marquis Beccaria § 46. that pardons should be excluded." At another place he noted: "this confirms the conjecture in the margin that he does not think a power of pardon necessary but in monarchical governments." *Ibid.*, item 780.

[19] U.S. v. Wilson, 7 Pet. 150, 160 (1833). "A pardon is a deed, to the validity of which, delivery is essential, and delivery is not complete, without acceptance. It may then be rejected by the person to whom it is tendered; and if it be rejected, we have discovered no power in a court to force it on him. . . . A pardon may be conditional; and the condition may be more objectionable than the punishment inflicted by the judgment." *Ibid.*, 161.

[20] *Ibid.*, 160–61. But the courts must take judicial notice of a pardon by act of

benefit of a pardon must plead it or otherwise in some manner bring it to the attention of the court.[21]

On a previous occasion, during the proceedings against Aaron Burr in Richmond, a witness about to go before the grand jury, Dr. Eric Bollman, dramatically refused to accept a pardon tendered by President Jefferson. It had not been necessary for Chief Justice Marshall at the Burr trial in 1807 to decide what was the legal effect of such refusal; for the witness did not refuse to testify on the ground that it might incriminate him.[22] Bollman felt, according to his attorneys, that acceptance of a pardon might be "considered as an admission of guilt. Doctor Bollman does not admit that he has been guilty. He does not consider a pardon as necessary for an innocent man. . . . The man, who did so much to rescue the marquis la Fayette from his imprisonment . . . bears too great a regard for his reputation, to wish to have it sounded throughout Europe, that he was compelled to abandon his honour through a fear of unjust persecution."[23]

Marshall's concept of a pardon as a deed or charter, requiring delivery and acceptance, has the air of being a vestige of feudalism, smacking of a bygone era of English law. It views a pardon as a grant of an immunity from the normal processes of the administration of justice, akin to the chartered privileges of a medieval city or market place, or

Parliament. Such an act, unlike the king's charter, is considered as a public law "having the same effect on the case, as if the general law punishing the offence had been repealed or annulled." *Ibid.*, 163, quoting Blackstone, *Commentaries*, IV, 401.

[21] 7 Pet. at 163. In the Wilson case the defendant disclaimed reliance on the pardon. *Ibid.*, 158–59. The pardon remitted the death penalty on a charge of robbing the mail and putting the life of the carrier in jeopardy, but expressly stipulated "that this pardon shall not extend to any judgment . . . in any other case or cases now pending" for other offenses with which the defendant was charged. The pending indictment for simple robbery, however, was merged in the more serious offense and could not be separately prosecuted if the prior conviction had been pleaded. Since the conviction and pardon were not pleaded or relied upon by the defendant, the effect of the Supreme Court's decision was to permit sentence on the lesser charge, without deciding "whether a pardon of the greater offence, excluding the less, necessarily comprehends the less, against its own express terms." *Ibid.*, 153, 160.

[22] David Robertson, *Reports of the Trials of Colonel Aaron Burr*, I, 190–96.

[23] *Ibid.*, I, 196. In Burdick v. U.S., 236 U.S. 79, 85–87 (1915), a witness did refuse to testify on the ground that it might incriminate him, and also refused to accept a pardon tendered by President Wilson. The Supreme Court upheld the position of the witness, a city editor of the *New York Tribune*, who refused to divulge his sources for articles on frauds against the customs. But see Brown v. Walker, 161 U.S. 591, 599 (1896).

to an exemption from escheat and forfeiture of property upon conviction of felony.[24]

More in keeping with modern legal philosophy is the view expressed by Justice Holmes, which regards the issuance of a pardon as an official determination, in the normal course of operation of the machinery of government, that the public interest is best served in the particular case by imposition of a less severe penalty than would ordinarily be inflicted.[25] Thus a death sentence may be commuted to life imprisonment regardless of the wishes of the defendant.[26]

In support of this holding, Justice Holmes declared that: "A pardon in our day is not a private act of grace from an individual happening to possess power. It is a part of the Constitutional scheme. When granted it is the determination of the ultimate authority that the public welfare will be better served by inflicting less than what the judgment fixed. . . . Just as the original punishment would be imposed without regard to the prisoner's consent and in the teeth of his will, whether he liked it or not, the public welfare, not his consent, determines what shall be done."[27]

The President's power to pardon "Offences against the United States" is limited to offenses that have already been committed. It ex-

---

[24] Inhabitants of a city or visitors to fairs and markets often were exempted by charter from the normal jurisdiction of courts located elsewhere. The immunity from confiscation recognized by the custom of Kent was expressed in the rhyme "the father to the bough, the son to the plough." Robert von Keller, *Freiheitsgarantien*, 132–33, 177, 209, 229–37; Holdsworth, *History of English Law*, I, 219, 260.

[25] The contrast between the two attitudes of emphasizing, on the one hand, the privilege of the individual or, on the other hand, the operation of the institutions of government may be illustrated by the example of jury trial. With respect to jury trial, the Supreme Court held in Patton v. U.S., 281 U.S. 276, 296 (1930), that it is a privilege of the individual and may be waived; it is not a mandatory feature of the functioning of the judicial system.

[26] Biddle v. Perovich, 274 U.S. 480, 486–87 (1927).

[27] Of course it would not be a permissible exercise of the pardoning power to *increase* the original penalty, or to impose a punishment not warranted by law. No one doubts that a reduction in the term of imprisonment or the amount of a fine lessens the original penalty. "By common understanding imprisonment for life is a less penalty than death," though this is debatable because the nature of the penalties is different. But to deny the President the power to commute the death penalty would preclude clemency in the most important case and require him to permit an execution which he had decided ought not to take place "unless the change is agreed to by one who on no sound principle ought to have any voice in what the law should do for the welfare of the whole." *Ibid.*, 487.

tends to every offense known to the law, and may be exercised at any time after its commission, whether before, during, or after trial.[28] To pardon offenses not yet committed would be to grant a dispensation from the law, which was forbidden in 1689 by the English Bill of Rights.[29]

All offenses against the United States are included within the scope of the pardoning power, including criminal contempts.[30] A general pardon or amnesty may be used to deal with a large group or class of offenders.[31]

ART. II, SEC. 2, CL. 2

He shall have Power, by and with the Advice and Consent of the Senate, to make Treaties, provided two thirds of the Senators present concur; and he shall nominate, and by and with the Advice and Consent of the Senate, shall appoint Ambassadors, other public Ministers and Consuls, Judges of the supreme Court, and all other Officers of the United States, whose Appointments are not herein otherwise provided for, and which shall be established by Law: but the Congress may by Law vest the Appointment of such inferior Officers, as they think proper, in the President alone, in the Courts of Law, or in the Heads of Departments.

[28] Ex parte Garland, 4 Wall. 333, 380 (1867). The Court here said that the effect of a pardon is not only to relieve from punishment but to blot out guilt. On this, see Samuel Williston, "Does a Pardon Blot Out Guilt?" *Harvard Law Review*, Vol. XXVIII, No. 7 (May, 1915), 647, 653.

[29] Dumbauld, *The Bill of Rights and What It Means Today*, 167. For prior controversies regarding the dispensing power, see note 18, page 7, above.

[30] Ex parte Grossman, 267 U.S. 87, 110 (1925). Contempt of court is classified in two varieties. Criminal contempts punish disrespect for or interference with the functioning of courts; civil contempts are a mode of enforcing court decrees for protection of the rights of litigants. Where contempt proceedings are used to coerce parties into compliance with their obligations as determined in a civil decree, the pardoning power cannot be invoked. In both civil and criminal contempt proceedings the right to trial by jury exists only where it has been granted by modern statutes in particular cases.

[31] U.S. v. Klein, 13 Wall. 128, 139–42 (1872). Apparently Congress may grant an amnesty without infringing upon the President's pardoning power. Brown v. Walker, 161 U.S. 591, 601 (1896). But it cannot compel the courts to deny to a pardon the legal effect which they hold it should have. U.S. v. Klein, 13 Wall. 128, 145–47 (1872).

HISTORY

Treaty Power

IN Randolph's draft in the Committee of Detail he had enumerated among the legislative powers: "To make treaties of commerce"; "To make treaties of peace or alliance";[32] and "To send embassadors."[33] Further on, specifying the powers "destined for the Senate peculiarly,"[34] he enumerated: "To make treaties of commerce"; "to make peace";[35] and "to appoint the judiciary."[36] In a draft in the handwriting of James Wilson these provisions were combined to read: "The Senate shall be empowered to make Treaties of Peace, of Alliance, and of Commerce, to send Ambassadors, and to appoint the Judges of the Supreme national Court."[37] As reported by the Committee of Detail, this provision read: "The Senate of the United States shall have power to make treaties, and to appoint Ambassadors, and Judges of the supreme Court."[38]

The treaty-making power (as well as that of appointing ambassadors and members of the Supreme Court) was transferred to the President (by and with the advice and consent of the Senate) in recommendations later made by the Committee on Postponed Parts.[39] This proposal was accepted by the convention.[40] The Committee of Style

---

[32] Farrand, *Records*, II, 143. There were suggested restrictions upon exercise of these powers. A marginal note read "qu: as to senate."

[33] *Ibid.*, II, 144. All three clauses were stricken through, indicating that they had been transferred to the provisions regarding the Senate.

[34] *Ibid.*, II, 144.

[35] *Ibid.*, II, 145. In Rutledge's handwriting this was amended to read "to make Treaties of peace & Alliance."

[36] Rutledge added as a fourth item "to send Embassadors." *Ibid.*, II, 145.

[37] *Ibid.*, II, 155. The words "shall be empowered" were replaced by "of the United States shall have power," and the three specific types of treaties were stricken out, leaving a general power to make treaties.

[38] Art. IX, sec. 1. *Ibid.*, II, 183 (August 6).

[39] *Ibid.*, II, 495, 498 (September 4). There was added the restriction: "But no Treaty shall be made without the consent of two thirds of the Members present." This method of appointing the Supreme Court (based on the practice in Massachusetts) had been previously proposed by Gorham, but not adopted. *Ibid.*, II, 38, 41–44 (July 18); II, 80–83 (July 21).

[40] *Ibid.*, II, 533, 538 (September 7). A motion by Madison to delete the two-thirds requirement in the case of treaties of peace was adopted, but deleted on the following day. *Ibid.*, II, 533, 540–41 (September 7); II, 544, 547–49 (September 8). After various other proposed amendments had been defeated, the clause was adopted. *Ibid.*,

then reworded the provision in the form which now appears in the Constitution.[41]

Appointing Power

When the seventh resolution of the Virginia Plan was under consideration by the Committee of the Whole, an amendment by Madison was adopted giving the "national executive" power "to appoint to offices in cases not otherwise provided for."[42] Randolph's draft in the Committee of Detail incorporated it, adding the power of "commissioning officers."[43] That committee's report provided that the President "shall commission all the officers of the United States; and shall appoint officers in all cases not otherwise provided for by this Constitution."[44] In convention Madison's motion to substitute the phrase "appoint to offices" for "appoint officers" was adopted "in order to obviate doubts that he might appoint officers without previous creation of the offices by the Legislature."[45]

549–50 (September 8). Twice defeated was a proposal sponsored by Gouverneur Morris and Wilson to require assent of the House of Representatives to treaties. *Ibid.*, II, 382–83, 392–94 (August 23); II, 532, 538 (September 7). See also *ibid.*, II, 297 (August 15), where Mercer first raised this point.

[41] *Ibid.*, II, 599 (September 12).

[42] *Ibid.*, I, 63, 67 (June 1). This provision stood unchanged in the resolutions reported by the Committee of the Whole. *Ibid.*, I, 226, 236 (June 13). It was accepted in convention. *Ibid.*, II, 23, 33 (July 17); II, 116, 121 (July 26). Judges of the Supreme Court were to be appointed by the Senate, under Madison's suggestion accepted by the Committee of the Whole. *Ibid.*, I, 116, 119–21 (June 5); I, 224, 232–33, 236–37, 238 (June 13).

[43] *Ibid.*, II, 145, 146. Randolph enumerated the power "to appoint the judiciary" as one "destined for the senate peculiarly." *Ibid.*, II, 145.

[44] Art. X, sec. 2. *Ibid.*, II, 185 (August 6). Art. IX, sec. 1, provided that "The Senate of the United States shall have power . . . to appoint Ambassadors, and Judges of the supreme Court." *Ibid.*, II, 183. An amendment adding "and other public Ministers" after "Ambassadors" was adopted in convention, and the article was referred back to the Committee of Detail. *Ibid.*, II, 383, 394 (August 23). There was no further action until the Committee on Postponed Parts reported a new plan on September 4. See notes 45 and 46 just below.

[45] *Ibid.*, II, 398, 405 (August 24). An amendment of similar import by Dickinson was also accepted, covering appointment "to all offices established by this Constitution, except in cases herein otherwise provided for, and to all offices which may hereafter be created by law." *Ibid.*, II, 398, 405. "Officers" was restored in the proposal of the Committee on Postponed Parts transferring to the President power to appoint ambassadors and members of the Supreme Court. *Ibid.*, II, 495, 498 (September 4). A motion by Gerry similar to Madison's was then defeated as unnecessary; but during considera-

When the Committee on Postponed Parts submitted its plan of choosing the President by an electoral college, the scheme included a provision transferring to him, from the Senate, the power of appointing "Ambassadors and other public Ministers" as well as members of the Supreme Court.[46] But the President's appointing power was restricted by making it subject to the Senate's advice and consent. After debate (in which Wilson "objected to the mode of appointing, as blending a branch of the Legislature with the Executive . . . and there can be no good Executive without a responsible appointment of officers to execute") the clause giving the appointment power (as thus enlarged and at the same time diluted) to the President was adopted.[47]

Following the report of the Committee of Style,[48] some changes were made in convention.[49] Upon motion of Gouverneur Morris, a provision was added: "but the Congress may by law vest the appointment of such inferior Officers as they think proper, in the President alone, in the Courts of law, or in the heads of Departments."[50]

INTERPRETATION

Treaty Power

A TREATY is a contract or agreement between sovereign states, which derives its binding force from international law. The treaty-making power vested in the President extends to all proper subjects of negotiation between the United States and the governments of other nations.[51] There is language in opinions of the Supreme Court intimating that

tion of the draft of the Committee of Style the words "and which shall be established by law" were added. *Ibid.*, II, 545, 550 (September 8); II, 621, 628 (September 15).

[46] *Ibid.*, II, 495, 498 (September 4). See note 39, page 287, above.

[47] *Ibid.*, II, 533, 538–40 (September 7). An amendment adding "Consuls" to the officers to be appointed by the President was accepted. *Ibid.*, II, 533, 539.

[48] *Ibid.*, II, 599 (September 12). The Committee of Style overlooked the point that offices must be established by law before the President can fill them. See note 45, page 288, above. Perhaps this was another attempt by Gouverneur Morris to enlarge the scope of executive power, although it is more likely that the committee merely followed the new wording of the Committee on Postponed Parts.

[49] To meet the point mentioned in the preceding note, the words "and which shall be established by law" were added. *Ibid.*, II, 621, 628 (September 15).

[50] *Ibid.*, II, 627–28 (September 15). At first this motion was lost by an equal division of votes. "It was urged that it be put a second time, some such provision being too necessary to be omitted, and on a second question it was agreed to nem. con."

[51] Geofroy v. Riggs, 133 U.S. 258, 266 (1890); *In re* Ross, 140 U.S. 453, 463 (1891); Santovicenza v. Egan, 284 U.S. 30, 40 (1931).

even if nothing had been said in the Constitution regarding the President's treaty-making power, such power would nevertheless have been vested in the federal government as one of the "necessary concomitants of nationality" or incidents of sovereignty which must be found somewhere in every civilized government.[52]

But in the United States, by virtue of constitutional command,[53] treaties are more than political compacts with foreign states. They are also internal law, part of the supreme law of the land.[54] Hence if they contain self-executing provisions, they become immediately operative, without any further legislative or executive action, and the private rights which they create are judicially enforceable.[55]

Where a treaty has been validly made dealing with a proper subject for international regulation, Congress under the "necessary and proper" clause may legislate to enforce the treaty provisions, even if they deal with a subject-matter over which Congress would have no legislative authority in the absence of the treaty.[56]

Treaty stipulations, as part of the supreme law of the land, supersede conflicting provisions of state law.[57] Treaties are to be construed

[52] U.S. v. Curtiss-Wright Corp., 299 U.S. 304, 318 (1936); Missouri v. Holland, 252 U.S. 416, 433 (1920). Compare James Wilson's argument on the power of the Continental Congress to incorporate the Bank of North America under the Articles of Confederation. Randolph G. Adams, ed., *Selected Political Essays of James Wilson*, 132; James Wilson, *Works*, III, 406. See also Knox v. Lee, 12 Wall. 457, 535, 555 (1871); Jones v. U.S., 137 U.S. 202, 212 (1890); Fong Yue Ting v. U.S., 149 U.S. 698, 705, 711 (1893); Mackenzie v. Hare, 239 U.S. 299, 311 (1915); Burnet v. Brooks, 288 U.S. 378, 396 (1933).

[53] Art. VI, cl. 2.

[54] The Peggy, 1 Cr. 103, 109–10 (1801); Head Money Cases, 112 U.S. 580, 598 (1884).

[55] Foster v. Neilson, 2 Pet. 253, 314 (1829). The Court construed Art. 8 of the treaty with Spain of February 22, 1819, however, as contemplating and requiring further action in order to validate the land claims involved. *Ibid.*, 315. But in U.S. v. Percheman, 7 Pet. 51, 88–89 (1833), involving the same treaty language, the Court, upon having the wording of the Spanish version of the text brought to its attention, concluded that the provision was self-executing. See Edward Dumbauld, "John Marshall and Treaty Law," *American Journal of International Law*, Vol. L, No. 1 (January, 1956), 76–78.

[56] Missouri v. Holland, 252 U.S. 416, 432 (1920). See also Trade-Mark Cases, 100 U.S. 82, 99 (1879), and Baldwin v. Banks, 120 U.S. 678, 683 (1887). The treaty involved in Missouri v. Holland was for the protection of migratory birds. See Edwin M. Borchard, "Treaties and Executive Agreements," *Yale Law Journal*, Vol. LIV, No. 3 (June, 1945), 632–33.

[57] Ware v. Hylton, 3 Dall. 199, 243–44 (1796); Fairfax's Devisee v. Hunter's

liberally, to give effect to the intention of the negotiators. This rule prevails even where its application would result in conflict with state law; for state law must yield to the treaty which is part of the supreme law of the land.[58]

Treaties and acts of Congress are on a parity as part of the supreme law of the land;[59] hence the later in date prevails.[60] Unilateral repudiation of a treaty by one party, however, would not relieve the abrogating state of its duly incurred obligations under international law to the other party or parties, even though the treaty had ceased to be binding on the judicial organs of the abrogating state as a part of its internal law.[61] It is a political, not a judicial, question to determine whether or not a treaty is in force.[62]

Lessee, 7 Cr. 603, 627 (1813); Chirac v. Chirac, 2 Wheat. 259, 270–71, 274–75 (1817); Hauenstein v. Lynham, 100 U.S. 483, 488 (1880); Geofroy v. Riggs, 133 U.S. 258, 267 (1890); Clark v. Allen, 331 U.S. 503, 508 (1947).

[58] Nielsen v. Johnson, 279 U.S. 47, 52 (1929). But internal law is to be construed so as to avoid conflict with international law. Talbot v. Seeman, 1 Cr. 1, 43–44 (1801); Murray v. The Charming Betsey, 2 Cr. 64, 118 (1804); Cook v. U.S., 288 U.S. 102, 119–20 (1933).

[59] Jefferson at one time believed that a treaty was "a law of superior order, because it not only repeals past laws, but cannot itself be repealed by future ones." Opinion on Indian Trade, July 29, 1790. Jefferson, *Works*, VI, 111; cf. to Madison, May 31, 1798, in *ibid.*, VIII, 428. In a sense there is a superiority accorded to treaties in the rule that they will be interpreted liberally, whereas legislation will be construed restrictively so as not to conflict with international obligations. See note 58 just above.

[60] In Cook v. U.S., 288 U.S. 102, 118–19 (1933), the treaty with Great Britain of May 22, 1924, was held to have superseded conflicting provisions of the Tariff Act of 1922, even though they were re-enacted by the Tariff Act of 1930. For repeal of treaties by legislation later in date, see Chirac v. Chirac, 2 Wheat. 259, 272 (1817); Head Money Cases, 112 U.S. 580, 599 (1884); Whitney v. Robertson, 124 U.S. 190, 194–95 (1888); Chinese Exclusion Case, 130 U.S. 581, 600 (1889).

[61] Whitney v. Robertson, 124 U.S. 190, 194 (1888). The distinction between the international obligation of a treaty and its effect as internal law is also illustrated by the date when it takes effect. Internationally a treaty is binding retroactively from the time of signature; but as to private rights it does not become effective until after ratification. Haver v. Yaker, 9 Wall. 32, 34–35 (1870).

[62] Doe v. Braden, 16 How. 635, 657 (1853); Terlinden v. Ames, 184 U.S. 270, 286–88 (1902); Charlton v. Kelly, 229 U.S. 447, 473–75 (1913); Foster v. Neilson, 2 Pet. 253, 307, 309 (1829). See Edward Dumbauld, "John Marshall and the Law of Nations," *University of Pennsylvania Law Review*, Vol. CIV, No. 1 (October, 1955), 47. The treaty of February 6, 1778 (David Hunter Miller, *Treaties and Other International Acts of the United States of America*, II, 3), was abrogated by the Act of July 7, 1798, 1 St. 578, which contained recitals that there had been repeated violations on the part of France. This was the first treaty made by the United States, and antedated the Constitution. It was signed by Benjamin Franklin.

Besides treaties, other types of international agreements or compacts are recognized by international law.[63] As the sole organ of the nation in the conduct of international relations,[64] the President often has occasion to enter into agreements with the governments of foreign states. These are commonly called "executive agreements."[65] They are valid constitutionally insofar as they are confined to matters falling within the scope of the President's executive powers, or incident to the exercise thereof.[66] Because of the ease of consummating such agreements, in comparison with the requirement of obtaining a two-thirds vote of the Senate in order to conclude a treaty, there has been a growing tendency to use executive agreements instead of treaties wherever feasible.[67]

[63] There is also a distinction recognized in the Constitution between a "treaty" (referred to in Art. I, sec. 10, cl. 1) and an "agreement or compact" (referred to in Art. I, sec. 10, cl. 3). But neither term is defined in the Constitution. Some writers believe that the only distinction between the two types of instrument is procedural: that one which has been submitted to the Senate and approved by the constitutionally prescribed majority is a treaty; others are agreements or compacts. Edward S. Corwin, *The Constitution and World Organization*, 32; Quincy Wright, "The United States and International Agreements," *American Journal of International Law*, Vol. XXXVIII, No. 3 (July, 1944), 345. See pages 249–50 above.

[64] That the President is "the sole organ of the nation in its external relations" was asserted by John Marshall in his famed speech in the House on March 7, 1800, on the extradition of Jonathan Robbins. Dumbauld, "John Marshall and Treaty Law," *loc. cit.*, 75. See also U.S. v. Curtiss-Wright Corp., 299 U.S. 304, 319 (1936). This status of the executive branch in the international field results from the power to send and receive diplomatic representatives, as well as from the treaty power. Art. II, sec. 2, cl. 2; Art. II, sec. 3. Jefferson, the first secretary of state under the Constitution, had occasion to state forcefully to the French envoy Genêt that the President "being the only channel of communication between this country and foreign nations, it is from him alone that foreign nations or their agents are to learn what is or has been the will of the nation." To E. C. Genêt, November 22, 1793, in Jefferson, *Works*, VIII, 73. On another occasion Jefferson said: "The transaction of business with foreign nations is executive altogether." Opinion on the powers of the Senate, April 24, 1790, in *ibid.*, VI, 50.

[65] See Wallace McClure, *International Executive Agreements, passim*; and the articles by John Bassett Moore, Charles C. Hyde, Edwin M. Borchard, Quincy Wright, and Myres McDougal and Asher Lans listed in the Bibliography of this volume.

[66] For whatever the President can do of his own accord *sua sponte*, he can do pursuant to agreement with a foreign government. Corwin, *The Constitution and World Organization*, 41. See page 251 above.

[67] McClure, *International Executive Agreements*, 32; Wright, "The United States and International Agreements," *loc. cit.*, 343, 345, 354–55. See statistics compiled by John Bassett Moore in Borchard, "Treaties and Executive Agreements—A Reply," *loc. cit.*, 627. Opposition by Senators to the practice is sometimes a circumstance rendering use of an executive agreement not feasible. *Ibid.*, 634. Borchard lists ten differences

The Supreme Court, in several cases arising out of the so-called Litvinov Assignment of November 16, 1933, executed in connection with the recognition by the United States of the Soviet government of Russia, has held that an agreement thus incident to exercise of an executive function, while not constituting a treaty,[68] is nevertheless entitled to the "dignity" of a treaty[69] in that it supersedes and overrides state law and policy.[70]

Unquestionably the recognition of foreign governments is a political question for executive determination.[71] In the exercise of that executive function it was only "a modest implied power" attributed to the President by the Supreme Court when it held that he had power to determine policy with respect to matters incident to recognition, such as whether it shall be conditional or unconditional, and the terms upon which it should take place, as well as power to remove obstacles or impediments to recognition, and in that connection to provide for the settlement of claims of American citizens against Russia.[72]

between the two types of transactions (*ibid.*, 628–29) in reply to the contention of McDougal and Lans that the legal consequences of both are the same in domestic as well as in international law. Myres McDougal and Asher Lans, "Treaties and Congressional-Executive or Presidential Agreements: Interchangeable Instruments of National Policy," *Yale Law Journal*, Vol. LIV, No. 2 (March, 1945), 307.

[68] U.S. v. Belmont, 301 U.S. 324, 330 (1937); U.S. v. Pink, 315 U.S. 203, 229 (1942).

[69] 315 U.S. at 230. Similarly, in B. Altman & Co. v. U.S., 224 U.S. 583, 600–601 (1912), the Court held that a reciprocal tariff agreement concluded with France under statutory authority was not a treaty but was an international compact of sufficient importance to be interpreted by the Court under a statute giving the Court jurisdiction over cases in which the "construction of any treaty" made under the authority of the United States was drawn in question.

[70] 315 U.S. at 231. The same rule as in the case of treaties applies because the agreement is "an incident of recognition, an executive function." Borchard, "Treaties and Executive Agreements—A Reply," *loc. cit.*, 647. Since complete power over international affairs is vested in the national executive, there can be no interference by a state's law or policy with the policy determined by the national executive. 301 U.S. at 331. The reasoning is similar to that adopted in Board of Trustees of the University of Illinois v. U.S., 289 U.S. 48, 56–57 (1933), with respect to the commerce power of Congress: "As an exclusive power, its exercise may not be limited, qualified or impeded to any extent by state action." The Court cites Gibbons v. Ogden, 9 Wheat. 1, 196–200 (1824).

[71] This was established as early as Chief Justice Marshall's time. Rose v. Himely, 4 Cr. 241, 272 (1808); U.S. v. Palmer, 3 Wheat. 610, 634–35 (1818).

[72] U.S. v. Pink, 315 U.S. 203, 229 (1942). Settlement of claims against a foreign state is also a well-established executive function. John Bassett Moore, "Treaties and Executive Agreements," *Political Science Quarterly*, Vol. XX, No. 3 (September, 1905), 403–408.

Two of the reasons which had theretofore prevented recognition of the Soviet government were its propaganda program and its confiscatory nationalization of property without compensation to American citizens adversely affected thereby.[73] In his notes of November 16, 1933, Maksim Maksimovich Litvinov, the Soviet commissar for foreign affairs, undertook to give assurances regarding both of these controversial issues. With respect to the second, he released and assigned to the United States all claims of Russia against American citizens. Thereby a fund was created, to the extent of collections by the United States, out of which to pay claims of Americans against Russia.[74]

Pursuant to the Litvinov Assignment, the United States brought suit against a New York bank to collect the balance of an account opened by the Czar's government, and replenished by the deposit of five million dollars by the Provisional government which preceded the Soviet regime and was recognized by the United States. While so recognized, the Provisional government was notified by the bank that it had set off the balance against debts arising from seizure of ruble accounts in Russia. Following this notification, no suit had been brought against the bank until after the New York statute of limitations had run, although the courts were open to the recognized Provisional government of Russia. Upon these facts the Supreme Court held that the United States was in no better position than its predecessor in interest; that the recognition of the Soviet regime validated retroactively its acts in Russia but did not nullify or undo transactions consummated in the United States which had released the bank from liability before such recognition took place.[75]

[73] 315 U.S. at 239–40 (concurring opinion of Justice Frankfurter).

[74] This release and assignment would seem to be a unilateral grant, rather than an international compact, as the Court regarded it. 315 U.S. at 229. All that the United States agreed to do, by the exchange of notes, was to notify the Soviet government of the amount collected by the United States, in order that it could be credited against Russia's obligations to Americans. *Ibid.*, 213. For the text of the Litvinoff-Roosevelt correspondence, see *American Journal of International Law* (Supplement), Vol. XXVIII, No. 1 (January, 1934), 2–11. For the note of November 16, 1933, containing the Assignment, see *ibid.*, 10. For President Roosevelt's reply, stating that he would be pleased to transmit notification regarding the amount realized, see *ibid.*, 10–11.

[75] Guaranty Trust Co. v. U.S., 304 U.S. 126, 140–42 (1938). The opinion was by Justice Stone, who had also spoken for the Court in Compañía Española v. Navemar, 303 U.S. 68, 75 (1938). There an entry in the ship's roll made by the Spanish consul in an Argentine port, upon cabled advice of a Spanish confiscation decree, but without actual seizure, was held insufficient to confer exemption from United States admiralty jurisdiction as a Spanish public ship.

In another case the United States sued a private banker in New York to collect money which had been deposited by a Russian corporation. The corporation had been nationalized by Soviet decree, and the Soviet government's claim transferred to the United States by the Litvinov Assignment. Here the question arose whether the Soviet confiscation decree could have extraterritorial operation and affect the ownership of property situated in New York, not in Russia. Under the customary rules of "conflict of laws," this question would be decided by applying the law of New York; and the ordinary rule is that such transfers of property owned by a corporation will be recognized unless contrary to the public policy of the law of the place where the property is situated.[76] With respect to Soviet confiscation decrees, New York law took the view that they were against public policy and would not be recognized as affecting the ownership of property having its situs in New York. The Supreme Court held that New York law and policy was to be disregarded.[77] The United States was entitled to the money by virtue of the Litvinov Assignment and the recognition of the Soviet government. Such recognition validated retroactively the Soviet confiscation decree. The Court said:

> We do not pause to inquire whether in fact there was any policy of the State of New York to be infringed, since we are of opinion that no state policy can prevail against the international compact here involved. . . .
>
> We take judicial notice of the fact that coincident with the assignment set forth in the complaint, the President recognized the Soviet Government, and normal diplomatic relations were established between that government and the Government of the United States, followed by an exchange of ambassadors. The effect of this was to validate, so far as this country is concerned, all acts of the Soviet Government here

[76] For example, it might be contrary to public policy to recognize a transfer unless priority were given to creditors located in New York to obtain satisfaction out of the property situated there before it could be withdrawn from the state for distribution to creditors elsewhere. Discontogesellschaft v. Umbreit, 208 U.S. 570, 580 (1908); Clark v. Williard, 292 U.S. 112, 123 (1934). The Court remarked that the status of a statutory liquidator of an Iowa insurance company was "a succession established for the company by the law of its creation." *Ibid.*, 121.

[77] U.S. v. Belmont, 301 U.S. 324, 327 (1937). Justices Stone, Brandeis, and Cardozo concurred separately, on the ground that there was no proof of state policy conflicting with the Assignment or of any Presidential action conflicting with state policy. *Ibid.*, 334, 336.

involved from the commencement of its existence. The recognition, establishment of diplomatic relations, the assignment, and agreements with respect thereto, were all parts of one transaction, resulting in an international compact between the two governments.[78]

The Court conceded that the Litvinov Assignment was not a treaty, but it held that the same rule would apply as in the case of treaties, with respect to overriding state law. The Court declared that "while this rule in respect of treaties is established by the express language of cl. 2, Art. VI, of the Constitution, the same rule would result in the case of all international compacts and agreements from the very fact that complete power over international affairs is in the national government and is not and cannot be subject to any curtailment or interference on the part of the several states. . . . In respect of all international negotiations and compacts, and in respect of our foreign relations generally, state lines disappear. As to such purposes, the State of New York does not exist."[79]

The Supreme Court's ruling was elaborated in a third case, involving a suit by the United States to recover the remaining assets of a nationalized Russian insurance company after all claims of local creditors arising out of business done in New York had been provided for. The New York liquidation proceedings contemplated application of the fund to payment of certain foreign creditors of the company, and payment of the surplus, if any, to the remaining directors of the company.[80]

Viewed realistically, the issue therefore was whether the American

[78] 301 U.S. at 330.

[79] *Ibid.*, 331. See note 70, page 293, above. In other words, the Court is not relying upon Art. VI, cl. 2, and treating executive agreements as equivalent to treaties and hence as part of the supreme law of the land, but is using reasoning similar to that in Gibbons v. Ogden, 9 Wheat. 1, 196–200 (1824), to show that an exclusively federal power (such as that of the President over foreign relations) cannot be impeded to any extent by state action. Justice Stone's dissent pointed out that it was unnecessary dictum to consider whether the Litvinov agreement could rightly be given the same effect as a treaty. 301 U.S. at 336.

[80] U.S. v. Pink, 284 N.Y. 555 (1940); 315 U.S. 203, 210–11 (1942). The Court intimated no opinion concerning the validity of this preference to claims arising out of local business. *Ibid.*, 226–27. See note 76, page 295, above. The New York Court of Appeals had affirmed *per curiam* the decision of the lower courts of the state, in reliance upon Moscow Fire Ins. Co. v. Bank of N.Y., 280 N.Y. 286 (1939), affirmed by a divided court (Justices Harlan F. Stone, Stanley F. Reed, and Frank Murphy abstaining) on February 12, 1940. 309 U.S. 624.

assets should be used exclusively for the payment of American claims against the Russian government or whether foreign creditors of the company having claims against it based on business done outside of the United States should be allowed to participate.[81] To give such priority to its own nationals was a legitimate policy for the American government to adopt, and it did adopt it, in the Court's opinion, by accepting the Litvinov Assignment and recognizing the Soviet government.[82] State law and policy must yield to federal control of foreign relations, as expressed in a treaty, or in an international compact or agreement such as the Litvinov Assignment. The New York court's nonrecognition of the Soviet confiscation decree would definitely conflict with the federal government's recognition of the Soviet government, one consequence of which is the retroactive validation of that government's acts, including its acts of confiscation.[83]

The Court was undoubtedly correct in saying that the interpretation of the Litvinov Assignment, and determination of the rights acquired thereunder by the United States, was a federal question, not one of state law.[84] But if the correct construction of the Assignment was that it merely transferred to the United States whatever rights the Soviet government had,[85] and did not itself contain a self-executing independent determination of the scope of those rights,[86] then it is difficult

[81] 315 U.S. at 227–28.

[82] "It was the judgment of the political department that full recognition of the Soviet Government required the settlement of all outstanding problems including the claims of our nationals. Recognition and the Litvinov Assignment were interdependent. We would usurp the executive function if we held that that decision was not final and conclusive in the courts." *Ibid.*, 230.

[83] "Enforcement of New York's policy would collide with and subtract from the Federal policy," for the New York court "refuses to give effect or recognition in New York to acts of the Soviet Government which the United States by its policy of recognition agreed no longer to question. Enforcement of such state policies would indeed tend to restore some of the precise impediments to friendly relations which the President intended to remove. . . . Thus the action of New York tends to restore some of the precise irritants which had long affected the relations between these two great nations and which the policy of recognition was designed to eliminate." *Ibid.*, 231–32. See also the concurring opinion of Justice Frankfurter. *Ibid.*, 240.

[84] *Ibid.*, 217. See note 96, page 301, below.

[85] This construction had been given to the Assignment by the Court in Guaranty Trust Co. v. U.S., 304 U.S. 126, 141–42 (1938), and was accepted by the majority of the Court in the Pink case, 315 U.S. at 217.

[86] In Doe v. Braden, 16 How. 635, 658 (1853), a treaty with Spain transferred land to the United States as public domain, and expressly declared that a prior grant

to see why New York law would not govern in deciding what rights, if any, the Soviet government had obtained to the insurance company's New York assets by virtue of the Soviet government's confiscation decree.[87]

It is true that, as a practical matter, it may be thought that "gossamer" legal conceptions such as those regarding the "situs" of a debt are "too tenuous a thread" upon which to support a decision which in fact might produce serious international consequences by reason of its conflict with the President's policies regarding foreign affairs.[88]

To speak of a debt owed by a New York bank to a Russian corporation as "property" having a geographical location or "situs" in New York involves, indeed, the performance of a considerable feat of legal legerdemain.[89] The debt itself has no physical existence and is nothing more than an obligation existing by virtue of the law of some state which requires the debtor to pay the amount due. Such compulsion to

---

to the Duke of Alagon, made during negotiations for the treaty, was null and void. This declaration was accepted as conclusive upon United States courts. Thus if the Litvinov Assignment had contained a declaration concerning the effect of the Soviet confiscation upon assets in New York, the question whether an executive agreement overrides state law would have actually arisen. See 315 U.S. at 249–53. There would then also have been presented a due process question. Cf. 301 U.S. at 332, 335; 315 U.S. 228.

[87] If the question of the extraterritorial effect of the decree of confiscation is one of state law, the comment in Chief Justice Stone's dissenting opinion is pertinent: "State questions do not become federal questions because they are difficult or because we may think that the state courts have given wrong answers to them." 315 U.S. at 244. Likewise the mere fact that the state policy may conflict with the President's foreign policy would not be a ground for disregarding the state law. State law cannot be superseded in the absence of valid federal action, such as a treaty provision, or perhaps even conflicting executive action in a field exclusively committed to the federal government. See notes 79 and 86, pages 296 and 297, above.

[88] 315 U.S. at 238, 239 (concurring opinion of Justice Frankfurter). Even as between the states of the Union the problem of deciding "when may the policy of one state deny the consequences of a transaction authorized by the laws of another" has given rise to "a long history of judicial subtleties which hardly commend themselves for transfer to the solution of analogous problems between friendly nations." *Ibid.*, 239. See notes 76, page 295, above, and 90, page 299, below.

[89] While it is true that all property is created by law, nevertheless estates in land and tangible chattels have been regarded as possessing higher dignity than mere rights enforceable by legal proceedings in court. Truax v. Corrigan, 257 U.S. 312, 342 (1921); Mercoid Corp. v. Mid-Continent Co., 320 U.S. 661, 678 (1944). The latter type of rights are called "choses in action" and at common law were not assignable at all. Holdsworth, *History of English Law*, VII, 516, 531.

pay can be exerted only by a state where the debtor can be found and sued. In this sense the debt can be regarded as "property" having a "situs" in New York, where the debtor bank can be brought into court and compelled to make payment.

But would it not be equally logical to regard the "situs" of the property as located in the jurisdiction where the creditor can be found and subjected to the power of the courts and laws of the state? Particularly with respect to the transfer or devolution of the creditor's rights would there seem to be propriety in recognizing the effect of the law of the state where the creditor can be reached. Thus normally the estate of a deceased person is administered in the state of his domicile, even though the process of settlement may involve the collection of debts due from debtors located elsewhere. Similarly an insolvent corporation is usually liquidated in the state where it was organized.

Much litigation in the United States Supreme Court has arisen regarding the situs of a debt, particularly with reference to the power of states to impose a property or inheritance tax on such obligations.[90] In view of the intangible and "gossamer" qualities of the conflicting ratiocinations on this subject, it is readily understandable that the Court may have been reluctant, in a matter of serious international import and involving approximately one million dollars, to render a decision based upon the rule holding that New York law governed because the

[90] In Blackstone v. Miller, 188 U.S. 189, 205 (1903), it was held that New York could impose a transfer tax on a debt due from a New York bank to a decedent domiciled in Illinois (although Illinois also collected a similar tax). Justice Holmes said: "But it is plain that the transfer does depend upon the law of New York, not because of any theoretical speculation concerning the whereabouts of the debt, but because of the practical fact of its power over the person of the debtor. . . . What gives the debt validity? Nothing but the fact that the law of the place where the debtor is will make him pay." This case was overruled in Farmers Loan & Trust Co. v. Minnesota, 280 U.S. 204, 209 (1930), where Minnesota was forbidden to tax its negotiable bonds kept in New York. Justice Stone concurred on the ground that Minnesota law was not needed to transfer the bonds. Holmes thought it was that law which kept the obligation alive. *Ibid.*, 214, 217–18. In Baldwin v. Missouri, 281 U.S. 586, 591, 593 (1930), another Illinois testator escaped payment of Missouri's transfer tax on bank deposits, promissory notes signed by Missourians, and United States coupon bonds, all kept in Missouri. The Court held that the situs of bank deposits is at the domicile of the creditor. The rule of Blackstone v. Miller was rehabilitated following Curry v. McCanless, 307 U.S. 357, 366–68 (1939). The state where the debtor is located can also impose a property tax. Liverpool Ins. Co. v. Orleans Assessors, 221 U.S. 346, 354 (1911). The state where the creditor is domiciled can likewise impose both property tax and transfer tax. Kirtland v. Hotchkiss, 100 U.S. 491, 499 (1879); Blodgett v. Silverman, 277 U.S. 1, 14, 18 (1928).

"situs" of the Russian corporation's "property" was in that state, and that "comity" did not compel New York to recognize a foreign decree conflicting with the state's public policy.[91]

May not the Soviet confiscation decree be regarded as similar to the settlement of a deceased person's estate or the liquidation of a defunct corporation? Or to the forfeiture of a charter by quo warranto proceedings? If the President's executive decision to recognize the Soviet regime necessarily involved retroactive validation, insofar as American courts were concerned, of all the Soviet government's actions in Russia,[92] why not take the further step of saying that the confiscation decrees thus recognized as valid were applicable to all debts owed to the corporation, even though the debtor was located in New York? Should New York courts be permitted to continue to denounce as confiscatory and to ignore the legal effect of acts which the foreign policy of the nation no longer regarded as just cause for withholding recognition?[93]

The foregoing analysis of the Supreme Court's decisions involving the Litvinov Assignment indicates that although there is a substantial justification for the Court's conclusions when the issues involved are viewed from the standpoint of practical consequences and effect upon national policy in the conduct of foreign affairs, nevertheless from the standpoint of legal reasoning the Court appears to have gone astray. It ignored the fact that under the terms of the Litvinov Assignment the United States obtained only such rights as the Soviet government had, and that the extent of such rights depended upon the law of New York with respect to the extraterritorial effect of the Soviet confiscation decrees.[94]

Most of the severe criticism directed at the decisions was focused upon the supposed holding that an executive agreement could supplant

[91] For the "judicial subtleties" developed with respect to these problems in relation to interstate relationships in the constitutional law of the United States, see notes 76 and 90, pages 295 and 299, above.

[92] See note 83, page 297, above. There was no dispute over the fact that, under established precedents, recognition did have the effect of retroactively validating confiscations occurring in Russia. Guaranty Trust Co. v. U.S., 304 U.S. 126, 140 (1938).

[93] The Court regarded the case as one where the government was seeking "enforcement of its foreign policy in the courts." In such a case state policy was "wholly irrelevant." 315 U.S. at 233–34.

[94] These points were emphasized in Chief Justice Harlan F. Stone's dissenting opinion, in which Justice Owen J. Roberts joined. 315 U.S. at 244–45, 248–49.

state law to the same extent as a treaty.[95] Actually, the Court did not make such a holding. Indeed, it has been urged that the only proposition actually decided was "that the United States can by executive agreement acquire from a foreign sovereign property to which that government had, in the opinion of the Supreme Court, good title. The principle of Federal jurisdiction over Federal questions permitted the Supreme Court to decide finally on the Soviet Government's claim to title of the property in question, even though the State court had taken a different view."[96] As so restricted, the exuberant expressions of the Court regarding the "dignity" and effect of executive agreements shrink to the status of elaborate obiter dicta.

Besides executive agreements concluded by the President in the exercise of his own powers granted by the Constitution, many international agreements are made by the President in execution of laws enacted by the Congress. The earliest use of such compacts was in connection with the postal service. In 1792 the Postmaster General was empowered to "make arrangements with the postmasters in any foreign country for the reciprocal receipt and delivery of letters and packets, through the postoffices."[97] Another field in which such statutory au-

[95] The Belmont and Pink cases, as well as Missouri v. Holland, 252 U.S. 416 (1920), discussed at note 56, page 290, above, were often cited by proponents of the so-called "Bricker Amendment," a proposal to modify the effect of Art. VI, cl. 2. See, e.g., George A. Finch, "Observations on Proposed Amendments to United States Constitution," *Proceedings of the American Society of International Law* (1954), 136–38. On the other hand, writers favoring the use of executive agreements instead of treaties hailed the Belmont and Pink decisions as supporting their thesis that the two types of international compacts were interchangeable. McDougal and Lans, "Treaties and Congressional-Executive or Presidential Agreements," *loc. cit.*, 308–13. See note 67, page 292, above.

[96] Quincy Wright, "Congress and the Treaty-making Power," *Proceedings of the American Society of International Law* (1952), 45; 315 U.S. at 234. See notes 70, 79, and 84, pages 293, 296, and 297, above. In U.S. v. Allegheny Co., 322 U.S. 174, 182–83 (1944), the Court said: "Every acquisition, holding, or disposition of property by the Federal Government depends upon proper exercise of a constitutional grant of power. . . . The validity and construction of contracts through which the United States is exercising its constitutional functions, their consequences on the rights and obligations of the parties, the titles or liens which they create or permit, all present questions of federal law not controlled by the law of any State." See also U.S. v. Fullard-Leo, 331 U.S. 256, 269–70 (1947); Clearfield Trust Co. v. U.S., 318 U.S. 363, 366 (1943).

[97] Act of February 20, 1792, sec. 26, 1 Stat. 232, 239. Current legislation contains a provision that: "for the purpose of making better postal arrangements with foreign countries, or to counteract their adverse measures affecting our postal intercourse with them, the Postmaster-General, by and with the advice and consent of the President, may

thorization to make agreements with other nations has been used extensively is the regulation of foreign trade and tariffs.[98] Existing legislation continues in effect the reciprocal trade program inaugurated by Secretary of State Cordell Hull in 1934.[99] In view of the increasing impact of world affairs upon the national welfare, the enactment of legislation dealing with international matters is becoming more and more frequent.[100] As the legislative organ of a sovereign nation Congress has "indefinite power in the field of foreign relations";[101] and "if the subject-matter to be regulated falls within the powers of Congress, the latter may constitutionally authorize the President to deal with it by negotiation and agreement with other governments, the treaty-making power to the contrary notwithstanding."[102] Thus in the spheres of military assistance[103] and financial aid,[104] as well as educational ex-

---

negotiate and conclude postal treaties or conventions, and may reduce or increase the rates of postage on mail-matter conveyed between the United States and foreign countries." Act of June 8, 1872, 17 Stat. 304; 5 U.S.C.A. 372. Such a "postal treaty" was referred to as "the law of the land" in Cotzhausen v. Nazro, 107 U.S. 215, 217 (1882).

[98] Laws authorizing the President to modify applicable tariff rates were sustained as constitutional in Field v. Clark, 143 U.S. 649, 692 (1892); and Hampton & Co. v. U.S., 276 U.S. 394, 409 (1928).

[99] Act of June 12, 1934, 48 Stat. 943. The effective date of authority to conclude trade agreements thereby conferred was extended to July 1, 1967, by Act of October 11, 1962, 76 Stat. 872, 19 U.S.C.A. 1821.

[100] Walter S. Surrey, "The Legislative Process and International Law," *Proceedings of the American Society of International Law* (1958), 13–15.

[101] Corwin, *The Constitution and World Organization*, 46.

[102] *Ibid.*, 44. See also Charles C. Hyde, "Constitutional Procedures for International Agreement by the United States," *Proceedings of the American Society of International Law* (1937), 52, and Wright, "The United States and International Agreements," *loc. cit.*, 355. But Congress could not deal in this manner with matters outside its legislative powers. *Ibid.*, 347. In other words, Missouri v. Holland, 252 U.S. 416, 432 (1920), would not be applicable to such a case. See note 56, page 290, above.

[103] The Lend-Lease Act of March 11, 1941, 55 Stat. 31–33, was a notable example of such legislation authorizing transactions with foreign governments. It authorized the President to "sell, transfer title to, exchange, lease, lend, or otherwise dispose of" defense articles to "any country whose defense the President deems vital to the defense of the United States," upon such terms as he "deems satisfactory." Sections 4 and 7 of the Act contemplated the making of "contracts or agreements" for the disposition of such articles, and required the inclusion of certain provisions therein. Mutual aid agreements were negotiated pursuant to this Act whereby the United States furnished over forty billion dollars worth of munitions and supplies to its allies in World War II.

[104] Examples of legislation providing for conclusion of agreements with foreign nations (requiring their assent to certain terms prescribed by Congress as a condition of receiving aid) are the act to provide assistance for Greece and Turkey of May 22,

change,[105] extensive programs have been carried out, in the administration of which the conclusion of agreements with foreign nations was a necessary step.

Appointing Power

The language of the Constitution apparently distinguishes between three types of federal officials to be appointed by the President. The first group is composed of "Ambassadors, other public Ministers and Consuls." These are conceived of as holders of offices existing under international law, as an inherently necessary means of carrying on business between sovereign nations. For many years it was customary practice for the President to appoint officers with diplomatic functions whenever in his opinion they were needed, and for Congress simply to appropriate a lump sum "for the expenses of intercourse with foreign nations."[106] According to a written opinion rendered by Secretary of State Jefferson to President Washington, the determination of the need for a diplomatic mission and of the proper rank or grade of diplomat to be sent is exclusively an executive function.

In Jefferson's view, even the Senate had no share in deciding whether a diplomat of a particular rank or grade should be sent to a particular foreign post: "The transaction of business with foreign nations is executive altogether; it belongs, then, to the head of that department, except as to such portions of it as are specially submitted to the senate. Exceptions are to be construed strictly; the constitution itself,

1947, 61 Stat. 103; the Foreign Aid Act of December 17, 1947, 61 Stat. 934; the Foreign Assistance Act of April 3, 1948, 62 Stat. 138; the Mutual Defense Assistance Act of October 6, 1949, 63 Stat. 74; the Foreign Economic Assistance Act of June 5, 1950, 64 Stat. 198; the Yugoslav Emergency Relief Assistance Act of December 29, 1950, 64 Stat. 1122; the Mutual Security Act of October 10, 1951, 65 Stat. 373; the Mutual Security Act of August 26, 1954, 68 Stat. 832 (amended and carried forward by later acts and now replaced by the Foreign Assistance Act of September 4, 1961, 75 Stat. 424, 456, and the Foreign Assistance Act of August 1, 1962, 76 Stat. 255). The Mutual Defense Assistance Control Act of October 26, 1951, 65 Stat. 644, required recipient nations to take certain action (rather than merely to agree to do so) against trade with Iron Curtain areas as a condition of receiving aid. The Atomic Energy Act of August 20, 1954, 68 Stat. 919, is another important instance of legislation contemplating conclusion of agreements with other nations.

[105] The Fulbright educational exchange program was based on the Act of August 1, 1946, 60 Stat. 754, providing for executive agreements to use for that purpose the proceeds of surplus property on hand abroad at the end of World War II.

[106] See, e.g., Act of May 7, 1800, 2 Stat. 66; Act of March 3, 1801, 2 Stat. 120; Act of May 1, 1802, 2 Stat. 188.

indeed, has taken care to circumscribe this one within very strict limits; for it gives the nomination of the foreign agent to the president, the appointment to him and the senate jointly, and the commissioning to the president. . . . If appointment does not comprehend the neighboring acts of nomination or commission, (and the constitution says it shall not, by giving them exclusively to the president) still less can it pretend to comprehend those previous and more remote of destination and grade. . . . The senate is not supposed by the constitution to be acquainted with the concerns of the executive department. It was not intended that these should be communicated to them; nor can they, therefore, be qualified to judge of the necessity which calls for a mission to any particular place, or of the particular grade, more or less marked, which special and secret circumstances may call for. All this is left to the president; they are only to see that no unfit person be employed."[107]

Nevertheless, in 1855, Congress undertook to direct that the President "shall" appoint envoys of a certain rank to certain posts at prescribed compensation.[108] In 1909, Congress enacted that "hereafter no new ambassadorship shall be created unless the same shall be provided by Act of Congress."[109] In recent years, recognizing the importance of the foreign service and the need for a comprehensive merit system in that field, Congress has provided a detailed code of personnel administration.[110]

[107] Opinion of April 24, 1790, in Jefferson, *Works*, VI, 50–51. Hamilton likewise believed that the exceptions derogating from the President's executive power with respect to foreign affairs should be strictly construed. *Pacificus*, No. 1 (June 29, 1793), reproduced in Edward S. Corwin, *The President's Control of Foreign Relations*, 12, 14.

[108] Act of March 1, 1855, 10 Stat. 619. Attorney General Caleb Cushing construed the effect of this act to be merely that if and when the President should appoint an envoy of the specified grade to a specified station, he would be entitled to receive the compensation prescribed. 7 Op. 220.

[109] Act of March 2, 1909, 35 Stat. 672. This act may be interpreted as expressive of unwillingness that an American diplomat hold a post of high rank without appropriated funds being available to maintain the inevitable expenses of the office.

[110] The Rogers Act of May 24, 1924, 43 Stat. 140, established a unified "foreign service" to combine the previously separated diplomatic and consular services. The system thus inaugurated was codified by the Foreign Service Act of August 13, 1946, 60 Stat. 999. Various classes of foreign service officers were created, appointment to a higher class ordinarily requiring prior satisfactory service in the next lower class. Appointment after examination and probation was to be made to the lowest class, and not to a particular post. Promotions to a higher class likewise required advice and consent of the Senate. Hearing was to be accorded before dismissal for poor work or bad conduct.

The second group of officers recognized by the Constitution is composed of "Judges of the supreme Court." Probably this group is separately mentioned in the Constitution not in order to confer upon it a constitutional status but because originally it had been planned that the members of the Supreme Court, as well as diplomatic functionaries, were to be appointed by the Senate.[111] When the power was transferred to the President, the specific enumeration of those offices was preserved. Notwithstanding whatever constitutional status members of the Supreme Court may possess, the size of the Court, its jurisdiction, salaries, and other aspects of its operation are regulated by Congress.[112]

The third group is composed of all officers of the United States (other than those in the first two groups) "whose Appointments are not herein otherwise provided for, and which shall be established by Law." This language was preserved without change when the appointive power of the Senate over the diplomatic and judicial officers above referred to was transferred to the President. In fact there are now no officers of the United States whose appointments are "otherwise provided for" in the Constitution, unless one takes the view that the "Speaker and other Officers" of the legislative branch of the government are officers of the United States.[113] The President appoints all officers to whose appointment the advice and consent of the Senate is requisite.[114] The significant feature about this third group of officers is that the office must have been established by law before the appointment is made.

Besides the foregoing three groups of officers appointed by the President with the advice and consent of the Senate, the Constitution recognizes the potential existence of a class of "inferior" officers, estab-

[111] See page 289 above. This court is recognized in Art. III, sec. 1, and its Chief Justice is referred to in Art. I, sec. 3, cl. 6 (providing that he shall preside when the President is impeached).

[112] Durousseau v. U.S., 6 Cr. 307, 314 (1810); Wayman v. Southard, 10 Wheat. 1, 22 (1825); Ex parte McCardle, 7 Wall. 506, 513–15 (1869). See also pages 360–61 below.

[113] See Art. I, sec. 2, cl. 5; Art. I, sec. 3, cl. 5. In practice the Supreme Court also appoints its clerk, marshal, and other employees; but this is done by statutory authority, as there is no constitutional provision authorizing it. Matter of Hennen, 13 Pet. 230, 258 (1839).

[114] The President nominates such officers, and also appoints them (by and with the advice and consent of the Senate, which is a condition precedent to his exercise of the function of appointment). He also commissions "all the Officers of the United States." Art. II, sec. 3; Marbury v. Madison, 1 Cr. 137, 155–56 (1803).

lished by law, whose appointment is subject to the legislative pleasure of Congress. Congress is empowered to vest the appointment of such inferior officers "in the President alone, in the Courts of Law, or in the Heads of Departments."

Apart from the above-mentioned categories of officers, everyone on the federal payroll is to be regarded as an "employee," not an officer.[115]

The term "office," the Supreme Court has said, embraces the ideas of "tenure, duration, emolument, and duties."[116] Hence, a surgeon employed to examine applicants for pensions, at a fixed fee for each examination, was held not to be an officer.[117] The same conclusion was reached with respect to a merchant selected to appraise the value of dutiable goods for tariff purposes.[118]

Since the appointing power in the case of inferior officers must be vested in the President, in the courts, or in the "Heads of Departments,"[119] an appointment in fact made by a subordinate official will be presumed to have been made by his superior who is head of the department.[120] It is not necessary, however, that it be made by the head of the very department in which the appointee is to serve.[121]

It would doubtless be unconstitutional if Congress undertook to establish an office and require the President to fill it by appointing a particular person. But Congress may lawfully create a classified civil service, requiring appointments to be made from a list of persons who have by examinations demonstrated their ability to perform the duties of the office, and may establish appropriate professional or other qualifications to be required in the appointee.[122] Legislation to promote

[115] U.S. v. Germaine, 99 U.S. 508, 509 (1879).

[116] U.S. v. Hartwell, 6 Wall. 385, 393 (1868).

[117] U.S. v. Germaine, 99 U.S. 508, 511 (1879).

[118] Auffmordt v. Heden, 137 U.S. 310, 326–27 (1890).

[119] These are the same as the principal officers in each of the executive departments whose opinions in writing the President is entitled to call for under Art. II, sec. 2, cl. 1. U.S. v. Germaine, 99 U.S. 508, 511 (1879).

[120] Ekiu v. U.S., 142 U.S. 651, 663 (1892).

[121] Ex parte Siebold, 100 U.S. 371, 397 (1880). There Congress had vested in the courts the appointment of supervisors of elections.

[122] Myers v. U.S., 272 U.S. 52, 128 (1926). Justice Brandeis, in his dissenting opinion in that case (272 U.S. at 265–73), enumerates many laws restricting the President's appointing power by requirements of age, sex, race, politics, citizenship, residence, occupation, professional attainments, and the like. Congress has often named individuals to perform particular tasks: 3 Stat. 400 (John Trumbull to paint pictures); 19 Stat. 216 (committee to restore the parchment manuscript of the Declaration of Inde-

efficiency and integrity in the public service by prohibiting conflict of interests or political activity is also legitimate.[123]

Congress may also change the title or duties of an office,[124] and may add to the duties of an office by naming its incumbent as a member of a commission created to perform certain tasks.[125] Such action is not an attempt to usurp the President's appointing power.

Incident to the power of appointment is the power of removal.[126] In the case of inferior officers who are not appointed by and with the advice and consent of the Senate, Congress may provide, in the exercise of its power under the "necessary and proper" clause, how they shall be removed.[127] But in the case of officers appointed by and with the advice and consent of the Senate, Congress cannot take away from the President his power to remove them at pleasure, such authority being an incident to the appointing power and constituting an inherent part

pendence). See "Power of Appointment to Public Office under the Federal Constitution," *Harvard Law Review*, Vol. XLII, No. 3 (January, 1929), 430–31n.

[123] Civil Service Act of January 16, 1883, 22 Stat. 403; Hatch Act of August 2, 1939, 53 Stat. 1147; Ex parte Curtis, 106 U.S. 371, 372–73 (1882); United Public Workers v. Mitchell, 330 U.S. 75, 99 (1947).

[124] Crenshaw v. U.S., 134 U.S. 99, 109 (1890); Matter of Hennen, 13 Pet. 230, 258 (1839).

[125] Shoemaker v. U.S., 147 U.S. 282, 301 (1893). Cf. Springer v. Philippine Islands, 277 U.S. 189, 202 (1928), where the Court said that "the legislature cannot engraft executive duties upon a legislative office, since that would be to usurp the power of appointment by indirection." Voting power of stock in government-controlled corporations had there been entrusted to a committee composed of the President of the Philippine Senate, the Speaker of its House of Representatives, and the Governor General. *Ibid.*, 198. The Court regarded the duty of voting stock as executive, since it was clearly neither legislative nor judicial. *Ibid.*, 202. Justice Holmes, dissenting, pointed to the Smithsonian Institution, "to question which would be to lay hands on the Ark of the Covenant," as a parallel case. *Ibid.*, 211.

[126] Matter of Hennen, 13 Pet. 230, 259 (1839); Blake v. U.S., 103 U.S. 227, 231 (1881); Shurtleff v. U.S., 189 U.S. 311, 314–16 (1903); Wallace v. U.S., 257 U.S. 541, 544 (1922); Myers v. U.S., 272 U.S. 52, 164 (1926). The silence of the Constitution with respect to removal (except for the provisions of Art. II, sec. 4, in cases of impeachment) was never construed as prohibiting removal for other grounds, or as vesting in officers a life tenure in their offices. 13 Pet. at 259; 189 U. S. at 317. In early English Law the notion that an incumbent had a proprietary right to an office (for life or even transmissible by hereditary succession) was widely accepted. Holdsworth, *A History of English Law*, I, 19; Koenraad W. Swart, *Sale of Offices in the Seventeenth Century*, 45–67.

[127] U.S. v. Perkins, 116 U.S. 483, 485 (1886). This case did not involve the question whether the President's power to remove officers appointed by and with the advice and consent of the Senate could be curtailed by Congress. *Ibid.*, 484. See Myers v. U.S., 272 U.S. 52, 161–62 (1926).

of his executive function to take care that the laws be faithfully executed.[128] Congress had sought to impose restrictions on the President's removal power by the Tenure of Office Act[129] and other legislation[130] enacted during the "Reconstruction" controversy with President Andrew Johnson,[131] but the constitutionality of such laws was never upheld by the Supreme Court.[132]

The Court has, however, sought to impose restrictions on the President's power to remove members of "quasi-legislative or quasi-judicial agencies," such as the Interstate Commerce Commission or Federal Trade Commission, which are expected to act independently of and free from executive control.[133] The utilization of such agencies as part of the administrative process is probably desirable, or at least necessary, in modern society. But it is difficult to fit them into an appropriate legal niche in a system of government recognizing only a tripartite separation of powers.[134]

ART. II, SEC. 2, CL. 3

The President shall have Power to fill up all Vacancies that may

[128] Art. II, sec. 3; Myers v. U.S., 272 U.S. 52, 163–64 (1926). This notable decision adhered to the legislative interpretation adopted in 1789 by the first Congress. 272 U.S. at 111–36.

[129] Act of March 2, 1867, 14 Stat. 430.

[130] The Act of July 13, 1866, 14 Stat. 92, and the Act of March 2, 1867, 14 Stat. 487, restricted the removal of military officers.

[131] In Blake v. U.S., 103 U.S. 227, 236 (1881), the Act of July 13, 1866, 14 Stat. 92, prohibiting the dismissal of an army officer in time of peace except upon court martial, was interpreted as not intended to prevent his removal by the appointment of someone else to his place with the advice and consent of the Senate. Regarding the same rule, see also Quackenbush v. U.S., 177 U.S. 20, 23–24 (1900); and Wallace v. U.S., 257 U.S. 541, 545–46 (1922).

[132] Wallace v. U.S., 257 U.S. 541, 545 (1922). In Shurtleff v. U.S., 189 U.S. 311, 314–16 (1903), the Court assumed *arguendo* that Congress might impose restrictions but found that the language used was not sufficient to evidence an intent to limit the President's powers. In Parsons v. U.S., 167 U.S. 324, 342 (1897), the Court interpreted a provision that a United States attorney should be appointed for a four-year term as merely meaning that he should not serve for a longer period, but should serve for four years unless sooner removed by the President. By means of such restrictive constructions of the legislation, as well as the rule mentioned in the preceding note, the Court avoided passing on the constitutional question until the Myers case in 1926.

[133] Humphrey v. U.S., 295 U.S. 602, 628–29 (1935); Wiener v. U.S., 357 U.S. 349, 353 (1958).

[134] James M. Landis, *The Administrative Process*, 4.

happen during the Recess of the Senate, by granting Commissions which shall expire at the End of their next Session.

HISTORY

THIS clause originated in a proposal offered by Spaight of North Carolina: "That the President shall have power to fill up all vacancies that may happen during the recess of the Senate by granting commissions which shall expire at the end of the next session of the Senate."[135] A slight change in wording was made by the Committee of Style.[136]

INTERPRETATION

THIS clause has been construed in official practice as if it read "happen to exist" rather than "happen to occur." Efficient operation of the government would be hampered if an office had to remain vacant until the next session of the Senate and the President were unable to fill it during a recess merely because the vacancy had existed before the recess began.[137] However, the power of the purse in the hands of Congress[138] apparently warrants legislation withholding the salary of an interim appointee until he has obtained requisite Senate approval.[139]

ART. II, SEC. 3

He shall from time to time give to the Congress Information of the State of the Union, and recommend to their Consideration such Measures as he shall judge necessary and expedient; he may, on extraordinary Occasions, convene both Houses, or either of them, and in Case of Disagreement between them, with Respect to the Time of Adjournment, he may adjourn them to such Time as he

[135] Farrand, *Records*, II, 533, 540 (September 7).

[136] *Ibid.*, II, 600 (September 12).

[137] U.S. v. Allocco, 200 F. Supp. 868 (S.D.N.Y. 1961).

[138] See Art. I, sec. 8, cl. 1, and Art. I, sec. 9, cl. 7.

[139] The Act of February 9, 1863, 12 Stat. 642, 646, as amended by the Act of July 11, 1940, 54 Stat. 751, 5 U.S.C.A. 56, provides, subject to certain exceptions, that no money shall be paid out of the treasury as salary "to any person appointed during the recess of the Senate, to fill a vacancy in any existing office, which vacancy existed while the Senate was in session and is by law required to be filled by and with the advice and consent of the Senate, until such appointee shall have been confirmed by the Senate."

shall think proper; he shall receive Ambassadors and other public Ministers; he shall take Care that the Laws be faithfully executed, and shall Commission all the Officers of the United States.

THE essence of the President's executive power under the Constitution is the mandate that "he shall take Care that the Laws be faithfully executed."[140] In varying form, this provision goes back to the Virginia Plan.[141] Randolph's draft in the Committee of Detail empowered the executive "to carry into execution the national laws," and Rutledge added "receiving embassadors," "commissioning officers," and "convene legislature."[142]

The report of the Committee of Detail provided: "He shall, from time to time, give information to the Legislature, of the state of the Union: he may recommend to their consideration such measures as he shall judge necessary, and expedient: he may convene them on extraordinary occasions. In case of disagreement between the two Houses, with regard to the time of adjournment, he may adjourn them to such time as he thinks proper: he shall take care that the laws of the United States be duly and faithfully executed: he shall commission all the officers of the United States; and shall appoint officers in all cases not otherwise provided for by this Constitution. He shall receive Ambassadors and may correspond with the supreme Executives of the several States."[143]

In convention several verbal changes were made, one for the purpose of making it the *duty* of the President to recommend measures to Congress.[144] Other amendments added "other public Ministers" after

---

[140] See page 264 above.

[141] Randolph's seventh resolution conferred on the National Executive "a general authority to execute the National laws." Farrand, *Records*, I, 21 (May 29). In Committee of the Whole this was changed to "with power to carry into execution the national laws." *Ibid.*, I, 63, 67 (June 1). This was approved in convention. *Ibid.*, II, 23, 32 (July 17); II, 116, 121 (July 26).

[142] *Ibid.*, II, 145–46. For drafts in Wilson's hand, see *ibid.*, II, 158, 171.

[143] Art. X, sec. 2. *Ibid.*, II, 185 (August 6). The "take care" clause may have been based on the Pennsylvania Frame of Government of 1683. Thorpe, *Federal and State Constitutions*, VI, 3065.

[144] Farrand, *Records*, II, 398, 404–405 (August 24). Nevertheless there was grumbling when President Franklin D. Roosevelt frequently submitted fully elaborated drafts of proposed legislation to Congress.

"Ambassadors," and deleted as unnecessary, on motion of Gouverneur Morris, the provision about correspondence with state executives.[145] A motion by McHenry empowered the President to convene the Senate separately.[146]

INTERPRETATION

A NUMBER of routine administrative powers are here interspersed with several of major importance. The duty to furnish information and recommend measures to Congress makes it plain that it is not an officious intrusion upon the functions of the legislative branch, violative of the principle of separation of powers, when the President proposes a program of lawmaking to meet the needs of the nation.[147] In keeping with English custom when the king opens Parliament,[148] the first two Presidents delivered messages to Congress in person. President Jefferson, being only a mediocre orator and desiring to maintain an atmosphere of democratic simplicity, adopted the practice of transmitting messages in writing. This custom was continued until President Wilson resumed the habit of personal appearance.[149]

The duty of furnishing information to Congress is limited to information useful in connection with the enactment of legislation, and does not require the communication of confidential data (including FBI reports) which the President concludes it would be contrary to the public interest to disclose.[150]

The President's power to convene a special session of Congress "on extraordinary Occasions" (or to summon either house separately, as

[145] Farrand, *Records*, II, 411, 419 (August 25).

[146] *Ibid.*, II, 547, 553 (September 8). Wilson thought it improper for the Senate to be in session when the Congress as a whole was not. But there might be occasion for the Senate to act upon an important treaty without need for convening the entire Congress. The Committee of Style made only verbal change. *Ibid.*, II, 600 (September 12).

[147] See note 144, page 310, above.

[148] For a description of the opening of Parliament in 1593 when Lord Coke was speaker, see Catherine D. Bowen, *The Lion and the Throne*, 13–23.

[149] Charles Warren, "Why Jefferson Abandoned the Presidential Speech in Congress," *Massachusetts Historical Society Proceedings*, Vol. LVII (1924), 123. Regarding the policy of "Jeffersonian simplicity," in the course of which the President received the British Minister in carpet slippers, see Henry Adams, *History of the United States*, II, 363–76.

[150] See Watkins v. U.S., 345 U.S. 178, 208–209 (1957); letter of April 30, 1941, from Attorney General Robert H. Jackson to Congressman Carl Vinson, 40 Op. 45.

for the purpose of procuring speedy Senate approval of an important treaty)[151] supplements the provision[152] that Congress must assemble at least once a year. That regular and frequent meetings of the representatives chosen by the people should be provided for was a part of America's heritage from the struggles between crown and Parliament in England. To summon and to dissolve Parliament had been a royal prerogative; and the Stuart kings tried to make the meetings of Parliament as infrequent, short, and innocuous as possible. They summoned Parliament only when they were in need of revenue, and abruptly dismissed the representatives of the people when they began to discuss grievances or other topics displeasing to the monarch.[153]

Likewise the arbitrary dissolution of colonial legislatures by royal governors was a grievance enumerated in the Declaration of Independence: "He has dissolved Representative Houses repeatedly, for opposing with manly Firmness his Invasions on the Rights of the People. He has refused for a long Time, after such dissolution, to cause others to be elected."[154]

Mindful of these lessons of the past, the Constitution of the United States entrusted to Congress, not to the President, the power to decide when Congress should adjourn.[155] But in the event that they were unable to agree, the President was given the authority to adjourn them.

The President's power to receive ambassadors and other public ministers is one of major importance; for this power, together with the treaty power and the power to appoint ambassadors and other public ministers,[156] is the source of his control over foreign policy.[157] The power to recognize foreign states has long been recognized as an executive function.[158] Notable examples of nonrecognition were Soviet Russia

[151] See note 146, page 311, above.   [152] Art. I, sec. 4, cl. 2.

[153] Tanner, *English Constitutional Conflicts*, 45, 47, 49, 59, 64, 68–70. For eleven years (1629 to 1640) Charles I governed without a meeting of Parliament at all. *Ibid.*, 70.

[154] Dumbauld, *The Declaration of Independence and What It Means Today*, 102–105.

[155] Art. I, sec. 5, cl. 4.   [156] Art. II, sec. 2, cl. 2.

[157] See notes 64, page 292, and 107, page 304, above. Madison's polemic assertion as "Helvidius" in 1793 that the power to receive foreign ministers was simply a ceremonial function was never accepted in practice. Corwin, *The President's Control of Foreign Relations*, 24. The President's power to receive is a power not to receive.

[158] See note 71, page 293, above; Mexico v. Hoffman, 324 U.S. 30, 35 (1945); Compañía Española v. The Navemar, 303 U.S. 68, 74 (1938); *In re* Baiz, 135 U.S. 403, 432 (1890).

prior to November 16, 1933; the Chinese Communist government; and the "Stimson doctrine" of refusal to recognize the Japanese puppet government in Manchuria, established by aggression in 1932. An example of hasty recognition was President Theodore Roosevelt's action in 1903 when revolutionists in Colombia were promptly recognized as an independent state and a treaty was negotiated enabling the United States to construct the Panama Canal.[159]

The President's power to take care that the laws be faithfully executed constitutes the essence of his executive power. This, like the power over foreign affairs, involves a function of major importance. It does not deal with mere formalities of administrative routine.

This provision recognizes that the President is not required or expected to exercise all his powers personally, but is authorized to act through his subordinates. Their acts are ordinarily regarded in law as being his acts, and he may direct their decisions.[160]

The "laws" to be executed are not merely statutes of the United States. The entire legal order established by the Constitution is to be maintained.[161] The President may use troops to ensure transportation of the mails during a railroad strike.[162] Troops were also used by President Eisenhower in Little Rock, Arkansas, in 1957 and by President Kennedy in Oxford, Mississippi, in 1962 in order to enforce compliance with judicial decisions requiring racial integration in the public schools.[163] Use of the armed forces abroad in order to protect the rights

[159] Roosevelt, *Autobiography*, 524.

[160] Williams v. U.S., 1 How. 290, 297 (1843). See also Act of October 31, 1951, 65 Stat. 713, 3 U.S.C.A. 301. Of course there can be instances where the law confers discretion specifically upon a particular official, not subject to control by the President. President Jefferson's attempt to direct all collectors of revenue in enforcement of the embargo was thwarted by the wording of such a provision. Gilchrist v. Collector of Charleston, 10 Fed. Cas. No. 5420 (1808). See also Kendall v. U.S., 12 Pet. 534, 611 (1838).

[161] Thus a marshal who had killed a person assaulting a federal judge was held to be entitled to habeas corpus as being in state custody for an act done "in pursuance of a law of the United States." *In re* Neagle, 135 U.S. 1, 41, 59, 64 (1890). See also Cooper v. Aaron, 358 U.S. 1, 18 (1958); and Romero v. Int. Terminal Co., 358 U.S. 354, 393 (1959).

[162] *In re* Debs, 158 U.S. 564, 582 (1895).

[163] Brown v. Board of Education, 347 U.S. 483, 495 (1954); Cooper v. Aaron, 358 U.S. 1, 12 (1958); Alfred J. Schweppe, "Enforcement of Federal Court Decrees," *American Bar Association Journal*, Vol. XLIV, No. 2 (February, 1958), 113–16; Charles Warren, *The Supreme Court and Sovereign States*, 77. See also note 72, page 339, and pages 335 and 445, below.

of United States citizens under international law is also a matter committed to the care of the President as commander in chief.[164]

Executive action by the President cannot be ordered or prohibited by the courts;[165] but judicial relief against subordinate officers may be obtained.[166]

The provision that the President shall commission all the officers of the United States is a matter dealing with administrative routine. Issuance and delivery of an officer's commission is the final stage in the appointment process. To the President is committed the threefold task of nominating, of appointing, and finally of commissioning all officers of the United States.[167]

[164] See Art. II, sec. 2, cl. 1.

[165] Mississippi v. Johnson, 4 Wall. 475, 499 (1867).

[166] Youngstown Sheet and Tube Co. v. Sawyer, 343 U.S. 579, 584, 589 (1952); Larson v. Domestic & Foreign Commerce Corp., 337 U.S. 682, 689–90, 702 (1949); Philadelphia Co. v. Stimson, 223 U.S. 605, 619–20 (1912); Little v. Bareme, 2 Cr. 170, 178–79 (1804). See note 24, page 329, and note 106, page 345, below.

[167] See Art. II, sec. 2, cl. 2 and cl. 3; and notes 107, page 304, and 114, page 305, above.

ART. II, SEC. 4

The President, Vice President and all civil Officers of the United States, shall be removed from Office on Impeachment for, and Conviction of, Treason, Bribery, or other high Crimes and Misdemeanors.

HISTORY

TRIAL of "impeachments of any National officers" was one of the functions assigned to the national judiciary under the Virginia Plan.[1] In Committee of the Whole, on motion of Williamson of North Carolina, a provision was added that the executive was "to be removable on impeachment and conviction of mal-practice or neglect of duty."[2] Randolph's draft in the Committee of Detail expanded this to read: "to be removeable [*sic*] on impeachment, made by the house of representatives and on conviction of mal-practice or neglect of duty; before the supreme judiciary." In Rutledge's hand "Treason, Bribery or Corruption" was substituted for "mal-practice or neglect of duty."[3] The report of the Committee of Detail provided that the executive "shall be removed from his office on impeachment by the House of Representatives, and conviction in the supreme Court, of treason, bribery, or corruption."[4]

[1] Farrand, *Records*, I, 22 (May 29). Madison later said that this reference of impeachments to the judicial department "may be presumed to have been suggested by the example in the Constitution of Virg[ini]a." *Ibid.*, III, 528. See Thorpe, *Federal and State Constitutions*, VII, 3818.

[2] Farrand, *Records*, I, 78, 88 (June 2). This was accepted in convention after considerable discussion, during the course of which Gouverneur Morris changed his mind. *Ibid.*, II, 61, 64–69 (July 20); II, 116, 121 (July 26).

[3] *Ibid.*, II, 145. See also *ibid.*, II, 172.

[4] Art. X, sec. 2. *Ibid.*, II, 186 (August 6). On motion of Gouverneur Morris and Charles Pinckney proposals regarding the impeachment of other executive officers were referred to the Committee of Detail, and on motion of Gerry the committee was instructed to devise "a mode for trying the supreme Judges in cases of impeachment." *Ibid.*, II, 337, 344 (August 20). The Committee of Detail reported a provision that "The Judges of the Supreme Court shall be triable by the Senate, on impeachment by the House of representatives." *Ibid.*, II, 367 (August 22). See page 87 above.

At the instance of Gouverneur Morris, "who thought the tribunal an improper one" for trying such issues, this provision was postponed.[5] The Committee on Postponed Parts reported a plan for trial of all impeachments by the Senate, with a two-thirds vote required to convict. The Chief Justice was to preside when the President was on trial.[6]

In convention Mason inquired: "Why is the provision restrained to Treason & bribery only? Treason as defined in the Constitution will not reach many great and dangerous offences. . . . As bills of attainder . . . are forbidden, it is the more necessary to extend the power of impeachments." Accordingly he moved to add "or maladministration." Madison argued that this term was too vague. Mason withdrew that word and substituted "other high crimes and misdemeanors against the State." This addition was adopted,[7] as well as a further provision that "The Vice President and other civil Officers of the United States shall be removed from Office on impeachment and conviction as aforesaid."[8] The Committee of Style consolidated these clauses to read: "The president, vice-president, and all civil officers of the United States, shall be removed from office on impeachment for, and conviction of treason, bribery, or other high crimes and misdemeanors."[9]

INTERPRETATION

MEMBERS of Congress are not civil officers of the United States subject to impeachment under this clause.[10]

[5] Ibid., II, 422, 427 (August 27).

[6] Ibid., II, 493, 495, 497, 499 (September 4). The committee eliminated "corruption" as a ground for impeachment.

[7] Ibid., II, 545, 550 (September 8). Thereafter "United States" was substituted for "State" in the addition. Ibid., II, 545, 551 (September 8). A motion by Madison to strike out "by the Senate" in order to provide for trial of the President by a tribunal composed of or including the Supreme Court was defeated. Ibid., II, 545, 551 (September 8).

[8] Ibid., II, 545, 552 (September 8).

[9] Ibid., II, 600 (September 12). A proposal that impeached officers be suspended pending trial and acquittal was defeated. Ibid., II, 612 (September 14). For the Committee of Style's version of Art. I, sec. 3, cl. 6, see ibid., II, 592.

[10] See Art. I, sec. 6, cl. 2, which draws a clear line of distinction between persons holding an office under the United States and members of either house. The latter, however, are punishable by their own house. Art. I, sec. 5, cl. 2. The case of Lamar v. U.S., 241 U.S. 103, 112–13 (1916), upheld a conviction for pretending to be an officer of the United States, to wit A. Mitchell Palmer, a member of Congress. This case involved only a question of statutory construction, not one of constitutional interpretation.

It is doubtful what type of misconduct by officers is condemned by the term "other high Crimes and Misdemeanors." During the impeachments of Justice Samuel Chase in 1805 and of President Andrew Johnson in 1867 it was argued that the term includes only indictable offenses for which the defendant could be punished under the criminal law as it existed at the time when the acts complained of were committed. Some weight was given to this contention by the acquittal of Chase and Johnson.[11]

However, it is clear from the discussion by Mason when these words were substituted for his first expression "maladministration"[12] that a broader significance should be given to the language used. An effective equivalent was intended for the impeachments and bills of attainder which had been used in England as a means of political control.[13] On the other hand, it seems unlikely that the view is correct which regards impeachment merely as an inquiry whether the incumbent's office could better be filled by someone else.[14]

[11] Evans, *Report of the Trial of the Hon. Samuel Chase*, 118–21, 162, 175–79, 206–12; *Proceedings in the Trial of Andrew Johnson*, 97, 274. But in the twentieth century judges have been removed for unethical conduct which did not amount to a violation of criminal law. Felix Frankfurter and James M. Landis, *The Business of the Supreme Court*, 171; William S. Carpenter, *Judicial Tenure in the United States*, 145–53. In the case of judges holding office during "good behavior," impeachment is the only procedure available for determining whether the incumbent has complied with the proper standards of judicial behavior.

[12] See note 7, page 316, above.

[13] Chafee, *Three Human Rights in the Constitution of 1787*, 103–44; Tanner, *English Constitutional Conflicts*, 50, 66.

[14] This was in substance the position of the House managers in the impeachments of Chase and Johnson. Evans, *Report of the Trial of the Hon. Samuel Chase*, 108, 171, 238–39, 244–46, 256–57; *Proceedings in the Trial of Andrew Johnson*, 58, 82–102.

Article III—The Judicial Branch

Judicial Power and Tenure

ART. III, SEC. 1

The judicial Power of the United States, shall be vested in one supreme Court, and in such inferior Courts as the Congress may from time to time ordain and establish. The Judges, both of the supreme and inferior Courts, shall hold their Offices during good Behaviour, and shall, at stated Times, receive for their Services, a Compensation, which shall not be diminished during their Continuance in Office.

HISTORY

THE Virginia Plan contained as its ninth resolution a provision for the establishment of a federal court system: "that a National Judiciary be established to consist of one or more supreme tribunals, and of inferior tribunals to be chosen by the National Legislature, to hold their offices during good behaviour; and to receive punctually at stated times fixed compensation for their services, in which no increase or diminution shall be made so as to affect the persons actually in office at the time of such increase or diminution."[1]

In Committee of the Whole this was amended to read: "to consist of one supreme tribunal, and of one or more inferior tribunals."[2] Later the words "one or more" were eliminated.[3] A motion by Rutledge to delete "and of inferior tribunals" was adopted, after discussion. But a motion of Wilson and Madison was then accepted, providing "that the National Legislature be empowered to institute inferior tribunals." They observed that "there was a distinction between establishing such

---

[1] Farrand, *Records*, I, 21–22 (May 29). As to the text of this resolution, see also *ibid.*, III, 593–94. If the text referred to "one or more supreme tribunals," this may have been derived from the Virginia practice of separate co-ordinate courts for chancery, admiralty, and the like. Jefferson, *Papers*, I, 605–52; II, 566–82. William Waller Hening, *Statutes*, IX, 202–206, 389–99, 401–19, 522–25. When Dr. Johnson suggested "that the judicial power ought to extend to equity as well as law," Read of Delaware "objected to vesting these powers in the same Court." Farrand, *Records*, II, 428 (August 27).

[2] Farrand, *Records*, I, 95, 104–105 (June 4).   [3] *Ibid.*, I, 116, 119 (June 5).

tribunals absolutely, and giving a discretion to the Legislature to Establish them."[4]

During debate on the method of selecting judges, Benjamin Franklin "in a brief and entertaining manner related a Scotch mode, in which the nomination proceeded from the lawyers, who always selected the ablest of the profession in order to get rid of him, and share his practice among themselves."[5] After discussion of this subject, in which Wilson, Madison, Gorham, and Randolph spoke in favor of appointment by the executive, it was decided to vest the appointing power in the Senate.[6]

With respect to the judges' compensation, Gouverneur Morris was successful in eliminating the prohibition against increase of salary. Madison urged that variations in the value of money could be guarded against "by taking for a standard wheat or some other thing of permanent value." Morris replied that not only might the value of money alter, but the manners and style of living in the country might alter. Hence "the same value would not be the same compensation."[7]

The Committee of Style reported this clause as follows: "The judicial power of the United States, both in law and equity, shall be vested in one supreme court, and in such inferior courts as the Congress may

[4] *Ibid.*, I, 118, 124–25 (June 5). Rutledge argued "that the State Tribunals might and ought to be left in all cases to decide in the first instance," believing that "the right of appeal to the supreme national tribunal" was sufficient to secure the national rights and uniformity of judgments. He feared that needless encroachment upon state jurisdiction would create unnecessary obstacles to the adoption of the new Constitution. Sherman emphasized the expensiveness "of having a new set of Courts, when the existing State Courts would answer the same purpose." On the other hand, Madison declared that "An effective Judiciary establishment commensurate to the legislative authority, was essential"; and Dickinson "contended strongly that if there was to be a National Legislature, there ought to be a national Judiciary, and that the former ought to have authority to institute the latter." Wilson asserted that "admiralty jurisdiction ought to be given wholly to the national Government." (Indeed, such federal tribunals were already in existence under the Articles of Confederation.) There was similar debate, with the same result, in convention. *Ibid.*, II, 38–39, 45–46 (July 18). For the judiciary article (Art. XI), as reported by the Committee of Detail, see *ibid.*, II, 186–87 (August 6).

[5] *Ibid.*, I, 120 (June 5).

[6] *Ibid.*, I, 224, 232–33, 238 (June 13); II, 37–38, 41–44 (July 18); II, 72, 80–83 (July 21). The Committee of Detail retained this method of appointing Supreme Court judges. Art. IX, sec. 1. *Ibid.*, II, 183 (August 6). The Committee on Postponed Parts proposed to transfer the appointing power to the President, and this was agreed to. *Ibid.*, II, 495, 498 (September 4); II, 533, 539–40 (September 7). See Art. II, sec. 2, cl. 2, and notes 38–39, page 287, and 46, page 289, and page 287, above.

[7] *Ibid.*, II, 38, 44–45 (August 18); II, 423, 429–30 (August 27).

from time to time ordain and establish. The judges, both of the supreme and inferior courts, shall hold their offices during good behaviour, and shall, at stated times, receive for their services, a compensation, which shall not be diminished during their continuance in office."[8]

INTERPRETATION

"THE judicial Power of the United States," like the legislative and executive powers, is one of the three major branches of government provided for by the Constitution. The framers were influenced by the political system of "separation of powers" expounded by the famous French publicist Montesquieu, who considered such separation as the key to the maintenance of political liberty and as the characteristic feature of English polity.[9] Madison and Jefferson held the same view.[10]

The constitutional language that the judicial power shall be vested in specified tribunals, therefore, is merely a provision effecting a suitable distribution of governmental powers among the three branches of the government established by the Constitution. It is not a mandate to Congress requiring that body to confer upon federal courts the entire judicial power as defined in Article III, section 2, clause 1.[11] The words "shall be vested" do not have an imperative or mandatory sense, obligating Congress to "vest" the judicial power in federal courts, but are rather descriptive and self-executing, as if the clause read "The judicial power of the United States is delegated to one Supreme Court and

[8] *Ibid.*, II, 600 (September 12). The words "both in law and equity" were deleted in convention. *Ibid.*, II, 621 (September 15). They had been inserted at the suggestion of Dr. Johnson of Connecticut. *Ibid.*, II, 422, 428 (August 27). Doubtless they were regarded as repetitious in view of the more appropriate reference to law and equity in Art. III, sec. 2. *Ibid.*, II, 425 (August 27). For Art. XI, sec. 1 and sec. 2, as reported by the Committee of Detail, see *ibid.*, II, 186 (August 2).

[9] Montesquieu, *Esprit des Lois*, l. XI, c. vi.

[10] Madison wrote, in *The Federalist*, No. 47 (Lodge ed.), 300: "The accumulation of all powers, legislative, executive, and judiciary, in the same hands, whether of one, a few, or many, and whether hereditary, self-appointed, or elective, may justly be pronounced the very definition of tyranny." In his *Notes on Virginia*, Jefferson pointed out as a defect of that state's constitution the fact that "All the powers of government, legislative, executive, and judiciary, result to the legislative body. The concentrating of these in the same hands is precisely the definition of despotic government." Dumbauld, *The Political Writings of Thomas Jefferson*, 103. See also Edward M. Burns, *James Madison*, 41–42, 182.

[11] Justice Story's contrary view in Fairfax's Devisee v. Hunter's Lessee, 1 Wheat. 304, 328–31 (1816), has found no support in subsequent decisions or practice. See pages 158–60 above and pages 360–61 below.

320

such inferior courts as the Congress may from time to time ordain and establish, and is to be exercised solely by such judicial tribunals, and not by the Congress or President."[12]

The mandatory or imperative theory, that Congress must vest the entire judicial power in federal courts, is likewise disproved by the history of this clause. The power to create inferior courts was clearly made optional and discretionary with Congress. It was accepted as a compromise, Rutledge having opposed the establishment of any inferior federal courts at all.[13]

Judicial power consists of authority to decide "cases" and "controversies" of a justiciable character, as specified in Article III, section 2, clause 1. Such adjudication must be an authoritative and final determination of the litigation, and must be conclusive and binding upon the parties thereto. It cannot be ancillary or advisory. A court exercising the judicial power of the United States cannot be authorized or required to perform any nonjudicial functions.[14]

Judicial power also includes such ancillary and incidental powers as that of controlling the orderly conduct of judicial business,[15] adopting rules of procedure, and punishing contempts.[16]

The judicial power does not extend to political questions.[17] Con-

[12] This is proved by the fact that legislative and executive powers are conferred in similar terms: "shall be vested in a Congress" (Art. I, sec. 1), and "shall be vested in a President" (Art. II, sec. 1, cl. 1). Story's mandatory or imperative theory that these words impose a duty upon Congress is reduced to absurdity when applied to legislative powers. Congress cannot vest these in itself.

[13] See note 4, page 319, above. Under Rutledge's plan, all cases would have had to be instituted in state courts, with an appeal to the Supreme Court of the United States.

[14] Hayburn's Case, 2 Dall. 409 (1792); Gordon v. U.S., 117 U.S. 697, 700, 702 (1865); U.S. v. Ferreira, 13 How. 40, 49–53 (1852); Muskrat v. U.S., 219 U.S. 346, 361 (1911); La Abra Silver Mining Co. v. U.S. 175 U.S. 423, 458 (1899). The last-cited case shows that, notwithstanding Chief Justice Taney's statement in the Gordon case that execution is an essential element of judicial power, it is sufficient if the decision of the court determines conclusively the duty of an executive officer with respect to disbursement of a fund in his hands.

[15] McDonald v. Pless, 238 U.S. 264, 266 (1915). In this connection courts have inherent power to admit and disbar attorneys, as well as to appoint masters, referees, auditors, and other assistants necessary in the administration of justice. Ex parte Secombe, 19 How. 9, 13 (1857); Ex parte Peterson, 253 U.S. 300, 312 (1920).

[16] Michaelson v. U.S., 266 U.S. 42, 65 (1924); U.S. v. Hudson, 7 Cr. 32, 34 (1812).

[17] The distinction between judicial and political questions will be discussed in connection with the definition of "cases" and "controversies" under Art. III, sec. 2, cl. 1, below.

versely, neither Congress[18] nor the President[19] may exercise judicial power. "Legislative courts" established by Congress by virtue of its power to govern territories[20] do not exercise the "judicial power" delineated in Article III.[21] Hence Congress may confer upon such "legislative courts" administrative powers and other nonjudicial authority.[22] There can be no review by the Supreme Court, however, of a

[18] Thus Congress may not set aside judgments of a court, or order new trials, or direct what steps shall be taken in the course of a judicial inquiry. Stephens v. Cherokee Nation, 174 U.S. 445, 478 (1899). Special legislation permitting retroactive judicial review of a compensation award when subsequent disability was found to exist after expiration of the usual time for review did not constitute usurpation of judicial power. Paramino Co. v. Marshall, 309 U.S. 370, 378, 381 (1950). See also Johannesen v. U.S., 225 U.S. 227, 241 (1912).

[19] But the President may establish military tribunals, and provisional courts in occupied territory pending the establishment of civil government. These do not form part of the judicial system of the United States established under Art. III. Kurtz v. Moffitt, 115 U.S. 487, 500 (1885); Santiago v. Nogueras, 214 U.S. 260, 265–66 (1909). See also Ex parte Quirin, 317 U.S. 1, 25–29 (1942); and In re Yamashita, 327 U.S. 1, 7 (1946), regarding military tribunals established by the President under authority of Congress to punish violations of the laws of war as offenses against the law of nations (Art. I, sec. 8, cl. 10). Concerning international war crimes tribunals, see Hirota v. MacArthur, 338 U.S. 197, 198 (1948).

[20] Art. I, sec. 8, cl. 17, and Art. IV, sec. 3, cl. 2. Legislative courts can also be established by virtue of other powers, such as that of governing the District of Columbia, or that of paying the debts of the United States. Courts of the District of Columbia, it was finally held in O'Donoghue v. U.S., 289 U.S. 516, 545–46 (1933), have a dual status. They are Art. III courts (hence their judges have life tenure and their salary cannot be reduced), although they may also be vested with nonjudicial functions as legislative courts by virtue of the general legislative power of Congress to govern the District of Columbia. Art. I, sec. 8, cl. 17. See note 21, which follows.

[21] American Ins. Co. v. Canter, 1 Pet. 511, 546 (1828); Ex Parte Bakelite Corp., 279 U.S. 438, 449 (1929); Williams v. U.S., 289 U.S. 553, 565, 579 (1933). The same is true of military tribunals established in the exercise of executive power. See note 19 just above.

[22] Keller v. Potomac Electric Power Co., 261 U.S. 428, 443–44 (1923); Federal Radio Commission v. General Electric Co., 281 U.S. 464, 468 (1930); Williams v. U.S., 289 U.S. 553, 579–80 (1933). It is not the nature of the subject-matter involved but the nature of the procedure prescribed for dealing with it which makes a proceeding judicial or not. Tutun v. U.S., 270 U.S. 568, 576 (1926); Murray's Lessee v. Hoboken Land & Improvement Co., 18 How. 272, 284 (1856). Thus Congress can delegate to executive or state officials the power to arrest deserting seamen, naturalize aliens, take affidavits, and perform "such other duties as may be regarded as incidental to the judicial power rather than a part of the judicial power itself." Robertson v. Baldwin, 165 U.S. 275, 279 (1897). Such executive functions may include collection of a penalty and determination of the heirs of a decedent as ascertained by state law. Oceanic Navigation Co. v. Stranahan, 214 U.S. 320, 339 (1909); Hallowell v. Commons, 239 U.S. 506, 508 (1916).

legislative court's nonjudicial activities.[23] But the exercise of judicial functions by such a court is reviewable by the Supreme Court.[24]

The requirement that there be "one" Supreme Court was invoked by Chief Justice Hughes in 1937, during discussion of President Roosevelt's court reorganization plan, in response to suggestions that to expedite business the Court should sit in separate sections or divisions.[25]

Whether federal judges continue to hold their "Offices" as judicial magistrates even after abolition of the courts of which they are members has never been authoritatively determined.[26] The issue was debated fiercely[27] in President Jefferson's administration, when the "midnight judges" appointed by President John Adams were relegated to private life by repeal of the statute reorganizing the federal courts and creating sixteen additional judgeships which was enacted in the closing weeks of the Adams administration.[28]

On the other hand, when the ill-starred Commerce Court was abolished in 1913, the judges were retained in the federal service as circuit judges.[29]

The provisions of this clause of the Constitution regarding the tenure and compensation of judges were designed to ensure their independence by relieving them of "the temptation to cultivate the favor

[23] Gordon v. U.S., 117 U.S. 697, 699 (1865); U.S. v. Ferreira, 13 How. 48, 52 (1852); Federal Radio Commission v. General Electric Co., 281 U.S. 464, 469 (1930).

[24] Pope v. U.S., 323 U.S. 1, 13 (1944); Williams v. U.S., 289 U.S. 553, 565 (1933).

[25] Chief Justice Hughes stated that "the Constitution does not appear to authorize two or more Supreme Courts or two or more parts of a Supreme Court functioning in effect as separate courts." 75 Cong., 1 sess., Sen. Jud. Committee Hearings on Reorganization of the Federal Judiciary, Pt. III, 491.

[26] In Stuart v. Laird, 1 Cr. 299, 303–306 (1803), Charles Lee argued that the Act of March 8, 1802, 2 Stat. 132, was totally unconstitutional, though admitting that Congress had power to transfer cases from one court to another. That was the only aspect of the Act of 1802 actually involved and upheld in Stuart v. Laird, apart from the subsidiary question concerning the legality of requiring justices of the Supreme Court to sit in circuit courts. Long acquiescence in that custom made it too late to disturb the practice. 1 Cr. at 309.

[27] See *Debates . . . on the Bill*, 30, 33, 55, 300, 330–34, 394.

[28] The Act of February 13, 1801, 2 Stat. 89, was repealed by the Act of March 8, 1802, 2 Stat. 132. See Frankfurter and Landis, *The Business of the Supreme Court*, 24–29; Henry Adams, *History of the United States*, I, 274–78; Warren, *The Supreme Court in United States History*, I, 185–94, 206–15.

[29] Act of October 22, 1913, 38 Stat. 208, 219; Frankfurter and Landis, *The Business of the Supreme Court*, 173.

or avoid the displeasure of that department which, as master of the purse, would otherwise hold the power to reduce their means of support."[30] In England tenure during good behavior was established in 1701 by the Act of Settlement.[31]

Insistence by the English government that the tenure of judges in the colonies should be at the king's pleasure was a widespread source of friction, and in the Declaration of Independence one of the grievances charged against the king was that "He has made Judges dependent on his Will alone, for the Tenure of their Offices, and the Amount and Payment of their Salaries."[32]

[30] O'Donoghue v. U.S., 289 U.S. 516, 531 (1933). Regarding taxation as a diminution of compensation, see note 81, page 78, above. Rhode Island judges who in 1786 decided Trevett v. Weeden, the first American case in which an act of legislation was declared unconstitutional (for denying trial by jury), were replaced by the legislature upon the expiration of their one-year terms. Coxe, *An Essay on Judicial Power and Unconstitutional Legislation*, 234–47. In England, before the Glorious Revolution, many judges had been removed from office because their decisions displeased the crown. Of these Lord Coke was the best-known example.

[31] Act of June 12, 1701, 12 and 13 Wm. III, c. 2, sec. 3. George B. Adams and H. Morse Stephens, *Select Documents of English Constitutional History*, 479.

[32] Dumbauld, *The Declaration of Independence and What It Means Today*, 112–15.

ART. III, SEC. 2, CL. 1 *and* CL. 2

*The judicial Power shall extend to all Cases, in Law and Equity,
arising under this Constitution, the Laws of the United States, and
Treaties made, or which shall be made, under their Authority;—to
all Cases affecting Ambassadors, other public Ministers and Consuls;—to all Cases of admiralty and maritime Jurisdiction;—to
Controversies to which the United States shall be a Party;—to Controversies between two or more States; between a State and Citizens of another State;—between Citizens of different States,—
between Citizens of the same State claiming Lands under Grants
of different States, and between a State, or the Citizens thereof, and
foreign States, Citizens or Subjects.*

*In all Cases affecting Ambassadors, other public Ministers and
Consuls, and those in which a State shall be Party, the supreme
Court shall have original Jurisdiction. In all the other Cases before
mentioned, the supreme Court shall have appellate Jurisdiction, both
as to Law and Fact, with such Exceptions, and under such Regulations as the Congress shall make.*

HISTORY

THE Virginia Plan contemplated a national judiciary having jurisdiction over "all piracies & felonies on the high seas, captures from an
enemy; cases in which foreigners or citizens of other States applying
to such jurisdictions may be interested, or which respect the collection
of the National revenue; impeachments of any National officers, and
questions which may involve the national peace and harmony."[1]

In substance, the federal judiciary was expected to handle cases
having interstate or foreign aspects, or arising out of the operation of
the federal system itself. In order to leave the Committee of Detail a
free hand in elaborating the details of the judicial system, the specific
provisions preceding that relating to revenue were stricken. As reported
by the Committee of the Whole the jurisdiction of the national judiciary was to include "cases which respect the collection of the national

[1] Farrand, *Records*, I, 22 (May 29).

revenue, impeachments of any national officers, and questions which involve the national peace and harmony."[2] In convention the established principle was then generalized to state: "That the jurisdiction of the national Judiciary shall extend to cases arising under laws passed by the general Legislature, and to such other questions as involve the National peace and harmony."[3]

Randolph's draft in the Committee of Detail expanded the skeleton provision:

7. The jurisdiction of the supreme tribunal shall extend
    1 to all cases, arising under laws, passed by the general Legislature
    2. to impeachments of officers, and
    3. to such other cases, as the national legislature may assign, as involving the national peace and harmony,
       in the collection of the revenue
       in disputes between citizens of different states
       in disputes between a State & a Citizen or Citizens of another State[4]
       in disputes between different states; and
       in disputes, in which subjects or citizens of other countries are concerned
       & in Cases of Admiralty Jurisd[ictio]n.[5]

But this supreme jurisdiction shall be appellate only, except in Cases of Impeachm[en]t.[6] & in those instances, in which the legislature shall make it original. and the legislature shall organize it[.]

8. The whole or a part of the jurisdiction aforesaid according to the discretion of the legislature may be assigned to the inferior tribunals, as original tribunals.[7]

The Committee of Detail reported the jurisdictional provision in the following form:

[2] *Ibid.*, I, 211–12, 220 (June 12); I, 223–24, 232, 237, 238 (June 13). The New Jersey Plan added several new matters: "cases touching the rights of Ambassadors" and "the construction of any treaty or treaties or which may arise on any of the Acts for regulation of trade, or the collection of the federal Revenue." *Ibid.*, I, 244 (June 15).

[3] *Ibid.*, II, 39, 46 (July 18).

[4] This clause is added in Rutledge's hand.

[5] Rutledge also added the admiralty provision.

[6] The reference to impeachment was inserted by Rutledge.

[7] Farrand, *Records*, II, 146–47; Meigs, *Growth of the Constitution*, plate VII opposite page 316. A further stage of development is shown in a draft in Wilson's handwriting, with emendations by Rutledge. Farrand, *Records*, II, 172–73.

The Jurisdiction of the Supreme Court shall extend to all cases arising under laws passed by the Legislature of the United States; to all cases affecting Ambassadors, other Public Ministers and Consuls; to the trial of impeachments of Officers of the United States; to all cases of Admiralty and maritime jurisdiction; to controversies between two or more States, (except such as shall regard Territory or Jurisdiction) between a State and Citizens of another State, between Citizens of different States, and between a State or the Citizens thereof and foreign States, citizens or subjects. In cases of impeachment, cases affecting Ambassadors, other Public Ministers and Consuls, and those in which a State shall be party, this jurisdiction shall be original. In all the other cases before mentioned, it shall be appellate, with such exceptions and under such regulations as the Legislature shall make. The Legislature may assign any part of the jurisdiction above mentioned (except the trial of the President of the United States) in the manner, and under the limitations which it shall think proper, to such Inferior Courts, as it shall constitute from time to time.[8]

In convention, the words "judicial power" were substituted for "jurisdiction of the Supreme Court" on motion of Madison, seconded by Gouverneur Morris.[9] After "cases" the words "both in law and equity" were added.[10] On motion of Dr. Johnson the words "this Constitution and the" were inserted before "laws."[11] After "laws" the words "passed by the Legislature" were deleted, on motion of Rutledge, and "treaties made or which shall be made under their authority" added, "conformably to a preceding amendment in another place."[12]

The provision regarding impeachments was postponed,[13] and ultimately eliminated when trial of impeachments was given to the Senate.[14] A clause giving jurisdiction of controversies "to which the

[8] Art. XI, sec. 3. *Ibid.*, II, 186–87 (August 6).

[9] *Ibid.*, II, 425, 431 (August 27).   [10] *Ibid.*, II, 425 (August 27).

[11] *Ibid.*, II, 423, 430 (August 27). This change was made in conformity with the wording previously adopted for Art. VI, cl. 2. *Ibid.*, II, 381–82, 389 (August 23). Madison doubted whether it was not going too far to extend the jurisdiction of the Court generally to cases arising under the Constitution, and "whether it ought not to be limited to cases of a Judiciary Nature. The right of expounding the Constitution in cases not of this nature ought not to be given to that Department." Dr. Johnson's motion was agreed to *nemine contradicente*, "it being generally supposed that the jurisdiction given was constructively limited to cases of a Judiciary nature."

[12] *Ibid.*, II, 423–24, 431 (August 27). See Art. VI, cl. 2, and Farrand, *Records*, II, 409, 417 (August 25).

[13] *Ibid.*, II, 424, 431 (August 27).

[14] Art. I, sec. 3, cl. 6, and Art. II, sec. 4. See pages 87 and 315–16 above.

United States shall be a Party" was added on motion of Madison, seconded by Gouverneur Morris.[15] On motion of Sherman a provision was inserted giving jurisdiction of controversies "between Citizens of the same State claiming lands under grants of different States."[16] The last sentence of the section, regarding assignment of jurisdiction, was eliminated.[17]

In the portion of the section relating to distribution of jurisdiction, amendments were adopted substituting "the supreme Court shall have original jurisdiction" for "this jurisdiction shall be original,"[18] and "the Supreme Court shall have appellate jurisdiction" for "it shall be appellate."[19] The words "both as to law and fact" were added on motion of Dickinson after a question had been raised by Gouverneur Morris regarding the scope of the language used.[20]

The Committee of Style eliminated the exception regarding disputes between two or more states regarding territory or jurisdiction,[21] and made a few purely verbal changes.[22] There is no record of how the word "all" came to be inserted before "Cases affecting Ambassadors" in Article III, section 2, clause 2.

INTERPRETATION

IN this section the extent of the federal judicial power is delineated and specified. No proceeding in any court of the United States is possible unless it is authorized by the terms of one or more of the categories of jurisdiction here enumerated.

[15] *Ibid.*, II, 423, 430 (August 27). A similar proposal had been submitted to the Committee of Detail by Charles Pinckney and reported by the committee, but not acted on. "The motion of Madison and Gouverneur Morris attained the same purpose in better language." Meigs, *The Growth of the Constitution*, 246. See Farrand, *Records*, II, 335, 342 (August 20); II, 367 (August 22). A verbal amendment was then made inserting "controversies" before "between two or more States." *Ibid.*, II, 424 (August 27).

[16] *Ibid.*, II, 425, 431–32 (August 27). This provision was probably based on Art. IX of the Articles of Confederation.

[17] *Ibid.*, II, 425, 431 (August 27).   [18] *Ibid.*, II, 425 (August 27).

[19] *Ibid.*, II, 434, 437–38 (August 28).   [20] *Ibid.*, II, 424, 431 (August 27).

[21] The Committee of Detail had proposed elaborate provisions, based on procedure under the Articles of Confederation, for adjudicating disputes between states relating to territory or jurisdiction. Article IX, sec. 2 and sec. 3. *Ibid.*, II, 183–85 (August 6). These had been stricken out on motion of Rutledge. *Ibid.*, II, 396, 400–401 (August 24).

[22] *Ibid.*, II, 600–601 (September 12). The word "both" before "in law and equity" was stricken in convention. *Ibid.*, II, 621 (September 15).

In the first place it should be noted that the power here described is "judicial power," as vested in the preceding section of Article III. Hence it does not extend to matters not appropriate for or susceptible of judicial determination at all, such as political questions falling within the sphere of legislative or executive cognizance.[23] In the second place, the federal judicial power is by this section limited to the adjudication of "cases" and "controversies" of the types enumerated. Unless a dispute is presented in the form of a case or controversy the federal judicial power is incapable of acting upon it.

In the famous case in which an act of Congress was first held unconstitutional by the Supreme Court, Chief Justice John Marshall declared that it was beyond the province of the Court "to inquire how the executive, or executive officers, perform duties in which they have a discretion. Questions in their nature political, or which are, by the constitution and laws, submitted to the executive, can never be made in this court."[24] In another famous case, involving Spanish land grants in an area claimed by Spain as part of West Florida but regarded by the United States as part of the Louisiana Purchase, the Court refused to embark upon an independent investigation of the boundary dispute. Such a question was a matter for the political departments of the government. "The judiciary is not that department of the government, to which the assertion of its interests against foreign powers is confided. . . . A question like this, regarding the boundaries of nations, is, as has been truly said, more a political than a legal question and in its discussion, the courts of every country must respect the pronounced will

---

[23] Madison held the view that "a question, the moment it assumes the character of mere expediency or policy," is "evidently beyond the reach of Judicial cognizance." Madison to Spencer Roane, September 2, 1819, in *The Writings of James Madison*, VIII, 449.

[24] Marbury v. Madison, 1 Cr. 137, 170 (1803). Similar views had been expressed by Marshall as a member of Congress in his famous speech on the Jonathan Robbins case. John E. Oster, *The Political and Economic Doctrines of John Marshall*, 238–39. In the Burr treason trial, Marshall issued a subpoena to President Jefferson, who ignored it. For a photographic reproduction of it, see Worthington C. Ford (ed.), *Thomas Jefferson Correspondence*, opposite page 144. It is now settled that the President is not subject to restraint by injunction. Mississippi v. Johnson, 4 Wall. 475, 500 (1867). Nor can the head of an executive department be controlled by the courts in the exercise of his discretion. Georgia v. Stanton, 6 Wall. 50, 76–77 (1868). *Ultra vires* action, however, may be enjoined. Philadelphia Co. v. Stimson, 223 U.S. 605, 619–20 (1912); Harmon v. Brucker, 355 U.S. 579, 582 (1958). See also note 106, page 345, below.

of the legislature."[25] Another field in which Marshall established the rule of political rather than judicial determination was with regard to recognition of foreign governments.[26]

Besides matters relating to foreign affairs, there are many domestic issues where the courts will not interfere with the functioning of the political departments of government.[27] The guarantee to states of a republican form of government, and their protection by federal troops against domestic insurrection (Article IV, section 4), are matters with which the courts will not interfere.[28] The same is true with respect to the obligation imposed by Article IV, section 2, clause 2 and clause 3, regarding the interstate rendition of fugitives from justice and runaway slaves.[29]

---

[25] Foster v. Neilson, 2 Pet. 253, 307–309 (1829).

[26] U.S. v. Palmer, 3 Wheat. 610, 634–35 (1818). The same rule applies to determination whether a particular individual is entitled to diplomatic status or whether a treaty is in force. For later cases following the doctrine of political questions with respect to foreign affairs, see Gelston v. Hoyt, 3 Wheat. 246, 324 (1818); Doe v. Braden, 16 How. 635, 656 (1853); In re Baiz, 135 U.S. 403, 432 (1890); Fong Yue Ting v. U.S., 149 U.S. 698, 712–14 (1893); Terlinden v. Ames, 184 U.S. 270, 288 (1902); Charlton v. Kelly, 229 U.S. 447, 476 (1913); Compañía Española v. Navemar, 303 U.S. 68, 74 (1938); Ex parte Peru, 318 U.S. 578, 588–89 (1943); U.S. v. Pink, 315 U.S. 203, 229–30 (1942); Chicago & Southern Airlines v. Waterman Steamship Corp., 333 U.S. 103, 111 (1948). The last-named case also serves as a recent reaffirmation of the rule that a federal court cannot be called upon for an advisory opinion. 333 U.S. at 113.

[27] See on political questions, the articles by Oliver P. Field, Charles E. Martin, and Melville F. Weston listed in the Bibliography of this volume. Generally speaking, a question is political if it has been committed to the executive or legislative departments, or if no rules of law exist by which it can be resolved, but the decision must be based entirely upon policy, expediency, or statecraft. Questions regarding the existence or exercise of political authority usually fall within these categories. But see Baker v. Carr, 369 U.S. 186, 210 (1962), which emphasizes the first criterion, and regards the doctrine of political questions as an outgrowth of the principle of separation of powers. This case contains a comprehensive review of the authorities.

[28] Luther v. Borden, 7 How. 1, 39, 43 (1849); Cherokee Nation v. Georgia, 5 Pet. 1, 20 (1831); Georgia v. Stanton, 6 Wall. 50, 76 (1868); Taylor v. Beckham, 178 U.S. 548, 578 (1900); Pacific States Tel. & Tel. Co. v. Oregon, 223 U.S. 118, 142, 151 (1912); Davis v. Ohio, 241 U.S. 565, 569 (1916).

[29] Kentucky v. Dennison, 24 How. 66, 109–10 (1861). Attempts to enforce the fugitive slave law (Act of February 12, 1793, 1 Stat. 302) met with opposition in free states, although its constitutionality was upheld by the Supreme Court. See Prigg v. Pennsylvania, 16 Pet. 539, 621–22 (1842); Ableman v. Booth, 2 How. 506, 526 (1859). There appear to be no instances, however, of judicial action to enforce this constitutional provision in the absence of legislation.

Likewise disputes whether a statute has been duly enacted[30] or an amendment to the Constitution adopted[31] or electoral districts properly established[32] are regarded as political questions not subject to judicial determination. Whether it was lawful to build the Panama Canal is also a question of political nature.[33] However, the fact that the Supreme Court would have to exercise administrative functions in enforcing a decree regulating the allocation of water among several riparian states does not prevent its exercise of judicial power over a controversy between states.[34] Nor is it a political function to make findings, unreviewable by any other agency of government, as to whether a strike in the steel industry is injurious to the national health and safety.[35]

With regard to the nature of the cases and controversies with which the federal judicial power may deal, it is necessary that there be a bona fide clash or conflict between adverse parties with regard to their respective legal rights in a specific situation where a conclusive and effective determination can be made by the court.

In the frequently quoted language of Justice Field: "By cases and controversies are intended the claims of litigants brought before the courts for determination by such regular proceedings as are established by law or custom for the protection or enforcement of rights, or the prevention, redress, or punishment of wrongs. Whenever the claim of a party under the constitution, laws, or treaties of the United States takes such a form that the judicial power is capable of acting upon it, then it has become a case. The term implies the existence of present or possible adverse parties whose contentions are submitted to the court for adjudication."[36]

---

[30] Field v. Clark, 143 U.S. 649, 672 (1892). However, the effect of the Senate rules on outsiders was considered as raising a judicial question in U.S. v. Smith, 286 U.S. 6, 33 (1932). In that case the Court held that the Senate could not reconsider and withdraw its approval of an appointment after the President had commissioned the officer.

[31] Coleman v. Miller, 307 U.S. 433, 447–50, 457–59 (1939); Leser v. Garnett, 258 U.S. 130, 137 (1922).

[32] Colegrove v. Green, 328 U.S. 549, 554 (1946); South v. Peters, 339 U.S. 276, 277 (1950). But see Baker v. Carr, 369 U.S. 186, 209 (1962).

[33] Wilson v. Shaw, 204 U.S. 24, 31 (1907).

[34] Nebraska v. Wyoming, 325 U.S. 589, 616 (1945). See also U.S. v. California, 332 U.S. 19, 26 (1947), regarding difficulty in determining the location of a sinuous coast line.

[35] United Steelworkers v. U.S., 361 U.S. 39, 43 (1959).

[36] *In re* Pacific Ry. Commission, 32 Fed. 241, 255 (N.D. Calif. 1887). He adds

Chief Justice Marshall had declared that the judiciary could receive jurisdiction only when a question "shall assume such a form that the judicial power is capable of acting on it. That power is capable of acting only when the subject is submitted to it by a party who asserts his rights in the form prescribed by law. It then becomes a case."[37]

The Supreme Court's "most important and delicate duty," that of declaring unconstitutional a law enacted by Congress, is merely a consequence sometimes necessarily arising in the normal course of exercising the ordinary judicial function of deciding actual controversies between adverse litigants.[38] The Court's views on constitutional questions cannot be elicited, in the absence of an actual justiciable controversy, by a proceeding which is in substance a mere request for an advisory opinion.[39]

Likewise the Court will not render an opinion in a "moot" case, that is to say one where the Court's decision, by reason of events, would be denuded of practical effect. For example, a citizen's right to vote could not be effectively adjudicated after the election at which he desired to exercise his suffrage had already been held.[40]

---

that if there is any difference between cases and controversies, it is that the latter term applies only to civil suits, whereas the former would include criminal proceedings. The passage is discussed in Muskrat v. U.S., 219 U.S. 346, 356 (1911).

[37] Osborn v. Bank of the United States, 9 Wheat. 738, 819 (1824). *In re* Summers, 325 U.S. 561, 565–68 (1945), quoting Marshall's definition, held that a "case," with adversary parties, arose when the Illinois Supreme Court informally denied an applicant's right to practice law on the ground that he was a conscientious objector. The Illinois Court treated the proceeding not as an adjudication but simply as administrative action upon an application for appointment as an "officer of the court." In Cohens v. Virginia, 6 Wheat. 264, 405 (1821), Marshall had said, "If the question cannot be brought into a court, then there is no case in law or equity." See also his comments in the case of Jonathan Robbins, note 24, page 329, above.

[38] Muskrat v. U.S., 219 U.S. 346, 361 (1911). Hence the Court there held unconstitutional an act of Congress designed to test the constitutionality of certain other acts of Congress. The Act of March 1, 1907, 34 Stat. 1028, purported to authorize bringing suit to determine the validity of any acts of Congress passed since 1902 attempting to increase the number of persons then entitled to share in Cherokee lands. *Ibid.*, 362.

[39] As early as 1793 the Court refused to give President Washington the benefit of their legal advice. As they pointed out, Art. II, sec. 2, cl. 1, provides a method by which the President can obtain the opinion of the Attorney General of the United States as a guide to executive policy and action. Warren, *The Supreme Court in United States History*, I, 108–11.

[40] Mills v. Green, 159 U.S. 651, 653, 657 (1895). A suit to enjoin the Secretary of the Treasury from making payments for construction of the Panama Canal is moot

Similarly a feigned or fictitious issue will not suffice,[41] although the rule is often strained in cases where a stockholder sues his corporation to restrain it from paying a tax or complying with some other allegedly unconstitutional requirement imposed by legislation.[42]

Besides being genuine, the litigant's interest in the case must also be substantial. A citizen or taxpayer, merely as a member of the general public, does not have standing to challenge the expenditure of public funds or the validity of governmental action.[43] A mere difference of opinion with respect to an abstract question of law does not give rise to a controversy; there must be actual or threatened action adversely affecting the complainant's legal rights.[44]

It is now settled that the declaratory judgment is a remedy available under the federal judicial power.[45] The fact that no injunctive relief is sought and that no execution follows upon the court's judgment does not negate the existence of a genuine case or controversy, between adverse parties, and resulting in a conclusive and binding determination of the issues involved.

Federal Questions

The Judicial power of the United States does not extend to all types

after the payments have been made. Wilson v. Shaw, 204 U.S. 24, 30 (1907). After a child's graduation from school, questions regarding the propriety of the curriculum are moot. Doremus v. Bd. of Education, 342 U.S. 429, 432–33 (1952). An appeal by the government to test the trial court's rulings is moot after a verdict of not guilty. U.S. v. Evans, 213 U.S. 297, 299 (1909). Legislation enacted while a case is pending may make judicial relief unnecessary. The case is then moot. Berry v. Davis, 242 U.S. 468, 470 (1917); U.S. v. Alaska S.S. Co., 253 U.S. 113, 115–16 (1920).

[41] New Hampshire v. Louisiana, 108 U.S. 76, 88, 91 (1883). Cf. South Dakota v. North Carolina, 192 U.S. 286, 310 (1904).

[42] Dodge v. Woolsey, 18 How. 331, 346 (1856); Carter v. Carter Coal Co., 298 U.S. 238, 287 (1936).

[43] Fairchild v. Hughes, 258 U.S. 126, 129–30 (1922); Massachusetts v. Mellon, 262 U.S. 447, 488 (1923); Alabama Power Co. v. Ickes, 302 U.S. 464, 478–81 (1938).

[44] U.S. v. West Virginia, 295 U.S. 463, 473 (1935). Cf. U.S. v. California, 332 U.S. 19, 25 (1947). See also note 55, page 336, below.

[45] Aetna Life Ins. Co. v. Haworth, 300 U.S. 227, 240–42 (1937). Doubt had existed before this decision, because of language in Gordon v. U.S., 117 U.S. 697, 702 (1864); Liberty Warehouse v. Grannis, 273 U.S. 70, 74, 76 (1927); and Willing v. Chicago Auditorium Assn., 277 U.S. 274, 289 (1928). Cf. Fidelity Natl. Bank v. Swope, 274 U.S. 123, 132 (1927); and N., C. & St. L. R. Co. v. Wallace, 288 U.S. 249, 263–64 (1933).

of cases and controversies, but only to those specified in the ten categories set forth in Article III, section 2, clause 1. These categories fall into two groups: those classified according to the subject matter of the litigation, and those classified according to the parties thereto. In the first group are cases involving federal questions and admiralty jurisdiction; in the second group are all other types of cases falling within the scope of the federal judicial power.

As stated by Chief Justice Marshall: "The second section of the third article of the constitution defines the extent of the judicial power of the United States. Jurisdiction is given to the courts of the Union in two classes of cases. In the first, their jurisdiction depends on the character of the cause, whoever may be the parties. . . . In the second class, the jurisdiction depends entirely on the character of the parties. . . . If these be the parties, it is entirely unimportant what may be the subject of controversy. Be it what it may, these parties have a constitutional right to come into the courts of the Union."

Further elaborating this point, Marshall said: "In one description of cases, the jurisdiction of the court is founded entirely on the character of the parties; and the nature of the controversy is not contemplated by the constitution. The character of the parties is everything, the nature of the case nothing. In the other description of cases, the jurisdiction is founded entirely on the character of the case, and the parties are not contemplated by the constitution. In these, the nature of the case is everything, the character of the parties nothing."[46]

Marshall likewise declared that: "A case in law or equity consists of the right of the one party, as well as of the other, and may truly be said to arise under the constitution or a law of the United States, whenever its correct decision depends on the construction of either."[47]

He also emphasized that: "The article does not extend the judicial power to every violation of the constitution which may possibly take place, but to 'a case in law or equity,' in which a right, under such law, is asserted in a court of justice. If the question cannot be brought into

[46] Cohens v. Va., 6 Wheat. 264, 378, 393 (1821).

[47] *Ibid.*, 379. In Osborn v. Bank of the U.S., 9 Wheat. 738, 825–27 (1824), Marshall held that any suit brought by the bank was a case arising under the laws of the United States since the bank was incorporated by an act of Congress. A similar holding was made in Pacific Railroad Removal Cases, 115 U.S. 1, 11 (1885). Congress has since eliminated this ground of litigation in federal courts. Romero v. International Terminal Co., 358 U.S. 354, 379 (1959).

a court, then there is no case in law or equity, and no jurisdiction is given by the words of the article. But if, in any controversy depending in a court, the cause should depend on the validity of such a law, that would be a case arising under the constitution, to which the judicial power of the United States would extend."[48]

The meaning of the terms "law" and "equity" (as well as of "admiralty and maritime jurisdiction") must be discovered by resort to the principles of the English common law.[49]

In early times the chancellor was usually an ecclesiastical dignitary, and as "keeper of the king's conscience" undertook to mitigate the strictness of common law rules by applying ethical and moral standards more adequate to the exigencies of justice. In Lord Coke's day the chancery and common law courts were separate and rival tribunals. Modern law seeks to amalgamate in a single body of law the doctrines developed by both types of courts in the course of their history.[50]

The "Laws of the United States" are the legislative enactments passed by Congress and approved by the President, or which otherwise "shall become.a Law" by virtue of the provisions of Article I, section 7, clause 2. Perhaps the term also includes judicial decisions rendered by federal courts, as it apparently does in Article II, section 3, clause 4.

The distinction between treaties "made" and those "which shall

[48] 6 Wheat. at 405. In his famous speech in Congress on the Jonathan Robbins case, Marshall had earlier stressed the same distinction. Oster, *The Political and Economic Doctrines of John Marshall*, 238. Madison had favored the same restriction in convention. Farrand, *Records*, II, 430 (August 27). It was Dr. Johnson who moved to add the words "in law and equity." *Ibid.*, II, 428. See note 8, page 320, and note 11, page 327, above (Art. III, sec. 2, cl. 1).

[49] This clause is an excellent example of the often-stressed truth that the language of the Constitution itself cannot be understood or interpreted without reference to the common law. Smith v. Alabama, 124 U.S. 465, 478 (1888); U.S. v. Wong Kim Ark, 169 U.S. 649, 654 (1898); McNally v. Hill, 293 U.S. 131, 136 (1934); D'Oench, Duhme & Co. v. F.D.I.C., 315 U.S. 447, 470–71 (1942). In Ex parte State of New York, 256 U.S. 490, 498 (1921), the words "law and equity" in the Eleventh Amendment were interpreted as impliedly including "admiralty" also.

[50] In Roman law the praetor likewise acted *juris civilis adjuvandi aut supplendi aut corrigendi causa* to mitigate the rigor of the strict civil law. A renowned historian of English law writes: "Equity now is that body of rules administered by our English courts of justice which, were it not for the operation of the Judicature Acts, would be administered by those courts which would be known as Courts of Equity. . . . Equity is a certain portion of our existing substantive law, yet in order that we may describe this portion and mark it off from other portions we have to make reference to courts that are no longer in existence. Still I fear that nothing better than this is possible." Frederic W. Maitland, *Equity*, 1.

be made" under the authority of the United States is that the former were negotiated while the Articles of Confederation were in effect, before the Constitution became operative.[51] Both types of treaties, regardless of date, are recognized by the Constitution as equally valid and binding.

This clause, extending the federal judicial power to all cases involving federal questions (in conjunction with the "supremacy" clause),[52] is the legal basis of the claim of the Supreme Court of the United States to possess authority to declare acts of Congress and of state legislatures unconstitutional and void by reason of conflict with the federal Constitution.[53] It must be emphasized in this connection that the courts have no substantive power to veto legislation, such as that in which they would have participated as members of a council of revision modeled after the New York constitution of 1777, if proposals to establish such a scheme had been accepted by the convention in 1787.[54] The judicial power to pass upon the constitutionality of legislation is simply one aspect of the normal judicial function of ascertaining what the law is which is applicable to a case or controversy pending before a court.[55]

[51] Worcester v. Georgia, 6 Pet. 515, 559 (1832). The same wording appears in Art. VI, cl. 2 (the "supremacy clause"). See page 327 above and page 444 below. See Dumbauld, "John Marshall and Treaty Law," loc. cit., 80.

[52] Art. VI, cl. 2, which provides that "This Constitution, and the Laws of the United States which shall be made in pursuance thereof; and all Treaties made, or which shall be made, under the Authority of the United States, shall be the supreme Law of the Land."

[53] The first time that an act of Congress was actually held unconstitutional was in the famous case of Marbury v. Madison, 1 Cr. 137, 176–80 (1803). See David H. Miller, "Some Early Cases in the Supreme Court of the United States," Virginia Law Review, Vol. VIII, No. 2 (December, 1921), 120. The doctrine was not a novelty, however. Dumbauld, "Thomas Jefferson and American Constitutional Law," loc. cit., 385. For earlier intimations of the principle, see Chisholm v. Georgia, 2 Dall. 419, 433 (1793); Vanhorne's Lessee v. Dorrance, 2 Dall. 304, 308–309 (1795); Cooper v. Telfair, 4 Dall. 14, 19 (1800). See page 20 above.

[54] Farrand, Records, I, 21 (May 29); I, 131, 138–40 (June 6); II, 71, 73–80 (July 21); II, 294–95, 298 (August 15). See pages 40–41 and 103–104 above.

[55] See page 332 above. Muskrat v. U.S., 219 U.S. 346, 361 (1911); Adkins v. Children's Hospital, 261 U.S. 525, 544 (1923); Massachusetts v. Mellon, 262 U.S. 447, 488 (1923). Hence an injunction cannot be obtained merely because a law is unconstitutional. The traditional requisites of equity jurisdiction must be shown, such as irreparable injury and lack of an adequate remedy at law. Cruickshank v. Bidwell, 176 U.S. 73, 80 (1900). No one who is not adversely affected by it may challenge the constitutionality of a law. Premier-Pabst Sales Co. v. Grosscup, 298 U.S. 226, 227 (1936); Ex parte Albert Levitt, 302 U.S. 633, 638 (1937); Tileston v. Ullman, 318 U.S. 44, 46 (1943); Doremus v. Bd. of Education, 342 U.S. 429, 433–34 (1952).

In exercising the power to construe and pass upon the constitutionality of laws where a federal question is involved, the Supreme Court has evolved a number of maxims or rules of interpretation: such as that a ruling whether a law is constitutional will not be made unless it is actually necessary to do so;[56] that a law will be presumed to be constitutional and will not be held void unless its invalidity is clear and indubitable;[57] that whenever possible[58] a law will be interpreted so as to avoid conflict with the Constitution[59] or with the nation's obligations under international law;[60] and numerous other rules of statutory construction.[61]

Where a question under the Constitution, laws, or treaties of the United States is concerned, the Supreme Court has the last word,

[56] Harmon v. Brucker, 355 U.S. 579, 581 (1958); Barr v. Matteo, 355 U.S. 171, 172 (1957); Peters v. Hobby, 349 U.S. 331, 338 (1955); Rice v. Sioux City Cemetery, 349 U.S. 70, 74 (1955); Rescue Army v. Municipal Court, 331 U.S. 549, 568–75 (1947); Ashwander v. T.V.A., 297 U.S. 288, 345–48 (1936).

[57] Hylton v. U.S., 3 Dall. 171, 175 (1796); U.S. v. Carolene Products Co., 304 U.S. 144, 152 (1938).

[58] Of course where the meaning of a statute is clear and unambiguous, the Court will not adopt a tortured construction of it merely in order to uphold its validity. U.S. v. Automobile Workers, 352 U.S. 567, 589 (1957); Jay v. Boyd, 351 U.S. 345, 357 (1956); U.S. v. Sullivan, 332 U.S. 689, 693 (1948); Hopkins Savings Assn. v. Cleary, 296 U.S. 315, 334–35 (1935); Moore Ice Cream Co. v. Rose, 289 U.S. 373, 379 (1933).

[59] Harmon v. Brucker, 355 U.S. 579, 583 (1958); Employees v. Westinghouse Corp., 348 U.S. 437, 453, 459–60 (1955); U.S. v. Harriss, 347 U.S. 612, 623–24, 633 (1954); Crowell v. Benson, 285 U.S. 22, 62 (1932); Panama R.R. Co. v. Johnson, 264 U.S. 375, 390 (1924).

[60] Talbot v. Seeman, 1 Cr. 1, 43–44 (1801); Murray v. The Charming Betsey, 2 Cr. 64, 118 (1804); Lauritzen v. Larsen, 345 U.S. 571, 578 (1953).

[61] Such as the rule that legislative history may be utilized to resolve, but not to create, an ambiguity. Gemsco Inc. v. Walling, 324 U.S. 244, 263–64 (1945). So too where literal application of the words used would result in absurd or unjust consequences, or conflict with the purpose and policy of the legislation, effect should be given to the legislative intent. Holy Trinity Church v. Madigan, 143 U.S. 457, 472 (1892); U.S. v. A.T.A., 310 U.S. 534, 543, 553 (1940); U.S. v. Rosenblum Truck Lines, 315 U.S. 50, 55 (1942); Markham v. Cabell, 326 U.S. 404, 409 (1945); Vermilya-Brown Co. v. Cornell, 335 U.S. 377, 388 (1948); Feres v. U.S., 340 U.S. 135, 139, 141 (1950); Johansen v. U.S., 343 U.S. 427, 431 (1952); Lauritzen v. Larsen, 345 U.S. 571, 577 (1953); Cox v. Roth, 348 U.S. 207, 209 (1955); Textile Workers Union v. Lincoln Mills, 353 U.S. 448, 456 (1957); F.T.C. v. Mandel Bros., 359 U.S. 385, 389–90 (1959). In McMahon v. U.S., 342 U.S. 25, 27 (1951), there was a conflict between the rules that legislation for the benefit of seamen should be construed liberally and that statutes waiving the immunity of the government from suit should be strictly construed.

whether the case originates in a state court, a lower federal court, or in the Supreme Court itself,[62] and whether the case is criminal or civil.[63]

In cases of this type, as Chief Justice Marshall observed, an important object of the framers "was the preservation of the constitution and laws of the United States, so far as they can be preserved by judicial authority; and therefore the jurisdiction of the courts of the Union was expressly extended to all cases arising under that constitution and those laws . . . ; and we think that the judicial power, as originally given, extends to all cases arising under the constitution or a law of the United States, whoever may be the parties."[64]

"Cases affecting Ambassadors" are a category where federal jurisdiction arises by virtue of the character of the parties involved, rather than by reason of the subject matter of the litigation.[65] These matters are of the sort which might adversely affect the international relations of the United States, and which cannot safely be relegated to the care of state courts.[66] The public ministers protected by this clause are those accredited *to* the United States by foreign nations, not those sent *by* the United States to other countries.[67]

Admiralty

"Cases of admiralty and maritime Jurisdiction" constitute a second group (similar to those where a federal question is involved) of cases in which the criterion of federal jurisdiction is the character of the subject-matter rather than of the parties to the litigation.

The law of the sea (like the law merchant and the law of nations) is a peculiar body of law, international in its origin and nature, which has been adopted as part of the law of the United States.[68]

[62] Fairfax's Devisee v. Hunter's Lessee, 1 Wheat. 304, 340–42, 347–51 (1816); Cohens v. Virginia, 6 Wheat. 264, 413, 416 (1821); Ableman v. Booth, 2 How. 506, 518 (1859).

[63] Tennessee v. Davis, 100 U.S. 257, 264–66 (1880); Ames v. Kansas, 111 U.S. 449, 471 (1884).

[64] Cohens v. Va., 6 Wheat. 264, 391–92 (1821).   [65] See page 334 above.

[66] A well-known incident under the Articles of Confederation, concerning which Jefferson sought to inform himself before going as American envoy to the French court, was the assault by one Longchamps upon François Barbé de Marbois, the French consul general in Philadelphia. Respublica v. Longchamps, 1 Dall. 111, 115–18 (Pa. 1784). Jefferson, *Papers*, VII, 279, 305–308, 393, 446, 461–62; VIII, 99, 374, 519.

[67] Ex parte Gruber, 269 U.S. 302, 303 (1925).

[68] Lauritzen v. Larsen, 345 U.S. 571, 578 (1953); Farrell v. U.S., 336 U.S. 511,

James Wilson (1742–1798)

From a miniature attributed to James Peale
Courtesy Independence National Historical Park

Chief Justice John Marshall (1755–1835)

Courtesy Architect of the Capitol

In England the jurisdiction of the admiral was restrained within relatively narrow limits by the rivalship of the common law courts. In the colonies the power of the crown was less restricted by the local popular legislative assemblies. Admiralty courts were reorganized after 1696,[69] and again their jurisdiction was extended in 1764 and 1768. Americans protested against this extension of the powers of the admiralty courts "beyond their ancient limits," and in the Declaration of Independence one of the grievances enumerated was the consequent deprivation "in many cases, of the benefits of trial by jury."[70]

After independence and before adoption of the Constitution, the states established admiralty courts.[71] Under the Articles of Confederation a federal Court of Appeals in Cases of Capture was created, to hear appeals from state admiralty courts.[72]

States' rights advocates who opposed the establishment of inferior federal courts except for admiralty matters apparently were willing to concede the propriety of continuing the existence of federal jurisdiction in that field.[73]

Prize jurisdiction, to determine the lawfulness of captures by bellig-

517 (1949); Robertson v. Baldwin, 165 U.S. 275, 283 (1897); The Lottawanna, 21 Wall. 558, 572 (1875); Holdsworth, *History of English Law*, V, 60–65, 120–28.

[69] Regarding early admiralty courts in the colonies, see the works of Helen J. Crump, Charles M. Hough, Dorothy S. Towle, and Carl Ubbelohde listed in the Bibliography of this volume.

[70] Dumbauld, *The Declaration of Independence and What It Means Today*, 132–33.

[71] The state laws establishing such courts are listed by J. C. Bancroft Davis, "Federal Courts Prior to the Adoption of the Constitution," 131 U.S. at xx–xxii. In Virginia a bill drafted by Thomas Jefferson to establish a court of admiralty was speedily enacted into law in 1776. Jefferson, *Papers*, I, 645–49; Hening, *Statutes*, IX, 202–206.

[72] See 131 U.S. xxv–xxvi. The authority of decisions by that court was upheld by the Supreme Court in Penhallow v. Doane's Admrs., 3 Dall. 54, 85, 96, 113, 116 (1795). A similar case led to armed resistance by Pennsylvania. See U.S. v. Peters, 5 Cr. 115, 140 (1809); Warren, *The Supreme Court in United States History*, I, 374–86; Hampton L. Carson, "The Case of the Sloop 'Active,'" *Pennsylvania Magazine of History and Biography*, Vol. XVI, No. 4 (1892), 385, 394–96. In connection with this case, President Madison wrote to Governor Simon Snyder of Pennsylvania on April 13, 1809, "that the Executive of the United States is not only unauthorized to prevent the execution of a decree sanctioned by the Supreme Court of the United States but is expressly enjoined, by statute, to carry into effect any such decree where opposition may be made to it." *Debates* (11 Cong., 1 and 2 sess.), 2269.

[73] See note 4, page 319, above, and Dumbauld, *The Bill of Rights and What It Means Today*, 25, 29, 42, 44, 47, 175, 187, 197.

erents, has remained one of the distinctive prerogatives of admiralty courts. Other characteristic features of admiralty procedure are the absence of jury trial,[74] and the use of proceedings in rem against a ship[75] rather than in personam against its owner. In case of collision, the liability of the vessels involved is apportioned on the basis of their comparative fault, rather than in accordance with the common law doctrine that any contributory negligence on the part of a claimant prevents recovery. Admiralty rules regarding the powers of the master of a vessel to bind the owner, as for repairs in a foreign port, differ from the ordinary rules of agency; and liability for an injured sailor's "maintenance and cure" is unlike the responsibilities of an employer to employees on land.[76]

Admiralty jurisdiction is a branch of the federal judicial power entirely separate and distinct from that relating to cases involving federal questions.[77]

By virtue of the admiralty provision in Article III, section 2, clause 1, together with the "necessary and proper" clause (Article I, section 8, clause 18) and the "commerce" clause (Article I, section 8, clause 3), Congress has power to modify the traditional law of the sea and adapt it to meet the needs of present-day conditions.[78]

[74] Congress can provide jury trial in admiralty if it sees fit to do so, just as it can limit appellate review in admiralty cases to the same type of narrow review that is permitted in the case of jury verdicts. The Genesee Chief, 12 How. 443, 459–60 (1852). See note 10, page 361, below.

[75] The Genesee Chief, 12 How. 443, 460 (1852). The Moses Taylor, 4 Wall. 411, 427, 430 (1867), struck down a California statute which gave jurisdiction in rem to state courts in suits involving nonperformance of contracts for water transportation. The Court held that proceedings in rem were a distinctive feature of admiralty jurisdiction, and that admiralty jurisdiction was exclusively granted to federal courts and could not be exercised by state courts. Cf. Hendry Co. v. Moore, 318 U.S. 133, 153 (1943). See also Madruga v. Superior Court, 346 U.S. 556, 560–611 (1954).

[76] Regarding "maintenance and cure," see The Osceola, 189 U.S. 158, 169, 175 (1903); Mahnich v. Southern Steamship Co., 321 U.S. 96, 99–102 (1944); Farrell v. U.S., 336 U.S. 511, 517 (1949).

[77] American Ins. Co. v. Canter, 1 Pet. 511, 545 (1828); Romero v. Int. Terminal Co., 358 U.S. 354, 367 (1959). In the latter case, doubtless in order to obtain the advantage of jury trial, plaintiff attempted, in the absence of diversity of citizenship, to bring suit for a maritime tort on the "law side" of a United States district court under 28 U.S.C. 1331, as a case arising under the Constitution and laws of the United States, rather than on the "admiralty side" of the court.

[78] The Lottawanna, 21 Wall. 558, 573, 577 (1875); In re Garnett, 141 U.S. 1, 14 (1891); Southern Pacific Co. v. Jensen, 244 U.S. 205, 215 (1917); Knickerbocker Ice Co. v. Stewart, 253 U.S. 149, 160 (1920); Panama R.R. Co. v. Johnson, 264 U.S.

One noteworthy modernization of admiralty jurisdiction by Congress, with the approval of the Supreme Court, was its extension to inland lakes[79] and navigable rivers.[80] In England the ebb and flow of the tide marked the limit of admiralty jurisdiction. This restriction was perhaps a result of the rivalry between the admiralty courts and the common law courts. At first it was accepted also in America,[81] but later was found unsuited to the geographical and commercial conditions prevailing in the United States.

Contracts fall within the admiralty jurisdiction only when their subject-matter is maritime in nature (as in the case of marine insurance policies, agreements for transportation of goods by ship, for service as seamen, and the like). Locality, rather than subject-matter, is the criterion for determining whether torts are maritime in character. Wrongful acts occurring on navigable waters of the United States are maritime torts, and fall within the jurisdiction of admiralty.[82]

When no distinctive rule of maritime law applies to wrongful acts committed on navigable waters of the United States situated within the territorial jurisdiction of a state, it is permissible to apply state law in admiralty courts.[83]

It is also permissible for state courts (or federal courts exercising diversity of citizenship jurisdiction) to apply state law in cases involving maritime torts, if such action does not disrupt the uniformity of the national system of admiralty law.[84]

The most usual occasion for applying state law in a maritime tort
375, 385–87 (1924); Crowell v. Benson, 285 U.S. 22, 39 (1932); Detroit Trust Co. v. The Thomas Barlum, 293 U.S. 21, 43–44 (1934); O'Donnell v. Great Lakes Dredge & Dock Co., 318 U.S. 36, 39–41 (1943); Swanson v. Marra Bros., 328 U.S. 1, 5 (1946).

[79] The Propeller Genesee Chief v. Fitzhugh, 12 How. 443, 453–69 (1852).

[80] The Daniel Ball, 10 Wall. 557, 563 (1871). See also U.S. v. Appalachian Power Co., 311 U.S. 377, 408 (1940).

[81] The Thomas Jefferson, 10 Wheat. 428, 429 (1825). This case was overruled by The Genesee Chief, 12 How. 443, 459 (1852). See also Detroit Trust Co. v. The Thomas Barlum, 293 U.S. 21, 43 (1934), for the proposition that admiralty jurisdiction is not confined within the limits in force in England at the time of the adoption of the Constitution.

[82] Ex parte Easton, 95 U.S. 68, 72–73 (1877); Southern Pacific Co. v. Jensen, 244 U.S. 205, 252 (1917); P. R.R. v. O'Rourke, 344 U.S. 334, 342 (1953); Wilburn Boat Co. v. Fireman's Fund Ins. Co., 348 U.S. 310, 313, 321 (1955).

[83] Just v. Chambers, 312 U.S. 383, 385, 389 (1941); The Tungus v. Skovgaard, 358 U.S. 588, 590–92 (1959).

[84] United Pilots Assn. v. Halecki, 358 U.S. 613, 615 (1959).

action is where a wrongful act committed on navigable waters has caused death. Under admiralty law damages cannot be recovered for wrongful death.[85] Congress did not modify the admiralty rule by establishing a comprehensive cause of action for wrongful death.[86] Instead, admiralty courts proceeded to apply state wrongful death and survival statutes whenever possible.[87]

Notwithstanding the fact that the application of state laws dealing with wrongful death has been regarded with approval by the Supreme Court, the application of state workmen's compensation laws has been condemned as disruptive of the uniformity and harmony of the maritime law.[88] It is difficult to perceive any rational basis for the distinction thus established between the two types of legislation. Acquiescence in the doctrine of the Court by Congress has resulted in delicate adjustments leaving a "shadowy area" or "twilight zone" where there is much confusion and uncertainty whether state or federal legislation governs.[89]

Congress did extend to seamen suffering personal injury in the course of their employment an election to bring an action at law for damages, with the right of jury trial; and in case of death a similar action by the seaman's executor or administrator was authorized.[90]

Thus a seaman often finds himself in the advantageous position of

[85] The Harrisburg, 119 U.S. 199, 213 (1886). Nor was there originally any cause of action for wrongful death at common law, but the situation was remedied in most jurisdictions by widespread adoption of wrongful death and survival statutes following the pattern of Lord Campbell's Act, 9 & 10 Victoria c. 93 (1846). See page 391 below.

[86] The Tungus v. Skovgaard, 358 U.S. 588, 590, 599–611 (1959).

[87] The Tungus v. Skovgaard, 358 U.S. 588, 590 (1959); Just v. Chambers, 312 U.S. 383, 388–89 (1941); Western Fuel Co. v. Garcia, 257 U.S. 233, 242 (1921); The Hamilton, 207 U.S. 398, 405–406 (1907).

[88] Southern Pacific Co. v. Jensen, 244 U.S. 205, 217 (1917). A later decision condemned as an invalid delegation of power an effort by Congress to sanction such application of state laws. Knickerbocker Ice Co. v. Stewart, 253 U.S. 149, 164 (1920).

[89] Parker v. Motor Boat Sales, 314 U.S. 244, 250 (1941); Davis v. Dept. of Labor, 317 U.S. 249, 253, 256 (1942); P. R.R. v. O'Rourke, 344 U.S. 334, 337–38 (1953).

[90] In such actions all federal statutes applicable to similar remedies available in the case of railway employees shall apply. Act of March 4, 1915, 38 Stat. 1185, as amended by Act of June 5, 1920, 41 Stat. 1007, commonly called the "Jones Act." This awkward method of legislating indirectly for seamen by incorporating statutes relating to railroad workers calls for ingenuity on the part of courts applying incongruous pro-

being able to bring, either in a state[91] or federal[92] court, a threefold action:[93] claiming damages in a common-law action for negligence,[94] and also maintenance, cure, and wages under the rule peculiar to admiralty,[95] as well as indemnity for injury due to the unseaworthy condition of the vessel (which may or may not be due to negligence).[96] A seaman may recover although the injury occurred on land in the course of his employment.[97] However, a longshoreman, stevedore, or other landsman may not recover unless the injury occurred on navigable waters and while the work being performed was of a maritime nature, of the sort ordinarily or historically forming part of the tasks of the vessel's crew.[98] Longshoremen, stevedores, and other harbor workers are covered by a federal compensation law[99] which is exclusive and takes

visions of law. Lindgren v. U.S., 281 U.S. 38, 42 (1930); Cox v. Roth, 348 U.S. 207, 209 (1955); Kernan v. Am. Dredging Co., 355 U.S. 426, 431–32, 438–39 (1958).

[91] Suits in personam governed by rules of admiralty law can be brought in a state court. Garrett v. Moore-McCormack Co., 317 U.S. 239, 243 (1942).

[92] The law of the sea may be enforced in a common-law action in personam on the "law side" of a federal court, as well as by proceedings in admiralty. Panama R.R. Co. v. Johnson, 264 U.S. 375, 388–89 (1924).

[93] McAllister v. Magnolia Petroleum Co., 357 U.S. 221, 222 (1958). Earlier suggestions that the "election" afforded by the Jones Act makes the actions for negligence and for unseaworthiness alternative have been abandoned. See Pacific Steamship Co. v. Peterson, 278 U.S. 130, 138–39 (1928); Lindgren v. U.S., 281 U.S. 38, 47 (1930). The election is between a suit on the "law side" of a federal court, where jury trial can be had, or on the admiralty side, without a jury. Romero v. Int. Terminal Co., 358 U.S. 354, 363 (1959).

[94] Until the Jones Act of 1920, negligence was not a ground of liability in maritime law. The Osceola, 189 U.S. 158, 175 (1903); Chelentis v. Luckenbach S.S. Co., 247 U.S. 372, 382–84 (1918). But recovery of maintenance, cure, and wages, as well as an indemnity for unseaworthiness, was allowed whether or not there was negligence.

[95] See notes 76 and 94, pages 340 and 343, above.

[96] The Osceola, 189 U.S. 158, 175 (1903); Mahnich v. So. S.S. Co., 321 U.S. 96, 99–102 (1944); Mitchell v. Trawler Racer, 362 U.S. 539, 546–49 (1960). Unseaworthiness may be due to personnel as well as equipment. Boudoin v. Lykes Bros., 348 U.S. 336, 339 (1955).

[97] O'Donnell v. Great Lakes Co., 318 U.S. 36, 42 (1943); Braen v. Pfeifer Transp. Co., 361 U.S. 129, 131–33 (1959).

[98] International Stevedoring Co. v. Haverty, 272 U.S. 50, 52 (1926); Swanson v. Marra Bros., 328 U.S. 1, 4 (1946); Seas Shipping Co. v. Sieracki, 328 U.S. 85, 93–99 (1948); P. R.R. v. O'Rourke, 344 U.S. 334, 338, 342 (1953); Pope & Talbot v. Hawn, 346 U.S. 406, 411–13 (1953); The Tungus v. Skovgaard, 358 U.S. 588, 590 (1959); United Pilots Assn. v. Halecki, 358 U.S. 613, 617 (1959); Kermarec v. Compagnie Generale, 358 U.S. 625, 629 (1959).

[99] Longshoremen's and Harbor Workers' Act of March 4, 1927, 44 Stat. 1424,

the place of the common-law action for negligence against their employers.[100] They may still bring such action, however, against other parties whose negligence contributed to the injury.[101]

Cases Affecting Ambassadors; United States a Party

The first group of categories of cases and controversies which are specified in Article III, section 2, clause 1, as falling within the judicial power of the United States contains those classified according to the subject matter of the litigation. This group is composed of cases involving federal questions and admiralty jurisdiction. The second group of cases and controversies contains those classified according to the character of the parties to the litigation. In this group, as Chief Justice Marshall observed, "it is entirely unimportant what may be the subject of controversy. Be it what it may, these parties have a constitutional right to come into the courts of the Union."[102]

"Cases affecting Ambassadors, other public Ministers and Consuls" comprise the first category where federal judicial power is brought into play by reason of the character of the parties.[103]

---

33 U.S.C. 901. This legislation promptly followed International Stevedoring Co. v. Haverty, 272 U.S. 50, 52 (1926), which treated stevedores as "seamen" for the purpose of permitting them to bring action under the Jones Act against their employers. See Pope & Talbot v. Hawn, 346 U.S. 406, 415, 421 (1953).

[100] Compensation is payable under this Act "only if the disability or death results from injury occurring upon the navigable waters of the United States (including any dry dock) and if recovery for the disability or death through workmen's compensation proceedings may not validly be provided by State laws." Sec. 3(a), 44 Stat. 1426, 33 U.S.C. 903. Every case under this Act thus involves a constitutional question as to the extent of the Jensen doctrine. See note 88, page 342, above. Moreover the boundaries between this statute, other federal legislation, and state laws are often difficult to trace. See notes 89, 97, and 98, pages 342 and 343, above.

[101] Pope & Talbot v. Hawn, 346 U.S. 406, 413 (1953); Seas Shipping Co. v. Sieracki, 328 U.S. 85, 101–102 (1948).

[102] Cohens v. Va., 6 Wheat. 264, 378 (1821). See note 46, page 334, above.

[103] This category has already been discussed. See page 338 above. Its insertion between cases involving federal questions and cases in admiralty may seem to depart from logical order; but perhaps the sequence followed in the Constitution is justified by the fact that the three types of "cases" first mentioned in Art. III all relate to affairs involving the international responsibilities of the United States as a member of the family of nations: treaties, matters affecting the official representatives of foreign countries, and admiralty litigation. Under the Articles of Confederation the lack of judicial power in the national government had been keenly felt as a hindrance to the proper enforcement of international obligations. Dumbauld, "John Marshall and Treaty Law," loc. cit., 70.

"Controversies to which the United States shall be a Party" constitute the second category of litigation where the character of the parties thereto brings it within the ambit of the federal judicial power.

Under the wording of this provision it is immaterial, so far as the extent of the judicial power is concerned, whether the United States is a party plaintiff or a party defendant.[104] In either case the courts have capacity to receive jurisdiction. But no actual jurisdiction over the United States as a defendant exists unless the United States has consented to be sued. Not even a state may sue the United States without its consent, expressed in an act of Congress.[105] The nation is protected against suit by the doctrine of sovereign immunity.[106]

In any case the United States cannot be a party defendant except in such courts and in strict accordance with such terms and conditions as Congress may prescribe when consent is given to a suit against the United States.[107] When the United States is by statute made a party defendant, the Supreme Court has stated, the case is not necessarily one embraced within the judicial power of the United States as established by Article III.[108] The Court emphasized that in the wording of Article

[104] Minnesota v. Hitchcock, 185 U.S. 373, 383 (1902).

[105] Arizona v. California, 298 U.S. 558, 568 (1936).

[106] U.S. v. Lee, 106 U.S. 196, 204 (1882). The same immunity is enjoyed by the states except where it is waived by the plan of government which the Constitution establishes. Monaco v. Mississippi, 292 U.S. 313, 322, 330 (1934). It is often difficult to determine whether a suit against public officers is in reality a suit against the state. The general rule is that it is unless the officers exceed their statutory powers or act under an unconstitutional statute. Larson v. Domestic and Foreign Commerce Corp., 337 U.S. 682, 689–90 (1949); Land v. Dollar, 330 U.S. 731, 738 (1947); U.S. v. Lee, 106 U.S. 196, 219–20 (1882); Gen. Oil Co. v. Crane, 209 U.S. 211, 226 (1908). See also note 24, page 329, above.

[107] Soriano v. U.S., 352 U.S. 270, 276 (1957); U.S. v. Sherwood, 312 U.S. 584, 586, 591 (1941). A general provision authorizing suits against the United States not involving tort liability was provided by the Tucker Act of March 31, 1887, 24 Stat. 505. Besides the jurisdiction given to the Court of Claims, concurrent jurisdiction in case of claims not exceeding $10,000 was given to district courts. Consent to suits in tort for money damages was not granted until the Federal Tort Claims Act of August 2, 1946, 60 Stat. 842. Both of these enactments are now codified in 28 U.S.C. 1346. Suits in admiralty against the United States arising out of operation of merchant ships and public vessels are authorized by the Acts of March 9, 1920, 41 Stat. 575, and of March 3, 1925, 43 Stat. 1112, 46 U.S.C. 742, 781.

[108] Williams v. U.S., 289 U.S. 553, 577 (1933). The reason given is that settlement of claims against the United States is a political function which Congress could exercise itself or delegate to the executive rather than the judicial branch of the government. *Ibid.*, 580. Hence the Court of Claims, though exercising a species of judicial

345

III dealing with "controversies" the word "all" was omitted, apparently *ex industria*, whereas in the prior portion dealing with "cases" the judicial power was expressly extended to "all cases" of the categories specified.[109]

Nevertheless, there are controversies to which the United States is a party defendant which do fall within the scope of the judicial power as delineated in Article III.[110] For it is not the inherent nature of the subject-matter involved but the nature of the procedure prescribed for dealing with it which makes a particular proceeding judicial in its character or otherwise;[111] and certainly Congress can, when it chooses to do so, authorize suits against the United States to be heard and determined by courts exercising the judicial power of the United States under Article III of the Constitution rather than by "legislative" courts.

But the controversies to which the United States is a party plaintiff are more numerous and important than those to which it is a party defendant.

All criminal prosecutions for federal offenses may be regarded as controversies to which the United States is a party.[112] The Constitution in Article III, section 2, clause 3, speaks of the "trial" of crimes, thus evincing clearly the understanding that such criminal trials constitute a proper exercise of the judicial power conferred by Article III.[113]

---

power, was not exercising power under Art. III. *Ibid.*, 565. Cf. Minnesota v. Hitchcock, 185 U.S. 373, 383, 386 (1902); and the critical comments of Chief Justice Fred M. Vinson in National Mutual Ins. Co. v. Tidewater Transfer Co., 337 U.S. 582, 640–41 (1949). The dubious assertion in the Williams case that suits against the United States do not fall within the judicial power conferred by Art. III was repudiated by the Supreme Court in Glidden Co. v. Zdanok, 370 U.S. 530, 562–65 (1962).

[109] 289 U.S. at 572.

[110] Tort claims, contract cases involving less than $10,000, and admiralty suits against the United States litigated in district courts would be examples. See note 107, page 345, above.

[111] Tutun v. U.S., 270 U.S. 568, 576 (1926). See note 22, page 322, above.

[112] However, Justice Field has said that if there is any distinction between "cases" and "controversies," it is that the latter embrace only suits of a civil nature. See note 36, page 331, above. Justice Iredell, dissenting in Chisholm v. Georgia, 2 Dall. 419, 431–32 (1793), made a similar comment.

[113] Apart from Art. I, sec. 8, cl. 10, Art. I, sec. 8, cl. 6, and Art. III, sec. 3, cl. 2, relating to the punishment of specific offenses (piracy, counterfeiting, treason), the constitutional basis for federal criminal law must be found in the "necessary and proper" clause (Art. I, sec. 8, cl. 18). Not until after U.S. v. Hudson, 7 Cr. 32 (1812), and U.S. v. Coolidge, 1 Wheat. 415 (1816), was it established that nothing could be a federal crime until it was made so by Congress. See note 9, page 361, below.

Suits of a civil nature where the United States is party plaintiff are also authorized by this provision of Article III. They may relate to the public lands or other property interests of the government, or may be brought in order to acquire land by eminent domain, or to cancel a grant or patent or certificate of naturalization obtained by fraud, or to enforce a contract, redress a wrong, or for any other appropriate purpose.[114]

An important category of cases where the United States is party plaintiff consists of suits against states. The Supreme Court has held that the Constitution authorizes such suits, and that the states impliedly gave their consent to such suits as an incident to their admission into the Union.[115] It would perhaps be more accurate to acknowledge that "a State may be sued by the United States without its consent."[116] A well-known instance of proceedings instituted by the United States against a number of states is furnished by the recent litigation regarding ownership of offshore oil deposits underlying the marginal sea adjacent to California and several Gulf states.[117]

[114] U.S. v. San Jacinto Tin Co., 125 U.S. 273, 279 (1888): "The Constitution itself declares that the judicial power shall extend to all cases to which the United States shall be a party, and that this means mainly where it is a party plaintiff is a necessary result of the well-established proposition that it cannot be sued in any court without its consent."

[115] U.S. v. Texas, 143 U.S. 621, 644–46 (1892). This case involved interpretation of a treaty with Spain to determine the boundary between the state of Texas and the territory of Oklahoma. *Ibid.*, 636, 643. Texas claimed that the question was political, under Foster v. Neilson, 2 Pet. 253 (1829). See note 25, page 330, above. But the Court limited that doctrine to international disputes between independent nations. 143 U.S. at 639. In U.S. v. N.C., 136 U.S. 211 (1890), an original suit by the United States against a state had been adjudicated on its merits, but the question of jurisdiction had not been raised. The Court's reasoning in the Texas case is largely ipse dixit. Since it had jurisdiction of suits between states (143 U.S. at 640), and since it could not assume that the framers had ignored the possibility that similar disputes would arise between the United States and a state which might seriously endanger the permanence of the Union if there were no tribunal to decide them, and since no better tribunal for that purpose than itself was available, the Court held that the states had impliedly consented to its exercise of jurisdiction in such cases. *Ibid.*, 644–46.

[116] "It does not follow that because a State may be sued by the United States without its consent, therefore the United States may be sued by a State without its consent. Public policy forbids that conclusion." Kansas v. U.S., 204 U.S. 331, 342 (1907). See also Monaco v. Mississippi, 292 U.S. 313, 329 (1934).

[117] U.S. v. California, 332 U.S. 19, 25, 38–39 (1947); U.S. v. Louisiana, 339 U.S. 699, 701, 704 (1950); U.S. v. Texas, 339 U.S. 707, 718–19 (1950); Alabama v. Texas, 347 U.S. 272, 273 (1954); U.S. v. Louisiana, 363 U.S. 1, 64, 68, 82 (1960);

Suits between States

"Controversies between two or more States" form the third, and perhaps the most distinctive[118] category of controversies where the character of the parties thereto makes applicable the federal judicial power. Disputes between states had been adjudicated by federal authority under the Articles of Confederation.[119] Need for effective machinery to handle interstate controversies was keenly felt by the framers of the Constitution. Among independent nations such differences, if not settled by agreement, might lead to war. But war and diplomacy were both banned by the Constitution as a means of settling disputes between states. Judicial procedure was the only remaining alternative.[120]

Accordingly, the Court has developed a body of legal rules appropriate to the decision of interstate disputes, occasionally drawing upon international law for pertinent analogies.[121]

Most of the litigation between states has involved boundaries[122]

U.S. v. Florida, 363 U.S. 121, 124–25 (1960). A vain attempt was made in 1950 by Texas and Louisiana (339 U.S. at 701, 709–10) to persuade the Court to overrule U.S. v. Texas, 143 U.S. 621.

[118] American experience with judicial settlement of disputes between states by the Supreme Court was regarded by Dr. James Brown Scott as so useful a precedent for the establishment of an international court to decide disputes between nations that he collected the Supreme Court's opinions in cases of that type up through 1918 in a two-volume work, *Judicial Settlement of Controversies between States of the American Union.* See also James Brown Scott, *Sovereign States and Suits*, 213–14, 249. For a list of such cases through 1924, see *ibid.*, 267–71.

[119] A lengthy paragraph in Art. IX regulated the cumbersome procedure to be followed. A boundary dispute between Connecticut and Pennsylvania was the only case actually decided (on December 30, 1782, in favor of Pennsylvania) by a court established under this procedure. See 131 U.S. l–lxiii.

[120] Rhode Island v. Massachusetts, 12 Pet. 657, 726 (1838). The Court pointed out that although this clause does not apply to "all" controversies between states (see note 109, page 346, above), it excludes none (*ibid.*, 721); that it would be absurd to suppose that the jurisdiction conferred by the Constitution was less extensive than that granted under the Articles of Confederation (*ibid.*, 728); and that political controversies between independent nations become judicial questions when submitted to a court for decision (*ibid.*, 737). See also Missouri v. Illinois, 180 U.S. 208, 241 (1901); Kansas v. Colorado, 185 U.S. 125, 143 (1902); Kansas v. Colorado, 206 U.S. 46, 97 (1907).

[121] Kansas v. Colorado, 185 U.S. 125, 146–47 (1902); Kansas v. Colorado, 206 U.S. 46, 97 (1907); New Jersey v. New York, 283 U.S. 336, 342 (1931); Washington v. Oregon, 297 U.S. 517, 523 (1936).

[122] The first case brought before the Court, as well as the first to be decided, involved boundary disputes. New York v. Connecticut, 4 Dall. 1 (1799); Rhode Island

or the use of natural resources[123] (especially rivers).[124] Other suits have involved debts[125] and jurisdiction to tax.[126]

Suits between a State and Citizens of Another State

Controversies "between a State and Citizens of another State" make up the fourth category of cases brought within the scope of the federal judicial power by reason of the character of the parties.

Suits by a state as *parens patriae* to protect the health and welfare of its citizens against nuisances such as the discharge of noxious gases from an industrial plant outside the state are quite similar to those brought by a state against another state to prevent pollution of a river by sewage.[127] Regarding this type of complaint, the Supreme Court said: "When the States by their union made the forcible abatement of outside nuisances impossible, they did not thereby agree to submit to whatever might be done. They did not renounce the possibility of making reasonable demands on the ground of their still remaining *quasi*-sovereign interests; and the alternative to force is a suit in this Court."[128] Likewise a state may seek relief when its economy is threat-

v. Massachusetts, 12 Pet. 657 (1838). For a more recent instance, see Georgia v. South Carolina, 257 U.S. 516 (1922).

[123] In Pennsylvania v. West Virginia, 262 U.S. 553, 597 (1923), it was held that a state could not withdraw natural gas from the established current of interstate commerce in order to give priority to its own consumers. Missouri v. Illinois, 180 U.S. 208 (1901), and New York v. New Jersey, 256 U.S. 296 (1921), involved pollution of rivers by sewage.

[124] "A river is more than an amenity, it is a treasure," Justice Holmes observed in New Jersey v. New York, 283 U.S. 336, 342 (1931), involving equitable apportionment of water. This problem is of particular importance in arid areas where irrigation is essential. Kansas v. Colorado, 185 U.S. 125 (1902), 206 U.S. 46 (1907); Wyoming v. Colorado, 259 U.S. 419 (1922); Nebraska v. Wyoming, 325 U.S. 589, 599 (1945); Arizona v. California, 373 U.S. 546, 588–90 (1963).

[125] South Dakota v. North Carolina, 192 U.S. 286, 310 (1904); Virginia v. West Virginia, 246 U.S. 565, 589 (1918). The Court will not take jurisdiction if the state is merely lending its name as a formal party to what is in fact a claim where private citizens are the real parties in interest. New Hampshire v. Louisiana, 108 U.S. 76, 88, 91 (1883).

[126] In Texas v. Florida, 306 U.S. 398, 407–10 (1939), the Court took jurisdiction when it appeared that the total tax claims of four states claiming to be the domicile of a decedent exceeded the assets of the estate. Where the property is ample to satisfy all claimant states, the Court says that no justiciable controversy is presented. Massachusetts v. Missouri, 308 U.S. 1, 15 (1939).

[127] See note 123 just above.

[128] Georgia v. Tennessee Copper Co., 206 U.S. 230, 237 (1907). See also Georgia

ened by discriminatory freight rates. "They may cause a blight no less serious than the spread of noxious gas over the land or the deposit of sewage in the streams. They may affect the prosperity and welfare of a State as profoundly as any diversion of waters from the rivers."[129] Moreover, a state may vindicate its own proprietary interests by bringing suit.[130]

However, if the state is not the real party in interest, but is acting for the benefit of others, even if it holds legal title, the Court will refuse to take jurisdiction. Thus, where the state takes over the affairs of an insolvent bank, and sues to enforce the statutory liability of a stockholder, the Court will regard the state's ownership of legal title to the bank's assets as a mere trusteeship for the benefit of the bank's creditors, as a "mere expedient for the purpose of collection," which could logically be extended to the point of authorizing suits in the Supreme Court against every debtor owing money to the bank. This would saddle upon the Court "an enormous burden foreign to the purpose of the constitutional provision" involved in the grant of original jurisdiction. "These considerations emphasize the importance of strict adherence to the governing principle that the State must show a direct interest of its own and not merely seek recovery for the benefit of individuals who are the real parties in interest."[131]

Another limitation on a state's right to resort to the original jurisdiction of the Supreme Court is that such procedure is not available in criminal cases.[132] Moreover, a state cannot invoke the original jurisdic-

---

v. Pennsylvania R.R. Co., 324 U.S. 439, 450 (1945). Note the similarity of the reasoning in support of this type of suit to that upholding the necessity for judicial settlement of suits between states. See note 120, page 348, above.

[129] Georgia v. Pennsylvania R.R. Co., 324 U.S. 439, 450 (1945).

[130] Georgia v. Evans, 316 U.S. 159, 162 (1942). Here the state, as a purchaser of asphalt, was held to be a "person" entitled to triple damages under the Sherman Antitrust Law. In Oklahoma v. A., T. & S.F. Ry. Co., 220 U.S. 277, 286–87, 289 (1911), the state was held to have no standing to sue to enjoin unreasonable freight rates because it was not a shipper of the commodities involved.

[131] Oklahoma v. Cook, 304 U.S. 387, 392–96 (1938). See also Massachusetts v. Missouri, 308 U.S. 1, 18–19 (1939), involving tax claims. Of course the more time and effort the Supreme Court devotes to cases (such as the routine collection of debts) which should not be brought before it, the less effectively can it discharge its essential functions in connection with important litigation involving constitutional problems and affecting the public interest. Ex parte Peru, 318 U.S. 578, 602–603 (1943); Ferguson v. Moore-McCormack Lines, 352 U.S. 521, 546–48 (1957); Dick v. N.Y. Life Ins. Co., 359 U.S. 437, 458–59 (1959).

[132] In Cohens v. Va., 6 Wheat. 264, 399 (1821), Chief Justice Marshall said:

tion of the Court in a suit against its own citizens,[133] or where a citizen of the plaintiff state is a necessary party.[134]

It was originally held by the Supreme Court in 1793 that a state could be sued as a defendant by citizens of another state under the provision giving the Supreme Court jurisdiction of controversies "between a State and Citizens of another State."[135] This decision, disregarding the English common law rule which recognized the sovereign's immunity from suit,[136] caused widespread alarm, and the Eleventh Amendment was speedily adopted.[137] Under the terms of this amendment "The Judicial power of the United States shall not be construed to extend to any suit in law or equity, commenced or prosecuted against one of the United States by Citizens of another State, or by Citizens or Subjects of any Foreign State."

Later Supreme Court decisions have expanded the effect of this amendment far beyond the scope of its language. It will be noted that the words used do not prohibit suits against a state in admiralty,[138] or suits against a state by its own citizens,[139] or suits against a state by a

"Of the last description [cases in which an original suit might not be instituted in a federal court], is every case between a state and its citizens, and, perhaps, every case in which a state is enforcing its penal laws. In such cases, therefore, the Supreme Court cannot take original jurisdiction." In Wisconsin v. Pelican Ins. Co., 127 U.S. 265, 290 (1888), where the state sued a foreign corporation upon a judgment obtained in its own courts, the Supreme Court held that there could be no recovery, on the principle that the original judgment was of a penal character, and hence could not be enforced except by the state's own tribunals. Here, too, the Court emphasized that a contrary decision would mean that every fine imposed by a state, no matter how petty the offense, could be collected by a proceeding in the Supreme Court. *Ibid.*, 300. See note 131, page 350, above.

[133] Pennsylvania v. Quicksilver Co., 10 Wall. 553, 556 (1871).

[134] Minnesota v. Northern Securities Co., 184 U.S. 199, 247 (1902); California v. Southern Pacific Co., 157 U.S. 229, 261 (1895).

[135] Chisholm v. Georgia, 2 Dall. 419, 450, 467, 472 (1793).

[136] *Ibid.*, 437 (dissent of Justice Iredell). Proponents of ratification of the Constitution had contended that it did not deprive the states of the benefit of this rule. Hamilton, in *The Federalist*, No. 32, and Marshall in the Virginia ratifying convention, took that position. Thorpe, *Constitutional History*, II, 266–67.

[137] Its ratification was proclaimed by President John Adams on January 8, 1798. *Ibid.*, II, 291.

[138] Ex parte State of New York, 256 U.S. 490, 498 (1921), applied the prohibition in admiralty. See also Monaco v. Mississippi, 292 U.S. 313, 322 (1934).

[139] Of course, regardless of the Eleventh Amendment, such a suit would not be one falling within the scope of the judicial power by reason of the character of the parties. See note 132, page 350, above. Jurisdiction would have to be based upon the subject

foreign state.[140] Yet all of these have been held by the Supreme Court to be forbidden.[141]

Diversity of Citizenship

Controversies "between Citizens of different States" constitute the fifth, and most numerous, category of matters to which the federal judicial power extends by reason of the character of the parties.

This jurisdiction based on "diversity of citizenship" has had many critics and few defenders ever since its establishment. Its only justification is the suspicion that state courts may be unfair to litigants from other states.[142] Whether there is any substantial basis in fact at the present time for such distrust is a debatable question. As no original jurisdiction in the Supreme Court is involved in connection with this class of cases, Congress could abolish diversity jurisdiction entirely if it chose to do so, and relegate litigants to state courts. As a step toward curtailing the volume of this type of litigation, Congress has recently raised from $3,000 to $10,000 the minimum amount which must be involved in order to bring a case based upon diversity of citizenship into a federal court.[143]

It is now definitely settled that the law applicable in a diversity case is the pertinent state law which would be applied if the case were

---

matter, as in a case arising under the "federal question" clause. The Eleventh Amendment, its terms not being applicable, would not be operative to defeat jurisdiction so acquired. But the Court held that "This amendment . . . actually reversed the decision of the Supreme Court" in Chisholm v. Georgia, and adopted Iredell's dissenting views on sovereign immunity as controlling. Hans v. Louisiana, 134 U.S. 1, 10–11, 19 (1890). See also Duhne v. New Jersey, 251 U.S. 311, 313 (1920).

[140] Monaco v. Mississippi, 292 U.S. 313, 330 (1934). Chief Justice Marshall in Cohens v. Virginia, 6 Wheat. 264, 406 (1821), had said that the Eleventh Amendment did not forbid suit by a foreign state. "It does not comprehend controversies between two or more states, or between a state and a foreign state. The jurisdiction of the court still extends to these cases; and in these a state may still be sued."

[141] The Court's reasoning seems to be that states are immune from suit except where the plan of government embodied in the Constitution provides differently (as in the case of suits by other states and by the United States). But foreign states are not participants in the constitutional plan. 292 U.S. at 322, 330.

[142] Bank of the U.S. v. Deveaux, 5 Cr. 61, 87 (1809). On the merits of abolishing diversity jurisdiction, see National Mutual Ins. Co. v. Tidewater Transfer Co., 337 U.S. 582, 622, 651 (1949); and Robert H. Jackson, *The Supreme Court in the American System of Government*, 37.

[143] Act of July 25, 1958, 72 Stat. 415, 28 U.S.C. 1332.

brought in a state court.[144] Under this rule a federal court in a diversity case functions in effect as simply one of the courts of the state in which it sits.[145]

It is now also settled that, for purposes of diversity jurisdiction, a corporation is to be deemed a "citizen" of the state where it is incorporated.[146] A corporation can thus obtain for itself the real or supposed advantages available to litigants in federal courts and can escape the burdens of litigation in the courts of the states where it does business by the simple device of securing its charter in another state.[147] The political climate favorable to corporate interests which prevailed in the Senate during the decades following the Civil War condemned to defeat the numerous attempts which were made in Congress to relieve congestion in the federal courts by preventing corporations from finding a haven there.[148]

Another important rule in diversity cases is that all the parties on

---

[144] Erie R.R. Co. v. Tompkins, 304 U.S. 64, 78 (1938). This case overruled a long-standing and much-criticized decision by Justice Story in Swift v. Tyson, 16 Pet. 1, 18–19 (1842), according to which the federal courts would decide independently on matters of general commercial law, although professing to follow state decisions construing statutes or constituting "local rules of property." See Robert H. Jackson, "The Rise and Fall of Swift v. Tyson," *American Bar Association Journal*, Vol. XXIV, No. 8 (August, 1938), 611.

[145] Guaranty Trust Co. v. York, 326 U.S. 99, 108–109 (1945). Later refinements of the Erie rule have made it clear that the state law to be applied includes state rules on conflict of laws, *res judicata*, statutes of limitations, burden of proof, and similar matters which would substantially affect the outcome of the litigation. Klaxon Co. v. Stentor, 313 U.S. 487, 496 (1947); Angel v. Bullington, 330 U.S. 183, 189 (1947); Ragan v. Merchants Transfer & Warehouse Co., 337 U.S. 530, 533 (1949); Cities Service Oil Co. v. Dunlap, 308 U.S. 208, 212 (1939).

[146] Wisconsin v. Pelican Ins. Co., 127 U.S. 265, 287 (1888); 28 U.S.C. 1332 (providing that a corporation shall be deemed a citizen of the state where it is incorporated or where its principal place of business is located). Chief Justice Marshall in Bank of U.S. v. Deveaux, 5 Cr. 61, 86–88 (1809), had held that a corporation "is certainly not a citizen," but permitted suit on the assumption that the real plaintiffs were the individual members of the corporation, who were citizens of a different state than the defendant. This theory became unworkable when corporations grew in size and came to have stockholders in many states. It was abandoned in Louisville R.R. Co. v. Letson, 2 How. 497, 554–55 (1844).

[147] Apart from any difference in the psychology or attitude of the judges and juries, there were real advantages while the rule of Swift v. Tyson prevailed. Black & White Taxicab Co. v. Brown & Yellow Taxicab Co., 276 U.S. 518, 528–29 (1923).

[148] Frankfurter and Landis, *The Business of the Supreme Court*, 65, 88–95, 136–41.

one side of the case must be citizens of different states from all the parties on the other side.[149]

The District of Columbia is not a "state" for purposes of diversity jurisdiction.[150] However, the constitutionality of legislation making available to citizens of the District the diversity jurisdiction of federal courts has been upheld.[151]

Land Grants of Different States

Controversies "between Citizens of the same State claiming Lands under Grants of different States" compose the sixth category of cases which fall within the scope of federal judicial power by reason of the character of the parties.

This class of litigation is of no present practical importance. At the time of the adoption of the Constitution, it was a matter of general knowledge that, besides the controversial status of the Northwest Territory,[152] there were several boundary disputes between individual states,[153] and this provision was made to facilitate the impartial disposal of lawsuits arising out of conflicting land grants made by different states. The interstate character of such disputes would warrant their decision by a federal tribunal, even if the rival claimants happened to be citizens of the same state.[154]

[149] Strawbridge v. Curtiss, 3 Cr. 267 (1806); Indianapolis v. Chase Natl. Bank, 314 U.S. 63, 69 (1941).

[150] Hepburn v. Ellzey, 2 Cr. 445, 451 (1805).

[151] The Act of April 20, 1940, 54 Stat. 143, 28 U.S.C. 1332, was sustained in National Mutual Ins. Co. v. Tidewater Transfer Co., 337 U.S. 582, 589, 604 (1949), by a combination of conflicting minorities among the members of the Court. Three judges held that the legislation was valid by virtue of the power of Congress to legislate for the District in conjunction with the "necessary and proper" clause. Two judges favored overruling Marshall's decision in the Hepburn case. Four judges thought the law was unconstitutional.

[152] Maryland's hostility to ownership of large territories by other states had prevented the Articles of Confederation from going into force until 1781. See page 30 above.

[153] "When the Federal Convention met in 1787 for the framing of the Constitution, serious interstate disputes over lands, boundaries, and river rights were pending, involving at least ten states, as well as Vermont which had declared its independence." Charles Warren, "The Supreme Court and Disputes between States," *Bulletin of the College of William and Mary*, Vol. XXXIV, No. 5 (June, 1940), 10.

[154] Examples are the dispute between Connecticut and Pennsylvania, involved in Van Horne's Lessee v. Dorrance, 2 Dall. 304 (1795), and that between Pennsylvania

As Justice Story said, in a case arising under this provision: "The constitution intended to secure an impartial tribunal for the decision of causes arising from the grants of different states; and it supposed that a state tribunal might not stand indifferent in a controversy where the claims of its own sovereign were in conflict with those of another sovereign."[155]

Foreign States and Nationals

Controversies "between a State . . . and Foreign States, Citizens or Subjects" form the seventh category of cases to which the federal judicial power is extended by reason of the character of the parties.[156]

In the case of suits between a state and a foreign state, the consent of both parties is required before jurisdiction can be exercised. If a foreign state is defendant, the doctrine of sovereign immunity from suit without its consent would be applicable.[157] If a state is defendant, the same rule applies.[158] The same privilege is available to a state if sued by foreign individuals or corporations.[159]

and Virginia mentioned in Marlett v. Silk, 11 Pet. 1 (1837). See also note 119, page 348, above. A similar provision was contained in the Articles of Confederation, concerning which Thomas McKean wrote to George Reed on April 3, 1778: "The third section of the ninth article seems to have been calculated for the disputed lands of purchasers under Maryland and Delaware, and Maryland and Pennsylvania; but upon the whole, it may not be an improper method of adjusting such controversies." Burnett, *Letters of Members of the Continental Congress*, III, 149.

[155] Town of Pawlet v. Clark, 9 Cr. 292, 322 (1815). See page 352 above.

[156] For convenience of analysis, since Art. III, sec. 2, cl. 2, for jurisdictional purposes refers generally to cases "in which a State shall be Party," it seems advisable to treat separately suits between states and foreign states, citizens, or subjects, disregarding for the time being the words "or the Citizens thereof" in the language of Art. III, sec. 2, cl. 1. Controversies between citizens of a state and foreign states, citizens, or subjects will be treated subsequently as a separate category of controversies. More minute subdivision is not warranted since the number of suits involving foreign states or nationals is small. Thus the total number of categories of cases in our analysis is ten (rather than nine or twelve).

[157] Schooner Exchange v. McFaddon, 7 Cr. 116, 137 (1812); Guaranty Trust Co. v. U.S., 304 U.S. 126, 134 (1938); National City Bank v. Republic of China, 348 U.S. 356, 358–59 (1955).

[158] Monaco v. Mississippi, 292 U.S. 313, 330 (1934). A contrary conclusion would have been reached under Chisholm v. Georgia, 2 Dall. 419 (1792), but the Supreme Court regards that case as overruled by the Eleventh Amendment. See notes 139–41, pages 351–52, above.

[159] A state cannot be sued without its consent except where otherwise implicit in

A friendly foreign nation, recognized by the political department of the federal government,[160] has the right to sue in courts of the United States as a matter of international comity.[161] But an enemy state or national is excluded from the courts during the existence of hostilities.[162]

Indian tribes have never been regarded as foreign states within the meaning of this clause of the Constitution.[163]

Controversies between "Citizens [of a state] and foreign States, Citizens or Subjects" constitute the eighth and final category of cases which fall within the federal judicial power by reason of the character of the parties.[164]

Here, too, suit cannot be brought against a foreign state without its consent.[165] A foreign state may sue citizens of a state[166] under the recognized practices of international comity.[167] Suits between citizens of a state and aliens are authorized by this clause, but the Constitution does not authorize suits between two or more aliens *inter sese*.[168] Access to courts by aliens against other aliens could be accorded by treaty,

---

the plan of government established by the Constitution (that is to say, in the case of suits by other states or the United States). 292 U.S. at 322. Neither foreign states nor nationals are participants in that plan. See note 141, page 352, above.

[160] Recognition is a political question. See note 26, page 330, above.

[161] The Sapphire, 11 Wall. 164, 167 (1871). To deny this privilege, the Court said, "would manifest a want of comity and friendly feeling." During the existence of war, however, suit by an enemy state is prohibited. Ex parte Colonna, 314 U.S. 510, 511 (1942).

[162] This strict common law rule is relaxed in the case of resident aliens, where resort to the courts is barred only when permitting suit would aid the enemy's war effort. Ex parte Kawato, 317 U.S. 69, 72, 75 (1942).

[163] They are rather to be deemed "domestic dependent nations." Cherokee Nation v. Georgia, 5 Pet. 1, 16–17, 20 (1831).

[164] See note 156, page 355, above.

[165] See notes 157 and 159, page 355, above.

[166] Including citizens of the District of Columbia? See notes 150 and 151, page 354, above.

[167] See note 161 just above.

[168] Section 11 of the Judiciary Act of September 24, 1789, 1 Stat. 73, 78, conferred jurisdiction in cases where an alien is a party. The Court limited this language to cases where one party is an alien and a citizen of a state is shown by the record to be the adverse party. Mossman v. Higginson, 4 Dall. 12, 14 (1800); Montalet v. Murray, 4 Cr. 46 (1807); Hodgson & Thompson v. Bowerbank, 5 Cr. 303, 304 (1809); Jackson v. Twentyman, 2 Pet. 136 (1829). Cf. Pang-Tsu Mow v. Republic of China, 201 F. (2d) 195, 198 (D.C. App. 1952). See note 151, page 354, above.

enforced by legislation.[169] It could possibly also be accorded in the exercise of other powers of Congress, such as that of governing the District of Columbia.[170]

[169] Missouri v. Holland, 252 U.S. 416 (1920). See note 56, page 290, above.
[170] See note 151, page 354, above.

ARTICLE III—THE JUDICIAL BRANCH

Distribution of Jurisdiction

ARTICLE III, section 2, clause 2, does not add anything to the judicial power as defined in Article III, section 2, clause 1. It merely distributes jurisdiction over the categories of cases previously enumerated by providing that in two categories (cases affecting public representatives of foreign nations and those in which a state shall be party), the Supreme Court shall have original jurisdiction; and that in "all the other cases *before mentioned*" the Supreme Court "shall have appellate jurisdiction, both as to Law and Fact, with such Exceptions, and under such Regulations as the Congress shall make."

This distributive character of Article II, section 2, clause 2, is confirmed by the history of its drafting. Originally the preceding clause dealt with the jurisdiction of the Supreme Court,[1] and with respect to the cases specified in what became Article III, section 2, clause 2, it was simply provided that "this jurisdiction shall be original. In all the other cases before mentioned, it shall be appellate."[2] This origin makes it plain that the function of Article III, section 2, clause 2, is merely to distribute jurisdiction over categories of litigation previously enumerated.

The Supreme Court has uniformly adhered to this construction, and held that nothing is added to the judicial power by Article III, section 2, clause 2.[3] A clear statement of the proposition was given by the Supreme Court in a case where a state sued the Secretary of Interior and the Commissioner of Lands (who happened to be citizens of other states) to restrain them from selling lands in an Indian reservation which the state claimed should be allocated to its use for school purposes. With

---

[1] The words "judicial power" were substituted in convention for "jurisdiction of the Supreme Court." See note 9, page 327, above.

[2] See note 8, page 327, above.

[3] The Court has rebuffed attempts to expand the judicial power to include all cases "in which a State shall be Party," even if the other party is a citizen of the same state. Pennsylvania v. Quicksilver Co., 10 Wall. 553, 556 (1871); California v. S.P. Co., 157 U.S. 229, 257 (1895). The proposition has been emphasized also in cases which were held to be outside the judicial power by reason of lack of a justiciable controversy or because a political question was involved. Louisiana v. Texas, 176 U.S. 1, 16 (1900); Massachusetts v. Mellon, 262 U.S. 447, 480 (1923); U.S. v. West Virginia, 295 U.S. 463, 470–71 (1935); Massachusetts v. Missouri, 308 U.S. 1, 19 (1939). See also Monaco v. Mississippi, 292 U.S. 313, 321 (1934); and Georgia v. Penn. R.R. Co., 324 U.S. 439, 464 (1945).

reference to Article III, section 2, the Court said: "The first of these paragraphs defines the matters to which the judicial power of the United States extends, and the second divides the original and appellate jurisdiction of this court. By the latter paragraph this court is given original jurisdiction of all cases 'in which a State shall be a party'. This paragraph, distributing the original and appellate jurisdiction of the court, is not to be taken as enlarging the judicial power of the United States or adding to the cases or matters to which by the first paragraph the judicial power is declared to extend. The question is, therefore, not finally settled by the fact that the State of Minnesota is a party to this litigation. It must also appear that the case is one to which by the first paragraph the judicial power of the United States extends."[4]

[4] Minnesota v. Hitchcock, 185 U.S. 373, 383 (1902). The Court found no genuine controversy between the state and the government officials sued, but found that in substance the case was one to which the United States was a party. "It is one, therefore, to which the judicial power of the United States extends" under Art. III, sec. 2, cl. 1. The Court regarded it as immaterial for this purpose whether the United States is a party plaintiff or defendant (so long as Congress has authorized the suit to be brought). See note 108, page 345, above. In the Hitchcock case the Court also observed that its original jurisdiction in a case where a state is a party was not affected by the circumstance whether it is party plaintiff or defendant. 185 U.S. at 388.

ARTICLE III—THE JUDICIAL BRANCH

Congress and the States

THE original jurisdiction vested in the Supreme Court by the Constitution cannot be added to by Congress.[1] But it is not exclusive,[2] and Congress can authorize other courts to handle routine cases involving foreign ministers or states.[3] No affirmative action by Congress is necessary in order for the Supreme Court to exercise its original jurisdiction.[4]

Legislation is necessary, however, to organize the judicial system and to vest jurisdiction in the several inferior federal courts.[5] Congress may regulate the process of the federal courts (including execution).[6]

[1] This was decided in Marbury v. Madison, 1 Cr. 137, 174–76 (1803), the famous case in which Chief Justice Marshall established the Court's power to hold legislation unconstitutional. He adroitly executed a significant political coup by side-stepping the onus of issuing a mandamus to Secretary of State Madison (which would certainly have been disregarded) upon the ground that Congress could not empower the issuance of such a writ since that would unconstitutionally add to the Court's original jurisdiction. This holding is of questionable correctness. The language of the Constitution may have been designed merely to prevent Congress from withdrawing original jurisdiction over the cases specified in Art. III, sec. 2, cl. 2. Corwin, *John Marshall and the Constitution*, 65–66. See pages 20 and 332 above.

[2] Börs v. Preston, 111 U.S. 252, 260 (1884); U.S. v. Ravara, 2 Dall. 297, 298–99 (1793).

[3] Ames v. Kansas, 111 U.S. 449, 464–69 (1884); U.S. v. Louisiana, 123 U.S. 32, 35–37 (1887); U.S. v. California, 297 U.S. 175, 187 (1936); Georgia v. Penna. R.R. Co., 324 U.S. 439, 464 (1945); Case v. Bowles, 327 U.S. 92, 97 (1946).

[4] Kentucky v. Dennison, 24 How. 66, 98 (1861). Cf. Justice Iredell, dissenting, in Chisholm v. Georgia, 2 Dall. 419, 432–33 (1793).

[5] As Justice Chase observed, in a frequently quoted comment made during argument in Turner v. Bank of North America, 4 Dall. 8, 10 (1799): "The notion has frequently been entertained, that the federal courts derive their judicial power immediately from the constitution; but the political truth is, that the disposal of the judicial power (except in a few specified instances) belongs to congress. If congress has given the power to this court, we possess it, not otherwise: and if congress has not given the power to us, or to any other court, it still remains at the legislative disposal. Besides, congress is not bound, and it would, perhaps, be inexpedient, to enlarge the jurisdiction of the federal courts, to every subject, in every form, which the constitution might warrant." See pages 159–60, 320–21 above, and 361 below.

[6] On this point the Court said: "That a power to make laws for carrying into execution all the judgments which the judicial department has power to pronounce, is expressly conferred by this ["necessary and proper"] clause, seems to be one of those plain propositions which reasoning cannot render plainer." Wayman v. Southard, 10 Wheat. 1, 22 (1824). To the same effect, regarding enforcement of judgments in suits between states, see Virginia v. West Virginia, 246 U.S. 565, 591 (1918).

Likewise, "Congress have constitutional authority to establish, from time to time, such inferior tribunals as they may think proper; and to transfer a cause from one such tribunal to another."[7] Congress may assign to (or withhold from) the inferior courts which it creates such portions of the constitutionally defined judicial power as it sees fit.[8] As the Supreme Court has said: "Of all the courts which the United States may, under their general powers, constitute, only one, the supreme court, possesses jurisdiction derived immediately from the Constitution, and of which the legislative power cannot deprive it. All other courts created by the general government possess no jurisdiction but what is given to them by the power that creates them, and can be vested with none but what the power ceded to the general government will authorize them to confer."[9] The Constitution simply endows inferior federal courts with capacity to receive jurisdiction in certain specified cases, but an act of Congress is needed to confer it.

Moreover, with respect to the Supreme Court's appellate jurisdiction Congress has as unlimited powers of regulation as it has with respect to the jurisdiction of inferior courts.[10] A striking instance of such Congressional control was shown during the Reconstruction era when Congress went so far as to withdraw jurisdiction over a pending case, in which it feared that the Court might hold certain Reconstruction legislation to be unconstitutional.[11]

[7] Stuart v. Laird, 1 Cr. 299, 309 (1803). On the historical significance of this case, see note 26, page 323, above. The Alicia, 7 Wall. 571, 573 (1868), held that the Act of June 30, 1864, 13 Stat. 311, inadvertently attempted to add to the Supreme Court's original jurisdiction by authorizing transfer of a pending prize case where no decision had been rendered in the court below.

[8] Sheldon v. Sill, 8 How. 441, 448–49 (1850); Kline v. Burke Construction Co., 260 U.S. 226, 233–34 (1922); Lockerty v. Phillips, 319 U.S. 182, 187 (1943); Yakus v. U.S. 321 U.S. 414, 429, 439–40, 468 (1944). See also pages 159–60 and 320–21 above.

[9] U.S. v. Hudson, 7 Cr. 32, 33 (1812). This was the case holding that no common law crimes could be punished in federal courts, but that Congress must first define the offense, fix the punishment, and declare what court has jurisdiction to try it. *Ibid.*, 34. See note 113, page 346, above.

[10] Thus Congress may provide for exercise of appellate jurisdiction in admiralty cases by writ of error rather than by appeal. Review is then limited to questions of law arising on the record and does not extend to a re-examination of the facts. Wiscart v. Dauchy, 3 Dall. 321, 327–28 (1796); The Francis Wright, 105 U.S. 381, 385–86 (1882). Cf. the fears of Patrick Henry that such limitation would be unconstitutional. Elliot, *Debates*, II, 396.

[11] Ex parte McCardle, 7 Wall. 506, 514 (1869). See page 160 above. Likewise

In its power to establish a judicial system, Congress could provide, if it chose to do so, that the judicial power of any federal court could be exercised throughout the entire nation.[12] Opponents of the Constitution, during debates on ratification, had dwelt on the plight of an oppressed citizen being dragged from remote regions to the national capital for trial.[13] In practice, however, in order to accommodate the convenience of litigants, courts have been established with a restricted geographical jurisdiction.[14] Ever since the original Judiciary Act of 1789,[15] there has been at least one judicial district in every state.[16]

Another power conferred by the Constitution which has not proved oppressive in actual exercise, under the political responsibility of Congress to its constituents, is that of providing for appellate review "both as to Law and Fact." Congress has in fact respected popular sentiment in favor of trial by jury.[17]

---

the Supreme Court had no general appellate jurisdiction in criminal cases until 1891. Act of March 3, 1891, 26 Stat. 827; Fay v. Noia, 372 U.S. 391, 413 (1963); Frankfurter and Landis, *The Business of the Supreme Court*, 109–20.

[12] Toland v. Sprague, 12 Pet. 300, 328 (1838); U.S. v. Union Pacific R.R. Co., 98 U.S. 569, 603 (1879); Robertson v. Labor Board, 268 U.S. 619, 622 (1925).

[13] *Writings of James Madison*, V, 387; Elliot, *Debates*, II, 384, 386, 388 (George Mason), 399, 422–23 (Patrick Henry). The western Pennsylvania farmers tried in Philadelphia for participation in the Whisky Rebellion furnish perhaps the best instance of actual hardship by reason of being brought to a distant point for trial. See page 376 below.

[14] It might be thought burdensome that in some types of litigation, such as antitrust cases, Congress as a matter of policy has subjected defendants to suit in a multiplicity of districts. 15 U.S.C. 5, 22; U.S. v. National City Lines, 334 U.S. 573, 578, 581, 588 (1948). But no matter where such cases were to be tried there would be inconvenience for some of the parties involved, since numerous large companies, doing a nationwide business, are usually named as defendants. *Ibid.*, 591–93. Even in such cases, however, transfer to a more convenient place by order of the court is now permitted under 28 U.S.C. 1404(a). U.S. v. National City Lines, 337 U.S. 78, 80, 84 (1949). But even apart from statute the doctrine of *forum non conveniens* is always available. Gulf Oil Co. v. Gilbert, 330 U.S. 501, 508 (1947).

[15] Section 2 of an Act to establish the Judicial Courts of the United States, approved September 24, 1789, 1 Stat. 73, established thirteen judicial districts. Section 11 provided that defendants must be sued in the district where they are inhabitants or are found. The same principles apply in general to existing legislation. See note 14 just above and 16 just below.

[16] District Courts are created by 28 U.S.C. 81–133, and rules of venue are given by 28 U.S.C. 1391–1403. Eleven Circuits in which Courts of Appeal are established are created by 28 U.S.C. 41.

[17] Great fears were expressed with respect to this point by opponents of the Con-

It must be remembered that the federal courts established pursuant to the Constitution are simply one part of the dual system of judicial tribunals prevailing in America. In spite of the vast expansion of federal activities that began under President Franklin D. Roosevelt, federal legislation is still limited to matters of genuinely nationwide concern, and the bulk of litigation is still handled by the state courts. In appropriate cases, state courts apply federal law,[18] and federal courts apply state law.[19] At first the adversaries of a strong national government sought to curtail the jurisdiction of federal courts, and wished all cases (or all but admiralty cases) to originate in state courts, subject to appellate review by the United States Supreme Court.[20] Even in criminal proceedings early legislation made use of state courts for the enforcement of federally created duties. Later, especially when opposition to the fugitive slave act was at its height, the notion grew that the federal government should not use state courts for that purpose but must depend upon its own instrumentalities.[21]

In a case involving specific property, the practice of comity requires that whichever court (whether federal or state) first gets jurisdiction

stitution. Farrand, *Records*, III, 221; Charles Warren, "New Light on the History of the Federal Judiciary Act of 1789," *Harvard Law Review*, Vol. XXXVII, No. 1 (November, 1923), 81–85; Dumbauld, *The Bill of Rights and What It Means Today*, 25. In practice, even in admiralty cases, where the Seventh Amendment does not apply, reexamination of facts was forbidden by Congress. See note 10, page 361, above.

[18] Art. VI, cl. 2; see note 91, page 343, above.

[19] See note 144, page 353, above.

[20] In the convention they had opposed giving Congress power to establish inferior courts at all. See note 4, page 319, above; and Warren, "New Light on the History of the Federal Judiciary Act of 1789," *loc. cit.*, 65, 123–24. The Judiciary Act of 1789 was a compromise between those who wished to vest the entire federal judicial power in federal courts and those who wished no federal courts at all except the Supreme Court. *Ibid.*, 131.

[21] *Ibid.*, 70–71; Charles Warren, "Federal Criminal Laws and State Courts," *Harvard Law Review*, Vol. XXXVIII, No. 5 (March, 1925), 553–54, 570–73; Prigg v. Pennsylvania, 16 Pet. 539, 615–16 (1842). Cf. Testa v. Katt, 330 U.S. 386, 389 (1947). The latter case ignores the principle that the criminal law of any jurisdiction should be enforced only by its own courts. The Antelope, 10 Wheat. 66, 123 (1825); Wisconsin v. Pelican Ins. Co., 127 U.S. 265, 290 (1888). See note 132, page 350, above. Each state also has the right to fashion its own judicial system and is not obliged to create any particular type of tribunals (such as equity courts). But whenever there exists an appropriate state court having jurisdiction of a matter governed by federal law, the state court must give full effect to all federally created rights. Second Employers' Liability Cases, 223 U.S. 1, 55–57 (1912). See page 390 below.

of the *res* shall retain exclusive jurisdiction.[22] Logically, the same principle should apply to detention of a prisoner. If the state court first obtains custody, it is bound to respect the defendant's constitutional and other federally created rights, and orderly procedure would dictate that, subject to appellate review by the Supreme Court of the United States, the case should proceed without interruption in the state court. However, a recent practice has grown up of bringing habeas corpus in an inferior federal court to procure the release of a prisoner held in custody by virtue of conviction for a crime under state law, even where the sentence has been upheld by the highest court of the state.[23] In these cases the contention is that the prisoner is detained in violation of his federal constitutional rights.[24] A favorite argument is that he has been denied due process of law by reason of lack of adequate representation by counsel at his trial or when he entered a plea of guilty.[25]

Usually these claims of denial of federal constitutional rights are entirely frivolous and without merit.[26] Most of the habeas corpus applications involve only disputed questions of fact. The prisoner hopes that his story will convince a federal judge even after it has been disbelieved by a state judge or jury.[27] The multiplicity of such applications for

[22] Kline v. Burke Construction Co., 260 U.S. 226, 230 (1922); Princess Lida v. Thompson, 305 U.S. 456, 466 (1939).

[23] Before the Civil War, state courts often undertook to release by habeas corpus prisoners held in custody under the authority of the United States. In Ableman v. Booth, 2 How. 506, 523–24 (1859), the Supreme Court held that no state court possesses such power. The same rule applies if confinement is under color of purported federal authority, the validity of which is to be determined under the Constitution and laws of the United States, (*i. e.*, ultimately by the Supreme Court). Tarble's Case, 13 Wall. 397, 410–11 (1872).

[24] Strong antipathy is aroused by these rulings. In 1952 the conference of state Chief Justices urged that decisions of the highest court of a state should be subject to review only by the United States Supreme Court. It is unseemly for a ruling by a state's top court to be upset by a single federal District Court judge. Darr v. Burford, 339 U.S. 200, 204, 217 (1950). Yet this cannot be avoided, since the Act of February 5, 1867, 14 Stat. 385, 22 U.S.C. 2242, permits habeas corpus in the case of all persons restrained in violation of the Constitution, laws, or treaties of the United States. Brown v. Allen, 344 U.S. 443, 499, 539 (1953). The opinion of Justice Robert H. Jackson in this case is particularly illuminating with regard to the evils of the current practice, which cheapens and trivializes the great writ of habeas corpus, long a cherished remedy against arbitrary executive action. *Ibid.*, 536.

[25] Dumbauld, *The Bill of Rights and What It Means Today*, 69.

[26] 344 U.S. at 496–97, 536–37.

[27] 344 U.S. at 545. In some cases the federal court is free to accept the facts as found by the state court. Townsend v. Sain, 372 U.S. 293, 312–13 (1963).

habeas corpus is burdensome to federal courts as well as annoying to state courts.

In 1948, Congress enacted legislation designed to curtail to some extent the number of habeas corpus applications considered by federal courts. One provision relieves the federal judiciary from considering on its merits an application for habeas corpus by a prisoner held under a judgment whose legality has previously been upheld by a federal court or judge if no new ground is advanced.[28] Another provision codifies in statutory form the rule enunciated by the Supreme Court requiring exhaustion of available state remedies before resort to federal habeas corpus.[29] In 1944 the Supreme Court had declared that: "Ordinarily an application for habeas corpus by one detained under a state court judgment of conviction for crime will be entertained by a federal court only if all state remedies available, including appellate remedies in the state courts and in this Court by appeal or writ of certiorari, have been exhausted."[30] If alternative modes of seeking a state remedy are available, exhaustion of one of them will suffice.[31] If state law does not afford any adequate remedy, immediate application to the federal court is permissible.[32]

Exhaustion of available state remedies for enforcement of federal rights is not merely a condition precedent to application for federal habeas corpus but is often a means of relieving the federal court from reconsidering issues adequately litigated in state courts. Before any relief can be granted to a state prisoner by means of federal habeas

[28] Section 2244 of the Revised Judicial Code of 1948. Act of June 25, 1948, 62 Stat. 967, 28 U.S.C. 2244.

[29] 28 U.S.C. 2254. But in Fay v. Noia, 372 U.S. 391, 435 (1963), it was held "that § 2254 is limited . . . to failure to exhaust state remedies still open to the habeas applicant at the time he files his application in federal court."

[30] Ex parte Hawke, 321 U.S. 114, 116–17 (1944). Darr v. Burford, 339 U.S. 200, 216 (1950), reaffirmed the Hawke requirement of application for certiorari, although it was recognized as an illogical and meaningless but usually necessary formality in Brown v. Allen, 344 U.S. 443, 456, 491, 542–43 (1953). A dictum in Fay v. Noia, 372 U.S. 391, 435–38 (1963), overrules Darr v. Burford and dispenses with this futile preliminary step.

[31] Wade v. Mayo, 334 U.S. 672, 677 (1948). This case was unusual in that it was not known until a later decision of the state court that its denial of habeas corpus had been based upon its view of the constitutional question raised. Hence the prisoner's failure to seek certiorari was excusable, since at the time it seemed that it would have been denied on the ground that the state court's decision was not based upon its determination of a federal question. *Ibid.*, 679, 682.

[32] 334 U.S. at 692.

corpus, there must be a substantial showing that the state procedure has resulted in denial of a fundamental federal right. Where the merits of the federal question involved have been fairly considered and adequately adjudicated by the state courts, and have been reviewed by the United States Supreme Court (or review denied), habeas corpus will ordinarily not be granted.[33] Likewise if the applicant has disentitled himself to relief by his own conduct and has deliberately elected to ignore available state remedies or has "inexcusably failed to tender the federal questions to the state courts," habeas corpus may be denied.[34]

Congress has also provided a special procedure to regulate another source of friction with the state governments—namely, the use of injunctions in federal courts to prevent enforcement of state legislation. This practice was often resorted to by railroads, during their heyday, to nullify laws regulating public utility rates.[35] Its abuse led to adoption of the requirement that such cases must be heard by a specially convened court of three judges, one of whom must be a circuit judge, and provision was made for expediting appeals to the Supreme Court from any injunction granted.[36]

Another expedient sometimes,[37] but not always,[38] adopted to avoid conflict with state courts is the practice known as "abstention." Under this practice a federal court confronted with a case which is pending in a state court or which turns upon a doubtful question of state law abstains from exercise of its jurisdiction until after a decision upon the

[33] Ex parte Hawke, 321 U.S. 114, 118 (1944); Townsend v. Sain, 372 U.S. 293, 312 (1963). To be sure, the federal court must independently decide questions of law. *Ibid.*, 318. But if the state court has applied the correct federal legal standard, and has adequately found the facts, the federal court's task is simple.

[34] Fay v. Noia, 372 U.S. 391, 425, 433, 438 (1963). The principle here recognized may prove an inadequate "attempted palliative" for the havoc wrought by this revolutionary decision. *Ibid.*, 470. Further legislation may be needed to restore some semblance of finality to sentences imposed by state courts. Noia was convicted in 1942. He knowingly elected not to appeal, fearing that a new trial might result in a severer sentence (death instead of life). *Ibid.*, 394, 397.

[35] Ex parte Young, 209 U.S. 123, 148 (1908).

[36] Act of June 18, 1910, 36 Stat. 557, 28 U.S.C. 2281; Frankfurter and Landis, *The Business of the Supreme Court*, 143, 278, 284; Florida Lime Growers v. Jacobsen, 362 U.S. 73, 75–85 (1960).

[37] Ex parte Royall, 117 U.S. 241, 251 (1886); Thompson v. Magnolia Petroleum Co., 309 U.S. 478, 483–84 (1940); Ala. P.S.C. v. Southern Ry., 341 U.S. 341, 345, 349–51 (1951).

[38] Allegheny Co. v. Frank Mashuda Co., 360 U.S. 185, 187 (1959).

question can be obtained from a state court. Unless circumstances really justify such referral to a state tribunal, the federal court might be criticized for denial of justice, an evil condemned by Magna Charta.[39]

[39] Other instances where a court having jurisdiction declines to exercise it are found in connection with the Supreme Court's original jurisdiction and the doctrine of *forum non conveniens*. See notes 131, page 350, 3 and 4, page 360, and 14, page 362, above.

Trial by Jury

The Trial of all Crimes, except in Cases of Impeachment, shall be by Jury; and such Trial shall be held in the State where the said Crimes shall have been committed; but when not committed within any State, the Trial shall be at such Place or Places as the Congress may by Law have directed.

HISTORY

THIS provision first appears in an addition by Rutledge to Randolph's working draft in the Committee of Detail: "That Trials for Criml. Offences be in the State where the Offe[nse] was com[mitte]d—by Jury."[1] As reported by the Committee of Detail, the language was: "The trial of all criminal offences (except in cases of impeachments) shall be in the State where they shall be committed; and shall be by Jury."[2] In convention this was amended to read: "The trial of all crimes (except in cases of impeachment) shall be by jury, and such trial shall be held in the State where the said crimes shall have been committed; but when not committed within any State, then the trial shall be at such place or places as the Legislature may direct."[3]

The Committee of Style changed the last clause to "the trial shall be at such place or places as the Congress may by law have directed."[4]

[1] Farrand, *Records,* II, 144.

[2] Art. XI, sec. 4. *Ibid.,* II, 187 (August 6). The exception in case of impeachments had been inserted by Rutledge in a working draft in the handwriting of Wilson. *Ibid.,* II, 173.

[3] *Ibid.,* II, 434, 438 (August 28). Madison comments that "The object of this amendment was to provide for trial by jury of offences committed out of any State."

[4] *Ibid.,* II, 601 (September 12). Attempts to provide for jury trial in civil cases were unsuccessful. *Ibid.,* II, 587–88 (September 12); II, 628 (September 15). See Dumbauld, *The Bill of Rights and What It Means Today,* 4–5. The omission was not due to hostility to jury trial in civil cases, but to the lack of uniformity among the laws of the several states with respect to the subject matter, and to the fact that jury trial in admiralty and equity matters was not customary. The diversity of state practice was also a problem when the Sixth Amendment was being drafted. *Ibid.,* 49. See also Farrand, *Records,* III, 298, 349.

INTERPRETATION

PROVISION having been made elsewhere in the Constitution[5] for trial of impeachments by the Senate, such cases are excluded from the guarantee of jury trial. Since criminal prosecution and impeachment can both result from the commission of the same offense,[6] the requirement of jury trial would be applicable in the event of proceedings to subject an officer to "Indictment, Trial, Judgment, and Punishment, according to Law," as well as to impeachment.

The requirement that trial shall be by jury does not make such trial a mandatory feature of the functioning of the federal judicial system; it merely gives accused persons a right to that mode of trial, which they can waive (as by entering a plea of guilty).[7]

Trial by jury, as that term is used in the Constitution, means jury trial as it was understood and practiced at common law. This includes three features: (1) there must be twelve jurors, neither more nor less; (2) the trial must be conducted in the presence and under the superintendence of a judge to instruct the jury concerning the law; and (3) the verdict must be unanimous.[8]

Notwithstanding the fact that the Constitution prescribes that the trial of "all" crimes shall be by jury, there has always been a class of

[5] Art. I, sec. 3, cl. 6.

[6] Art. I, sec. 3, cl. 7. Hence no inference can be drawn from Art. III, sec. 2, cl. 3, regarding the controversial issue whether impeachment is available for offenses which are not punishable as crimes. This question was debated at the impeachments of Judge Chase and President Johnson. No conclusion was established, though both officers were acquitted of the charges preferred.

[7] Patton v. U.S., 281 U.S. 276, 298 (1930). In that case one juror became ill, and the defendant and prosecution agreed to proceed with eleven jurors. The language of the Sixth Amendment clearly shows that jury trial is there described as a "right" of the accused. If there is any conflict on this point between that amendment and Art. III, sec. 2, cl. 3, the amendment, being later in date, would prevail. See Schick v. U.S., 195 U.S. 65, 68 (1904).

[8] 281 U.S. at 288. Thus the ex post facto clause (Art. I, sec. 10, cl. 1) prevented conviction by a jury of eight for a crime committed while Utah was a federal territory. Thompson v. Utah, 170 U.S. 343, 349–51 (1898). But crimes committed after Utah attained statehood can be punished upon conviction by a jury of eight in the state courts. Maxwell v. Dow, 176 U.S. 581, 586, 595, 602 (1900). It would seem that the service of alternate jurors, discharged before the jury begins its deliberations unless called upon to replace jurors withdrawn because of illness, is not forbidden, since the verdict would be rendered by a jury of twelve. Robinson v. U.S., 144 F.(2d) 392, 397 (C.C.A. 6, 1944), aff'd. 324 U.S. 282. See Rule 28(c) of the Federal Rules of Criminal Procedure. For the requirement of a judge, see also Capital Traction Co. v. Hof, 174 U.S. 1, 13–14 (1899). For unanimity, see also Andres v. U.S., 333 U.S. 740, 748 (1948).

"petty offenses" which are punishable without trial by jury.[9] To be included in this category, the offense must not be serious in its nature,[10] and the punishment must not be severe.[11]

In a criminal case, where the crime charged is not a petty offense but one requiring jury trial, it will not suffice if the jury trial is available only on appeal, after the case has first been heard without a jury.[12]

The right to jury trial is also inapplicable to proceedings before a court-martial or other form of military tribunal.[13] It is also usually unavailable in proceedings for contempt of court.[14]

The provisions of Article III, section 2, clause 3, have been supplemented, but not superseded,[15] by the Sixth Amendment. The amendment requires not merely a jury trial, but a speedy and public trial by an impartial jury.[16] It likewise prescribes, more specifically than the original constitutional provision, that such trial must take place in "the State and district" where the offense occurred.[17] The district must be established in advance of the trial.[18]

When a crime is committed at a place which is not within a state,

[9] District of Columbia v. Clawans, 300 U.S. 617, 624 (1937); Schick v. U.S., 195 U.S. 65, 68–70 (1904).

[10] Thus in Callan v. Wilson, 127 U.S. 540, 552, 555 (1888), while recognizing the rule that petty offenses could be punished without trial by jury, the Court held that the offense there involved (conspiracy) was too serious to be treated as a petty offense, even if the prescribed penalty was slight. Driving recklessly so as to endanger life and property was classified as a "grave" offense requiring jury trial in District of Columbia v. Colts, 282 U.S. 63, 72–74 (1930).

[11] In colonial times imprisonment up to twelve months was sometimes imposed for petty offenses. Hence in the Clawans case a term of ninety days for selling unused railroad tickets without a license was not too severe. 300 U.S. at 625–27.

[12] Callan v. Wilson, 127 U.S. 540, 557 (1888). The rule is otherwise in a civil case. Capital Traction Co. v. Hof, 174 U.S. 1, 45 (1899).

[13] Ex parte Quirin, 317 U.S. 1, 39 (1942).

[14] Green v. U.S., 356 U.S. 165, 183 (1958).

[15] Callan v. Wilson, 127 U.S. 540, 548–49 (1888). Cf. Schick v. U.S., 195 U.S. 65, 68 (1904).

[16] Whether a jury is "impartial" when government employees in the District of Columbia serve as jurors has often been the subject of dispute. See Dumbauld, *The Bill of Rights and What It Means Today*, 68. Jurors must be interrogated to determine actual bias. Morford v. U.S., 339 U.S. 258, 259 (1950).

[17] Hence the Sixth Amendment does not apply if the place where the offense was committed was not within a state. U.S. v. Dawson, 15 How. 467, 487 (1853); Cook v. U.S., 138 U.S. 157, 181 (1891).

[18] The district need not have been established before the crime was committed. If Congress changes the district boundaries, the trial will be in the new district embracing the locality where the offense was committed. Cf. note 19, which follows.

Justice Oliver Wendell Holmes, Jr. (1841–1935)

Supreme Court Building, where the Court has sat since 1935.

Courtesy Architect of the Capitol

the trial may be held wherever Congress directs.[19] The trial cannot be held until after Congress has specified where it is to be held; but Congress may designate the place of trial (or change such disposition) at any time before the trial begins.[20]

The guarantee of a jury trial applies wherever the Constitution is in force. The question whether "the Constitution follows the flag" affects the availability of the right to jury trial. It is not mandatory in "unincorporated territories" such as were Hawaii and the Philippines.[21] In "incorporated territories," such as was Alaska, jury trial must be accorded.[22] Moreover, there is a growing tendency to hold that wherever the United States government acts, in any part of the world, its action must be in accordance with the fundamental law upon which its legal existence depends.[23]

[19] Jones v. U.S., 137 U.S. 202, 211 (1890). In the case of crimes not committed within any state, Congress can at any time change the place of trial. A defendant has no vested right to be tried at the place which at the time of the offense was the place fixed by Congress for trying such offenses. Cook v. U.S., 138 U.S. 157, 182 (1891).

[20] 138 U.S. at 182.

[21] Balzac v. Porto Rico, 258 U.S. 298, 305, 312 (1922); Dorr v. U.S., 195 U.S. 138, 143 (1904).

[22] Rasmussen v. U.S., 197 U.S. 516, 528 (1905); Thompson v. Utah, 170 U.S. 343, 346 (1898). Jury trial is also guaranteed in the District of Columbia. Callan v. Wilson, 127 U.S. 540, 550 (1888).

[23] Reid v. Covert, 354 U.S. 1, 7 (1957). This case, followed in Kinsella v. Singleton, 361 U.S. 234, 248 (1960), overruled Madsen v. Kinsella, 343 U.S. 341, 360 (1952), and *In re* Ross, 140 U.S. 453, 464 (1891). Cf. Johnson v. Eisentrager, 339 U.S. 763, 783–84 (1950).

ART. III, SEC. 3, CL. 1 *and* CL. 2

Treason against the United States, shall consist only in levying War against them, or in adhering to their Enemies, giving them Aid and Comfort. No Person shall be convicted of Treason unless on the Testimony of two Witnesses to the same overt Act, or on Confession in open Court.

The Congress shall have Power to declare the Punishment of Treason, but no Attainder of Treason shall work Corruption of Blood, or Forfeiture except during the Life of the Person attainted.

HISTORY

THESE provisions regarding treason originated in the Committee of Detail. Randolph's working draft contained, among the legislative powers to be conferred upon Congress, the authority "To declare it to be treason to levy war against or adhere to the enemies of the U.S."[1] An addition by Rutledge to a draft in Wilson's hand would have empowered Congress to declare the punishment of treason against the United States "or any of them; not to work Corruption of Blood or Forfeit except during the life of the Party."[2]

The Committee of Detail reported: "Treason against the United States shall consist only in levying war against the United States, or any of them; and in adhering to the enemies of the United States, or any of them. The Legislature of the United States shall have power to declare the punishment of treason. No person shall be convicted of treason, unless on the testimony of two witnesses. No attainder of treason shall work corruption of blood nor forfeiture, except during the life of the person attainted."[3]

[1] Farrand, *Records*, II, 144.   [2] *Ibid.*, II, 168.

[3] Art. VII, sec. 2. *Ibid.*, II, 182 (August 6); IV, 5. In debate, the words "or any of them" were stricken. *Ibid.*, II, 338, 346 (August 20). Likewise, at Madison's suggestion, "and" was changed to "or" before "in adhering to their enemies." On motion of Mason, "giving them aid and comfort" was added. *Ibid.*, II, 339, 349. On motion of Martin, "or on confession in open court" was added. *Ibid.*, II, 339, 349–50. At the suggestion of Dickinson, supported by Franklin, "to the same overt act" was added

Various changes were made during debate.[4] There was considerable discussion, particularly with respect to the question whether treason could be an offense both against the United States and against a particular state.[5]

The Committee of Style reported the provisions in their present form.[6]

INTERPRETATION

THE definition of treason embodied in the Constitution was derived from the basic English statute of 1351,[7] with limitations designed to prevent the extension which had been given to the crime of treason during the course of English history. Seven categories of treason were enumerated in the statute: (1) to compass or imagine the death of the king, or certain members of the royal family; (2) to violate the queen,

after "two witnesses." *Ibid.*, II, 338, 346, 348. The words "of the United States" were deleted after "Legislature." *Ibid.*, II, 338.

[4] In addition to the changes mentioned in note 3 just above, "against the United States" was stricken and then reinserted. *Ibid.*, II, 338, 348, 349 (August 20). Likewise "some overt act of" was inserted before "levying war," and then eliminated. *Ibid.*, II, 337, 338. A number of other proposed amendments were defeated. On motion of Gerry there was adopted an additional prohibition: "The Legislature shall pass no bill of attainder, nor any ex post facto laws." *Ibid.*, II, 368, 375 (August 22). This later became Art. I, sec. 9, cl. 3.

[5] Dr. Johnson contended that treason could only be an offense against the supreme sovereignty, namely the United States. Madison, Mason, Sherman, and Ellsworth took the contrary view. *Ibid.*, II, 346–47 (August 20). Gouverneur Morris perceptively noted that in case of a contest between the United States and a particular state, the people of the latter must be traitors to one or the other authority. *Ibid.*, II, 345. Luther Martin offered a proviso exempting acts done by authority of a state from punishment as treason, but this was not accepted. *Ibid.*, III, 158–59, 223. For an analogous situation resulting in the imprisonment and exile of the famous Dutch jurist Hugo Grotius, see Edward Dumbauld, "Grotius' Defence of the Lawful Government of Holland," *Journal of Public Law*, Vol. III, No. 1 (Spring, 1954), 192, 198, 206.

[6] *Ibid.*, II, 601 (September 12). Apparently "nor" before "forfeiture" in the report of the Committee of Style became "or" in the Constitution without any recorded action in convention.

[7] 25 Edward III st. 5 c. 2. The statute contained a provision that the judges should consult Parliament before holding other acts to be treason. Holdsworth, *History of English Law*, I, 377–78. In periods of stress the scope of treason was often extended, but in calmer times the provisions of the act of 1351 were reinstated as the proper standard. *Ibid.*, VIII, 310; Cramer v. U.S., 325 U.S. 1, 17 (1945). Blackstone, *Commentaries*, IV, 87–92, criticized "new-fangled treasons" not enumerated in the statute of 1351. The framers of the Constitution also drew from the statute of 1698 regulating trials for treason, 7 & 8 Wm. III, c. 3. Charge of Justice Iredell in U.S. v. Fries, 9 Fed. Cas. at 911.

or certain members of the royal family; (3) to levy war against the king; (4) to "be adherent to the king's enemies in his realm, giving to them aid and comfort in the realm, or elsewhere";[8] (5) to counterfeit the king's seal or money; (6) to bring false money into the realm; (7) to slay the chancellor or the king's judges while performing their duties.[9]

In times of national peril or political passion, the scope of treasonable conduct was often broadened by extension of the crime to embrace other acts than those specified in the statute of 1351. Besides a number of temporary extensions by statute,[10] many acts were declared by the courts to be "constructive treason."[11] Mere words, even unspoken or unpublished, could constitute the crime of treason.[12]

The framers of the Constitution effectively forestalled any such legislation or judicial extension of the crime of treason in America by adopting an exclusive definition, which neither Congress nor the courts were authorized to modify. "The concern uppermost in the framers' minds, that mere mental attitudes or expression should not be treason, influenced both definition of the crime and procedure for its trial."[13] Procedural requirements were proof of an overt act,[14] and the two-witness rule.[15]

[8] In Rex v. Casement, [1917] 1 K.B. 98, 122–25, the contention was rejected that under this ambiguous wording aid given out of the realm by Sir Roger Casement when he was himself abroad did not constitute treason. It is clear that treason can be committed by a citizen of the United States outside the country. Kawakita v. U.S., 343 U.S. 717, 733 (1952).

[9] For the text of items (1) and (4) in law French as well as English, see [1917] 1 K.B. at 98–99. For the complete text in English, see Cramer v. U.S., 325 U.S. 1, 16–17 (1945). See also Blackstone, *Commentaries*, IV, 76–85. And see Holdsworth, *History of English Law*, II, 449; III, 287–93.

[10] Holdsworth, *History of English Law*, II, 450; IV, 498–500.

[11] *Ibid.*, VIII, 307–22. The concept of "imagining the king's death" was capable of indefinite extension. Thus the regicides who condemned Charles I were charged with that species of treason, the actual killing of the king being pleaded merely as an overt act. *Ibid.*, VIII, 309.

[12] Thus Algernon Sidney, considered as a patriotic martyr by American statesmen of the eighteenth century, was condemned because of sentiments contained in an unpublished book. *Ibid.*, VIII, 315; Howell, *State Trials*, IX, 817, 854–58, 868, 892–93, 898, 901 (1683); Dumbauld, *The Political Writings of Thomas Jefferson*, 8, 192.

[13] Cramer v. U.S., 325 U.S. 1, 28 (1945).

[14] Except in cases of plotting the king's death, an overt act was required in English practice. Holdsworth, *History of English Law*, III, 291.

[15] In England the two-witness rule, which had its inception in 1551–52 (5, 6 Edward VI c. 11 § 9), became indubitably established in 1696 (7, 8 William III c. 3

The Constitution, likewise mindful of English experience, forbade bills of attainder, which had been a favorite mode of securing condemnations for treason in England. In the United States, judicial procedure (with the right of trial by jury) was to be the only permissible method of inflicting punishment for treason.[16]

Moreover, the freedom of Congress to prescribe the punishment for treason was limited by the restriction preventing imposition of the familiar English penalty known as "corruption of blood." For the protection of the innocent heirs of persons guilty of treason, it was ordained by the Constitution that if forfeiture of property were prescribed by Congress as part of the penalty for treason, such forfeiture should continue no longer than during the life of the condemned traitor.[17]

In language somewhat reminiscent of Blackstone,[18] Madison succinctly summarized the work of the framers with respect to treason: "As treason may be committed against the United States, the authority of the United States ought to be enabled to punish it. But as new-fangled and artificial treasons have been the great engines by which violent factions, the natural offspring of free government, have usually wreaked their alternate malignity on each other, the convention have, with great judgment, opposed a barrier to this peculiar danger, by inserting a constitutional definition of the crime, fixing the proof necessary for conviction of it, and restraining the Congress, even in punishing it,

§§ 2 and 4). *Ibid.*, IV, 499; IX, 233–34. Art. III, sec. 3, cl. 1, was stricter than the English statutes in requiring that two witnesses must testify to the same overt act. English law permitted an alternative, the testimony of one witness each to two overt acts of the same type of treason. *Ibid.*, IX, 235; Cramer v. U.S., 325 U.S. 1, 24, 76 (1945); Algernon Sidney's case, in Howell, *State Trials*, IX, 817, 889 (1683).

[16] Art. I, sec. 9, cl. 3; Art. I, sec. 10, cl. 1; Art. III, sec. 2, cl. 3. "Congress can neither define nor try the crime," James Wilson observed in the Pennsylvania ratifying convention. Farrand, *Records*, III, 163. The legislative branch does have jurisdiction to try impeachments, but the penalty is limited to exclusion from office. Art. I, sec. 3, cl. 6 and cl. 7. In England impeachment and attainder were interchangeable weapons in the hands of Parliament. Chafee, *Three Human Rights in the Constitution*, 104–33.

[17] Hence, if the death penalty is applicable, there can be no forfeiture at all (except from the date of the treason to the date of execution). For the English precedents regarding forfeiture, escheat, and corruption of blood, see page 195 above. Blackstone favored abolition of these penalties, as well as a precise definition of treason. Blackstone, *Commentaries*, IV, 384, 388–89; IV, 75, citing Montesquieu, *Esprit des Lois*, l. XII, c. 7. Corruption of blood was finally abolished in England in 1834. 3, 4 Wm. IV c. 106. In 1800 it had been abolished in cases of felony, but not in those of treason or murder. 54 Geo. III c. 145. Holdsworth, *A History of English Law*, XIII, 391.

[18] See notes 7 and 17, pages 373 and 375, above.

from extending the consequences of guilt beyond the person of its author."[19]

The first cases in which the courts were required to interpret the scope of treason as defined by the Constitution arose out of the Whisky Rebellion of 1794.[20] That was an uprising of western Pennsylvania farmers in protest against a federal excise tax on whisky. The primitive state of transportation facilities made it impossible for grain to be profitably marketed otherwise than in distilled form. President Washington took the field with troops to suppress the insurrection. After reaching Carlisle, he returned to the seat of government, but Alexander Hamilton continued industriously to ferret out insurgents, hoping to find incriminating evidence against Albert Gallatin, Congressman William Findley, and other Jeffersonian sympathizers. Many inoffensive citizens were seized and brought to Philadelphia for trial, where they were paraded through the streets as a spectacle on their way to jail. Only two were convicted, and were later pardoned.[21]

In the course of these cases the rule was established that it was levying war for an assembly to use violence for the purpose of resisting the general execution of a law. The same rule was followed in a later uprising in the eastern part of the state led by John Fries against the enforcement of a tax on windows.[22] However, if there was no intent to prevent in its entirety the enforcement of a law but merely to resist it in a particular case, the crime was not treason but simply the lesser

[19] *The Federalist*, No. 43, (Lodge ed., 1888), 269; quoted in 325 U.S. at 76. As stated by Justice Robert H. Jackson, "the basic law of treason in this country was framed by men who . . . were taught by experience and by history to fear abuse of the treason charge almost as much as they feared treason itself." 325 U.S. at 21.

[20] U.S. v. Vigol, 2 Dall. 346, 347 (1795); U.S. v. Mitchell, 2 Dall. 348, 355 (1795). See also various charges to grand juries during the Civil War. Fed. Cas. Nos. 18271–18277. After that conflict an abortive attempt was made to try Jefferson Davis for treason. Case of Davis, Fed. Cas. No. 3621a; David K. Watson, "The Trial of Jefferson Davis," *Yale Law Journal*, Vol. XXIV, No. 8 (June, 1915), 669, 676.

[21] See William Findley, *History of the Insurrection*, 187, 210, 218–22, 245. Albert Gallatin, *Writings*, I, 3; III, 3–67. Henry M. Brackenridge, *History of the Western Insurrection*, 330.

[22] U.S. v. Mitchell, 2 Dall. 348, 355 (1795); U.S. v. Fries, Fed. Cas. No. 5126 (1799). Justice Iredell and Judge Peters conducted the first trial, but granted a new trial, at which Justice Samuel Chase presided. His conduct at this trial led William Lewis and Alexander J. Dallas to withdraw as counsel for the defendant, and was the subject of animadversion at Chase's impeachment. Fed. Cas. No. 5127 (1800); Evans, *Report of the Trial of the Hon. Samuel Chase*, 18–32, 61–62; App. 8–17, 42–48.

offense of riot. To amount to treason the resistance had to be of a public rather than private character.[23] Thus, during the period when public opinion in the Northern states opposed enforcement of the fugitive slave law, it was held not to be treason when a defendant merely refused to assist a federal officer acting in pursuance of that odious statute.[24]

The Burr conspiracy in 1807 gave rise to several important cases in which Chief Justice John Marshall expounded the effect of the constitutional provisions relating to treason. Two of Burr's confederates, Justus Erich Bollman and Samuel Swartwout, were seized in New Orleans by General James Wilkinson (a scoundrel later disclosed to be a Spanish pensioner) and transported to the nation's capital by military force. There the United States Attorney, at the direction of President Jefferson, who desired their surrender to the civil authority, moved for a bench warrant to commit them on a charge of treason. The prisoners sought discharge by writ of habeas corpus, but were held for trial and not released on bail.[25] They renewed their application for habeas corpus before the Supreme Court.[26] Their discharge was ordered by that tribunal. It was clear that the District of Columbia had no jurisdiction to try them; whatever offense, if any, they had been guilty of had been committed in New Orleans, where they had been arrested by Wilkinson, and they should be tried there.[27] But Marshall also pointed out that there was no sufficient evidence of conduct amounting to treason.[28] He emphasized that "conspiracy is not treason."[29] War

[23] This distinction was recognized in English law. Holdsworth, *A History of English Law*, VIII, 319.

[24] U.S. v. Hanway, Fed. Cas. No. 15299 (E.D. Pa. 1851). The Court held that it was for the jury to decide whether the defendant had abetted or acted in concert with slaves who shot their owner who accompanied the federal officer seeking to seize them. The defendant was acquitted.

[25] U.S. v. Bollman, Fed. Cas. No. 14622 (Circt. Ct. D.C. 1807). Judges Allen Bowie Duckett and Nicholas Fitzhugh held that probable cause had been shown; Chief Judge Cranch contended that to constitute levying war there must be an assemblage of men, armed in warlike manner, or assembled in such numbers as to make arms unnecessary, and ready to act and with intent to do some treasonable act. Cranch's view was followed by Marshall in U.S. v. Burr, 4 Cr. 470, 487 (1807).

[26] An attempt was made in Congress to suspend habeas corpus. An act to that effect was passed by the Senate but rejected by the House of Representatives. Beveridge, *Life of John Marshall*, III, 346–48.

[27] Ex parte Bollman and Swartwout, 4 Cr. 125, 136 (1807).

[28] *Ibid.*, 135.

[29] *Ibid.*, 126. This was the English law. Holdsworth, *A History of English Law*,

must actually be levied. There must be "an actual assemblage of men for the purpose of executing a treasonable design."[30]

Marshall went on to explain that: "It is not the intention of the court to say that no individual can be guilty of this crime who has not appeared in arms against his country. On the contrary, if war be actually levied, that is, if a body of men be actually assembled for the purpose of effecting by force a treasonable purpose, all those who perform any part, however minute, or however remote from the scene of action, and who are actually leagued in the general conspiracy, are to be considered as traitors. But there must be an actual assembling of men for the treasonable purpose, to constitute a levying of war."[31]

This language gave Marshall considerable difficulty when Aaron Burr himself was tried for treason in 1807. During the course of lengthy proceedings in Richmond, Marshall wrote many opinions on points of law that arose; but the climax of the case, which brought about the collapse of the prosecution, was Marshall's ruling that no overt act of levying war had been proved against Burr.[32]

There had been evidence that twenty or thirty men had assembled, some of them with rifles, at Blennerhassett's Island on the Ohio River in Wood County, Virginia. It was conceded that Burr was not present at that time, but was in another state.

Marshall held that this assemblage was insufficiently belligerent to constitute an overt act of levying war. A secret, unarmed meeting, although with treasonable intent, would not amount to an actual levying of war.[33] Marshall took great pains to repudiate the interpretation of his language in the case of Bollman and Swartwout as meaning "that

III, 462; VIII, 318. Likewise Marshall pointed out that merely enlisting men, without assembling them in warlike array, does not amount to levying war. 4 Cr. 134.

[30] 4 Cr. 127.

[31] *Ibid.*, 126. Judge Chase in the Fries case said that weapons were not necessary, that numbers might supply the want of arms. He said that "some actual force or violence must be used," though the quantum of force is immaterial, and it need not be enough to effect its object. 9 Fed. Cas. 930.

[32] "The opinion of the Chief Justice was one of the longest ever rendered by him, and the only one in which an extensive examination of authorities is made. Indeed, a greater number of decisions, treatises, and histories are referred to than in all the rest of Marshall's foremost Constitutional opinions." Beveridge, *Life of John Marshall,* III, 504. This opinion was delivered on August 31, 1807. The next day Burr was acquitted.

[33] U.S. v. Burr, 4 Cr. 470, 486 (1807). For this opinion, see also Robertson, *Trials,* II, 401–45.

any assemblage whatever for a treasonable purpose, whether in force, or not in force, whether in a condition to use violence, or not in that condition, is a levying of war."[34] Explaining the embarrassing paragraph in his prior opinion, Marshall pointed out that "Although it is not expressly stated that the assemblage of men for the purpose of carrying into operation the treasonable intent, which will amount to levying war, must be an assemblage in force, yet it is fairly to be inferred from the context." A lengthy and laborious effort was made to show that this was a natural, not a strained, explanation of the quoted words.[35]

Perhaps Marshall's explanation was not unduly strained. His prior language may have implied the necessity of an assemblage in a position actually to use force, although his words simply spoke of an assemblage *"for the purpose* of effecting by force" a treasonable design.[36] He did characterize as traitors in his earlier dictum only those "who perform any part" in prosecuting the war "and who are actually leagued in the general conspiracy."[37]

Not only did Marshall hold that the overt act at Blennerhassett's Island charged against Burr did not amount to levying war; he also held that Burr, not being present, was not responsible as a participant

---

[34] 4 Cr. at 476. The contention of the prosecution, based upon Marshall's language, was "that an assemblage of men convened for the purpose of effecting by force a treasonable design, which force is intended to be employed before their dispersion, is treasonable; and the persons engaged in it are traitors." Marshall's language was interpreted as meaning "that a bare assemblage of men, met to carry into forcible execution, before their separation, a treasonable design, was an overt act of levying war against the United States." Robertson, *Trials*, I, 435–36. It was emphasized that this definition excluded the requirement that the assemblage be armed or actually use force; and that a person not present at the scene could be guilty of levying war. *Ibid.*, 437, 440, 448.

[35] 4 Cr. at 482.

[36] 4 Cr. at 126. Corwin says that "Marshall's effort to square this previous opinion with his later position was as unconvincing as it was labored" and that "Marshall's conduct of Burr's trial for treason is the one serious blemish in his judicial record." Corwin, *John Marshall and the Constitution*, 108–109, 111.

[37] Marshall correctly interpreted his Bollman language in the Burr case when he said: "Those only who perform a part, and who are leagued in the conspiracy, are declared to be traitors. To complete the definition both circumstances must concur." 4 Cr. at 474. He conceded in the Burr case that "it does not follow that he alone can have levied war who has borne arms." War is a complex operation, composed of many parts, and all those who perform any part in the prosecution of the war "may correctly be said to levy war." *Ibid.*, 472, 502.

in that act.[38] "The whole treason laid in this indictment is the levying of war in Blennerhassett's island," and "the prisoner can only be convicted on the overt act laid in the indictment."[39] Without proof of Burr's presence "by two witnesses, the overt act laid in this indictment cannot be proved."[40]

If a person could be convicted for levying war, not because he did so in person but because he procured it to be done by others, it would be necessary to charge such procurement as an overt act, and prove it by two witnesses, rather than to charge against the defendant a different overt act committed by other persons, as was the case in the indictment against Burr.[41]

Under English authorities, including Lord Coke, a person procuring or causing treason to be committed by others is himself guilty of treason. But this is not because he is deemed to be present and participating in overt acts committed by others when in fact he is absent but because, under a rule of English common law, in treason all parties involved are principals. Indirect connection with a crime, which in the case of a felony would result in conviction as an accessory rather than as a principal, would in the case of treason result in conviction as a principal offender.[42]

Whether a person guilty of procurement could be convicted under this doctrine in the United States is a question of importance which in Marshall's view would be proper for decision by the Supreme Court.[43]

[38] William Wirt, one of the prosecuting attorneys, summarized Marshall's opinion as holding "that our evidence is irrelevant, Burr not having been present at the island with the assemblage, and the act itself not amounting to levying war." Wirt to Dabney Carr, September 1, 1807. Warren, *The Supreme Court in United States History*, I, 310.

[39] 4 Cr. at 493. For the indictment, see Robertson, *Trials*, 430–32. It is similar to that in U.S. v. Fries, 9 Fed. Cas. 847.

[40] 4 Cr. at 496.

[41] *Ibid.*, 500. Marshall's own view seems to be that "To advise or procure a treason is in the nature of conspiring or plotting treason, which is not treason in itself." *Ibid.*, 501 .

[42] *Ibid.*, 491, 502. Marshall argues also that the person procuring the treason could not be tried until after conviction of the persons committing it. *Ibid.*, 504.

[43] *Ibid.*, 472. "It may possibly be the opinion of the Supreme Court, that those who procure a treason, and do nothing further, are guilty under the Constitution; I only say that opinion has not yet been given." *Ibid.*, 502. However, Justice Chase treated the English doctrine as applicable in the Fries case. He also charged the jury that they could convict if satisfied "that the prisoner at the bar incited, encouraged, promoted, or assisted in the insurrection . . . and that some force was used by some of the people assembled." 9 Fed. Cas. at 931. President Jefferson in a draft of a mes-

But Marshall points out that the doctrine making accessories principals in case of treason is one that depends upon the operation of the common law. "It is an operation, then, which can only be performed where the common law exists to perform it." Hence to decide that this doctrine is applicable in the United States would necessarily presuppose "that the United States, as a nation, have a common law which creates and defines the punishment of crimes accessorial in their nature."[44] It would further imply "that these accessorial crimes are not, in the case of treason, excluded by the definition of treason" given in the Constitution.[45]

The precise posture of the case against Burr at the time of Marshall's opinion was that the events on Blennerhassett's Island had been proved, and the prosecution proposed to offer testimony regarding Burr's treasonable activities at a subsequent time and a different place in order to connect him as a coconspirator with those who had committed the overt act which had been proved. The defense objected to such testimony as irrelevant, and insisted that no collateral testimony be offered until all the testimony intended to prove the overt acts had been received, at which time the defense intended to ask the court to rule whether there had been sufficient proof of any overt acts of levying war.[46]

The effect of Marshall's rulings was to uphold Burr's objection. Admittedly, under the Constitution, if the overt act charged against the defendant is not proved by two witnesses, "all other testimony must be

sage to Congress made the comment that "the pliability of the law as construed in the case of Fries, and it's wonderful refractoriness as construed in that of Burr . . . induce an awful doubt whether we all live under the same law." Jefferson, *Works*, X, 524. To the Senator from Virginia he wrote: "If there ever had been an instance in this or the preceding administrations, of federal judges so applying principles of law as to condemn a federal or acquit a republican offender, I should have judged them in the present case with more charity." *Ibid.*, X, 387.

[44] Hence with the downfall in U.S. v. Hudson, 7 Cr. 32 (1812), and U.S. v. Coolidge, 1 Wheat. 415 (1816), of the Federalist doctrine of a federal common law the doctrine of treason by procurement was rendered untenable. See note 113, page 346, and note 9, page 361, above.

[45] 4 Cr. at 501. Marshall adds: "I will not pretend that I have not individually an opinion on these points, but it is one which I should give only in a case absolutely requiring it, unless I could confer respecting it with the judges of the Supreme Court." Probably his opinion was that the narrow definition of treason in the Constitution forbade making accessorial crimes treason. See note 41, page 380, above.

[46] 4 Cr. at 469. The objections were made on August 20, 1807. Robertson, *Trials*, I, 526–31. Lengthy arguments were then heard before Marshall's opinion was rendered on August 31, 1807.

irrelevant" and inefficacious because no other testimony would suffice to prove treason. But under Marshall's opinion, since Burr could not be shown to have been present when the overt act occurred (even if such act amounted to treason, which Marshall also denied, because an assemblage in sufficiently warlike array had not been shown), "the overt act is not proved by a single witness" (although two are necessary), and consequently "all other testimony must be irrelevant."[47]

Marshall's conclusion was: "No testimony relative to the conduct or declarations of the prisoner elsewhere, and subsequent to the transaction on Blennerhassett's island, can be admitted, because such testimony, being merely corroborative, and incompetent to prove the overt act in itself, is irrelevant, until there be proof of the overt act by two witnesses."[48]

Marshall's opinion had the effect of bringing Burr's trial to a close. The following day, after the prosecuting attorney had studied the opinion, he informed the court that he had no further evidence or argument to offer, "and must leave the case with the jury," who returned in a short time with a verdict of acquittal.[49]

Besides levying war,[50] a second type of treason is recognized by the Constitution. This consists of adhering to the enemies of the nation, giving them aid and comfort.[51] This offense likewise consists of two elements: disloyal intent and conduct beneficial to the enemy.

"Thus the crime of treason consists of two elements: adherence to

[47] 4 Cr. at 506–507.

[48] *Ibid.*, 508. Marshall invited the prosecution to offer "proof by two witnesses that the meeting on Blennerhassett's island was procured by the prisoner," if such testimony were available. That would raise the questions regarding the existence of a federal common law and the permissibility under the Constitution of applying the English rule that in treason all parties are principals, which Marshall had discussed without deciding. See notes 43–45, pages 380–81, above.

[49] The verdict read: "We of the jury say that Aaron Burr is not proved to be guilty under this indictment by any evidence submitted to us. We therefore find him not guilty." Marshall directed that the verdict stand on the bill in that form and that an entry of "not guilty" be made on the record. Robertson, *Trials*, II, 446–47.

[50] Levying war (a common practice under feudalism) was not recognized as a species of treason until the statute of 1351. Holdsworth, *History of English Law*, III, 461; Sir Frederick Pollock and Frederic W. Maitland, *History of the English Law*, II, 505.

[51] Many acts (such as enlisting troops—see note 29, page 377, above) constituting aid and comfort to the enemy would not amount to levying war. Charles Warren, "What Is Giving Aid and Comfort to the Enemy?" *Yale Law Journal*, Vol. XXVII, No. 3 (January, 1918), 331, 333. For examples of aid and comfort, see *ibid.*, 333–43.

the enemy; and rendering him aid and comfort. A citizen intellectually or emotionally may favor the enemy and harbor sympathies or convictions disloyal to the country's policy or interest, but so long as he commits no act of aid and comfort to the enemy, there is no treason. On the other hand, a citizen may take actions which do aid and comfort the enemy—making a speech critical of the government or opposing its measures, profiteering, striking in defense plants or essential work, and the hundred other things which impair our cohesion and diminish our strength—but if there is no adherence to the enemy in this, if there is no intent to betray, there is no treason."[52]

The two-witness rule applies to the overt act of aid and comfort to the enemy, while the treasonable intent may be proved by other evidence.[53] The overt act must be proved directly by two witnesses, "not by the establishment of other facts from which the jury might reason to this fact."[54]

The treasonable intent to adhere to the enemy need not be proved by two witnesses, but that aid and comfort has in fact been given must be so proved.[55] It is not enough to prove by two witnesses some trivial or indifferent act, and then from other circumstances attach to such act a treasonable significance or character. Such a rule would reduce to zero the function of the overt-act requirement imposed by the Constitution. "The very minimum function that an overt act must perform in a treason prosecution is that it show sufficient action by the accused, in its setting, to sustain a finding that the accused actually gave aid and

---

[52] Cramer v. U.S., 325 U.S. 1, 29 (1945); Kawakita v. U.S., 343 U.S. 717, 736 (1952).

[53] 325 U.S. at 31, 33; Kawakita v. U.S., 343 U.S. 717, 742 (1952). This rule is in accord with that applied in the case of levying war. See Justice James Iredell's charge in the Fries case, 9 Fed. Cas. 914. Judge Richard Peters added that "the overt act and the intention constitute the treason; for without the intention the treason is not complete." *Ibid.*, 916.

[54] Chief Justice Marshall in the Burr case, 4 Cr. at 506; Cramer v. U.S., 325 U.S. at 33.

[55] Of course in some cases where actual aid to the enemy is given, the lack of disloyal intent may prevent the existence of treason. 325 U.S. at 35; see also note 52 just above. Thus if a Japanese subject born in the United States, hence having dual nationality, honestly believed that his registration in 1943 as Japanese constituted an effective renunciation of his American citizenship, there would be no treasonable intent when he committed eight overt acts of brutality toward American prisoners of war in Japan. The question of intent is for the jury to decide. Kawakita v. U.S., 343 U.S. 717, 724, 727, 732, 737 (1952).

comfort to the enemy. Every act, movement, deed, and word of the defendant charged to constitute treason must be supported by the testimony of two witnesses. The two-witness principle is to interdict imputation of *incriminating acts* to the accused by circumstantial evidence or by the testimony of a single witness. The prosecution cannot rely on evidence which does not meet the constitutional test for overt acts to create any inference that the accused did other acts or did something more than was shown in the overt act, in order to make a giving of aid and comfort to the enemy."[56]

The testimony of the two witnesses to the same overt act need not be identical. Thus if the act charged were a shooting, one witness might be deaf but see the smoke from the gun, and another witness might hear the explosion.[57]

In holding that it is "aid and comfort" which constitutes the treason and must be proved by two witnesses, the Supreme Court apparently accepts the view that the addition of those words restricts, rather than extends, the scope of the preceding language about "adhering" to the enemy.[58] The restriction doubtless effects the intention of the framers

[56] 325 U.S. at 34–35. On the other hand, the overt act need not itself show treasonable intent. In the Cramer case the overt acts relied on were drinking with saboteurs in a tavern and lying to the FBI. These acts did not necessarily aid the enemy. An allegation that defendant kept large sums of money safely available to the saboteurs, which would have shown aid to the enemy, was withdrawn from the case. If it had not been, the Court would have had to decide whether defendant's own testimony on that point constituted a confession in open court, or whether a defendant himself can be one of the two witnesses required to prove an overt act. *Ibid.*, 36, 39.

[57] Haupt v. U.S., 330 U.S. 631, 640 (1947). In this case there was proof by two witnesses of three overt acts which undoubtedly aided defendant's son, a saboteur, in his hostile mission: defendant gave him shelter in an apartment, bought him an automobile, and helped him get a job in a factory manufacturing Norden bombsights. *Ibid.*, 634. These acts differed from the mere convivial association with enemy agents proved in the Cramer case. In the Haupt case the acts proved constituted substantial aid and comfort to the enemy. *Ibid.*, 635. The jury's verdict determined that defendant's hospitality did not flow from mere parental interest in his son as an individual but was extended in furtherance of the son's mission as a German agent. *Ibid.*, 641.

[58] Randolph had remarked that the English statute of 25 Edward III, containing the phrase about "aid and comfort," had "a more extensive meaning" than the draft eliminating those words. Farrand, *Records*, II, 345. Mason proposed the addition as "restrictive," since the language would otherwise be "too indefinite." *Ibid.*, II, 349. Gouverneur Morris pointed out that, whichever interpretation was accepted, the English statute was not being followed. Wilson thought that "aid and comfort" were "explanatory, not operative words; and that it was better to omit them." Dr. Johnson

that guilt of treason should not be imputed by reason of mere words or emotional attitudes, without overt acts.[59]

"Treason is a breach of allegiance, and can be committed by him only who owes allegiance, either perpetual or temporary."[60] Permanent allegiance is ordinarily owed only by citizens or nationals of a state. But aliens sojourning within a country owe temporary or secondary allegiance, and can be guilty of treason.[61]

The power of Congress to declare the punishment of treason is limited by the provision that if forfeiture of property is prescribed as part of the penalty the duration of such forfeiture shall not exceed the lifetime of the offender. Innocent members of the family are thus protected from destitution.

Because of President Lincoln's doubts about the validity of a law confiscating the property of Confederate supporters for a longer period than the owner's lifetime, Congress accepted such a limitation in enacting wartime legislation.[62] But although the heirs of the offender were protected under those provisions, the owner himself was deprived during his lifetime of all interest in his property, and retained nothing which he could convey.[63] But if he received a pardon, he could thereafter transfer his interest in the property so that it would not pass to his heirs upon his death.[64]

agreed. *Ibid.*, II, 346. In applying the English statute, it has been held that those words are in apposition to and explanatory of "adherent to the king's enemies." Rex v. Casement, [1917] 1 K.B. 98, 136.

[59] See page 374 above.

[60] U.S. v. Wiltberger, 5 Wheat. 76, 97 (1820).

[61] Carlisle v. U.S., 16 Wall. 147, 154–55 (1873).

[62] The confiscation Act of July 17, 1862, 12 Stat. 589, was accompanied by an explanatory joint resolution of the same date, 12 Stat. 627, providing that no punishment or proceedings under the act should be so construed as to "work a forfeiture of the real estate of the offender beyond his natural life." Bigelow v. Forrest, 9 Wall. 339, 350 (1870). This legislation was enacted under the war power, as well as under the power to punish treason, and hence may not have been in all respects subject to the limitations of Art. III, sec. 3, cl. 2. See Miller v. U.S., 11 Wall. 268, 305–307 (1871).

[63] Wallace v. Van Riswick, 92 U.S. 202, 208–10 (1870). These confiscation cases disregard the common law rule that the freehold must not be in abeyance. *Ibid.*, 212.

[64] Ill. Central R.R. v. Bosworth, 133 U.S. 92, 103 (1890). Regarding the effects of a pardon, see commentary on Art. II, sec. 2, cl. 1, above.

Full Faith and Credit

Full Faith and Credit shall be given in each State to the public Acts, Records, and judicial Proceedings of every other State. And the Congress may by general Laws prescribe the Manner in which such Acts, Records and Proceedings shall be proved, and the Effect thereof.

HISTORY

THIS clause originated in the Committee of Detail. It was based upon Article IV of the Articles of Confederation, which contained a provision that "Full faith and credit shall be given in each of these States to the records, acts, and judicial proceedings of the courts and magistrates of every other State."

The report of the Committee of Detail extended the coverage of the provision to include legislative as well as judicial acts: "Full faith shall be given in each State to the acts of the Legislatures, and to the records and judicial proceedings of the Courts and Magistrates of every other State."[1] In debate, Williamson of North Carolina moved to substitute "the words of the Articles of Confederation on the same subject." Charles Pinckney moved to commit the article, together with a provision which he offered regarding bankruptcy. Madison "wished the Legislature might be authorized to provide for the *execution* of Judgments in other States, under such regulations as might be expedient." Randolph "said there was no instance of one nation executing judgments of the Courts of another nation." He offered another proposition: "Whenever the Act of any State, whether Legislative Executive or Judiciary shall be attested & exemplified under the seal thereof, such attestation and exemplification, shall be deemed in other States as full proof of the existence of that act—and its operation shall be binding in every other State, in all cases to which it may relate, and which are within the cognizance and jurisdiction of the State, wherein the said Act was done." Gouverneur Morris offered a third formula: "Full

[1] Art. XVI. Farrand, *Records*, II, 188 (August 6).

faith ought to be given in each State to the public acts, records, and judicial proceedings of every other State; and the Legislature shall by general laws, determine the proof and effect of such acts, records, and proceedings."

The committee to which these propositions were referred was composed of Rutledge, Randolph, Gorham, Wilson, and Johnson.[2] On behalf of this committee, Randolph reported the following version: "Full faith and credit ought to be given in each State to the public Acts, Records, and Judicial proceedings of every other State, and the Legislature shall by general laws prescribe the manner in which such acts, records, and proceedings shall be proved, and the effect which judgments obtained in one State shall have in another."[3]

INTERPRETATION

THIS provision, unlike that in the Articles of Confederation, requires that full faith and credit be given in every state to all the public acts and records of any other state; it is not limited, as was the former language, to judicial proceedings. Legislative and executive acts and records are included within the operation of the constitutional command. Congress is also empowered to prescribe the manner in which such public acts, records, and proceedings shall be proved, and the effect which shall be given to them in the state where they are invoked.

In the exercise of the power thus conferred, Congress has prescribed the mode of authentication of legislative and judicial proceedings, and has ordained that the effect to be given to them in other jurisdictions shall be the same as they would have by law or usage in the jurisdiction from which they are taken.[4] Under this legislation, it

[2] *Ibid.*, II, 445, 447–48 (August 29).

[3] *Ibid.*, II, 483–85 (September 1). In debate, on motion of Gouverneur Morris, "thereof" was substituted for the words after "effect"; and on motion of Madison, "shall" was inserted in place of "ought to" in the first part of the provision, and "may" for "shall" in the latter part. *Ibid.*, II, 486, 488–89 (September 3). No change was made by the Committee of Style, except to divide the provision into two sentences. *Ibid.*, II, 601 (September 12).

[4] 28 U.S.C. 1738, 1739; Act of May 26, 1790, 1 Stat. 122. Until the Act of June 25, 1948, 62 Stat. 947, Congress had not prescribed the effect to be given to statutes. The legislation in force had been limited to judicial records and proceedings. Carroll v. Lanza, 349 U.S. 408, 411 (1955); Hughes v. Fetter, 341 U.S. 609, 613–14 (1951); Pacific Ins. Co. v. Industrial Accident Commission, 306 U.S. 493, 502 (1939); Alaska Packers Assn. v. Industrial Accident Commission, 294 U.S. 532, 547 (1935).

should be noted that full faith is given to the legislative acts and court proceedings not only of states but also of territories and possessions of the United States.[5] Likewise federal as well as state courts are bound by the obligation to give full faith and credit to action taken in other jurisdictions. However, Congress could go much further than it has gone in prescribing the extraterritorial effect of legislative, executive, and judicial proceedings.[6]

The full faith and credit clause establishes a rule of conflict of laws, since it regulates the effect to be given in the courts of one jurisdiction to the law of another jurisdiction.[7] Ordinarily, each state is free to adopt its own rules of conflict of laws. For example, a state may accept the rule that validity of a contract is to be determined by the place of contracting (*lex loci contractus*) or by the place of performance (*lex loci*

In 1948 the words "Such Acts, records and judicial proceedings" were substituted for "And the said records and judicial proceedings" in the provision prescribing that the same faith and credit shall be given them elsewhere "as they have by law or usage" in the jurisdiction of origin.

[5] Inclusion of territories began with the Act of March 27, 1804, 2 Stat. 298. The legislation, insofar as it related to the effect of decisions of federal rather than state courts, was sustainable under other powers of Congress, though not under that granted by Act. IV, sec. 1. Embry v. Palmer, 107 U.S. 3, 9 (1883); Alaska Packers Assn. v. Industrial Accident Commission, 294 U.S. 532, 546 (1935). United States courts are bound to give full faith to state decisions, just as other state courts are. Chicago & Alton R.R. Co. v. Wiggins Ferry Co., 108 U.S. 18, 22 (1883); Cooper v. Newell, 173 U.S. 555, 567 (1899); Bradford Electric Light Co. v. Clapper, 286 U.S. 145, 155 (1932); Davis v. Davis, 305 U.S. 32, 40 (1938).

[6] Walter W. Cook, "The Powers of Congress under the Full Faith and Credit Clause," *Yale Law Journal*, Vol. XXVIII, No. 5 (March, 1919), 421, 427–32; Edward S. Corwin, "The 'Full Faith and Credit' Clause," *University of Pennsylvania Law Review*, Vol. LXXXI, No. 4 (February, 1933), 371, 388; Robert H. Jackson, "Full Faith and Credit—The Lawyer's Clause of the Constitution," *Columbia Law Review*, Vol. XLV, No. 1 (January, 1945), 1, 18, 22.

[7] Conflict of laws, or private international law as it is sometimes called, is that branch of law which deals with the determination of what law is applicable to events and transactions that have a relationship or nexus connecting them with more than one jurisdiction. For example, suppose a resident of Pennsylvania dies owning land in Massachusetts. The generally accepted rule of conflict of laws declares that transfer of land must be governed by the law of the place where the land is situated (*lex rei sitae*). Hence a will made with only two witnesses, though it would be valid in Pennsylvania, could not pass land in Massachusetts, where a will must have three witnesses. Other familiar rules of conflict of laws are that liability for wrongful conduct is governed by the law of the place where the wrong occurred (for example, the state where an automobile collision took place involving tourists from other states) and that the validity of a contract is governed by the laws of the place where it is made or is to be performed.

388

solutionis). "The states are free to adopt such rules of conflict of laws as they choose ... subject to the Full Faith and Credit Clause and other constitutional restrictions."[8] No particular system of conflict of laws rules is mandatory upon the states.[9]

Even without the full faith and credit clause, the courts of one common law jurisdiction would under generally accepted principles regarding conflict of laws give effect in many instances to rights acquired by virtue of the laws and court decisions of another jurisdiction.[10] But such recognition of foreign-created rights would be subject to the restriction that it might be denied in any case where it would infringe strongly felt local policies prevailing in the forum state. Effect would be given to the foreign law as a matter of "comity" rather than of right. But as between the states of the United States, the full faith and credit clause replaced the conflict of laws rule of comity (which was subject to the overriding force of local policy) with a constitutional command that *full* (not merely some) faith and credit be given to the public acts

[8] Wells v. Simonds Abrasive Co., 345 U.S. 514, 516 (1953). Besides the requirements imposed by the full faith and credit clause with respect to the effect to be given in one state to the law of another state, there could be violation of the "due process" clause if a state sought to apply its own law to transactions occurring outside its boundaries. Hanson v. Denckla, 357 U.S. 235, 250–55 (1958). During the period when conservative economic views were dominant on the Supreme Court, there was a tendency to strike down such extraterritorial exertions of state power, especially in multiple taxation cases. The present tendency is to recognize the revenue needs of the states and to find a local "nexus" sufficient to sustain the tax as one imposed upon a "taxable event" within the state. Curry v. McCanless, 307 U.S. 357, 363–69 (1939); Nelson v. Sears, Roebuck & Co., 312 U.S. 359, 363(1941); Northwestern State Portland Cement Co. v. Minnesota, 358 U.S. 450, 452 (1959).

[9] It has been contended that the Supreme Court does, or should, to some extent seek to establish national uniformity with respect to conflict of laws rules. Edwin Merrick Dodd, Jr., "The Power of the Supreme Court to Review State Decisions in the Field of Conflict of Laws," *Harvard Law Review*, Vol. XXXIX, No. 5 (March, 1926), 533, 534, 560; Jackson, *The Supreme Court in the American System of Government*, 43.

[10] Conflict of laws rules would often give effect to the law of a sister state or foreign nation when expressed in judicial decisions as well as when embodied in statutory legislation. It would be farfetched to regard the full faith and credit clause as adopting the rule of *stare decisis*, and requiring a state to apply the case law established by the judicial decisions of another state. On this point Justice Robert H. Jackson took a different view. Jackson, "Full Faith and Credit—The Lawyer's Clause of the Constitution," *loc. cit.*, 1, 12. The clause requires recognition only of statutes and of the proceedings in a particular case as *res judicata*. Cf. Erie Railroad Co. v. Tompkins, 304 U.S. 64, 78 (1938), where a distinction formerly recognized between a state's statutory and decisional law was rejected.

and judicial proceedings of other states[11] without regard to local policy.

Nothing in the Constitution limits the power of an individual state to mold its judicial system in such form as it sees fit. A state is not obliged to provide courts of a particular character (such as separate courts of equity) in order to enforce out-of-state rights of that description.[12] It may outlaw all actions of a given sort (such as suits for breach of promise to marry or stockholders' derivative suits) by a general prohibition applying to all such proceedings, whether they originate within or outside of the state. However, where courts are established which are capable of granting the type of relief sought, a state cannot arbitrarily discriminate against other states by withdrawing jurisdiction with respect to such matters when they arise under the law of another state. For a state cannot escape its constitutional obligation to enforce the rights and duties validly created under the laws of other states "by the simple device of denying jurisdiction in such cases to courts otherwise competent."[13]

Similarly, a state cannot escape the effect of the principle that no jurisdiction will enforce the penal laws of another by the simple device

[11] Hilton v. Guyot, 159 U.S. 113, 163, 181 (1895); Johnson v. Muelberger, 340 U.S. 581, 584 (1951); Estin v. Estin, 334 U.S. 541, 546 (1948); Williams v. North Carolina, 317 U.S. 287, 294 (1942); Milwaukee County v. White Co., 296 U.S. 268, 276–77 (1935); Broderick v. Rosner, 294 U.S. 629, 643 (1935); Mills v. Duryee, 7 Cr. 481, 485 (1813). In the Brosner case Justice Brandeis stated that "For the States of the Union the constitutional limitation imposed by the full faith and credit clause abolished, in large measure, the general principle of international law by which local policy is permitted to dominate rules of comity." The full faith and credit clause does not apply to judgments of the courts of a foreign nation. Aetna Life Ins. Co. v. Tremblay, 223 U.S. 185, 190 (1912). Doubtless legislation or treaty provisions regarding enforcement of foreign judgments would be constitutional.

[12] Anglo-American Provision Co. v. Davis Provision Co., 191 U.S. 373, 374 (1903); Chambers v. B. & O. R.R. Co., 207 U.S. 142, 148 (1907); Bradford Electric Light Co. v. Clapper, 286 U.S. 145, 160 (1932); Herb v. Pitcairn, 324 U.S. 117, 120 (1945). For an unsound decision to the effect that a state could not forbid injunctive relief in labor disputes, see Truax v. Corrigan, 257 U.S. 312, 334 (1921). A contrary conclusion with respect to federal courts was reached in Lauf v. Shinner & Co., 303 U.S. 323, 330 (1938).

[13] Kenney v. Supreme Lodge, 252 U.S. 411, 415 (1920); Broderick v. Rosner, 294 U.S. 629, 642–44 (1935); Hughes v. Fetter, 341 U.S. 609, 611 (1951); First National Bank v. United Air Lines, 342 U.S. 396, 398 (1952). For the significance of discrimination as a factor, see Wells v. Simonds Abrasive Co., 345 U.S. 514, 518–19 (1953). For an example of inability to furnish the type of remedy granted by the law of the place where the liability arose, see Slater v. Mexican National R.R. Co., 194 U.S. 120, 126, 128 (1904).

of reducing the penalty to a judgment and bringing suit on the judgment.[14]

Likewise nothing in the Constitution requires a state to disregard its own statutes in order to apply those of another state dealing with the same subject-matter.[15] Literal application of the full faith and credit clause would result in an absurd paradox if it were interpreted as requiring the courts of each state to lay aside its own laws in order to give effect to those of the other.[16]

One type of case where a question often arises regarding the effect to be accorded under the full faith and credit clause to statutes of another state by the courts of the forum state is that where suit is brought for wrongful death and the plaintiff invokes the wrongful death statute of the locality where the injury occurred. At common law no action for damages arising from wrongful death was recognized; the action is purely of statutory origin.[17] Before such statutes became common in all jurisdictions, it might often happen that the law of the forum state where suit was brought did not have such a statute, and if the plaintiff were to have any remedy at all it would be the statutory remedy provided by the wrongful death statute of another jurisdiction, where the injury was inflicted. The effect to be given to such a statute under the full faith and credit clause was therefore important.

Such statutes sometimes provided that the right to damages for wrongful death was given only for deaths occurring within the state,[18]

[14] The Antelope, 10 Wheat. 66, 123 (1825); Wisconsin v. Pelican Insurance Co., 127 U.S. 265, 290 (1888); Huntington v. Attrill, 146 U.S. 657, 673–74, 683 (1892). A judgment for taxes due, however, is entitled to full faith and credit. Milwaukee County v. White Company, 296 U.S. 268, 275–79 (1935). Cf. Testa v. Katt, 330 U.S. 386, 389, 393 (1947), a case not involving the full faith and credit clause.

[15] "We have recognized, however, that full faith and credit does not automatically compel a forum state to subordinate its own statutory policy to a conflicting public act of another state; rather, it is for this Court to choose in each case between the conflicting public policies involved." Hughes v. Fetter, 341 U.S. 609, 611 (1951).

[16] Alaska Packers Assn. v. Industrial Accident Commission, 294 U.S. 532, 547 (1935); Milwaukee County v. White Company, 296 U.S. 268, 273 (1935); Pacific Employees Ins. Co. v. Industrial Accident Commission, 306 U.S. 493, 501 (1939); Pink v. A.A.A. Highway Express, 314 U.S. 201, 209–10 (1941); Watson v. Employees Liability Corporation, 348 U.S. 66, 73 (1954); Carroll v. Lanza, 349 U.S. 408, 412 (1955).

[17] Lord Campbell's Act, 9 & 10 Vict. c. 93 (1846), was the pioneer and parent of this type of legislation. The Harrisburg, 119 U.S. 199, 204 (1886). See note 85, page 342, above.

[18] See the Wisconsin and Illinois statutes involved in Hughes v. Fetter, 341 U.S.

or was enforceable only by suit brought in the courts of the state,[19] or within a certain time.[20] These restrictions are ordinarily disregarded, and by virtue of the full faith and credit clause the remedy granted by a statute creating a transitory cause of action can be enforced in any court of competent jurisdiction in another state.[21]

A second type of case involving the full faith and credit to be given to statutes occurs where there is a comprehensive statutory scheme regulating a complex and continuing relationship, such as that between a stockholder and a corporation, or between a policyholder and a fraternal insurance organization, or between employee and employer.

Thus a Minnesota statute imposing double liability upon stockholders, and prescribing a liquidation procedure for the corporation pursuant to which the statutory liquidator was authorized to bring suit in other jurisdictions, was held binding upon Wisconsin courts when suit was brought against a stockholder in the latter state. The Supreme Court declared that the subject-matter of the liquidation of a Minnesota corporation was "peculiarly within the regulatory power of the State of Minnesota; so much so that no other State properly can be said to have any public policy thereon." Wisconsin's policy concerning the rights and obligations of creditors and stockholders of its own corporations was irrelevant under the circumstances. The Minnesota statute was entitled to full faith and credit in Wisconsin.[22]

Similarly, the New York superintendent of banks was permitted to collect in New Jersey an assessment made against the bank's stockholders pursuant to New York legislation, even though New Jersey law sought to limit the jurisdiction of its courts in such suits involving

---

609, 610 (1951); and First Natl. Bank v. United Airlines, 342 U.S. 396, 397–98 (1952).

[19] Tennessee Coal, Iron & R.R. Co. v. George, 233 U.S. 354, 359–60 (1914). "A State cannot create a transitory cause of action and at the same time destroy the right to sue on that transitory cause of action in any court having jurisdiction." See also Wells v. Simonds Abrasive Co., 345 U.S. 514, 515 (1953); Kenney v. Supreme Lodge, 252 U.S. 411, 415 (1920); and A., T. & S. F. Ry. Co. v. Sowers, 213 U.S. 55, 70 (1909).

[20] Wells v. Simonds Abrasive Co., 345 U.S. 514, 515–17 (1953).

[21] The authorities on this point and the general subject of giving full faith to foreign statutes are collected and analyzed in Justice Frankfurter's dissent in Carroll v. Lanza, 349 U.S. 408, 414 (1955). For purposes of the full faith and credit clause, a state constitution is regarded, like a statute, as a "public act" of the state. Smithsonian Institution v. St. John, 214 U.S. 19, 24 (1909).

[22] Converse v. Hamilton, 224 U.S. 243, 260–61 (1912).

statutory liability created by the law of states other than New Jersey. The Supreme Court held that "the statutory liability sought to be enforced is contractual in character. The assessment is an incident of the incorporation. Thus the subject matter is peculiarly within the regulatory power of New York, as the state of incorporation."[23] The Court decided that the fact that the assessment was made by an administrative official pursuant to statutory direction did not preclude application of the full faith and credit clause;[24] but it did not need to pass upon the contention that the superintendent's assessment was itself a "public act" entitled to full faith and credit under that clause.[25]

The rights and liabilities of a member of a fraternal organization under the insurance feature incident to such membership are likewise controlled by the law pursuant to which the organization is incorporated.[26] In the case of such organizations, the Court says: "The act of becoming a member is something more than a contract, it is entering into a complex and abiding relation, and as marriage looks to domicil, membership looks to and must be governed by the law of the State granting the incorporation."[27]

Where an insurance policy is not an incident of membership in an organization, however, but arises merely from a contractual relationship, the forum state is free to apply its own law of contracts and is not bound to give effect to the law of the state where the insurance company was incorporated, or where the policy was issued.[28] Similarly, a

[23] Broderick v. Rosner, 294 U.S. 629, 643 (1935). The Court followed Converse v. Hamilton, as well as the rule stated in Kenney v. Supreme Lodge, note 13, page 390, above. Probably Morris v. Jones, 329 U.S. 545, 548–49 (1947), does not conflict with the Broderick and Converse cases. There a creditor who obtained a Missouri judgment, in spite of an Illinois stay order, was allowed to present it in Illinois liquidation proceedings. The ruling may be explained on the technical ground that the Missouri court did not deny full faith and credit to the Illinois stay order since that question was not raised in the Missouri court. *Ibid.*, 552.

[24] 294 U.S. at 644.

[25] *Ibid.*, 646–47. As to whether a workmen's compensation award is a "record" entitled to full faith and credit, see Magnolia Petroleum Co. v. Hunt, 320 U.S. 430, 443 (1943).

[26] Supreme Council of the Royal Arcanum v. Green, 237 U.S. 531, 542–46 (1915); Modern Woodmen v. Mixer, 267 U.S. 544, 551 (1925); Order of Commercial Travelers v. Wolfe, 331 U.S. 586, 592, 602, 606 (1947).

[27] 267 U.S. at 551. See also 331 U.S. at 606.

[28] American Fire Ins. Co. v. King Lumber Co., 250 U.S. 2, 10 (1919); Pink v. A.A.A. Highway Express, 314 U.S. 201, 205–208 (1941). In the Pink case the policy contained a notice stating that the policy-holder was a member of the mutual company,

state in which a mutual insurance company does business may require more stringent standards of financial soundness than those required by the state where the company is chartered.[29]

Whether the issuance of an insurance policy did or did not create a valid and binding contract (or, stated differently, whether the company had a valid defense by reason of misstatement by the company's agent in the application of the insured's answers to questions relating to his health) has been held to be a question of substantive law conclusively determined by the legislation of the place where the contract was entered into, and not a question of procedure or remedy, as to which the courts of the forum state where the suit is brought are free to follow their own rules.[30] Whether a court's judgment should add to the amount of a verdict interest thereon from the date suit was filed, on the other hand, has been held to be a question of procedure, governed by the law of the forum where the action was brought.[31]

---

but nothing to that effect was stated in the body of the policy. The Supreme Court held that Georgia could determine whether or not one of its citizens had in fact become a member and assumed the obligations of membership imposed by the laws of another state. *Ibid.*, 208, 211. See also Griffin v. McCoach, 313 U.S. 498, 503 (1941); Hoopeston v. Cullen, 318 U.S. 313, 316–17 (1943); McGee v. Int. Life Ins. Co., 355 U.S. 220, 223 (1957); and note 37, page 396, below.

[29] Such regulation, designed to afford proper protection to citizens of the state where the company does business, violates neither the due process clause nor the full faith and credit clause. State Farm Ins. Co. v. Duel, 324 U.S. 154, 159 (1945).

[30] John Hancock Mutual Life Ins. Co. v. Yates, 299 U.S. 178, 181–83 (1936). The Court said that this decision did not give extraterritorial effect to the New York statute. That law applied to a transaction occurring in New York, and determined whether or not a valid and binding contract of insurance had come into existence. There was nothing upon which the law of Georgia (where suit was brought) could operate. *Ibid.*, 183. Although the Court points out that the New York statute is a "public act" entitled to full faith and credit, the decision comes close to being a determination by the Supreme Court of the question what conflict of laws rule should be applied by the Georgia court.

[31] Klaxon Co. v. Stentor Co., 313 U.S. 487, 497–98 (1941). The John Hancock case was distinguished on the ground that the New York law authorizing addition of interest does not relate to the validity of the contract sued upon but is an incidental item of damages. Hence the Delaware forum is not obliged to give full faith and credit to that statute. But whether "such damages may be given as under all the circumstances of the case may be just" or merely $5,000 damages as specified in a Minnesota statute was held to be substantive, not procedural, and to be governed by the law of Montana where the wrongful death occurred. Northern Pacific R.R. Co. v. Babcock, 154 U.S. 190, 199 (1894). See also Slater v. Mexican National R.R. Co., 194 U.S. 120, 126 (1904), and Western Union Tel. Co. v. Brown, 234 U.S. 542, 547 (1914), for the

Workmen's compensation laws can also be interpreted as a regulation of the complex and continuing relationship between employee and employer. The statutory liability of the employer may extend to accidents occurring wherever the employee performs work under his contract of employment. When so viewed, the legislation of the state where the contract of employment was entered into is entitled, under the full faith and credit clause, to extraterritorial recognition in the state where the industrial accident or personal injury occurs as a legal ground for recovery of compensation by the employee.[32]

But with equal logic it would be possible to interpret workmen's compensation laws as a new form of statutory relief for wrongful conduct causing injury within the state where the accident occurred, as a substitute remedy for the common law tort action. Viewed as a tort rather than as a contract, the imposition of liability arising out of transactions occurring within the state would seem to be a prerogative clearly within the power of the state where the accident took place.[33]

In later cases the Supreme Court has recognized that the state where the accident occurred has a legitimate interest in regulating the legal consequences thereof.[34] Thus where an employee of a company subject

rule that the *lex loci* determines the extent, as well as the existence, of liability for wrongful conduct. Is this another instance of establishment of conflict of laws rules by the Supreme Court?

[32] Bradford Electric Light Co. v. Clapper, 286 U.S. 145, 158 (1932). Justice Brandeis emphasizes that to deny a defense based on Vermont law and to impose liability under the law of New Hampshire (where the injury occurred) is more serious and irremediable than merely denying relief based on the out-of-state law, leaving unimpaired the right of the party claiming such relief to seek it elsewhere. *Ibid.*, 160. He also remarks that the interest of New Hampshire in the transaction is casual. *Ibid.*, 162. Likewise there was no showing that enforcement of the Vermont law offended the public policy of New Hampshire. *Ibid.*, 161. In Alaska Packers Assn. v. Industrial Accident Commission, 294 U.S. 532, 547 (1935), Justice Stone denied the importance of the distinction between use of a judgment as a defense and as the basis of a suit to enforce it. "In either case the conflict is the same" between the policies of the states involved. He stressed the fact that in the Clapper case there was no showing of conflict with New Hampshire policy. *Ibid.*, 548. See note 34 just below.

[33] See the dissent of Justice Stone. *Ibid.*, 164. The Supreme Court is here again imposing a conflict of laws rule on the New Hampshire court in determining that the contract rule rather than the tort rule should be applied.

[34] Pacific Employers Ins. Co. v. Industrial Accident Commission, 306 U.S. 493, 507 (1939). Justice Stone distinguished the Clapper case by saying that there the application of Vermont law was not shown to be contrary to the policy of New Hampshire, whereas in the Pacific case California law clearly claimed exclusive application to accidents occurring in that state. *Ibid.*, 504.

to the Massachusetts workmen's compensation law (which claims to be the exclusive remedy for injuries within or without the state)[35] was injured during a temporary assignment in California (whose statute has similar coverage),[36] the Supreme Court held that the full faith and credit clause did not compel California to substitute the Massachusetts statute for its own with respect to transactions and events taking place within its own boundaries.[37] The Court said that "The very nature of the federal union of states . . . precludes resort to the full faith and credit clause as a means for compelling a state to substitute the statutes of other states for its own statutes dealing with a subject matter concerning which it is competent to legislate."[38] The Court regarded as unavoidable the conclusion that "the full faith and credit clause does not require one state to substitute for its own statute, applicable to persons and events within it, the conflicting statute of another state, even though that statute is of controlling force in the courts of the state of its enactment with respect to the same persons and events."[39]

The state of the authorities seems to indicate that the state where events occur or persons are present has the power to regulate such persons and events by its own rules, particularly where it expresses a strong public policy and insistence that its own interests in the matter at issue are sufficiently important to justify its refusal to permit the law of another jurisdiction to be applied. Earlier efforts to determine, as a matter of conflict of laws, which state shall have exclusive jurisdiction to regulate a particular matter, have largely been abandoned.

[35] *Ibid.*, 498.   [36] *Ibid.*, 499.

[37] *Ibid.*, 501. The Court recognized that the Massachusetts court would likewise be free to apply its own statute. *Ibid.*, 502. The Court thus recognized that it is constitutionally possible for two states to enact conflicting legislation regarding the same persons and events, and for each statute to be enforced in its own state. The same conclusion is expressly stated in Alaska Packers Assn. v. Industrial Accident Commission, 294 U.S. 532, 548 (1935). The same problem arises with respect to divorce and multiple taxation. Earlier efforts to limit legislative jurisdiction to a single state have now been abandoned. See note 8, page 389, and note 40, page 397, below.

[38] 306 U.S. at 501. Nevertheless there is great force in the observation of Justice Jackson that "The whole purpose and the only need for requiring full faith and credit to foreign law is that it does differ from that of the forum." Wells v. Simonds Abrasive Co., 345 U.S. 514, 521 (1953). See also Morris v. Jones, 329 U.S. 545, 553 (1947).

[39] 306 U.S. at 502. See also Milwaukee County v. White Co., 296 U.S. 268, 273 (1935). Carroll v. Lanza, 349 U.S. 408, 412 (1955), likewise recognizes the right of the state where the injury occurred to apply its own rule (either statutory or common law). Cf. note 42, page 397, below.

Where statutory (or common law) rules of different states conflict, therefore, the problem is to be solved in accordance with the general conflict of laws principles of comity as curtailed by public policy, rather than by means of any special solution derived from the full faith and credit clause. Of course where a state endeavors to apply its own law (either by legislation or by the exercise of adjudication) under circumstances where the state lacks jurisdiction under generally accepted conflict of laws principles, its action may be declared unconstitutional and invalid under the due process clause (without regard to the full faith and credit clause).[40] A statute or judgment which is void for lack of due process of law, being invalid even in the jurisdiction from which it is taken, is of course not entitled to extrastate recognition under the full faith and credit clause.[41]

The principal function of the full faith and credit clause is to facilitate enforcement of *judgments* rendered in another jurisdiction, rather than to give effect to statutes enacted in other states. Congress in its enactments pursuant to this clause dealt with judgments as early as 1790 but did not include statutes within the scope of its legislation until 1948.[42]

It was held in several early cases under the legislation enacted by Congress that when suit was brought on a judgment in another state

[40] The present tendency, as shown by the cases cited in note 8, page 389, above, is to find the existence of the necessary minimal contacts to justify exercise of the state's power. Lack of due process was found in Pennoyer v. Neff, 95 U.S. 714, 733 (1878); Old Wayne Life Assn. v. McDonough, 204 U.S. 8, 15, 23 (1907); McDonald v. Mabee, 243 U.S. 90, 92 (1917); Griffin v. Griffin, 327 U.S. 220, 228 (1946). Cf. Milliken v. Meyer, 311 U.S. 457, 462–63 (1940); Riley v. N.Y. Trust Co., 315 U.S. 343, 349–50, 354 (1942).

[41] See cases cited in the note just above. The due process clause also forbids extraterritorial recognition on the basis of comity of a judgment rendered without due process. Griffin v. Griffin, 327 U.S. 220, 229 (1946). But there are situations where a judgment may be valid in the state where it was rendered and yet not enforceable elsewhere under the full faith and credit clause. Haddock v. Haddock, 201 U.S. 562, 569 (1906); Yarborough v. Yarborough, 290 U.S. 202, 214–15 (1933); Williams v. North Carolina, 317 U.S. 287, 298–99 (1942); Williams v. North Carolina, 325 U.S. 226, 261 (1945); Vanderbilt v. Vanderbilt, 354 U.S. 416, 429 (1957).

[42] See note 4, page 387, above. It will be remembered that the corresponding provision in the Articles of Confederation dealt only with judgments, not with statutes. Chief Justice Stone drew a sharp distinction between the full faith due to statutes and that due to judgments in Magnolia Petroleum Company v. Hunt, 320 U.S. 430, 436–37 (1943). Cf. notes 34–39, pages 395–96, above. The effect of this distinction may have been weakened by the 1948 revision. See Hughes v. Fetter, 341 U.S. 609, 613 (1951); Carroll v. Lanza, 349 U.S. 408, 422 (1955).

the judgment was entitled to the same effect as it was given in the state where it was rendered.[43] Rejecting the contention that the judgment was prima-facie evidence only, and not conclusive evidence of record, the Supreme Court said that if judgments were prima-facie evidence only, "this clause in the Constitution would be utterly unimportant and illusory. The common law would give such judgments precisely the same effect."[44]

After an adjudication is made in another state, its enforcement cannot be denied because the court where suit is brought disagrees with the reasoning of the court which rendered the judgment. The full faith and credit clause "precludes any inquiry into the merits of the cause of action, the logic or consistency of the decision, or the validity of the legal principles on which the judgment is based."[45] The fact that a judgment may be considered to be erroneous or based upon a mistake of law does not withdraw it from the operation of the full faith and credit clause.[46] Likewise, even where by reason of the law or public policy of a state an original action could not be brought there, a judgment rendered in another state based upon such a cause of action must be accorded full faith and credit.[47]

[43] Hence, if in a suit on the judgment in the state where it was rendered the proper plea was *nul tiel record* rather than *nil debet*, the same rule applied in a suit on the judgment in another state. Mills v. Duryee, 7 Cr. 481, 484 (1813); Hampton v. McConnell, 3 Wheat. 234, 235 (1818); McElmoyle v. Cohen, 13 Pet. 312, 324–26 (1839). Of course a judgment is not entitled to greater effect in another state than it has where rendered; and if it is subject to modification at home (as in alimony or custody orders), it is subject to the same treatment in the court of another state where its enforcement is sought. Halvey v. Halvey, 330 U.S. 610, 614 (1947); Sistare v. Sistare, 218 U.S. 1, 17 (1910).

[44] 7 Cr. at 485.

[45] Milliken v. Meyer, 311 U.S. 457, 462 (1940).

[46] Fauntleroy v. Lum, 210 U.S. 230, 237 (1908). On the other hand, a merely erroneous interpretation of a statute of another state, construing it as inapplicable to the case at bar, does not constitute a violation of the full faith and credit clause. Pa. Fire Ins. Co. v. Gold Issue Mining Co., 243 U.S. 93, 96 (1917). Similarly, there is no denial of full faith and credit when a sister state judgment, though given its full effect, does not dispose of the matter at issue. Thus there is no denial of full faith and credit to a Louisiana adoption proceeding when Alabama holds that land situated there does not pass to adopted children. Hood v. McGehee, 237 U.S. 611, 615 (1915). So in Armstrong v. Armstrong, 350 U.S. 568, 569 (1956), the Supreme Court interpreted a Florida divorce decree as not passing upon the question whether alimony should be granted, rather than as denying alimony.

[47] Titus v. Wallick, 306 U.S. 282, 291 (1939); Milwaukee County v. White Co., 296 U.S. 268, 275 (1935); Kenney v. Supreme Lodge, 252 U.S. 411, 415 (1920);

The principal loophole in the operation of the full faith and credit clause is the rule which permits the court to which a judgment from another state is presented to inquire into the jurisdiction of the court which rendered the judgment. In the eyes of the law a judgment rendered without jurisdiction is a nullity, and is not a judgment at all, and hence is not entitled to receive full faith and credit in another court.[48]

It is in connection with judgments in divorce proceedings that troublesome questions of jurisdiction most frequently arise in practice. Persons seeking to circumvent strict divorce laws in their home state often obtain a divorce decree in a state with laxer requirements, and then resume residence in their home state. When must the home state recognize as valid a divorce obtained elsewhere?

The orthodox conflict of laws rule is that divorce is a matter pertaining to personal status and is governed by the law of the person's domicile.[49] Since domicile requires a certain degree of physical presence within a state as well as a certain degree of mental intention with respect to maintaining permanent residence there, it is inevitable that close questions will arise and that different courts may evaluate differently the intangible factors involved.[50] Hence complications are bound to occur.[51]

Under the orthodox theory, marriage is a relationship between two persons, and a suit to dissolve this relationship is an action in rem, directed against the status or relationship itself rather than against the

Fauntleroy v. Lum, 210 U.S. 230, 237 (1908); Christmas v. Russell, 5 Wall. 290, 301–302 (1886).

[48] Hanson v. Denckla, 357 U.S. 235, 250–53, 255 (1958); Milliken v. Meyer, 311 U.S. 457, 462 (1940); Hansberry v. Lee, 311 U.S. 32, 40 (1940); Old Wayne Life Assn. v. McDonough, 204 U.S. 8, 14 (1907); Hanley v. Donoghue, 116 U.S. 1, 3, 7 (1885); D'Arcy v. Ketchum, 11 How. 165, 176 (1850).

[49] Bell v. Bell, 181 U.S. 175, 177 (1901); Andrews v. Andrews, 188 U.S. 14, 38 (1903); Williams v. North Carolina, 317 U.S. 287, 297–99 (1942); Williams v. North Carolina, 325 U.S. 226, 229–30 (1945).

[50] Conflicting decisions on the issue of domicile, where it is the basis for the exertion of state power, are not forbidden either by the Fourteenth Amendment or by the full faith and credit clause. Worcester Trust Co. v. Riley, 302 U.S. 292, 299 (1937); Williams v. North Carolina, 325 U.S. 226, 230, 234–37 (1945). On the vagueness of domicile as a criterion of state power, see Justice Rutledge's dissent. *Ibid.*, 258.

[51] Since in divorce and tax matters a person may wish to be considered as domiciled in one state (where the laws are favorable) while actually living in another state, many self-serving declarations and circumstances regarding the person's affairs have to be sifted out in order to determine domicile.

individuals involved.[52] Hence, with respect to divorce decrees, the rule that a judgment rendered against a nonresident without personal appearance or service of process is invalid does not apply.[53] The nonresident spouse who has not appeared or been served with process is bound if the court granting the divorce has jurisdiction over the marital relationship or *res*.[54] Such jurisdiction, it was formerly held, was vested only in the court where the "matrimonial domicile" was located.[55] This was the last common domicile where both spouses lived together as man and wife. The wife's domicile was presumed to be the same as her husband's; hence if she deserted him, he could get a valid divorce at the matrimonial domicile; but if he abandoned her, his subsequent domicile was not a new matrimonial domicile and he could not obtain an ex parte divorce there. The wife, however, could obtain such a divorce at her subsequent domicile if she were not the party at fault in causing the separation.[56] This doctrine made the jurisdiction or power of the state to grant a divorce dependent upon the merits of the case. It required determination of the domestic dispute between the spouses regarding which one was at fault as a preliminary condition precedent to establishment of the court's jurisdiction.[57] A divorce granted by the court where only one person was domiciled was regarded as valid in that state, however, although it was not entitled to full faith and credit elsewhere.[58]

Later the Supreme Court abandoned the "confusing refinement" of matrimonial domicile, and the attempt to determine where the *res* or

[52] Haddock v. Haddock, 201 U.S. 562, 567, 569, 576 (1906).

[53] Atherton v. Atherton, 181 U.S. 155, 163 (1901). "In other words, settled family relationships may be destroyed by a procedure that we would not recognize if the suit were one to collect a grocery bill," as Justice Jackson says in his dissent in Williams v. North Carolina, 317 U.S. 287, 316 (1942). See note 40, page 397, and note 48, page 399, above.

[54] Later cases discarded the "in rem" terminology, but persisted in treating the divorce proceeding as something different from an ordinary suit in personam. Williams v. North Carolina, 317 U.S. 287, 297, 317 (1942); Williams v. North Carolina, 325 U.S. 226, 232 (1945).

[55] Haddock v. Haddock, 201 U.S. 562, 570–72 (1906). The concept of "matrimonial domicile" was characterized by Justice Frankfurter as a "cloudy abstraction" involving many "confusing refinements." Williams v. North Carolina, 317 U.S. 287, 305 (1942); Williams v. North Carolina, 325 U.S. 226, 230 (1945).

[56] Atherton v. Atherton, 181 U.S. 155, 164 (1901); Haddock v. Haddock, 201 U.S. 562, 571, 583 (1906).

[57] 317 U.S. at 301; 201 U.S. at 628, 631.   [58] 201 U.S. at 569, 605–606.

marital relationship was located when the spouses were domiciled in different states. The present rule is that the state where either spouse has a bona fide domicile has jurisdiction to grant an ex parte divorce,[59] effective to change the marital status of the absent spouse.[60]

This doctrine is based upon the view that since the state where either party to the marriage relationship is domiciled has an interest in regulating the personal status of all persons within its boundaries, it has power to grant a divorce; and that since marriage is a relationship between two people, it can be terminated by whichever state first acts to sever the bond uniting them.[61]

However, since jurisdiction can always be challenged, and jurisdiction to grant a divorce depends upon domicile, it follows that if the court of the home state finds that the divorced party has never lost his or her original domicile in the home state or acquired a bona fide domicile in the state where the divorce was granted, then the consequence is that the court granting the divorce had no jurisdiction, and its decree of divorce is therefore null and void, and not entitled to full faith and credit.[62]

The disturbing consequences of this principle are somewhat mitigated by decisions to the effect that if a personal appearance is entered in the divorce proceedings on behalf of the defendant spouse, so that the court has jurisdiction in personam over the defendant and not

[59] By the term "ex parte divorce" is meant one where a nonresident defendant did not appear and was not personally served with process in the state, but service was by publication. Justice Jackson says: "To me *ex parte* divorce is a concept as perverse and unrealistic as an *ex parte* marriage." Rice v. Rice, 336 U.S. 674, 678 (1949).

[60] The new rule that domicile of either spouse is sufficient to establish jurisdiction to grant a divorce was enunciated in Williams v. North Carolina, 317 U.S. 287, 298–99, 304 (1942), overruling Haddock v. Haddock. See Williams v. North Carolina, 325 U.S. 226, 229–30 (1945); and Estin v. Estin, 334 U.S. 541, 543 (1948). An earlier case relied on to support the holding, Maynard v. Hill, 125 U.S. 190, 193 (1888), was explained by Justice Jackson as merely relating to rights in land in Oregon Territory, where a husband had settled after abandoning his wife in Ohio. 317 U.S. at 318. See note 70, page 403, below.

[61] The fact that there is a race of diligence in which the state having the laxest requirements for divorce and the speediest procedure for granting it prevails is merely part of the price of a federal system where full faith and credit is given to judgments of other states. 317 U.S. at 302. Cf. 201 U.S. at 574, 616. It could be argued with equal logic that only a state having jurisdiction of both parties to the marriage could alter the relationship between them.

[62] Williams v. North Carolina, 325 U.S. 226, 229, 232, 234 (1945); Rice v. Rice, 336 U.S. 674, 675–76 (1949).

merely jurisdiction in rem over the marriage relationship, then the defendant who has appeared and litigated the issue of domicile is bound by the court's finding with respect to that issue. From this it follows that the question whether the court granting the divorce had jurisdiction becomes *res judicata*, and its decree is entitled to full faith and credit.[63]

A further refinement is the doctrine of "divisible divorce." In a case where a New York court had granted separation and alimony (the husband making a general appearance giving the court jurisdiction over him personally), it was held that this alimony decree survived an ex parte divorce decree obtained by the husband in Nevada, where he was then domiciled.[64] It was conceded that the Nevada divorce was effective to change the marital status of the parties in a manner entitled to recognition everywhere in the United States by virtue of the full faith and credit clause.[65]

But that does not mean, said the Supreme Court, that every incident of the marriage was affected by its termination.[66] The wife's rights to monetary payments under the terms of the New York decree maintained a separate existence, and were not affected by the Nevada divorce, since the wife made no personal appearance in the Nevada court so as to empower it to adjudicate her rights other than with respect to her marital status.[67] This makes the effects of the divorce decree divisible. It must be given full faith and credit insofar as it pronounces the dissolution of the marriage between the parties. But (as an ex parte decree in rem, without jurisdiction in personam over the wife) it cannot be given such faith and credit with respect to the wife's legal rights to alimony payments due from the former husband.[68]

[63] Davis v. Davis, 305 U.S. 32, 40–43 (1938); Williams v. North Carolina, 325 U.S. 226, 230 (1945); Sherrer v. Sherrer, 334 U.S. 343, 348–50 (1948); Coe v. Coe, 334 U.S. 378, 384 (1948); Johnson v. Muelberger, 340 U.S. 581, 585 (1951). For the same rule in another type of case, see Treinies v. Sunshine Mining Co., 308 U.S. 66, 78 (1939).

[64] Estin v. Estin, 334 U.S. 541, 547–49 (1948).

[65] *Ibid.*, 544.   [66] *Ibid.*, 545.

[67] *Ibid.*, 547–48. The Supreme Court held that jurisdiction over a debtor does not give jurisdiction to determine the rights of the creditor without personal service or an appearance giving the Court jurisdiction in personam over the creditor. Hence the Nevada divorce decree need not be given full faith and credit with respect to the financial rights of the wife under the New York alimony decree.

[68] *Ibid.*, 549. Justice Jackson, dissenting, said: "The court reaches the Solomon-like conclusion that the Nevada decree is half good and half bad under the full faith

The same notion of "divisibility" seems to be applicable with respect to property rights of a widow in her former husband's estate.[69] Unless explicable upon the theory that the state where the property is situated is free to determine as it sees fit to whom such property shall descend,[70] this rule seems anomalous. For if the law of the state where the property is situated ordains that it shall go to the widow of the owner, it would seem that a valid divorce, effectively terminating the marital relationship, would likewise *ipso facto* deprive the divorced wife of the marital status by virtue of which she becomes entitled to her husband's property. The doctrine of "divisible divorce" should be restricted to situations where the legal rights of the spouse over whom the divorce court has not obtained personal jurisdiction are rights which have been independently established as existent by a valid adjudication, and are not mere incidents of the marital status itself.[71]

A valid divorce decree, entitled to full faith and credit, would certainly terminate all marital rights which are really mere incidents of the marital status itself (for example, sexual privileges). The right of a spouse to financial support from the other spouse, or the right to custody of children born during the marriage, must be regarded as in

and credit clause. It is good to free the husband from the marriage; it is not good to free him from its incidental obligations. Assuming the judgment to be one which the Constitution requires to be recognized at all, I do not see how we can square this decision with the command that it be given *full* faith and credit." *Ibid.*, 554 (italics in the original).

[69] Rice v. Rice, 336 U.S. 674, 675–76 (1949). The Court held that a wife divorced in Nevada, where she did not appear, could challenge the decree upon jurisdictional grounds in a suit in Connecticut to obtain a declaratory judgment that she was the widow of her deceased husband and as such entitled to share in his estate. Justice Jackson, strongly dissenting, said that if Nevada was permitted to destroy the marriage, he could not see the propriety of a "compensating confusion in the device of divisible divorce" which would permit Rice "to have a wife who cannot become his widow and to leave a widow who was no longer his wife." He blamed the Court for "repudiating the usual requirements of procedural due process in divorce cases and compensating for it by repudiating the Full Faith and Credit Clause." *Ibid.*, 680.

[70] Compare Williams v. North Carolina, 317 U.S. 287, 294 (1942); Hood v. McGehee, 237 U.S. 611, 615 (1915). See note 46, page 398, above. Perhaps the Rice case is not to be regarded as an instance of a valid but "divisible" divorce, but simply as an instance of an invalid divorce, which the other spouse, who had not participated in the proceedings, could challenge on jurisdictional grounds for lack of domicile.

[71] See Justice Frankfurter's dissent in Vanderbilt v. Vanderbilt, 354 U.S. 416, 420 (1957). In that opinion he also points out that the expression "divisible divorce" is a misnomer. It is not the divorce that is divisible, but the judicial proceedings seeking divorce and property settlement. *Ibid.*, 425.

truth a separable right, not one derived directly from the marital status itself. Hence such rights (although they may be considered as incidental to the marriage relation in the sense that they grew out of it) are really independent of it and can survive divorce. Therefore such rights can be regulated by the law of states having a legitimate concern therewith without any denial of full faith and credit to the divorce decree terminating the marriage relation.

This analysis explains why the state where a divorced spouse is domiciled (and might become a public charge) has a legitimate interest in regulating the legal right of such spouse to receive support from a former mate, even if their marriage is admittedly terminated by a divorce decree entitled to full faith and credit.[72]

Similarly the state where a child is domiciled or is physically present has a legitimate interest in the child's maintenance and custody. It may therefore take action with respect to these matters even if a court in another state, when granting an ex parte divorce, has made a different decision. The welfare of the child, rather than the rights of the parents, is the controlling consideration in this type of case. Therefore (as in a case involving the level of public utility rates) a decision at one time is not *res judicata* at a later date (even in the same court) if conditions have changed and the best interests of the child call for a different decision.[73]

A judgment awarding support or alimony, however, is entitled to full faith and credit when, in the state where it was rendered, it has the effect of a final judgment requiring the payment of a certain sum of money. Thus where an order is made requiring the payment of fixed monthly installments, and a vested right accrues as future installments

[72] Vanderbilt v. Vanderbilt, 354 U.S. 416, 417–18 (1957). As Justice Frankfurter pointed out in his dissent, this case differs from Estin v. Estin, 334 U.S. 541 (1948), in that the New York support order was made *after*, and not *before*, the Nevada ex parte divorce. There was therefore no question of full faith and credit involved. 334 U.S. at 420. Justice Harlan would have remanded the case to determine whether the wife's New York domicile was acquired before or after the divorce. *Ibid.*, 434–35.

[73] Halvey v. Halvey, 330 U.S. 610, 612–14, 617 (1947); May v. Anderson, 345 U.S. 528, 534 (1953). The Court in the latter case followed Estin v. Estin, 334 U.S. 541 (1948), and held that a Wisconsin court granting an ex parte divorce and giving the children to the father could not cut off the mother's custodial rights without having jurisdiction in personam over her. Justice Frankfurter's concurring opinion properly lays greater stress on the welfare of the children. *Ibid.*, 536. Justice Jackson's dissent emphasizes the same point. *Ibid.*, 540–42. See also Justice Stone's dissent in Yarborough v. Yarborough, 290 U.S. 204, 221–22 (1933).

come due, the judgment is final and is entitled to full faith and credit. But if it is discretionary with the court to modify its order and relieve the defendant from payment of past installments, the judgment is not entitled to full faith and credit.[74] Even if the installments accrued under an original order could have been modified by the court, the amount payable becomes definite and certain if it is ascertained and determined by a subsequent order for a sum certain, and the second order is then a final judgment which is entitled to full faith and credit.[75] Where a second order is made, care must be taken to see that the defendant has notice and opportunity to present any defense which might move the court to exercise in his favor its discretionary power to modify the amount payable. Otherwise there is danger that it may be held that there has been a denial of due process.[76]

[74] Sistare v. Sistare, 218 U.S. 1, 8 (1910); Barber v. Barber, 323 U.S. 77, 80–84 (1944). In the latter case the Court found it unnecessary to decide whether accrued, modifiable but unmodified, installments are enforceable until modified. *Ibid.*, 81.

[75] Barber v. Barber, 323 U.S. 77, 84 (1944). This holding is similar to the principle embodied in Fauntleroy v. Lum, 210 U.S. 230 (1908), and other cases, distinguishing between suit on a judgment and suit on the original cause of action. See note 47, page 398, above.

[76] Griffin v. Griffin, 327 U.S. 220, 228 (1946). In his dissent Justice Rutledge made the sensible comment that where a judgment imposes a liability for future installments, and they accrue, without any action by defendant to modify the amount payable, there is no denial of due process, for the defendant had notice of the terms of the original order and the burden was on him to present to the court any subsequent defenses arising out of change in conditions. *Ibid.*, 238. Justice Rutledge also considers that where a judgment has sufficient finality to permit levy of execution in the state where it was rendered, it should be considered to have sufficient finality to entitle it to full faith and credit. *Ibid.*, 247.

Privileges and Immunities

The Citizens of each State shall be entitled to all Privileges and Immunities of Citizens in the several States.

HISTORY

THIS provision, often called the "comity" clause, originated in the Committee of Detail and was based upon Article IV of the Articles of Confederation, which declared that "the free inhabitants of each of these States . . . shall be entitled to all privileges and immunities of free citizens in the several States," together with other privileges of travel and trade.[1] This language was inserted by Rutledge in a paper in Wilson's handwriting which was apparently one of the working drafts used during the deliberations of the Committee of Detail.[2] The report of the Committee of Detail omitted the word "free."[3]

INTERPRETATION

THE persons entitled to protection under this clause are "Citizens" of a "State." State citizenship, rather than national citizenship,[4] is the

[1] Art. IV went on to provide that "the people of each State shall have free ingress and regress to and from any other State, and shall enjoy therein all the privileges of trade and commerce, subject to the same duties, impositions and restrictions as the inhabitants thereof respectively, provided that such restrictions shall not extend so far as to prevent the removal of property imported into any State, to any other State of which the owner is an inhabitant."

[2] Farrand, *Records*, II, 173–74. The words "free Citizens of each State" replaced "free inhabitants of each of these States."

[3] Art. XIV. *Ibid.*, II, 187 (August 6). See note 31, page 413, below. In convention the provision was accepted as reported. *Ibid.*, II, 437, 443 (August 28). "Genl. Pinkney was not satisfied with it. He seemed to wish some provision should be included in favor of property in slaves." No change was made by the Committee of Style. *Ibid.*, II, 601 (September 12).

[4] Regarding the distinctions between state and national citizenship, before the Fourteenth Amendment, see commentary on Art. I, sec. 8, cl. 4. The Fourteenth Amendment, besides defining national citizenship, forbade state laws "which shall abridge the privileges and immunities of citizens of the United States." The Supreme Court

indispensable factor which qualifies an individual[5] for the benefits of this clause.

It seems clear that the purpose and effect of this clause is to enable citizens of any state to enjoy in another state the same privileges and immunities (whatever they may be) that the law of the latter state accords to its own citizens.[6] In other words, by analogy with international law, it accords "national treatment," as distinguished from "most-favored nation treatment" or treatment in accordance with the "international law standard."[7] The noncitizen is not entitled to better treatment than the citizen,[8] but is entitled to be free from disabilities due to alienage and to be free from discrimination against noncitizens in favor of citizens of the state.

As stated by the Supreme Court in a frequently quoted passage: "It was undoubtedly the object of the clause in question to place the citizens of each State upon the same footing with citizens of other States, so far as the advantages resulting from citizenship in those States are concerned. It relieves them from the disabilities of alienage in other States; it inhibits discriminating legislation against them by other States; it gives them the right of free ingress into other States, and egress from them; it insures to them in other States the same freedom possessed by citizens of those States in the acquisition and enjoyment of property and in the pursuit of happiness; it secures to them in other States the equal protection of their laws. It has been justly said that

held that this amendment did not extend any additional protection to privileges and immunities derived from state citizenship. Slaughter-House Cases, 16 Wall. 36, 74 (1873). For examples of privileges of national citizenship, see *ibid.*, 79.

[5] Corporations and similar commercial organizations, not being citizens, derive no protection from this clause. Paul v. Virginia, 8 Wall. 168, 177 (1869); Waters-Pierce Oil Co. v. Texas, 177 U.S. 28, 45 (1900); Hemphill v. Orloff, 277 U.S. 537, 548 (1928).

[6] Paul v. Virginia, 8 Wall. 168, 180 (1869); Slaughter-House Cases, 16 Wall. 36, 77 (1873); U.S. v. Harris, 106 U.S. 629, 643–44 (1883); Detroit v. Osborne, 135 U.S. 492, 498 (1890); U.S. v. Wheeler, 254 U.S. 281, 293–98 (1920); Whitfield v. Ohio, 297 U.S. 431, 437 (1936); Hague v. C.I.O., 307 U.S. 496, 511 (1939); Toomer v. Witsell, 334 U.S. 385, 395–96 (1948); Mullane v. Anderson, 342 U.S. 415, 417–18 (1952).

[7] Robert R. Wilson, *The International Law Standard in Treaties of the United States*, 17–21, 91–97, 102–104, 246.

[8] Detroit v. Osborne, 135 U.S. 492, 498 (1890); Shaffer v. Carter, 252 U.S. 37, 53 (1920).

no provision in the Constitution has tended so strongly to constitute the citizens of the United States one people as this."[9] Or, as expressed in a more recent decision, this clause insures "to a citizen of State A who ventures into State B the same privileges which the citizens of State B enjoy."[10]

Legislation which has been stricken down as violative of this clause includes statutes giving local creditors preferential priority in the distribution of the assets of a foreign corporation doing business in the state;[11] those taxing nonresidents more heavily than citizens of the state;[12] and those discriminating in favor of citizens of the state with respect to the terms upon which access to the courts of the state is accorded for the enforcement of legal rights.[13]

Of course a distinction between residents and nonresidents is valid, where nonresident citizens of the state are given the same treatment as nonresident noncitizens.[14] Likewise there is no violation of the privi-

[9] Paul v. Virginia, 8 Wall. 168, 180 (1869). In Whitfield v. Ohio, 297 U.S. 431, 437 (1936), it was said that this clause "is directed against discrimination by a state in favor of its own citizens and against the citizens of other states." Hence an Ohio statute against prison-made goods, whether manufactured in Ohio or elsewhere, did not violate the clause. See also Hague v. C.I.O., 307 U.S. 496, 511 (1939).

[10] Toomer v. Witsell, 334 U.S. 385, 395 (1948). The Court further pointed out that "one of the privileges which the clause guarantees to citizens of State A is that of doing business in State B on terms of substantial equality with the citizens of that State." *Ibid.*, 396.

[11] Blake v. McClung, 172 U.S. 239, 254 (1898).

[12] Ward v. Maryland, 12 Wall. 418, 430–31 (1871); Chalker v. Birmingham & N.W. Ry. Co., 249 U.S. 522, 527 (1919); Travis v. Yale & Towne Mfg. Co., 252 U.S. 60, 79, (1920); Toomer v. Witsell, 334 U.S. 385, 389, 403 (1948); Mullaney v. Anderson, 342 U.S. 415, 416–18 (1952). Cf. Maxwell v. Bugbee, 250 U.S. 525, 534–38 (1919), and Shaffer v. Carter, 252 U.S. 37, 57 (1920), where the taxes were sustained as nondiscriminatory.

[13] The clause "requires a state to accord to citizens of other states substantially the same access to its courts as it accords to its own citizens." McKnett v. St. L. & S.F. Ry. Co., 292 U.S. 230, 233 (1934). This case is followed in Miles v. Ill. Central R.R. Co., 315 U.S. 698, 704–705 (1942), and Southern Ry. v. Mayfield, 340 U.S. 1, 4 (1950). In Chambers v. B. & O. R.R. Co., 207 U.S. 142, 148 (1907), the Court said that the right to sue and defend in the courts is a fundamental right and essential privilege of citizenship, "and must be allowed by each State to the citizens of all other States to the precise extent that it is allowed to its own citizens." The Court held, however, that there was no discrimination or inequality of treatment prescribed by the Ohio statute there involved. *Ibid.*, 149. Likewise upheld was the New York statute considered in Douglas v. N.Y., N.H. & H. R.R. Co., 279 U.S. 377, 385–87 (1929).

[14] In La Tourette v. McMaster, 248 U.S. 465, 470 (1919), there was upheld a South Carolina statute which regulated insurance brokers by requiring residence (as

leges and immunities clause if the difference of treatment is justified by a difference in circumstances, and hence is not "an unfriendly or unreasonable discrimination."[15] This point was elaborated in a recent case, where the Supreme Court explained that the clause "does bar discrimination against citizens of other States. But it does not preclude disparity of treatment where there are perfectly valid independent reasons for it." The clause outlaws "classifications based on the fact of noncitizenship unless there is something to indicate that non-citizens constitute a peculiar source of the evil at which the statute is aimed."[16]

Moreover, in the case of political privileges such as the right to vote, a residence requirement is not improper.[17] Similarly, citizens of a state are not obliged to share with outsiders the enjoyment of rights based upon their co-ownership of public property such as oyster beds,[18] or game *ferae naturae* belonging to the state.[19]

distinguished from citizenship), and thus applied equally to citizens and noncitizens of the state. In Douglas v. N.Y., N.H. & H. R.R. Co., 279 U.S. 377, 387 (1929), Justice Holmes said: "A distinction of privileges according to residence may be based upon rational considerations. . . . There are manifest reasons for preferring residents in access to often overcrowded Courts, both in convenience and in the fact that broadly speaking it is they who pay for maintaining the Courts concerned."

[15] Shaffer v. Carter, 252 U.S. 37, 57 (1920). Thus it would be proper to exact of nonresident litigants a bond for costs although citizens of the state were not subjected to that requirement. Blake v. McClung, 172 U.S. 239, 256 (1898).

[16] Toomer v. Witsell, 334 U.S. 385, 396, 398 (1948). Thus where there are added expenses of enforcement in the case of noncitizens, or where citizens of the state contribute (and noncitizens do not) by taxes to the conservation of natural resources, noncitizens could properly be required to pay a higher license fee than citizens. *Ibid.*, 399. See also Mullaney v. Anderson, 342 U.S. 415, 417 (1952).

[17] Blake v. McClung, 172 U.S. 239, 256 (1898). In Dred Scott v. Sandford, 19 How. 393, 422 (1857), Chief Justice Roger B. Taney said of the comity clause: "It gives them no political rights in the State, as to voting or holding office, or in any other respect. For a citizen of one State has no right to participate in the government of another." Justice Benjamin R. Curtis agreed that the clause covers only privileges which are attached to "mere naked citizenship." *Ibid.*, 583–84. See also Minor v. Happersett, 21 Wall. 162, 171, 174 (1875).

[18] Corfield v. Coryell, 4 Wash. C.C. 371, Fed. Cas. No. 3230 (1823). To the same effect, see McCready v. Virginia, 94 U.S. 391, 395 (1877).

[19] Geer v. Connecticut, 161 U.S. 519, 528–29 (1896). The same rule was applied in Hudson County Water Co. v. McCarter, 209 U.S. 349, 356–57 (1908), to water belonging to the state. But natural gas is treated differently, being regarded as private property rather than as part of the public domain. Oklahoma v. Kansas Natural Gas Co., 221 U.S. 229, 253–55 (1911); Pennsylvania v. West Virginia, 262 U.S. 553, 598 (1923). Moreover, in Toomer v. Witsell, 334 U.S. 385, 401–403 (1948), the Court held that shrimp in the coastal waters off Florida were different from fish that

It is now well settled, as indicated by the authorities reviewed above, that the measure of the rights to be enjoyed in State B by a citizen of State A is that which the citizens of State B enjoy. He cannot carry with him into State B the special privileges which would be available to him in his own state. The laws of State A are given no extraterritorial operation in State B by virtue of the comity clause.[20] Thus a defendant convicted of crime in New York is not entitled to release on bail pending appeal, merely because in his own state, or even in many other states, he would be entitled to that privilege.[21] New York is free, insofar as the federal Constitution is concerned, to adopt its own rule for such matters, regardless of what is the practice in other states.[22]

It is true that in an early case, decided by Justice Bushrod Washington while on circuit, language was used indicating that the comity clause protects only certain privileges and immunities "which are, in their nature, fundamental; which belong, of right, to the citizens of all free governments."[23]

This concept of fundamental privileges belonging, as of right, to the citizens of all free governments is akin to the "natural law" concept of "ordered liberty" which the Supreme Court has applied in interpreting the Fourteenth Amendment as imposing upon the states some (but not all) of the restrictions imposed upon the federal government by the Bill of Rights which are contained in the first ten amendments to the Constitution.[24]

---

would remain within the inland waters of a state unless removed by human intervention. Commercial shrimping was therefore held to be a common calling, protected by the privileges and immunities clause. *Ibid.*, 403.

[20] Paul v. Virginia, 8 Wall. 168, 180 (1868).

[21] McKane v. Durston, 153 U.S. 684, 687–88 (1894).

[22] Similarly, a pedestrian injured in Michigan by a defective sidewalk cannot hold the municipality (as well as the property owner) liable when that state's law provides differently, even though the Michigan law is not in harmony with the general rule prevailing in other states. Detroit v. Osborne, 135 U.S. 492, 498 (1890). See also Hague v. C.I.O., 307 U.S. 496, 511 (1939).

[23] Corfield v. Coryell, 4 Wash. C.C. 371, Fed. Cas. No. 3230 (1823). The American notion that certain rights were inherent in the citizen was the converse of the English royalist contention that certain prerogatives were inherent in the crown. See note 55, page 13, above.

[24] Adamson v. California, 332 U.S. 46, 70, 75, 90 (1947); Palko v. Connecticut, 302 U.S. 319, 323, 325 (1937); Hebert v. Louisiana, 272 U.S. 312, 316 (1926); Twining v. New Jersey, 211 U.S. 78, 101–102 (1908); Loan Assn. v. Topeka, 20 Wall. 655, 663 (1875). See Dumbauld, *The Bill of Rights and What It Means Today,* 135–36.

Justice Washington said: "The inquiry is, what are the privileges and immunities of citizens in the several states? We feel no hesitation in confining these expressions to those privileges and immunities which are, in their nature, fundamental; which belong, of right, to the citizens of all free governments; and which have, at all times, been enjoyed by the citizens of the several states which compose this Union, from the time of their becoming free, independent, and sovereign. What these fundamental principles are, it would perhaps be more tedious than difficult to enumerate. They may, however, be all comprehended under the following general heads: Protection by the government; the enjoyment of life and liberty, with the right to acquire and possess property of every kind, and to pursue and obtain happiness and safety; subject nevertheless to such restraints as the government may justly prescribe for the general good of the whole. The right of a citizen of one state to pass through, or to reside in any other state, for purposes of trade, agriculture, professional pursuits, or otherwise; to claim the benefit of the writ of habeas corpus; to institute and maintain actions of any kind in the courts of the states; to take, hold and dispose of property, either real or personal; and an exemption from higher taxes or impositions than are paid by the other citizens of the state; may be mentioned as some of the particular privileges and immunities of citizens, which are clearly embraced by the general description of privileges deemed to be fundamental: to which may be added the elective franchise, as regulated and established by the laws or constitution of the state in which it is to be exercised."[25]

No mention was made of the comity clause by Justice William Johnson, sitting on circuit, when he held unconstitutional (by reason of conflict with the commerce power of Congress and with a British treaty of 1815) the legislation which South Carolina enacted in 1822 to discourage the entry of free colored seamen into ports of that state.[26] Apparently alarmed by an anticipated uprising of slaves, the state decreed "That if any vessel shall come into any port or harbor of this

[25] 6 Fed. Cas. at 551–52.

[26] Elkison v. Deliesseline, Fed. Cas. No. 4366 (1823); Donald G. Morgan, *Justice William Johnson*, 192, 202. As legislation then in force did not permit the writ of habeas corpus in a federal court except where the applicant was held under color of authority of the United States, Justice Johnson held that the only remedy available was the writ *de homine replegiando*, which might be of no avail against the sheriff though it would against his vendee.

state, from any other state or foreign port, having on board any free negroes or persons of color, as cooks, stewards, or mariners, or in any other employment on board said vessel, such free negroes or persons of color shall be seized and confined in gaol until the vessel shall clear out and depart from this state; and that when said vessel is ready to sail the captain of said vessel shall be bound to carry away the said free negro, or free person of color, and to pay the expenses of his detention; and, in case of his neglect or refusal so to do, he shall be liable to be indicted . . . ; and such free negroes or persons of color shall be deemed and taken as absolute slaves, and sold."[27]

The imprisonment of British subjects who were guilty of no crime, and indeed were protected by the terms of a commercial treaty, led to acrimonious controversy. As Johnson observed, if color of skin were a sufficient ground for excluding a seaman, might not also the color of his eyes or hair permit the state to imprison Scotsmen? The law would likewise apply to naval vessels, and to Nantucket Indians aboard Massachusetts ships.[28]

When in 1843 a petition was presented to Congress by numerous prominent Boston citizens (mostly affected shipowners) remonstrating against the seamen's law, the comity clause was invoked.[29] Congress took no action, however, claiming that its legislative power could not provide a remedy. The Southern contention was that the free seamen from Massachusetts were entitled by virtue of that clause only to the same privileges as were accorded in South Carolina to persons of the same color (*i.e.*, to slaves).[30] But it would seem that if free persons of

[27] Section 3 of the Act of December 1, 1822, 8 Fed. Cas. at 493; 27 Cong., 3 sess., H. R. Doc. No. 80, 21–22. Attorney General William Wirt likewise concluded that the law was unconstitutional in his opinion of May 8, 1824. *Ibid.*, 35–36. A labored attempt to uphold the validity of such legislation as an exercise of police power was made by Attorney General John M. Berrien in his opinion of March 25, 1831. *Ibid.*, 49–58.

[28] Justice Johnson in a letter of July 31, 1824, to Secretary of State John Quincy Adams called attention to the case of Amos Daley, who claimed to be a Rhode Island Indian, but was held subject to the law because of his wooly hair. As he had not entered South Carolina voluntarily, however, he received only twelve lashes as punishment. *Ibid.*, 14, 18–21.

[29] 27 Cong., 3 sess., H. R. Doc. No. 80, 2: Jacobus ten Broek, *The Antislavery Origins of the Fourteenth Amendment*, 76–85.

[30] 27 Cong. 3 sess., H. R. Doc. No. 80, 39–41 (minority report). Even if the majority's interpretation of the comity clause is accepted, the minority argued that a free colored person is not a citizen within the meaning of the Constitution, that term

color in Massachusetts were citizens of that state,[31] then they would be entitled in South Carolina to the privileges and immunities which South Carolina granted to citizens of South Carolina, that is to say, to white citizens of that state, rather than to such restricted privileges as South Carolina granted to its noncitizens.[32] In other words, citizenship, rather than race, would be the controlling factor with respect to the operation of the comity clause.

The flagrant nonenforcement of the comity clause typified by the foregoing South Carolina incidents furnished ample practical justification for Congressman John A. Bingham's proposal to give to the federal government explicit power[33] to enforce the provisions of Article IV, being limited to persons enjoying all the rights and privileges conferred upon the highest class of society within the state. Regarding this point, Attorney General Edward Bates, in his opinion of November 29, 1862, 10 Op. 382, 407–408, justly observed that even if there are different classes of citizens within a state, the Constitution extends the protection of the comity clause to all citizens, even those of the lowest class.

[31] That is to say, if the view of Chief Justice Roger B. Taney in the ill-starred Dred Scott case, to the effect that even a free person of the "slave race" could not be a citizen of the United States or of a state, is rejected as unsound. Dred Scott v. Sandford, 19 How. 393, 406 (1857). It was convincingly refuted in the able dissenting opinion of Justice Benjamin R. Curtis. *Ibid.*, 571–88. Justice John McLean also disagreed with Taney. *Ibid.*, 531. It is noteworthy that both Taney and Curtis agreed that if such persons were citizens they could not be denied the privileges and immunities of citizenship in another state. *Ibid.*, 422–23, 582–84. But for Taney that consequence was so abhorrent that it served as an additional argument in support of his contention that they could not be citizens. He regarded it as significant that in Art. IV, sec. 2, "citizens" was substituted for "free inhabitants" in the corresponding provision in the Articles of Confederation. *Ibid.*, 419. But Curtis showed that these terms were equivalent, and that on June 25, 1778, the Continental Congress had rejected a proposal to insert "white" before "inhabitants." *Ibid.*, 575, 584–85.

[32] It might be argued that the South Carolina slaves were to be regarded as being citizens of the state, but citizens of a particular class or category, entitled to less extensive privileges and immunities than other citizens of the state. (Cf. 19 How. at 422, where Taney rejects this argument as incompatible with the comity clause). But could South Carolina classify Massachusetts citizens in this manner, when their own state did not? If each state is free to determine who shall be citizens of the state, the Massachusetts determination would have to be respected elsewhere. Moreover, it would seem that an individual is either a citizen of a state or a noncitizen. Slaves were simply regarded in slave states as noncitizens. See 19 How. at 412.

[33] The "necessary and proper" clause (Art. I, sec. 8, cl. 18) empowers Congress to make laws "for carrying into Execution" powers vested by the Constitution *in the federal government*. It does not authorize federal enforcement of rights directly vested by the Constitution in individual citizens. Art. IV, sec. 1, expressly empowers Congress to enforce that section; but Art. IV, sec. 2, does not. See pages 417 and 421 below. May Congress enforce provisions such as Art. I, sec. 10, which simply impose direct obligations upon the states?

section 2.[34] As finally worded, however, the Fourteenth Amendment failed to include such authorization.[35]

[34] In the Reconstruction Committee on February 3, 1866, Bingham proposed as a constitutional amendment: "The Congress shall have power to make all laws which shall be necessary and proper to secure to citizens of each State all privileges and immunities of citizens in the several States (Art. IV, Sec. 2); and to all persons in the several States equal protection in the rights of life, liberty, and property (5th Amendment)." Horace E. Flack, *The Adoption of The Fourteenth Amendment*, 62. Later the present wording of the Fourteenth Amendment was adopted. *Ibid.*, 66–68. Section 5 provides that "The Congress shall have power to enforce, by appropriate legislation, the provisions of this article."

[35] As adopted and as interpreted by the Supreme Court, the Fourteenth Amendment protects only privileges of *national* citizenship. See note 4, page 406, above. However, it might be argued that it is a privilege of national citizenship to enjoy without molestation the rights conferred directly by Art. IV, sec. 2, upon the "Citizens of each State." In other words there is a federally created right to the enjoyment of such privileges and immunities (whatever they may be) as are conferred by state law upon "Citizens in the several States." Being a right derived from the federal Constitution, it is a right of national citizenship. Moreover, the right to be a citizen of a state is also one conferred directly by the Fourteenth Amendment.

Fugitives from Justice; Fugitive Slaves

ART. IV, SEC. 2, CL. 2 *and* CL. 3

A Person charged in any State with Treason, Felony, or other Crime, who shall flee from Justice, and be found in another State, shall on Demand of the executive Authority of the State from which he fled, be delivered up, to be removed to the State having Jurisdiction of the Crime.

No Person held to Service or Labour in one State, under the Laws thereof, escaping into another, shall, in Consequence of any Law or Regulation therein, be discharged from such Service or Labour, but shall be delivered up on Claim of the Party to whom such Service or Labour may be due.

HISTORY

THE provision regarding delivery of fugitives from justice originated in the Committee of Detail, and was based upon Article IV of the Articles of Confederation, which contained language reading as follows: "If any person guilty of, or charged with treason, felony, or other high misdemeanor in any State, shall flee from justice, and be found in any of the United States, he shall upon demand of the Governor or Executive power, of the State from which he fled, be delivered up and removed to the State having jurisdiction of his offense."[1]

The Committee of Detail reported: "Any person charged with treason, felony or high misdemeanor in any State, who shall flee from justice, and shall be found in any other State, shall, on demand of the Executive power of the State from which he fled, be delivered up and removed to the State having jurisdiction of the offence."[2] In debate, the words "other crime" were substituted for "high misdemeanor." Butler and Charles Pinckney of South Carolina moved "to require fugitive slaves and servants to be delivered up like criminals." Wilson

[1] A substantially identical provision appears in a draft in Wilson's hand apparently used as a working paper in the Committee of Detail. Farrand, *Records*, II, 174. The New Jersey Plan had proposed a different method of regulating interstate offenders. *Ibid.*, I, 245, 247.

[2] Article XV. *Ibid.*, II, 187–88 (August 6).

retorted that such a provision would oblige the executive to do it at the public expense, and Sherman observed that he "saw no more propriety in the public seizing and surrendering a slave or servant, than a horse." Butler withdrew his proposition "in order that some particular provision might be made apart from this article."[3]

The Committee of Style substituted "A person charged in any state" for "Any person charged," deleted "in any State" after "crime," deleted "shall" before "be found," and substituted "crime" for "offence" at the end of the clause.[4] In convention the words "and removed" were replaced by "to be removed."[5]

In pursuance of his suggestion that provision be made for the delivery of fugitive slaves, Butler moved to add: "If any person bound to service or labor in any of the U[nited] States shall escape into another State, he or she shall not be discharged from such service or labor, in consequence of any regulations subsisting in the State to which they escape, but shall be delivered up to the person justly claiming their service or labor."[6] This addition was accepted, doubtless as a part of the compromise reached regarding navigation acts and the importation of slaves.[7]

The Committee of Style revised this clause to read: "No person legally held to service or labour in one state, escaping into another, shall in consequence of regulations subsisting therein be discharged from such service or labor, but shall be delivered up on claim of the party to whom such service or labour may be due."[8]

In convention the words "regulations subsisting" were replaced by "any law or regulations."[9] The word "legally" was also deleted and the phrase "under the laws thereof" inserted after "one State," in compliance with the wishes of some who thought that use of the word "legally" might imply "that slavery was legal in a moral view."[10]

---

[3] *Ibid.*, II, 437, 443 (August 28).

[4] *Ibid.*, II, 601 (September 12).

[5] *Ibid.*, II, 621 (September 15).

[6] *Ibid.*, II, 446, 453–54 (August 29).

[7] *Ibid.*, II, 414–15 (August 25); Meigs, *The Growth of the Constitution*, 260. See Art. I, sec. 9, cl. 1. In that clause, just as in Art. IV, sec. 2, cl. 3, a euphemistic paraphrase was used instead of mentioning the "slaves." See note 12, page 188, and note 24, page 190, above.

[8] *Ibid.*, II, 601–602 (September 12).

[9] *Ibid.*, II, 621 (September 15).

[10] *Ibid.*, II, 628 (September 15).

INTERPRETATION

LIKE other provisions of Article IV, dealing with interstate relations, this provision imposes on every state a duty to co-operate with other states in the administration of justice. There is no express grant to Congress of power to execute this provision,[11] and the Supreme Court has said that it is not in its nature self-executing; but contemporary construction and long acquiescence have established the validity of legislation to enforce the duty imposed by this provision of the Constitution.[12]

Such legislation was enacted in 1793[13] after Virginia had refused to honor a requisition from Pennsylvania on the ground that the Constitution did not specify with sufficient clarity the method of transmitting such demands.[14] The Supreme Court in 1861 declared, however, that

[11] As there is in Art. IV, sec. 1. In Kentucky v. Dennison, 24 How. 66, 107–10 (1861), the Court took the view that the federal government could not directly impose on any state official a duty and compel its performance. Cf. Prigg v. Pennsylvania, 16 Pet. 539, 616, 622 (1842).

[12] Roberts v. Reilly, 116 U.S. 80, 94 (1885). See also Prigg v. Pennsylvania, 16 Pet. 539, 615, 618–21 (1842); and Innes v. Tobin, 240 U.S. 127, 131 (1916).

[13] The Act of February 12, 1793, 1 Stat. 302, now embodied in 18 U.S.C. 3182, specified "That whenever the executive authority of any state [or territory] . . . shall demand any person as a fugitive from justice, of the executive authority of any such state or territory *to which such person shall have fled* and shall moreover produce the copy of an indictment found, or an affidavit made before a magistrate of any state or territory as aforesaid, charging the person so demanded, with having committed treason, felony or other crime, certified as authentic by the Governor or chief magistrate of the state or territory from whence the person so charged fled, it shall be the duty of the executive authority of the state or territory *to which such person shall have fled,* to cause him or her to be arrested and secured, and notice of the arrest to be given to the executive authority making such demand, or to the agent of such authority appointed to receive the fugitive, and to cause the fugitive to be delivered to such agent when he shall appear: But if no such agent shall appear within six months from the time of the arrest, the prisoner may be discharged. And all costs or expenses incurred in the apprehending, securing, and transmitting such fugitive to the state or territory making such demand, shall be paid by such state or territory." The italicized words in the statute, less broad than those of the Constitution, gave rise to an interesting contention in Innes v. Tobin, 240 U.S. 127, 133–35 (1916), that a defendant extradited from Oregon to Texas, and tried and acquitted there, could not be delivered up by Texas to Georgia, as she had not fled to Texas but had been brought into that state involuntarily. See note 36, page 421, below.

[14] Prigg v. Pennsylvania, 16 Pet. 539, 620, 666–67 (1842). See also President George Washington's message of October 27, 1791, and accompanying correspondence. *American State Papers* (Class X), I, 38–43. Attorney General James Innis of Virginia was of opinion that without additional legislation there was no power to arrest a

the duty imposed by the Constitution and statute to deliver up a fugitive was merely a moral duty, and that no branch of the federal government could use any coercive means to compel the governor of a state to perform such obligation if he refused to do so.[15]

A person is sufficiently "charged" with crime, for purposes of extradition, if a charge is sworn to before a magistrate in the demanding state. The magistrate before whom such charge is pending may be merely a committing magistrate, having no power to try the defendant for the offense charged, but only power to bind over for trial before a higher court.[16] An information is sufficient. There need not be an indictment returned by a grand jury.[17]

The charge may be any sort of "Crime," from the highest to the lowest.[18] Although the Constitution speaks only of charges pending "in any State," the provision in the legislation of 1793 making the obligation to extradite applicable to territories as well has been upheld by the Supreme Court.[19]

---

fugitive. United States Attorney General Edmund Randolph was of opinion that the duty to deliver, imposed by the Constitution, included the incidental power to arrest, but suggested that the President refer the matter to Congress. In Kentucky v. Dennison, 24 How. 66, 103 (1861), the Supreme Court said that the practice established under the Articles of Confederation of making the demand upon the governor of the state where the fugitive is found was carried over under the Constitution.

[15] Kentucky v. Dennison, 24 How. 66, 107–10 (1861). In that case (the converse of the Pennsylvania-Virginia situation) the fugitive was charged with aiding a slave to escape. The governor of Ohio refused to deliver him up, as in the attorney general's opinion the obligation to do so was limited to cases involving treason or felony by the common law at the time of adoption of the Constitution or offenses regarded as criminal by the usages and laws of all civilized nations. Ibid., 69. Kentucky invoked the original jurisdiction of the Supreme Court, seeking the remedy of mandamus. Ibid., 66. The Court rejected this narrow construction, holding that the obligation to extradite covered all crimes, from the highest to the lowest. Ibid., 99–102. Nevertheless the Court held that the duty was merely a moral one. Ibid., 107–10. This conclusion rests on a conception of the relationship between federal and state powers which is out of fashion today. See note 11, page 417, above. Cf. Testa v. Katt, 330 U.S. 386 (1947); and Robb v. Connolly, 111 U.S. 624, 635 (1884). See also Warren, "Federal Criminal Laws and the State Courts," loc. cit., 545.

[16] In the Matter of Strauss, 197 U.S. 324, 330 (1905).

[17] Pierce v. Creecy, 210 U.S. 387, 403 (1908). A fortiori there need not be a valid indictment. The legal sufficiency of the indictment as a pleading is a question for the trial court. However, an indictment might be so defective as not to constitute a charge of crime at all.

[18] Kentucky v. Dennison, 24 How. 66, 99, 102 (1861); Taylor v. Taintor, 16 Wall. 366, 375 (1873); Ex parte Reggel, 114 U.S. 642, 650 (1885).

[19] Ex parte Reggel, 114 U.S. 642, 650 (1885); Kopel v. Bingham, 211 U.S. 468, 474 (1909).

Besides showing that the person demanded is charged with crime, the demanding state must also show that he is a fugitive from justice,[20] that is to say that he was in the demanding state at the time when the alleged offense was committed,[21] and had departed therefrom at the time when he was wanted in connection with the criminal prosecution instituted against him.

Absolute accuracy with respect to the time of defendant's presence in the demanding state is not required, however; it suffices if he was there approximately at the time when the offense was committed.[22] Likewise it is not necessary that he be present during the completion of the entire crime; performance of one overt act or part of the crime is sufficient.[23]

Moreover, it is not necessary that the defendant fled from the state in order to avoid prosecution or escape trial. Mere absence when his presence is desired in connection with the criminal proceedings is sufficient to make him a fugitive from justice for the purposes of extradition. The motive for his departure is immaterial.[24]

The governor of the state where the fugitive is found need not hold a hearing, or demand proof apart from the papers submitted by the demanding state, but may act upon the basis of such evidence as he considers satisfactory.[25]

[20] Roberts v. Reilly, 116 U.S. 80, 95 (1885). The first question (whether the defendant is charged with a crime) is said to be one of law, the second (whether the defendant is a fugitive) is one of fact, which the governor of the state where the defendant is found must determine upon such evidence as he considers satisfactory.

[21] Ex parte Reggel, 114 U.S. 642, 651 (1885); Hyatt v. Corkran, 188 U.S. 691, 719 (1903). The constitutional requirement that the defendant "flee from Justice" could not be met if he had not been in the demanding state at the time of the crime. "How can a person flee from a place he was not in?" 188 U.S. at 713.

[22] Thus in Roberts v. Reilly, 116 U.S. 80, 97 (1885), the defendant was extradited when he denied being in New York only on the very day laid in the indictment as the date of offense; he did not deny being there about that time. In McNichols v. Pease, 207 U.S. 100, 110–11 (1907), defendant's alibi covered only part of the day, and the Court took judicial notice of the short distance between Chicago and the scene of the theft at Kenosha, Wisconsin. In Strassheim v. Daily, 221 U.S. 280, 286 (1911), Justice Holmes said that "when, as here, it appears that the prisoner was in the State in the neighborhood of the time alleged it is enough." Of course, if it conclusively appears that the defendant was not present at the time of the offense he should be released. Hyatt v. Corkran, 188 U.S. 691, 711 (1903).

[23] 221 U.S. at 285.

[24] Bassing v. Cady, 208 U.S. 386, 392–93 (1908); Drew v. Thaw, 235 U.S. 432, 439 (1914).

[25] Munsey v. Clough, 196 U.S. 364, 372 (1905); Pettibone v. Nichols, 203 U.S. 192, 204 (1906); Marbles v. Creecy, 215 U.S. 63, 68 (1909).

Although the executive determination is judicially reviewable by state[26] or federal[27] courts on habeas corpus, the governor's warrant is sufficient authority for detention of the prisoner until the presumption of its correctness is disproved.[28] Mere conflict in the evidence will not justify discharge of the person held, as the habeas corpus proceeding is not an appropriate means of trying his guilt or innocence of the crime charged.[29]

However, after the prisoner has been delivered up to the agent of the demanding state, it is too late to raise defenses which would have been valid if asserted earlier, such as the defendant's absence from the state at the time of the crime.[30] The Constitution and laws of the United States impose no duty on the state authorities to time their arrest and deportation of a prisoner in such a manner as to afford him a convenient opportunity for challenging in court the legality of their actions.[31]

The Act of February 12, 1793, relating to delivery of fugitives from justice, likewise made provision for delivering up fugitive slaves in accordance with Article IV, section 2, clause 2. The slaveowner, or his representative, was "empowered to seize or arrest such fugitive from labour, and to take him or her before any judge [of the United States] ... or magistrate ... and upon proof to the satisfaction of such judge or magistrate ... that the person so seized or arrested, doth, under the laws of the state or territory from which he or she fled, owe service or

---

[26] Robb v. Connolly, 111 U.S. 624, 637, 639 (1884); South Carolina v. Bailey, 289 U.S. 412, 420 (1933).

[27] Hyatt v. Corkran, 188 U.S. 691, 711 (1903).

[28] Munsey v. Clough, 196 U.S. 364, 372 (1905); South Carolina v. Bailey, 289 U.S. 412, 417 (1933).

[29] 196 U.S. at 375. See also Roberts v. Reilly, 116 U.S. 80, 96 (1885); Drew v. Thaw, 235 U.S. 432, 439–40 (1914); South Carolina v. Bailey, 289 U.S. 412, 420, 422 (1933). Nor will the reviewing court weigh the evidence independently. Ex parte Reggel, 114 U.S. 642, 653 (1885).

[30] Pettibone v. Nichols, 203 U.S. 192, 206 (1906); Cook v. Hart, 146 U.S. 183, 193 (1892). This follows a fortiori from the rule that even if a defendant is kidnapped and brought into a state he can be subjected there to a criminal trial. Ker v. Illinois, 119 U.S. 436, 441 (1886); Mahon v. Justice, 127 U.S. 700, 705 (1888). Similarly, a defendant extradited upon one charge may be tried for an entirely different crime. Lascelles v. Georgia, 148 U.S. 537, 542 (1893). The right of asylum which would exist in case of international extradition under a treaty does not apply between the states. Ibid., 545–46. See also Kentucky v. Dennison, 24 How. 66, 99–100 (1861).

[31] Pettibone v. Nichols, 203 U.S. 192, 205 (1906). In that case the fugitive was arrested at 11:30 P.M. on a Saturday night and immediately returned from Colorado to Idaho on a special train. Ibid., 219. The Court likewise felt that there would be

labour to the person claiming him or her, it shall be the duty of such judge or magistrate to give a certificate thereof to such claimant . . . which shall be sufficient warrant for removing the said fugitive from labour, to the state or territory from which he or she fled."[32]

In a case decided in 1842 which attracted considerable public attention and was criticized by both proslavery and antislavery forces, the Supreme Court held that this federal legislation was constitutional, and occupied the field to the exclusion of state laws on the subject.[33] Accordingly, a Pennsylvania statute under which one Prigg had been convicted for assault and battery by reason of seizing a slave and carrying her away to Maryland was held unconstitutional.[34] The fugitive slave clause of the Constitution[35] was interpreted as authorizing not only self-help by slaveowners in recapturing their slaves but also additional aid by means of legislation. Since the clause is worded in the passive voice, the natural inference is that the remedy for enforcement is to be provided by the national government.[36] Because the right is one derived from the federal Constitution and one requiring nationwide uniformity, the enforcement power is classified as exclusive and not concurrent.[37]

impropriety in considering the motives of the governors of the demanding and surrendering states and whether there was a conspiracy between them to extradite the defendant illegally. *Ibid.*, 216.

[32] Act of February 12, 1793, 1 Stat. 302–305, sec. 3.

[33] Prigg v. Pennsylvania, 16 Pet. 539, 617, 622 (1842).

[34] *Ibid.*, 625.

[35] Art. IV, sec. 2, cl. 3. As Justice Story pointed out, without this clause the Constitution could never have been adopted. 16 Pet. at 611. As Madison and other framers recognized, the clause increased the slaveowner's opportunity of recapturing runaway slaves. Farrand, *Records*, III, 84, 325.

[36] 16 Pet. at 615. Story observes that the Act of 1793 occupied the field, superseding state action, with regard both to fugitives from justice and fugitive slaves. *Ibid.*, 617. (On this point see Innes v. Tobin, 240 U.S. 127, 131 [1916].) The Act of 1793 had been generally accepted and acquiesced in with regard to both classes of fugitives until recently. 16 Pet. at 620–21. But even as *res integra* the statute is clearly constitutional. *Ibid.*, 622.

[37] *Ibid.*, 623. Justice McLean pointed out that the federal act permitted seizure of fugitive slaves, not for the purpose of taking them out of the state without any judicial hearing, but for the purpose of taking them before a judge or magistrate. Hence there was no conflict between the federal act and the Pennsylvania statute under which Prigg had been convicted. *Ibid.*, 669. The Court was unanimous in holding the federal act constitutional and the Pennsylvania act void; but Chief Justice Taney (along with Justices Thompson and Daniel) believed that the state had authority to enact laws (not conflicting with those of Congress) to aid slaveowners in recovering their property. *Ibid.*, 626.

ART. IV, SEC. 3, CL. 1 *and* CL. 2

New States may be admitted by the Congress into this Union; but no new State shall be formed or erected within the Jurisdiction of any other State; nor any State be formed by the Junction of two or more States, or Parts of States, without the Consent of the Legislatures of the States concerned as well as of the Congress.

The Congress shall have Power to dispose of and make all needful Rules and Regulations respecting the Territory or other Property belonging to the United States; and nothing in this Constitution shall be so construed as to Prejudice any Claims of the United States, or of any particular State.

HISTORY

CONSIDERABLE controversy marked the adoption of provisions for the admission of new states and for the government of the western lands. Eastern statesmen such as Gouverneur Morris did not want to permit the future transfer of dominant political power out of the hands of the seaboard states. Maryland's insistence that states having large territorial claims surrender them to the general government had delayed for a long time the going into effect of the Articles of Confederation. Maryland also favored the dismemberment of some of the larger states.[1] Moreover, the terms of the Ordinance of 1787 with respect to western territories were fresh in the minds of the members of the convention.

The Virginia Plan contained a resolution to the effect that "provision ought to be made for the admission of States lawfully arising within the limits of the United States, whether from a voluntary junction of Government & Territory or otherwise, with the consent of a number of voices in the National legislature less than the whole."[2]

[1] Farrand, *Records*, III, 223–27.

[2] Resolution X. *Ibid.*, I, 22 (May 29). The following resolution related to federal guarantee of republican government and of "the territory of each State, except in the instance of a voluntary junction of Government & territory." See also *ibid.*, I, 117, 121 (June 5); I, 237 (June 13); II, 39, 46 (July 18).

The Committee of Detail reported a provision that "New States lawfully constituted or established within the limits of the United States may be admitted, by the Legislature, into this Government; but to such admission the consent of two thirds of the members present in each House shall be necessary. If a new State shall arise within the limits of any of the present States, the consent of the Legislatures of such States shall be also necessary to its admission. If the admission be consented to, the new States shall be admitted on the same terms with the original States. But the Legislature may make conditions with the new States, concerning the public debt which shall be then subsisting."[3]

During debate, Gouverneur Morris moved to strike out the two last sentences. "He did not wish to bind down the Legislature to admit Western States on the terms here stated." Madison insisted "that the Western States neither would nor ought to submit to a Union which degraded them from an equal rank with the other States." Mason sagely observed that "If it were possible by just means to prevent emigration to the Western Country, it might be good policy. But go the people will as they find it for their interest, and the best policy is to treat them with that equality which will make them friends not enemies." After this motion had been adopted, Morris offered a substitute article which was accepted: "New States may be admitted by the Legislature into this Union: but no new State shall be erected within the limits of any of the present States, without the consent of the Legislature of such State, as well as of the Genl. Legislature."[4]

Carroll of Maryland opposed the requirement of a state's consent to its being divided. He considered it necessary to safeguard the rights of the United States to the territory ceded by the large states. "He suggested that it might be proper to provide that nothing in the Constitution should affect the Right of the U.S. to lands ceded by G. Britain in the Treaty of peace." Wilson was alarmed at the notion that a political society is to be torn asunder without its own consent.[5]

In order to deal with the case of Vermont, which was regarded as an existing state which should not have to procure the consent of New York as a prerequisite to its admission, Dr. Johnson proposed to insert the words "hereafter formed or" before "erected" in the Morris sub-

---

[3] Art. XVII. *Ibid.*, II, 188 (August 6). Stages in the elaboration of this provision are shown in the working drafts of Randolph and Wilson. *Ibid.*, II, 147–48, 159, 173.
   [4] *Ibid.*, II, 446, 454–55 (August 29).   [5] *Ibid.*, II, 462 (August 30).

stitute. This amendment was adopted, as was another offered by Morris himself to take care of the Vermont situation, substituting "jurisdiction" for "limits."[6] As amended, the proposition was adopted, after a substitute vehemently urged by Luther Martin of Maryland which would have empowered Congress to erect new states "within as well as without the territory claimed by the several States or either of them, and admit the same into the Union," was defeated.[7]

Dickinson thereupon proposed an additional clause, which was adopted: "Nor shall any State be formed by the junction of two or more States or parts thereof, without the consent of the Legislatures of such States, as well as of the Legislature of the United States."[8]

Carroll then revived his proposal to add a proviso that "nothing in this Constitution shall be construed to affect the claim of the United States to vacant lands ceded to them by the late Treaty of peace."[9] Wilson objected that it was best to leave everything "on that litigated subject in statu quo." Madison likewise "thought it best on the whole to be silent on the subject" but saw no harm in Carroll's proviso. But it should in fairness go further and "declare that the claims of particular States also should not be affected." Carroll thereupon withdrew his motion in favor of one that "Nothing in this Constitution shall be construed to alter the claims of the United States or of the individual States to the western territory but all such claims may be examined into and decided upon by the supreme Court of the United States."[10]

In lieu of this, Gouverneur Morris proposed: "The Legislature shall have power to dispose of and make all needful rules and regulations respecting the territory or other property belonging to the United States: and nothing in this Constitution contained shall be so construed as to prejudice any claims either of the United States or of any particular State." Luther Martin proposed to add "But all such claims may be examined into and decided upon by the Supreme Court of the United States." Morris objected to this as unnecessary since all suits to which the United States shall be a party "are already to be decided by the Supreme Court."[11] Martin's amendment was defeated, and the Morris

---

[6] *Ibid.*, II, 457, 463 (August 30).   [7] *Ibid.*, II, 457–58, 464 (August 30).
[8] *Ibid.*, II, 458, 465 (August 30).   [9] *Ibid.*, II, 458, 465 (August 30).
[10] *Ibid.*, II, 458, 465–66 (August 30).
[11] *Ibid.*, II, 458–59, 466 (August 30). Madison had previously offered a proposal which was referred to the Committee of Detail to empower Congress "To dispose of the unappropriated lands of the United States" and "To institute temporary govern-

version of Carroll's proposition adopted.[12] Only verbal changes were made by the Committee of Style,[13] although Morris later stated that in his opinion Congress could not admit as a new state territory which did not belong to the United States when the Constitution was adopted. He commented that "In wording the third section of the fourth article, I went as far as circumstances would permit to establish the exclusion. Candor obliges me to add my belief, that, had it been more pointedly expressed, a strong opposition would have been made."[14]

INTERPRETATION

BY this clause Congress is empowered to admit new states "into this Union"; and "this Union," as established by the Constitution among the states ratifying it, is a union of equals. Hence a new state, upon its admission, enters the union upon an equal footing with the other states composing the union.[15] The Supreme Court has uniformly applied this principle.[16]

ments for new States arising thereon." *Ibid.*, II, 321, 324 (August 18). For the report of that committee, see *ibid.*, II, 367 (August 22).

[12] *Ibid.*, II, 459, 466 (August 30).

[13] *Ibid.*, II, 602 (September 12). An amendment offered by Gerry in convention was rejected as unnecessary. *Ibid.*, II, 628 (September 15).

[14] Morris to Henry W. Livingston, December 4, 1803. *Ibid.*, III, 404. Morris must be referring to his amendments during debate rather than to his revision as a member of the Committee of Style. Yet it seems that the language offered by Morris is less explicit in effecting his intention than the original version reported by the Committee of Detail, which expressly confined the admission of new states to those established "within the limits of the United States." See note 3, page 423, above. Morris probably had in mind his amendment giving Congress power over "the territory or other property" of the United States. See note 11, page 424, above. This provision furnished a means of governing existing or after-acquired territories without admitting them as new states. He told Livingston: "I always thought that, when we should acquire Canada and Louisiana it would be proper to govern them as provinces, and allow them no voice in our councils."

[15] Coyle v. Oklahoma, 221 U.S. 559, 567 (1911). The equality of new states with the old, as contemplated by Madison and Mason in the convention, thus won general acceptance notwithstanding the success of Gouverneur Morris in eliminating express language recognizing such equality. See note 4, page 423, and note 14 just above.

[16] Pollard v. Hagan, 3 How. 212, 223–24 (1845), was the first case giving expression to the rule of equal footing. With respect to the state's ownership of land between high and low tide, that case was weakened by U.S. v. California, 332 U.S. 19, 30, 38 (1947), holding that the United States, rather than the states, had "dominion" of oil lands under the three-mile zone of marginal sea. The principle of equality among the states was not questioned, however, by the tidelands decision. See also Permoli v. First Municipality, 3 How. 609 (1845); Withers v. Buckley, 20 How.

Upon the admission of a new state, its legislative power supersedes territorial enactments, including the provisions of the Ordinance of 1787 enacted by the old Congress for the government of the Northwest Territory and continued in effect by federal authority after the adoption of the Constitution.[17] Likewise superseded are any provisions which Congress may have sought to impose on the new state which are inconsistent with the state's equal status or which Congress could not have validly enacted after the admission of the state or with respect to other states.[18]

Thus Oklahoma, after admission, could pass a law in 1910 providing for immediate transfer of the state's capital to Oklahoma City, although Congress had ordained that Guthrie should be the capital until 1913.[19] Likewise in 1911, Arizona was required, as a condition of admission, to adopt a proposed amendment to its constitution,[20] since President William H. Taft found objectionable a provision therein for recall of judges. At the general election of December 12, 1911, the people of Arizona approved the amendment proposed by Congress and inserted the words "except members of the judiciary" in the recall provision. Arizona was then admitted on February 14, 1912. At the general election of November 5, 1912, the words inserted in the constitution were deleted, and the provision as it had stood originally became effective on December 5, 1912. It was conceded in Congress, and by President Taft himself, that upon becoming a state Arizona could rid itself of the restriction imposed as a condition of admission, and that the federal government had no power to prevent such action.[21]

84, 92–93 (1858); Willamette Bridge Co. v. Hatch, 125 U.S. 1, 9 (1888); Ward v. Race Horse, 163 U.S. 504, 511 (1896); Coyle v. Oklahoma, 221 U.S. 559, 570 (1911); Skiriotes v. Florida, 331 U.S. 69, 77 (1941).

[17] Permoli v. First Municipality, 3 How. 609, 610 (1845); Willamette Bridge Co. v. Hatch, 125 U.S. 1, 9 (1888).

[18] Pollard v. Hagan, 3 How. 212, 229 (1845); Coyle v. Oklahoma, 221 U.S. 559, 573 (1911).

[19] 221 U.S. at 564–65, 579.

[20] Joint Resolution of August 21, 1911, 37 Stat. 39, 42. The Act of January 26, 1870, 16 Stat. 63, declared that Virginia "is admitted to representation in Congress as one of the States of the Union upon the following fundamental conditions: First, That the Constitution of Virginia shall never be so amended or changed as to deprive any citizen or class of citizens of the United States of the right to vote . . . [or] of the school rights and privileges secured by the Constitution of the said State."

[21] Edward Dumbauld, "Interstate Commerce and the Mode of Admission of States into the Union," *I.C.C. Practitioners' Journal*, Vol. XII, No. 9 (June, 1945), 915.

It is valid for Congress to provide, when admitting a new state, that the United States shall retain ownership of public lands.[22] Where no such reservation is made, all property rights of the predecessor government pass to the new state upon admission.[23] In the absence of any reservation for the benefit of Indian tribes, their hunting privileges under treaties with the United States are superseded by the regulations established by the new state.[24]

With regard to regulations respecting the territory or other property of the United States, the power of Congress is without limitation.[25] "With respect to the public domain, the Constitution vests in Congress the power of disposition and of making all needful rules and regulations. That power is subject to no limitations. Congress has the absolute right to prescribe the times, the conditions, and the mode of transferring this property, or any part of it, and to designate the persons to whom the transfer shall be made. No State legislation can interfere with this right or embarrass its exercise."[26]

With regard to governmental powers, as distinguished from proprietary rights, the power of the Congress must of course be exercised in accordance with applicable constitutional limitations. During the slavery controversy the Supreme Court asserted that the powers of Congress under Article IV, section 3, clause 2, related only to the Northwest Territory which had been ceded to the United States by

[22] Pollard v. Hagan, 3 How. 212, 223 (1845); Gibson v. Chouteau, 13 Wall. 92, 99 (1872); Van Brocklin v. Tennessee, 117 U.S. 151, 168 (1886); Stearns v. Minnesota, 179 U.S. 223, 244–45 (1900).

[23] Brown v. Grant, 116 U.S. 207, 212 (1886); U.S. v. Utah, 283 U.S. 64, 75 (1931). However, having held in U.S. v. California, 332 U.S. 19, 38–39 (1947), that the national government, and not the states, had "dominion" of lands lying below the low-water mark within the three-mile limit offshore, the Supreme Court in U.S. v. Texas, 339 U.S. 707, 718 (1950), applied the principle of equality and held that Texas, upon its admission, had relinquished to the federal government the right to such property which Texas had theretofore enjoyed as an independent sovereignty.

[24] Ward v. Race Horse, 163 U.S. 504, 505–507 (1896). Pointing out that the act admitting Wyoming (unlike the earlier act establishing it as a territory) made no reservation of Indian rights, the Court held that a treaty was superseded by later conflicting legislation by Congress, and that the hunting privilege terminated with respect to lands owned by the government which became part of the new state. *Ibid.*, 506, 511, 514.

[25] U.S. v. California, 332 U.S. 19, 27 (1947).

[26] Gibson v. Chouteau, 13 Wall. 92, 99 (1872). See also Pollard v. Hagan, 3 How. 212, 224 (1845); Van Brocklin v. Tennessee, 117 U.S. 151, 167–68 (1886). The last-named case holds that a state cannot tax property owned by the United States.

states at the time when the Constitution was adopted.[27] However, it seems clear that under earlier pronouncements in the time of Chief Justice Marshall the power of the United States to govern newly acquired territory (such as the Louisiana Purchase[28]) was recognized as unquestionable.[29] After the Spanish-American War of 1898, the Supreme Court developed the distinction between "incorporated" and "unincorporated" territories. With regard to the latter certain constitutional provisions (such as the guarantee of jury trial) were held to be inapplicable.[30] In a recent utterance the Court indicated that all activities of the United States government, in any part of the world, must be carried on in accordance with the fundamental law upon which its legal existence depends.[31]

By virtue of its power to govern territories, Congress can establish local courts which are "legislative courts" as distinguished from the "constitutional courts" established by virtue of Article III and exercising the judicial power of the United States.[32]

[27] Dred Scott v. Sandford, 19 How. 393, 432, 435–36 (1857). It was also said that the United States could acquire territory only with a view to its ultimate incorporation as a state or states. *Ibid.*, 447.

[28] Jefferson himself had been dubious regarding the constitutionality of acquiring this vast "empire for liberty." Dumbauld, *The Political Writings of Thomas Jefferson*, 50, 144. Federalists opposed the acquisition because, like Gouverneur Morris in the constitutional convention, they feared that the political predominance of the seaboard states would be destroyed.

[29] American Ins. Co. v. Canter, 1 Pet. 511, 543 (1828). Marshall declared that "the constitution confers absolutely on the government of the Union, the powers of making war, and of making treaties; consequently, that government possesses the power of acquiring territory, either by conquest or by treaty. . . . The right to govern may be the inevitable consequence of the right to acquire territory." Chief Justice Taney's attempt in his Dred Scott opinion to distinguish this case because it did not derive the power to govern territory from Art. IV, sec. 3, cl. 2, seems rather unconvincing. Marshall did mention that clause as an alternative source of the power. 1 Pet. at 546.

[30] Balzac v. Porto Rico, 258 U.S. 298, 304–305, 312 (1922). For comment on the Insular Cases, see Reid v. Covert, 354 U.S. 1, 13 (1957). See also page 371 above.

[31] Reid v. Covert, 354 U.S. 1, 12 (1957).

[32] American Insurance Co. v. Canter, 1 Pet. 511, 546 (1828); Balzac v. Porto Rico, 258 U.S. 298, 312 (1922). See pages 179–80 and 322 above.

Republican Government

ART. IV, SEC. 4

The United States shall guarantee to every State in this Union a Republican Form of Government, and shall protect each of them against Invasion; and on Application of the Legislature, or of the Executive (when the Legislature cannot be convened) against domestic Violence.

HISTORY

THE Virginia Plan contained a resolution "that a Republican Government & the territory of each State except in the instance of a voluntary junction of Government & territory, ought to be guaranteed by the United States to each State."[1] Read of Delaware "disliked the idea of guaranteeing territory." The provision was amended on motion of Madison to read "that a republican constitution, and it's existing laws ought to be guaranteed to each State by the United States."[2] Randolph emphasized that "republican government must be the basis of our national union; and no state in it ought to have it in their power to change its government into a monarchy."[3] In convention this wording likewise evoked strong objections. Gouverneur Morris was very unwilling to guarantee the laws of Rhode Island. Houston disfavored "perpetuating the existing Constitutions of the States. That of Georgia was a very bad one" which he hoped would be revised and amended. Wilson explained that the object was merely to secure the states against "dangerous commotions, insurrections, and rebellions." Mason feared that if the federal government could not suppress rebellions against particular states, it would "remain a passive Spectator of its own subversion." Randolph, Gorham, Carroll, and Rutledge spoke in favor of the power. At Wilson's suggestion the language was modified to

[1] Resolution XI. Farrand, *Records*, I, 22 (May 29). Consideration of this resolution in Committee of the Whole was postponed on June 5. *Ibid.*, I, 117, 121.

[2] *Ibid.*, I, 194, 202 (June 11). This was accepted in Committee of the Whole. *Ibid.*, I, 237 (June 13).

[3] *Ibid.*, I, 206 (June 11).

read: "That a republican form of Government shall be guaranteed to each State—and that each State shall be protected against foreign and domestic violence."[4]

Randolph's draft in the Committee of Detail analyzed the objective as follows:

> The guarantee is
> 1. to prevent the establishment of any government, not republican
> 2. to protect each state against internal commotion: and
> 3. against external invasion.
> 4. But this guarantee shall not operate in the last Case without an application from the legislature of a state.[5]

The Committee of Detail reported an article providing: "The United States shall guaranty to each State a Republican form of Government; and shall protect each State against foreign invasions, and, on the application of its Legislature, against domestic violence."[6] In convention the word "foreign" was stricken out as superfluous, and "or Executive" was added after "Legislature."[7] The Committee of Style made several verbal changes: "The United States shall guarantee to every state in this union a Republican form of government, and shall protect each of them against invasion; and on application of the legislature or executive, against domestic violence."[8] In convention the words "when the legislature cannot be convened" were added.[9]

INTERPRETATION

THE guarantee by the United States in this clause contemplates affirmative action, and the employment, if necessary, of armed force.[10]

[4] *Ibid.*, II, 39, 47–49 (July 18).

[5] *Ibid.*, II, 148. Rutledge noted that items 2 and 3 should be transposed, and added the words "in the last Case." The requirement for application therefore applies only to "internal commotion." A later working draft in Wilson's hand introduced the terms "foreign Invasion" and "domestic Violence." *Ibid.*, II, 159. Another such draft also listed among the powers of Congress one "to subdue a Rebellion in any State, on the Application of its Legislature." *Ibid.*, II, 168, 174, 182. This was deleted after debate. *Ibid.*, II, 313, 317–18 (August 17).

[6] Art. XVIII. *Ibid.*, II, 188 (August 6).   [7] *Ibid.*, II, 459, 466–67 (August 30).

[8] *Ibid.*, II, 602 (September 12).

[9] *Ibid.*, II, 621, 628–29 (September 5). This change had been accepted as an amendment to the moribund provision empowering Congress to subdue rebellions. *Ibid.*, II, 312, 317–18 (August 17). See note 5 just above.

[10] The guarantee is similar to that of an international alliance, or the much-

Accordingly, it was only natural that the Supreme Court should conclude that determination whether a state's form of government is republican or not is a political question, to be decided by the political branches of the government, rather than by the judiciary.[11] The principle that this issue presents only a political question, which the courts will not decide, has been consistently maintained.[12]

Presumably any type of government in vogue in the United States at the time of the adoption of the Constitution would be considered to be an acceptable variety of republican government.[13] It is not requisite that the state's governmental structure be similar in all respects to that of the federal government. A state may mold its own institutions as it sees fit, and need not follow the federal pattern with respect to delegation and distribution of power among the various branches of the government.[14]

publicized Article X of the League of Nations Covenant where "The Members of the League undertake to respect and preserve as against external aggression the territorial integrity and existing political independence of all Members of the League."

[11] Luther v. Borden, 7 How. 1, 42 (1849). The Court points out that it must be determined what government is established in a state before it can be determined whether it is republican in form. Apparently the reception of Senators and Representatives from a state in Congress is considered as recognizing the acceptability of the state's form of government. The Court says that this recognition by Congress is binding upon every other department of government. But it would seem that to "protect" a state against invasion might be an executive function, and the President might not be bound to accept the view of the Congress. See also Texas v. White, 7 Wall. 700, 730 (1869).

[12] Taylor and Marshall v. Beckham (No. 1), 178 U.S. 548, 578, 580 (1900); Pacific States Tel. & Tel. Co. v. Oregon, 223 U.S. 118, 151 (1912); Davis v. Ohio, 241 U.S. 565, 568 (1916); Cochran v. La. State Bd. of Education, 281 U.S. 370, 374 (1930); Baker v. Carr, 369 U.S. 186, 209, 218–29 (1962).

[13] Minor v. Happersett, 21 Wall. 162, 175–76 (1875). Hence, as women did not then vote, Missouri did not deviate from a republican form of government by confining suffrage to male citizens. For Jefferson's definition of republican government,

[14] South Carolina v. United States, 199 U.S. 437, 454 (1905); Michigan Central see Dumbauld, *The Political Writings of Thomas Jefferson,* 51–53, 55, 114–18. R.R. Co. v. Powers, 201 U.S. 245, 294 (1906); Highland Farms Dairy v. Agnew, 300 U.S. 608, 612 (1937). Hence a Virginia statute establishing a milk control commission was held not to be "a denial of a republican form of government." Even if it were, the Court points out, the enforcement of the guarantee contained in Art. IV, sec. 4, is a matter for Congress, not the courts. So, too, the use of initiative or referendum as part of a state's legislative process does not violate this provision of the Constitution. Davis v. Ohio, 241 U.S. 565, 568 (1916). See also page 390 above.

Congress may investigate Communism in aid of its legislative function to protect the states from potential threats against their republican form of government.[15]

[15] Barsky v. United States, 167 F.(2d) 241, 246 (D.C. App. 1948). Federal legislation against subversive activities (not shown to be directed specifically against the state government) was held to "occupy the field" to the exclusion of similar state legislation in Pennsylvania v. Nelson, 350 U.S. 497, 502 (1956).

ARTICLE V—THE AMENDING POWER

The Congress, whenever two thirds of both Houses shall deem it necessary, shall propose Amendments to this Constitution, or, on the Application of the Legislatures of two thirds of the several States, shall call a Convention for proposing Amendments, which, in either Case, shall be valid to all Intents and Purposes, as Part of this Constitution, when ratified by the Legislatures of three fourths of the several States, or by Conventions in three fourths thereof, as the one or the other Mode of Ratification may be proposed by the Congress; Provided that no Amendment which may be made prior to the Year One thousand eight hundred and eight shall in any Manner affect the first and fourth Clauses in the Ninth Section of the first Article; and that no State, without its Consent, shall be deprived of it's equal Suffrage in the Senate.

HISTORY

THE Virginia Plan contained a resolution "that provision ought to be made for the amendment of the Articles of Union whensoever it shall seem necessary, and that the assent of the National Legislature ought not to be required thereto."[1]

Randolph's working draft in the Committee of Detail, as revised by Rutledge, provided for the calling of a convention upon application by two-thirds of the state legislatures to Congress.[2] The Committee of Detail reported the same scheme,[3] which was agreed to in convention.[4] On reconsideration, Hamilton observed that the states would never seek amendments except to increase their own powers, and that Congress should be given power to call a convention.[5] Sherman moved to add a provision giving Congress power to propose amendments for acceptance by the states. Wilson's proposal to require the assent of

[1] Resolution XIII. Farrand, *Records*, I, 22 (May 29). The proposition was postponed on June 5. *Ibid.*, I, 117, 122. The latter part was again postponed on June 11. *Ibid.*, I, 194, 202–203, 237. The first part was accepted in convention. *Ibid.*, II, 84, 87 (July 23).

[2] *Ibid.*, II, 148. See also *ibid.*, II, 159, 174. [3] Art. XIX. *Ibid.*, II, 188 (August 6).

[4] *Ibid.*, II, 461, 468 (August 30). [5] *Ibid.*, II, 558 (September 10).

433

three-fourths of the states was agreed to. In lieu of the article as amended, language offered by Madison was accepted: "The Legislature of the United States, whenever two thirds of both Houses shall deem necessary, or on the application of two thirds of the Legislatures of the several States, shall propose amendments to this Constitution which shall be valid to all intents and purposes as part thereof, when the same shall have been ratified by three fourths at least of the Legislatures of the several States, or by Conventions in three fourths thereof, as one or the other mode of ratification may be proposed by the Legislature of the United States." Upon the insistence of Rutledge was added a proviso that no amendments made prior to the year 1808 should in any manner affect the provisions relating to protection of the slave trade.[6] The Committee of Style made only verbal changes.[7]

In convention Sherman expressed "fears that three fourths of the States might be brought to do things fatal to particular States," such as "abolishing them altogether or depriving them of their equality in the Senate." Accordingly he favored extension of the proviso in favor of the slave trade to provide "that no State should be affected in its internal police, or deprived of its equality in the Senate." Mason pointed out that it was "exceptionable & dangerous" to make amendments dependent upon the approval of Congress; Congress itself might become oppressive, and its own conduct occasion the need for amendments. Accordingly, Gouverneur Morris, seconded by Gerry, proposed to add language requiring a convention upon the application of two thirds of the states. This was adopted.[8] Several other proposed modifications were voted down,[9] but to conciliate "the circulating murmurs of the small States" a further proviso was agreed to without debate upon motion of Gouverneur Morris, "that no State without its consent shall be deprived of its equal suffrage in the Senate."[10]

[6] *Ibid.*, II, 555, 557–59 (September 10). The slave trade provisions were then in Art. VII, sec. 4 and sec. 5. Perhaps this change from calling a convention to proposing amendments directly was the incident referred to in the anecdote related by Mason to Jefferson. *Ibid.*, III, 367. Cf. *ibid.*, II, 629–30 (September 15).

[7] *Ibid.*, II, 602 (September 12). It substituted "Congress" for "Legislature of the United States," and left a blank for the slave trade provisions.

[8] *Ibid.*, II, 629–30 (September 15).

[9] *Ibid.*, II, 630. These included a proviso by Sherman regarding internal police and equal suffrage in the Senate, and his subsequent motion to strike out Art. V altogether.

[10] *Ibid.*, II, 631 (September 15).

INTERPRETATION

THE second of the two methods of proposing amendments to the Constitution provided in this article (namely a convention called at the request of the legislatures of two-thirds of the states) has never been used. Yet its existence continues to serve the purpose which Gouverneur Morris had in mind when he proposed it.[11] It places an effective remedy at the disposition of the people of the states if abuses on the part of Congress itself should become an evil requiring amendment and Congress should fail or refuse to act.

Two methods of ratification of amendments to the Constitution are also provided: by the legislatures of three-fourths of the states, or by conventions in the same number of states. It should be noted that the option of choosing between these modes of ratification is given to Congress.[12] Only "the one or the other" mode may be selected. Congress cannot leave it to the discretion of the states to employ whichever of the two modes best suits local convenience. A ratifying state must follow the procedure specified by Congress.

Only two restrictions limit the amending power. One of these (protecting the slave trade and requiring apportionment of direct taxes[13]) is obsolete. The provisions of Article I, section 9, clause 1, regarding the slave trade expired by their own terms in 1808. The provisions of Article I, section 9, clause 4, regarding direct taxes became unimportant after the Sixteenth Amendment in 1913 gave Congress power to provide for the nation's revenue needs by means of the income tax, without regard to apportionment among the states.

The other limitation on the amending power is a permanent prohibition against any amendment whereby any state, without its consent, would be deprived of its equal suffrage in the Senate.[14] If a proposed amendment eliminating equality of representation in the Senate were ratified by every state, it would be valid. For if every state assented to the amendment, no state would be deprived of equal representation

[11] See note 8, page 434, above.

[12] U.S. v. Sprague, 282 U.S. 716, 730 (1931).

[13] Art. I, sec. 9, cl. 1; Art. I, sec. 9, cl. 4.

[14] Such equality is provided by Art. I, sec. 3, cl. 1, under which each state has two Senators. Amendments increasing or decreasing the number of Senators allowed to each state would not violate Art. V so long as the same number was allowed to every state.

without its consent. Hence the proviso with respect to amendments affecting equal representation simply amounts to a requirement of unanimity in order to adopt an amendment affecting that basic feature of the original Constitution.

Without such unanimity, there is no method by which an amendment depriving any state of equal representation in the Senate could become effective[15] (short of revolutionary action by the people, of course, such as brought about the substitution of the Constitution for the earlier Articles of Confederation, which required unanimous consent of the states for their amendment).[16]

Popular acquiescence in a constitutional change, even if the change is effected in a manner contrary to pre-existing law, is an irresistible factor in establishing the legal validity of the innovation, particularly in a nation founded upon the political philosophy that all just government derives its rightful powers from the consent of the governed.[17]

In the process of adopting amendments to the Constitution, Congress is not exercising legislative power but is acting as the delegated agent of the people.[18] Similarly the state legislatures are not exercising

[15] Professor William Starr Myers of Princeton University used to assert that equality in the Senate could be eliminated in two stages: the first would be an amendment eliminating the proviso in Art. V, and the second would be the amendment changing representation in the Senate. But this position is clearly fallacious. The amendment eliminating the proviso would certainly be in itself a palpable violation of the terms of the proviso, and hence invalid.

[16] It was provided in Art. XIII of the Articles of Confederation that "the articles of this confederation shall be inviolably observed by every State, and the Union shall be perpetual; nor shall any alteration hereafter be made in any of them; unless such alteration be agreed to in a Congress of the United States, and be afterwards confirmed by the Legislatures of every State." It was recognized by the framers that adoption of the new Constitution would effect a revolution. See page 456 below.

[17] Dumbauld, *The Declaration of Independence and What It Means Today*, 73–82. Acquiescence acquires further force from the legal rules characterizing certain issues as political questions, as to which the courts will not interfere, and those with respect to standing to sue, whereby it often happens that no one is in a position to challenge the legality of political action. See note 28, page 101, and pages 329 and 333 above. See also Fairchild v. Hughes, 258 U.S. 126, 129–30 (1922); Coleman v. Miller, 307 U.S. 433, 450, 454 (1939). Doubts as to whether the Fourteenth Amendment was duly ratified and went into effect have been settled by long-continued popular acquiescence. 307 U.S. at 448–50.

[18] U.S. v. Sprague, 282 U.S. 716, 733 (1931). Hence an amendment is not submitted to the President and he has no veto power with respect thereto. Hollingsworth v. Virginia, 3 Dall. 378, 381–82 (1798).

legislative power but are merely expressing the assent of the state to the proposed amendment.[19] This is a federal function.[20]

Congress is not required to make a preliminary declaration that it deems an amendment "necessary" before proposing the amendment to the states for ratification. The action of Congress in voting to submit the proposed amendment to the states is a sufficient indication that Congress considers the proposal a "necessary" one.[21] The requirement of "two thirds of both Houses" in order to propose an amendment means, in the opinion of the Supreme Court, merely a two-thirds vote of the members present (a quorum being present), not two-thirds of the entire membership of each house.[22]

An amendment becomes effective on the date of the last necessary ratification by a state, not when it is proclaimed by the Secretary of State.[23] The states must ratify an amendment within a reasonable time after it is submitted for their consideration, in order for their ratifications to be effective[24]; and Congress in proposing the amendment may determine what period would be a reasonable time for ratification.[25] When no period has been fixed in advance, it is a political question whether an attempted ratification comes too late.[26] It is also a political question whether a state may ratify a proposed amendment after having once rejected it.[27] As to whether it is a political question whether

[19] Hawke v. Smith, 253 U.S. 221, 229 (1920).

[20] *Ibid.*, 230. Hence state law cannot provide for the submission of amendments to a popular referendum. Only the "Legislatures" are specified in the federal Constitution as the organs for expressing the assent of the states. To the same effect see Leser v. Garnett, 258 U.S. 130, 137 (1922); and National Prohibition Cases, 253 U.S. 350, 386 (1920).

[21] National Prohibition Cases, 253 U.S. 350, 386 (1920). Compare the interpretation of "necessary" in Art. I, sec. 8, cl. 18. McCulloch v. Maryland, 4 Wheat. 316, 413–20 (1819).

[22] 253 U.S. at 386.

[23] Dillon v. Gloss, 265 U.S. 368, 376 (1921).

[24] *Ibid.*, 375. Nothing in the Constitution says this. It is purely a judicial gloss.

[25] *Ibid.*, 376. Seven years was the time specified for ratification of the Eighteenth, Twentieth, Twenty-first, and Twenty-second Amendments. These cluttering transitory provisions, repeatedly embodied in the Constitution, detract from its dignity. Their purpose would be better served by specifying the period for ratification in the resolution of transmittal to the states, rather than in the text of the proposed amendment itself. Denys P. Myers, *The Process of Constitutional Amendment*, 28.

[26] Coleman v. Miller, 307 U.S. 433, 454 (1939).

[27] *Ibid.*, 450. Logic would indicate that it may. Art. V says that an amendment

the lieutenant governor of a state may vote in the state senate in order to break a tie (in other words whether such executive officials constitute part of the "Legislatures" referred to in Article V) the members of the Supreme Court were unable to muster a majority and necessarily left the point undecided.[28]

With respect to the content of amendments (as distinguished from the procedure for adopting them) no attempts to impose limitations on the amending power have ever been successfully urged.[29] With regard to the Eighteenth Amendment (prohibiting sale of intoxicating liquors), ingenious lawyers, including the eminent Elihu Root, contended in vain that the terms of this amendment were not within the amending power as established in Article V. Root argued that the amendment contained direct legislation, and thus conflicted with Article I, section 1, vesting all delegated legislative power in Congress; that an "amendment" must be germane to the original instrument, and not a complete innovation; and that the Eighteenth Amendment invaded the rights of the states under the federal system, in this respect differing from the post–Civil War amendments, which were germane to federal duties specified in the original Constitution.[30] These arguments failed to make any impression on the Supreme Court.[31] Likewise futile was the effort to upset the Nineteenth Amendment (providing for woman

becomes effective "when ratified," without specifying that a state has only one opportunity to act, once and for all, on the question of ratification. Whether a state may reject a proposed amendment after having once ratified it was apparently decided (politically) in the negative when the retracted ratifications of Ohio and New Jersey were counted in determining that the Fourteenth Amendment had been duly ratified. See *Documentary History of the Constitution of the United States*, II, 783–94; and note 17, page 436, above.

[28] *Ibid.*, 447. The Court found the issue to be a federal question (cf. note 20, page 437, above), although unable to determine whether it was a political or justiciable question. *Ibid.*, 438. Cf. Leser v. Garnett, 258 U.S. 130, 137 (1922).

[29] As succinctly stated by the renowned Judge Learned Hand in U.S. v. Dennis, 183 F.(2d) 201, 206 (C.A. 2, 1950): "Any amendment to the Constitution passed in conformity with Article V is as valid as though it had been originally incorporated in it; the only exception being that no state shall be denied 'its equal Suffrage in the Senate'."

[30] National Prohibition Cases, 253 U.S. 350, 363, 364, 367 (1920).

[31] *Ibid.*, 386. Another attack on the Eighteenth Amendment was unsuccessfully made in U.S. v. Sprague, 282 U.S. 716, 734 (1931). It was there contended that ratification by conventions rather than legislatures was requisite since the amendment affected individual rights as distinguished from regulating the machinery of government. *Ibid.*, 729–30, 734.

suffrage) on the ground that it destroyed the autonomy of the states as political bodies by reason of making a change in the electorate.[32]

The function of Congress in proposing amendments to the Constitution justifies its exercise of investigatory powers in order to obtain necessary information and pertinent data upon the basis of which it may intelligently act.[33]

[32] Leser v. Garnett, 258 U.S. 130, 136 (1922). The Court pointed out that the Fifteenth Amendment, which has been accepted as valid, had the same effect. The Fifteenth Amendment was not upheld simply as a war measure.

[33] Barsky v. U.S., 167 F.(2d) 241, 246 (D.C. App. 1948).

Validity of Prior Obligations

ART. VI, CL. 1

All Debts contracted and Engagements entered into, before the Adoption of this Constitution, shall be as valid against the United States under this Constitution, as under the Confederation.

HISTORY

THE Virginia Plan recommended the continuance of the old Congress during a transitional period until the new government could commence operation, and "that provision ought to be made . . . for the completion of all their engagements."[1] This was eliminated in convention, but Madison offered a proposal that Congress be given power "To secure the payment of the public debt."[2] This was referred to the Committee of Detail. At the same time a grand committee was appointed "to consider the necessity and expediency of the debts of the several States being assumed by the United States."[3] The committee reported a proposal that "The Legislature of the United-States shall have power to fulfil the engagements which have been entered into by Congress, and to discharge as well the debts of the United States, as the debts incurred by the several States during the late war, for the common defence and general welfare."[4] In convention this was amended on motion of Gouverneur Morris to read: "The Legislature shall fulfil the engagements and discharge the debts of the United States."[5] Mason objected to this mandatory requirement. Other members indicated that

[1] Resolution XII. Farrand, *Records*, I, 22 (May 29). This provision regarding engagements of the old Congress was accepted in Committee of the Whole. *Ibid.*, I, 117, 121 (June 5); I, 237 (June 13). After some discussion it was eliminated in convention. *Ibid.*, II, 39, 47 (July 18).

[2] *Ibid.*, II, 322, 326 (August 18).

[3] *Ibid.*, II, 322, 326–28 (August 18). The motion was made by Rutledge, Gerry having also remarked that "some provision ought to be made in favor of public Securities."

[4] *Ibid.*, II, 352, 355–56 (August 21).

[5] *Ibid.*, II, 368, 377, 394 (August 22). This clause was inserted at the beginning of the clause conferring the taxing power. *Ibid.*, II, 382, 392, 394 (August 23). See note 3, page 106, above.

they wished to do no more than "leave the Creditors in statu quo," neither increasing nor decreasing their security. On motion of Randolph the language was modified to provide that "all debts contracted and engagements entered into, by or under the authority of Congress shall be as valid against the United States under this constitution as under the confederation."[6] The Committee of Style substituted "before the adoption of this Constitution" for "by or under the authority of Congress."[7]

INTERPRETATION

THIS clause is now of merely historical importance. It was intended by its framers to protect public creditors by maintaining the status quo, and preserving the obligation of the United States under the new Constitution to pay debts incurred under the Confederation.

Although proponents of assumption by the federal government of state debts incurred during the Revolutionary War were not successful in obtaining inclusion in the Constitution of a provision authorizing such action, they were able to convince Congress to adopt Alexander Hamilton's financial program which included that item. Madison opposed the program because it would benefit speculators who had acquired the debt certificates at a bargain, at the expense of the war veterans to whom they had originally been issued. The plan was also unfair to those states that had made substantial payments on their own war debts, as it required them to bear a disproportionate share of the burden of national taxation in order to discharge the obligations of laggard states of whose war debts a relatively large part remained unpaid.

The assumption legislation was enacted as the result of a bargain with Southern leaders who desired the national capital to be located at a site on the Potomac.[8]

Unquestionably the war debts of the states were incurred for the common defense and general welfare of the United States, and Con-

---

[6] *Ibid.*, II, 408, 414 (August 25).

[7] *Ibid.*, II, 603 (September 12). The provision was transferred from the article dealing with the powers of Congress (Art. I, sec. 8, cl. 1) to a new Art. VI.

[8] Brant, *James Madison*, III, 292–318; Malone, *Jefferson and the Rights of Man*, 289–303. The Act of August 4, 1790, 1 Stat. 142, provided for assumption of state debts. The Act of July 16, 1790, 1 Stat. 130, provided for "establishing the temporary and permanent seat of the Government of the United States."

gress had power to pay them out of national revenues derived from the proceeds of federal taxes. In spite of the bitter political opposition to assumption as a matter of expediency, there was no constitutional question raised challenging the power of Congress to pass the legislation which it enacted dealing with this topic.

ART. VI, CL. 2

This Constitution, and the Laws of the United States which shall be made in Pursuance thereof; and all Treaties made, or which shall be made, under the Authority of the United States, shall be the supreme Law of the Land; and the Judges in every State shall be bound thereby, any Thing in the Constitution or Laws of any State to the Contrary notwithstanding.

HISTORY

THE "supreme law of the land" clause was developed as a substitute for the federal negative on state laws which Madison strongly favored.[1] As he explained in 1831, "The obvious necessity of a controul on the laws of the States, so far as they might violate the Constn. & laws of the U.S. left no option but as to the mode." The need for an effective means of guarding the Constitution and laws of the Union against violations of them by the laws of the states "was felt and taken for granted by all from the commencement, to the conclusion of the work performed by the Convention."[2]

The Virginia Plan proposed to give the national government power "to negative all laws passed by the several States, contravening in the opinion of the National Legislature the articles of Union."[3] To this was added on motion of Franklin "or any treaties subsisting under the authority of the Union."[4] After acceptance in Committee of the Whole,[5] the scheme of a federal negative was defeated in convention.[6]

In place of the rejected mode of control over state laws, a proposal containing language taken from the New Jersey Plan[7] was accepted,

[1] Dumbauld, "Thomas Jefferson and American Constitutional Law," *loc. cit.*, 387.

[2] Farrand, *Records*, III, 516, 527.

[3] Resolution VI. *Ibid.*, I, 21 (May 29).

[4] *Ibid.*, I, 47, 54 (May 31). An attempt by Charles Pinckney, seconded by Mason, to extend the veto to all "improper" laws was defeated. *Ibid.*, I, 162, 164–68 (June 8).

[5] *Ibid.*, I, 236 (June 13).

[6] *Ibid.*, II, 21–22, 27–28 (July 17). An attempt by Charles Pinckney to revive it also failed. *Ibid.*, II, 382, 390–91 (August 23).

[7] *Ibid.*, I, 245 (June 15).

on motion of Luther Martin. This provision declared that "the legislative acts of the United States made by virtue and in pursuance of the articles of Union and all Treaties made and ratified under the authority of the United States shall be the supreme law of the respective States as far as those acts or Treaties shall relate to the said States, or their Citizens and Inhabitants—and that the Judiciaries of the several States shall be bound thereby in their decisions, any thing in the respective laws of the individual States to the contrary notwithstanding."[8]

Martin's original plan went no further than to proclaim the supremacy of federal laws and treaties over state *laws*.[9] It was strengthened by the Committee of Detail by providing for supremacy over state *constitutions* as well.[10] In convention, on motion of Rutledge, it was further strengthened by providing for supremacy of "this Constitution" as well as of federal laws and treaties.[11]

Subsequently, on motion of Madison, the words "or which shall be made" were inserted after "treaties made."[12] As explained in his notes: "This insertion was meant to obviate all doubt concerning the force of treaties pre-existing, by making the words 'all treaties made' to refer to them, as the words inserted would refer to future treaties."[13] The Committee of Style substituted "supreme law of the land" for "supreme law of the several States, and of their citizens and inhabitants" and eliminated "in their decisions" after "bound thereby."[14]

INTERPRETATION

THIS clause, commonly called the "supremacy" clause, ordains that

[8] *Ibid.*, II, 22, 28–29 (July 17).   [9] *Ibid.*, III, 286–87.

[10] Art. VIII. *Ibid.*, II, 183 (August 6). This change appears in a draft in Wilson's handwriting. *Ibid.*, II, 169. The Committee of Detail, besides other verbal changes, simplified the wording after "supreme law" to read "of the several States, and of their citizens and inhabitants; and the judges in [the several states shall be bound thereby in their decisions]."

[11] Rutledge's amendment speaks of "This Constitution and the Laws of the United States made in pursuance thereof" rather than merely of "The Acts of the Legislature of the United States made in pursuance of this Constitution" as did the Committee of Detail. *Ibid.*, II, 381–82, 389 (August 23). A corresponding change was later made, on motion of Dr. Johnson, in Art. III, sec. 2. *Ibid.*, II, 423, 430 (August 27).

[12] With respect to laws, "made" was changed at the same time to "which shall be made."

[13] *Ibid.*, II, 409, 417 (August 25). A corresponding change was later made, on motion of Rutledge, in Art. III, sec. 2. *Ibid.*, II, 423–24, 431 (August 27).

[14] *Ibid.*, II, 603 (September 12). It also substituted "constitution or laws of any state" for "constitutions or laws of the several States."

federal law shall prevail over state law in case of conflict between them. The Constitution itself, laws of the United States made in pursuance thereof, and treaties "made, or which shall be made" under the authority of the United States, are all declared to be the supreme law of the land.

The Constitution itself, of course, prevails over statutes or treaties inconsistent with it. Between valid statutes and treaties *inter sese* there is no priority, and the one of most recent date prevails over earlier expressions of the lawgiver's will.[15]

A statute, in order to be entitled to be deemed part of the law of the land, must be made in pursuance of the Constitution. An act of Congress not so made will be disregarded as unconstitutional by the courts.[16]

A treaty is not expressly required by the terms of the Constitution to be made in pursuance thereof, but must be one "made, or which shall be made" under the authority of the United States. This language was adopted in order to make clear that not only treaties made after the adoption of the Constitution but also those made under the authority of the United States during preceding constitutional regimes should be valid as supreme law of the land.[17] After the Constitution became operative, a treaty would have to be made in pursuance of the Constitution in order to be made under the authority of the United States.

Apparently federal judicial decisions,[18] as well as statutes and treaties, constitute part of the supreme law of the land which overrides state law. Acts of the executive department, duly performed in accordance with constitutional authority, seem to enjoy a similar preference over state law.[19]

The supremacy clause first assumed importance in a case involving debts owed by Virginians to British creditors.[20] The Supreme Court held that, even with respect to debts previously discharged by payment into the state treasury in accordance with Virginia law, the British credi-

[15] See notes 59 and 60, page 291, above.

[16] Marbury v. Madison, 1 Cr. 137, 178 (1803).

[17] Reid v. Covert, 354 U.S. 1, 16 (1957). See also Dumbauld, "John Marshall and Treaty Law," *loc. cit.*, 80; and notes 12–13, page 444, above.

[18] Cooper v. Aaron, 358 U.S. 1, 18 (1958). See also page 313 above.

[19] See note 70, page 293, above.

[20] Ware v. Hylton, 3 Dall. 199 (1796). John Marshall and Patrick Henry were losing counsel in the case. Dumbauld, "John Marshall and Treaty Law," *loc. cit.*, 70–71. A similar case was Fairfax's Devisee v. Hunter's Lessee, 7 Cr. 603, 622 (1813).

tors were entitled to recover by virtue of the Peace Treaty of 1783.[21]

While John Marshall was Chief Justice a series of his memorable decisions firmly established the proposition that by virtue of the supremacy clause a state law, even if enacted under the police power or other valid power possessed by the state, must yield if it conflicts with a federal law constitutionally enacted by Congress in the exercise of its delegated powers.[22] As Marshall said, "it has been contended that if a law, passed by a State in the exercise of its acknowledged sovereignty, comes into conflict with a law passed by Congress in pursuance of the constitution, they affect the subject, and each other, like equal opposing powers.

"But the framers of our constitution foresaw this state of things, and provided for it, by declaring the supremacy, not only of itself, but of the laws made in pursuance of it. The nullity of any act, inconsistent with the constitution, is produced by the declaration that the constitution is the supreme law. The appropriate application of that part of the clause which confers the same supremacy on laws and treaties, is to such acts of the state legislatures as do not transcend their powers, but, though enacted in the execution of acknowledged state powers, interfere with, or are contrary to the laws of Congress, made in pursuance of the constitution, or some treaty made under the authority of the United States. In every such case, the act of Congress, or the treaty, is supreme; and the law of the state, though enacted in the exercise of powers not controverted, must yield to it."[23]

[21] 3 Dall. at 242–45, 256, 281, 282. Only Justice Iredell dissented. *Ibid.*, 272.
[22] McCulloch v. Maryland, 4 Wheat. 316, 405–406, 426 (1819); Cohens v. Virginia, 6 Wheat. 264, 381 (1821); Gibbons v. Ogden, 9 Wheat. 1, 210–11 (1824).
[23] 9 Wheat. at 210–11. In this case the Court found an actual collision between state law and an exercised power of Congress. *Ibid.*, 221. It was therefore not compelled to decide whether the power of Congress was exclusive and precluded state action even in the absence of exercise of the federal power. *Ibid.*, 209. In Cooley v. Board of Wardens, 12 How. 299, 318–20 (1851), it was held that the power of Congress is exclusive in matters requiring national uniformity of regulation. See Cloverleaf Butter Co. v. Patterson, 315 U.S. 148, 154–56 (1942); Southern Pacific Co. v. Arizona, 325 U.S. 761, 766–69, 781 (1945). When Congress does act, if it intends to "occupy the field" to the exclusion of additional regulation by the states, state regulation is invalid. Rice v. Santa Fe Elevator Corp., 331 U.S. 218, 234–37 (1947); Campbell v. Hussey, 368 U.S. 297, 300–302 (1961). Cf. Rice v. Chicago Bd. of Trade, 331 U.S. 247, 253–55 (1947). See note 36, page 421, above. The problem of interpreting the silence of Congress arises principally in connection with the interstate commerce power. See commentary on Art. I, sec. 8, cl. 3, above.

Many recent pronouncements of the Supreme Court enunciate the same principle. Thus a state selling timber from its school lands must obey the wartime price-control regulations enacted by Congress;[24] a state's regulation of transportation rates by means of a public utility commission's determinations must yield to the federal government's power to negotiate lower rates with the carriers;[25] a state's requirement that motor trucks be equipped with a certain type of mudguard flaps must give way if it burdens interstate commerce by reason of the fact that in most states a different type of flaps is required.[26]

Where there is no conflict between the state law and federal law, however, the state law remains operative unless federal law has "occupied the field."[27] Many close questions arise in determining whether Congress has occupied the field. The problem occurs particularly often in connection with the power of Congress to regulate interstate commerce.[28] For example, the scope of federal regulation of labor relations is so extensive that state action is largely ousted.[29] Another area of exclusive federal concern is the control of subversive activities (not directed specifically against a state).[30] In short, whenever state regulation conflicts with federal authority (whether expressly exercised or implicitly exerted through the doctrine of occupation of the field) the state law must yield, by virtue of the requirements of the supremacy clause.

Perhaps the supremacy clause, rather than "the supposed implications of our federal system," is the real basis of the rule striking down

[24] Case v. Bowles, 327 U.S. 92, 102–103 (1946). See also New York v. U.S., 326 U.S. 572, 575 (1946). In Morris v. Jones, 329 U.S. 545, 553 (1947), the Court said: "But where there is such a collision, the action of a State under its police power must give way by virtue of the Supremacy Clause."

[25] California P.U.C. v. U.S., 355 U.S. 534, 543 (1958); Paul v. U.S., 371 U.S. 245, 255 (1963); U.S. v. Georgia P.S.C., 371 U.S. 285, 287, 293 (1963).

[26] Bibb v. Navajo Freight Lines, 359 U.S. 520, 529 (1959).

[27] Thus in U.S. v. Burnison, 339 U.S. 87, 90 (1950), it was held that there was no violation of the supremacy clause when California forbade its citizens to leave property to the United States by will. The state was here curtailing the power of the individual to give, not that of the United States to take, a bequest. *Ibid.*, 91.

[28] See note 23, page 446, above.

[29] Bus Employees v. Wisconsin Board, 340 U.S. 383, 399 (1951).

[30] Pennsylvania v. Nelson, 350 U.S. 497, 502 (1956). With respect to broadcasting, the Supreme Court has said: "No state lines divide the radio waves, and national regulation is not only appropriate but essential to the efficient use of radio facilities." Federal Radio Commission v. Nelson Bros., 289 U.S. 266, 279 (1933).

447

state legislation deemed to obstruct or interfere with the due operation of the federal government.[31] Thus an Ohio law restricting the use of oleomargarine could not be applied to a federal home for old soldiers;[32] nor could Maryland require the driver of a mail truck to take an examination and obtain a license before performing his duties as prescribed by the Post Office Department.[33]

Determination of the extent and nature of the legal consequences flowing from federal legislation is a federal question; and in a domain where "the policy of the law is so dominated by the sweep of federal statutes" that legal relations which they affect are governed by rules of law derived therefrom, conflicting state law and policy must yield to the federal statute and policy, by virtue of the supremacy clause.[34]

[31] New York v. U.S., 326 U.S. 572, 575, 577 (1946); McCulloch v. Maryland, 4 Wheat. 316, 426, 431, 435–36 (1819). Nevertheless, some weight is still given to the principle that the American polity is "an indestructible Union, composed of indestructible States." Texas v. White, 7 Wall. 700, 725 (1869). Congress may not tax a state "as a state." 326 U.S. at 582. But the doctrine of "reciprocal immunity" of each government from taxation or crippling regulation by the other has lost its former potency. *Ibid.*, 576, 581. See note 81, page 78, above. State and municipal bonds are still exempt from federal income tax.

[32] Ohio v. Thomas, 173 U.S. 276, 284 (1899).

[33] Johnson v. Maryland, 254 U.S. 51, 56–57 (1920).

[34] Sola Electric Co. v. Jefferson Co., 317 U.S. 173, 176 (1942).

ARTICLE VI—FEDERAL-STATE RELATIONS
Oaths and Religious Tests

ART. VI, CL. 3

The Senators and Representatives before mentioned, and the Members of the several State Legislatures, and all executive and judicial Officers, both of the United States and of the several States, shall be bound by Oath or Affirmation, to support this Constitution; but no religious Test shall ever be required as a Qualification to any Office or public Trust under the United States.

HISTORY

THE Virginia Plan contained a provision "that the Legislative Executive & Judiciary powers within the several States ought to be bound by oath to support the articles of Union."[1] In Committee of the Whole considerable opposition was expressed, Gerry remarking that there was as much reason for requiring an oath of fidelity to the states from national officers as vice versa.[2] Williamson of North Carolina made the same point when the provision came up in convention. On motion of Gerry a similar oath was required of officials of the national government.[3] The Committee of Detail reported the article in the following form: "The members of the Legislatures, and the Executive and Judicial officers of the United States, and of the several States, shall be bound by oath to support this Constitution."[4]

In convention, on motion of Charles Pinckney, there was added the clause: "But no religious test shall ever be required as a qualification to any office or public trust under the authority of the United States."[5] The Committee of Style made only verbal changes.[6]

[1] Resolution XIV. Farrand, *Records*, I, 22 (May 29).

[2] *Ibid.*, I, 194, 203–204 (June 11); I, 237 (June 13). The topic had previously been postponed. *Ibid.*, I, 117, 123 (June 5).

[3] *Ibid.*, II, 84, 87–88 (July 23). [4] Art. XX. *Ibid.*, II, 188 (August 6).

[5] *Ibid.*, II, 461, 468 (August 30). The words "or affirmation" were also added after "oath." Pinckney had previously offered a clause that "No religious test or qualification shall ever be annexed to any oath of office under the authority of the United States." *Ibid.*, II, 335, 342 (August 20). This had been referred to the Committee of Detail, but no further action had been taken.

[6] *Ibid.*, II, 603 (September 12).

449

INTERPRETATION

REQUIRING state executive and judicial officers to take an oath to support the Constitution of the United States was one means of enforcing the provisions of the supremacy clause (Article VI, clause 2).

That federal officials should be bound by oath to support the Constitution seems so natural as to be almost a self-evident proposition, but in fact this requirement was added as a sort of retaliatory measure after it had been decided to exact such an oath of state officials.[7]

The form of oath to be taken by the President is specifically prescribed by the Constitution.[8] That oath is one to "preserve, protect and defend the Constitution." As the language of Article VI, clause 3, does not exclude the President when it speaks of "all executive" officers of the United States, it would seem that an oath to "preserve, protect and defend" the Constitution is regarded as equivalent to an oath to "support" it.

Since the Constitution has specifically prescribed the terms of the President's oath, it is questionable whether Congress may add anything to it or require an additional oath as a condition precedent to the exercise of executive functions.[9] With respect to other officers Congress has prescribed the form of oath to be taken, and such action is doubtless constitutional insofar as the oath prescribed by Congress is substantially equivalent to the oath of "support" required by Article VI, clause 3.

The fact that the inaugural ceremony at which a federal official commences his official duties takes the form of an oath does not make it a "religious Test."[10] The oath of office is merely the mode by which the official becomes "bound" to support the Constitution. If any additional consequences are attached to the oath by reason of the religious convictions of the incumbent, that is a private matter touching only his own conscience and having no significance from the standpoint of constitutional law.

The prohibition of any religious test as a qualification for federal officeholders was an expression of the distinctively American doctrine of separation between church and state which later led to the adoption of the First Amendment.[11] In the present connection it opened the door of

---

[7] See note 3, page 449, above. [8] Art. II, sec. 1, cl. 8.

[9] See pages 277–78 above. [10] See note 111, page 277, above.

[11] See Dumbauld, *The Bill of Rights and What It Means Today*, 103–15. Exclusion from public office was merely one form of civil disability formerly visited upon

public service to all otherwise qualified citizens without regard to their religious beliefs.[12]

Although the "new liberty" or "ordered liberty" theory of interpreting the "due process" clause of the Fourteenth Amendment as making applicable against the states certain basic provisions of the federal Bill of Rights (including the First Amendment's protection to religion)[13] has never explicitly been carried so far as to make Article VI, clause 3, enforceable against the states, yet in fact that is exactly what has been done in a recent decision.[14] A person appointed as a notary public in Maryland refused to take the oath required by that state's constitution[15] acknowledging belief in the existence of God. The Supreme Court held that this was a religious test.[16] Hence it was forbidden by the First Amendment provisions regarding religious liberty as made applicable against the states by the Fourteenth Amendment under the "ordered liberty" theory.[17] It may be doubted whether in this case the Court sufficiently heeded the force of Justice Holmes's quip[18]

---

dissenters from the established church in England. Tanner, *Constitutional Documents*, 109. They were also often required by law to pay for, or to participate in, the services of that church, and forbidden to engage in any other form of religious worship. Tanner, *Tudor Constitutional Documents*, 119–20, 153, 197. All of these restrictions were done away with by the First Amendment. Randolph at one time feared that prohibition of religious tests for public office might be construed as a "negative pregnant" recognizing the power of Congress over religion in other respects. Farrand, *Records*, III, 310.

[12] Supporters of President John F. Kennedy in the 1960 Presidential campaign pointed out that the practice of excluding an otherwise well-qualified candidate from the Presidency solely by reason of his adherence to the Roman Catholic faith was a violation of the principles embodied in Article VI, clause 3.

[13] Dumbauld, *The Bill of Rights and What It Means Today*, 132–34; Cantwell v. Connecticut, 310 U.S. 296, 303, (1940). First adumbrated in 1925, this theory has increasingly been in vogue with the Supreme Court ever since.

[14] Torcaso v. Watkins, 367 U.S. 488, 495–96 (1961).

[15] Art. 37 of the Maryland Bill of Rights provides "That no other test or qualification ought to be required on admission to any office of trust or profit than such oath of allegiance . . . and such oath of office and qualification as may be prescribed by this constitution, or by the laws of the State, and a declaration of belief in the Christian religion, or in the existence of God, and in a future state of rewards and punishments." Thorpe, *Federal and State Constitutions*, III, 1745. This is an amplification of Art. 35 of the Maryland Bill of Rights of 1776. *Ibid.*, 1690.

[16] 367 U.S. at 489. In other words, a violation of Art. VI, cl. 3, if applied to the states.

[17] 367 U.S. at 492, citing the Cantwell case. See note 13 just above.

[18] In McAuliffe v. New Bedford, 155 Mass. 216, 220 (1892).

that "The petitioner may have a constitutional right to talk politics [or to disbelieve in God], but he has no constitutional right to be a policeman [or a notary public]."[19]

With respect to federal employment, however, the prohibition of religious tests by Article VI, clause 3, is plain and indisputable.

[19] See 367 U.S. at 495–96.

ARTICLE VII—RATIFICATION

ART. VII

The Ratification of the Conventions of nine States, shall be sufficient for the Establishment of this Constitution between the States so ratifying the Same.

HISTORY

THE final resolution forming part of the Virginia Plan was one "that the amendments which shall be offered to the Confederation, by the Convention ought at a proper time, or times, after the approbation of Congress to be submitted to an assembly or assemblies of Representatives, recommended by the several Legislatures to be expressly chosen by the people, to consider & decide thereon."[1]

When this was first discussed in Committee of the Whole, Sherman opposed it, but Madison asserted that he "thought this provision essential." The Articles of Confederation themselves, he pointed out, were defective in this respect, having been in many states sanctioned only by the legislature. Hence later state legislation prevails over earlier acts of Congress. He therefore regarded it as "indispensable that the new Constitution should be ratified in the most unexceptionable form, and by the supreme authority of the people themselves." Wilson urged that the selfish opposition of a few states should not be permitted to defeat the desire of the majority "to confederate anew on better principles." He desired that "the provision for ratifying would be put on such a footing as to admit of such a partial union, with a door open for the accession of the rest." Charles Pinckney hoped that nine states would be permitted to unite under the new government if unanimity was not obtainable.[2]

In convention Mason, Randolph, Gorham, Williamson, and Gouverneur Morris adduced strong arguments of principle and expediency in favor of the requirement of ratification by the people. Ellsworth, Paterson, Gerry, and King favored ratification by the state legislatures. Madison again urged the necessity of ratification by the people of the

[1] Resolution XV. Farrand, *Records*, I, 22 (May 29).

[2] *Ibid.*, I, 122–23 (June 5). The resolution was adopted in Committee of the Whole. *Ibid.*, I, 209, 214 (June 12); I, 237 (June 13).

innovations to be proposed: "These changes would make essential inroads on the State Constitutions, and it would be a novel & dangerous doctrine that a Legislature could change the Constitution under which it held its existence. . . . He considered the difference between a system founded on the Legislatures only, and one founded on the people, to be the true difference between a *league* or *treaty*, and a *Constitution*." He pointed out that a law violating a treaty ratified by a previous law "might be respected by the Judges as a law, though an unwise or perfidious one"; but a law "violating a constitution established by the people themselves, would be considered by the Judges as null & void."[3]

Randolph's draft in the Committee of Detail set forth that "The ratification of the reform is—After the approbation of congress—to be made by a special convention in each State recommended by the assembly to be chosen for the express purpose of considering and approving or rejecting it in toto: and this recommendation may be used from time to time."[4] The Committee of Detail reported that "The ratifications of the Conventions of ———— States shall be sufficient for organizing this Constitution."[5] In convention Randolph proposed to fill the blank with nine, "that being a respectable majority of the whole, and being a number made familiar by the constitution of the existing Congress." Wilson favored seven or eight, observing that only the states "which ratify can be bound."[6] Nine was finally agreed to, after several votes were taken.[7] The Committee of Style changed the wording of the

[3] *Ibid.*, II, 84–85, 88–89 (July 23). See pages 16 and 41 above. The resolution was adopted and Ellsworth's proposal defeated. The delegates from Maryland were particularly insistent that their state constitution was an obstacle to the mode of ratification proposed. *Ibid.*, II, 475–76 (August 31); III, 229. Sherman and Gerry emphasized the requirement of unanimity prescribed in the Articles of Confederation for their amendment. *Ibid.*, II, 475, 560, 561 (August 31, September 10).

[4] *Ibid.*, II, 148. The words "in each State" are in Rutledge's handwriting. There was also a provision that "The assent of the major part of the people" should give operation to the Constitution. This was changed to provide that conventions in an unspecified number of states should have that effect. An alteration made implies that nine states would suffice. *Ibid.*, I, 149.

[5] Art. XXI. *Ibid.*, II, 189 (August 6).

[6] *Ibid.*, II, 468–69 (August 30). The words "between the said States" were inserted to make clear that the operation of the government was to be confined to the states ratifying the Constitution. *Ibid.*, II, 471, 475 (August 31). This action made it necessary to revise the clumsy preamble reported by the Committee of Detail. See note 103, page 56, and page 59 above.

[7] *Ibid.*, II, 471–72, 475–77 (August 31). On reconsideration the article was again accepted. *Ibid.*, II, 556, 563 (September 10).

article to its present form: "The ratification of the conventions of nine States, shall be sufficient for the establishment of this constitution between the States so ratifying the same."[8]

THE contingency anticipated by the framers of this article in fact occurred.[9] Only eleven states were participants in the newly established government when it began to function. The Constitution first went into effect between the eleven states which had ratified it, while two of the original thirteen states (Rhode Island and North Carolina) remained temporarily outside the union.[10]

Delaware was the first state to ratify the Constitution, on December 7, 1787.[11] Second was Pennsylvania, on December 12, 1787.[12] New Jersey quickly followed, on December 18, 1787.[13] Other states acted early in 1788: Georgia, on January 2;[14] Connecticut, a week later;[15] Massachusetts, on February 6;[16] Maryland, on April 26;[17] South Carolina, on May 23;[18] and New Hampshire, the ninth and last necessary state in order to ensure the establishment of the new government, on June 21.[19] The important states of Virginia[20] and New York[21] quickly fell into line on June 25 and July 26, respectively.

The Constitution was not ratified until after a vigorous political struggle. The contest was particularly close in Virginia and New York.[22]

---

[8] *Ibid.*, II, 603 (September 12).   [9] See note 2, page 453, above.

[10] Dumbauld, *The Bill of Rights and What It Means Today*, 10. North Carolina rejected the Constitution on August 2, 1788, but subsequently ratified it on November 21, 1789, after the new government had commenced to function. Rhode Island also ratified belatedly, on May 29, 1790. *Documentary History*, II, 276–90, 310–20. In August of that year, President Washington, accompanied by other high officials of the government, paid a ceremonial visit to Rhode Island, where they were enthusiastically received, as a manifestation of cordiality in the renewal of federal relationship. For an account of this trip, see Dumbauld, *Thomas Jefferson, American Tourist*, 156–58.

[11] *Documentary History*, II, 25–26.   [12] *Ibid.*, 44–45.

[13] *Ibid.*, 46–64.   [14] *Ibid.*, 65–84.

[15] *Ibid.*, 87–89.   [16] *Ibid.*, 93–96.

[17] *Ibid.*, 104–105. The vote was taken on April 26; the instrument of ratification itself was dated April 28. *Ibid.*, 121–22.

[18] *Ibid.*, 138–40.   [19] *Ibid.*, 141–44.

[20] *Ibid.*, 145–60.   [21] *Ibid.*, 190–203.

[22] Elliot's *Debates* is a convenient repository of the discussion for and against ratification in the state conventions. See also Warren, *The Making of the Constitution*, 744, 792, 799, 803, and Thorpe, *Constitutional History*, II, 18–198.

As a result of proposals for amendment which emerged during the debates on ratification, the first ten amendments, commonly called the Bill of Rights, came into existence.[23] Acceptance of these provisions for the protection of the liberties of the citizen was the price of ratification.[24]

It should be noted that establishment of the new government was a revolutionary act, subversive of the existing form of government under the Articles of Confederation.[25] State constitutions, as well as the federal constitution then in force, were violated by the innovations embodied in the instrument formulated at Philadelphia and accepted by the state conventions.[26] But under the American philosophy of government, the people could modify at any time their machinery and their agents for transacting public business. Exercising what John Milton called "the liberty and right of free born Men, to be governed as seems to them best," the Americans of 1789, like those of 1776, saw fit "to institute new Government, laying its Foundation on such Principles, and organizing its Powers in such Form, as to them shall seem most likely to effect their Safety and Happiness."[27]

[23] Dumbauld, *The Bill of Rights and What It Means Today*, 10–33.

[24] "Now the important fact about these ten Amendments is that *they* are the *essential portion* of the Constitution . . . the portion without which the Constitution itself would never have been accepted by the American people." Charles Warren, *Congress, the Constitution, and the Supreme Court*, 185. (Italics in the original).

[25] Farrand, *Records*, I, 249–53 (June 16), 314 (June 19); II, 560 (September 10).

[26] The delegates from Maryland were particularly aware of the conflict of the new form of government with the constitution of their state. Farrand, *Records*, II, 475–76 (August 31). Madison often had occasion to emphasize that the Constitution was ratified "by the people in each of the States, acting in their sovereign capacity," and hence was derived from "the same authority which formed the State Constitutions." Madison to Edward Everett, August 28, 1830, *Writings of James Madison*, IX, 385–86. See also Madison to Jefferson, December 29, 1798, in *ibid.*, VI, 328–29; and report on resolutions concerning the Alien and Sedition laws, in *ibid.*, VI, 348.

[27] Dumbauld, *The Declaration of Independence and What It Means Today*, 52, 74–82.

done in Convention by the Unanimous Consent of the States present the Seventeenth Day of September in the Year of our Lord one thousand seven hundred and Eighty seven and of the Independance of the United States of America the Twelfth   In witness whereof We have hereunto subscribed our Names,
Attest WILLIAM JACKSON *Secretary*   G°: WASHINGTON—*Presid*.
and deputy from Virginia
[There follow thirty-eight other signatures of representatives from twelve states.]

HISTORY

AFTER Randolph, Mason, and Gerry had indicated that they would not sign the Constitution as adopted,[1] Benjamin Franklin arose with a speech in his hand which was read for him by James Wilson.[2] The astute and amiable octogenarian humorously urged harmony and tolerance, observing that "the older I grow, the more apt I am to doubt my own judgment, and to pay more respect to the judgment of others." He accepted "this Constitution because I expect no better, and because I am not sure, that it is not the best." He hoped "that every member of the Convention who may still have objections to it, would with me, on this occasion doubt a little of his own infallibility—and to make manifest our unanimity, put his name to this instrument." He then moved that the Constitution be signed by the members, in the wording set forth in the attestation clause.[3] Under this formula a signer did not indicate his own approbation of the document but merely attested to the fact of its adoption by the unanimous consent of the states represented in the convention.[4] Notwithstanding Franklin's conciliatory proposal, the three recalcitrants still withheld their signatures. Randolph re-

[1] Farrand, *Records*, II, 631–33 (September 15).
[2] McHenry of Maryland noted that the speech was "plain, insinuating persuasive—and in any event of the system guarded the Doctor's fame." *Ibid.*, II, 649.
[3] *Ibid.*, II, 641–43 (September 17). This ambiguous wording had been drawn up by Gouverneur Morris, Madison notes, "in order to gain the dissenting members, and put into the hands of Docr. Franklin that it might have the better chance of success."
[4] *Ibid.*, II, 645.

457

garded "signing in the proposed form, as the same with signing the Constitution. The change of form therefore could make no difference with him."[5] Gerry also declared that "The proposed form made no difference with him."[6] Mason apparently did not express an opinion on this question but contented himself with refusal to sign.

It is of interest to lawyers, stenographers, printers, and other persons who are plagued by misprints and errors[7] in the preparation of written documents, to note that several corrections had to be made on the engrossed original copy of the Constitution.[8]

To the left of the attestation clause and above the signature of the Secretary, William Jackson, the following appears:

The Word, "the," being interlined between the seventh and eighth Lines of the first Page,[9] The Word "Thirty" being partly written on an Erazure in the fifteenth Line of the first Page,[10] The Words "is tried" being interlined between the thirty second and thirty third Lines of the first Page[11] and the Word "the" being interlined between the forty third and forty fourth Lines of the second Page.[12]

[5] *Ibid.*, II, 646. However, one member (Blount of North Carolina) was won over by the noncommittal formula so that he was willing to sign although he would not pledge his support to the Constitution.

[6] *Ibid.*, II, 647. General Pinckney and Butler, of South Carolina, disliked the equivocal form of signing and voted against it.

[7] The spelling "Independance" in the attestation clause is not an error but merely an eighteenth-century usage.

[8] The same was also true of the engrossed Declaration of Independence. See Dumbauld, *The Declaration of Independence and What It Means Today*, 18. The engrossed copy of the Constitution was made by Jacob Shallus, assistant clerk of the General Assembly of Pennsylvania, on four parchment sheets of 23½ by 27½ inches. Myers, *The Constitution of the United States of America*, 18; Farrand, *Records*, IV, 6.

[9] That is to say, before the word "Qualifications" in Art. I, sec. 2, cl. 1.

[10] This was not an error but an amendment made after the parchment was engrossed, substituting "thirty" for "forty" before the word "Thousand" in Art. I, sec. 2, cl. 3. See page 57 above.

[11] *I.e.*, after the words "President of the United States" in Art. I, sec. 3, cl. 6.

[12] *I.e.*, before the word "Congress" at the end of Art. I, sec. 10, cl. 2. This is really between lines 51 and 52 (rather than between lines 43 and 44), but by starting with the first full paragraph on page two, and disregarding a line containing only one word ("Discoveries" at the end of Art. I, sec. 8, cl. 8), the count as given can be obtained. It is noteworthy that the same omission has been silently corrected by interlineation between lines 49 and 50 (or 41 and 42) in Art. I, Sec. 10, cl. 2, where the word "Congress" appears for the first time in that clause.

PROCEEDINGS AFTER THE CONVENTION

O N Monday, September 17, 1787, besides adopting the final text of the Constitution itself, the convention adopted accompanying resolutions containing its recommendations regarding the procedure to be followed in connection with ratification of the Constitution and the mode of bringing into operation the new government established in pursuance thereof.[1]

These resolutions provided:

"Resolved, That the preceeding [*sic*] Constitution be laid before the United States in Congress assembled, and that it is the Opinion of this Convention, that it should afterwards be submitted to a Convention of Delegates, chosen in each State by the People thereof, under the Recommendation of its Legislature, for their Assent and Ratification; and that each Convention assenting to, and ratifying the Same, should give Notice thereof to the United States in Congress assembled.[2]

---

[1] Farrand, *Records*, II, 665–66; *Documentary History*, II, 20–21; Tansill, *Documents*, 1005–1006.

[2] This ratification procedure was the outgrowth of the debates on Art. VII of the Constitution. Elaborating Randolph's preliminary draft, the Committee of Detail reported in Art. XXII a provision that the Constitution be laid before Congress "for their approbation." Farrand, *Records*, II, 149, 174, 189 (August 6). On motion of Gouverneur Morris these words were deleted in convention. *Ibid.*, II, 472, 478–79 (August 31). FitzSimons of Pennsylvania said that this was done "in order to save Congress from the necessity of an Act inconsistent with the Articles of Confederation under which they hold their authority." King "thought it would be more respectful to Congress to submit the plan generally to them; than in such a form as expressly and necessarily to require their approbation or disapprobation." An attempt to reinstate the deleted requirement of approval by Congress was defeated. *Ibid.*, II, 560–63 (September 10). The Committee of Style amplified the provision as a separate resolution to accompany the Constitution. *Ibid.*, II, 604, 608–609 (September 13).

"Resolved, That it is the Opinion of this Convention, that as soon as the Conventions of nine States shall have ratified this Constitution, the United States in Congress assembled should fix a Day on which Electors should be appointed by the States which shall have ratified the same, and a Day on which the Electors should assemble to vote for the President, and the Time and Place for commencing Proceedings under this Constitution.

"That after such Publication the Electors should be appointed, and the Senators and Representatives elected: That the Electors should meet on the Day fixed for the Election of the President, and should transmit their Votes certified, signed, sealed and directed, as the Constitution requires, to the Secretary of the United States in Congress assembled, that the Senators and Representatives should convene at the Time and Place assigned; that the Senators should appoint a President of the Senate, for the sole Purpose of receiving, opening and counting the Votes for President; and, that after he shall be chosen, the Congress, together with the President, should, without Delay, proceed to execute this Constitution."[3]

The Constitution, together with these resolutions and a covering letter[4] to the President of Congress (Arthur St. Clair) from the President of the Convention, was promptly delivered by Major William Jackson, the secretary of the Convention.[5] Within a short time the next step was taken.

"Congress having received the report of the Convention lately assembled in Philadelphia

"Resolved Unanimously that the said Report with the resolutions and letter accompanying the same be transmitted to the several legisla-

---

[3] This resolution similarly sprang from Art. XXIII as reported by the Committee of Detail, which elaborated Randolph's preliminary draft. *Ibid.*, II, 149, 174–75, 189. After minor revision in convention, the provision was substantially altered and amplified by the Committee of Style as a separate resolution. *Ibid.*, II, 472–73, 479–81 (August 31); II, 604–605, 608–609 (September 13).

[4] Farrand, *Records*, II, 665–66; *Documentary History*, II, 1–2; Tansill, *Documents*, 1003–1004.

[5] He left Philadelphia by stage at 10 A.M. on September 18 and arrived in New York at 2 P.M. the next day. Myers, *The Constitution of the United States of America*, 19; see also Warren, *The Making of the Constitution*, 721. The documents were received in Congress on September 20, 1787, and considered on September 26–28, 1787. For comments on the debates, see Burnett, *Letters of Members of the Continental Congress*, VIII, 646–54, 660, 662, 665.

tures in Order to be submitted to a convention of Delegates chosen in each state by the people thereof in conformity to the resolves of the Convention made and provided in that case."[6] It should be noted that proponents of the Constitution availed themselves in Congress of the stratagem which Franklin had unsuccessfully employed in the convention, and in the resolution of September 28, 1787, inserted "the word *unanimously*, which applies only to simple transmission, hoping to have it mistaken for an unanimous approbation of the thing."[7]

Ratification followed in due course. When Congress learned on July 2, 1788, that nine states had ratified, a committee was directed to report an act for putting the Constitution into operation.[8] The act was not passed until September 13, 1788, however, due to disagreement concerning the place where the new government should be established.[9] The first Wednesday in January, 1789, was fixed as the day for appointing electors; the first Wednesday in February as the day they were to vote for a President; and the first Wednesday in March as the time, and "the present seat of Congress [New York]" as the place, for commencing proceedings under the Constitution.

March 4, 1789, was thus the official date for the beginning of the new government,[10] although it was not until April 6, 1789, that a quorum was present in the Senate, so that the electoral votes could be counted and George Washington declared to be President.[11] His

---

[6] *Documentary History*, II, 22; Tansill, *Documents*, 1007 (September 28, 1787).

[7] R. H. Lee to George Mason, October 1, 1787, in *Letters of Richard Henry Lee*, II, 439. Lee wrote to Samuel Adams, October 5, 1787, regarding the amendments proposed by Lee in Congress: "You will have been informed by other hands why these amendments were not considered and do not appear on the Journal, and the reasons that influenced a bare *transmission* of the Convention plan, without a syllable of approbation or disapprobation on the part of Congress." *Ibid.*, II, 444–45.

[8] *Documentary History*, II, 161; Tansill, *Documents*, 1060. The committee reported on July 8, 1788, proposing a time schedule but leaving blank the "place for commencing proceedings under the said Constitution." *Ibid.*, II, 171. Those who favored "the present seat of Congress" as the place where the new government should be established resorted to delaying tactics, since New York did not ratify the Constitution until July 26, 1788. See Burnett, *Letters of Members of the Continental Congress*, VIII, 758, 794–96.

[9] *Documentary History*, II, 263–64; Tansill, *Documents*, 1062.

[10] Owings v. Speed, 5 Wheat. 420, 422 (1820). October 10, 1788, was the last date on which a quorum was present in the old Congress.

[11] Thorpe, *Constitutional History*, II, 176–79. The House of Representatives had been able to organize five days earlier.

inauguration took place on April 30, 1789. The oath of office was administered by Chancellor Robert R. Livingston of New York, who then proclaimed in a loud voice: "Long live George Washington, the President of the United States." The President and the Congress were now prepared to "proceed to execute this Constitution."[12]

[12] Farrand, *Records*, II, 666.

BIBLIOGRAPHY

1. Judicial Decisions and Public Acts

The text of the Articles of Confederation, the first written federal constitution of the United States, appears in *Journals of the Continental Congress*, XIX, 214–23 (1912, edited by Gaillard Hunt), under date of March 1, 1781, when they went into force upon ratification by Maryland. They had been adopted by the Congress for submission to the states on November 15, 1777. *Journals*, IX, 907–25 (1907, edited by Worthington C. Ford, with frontispiece showing photographic reproduction of text). Eight states had ratified on July 9, 1778, and four others by May 5, 1779. *Journals*, XI, 677. A proposed amendment to Article VIII was embodied in the Act of April 18, 1783, which substituted the three-fifths ratio of slave to free population as a measure of apportioning expenses. *Journals*, XXIV, 260–61 (1922). An address to the states concerning this amendment was adopted on April 26, 1783. *Journals*, XXIV, 277–83. The proposal was ratified by eleven states. Quotations are ordinarily, unless otherwise indicated, taken from the text conveniently printed in U.S.C.A., Constitution 13–21 (1949 ed.).

Charters of Freedom. Washington, 1952. (National Archives Publication No. 53–14.) [Reproduces in facsimile the original Constitution of the United States, which is on permanent display in the National Archives Building along with the Bill of Rights and the Declaration of Independence.]

Coke, Sir Edward. *The Reports.* 4th edition. 13 vols. London, 1738. (Cited "Rep.") The acknowledged pre-eminence of Lord Coke as an oracle of the law and doughty champion of constitutional rights is such that when a lawyer cites simply "the Reports" (or, more briefly, "Rep.") the reference is to Coke's *Reports*. When any other reports are cited, the name of the reporter, or of the jurisdiction referred to, must be given. The first part of Coke's reports was published in 1600. Ten more were issued during the author's lifetime, the last in 1615. A second edition appeared before Coke's death on September 3, 1634. Parts Twelve and Thirteen were published posthumously, in 1656 and 1659 respectively, after most of Coke's papers (seized by the crown as seditious while he lay on his deathbed) had been returned to his heir in 1641. Of practically equal authority with Coke's *Reports* were his *Institutes*, a legal treatise of which the first part (commonly called "Coke on Littleton") was published in 1628, the second (a commentary on Magna Charta and other ancient statutes) in 1642, the third and fourth (dealing with criminal law and the jurisdiction of courts) in 1644. The edition used here is *The Second Part of the Institutes of the Laws of England*. London, 1817.

Federal Cases (cited "Fed. Cas.," with case number. Contains alphabetically cases from inferior federal courts through 1879).

Federal Reporter and Federal Supplement (cited "Fed." or "F.(2d)" or "F. Supp.," preceded by volume number and followed by page number. After October 31, 1932, cases from district courts [and the Court of Claims] are separately reported in the *Federal Supplement*, while the second series of the *Federal Reporter* contains cases from the Circuit Courts of Appeals).

Hening, William Waller. *The Statutes at Large [of Virginia]*. 13 vols. Richmond and Philadelphia, 1809–23.

Opinions of the Attorney General of the United States (cited "Op.," preceded by volume number and followed by page number).

Poore, Ben: Perley. *The Federal and State Constitutions, Colonial Charters, and Other Organic Laws of the United States*. 2nd ed. 2 vols. Washington, 1878.

Reports of the Supreme Court of the United States (cited "U.S.," preceded by volume number and followed by page number. For the period prior to 91 U.S., these reports are cited by the abbreviated names of the reporters, i.e., Dallas, Cranch, Wheaton, Peters, Howard, Black, and Wallace).

Statutes at Large of the United States (cited "St." or "Stat.," preceded by volume number and followed by page number).

Thorpe, Francis N. *The Federal and State Constitutions, Colonial Charters, and Other Organic Laws of the States, Territories, and Colonies Now or Heretofore Forming the United States of America*. 7 vols. Washington, 1909.

United States Code Annotated (cited "U.S.C.A.," preceded by title number and followed by section number).

Waters, Willard O. *Check List of American Laws, Charters and Constitutions of the 17th and 18th Centuries in the Huntington Library.* San Marino, Calif., 1936.

2. PUBLIC RECORDS

American State Papers. Edited by Walter Lowrie and Walter S. Franklin. Class X, Miscellaneous. Vol. I. Washington, 1834.

Debates and Proceedings in the Congress of the United States, The. Washington, 1853. [11 Cong.]

Debates in the Congress of the United States, on the Bill for Repealing the Law "For the More Convenient Organization of the Courts of the United States"; During the First Session of the Seventh Congress. And a List of the Yeas and Nays on that Interesting Subject. Albany, 1802.

Debates . . . of the Convention . . . of Massachusetts . . . for . . . Ratifying the Constitution. Boston, 1788.

Documentary History of the Constitution of the United States. 5 vols. Washington, 1894–1905.

Elliot, Jonathan. *The Debates . . . on the Adoption of the Federal Constitution.* 5 vols. Washington, 1827–45; 2nd ed., Philadelphia, 1881.

Farrand, Max (ed.). *The Records of the Federal Convention of 1787.* 4 vols. New Haven, 1911–37.

Ford, Worthington C. (ed.). *Journals of the Continental Congress.* 34 vols. Washington, 1904–37.

Journal, Acts and Proceedings, of the Convention, Assembled at Philadelphia, Monday, May 14, and Dissolved Monday, September 17, 1787, Which Formed the Constitution of the United States. Boston, 1819.

Tansill, Charles C. (ed.). *Documents Illustrative of the Formation of the Union of the American States.* Washington, 1927. (69 Cong., 1 sess., H. R. Doc. No. 398.)

3. BOOKS

Abernathy, Glenn. *The Right of Assembly and Association.* Columbia, S.C., 1961.

Abernethy, Thomas P. *The Burr Conspiracy.* New York, 1954.

Adams, George B. *The Origin of the English Constitution.* New Haven, 1912.

———. *An Outline Sketch of English Constitutional History.* New Haven, 1918.

———, and H. Morse Stephens. *Select Documents of English Constitutional History.* New York, 1908.

465

Adams, Henry. *A History of the United States during the Administration of Thomas Jefferson.* 4 vols. New York, 1889–90.

Adams, John. *The Adams Papers. Series I, Diary and Autobiography of John Adams.* Edited by Lyman H. Butterfield. 4 vols. Cambridge, Mass., 1961.

———. *The Works of John Adams.* Edited by Charles Francis Adams. 10 vols. Boston, 1850–56.

Adams, Randolph G. *Political Ideas of the American Revolution.* Durham, N.C., 1922.

——— (ed.). *Selected Political Essays of James Wilson.* New York, 1930.

Bancroft, George. *History of the Formation of the Constitution of the United States.* 2 vols. New York, 1882.

Barrett, Jay A. *Evolution of the Ordinance of 1787.* New York, 1891.

Barry, Richard H. *Mr. Rutledge of South Carolina.* New York, 1942.

Beccaria, Cesare B. *Dei delitti e delle pene.* Leghorn, 1764.

Berdahl, Clarence A. *War Powers of the Executive in the United States.* Urbana, Ill., 1921.

Beveridge, Albert J. *The Life of John Marshall.* 4 vols. Boston, 1916–19.

Blackstone, Sir William. *Commentaries on the Laws of England.* 4 vols. Oxford, 1765–69. Also edited by William Draper Lewis. 4 vols. Philadelphia, 1897.

Boswell, James. *The Life of Samuel Johnson.* 2 vols. London, 1906. [First published, 1791.]

Boutell, Lewis H. *The Life of Roger Sherman.* Chicago, 1896.

Bowen, Catherine D. *The Lion and the Throne: The Life and Times of Sir Edward Coke (1552–1634).* Boston, 1957.

Brackenridge, Henry M. *History of the Western Insurrection in Western Pennsylvania.* Pittsburgh, 1859.

Bracton. *De Legibus et Consuetudinibus Angliae.* Edited by George E. Woodbine. 4 vols. New Haven, 1915–42.

Brant, Irving. *James Madison.* 6 vols. Indianapolis, 1941–61.

Brown, William G. *The Life of Oliver Ellsworth.* New York, 1905.

Burnett, Edmund C. (ed.). *Letters of Members of the Continental Congress.* 8 vols. Washington, 1921–36.

Burns, Edward M. *James Madison, Philosopher of the Constitution.* New Brunswick, N.J., 1938.

Butzner, Jane. *Constitutional Chaff.* New York, 1941.

Cappon, Lester J. (ed.). *The Adams-Jefferson Letters.* 2 vols. Chapel Hill, N.C., 1959.

Carlyle, Alexander J. *Political Liberty.* Oxford, 1941.

Carpenter, William S. *Judicial Tenure in the United States.* New Haven, 1918.

Chafee, Zechariah, Jr. *Documents on Fundamental Human Rights.* 2 vols. New York, 1963.

————. *Freedom of Speech.* New York, 1920.

————. *How Human Rights Got into the Constitution.* Boston, 1952.

————. *Three Human Rights in the Constitution of 1787.* Lawrence, Kansas, 1956.

Churchill, Winston. *The New World.* New York, 1956.

Conway, Moncure D. *Omitted Chapters of History Disclosed in the Life and Papers of Edmund Randolph.* New York, 1888.

Corwin, Edward S. *The Commerce Power versus States Rights.* Princeton, 1936.

————. *The Constitution and What It Means Today.* 12th ed. Princeton, 1958.

————. *The Constitution and World Organization.* Princeton, 1944.

———— (ed.). *The Constitution of the United States of America: Analysis and Interpretation. Annotations of Cases Decided by the Supreme Court of the United States to June 30, 1952.* Washington, 1953. (82 Cong., 2 sess., *Sen. Doc. No. 170.*)

————. *John Marshall and the Constitution.* New Haven, 1919.

————. *National Supremacy: Treaty Power vs. State Power.* New York, 1913.

————. *The President: Office and Powers.* New York, 1940; 4th ed., 1957.

————. *The President's Control of Foreign Relations.* Princeton, 1917.

————. *Total War and the Constitution.* New York, 1947.

Coxe, Brinton. *An Essay on Judicial Power and Unconstitutional Legislation.* Philadelphia, 1893.

Cramer, Fritz. *Magna Carta.* Merano, 1937.

Cromwell, Oliver. *The Writings and Speeches of Oliver Cromwell.* Edited by Wilbur C. Abbott. 4 vols. Cambridge, Mass., 1937–47.

Crosskey, William W. *Politics and the Constitution in the History of the United States.* 2 vols. Chicago, 1953.

Crump, Helen J. *Colonial Admiralty Jurisdiction in the Seventeenth Century.* London, 1931.

Cushing, Harry A. *History of the Transition from Provincial to Commonwealth Government in Massachusetts.* New York, 1896.

Davies, Godfrey. *Bibliography of British History, Stuart Period, 1603–1714.* Oxford, 1928.

D'Ewes, Sir Simonds. *The Journal of Sir Simonds D'Ewes from the Be-*

ginning of the Long Parliament to the Opening of the Trial of the Earl of Strafford. Edited by Wallace Notestein. New Haven, 1923.

Dicey, Albert V. *Introduction to the Study of the Law of the Constitution*. 8th ed. London, 1915.

Dickinson, John. *The Political Writings of John Dickinson*. 2 vols. Wilmington, Del., 1801.

———. *The Writings of John Dickinson*. Edited by Paul L. Ford. Philadelphia, 1895.

Dickinson, John. *Administrative Justice and the Supremacy of Law in the United States*. Cambridge, Mass., 1927.

Dumbauld, Edward. *The Bill of Rights and What It Means Today*. Norman, 1957.

———. *The Declaration of Independence and What It Means Today*. Norman, 1950.

———. *The Political Writings of Thomas Jefferson*. New York, 1955.

———. *Thomas Jefferson, American Tourist*. Norman, 1946.

Evans, Charles. *Report of the Trial of the Hon. Samuel Chase*. Baltimore, 1805.

Farrand, Max. *The Framing of the Constitution*. New Haven, 1913.

Farrar, Timothy. *Report of the Case of the Trustees of Dartmouth College against William H. Woodward*. Portsmouth, N.H., 1819.

Fellman, David. *The Constitutional Right of Association*. Chicago, 1963.

Fenwick, Charles G. *International Law*. New York, 1924.

Figgis, John N. *Studies of Political Thought from Gerson to Grotius*. 2nd ed. Cambridge, Eng., 1916.

Findley, William. *History of the Insurrection, in the Four Western Counties of Pennsylvania*. Philadelphia, 1796.

Fisher, Sydney G. *The Evolution of the Constitution of the United States*. Philadelphia, 1897.

Flack, Horace E. *The Adoption of the Fourteenth Amendment*. Baltimore, 1908.

Flippin, Percy S. *The Royal Government in Virginia*. New York, 1919.

Ford, Paul L. *Bibliography and Reference List of the History and Literature Relating to the Adoption of the Constitution of the United States, 1787–8*. Brooklyn, 1888.

———. *Essays on the Constitution of the United States, Published during Its Discussion by the People, 1787–1788*. Brooklyn, 1892.

———. *Pamphlets on the Constitution*. Brooklyn, 1888.

Formation of the Union: An Exhibit, The. Washington, 1952. (National Archives Publication No. 53–15.)

468

Forster, John. *Arrest of the Five Members by Charles the First*. London, 1860.

Fortenbaugh, Robert. *The Nine Capitals of the United States*. York, Pa., 1948.

Frankfurter, Felix, and James M. Landis. *The Business of the Supreme Court*. New York, 1927.

Freeman, Douglas S. *George Washington*. 6 vols. New York, 1948–54.

Freeman, Edward A. *History of Federal Government, from the Foundation of the Achaian League to the Disruption of the United States*. London, 1863.

Gallatin, Albert. *The Writings of Albert Gallatin*. Edited by Henry Adams. 3 vols. Philadelphia, 1879.

Gardiner, Samuel R. *The First Two Stuarts and the Puritan Revolution, 1603–1660*. New York, 1898.

———. *History of England from the Accession of James I to the Disgrace of Chief-Justice Coke*. 2 vols. London, 1863.

———. *History of England from the Accession of James I to the Outbreak of the Civil War*. 10 vols. London, 1884–86.

Gellhorn, Walter. *Individual Freedom and Governmental Restraints*. Baton Rouge, 1956.

Gerould, James T. *Sources of English History of the Seventeenth Century, 1603–1689, in the University of Minnesota Library*. Minneapolis, 1921.

Gough, John W. *Fundamental Law in English Constitutional History*. Oxford, 1955.

Grigsby, Hugh Blair. *The History of the Virginia Federal Convention of 1788, with Some Account of the Eminent Virginians of That Era Who Were Members of the Body*. 2 vols. Richmond, 1890–91.

———. *The Virginia Convention of 1776*. Richmond, 1855.

Groce, George C. Jr. *William Samuel Johnson, A Maker of the Constitution*. New York, 1937.

Grose, Clyde L. *A Select Bibliography of British History, 1660–1760*. Chicago, 1939.

Haines, Charles G. *The American Doctrine of Judicial Supremacy*. 2nd ed. Berkeley, Calif., 1932.

———. *The Role of the Supreme Court in American Government and Politics, 1789–1835*. Berkeley, Calif., 1944.

———, and Foster H. Sherwood. *The Role of the Supreme Court in American Government and Politics, 1835–1864*. Berkeley, Calif., 1957.

Hallam, Henry. *The Constitutional History of England*. 2 vols. New York, 1893. [First published, 1827.]

Hamilton, Alexander. *The Papers of Alexander Hamilton.* Edited by Harold C. Syrett and Jacob E. Cooke. 6 vols. to date. New York, 1961–.

———. *The Works of Alexander Hamilton.* Edited by Henry C. Lodge. 12 vols. New York, 1904.

Harris, Robert J. *The Judicial Power of the United States.* University, La., 1940.

Haworth, Paul L. *The Hayes-Tilden Disputed Presidential Election of 1876.* Cleveland, 1906.

Henderson, Gerard C. *The Position of Foreign Corporations in American Constitutional Law.* Cambridge, Mass., 1918.

Henry, William W. *Patrick Henry: Life, Correspondence, and Speeches.* 3 vols. New York, 1891.

Hicks, Frederick C. *Men and Books Famous in the Law.* Rochester, N.Y., 1921.

Hill, Helen. *George Mason, Constitutionalist.* Cambridge, Mass., 1938.

Holdsworth, William S. *A History of English Law.* 13 vols. London, 1922–52.

———. *Sources and Literature of English Law.* Oxford, 1925.

Holmes, Oliver Wendell, Jr. *Collected Legal Papers.* New York, 1920.

Hough, Charles M. *Report of Cases in the Vice-Admiralty of the Province of New York and in the Court of Admiralty in the State of New York.* New Haven, 1925.

Howell, Thomas B. *A Complete Collection of State Trials and Proceedings for High Treason and Other Crimes and Misdemeanors from the Earliest Times to the Year 1783.* 21 vols. London, 1816.

Hulme, Harold. *Sir John Eliot, 1592 to 1632.* London, 1957.

Hunting, Warren B. *The Obligation of Contracts Clause of the United States Constitution.* Baltimore, 1919.

Jackson, Robert H. *The Nürnberg Case.* New York, 1947.

———. *The Struggle for Judicial Supremacy.* New York, 1941.

———. *The Supreme Court in the American System of Government.* Cambridge, Mass., 1955.

James, Charles W. *Chief Justice Coke, His Family and Descendants at Holkham.* London, 1929.

Jameson, J. Franklin (ed.). *Essays in the Constitutional History of the United States in the Formative Period, 1775–1789.* Boston, 1889.

Jefferson, Thomas. *Notes on the State of Virginia.* London, 1787. [First published in Paris in 1785, with an erroneous imprint of 1782. The most recent edition is that of William Peden, Chapel Hill, N. C., 1955.]

———. *The Papers of Thomas Jefferson.* Edited by Julian Boyd. 16 vols. to date. Princeton, 1950–.

————. *Thomas Jefferson Correspondence, Printed from the Originals in the Collections of William K. Bixby*. Edited by Worthington C. Ford. Boston, 1916.

————. *The Works of Thomas Jefferson*. Edited by Paul L. Ford. 12 vols. New York, 1904.

————. *The Writings of Thomas Jefferson*. Edited by Andrew A. Lipscomb and Albert E. Bergh. 20 vols. Washington, 1903–1904.

Jellinek, Georg. *Die Lehre von den Staatenverbindungen*. Berlin, 1882.

Jenks, Edward. *Law and Politics in the Middle Ages*. New York, 1898.

Jensen, Merrill. *The Articles of Confederation*. 2nd ed. Madison, Wis., 1948.

————. *The New Nation*. New York, 1950.

Johnson, Cuthbert W. *The Life of Sir Edward Coke*. 2 vols. London, 1837.

Judson, Margaret A. *The Crisis of the Constitution: An Essay in Constitutional and Political Thought in England, 1603–1645*. New Brunswick, N.J., 1949.

Keeler, Mary F. *The Long Parliament, 1640–1641*. Philadelphia, 1954.

Keller, Robert von. *Freiheitsgarantien für Person und Eigentum im Mittelalter*. Heidelberg, 1933.

Kingsbury, Susan M. (ed.). *The Records of the Virginia Company of London*. 4 vols. Washington, 1906–35.

Kunz, Josef. *Die Staatenverbindungen*. Stuttgart, 1929.

Labaree, Leonard W. *Royal Government in America*. New Haven, 1930.

————. *Royal Instructions to British Colonial Governors, 1670–1776*. 2 vols. New York, 1935.

Landis, James M. *The Administrative Process*. New Haven, 1938.

Lapsley, Arthur B. *The Writings of Abraham Lincoln*. 8 vols. New York, 1905–1906.

Laslett, Peter (ed.). *Patriarcha and Other Political Works of Sir Robert Filmer*. Oxford, 1949.

Lee, Guy C. *Source-Book of English History*. New York, 1901.

Lee, Richard Henry. *Letters of Richard Henry Lee*. Edited by James C. Ballagh. 2 vols. New York, 1911–14.

Lincoln, Charles H. *The Revolutionary Movement in Pennsylvania*. Philadelphia, 1901.

Lingley, Charles R. *The Transition in Virginia from Colony to Commonwealth*. New York, 1910.

Locke, John. *Two Treatises of Government*. London, 1690; edited by William S. Carpenter, London, 1924. [Citations are to the 1924 edition.]

Lodge, Henry Cabot (ed.). *The Federalist*. New York, 1888.

471

Lyon, Hastings, and Herman Block. *Edward Coke, Oracle of the Law.* Boston, 1929.

McClellan, George B., Jr. *The Gentleman and the Tiger.* Philadelphia, 1956.

McClure, Wallace. *International Executive Agreements.* New York, 1941.

McIlwain, Charles H. *The American Revolution: A Constitutional Interpretation.* New York, 1923.

———. *Constitutionalism: Ancient and Modern.* 2nd ed. Ithaca, N.Y., 1947.

———. *Constitutionalism and the Changing World.* Cambridge, Eng., 1939.

McKechnie, William S. *Magna Carta.* 2nd ed. Glasgow, 1914.

McLaughlin, Andrew C. *A Constitutional History of the United States.* New York, 1935.

———. *The Foundations of American Constitutionalism.* New York, 1932.

Maclay, William. *Journal of William Maclay, United States Senator from Pennsylvania, 1789–1791.* Edited by Edgar S. Maclay. New York, 1890.

McMaster, John B., and Frederick D. Stone. *Pennsylvania and the Federal Constitution, 1787–1788.* Philadelphia, 1888.

McRee, Griffith J. *Life and Correspondence of James Iredell.* 2 vols. New York, 1857–58.

Madison, James. *Letters and Other Writings of James Madison.* Edited by Henry D. Gilpin. 4 vols. Philadelphia, 1865.

———. *The Papers of James Madison.* Edited by William T. Hutchinson and William M. E. Rachal. 2 vols. to date. Chicago, 1962–.

———. *The Writings of James Madison.* Edited by Gaillard Hunt. 9 vols. New York, 1900–10.

Main, Jackson T. *The Antifederalists.* Chapel Hill, N.C., 1961.

Maitland, Frederic W. *The Constitutional History of England.* Cambridge, Eng., 1908.

———. *Equity; Also, the Forms of Action at Common Law.* Cambridge, Eng., 1913.

Malden, Henry E. (ed.). *Magna Carta Commemoration Essays.* [London], 1917.

Malone, Dumas. *Jefferson and the Rights of Man.* Boston, 1951.

Marriott, John A. R. *The Crisis of English Liberty: A History of the Stuart Monarchy and the Puritan Revolution.* Oxford, 1930.

———. *Federalism and the Problem of the Small State.* London, 1943.

Massachusetts State Papers. [Alden Bradford, ed.] *Speeches of the Governors of Massachusetts, from 1765 to 1775; and the Answers of the House of Representatives, to the Same; with Their Resolutions and Addresses for That Period. And Other Public Papers Relating to the Dispute between this Country and Great Britain, Which Led to the Independence of the United States.* Boston, 1818.

Mays, David J. *Edmund Pendleton, 1720–1803.* 2 vols. Cambridge, Mass., 1952.

Mearns, David C., and Verner W. Clapp. *The Chambers of the Supreme Court in Washington.* Washington, 1933 (Typewritten MS in the Library of Congress).

Meigs, William M. *The Growth of the Constitution in the Federal Convention of 1787.* Philadelphia, 1900.

Miller, David Hunter. *Treaties and Other International Acts of the United States of America.* 8 vols. Washington, 1931–48.

Minot, George R. *The History of the Insurrections, in Massachusetts, in the year MDCCLXXXVI, and the Rebellion Consequent Thereon.* Worcester, Mass., 1788.

Monaghan, Frank. *Heritage of Freedom.* Princeton, 1948.

Montesquieu, Charles Louis de. *L'Espirit des Lois.* 2 vols. Paris, 1748.

Morgan, Donald G. *Justice William Johnson.* Columbia, S. C., 1954.

Morris, Richard B. *Alexander Hamilton and the Founding of the Nation.* New York, 1957.

Mott, Rodney D. *Due Process of Law.* Indianapolis, 1926.

Mullett, Charles F. *Fundamental Law and the American Revolution.* New York, 1923.

Myers, Denys P. (ed.). *The Constitution of the United States of America.* Washington, 1954. (83 Cong., 2 sess., *Sen. Doc. No. 126.* A revised edition was issued in 1961 as 87 Cong., 1 sess., *Sen. Doc. No. 49.*) [A literal reproduction of the printed text of September 28, 1787, transmitted to the states by the Continental Congress for ratification.]

————. *The Process of Constitutional Amendment.* Washington, 1940. (76 Cong., 3 sess., *Sen. Doc. No. 314*).

Notestein, Wallace, and Frances H. Relf (eds.). *The Commons Debates for 1629.* Minneapolis, 1921.

————, and Frances H. Relf and Hartley Simpson (eds.). *Commons Debates, 1621.* 7 vols. New Haven, 1935.

Oster, John E. *The Political and Economic Doctrines of John Marshall.* New York, 1914.

Otis, James. *Some Political Writings of James Otis.* Edited by Charles F. Mullett. 2 vols. Columbia, Mo., 1929.

473

Padover, Saul K. *Thomas Jefferson and the National Capital*. Washington, 1946.

———. *To Secure These Blessings*. New York, 1962.

Patterson, Caleb P. *The Constitutional Principles of Thomas Jefferson*. Austin, Texas, 1953.

Pearson, Drew, and Robert S. Allen. *The Nine Old Men*. Garden City, 1936.

Pfeffer, Leo. *The Liberties of an American*. Boston, 1956.

Pollock, Sir Frederick, and Frederic W. Maitland. *The History of English Law before the Time of Edward I*. 2nd ed. 2 vols. Cambridge, 1898.

Post, Charles G. *The Supreme Court and Political Questions*. Baltimore, 1936.

Proceedings in the Trial of Andrew Johnson. Washington, 1868.

Randall, Henry S. *The Life of Thomas Jefferson*. 3 vols. New York, 1853.

Randall, James G. *Constitutional Problems under Lincoln*. New York, 1926.

Randolph, Sarah N. *The Domestic Life of Thomas Jefferson*. New York, 1871.

Read, Conyers. *Bibliography of British History, Tudor Period, 1485–1603*. Oxford, 1933.

Relf, Frances H. *The Petition of Right*. Minneapolis, 1917.

Richardson, James D. *Messages and Papers of the Presidents*. 10 vols. Washington, 1896–99.

Robertson, David. *Reports of the Trials of Colonel Aaron Burr*. 2 vols. Philadelphia, 1808.

Roosevelt, Theodore. *An Autobiography*. New York, 1913.

Root, Winifred T. *The Relations of Pennsylvania with the British Government, 1696–1765*. New York, 1912.

Rowland, Kate Mason. *The Life of George Mason*. 2 vols. New York, 1892.

Russell, Elmer B. *Review of American Colonial Legislation by the King in Council*. New York, 1915.

Sanders, Jennings B. *Evolution of the Executive Departments of the Continental Congress, 1774–1789*. Chapel Hill, 1935.

Schmeckebier, Laurence F. *Congressional Apportionment*. Washington, 1941.

Schramm, Percy E. *A History of the English Coronation*. Oxford, 1937.

Schulz, George J. (ed.). *Creation of the Federal Judiciary*. Washington, 1938. (75 Cong., 1 sess., *Sen. Doc. No. 91*.)

Scott, James Brown. *Judicial Settlement of Controversies between States of the American Union*. 2 vols. New York, 1918.

————. *Sovereign States and Suits before Arbitral Tribunals and Courts of Justice.* New York, 1925.

Selden, John. *The Table Talk of John Selden.* Edited by Samuel H. Reynolds. Oxford, 1892.

Selsam, John P. *The Pennsylvania Constitution of 1776.* Philadelphia, 1936.

Smith, Charles Page. *James Wilson, Founding Father, 1742–1798.* Chapel Hill, 1956.

————. *John Adams.* 2 vols. Garden City, N.Y., 1962.

Smith, Joseph H. *Appeals to the Privy Council from the American Plantations.* New York, 1950.

Stephenson, Carl, and Frederick G. Marcham. *Sources of English Constitutional History.* New York, 1937.

Stillé, Charles J. *The Life and Times of John Dickinson.* Philadelphia, 1891.

Story, Joseph. *Commentaries on the Constitution of the United States.* 5th ed. by Melville M. Bigelow. 2 vols. Boston, 1891.

Strayer, Joseph R. *The Delegate from New York, or Proceedings of the Federal Convention of 1787, from the Notes of John Lansing, Jr.* Princeton, 1939.

Street, Alfred B. *The Council of Revision of the State of New York.* Albany, 1859.

Stryker, Lloyd P. *Andrew Johnson.* New York, 1929.

Stubbs, William. *The Constitutional History of England.* 4th ed. 3 vols. Oxford, 1896.

Sutherland, George. *Constitutional Power and World Affairs.* New York, 1919.

Swart, Koenraad W. *Sale of Offices in the Seventeenth Century.* The Hague, 1949.

Syrett, Harold C. and Jean G. Cook. *Interview in Weehawken: The Burr-Hamilton Duel as told in the Original Documents.* Middletown, Conn., 1960.

Tanner, Joseph R. *Constitutional Documents of the Reign of James I, A.D. 1603–1625.* Cambridge, Eng., 1930.

————. *English Constitutional Conflicts of the Seventeenth Century, 1603–1689.* Cambridge, Eng., 1928.

————. *Tudor Constitutional Documents, A.D. 1485–1603.* 2nd ed. Cambridge, Eng., 1930.

Taswell-Langmead, Thomas P. *English Constitutional History.* 8th ed. by Coleman Phillipson. Boston, 1919.

Ten Broek, Jacobus. *The Antislavery Origins of the Fourteenth Amendment.* Berkeley, 1951.

Thompson, Faith. *The First Century of Magna Carta*. Minneapolis, 1925.
———. *Magna Carta*. Minneapolis, 1948.
——— (ed.). *Magna Carta*. Washington, 1950. (81 Cong., 2 sess., *Sen. Doc. No. 180.*)
Thorpe, Francis N. *The Constitutional History of the United States*. 3 vols. Chicago, 1901.
Towle, Dorothy S. *Records of the Vice-Admiralty Court of Rhode Island, 1716–1752*. Washington, 1936.
Towle, Nathaniel C. *A History and Analysis of the Constitution of the United States*. Boston, 1860.
Ubbelohde, Carl. *The Vice-Admiralty Courts and the American Revolution*. Chapel Hill, N.C., 1960.
Van Doren, Carl. *Benjamin Franklin*. New York, 1938.
———. *Benjamin Franklin's Autobiographic Writings*. New York, 1945.
Varnum, James M. *The Case, Trevett against Weeden: . . . Tried before the Honourable Superior Court, in the County of Newport, September Term, 1786. Also the Case of the Judges of Said Court, Before the Honourable General Assembly, at Providence, October Session, 1786, on Citation, for Dismissing Said Complaint*. Providence, 1787.
Vattel, Emmerich de. *Le droit des gens, ou principes de la loi naturelle appliqués à la conduite & aux affaires des nations & des souverains*. 3 vols. "London," 1758. [Actually published in Neuchâtel.]
———. *The Law of Nations or the Principles of Natural Law Applied to the Conduct and to the Affairs of Nations and Sovereigns*. Translated by Charles G. Fenwick. Washington, 1916.
Warren, Charles. *Bankruptcy in United States History*. Cambridge, Mass., 1935.
———. *Congress as Santa Claus*. Charlottesville, Va., 1932.
———. *Congress, the Constitution and the Supreme Court*. Boston, 1925; 2d ed., Boston, 1935.
———. *The Making of the Constitution*. Boston, 1928.
———. *Memorandum on the History and Scope of the Laws Prohibiting Correspondence with a Foreign Government, and Acceptance of a Commission to Serve a Foreign State in War*. Washington, 1915.
———. *Odd Byways in American History*. Cambridge, Mass., 1942.
———. *The Supreme Court and Sovereign States*. Princeton, 1924.
———. *The Supreme Court in United States History*. 3 vols. Boston, 1922.
Washburne, George A. *Imperial Control of the Administration of Justice in the Thirteen American Colonies, 1684–1776*. New York, 1923.
Wells, William V. *The Life and Public Services of Samuel Adams*. 3 vols. Boston, 1865.

Wertenbaker, Thomas J. *Virginia under the Stuarts*. Princeton, 1914.

Whiting, William. *War Powers under the Constitution of the United States*. 10th ed. Boston, 1864.

Wickham-Legg, John. *The Coronation Order of King James I*. London, 1902.

Wickham-Legg, Leopold G. *English Coronation Records*. Westminster [London], 1901.

Wilson, James. *The Works of the Honourable James Wilson*. 3 vols. Philadelphia, 1804.

Wilson, Robert R. *The International Law Standard in Treaties of the United States*. Cambridge, Mass., 1953.

Wright, Benjamin F. *The Contract Clause of the Constitution*. Cambridge, Mass., 1938.

————. *The Growth of American Constitutional Law*. New York, 1942.

Wright, Quincy. *The Control of American Foreign Relations*. New York, 1922.

4. ARTICLES

Adair, E. R. "The Petition of Right," *History* (New Series), Vol. V, No. 18 (July, 1920), 99–103.

————. "The Statute of Proclamations," *English History Review*, Vol. XXXII, No. 128 (October, 1917), 34–46.

Anderson, Chandler P. "The Extent and Limitations of the Treaty-making Power under the Constitution," *American Journal of International Law*, Vol. I, No. 3 (July, 1907), 636–70.

Andrews, Charles M. "The Royal Disallowance," *Proceedings of the American Antiquarian Society* (New Series), Vol. XXIV, Pt. 2 (October, 1914), 342–62.

Biklé, Henry W. "The Silence of Congress," *Harvard Law Review*, Vol. XLI, No. 2 (December, 1927), 200–24.

Bonfield, Arthur E. "The Guarantee Clause of Article IV, Section 4: A Study in Constitutional Desuetude," *Minnesota Law Review*, Vol. XLVI, No. 3 (January, 1962), 513–72.

Borchard, Edwin M. "Extraterritorial Confiscations," *American Journal of International Law*, Vol. XXXVI, No. 2 (April, 1942), 275–82.

————. "Shall the Executive Agreement Replace the Treaty?", *Yale Law Journal*, Vol. LIII, No. 4 (September, 1944), 664–83.

————. "Treaties and Executive Agreements—A Reply," *Yale Law Journal*, Vol. LIV, No. 3 (June, 1945), 616–64.

Brownell, Herbert. "Presidential Disability: The Need for a Constitutional

Amendment," *Yale Law Journal*, Vol. LXVIII, No. 2 (December, 1958), 189–211.

Bruce, Andrew A. "The Compacts and Agreements of States with One Another and with Foreign Powers," *Minnesota Law Journal*, Vol. II, No. 7 (June, 1918), 500–16.

Carpenter, William S. "Repeal of the Judiciary Act of 1801," *American Political Science Review*, Vol. IX, No. 3 (August, 1915), 519–28.

Carson, Hampton L. "The Case of the Sloop 'Active,' " *Pennsylvania Magazine of History and Biography*, Vol. XVI, No. 4 (1892), 385–98.

Celler, Emanuel. "Congressional Apportionment—Past, Present, and Future," *Law and Contemporary Problems*, Vol. XVII, No. 2 (Spring, 1952), 268–75.

Chafee, Zechariah, Jr. "Congressional Reapportionment," *Harvard Law Review*, Vol. XLII, No. 8 (June, 1929), 1015–47.

———. "Do Judges Make or Discover Law?" *Proceedings of the American Philosophical Society*, Vol. XCI, No. 5 (December, 1947), 405–20.

———. "Reapportioning the House of Representatives under the 1940 Census," *Proceedings of the Massachusetts Historical Society*, Vol. LXVI (1942), 364–408.

———. "Reapportionment of the House of Representatives under the 1950 Census," *Cornell Law Quarterly*, Vol. XXXVI, No. 4 (Summer, 1951), 643–65.

———. "The Test Oath Proposal," *Pennsylvania Bar Association Quarterly*, Vol. XXII, No. 3 (April, 1951), 221–39.

Chapin, Bradley. "Colonial and Revolutionary Origins of the American Law of Treason," *William and Mary Quarterly* (Third Series), Vol. XVII, No. 1 (January, 1960), 3–21.

Clulow, Ernest E., Jr., *et al.* "Constitutional Objections to the Appointment of a Member of a Legislature to Judicial Office," *George Washington Law Review*, Vol. VI, No. 1 (November, 1937), 46–91.

"Congressional Consent to Discriminatory State Legislation," *Columbia Law Review*, Vol. XLV, No. 6 (November, 1945), 927–52.

Cook, Walter W. "The Powers of Congress under the Full Faith and Credit Clause," *Yale Law Journal*, Vol. XXVIII, No. 5 (March, 1919), 421–49.

Corwin, Edward S. "The 'Full Faith and Credit' Clause," *University of Pennsylvania Law Review*, Vol. LXXXI, No. 4 (February, 1933), 371–89.

———. "The 'Higher Law' Background of American Constitutional Law," *Harvard Law Review*, Vol. XLII, No. 2 (December, 1928), 149–85; No. 3 (January, 1929), 365–409.

478

————. "The Progress of Constitutional Theory between the Declaration of Independence and the Meeting of the Philadelphia Convention," *American Historical Review*, Vol. XXX, No. 3 (April, 1925), 511–36.

Costigan, George P., Jr. "The History of the Adoption of Section I of Article IV of the United States Constitution and a Consideration of the Effect on Judgments of That Section and of Federal Legislation," *Columbia Law Review*, Vol. IV, No. 7 (November, 1904), 470–89.

Davis, J. C. Bancroft. "Federal Courts Prior to the Adoption of the Constitution," 131 U.S. xix–lxiii (1889) [Appendix].

DiLeva, Frank D. "Attempt to Hang an Iowa Judge," *Annals of Iowa* (Third Series), Vol. XXXII, No. 5 (July, 1954), 337–64.

Dodd, Edwin Merrick, Jr. "The Power of the Supreme Court to Review State Decisions in the Field of Conflict of Laws," *Harvard Law Review*, Vol. XXXIX, No. 5 (March, 1926), 533–62.

Dodd, Walter F. "Impairment of the Obligation of Contract by State Judicial Decisions," *Illinois Law Review*, Vol. IV, No. 3 (October, 1909), 155–73; No. 5 (December, 1909), 327–43.

————. "Judicially Non-enforcible Provisions of Constitutions," *University of Pennsylvania Law Review*, Vol. LXXX, No. 1 (November, 1931), 54–93.

Doe, Charles. "A New View of the Dartmouth College Case," *Harvard Law Review*, Vol. VI, No. 4 (November, 1892), 161–83; No. 5 (December, 1892), 213–22.

Dowling, Noel T. "Interstate Commerce and State Power," *Virginia Law Review*, Vol. XXVII, No. 1 (November, 1940), 1–28.

Dumbauld, Edward. "Grotius' Defence of the Lawful Government of Holland," *Journal of Public Law*, Vol. III, No. 1 (Spring, 1954), 192–213.

————. "Interstate Commerce and the Mode of Admission of States into the Union," *I.C.C. Practitioners' Journal*, Vol. XII, No. 9 (June, 1945), 908–19.

————. "John Marshall and the Law of Nations," *University of Pennsylvania Law Review*, Vol. CIV, No. 1 (October, 1955), 38–56.

————. "John Marshall and Treaty Law," *American Journal of International Law*, Vol. L, No. 1 (January, 1956), 69–80.

————. "Judicial Review and Popular Sovereignty," *University of Pennsylvania Law Review*, Vol. XCIX, No. 2 (November, 1950), 197–210.

————. "The Place of Philosophy in International Law," *University of Pennsylvania Law Review*, Vol. LXXXIII, No. 5 (March, 1935), 590–606.

————. "Thomas Jefferson and American Constitutional Law," *Journal of Public Law*, Vol. II, No. 2 (Fall, 1953), 370–89.

Dunham, Allison. "Congress, the States and Commerce," *Journal of Public Law*, Vol. VIII, No. 1 (Spring, 1959), 47–65.

Elton, G[eoffrey] R. "Henry VIII's Act of Proclamations," *English Historical Review*, Vol. LXXV, No. 295 (April, 1960), 208–22.

Farrand, Max. "Compromises of the Constitution," *The American Historical Review*, Vol. IX, No. 3 (April, 1904), 479–89.

————. "The Federal Constitution and the Defects of the Confederation," *American Political Science Review*, Vol. II, No. 4 (November, 1908), 532–44.

Farrier, Paul E. "Full Faith and Credit of Adjudication of Jurisdictional Facts," *University of Chicago Law Review*, Vol. II, No. 4 (June, 1935), 552–77.

Fenwick, Charles G. "The Authority of Vattel," *American Political Science Review*, Vol. VII, No. 3 (August, 1913), 395–410.

Field, Oliver P. "The Doctrine of Political Questions in the Federal Courts," *Minnesota Law Review*, Vol. VIII, No. 6 (May, 1924), 485–513.

————. "Ex post facto in the Constitution," *Michigan Law Review*, Vol. XX, No. 3 (January, 1922), 315–31.

————. "Judicial Notice of Public Acts under the Full Faith and Credit Clause," *Minnesota Law Review*, Vol. XII, No. 5 (April, 1928), 439–69.

Finch, George A. "Observations on Proposed Amendments to United States Constitution," *Proceedings of the American Society of International Law* (1954), 128–41.

Fisher, Sydney G. "The Suspension of Habeas Corpus during the War of the Rebellion," *Political Science Quarterly*, Vol. II, No. 3 (September, 1888), 454–88.

Ford, Worthington C. (ed.). "Alexander Hamilton's Notes in the Federal Convention of 1787," *American Historical Review*, Vol. X, No. 1 (October, 1904), 97–109.

Fox, Sir John C. "The Originals of the Great Charter of 1215," *English Historical Review*, Vol. XXXIX, No. 155 (July, 1924), 321–36.

Frankfurter, Felix, and James M. Landis, "The Compact Clause of the Constitution—A Study in Interstate Adjustments," *Yale Law Journal*, Vol. XXXIV, No. 7 (May, 1925), 685–758.

Garner, James W. "Acts and Joint Resolutions of Congress as Substitutes for Treaties," *American Journal of International Law*, Vol. XXXI, No. 1 (January, 1937), 482–88.

Grad, Frank P. "Federal-State Compact: A New Experiment in Cooperative Federalism," *Columbia Law Review*, Vol. LXIII, No. 5 (May, 1963), 825–55.

Greene, Evarts B. "American Opinion on the Imperial Review of Provincial Legislation, 1776–1787," *American Historical Review*, Vol. XXIII, No. 1 (October, 1917), 104–107.

Hale, Robert L. "The Supreme Court and the Contract Clause," *Harvard Law Review*, Vol. LVII, No. 4 (April, 1944), 512–57; No. 5 (May, 1944), 621–74; No. 6 (July, 1944), 852–92.

Hazeltine, Harold D. "Appeals from Colonial Courts to the King in Council, with Especial Reference to Rhode Island," *Annual Report of the American Historical Association for the year 1894*, 299–350.

————. "The Influence of Magna Carta on American Constitutional Development," *Columbia Law Review*, Vol. XVII, No. 1 (January, 1917), 1–33.

Holdsworth, William S. "Central Courts of Law and Representative Assemblies in the Sixteenth Century," *Columbia Law Review*, Vol. XII, No. 1 (January, 1912), 1–31.

Holt, J. C. "The Making of Magna Carta," *English Historical Review*, Vol. LXXII, No. 284 (July, 1957), 403–22.

Hudson, Manley O. "Advisory Opinions of National and International Courts," *Harvard Law Review*, Vol. XXXVII, No. 8 (June, 1924), 970–1001.

Hughes, Charles E. "War Powers under the Constitution," *Reports of the American Bar Association*, Vol. XLII (1917), 232–48. [Also printed as *Sen. Doc. No. 105*, 65 Cong., 1 sess.]

Hurst, Willard. "English Sources of the American Law of Treason," *Wisconsin Law Review*, Vol. [1945], No. 3 (May, 1945), 315–56.

————. "Treason in the United States," *Harvard Law Review*, Vol. LVIII, No. 2 (December, 1944), 226–72; No. 3 (February, 1945), 395–444; No. 6 (July, 1945), 806–57.

Hyde, Charles C. "Constitutional Procedures for International Agreement by the United States," *Proceedings of the American Society of International Law* (1937), 45–54.

Jackson, Robert H. "Full Faith and Credit—The Lawyer's Clause of the Constitution," *Columbia Law Review*, Vol. XLV, No. 1 (January, 1945), 1–34.

————. "The Rise and Fall of Swift v. Tyson," *American Bar Association Journal*, Vol. XXIV, No. 8 (August, 1938), 609–14, 644.

Jameson, John Franklin. "Portions of Charles Pinckney's Plan for a Constitution, 1787," *American Historical Review*, Vol. VIII, No. 3 (April, 1903), 509–11.

———. "Sketch of Pinckney's Plan for a Constitution, 1787," *American Historical Review*, Vol. IX, No. 4 (July, 1904), 735–47.

———. "Studies in the History of the Federal Convention of 1787," *Annual Report of the American Historical Association for the Year 1902*, Vol. I (Washington, 1903), 89–167.

Jenks, Edward. "The Story of the Habeas Corpus," *The Law Quarterly Review*, Vol. XVIII, No. 69 (January, 1902), 64–77.

Jessup, Philip C. "The Litvinoff Assignment and the Belmont Case," *American Journal of International Law*, Vol. XXXI, No. 3 (July, 1937), 481–84.

———. "The Litvinov Assignment and the Pink Case," *American Journal of International Law*, Vol. XXXVI, No. 2 (April, 1942), 282–88.

Katz, Wilber G. "Federal Legislative Courts," *Harvard Law Review*, Vol. XLIII, No. 6 (April, 1930), 894–924.

Keller, Charles R., and George W. Pierson. "A New Madison Manuscript Relating to the Federal Convention of 1787," *American Historical Review*, Vol. XXXVI, No. 1 (October, 1930), 17–30.

Langmaid, Stephen I. "The Full Faith and Credit Required for Public Acts," *Illinois Law Review*, Vol. XXIV, No. 4 (December, 1929), 383–422.

Lewis, H. H. Walker. "The Hayes-Tilden Election Contest," *American Bar Association Journal*, Vol. XLVII, No. 1 (January, 1961), 36–40; No. 2 (February, 1961), 163–67.

———. "The Impeachment of Andrew Johnson: A Political Tragedy," *American Bar Association Journal*, Vol. XL, No. 1 (January, 1954), 15–18, 80–87.

Lockhart, William B. "Gross Receipts Taxes on Interstate Transportation and Communication," *Harvard Law Review*, Vol. LVII, No. 1 (October, 1943), 40–95.

McDiarmid, John. "Government Corporations and Federal Funds," *American Political Science Review*, Vol. XXXI, No. 6 (December, 1937), 1094–1107.

McDougal, Myres, and Asher Lans. "Treaties and Congressional-Executive or Presidential Agreements: Interchangeable Instruments of National Policy," *Yale Law Journal*, Vol. LIV, No. 2 (March, 1945), 181–351; No. 3 (June, 1945), 534–615.

McHenry, Dr. James. "Papers . . . on the Federal Convention of 1787," edited by Bernard C. Steiner, *American Historical Review*, Vol. XI, No. 3 (April, 1906), 595–624.

McIlwain, Charles H. "Due Process of Law in Magna Carta," *Columbia Law Review*, Vol. XIV, No. 1 (January, 1914), 26–51.

McLaughlin, Andrew C. "The Background of American Federalism," *American Political Science Review*, Vol. XII, No. 2 (May, 1918), 215–40.

———. "James Wilson in the Philadelphia Convention," *Political Science Quarterly*, Vol. XII, No. 1 (March, 1897), 1–20.

Martin, Charles E. "Executive Determination of Legal Questions," *Proceedings of the American Society of International Law*, (1948), 53–70.

Miller, David H. "Some Early Cases in the Supreme Court of the United States," *Virginia Law Review*, Vol. VIII, No. 2 (December, 1921), 108–20.

Mishkin, Paul J. "The Federal 'Question' in the District Courts," *Columbia Law Review*, Vol. LIII, No. 2 (February, 1953), 157–96.

Moore, John Bassett. "Treaties and Executive Agreements," *Political Science Quarterly*, Vol. XX, No. 3 (September, 1905), 385–420.

Nadelmann, Kurt H. "Full Faith and Credit to Judgments and Public Acts," *Michigan Law Review*, Vol. LVI, No. 1 (November, 1957), 33–88.

Neale, John E. "The Commons' Privilege of Free Speech in Parliament," in *Tudor Studies Presented . . . to Albert Frederick Pollard*, edited by Robert W. Seton–Watson (London, 1924), 257–86.

Nutting, Helen A. "The Most Wholesome Law—The Habeas Corpus Act of 1679," *American Historical Review*, Vol. LXV, No. 3 (April, 1960), 527–43.

Painter, Sidney. "Magna Carta," *American Historical Review*, Vol. LIII, No. 1 (October, 1947), 42–49.

Paschal, Joel F. "The House of Representatives: 'Grand Depository of the Democratic Principle'?" *Law and Contemporary Problems*, Vol. XVII, No. 2 (Spring, 1952), 276–89.

Plucknett, Theodore F.T. "Bonham's Case and Judicial Review," *Harvard Law Review*, Vol. XL, No. 1 (November, 1926), 30–70.

Pierce, Major William. "Notes . . . on the Federal Convention of 1787," *American Historical Review*, Vol. III, No. 2 (January, 1898), 310–34.

"Power of Appointment to Public Office under the Federal Constitution," *Harvard Law Review*, Vol. XLII, No. 3 (January, 1929), 426–32.

"Proposed Anti-Communist Oath, The," *American Bar Association Journal*, Vol. XXXVII, No. 2 (February, 1951), 123–26.

Putnam, Harrington. "How the Federal Courts Were Given Admiralty Jurisdiction," *Cornell Law Quarterly*, Vol. X, No. 4 (June, 1925), 460–70.

Ratner, Leonard G. "Congressional Power over the Appellate Jurisdiction of the Supreme Court," *University of Pennsylvania Law Review*, Vol. CIX, No. 2 (December, 1960), 157–202.

Reeder, Robert P. "The First Homes of the Supreme Court of the United States," *Proceedings of the American Philosophical Society*, Vol. LXXVI, No. 4 (1936), 543–96.

Root, Elihu. "The Real Questions under the Japanese Treaty and the San Francisco School Board Resolution," *American Journal of International Law*, Vol. I, No. 2 (April, 1907), 273–86.

Ross, G.W.C. "Has the Conflict of Laws Become a Branch of Constitutional Law?" *Minnesota Law Review*, Vol. XV, No. 2 (January, 1931, 161–81.

Schlesinger, Arthur M. "Colonial Appeals to the Privy Council," *Political Science Quarterly*, Vol. XXVIII, No. 2 (June, 1913), 279–97; No. 3 (September, 1913), 433–50.

Schmeckebier, Laurence F. "The Method of Equal Proportions," *Law and Contemporary Problems*, Vol. XVII, No. 2 (Spring, 1920), 302–13.

Schweppe, Alfred J. "Enforcement of Federal Court Decrees: A 'Recurrence to Fundamental Principles,'" *American Bar Association Journal*, Vol. XLIV, No. 2 (February, 1958), 113–16, 187–90, 192.

Sherman, Gordon E. "The Case of John Chandler v. the Secretary of War," *Yale Law Journal*, Vol. XIV, No. 8 (June, 1905), 431–51.

Stevens, Theodore F. "Erie R.R. v. Tompkins and the Uniform General Maritime Law," *Harvard Law Review*, Vol. LXIV, No. 2 (December, 1950), 246–70.

Surrey, Walter S. "The Legislative Process and International Law," *Proceedings of the American Society of International Law* (1958), 11–17.

Thorne, Samuel E. "Dr. Bonham's Case," *The Law Quarterly Review*, Vol. LIV, No. 216 (October, 1938), 543–52.

Thornley, Isobel D. "Treason by Words in the Fifteenth Century," *English Historical Review*, Vol. XXXII, No. 128 (October, 1917), 556–61.

Turner, Kathryn. "The Midnight Judges," *University of Pennsylvania Law Review*, Vol. CIX, No. 4 (February, 1961), 494–523.

Usher, Roland G. "James I and Sir Edward Coke," *English Historical Review*, Vol. XVIII, No. 72 (October, 1903), 664–75.

Van Tyne, Claude H. "Sovereignty in the American Revolution," *American Historical Review*, Vol. XII, No. 3 (April, 1907), 529–45.

Warren, Charles. "Federal and State Court Interference," *Harvard Law Review*, Vol. XLIII, No. 3 (January, 1930), 345–78.

————. "Federal Criminal Laws and the State Courts," *Harvard Law Review*, Vol. XXXVIII, No. 5 (March, 1925), 545–98.

————. "New Light on the History of the Federal Judiciary Act of 1789," *Harvard Law Review*, Vol. XXXVII, No. 1 (November, 1923), 49–132.

————. "Political Practice and the Constitution," *University of Pennsylvania Law Review*, Vol. LXXXIX, No. 8 (June, 1941), 1003–1025.

————. "The Supreme Court and Disputes between States," *Bulletin of the College of William and Mary*, Vol. XXXIV, No. 5 (June, 1940), 1–32.

————. "What Is Giving Aid and Comfort to the Enemy?" *Yale Law Journal*, Vol. XXVII, No. 3 (January, 1918), 331–47.

————. "Why Jefferson Abandoned the Presidential Speech in Congress," *Massachusetts Historical Society Proceedings*, Vol. LVII (1924), 123–72.

Watson, David K. "The Trial of Jefferson Davis," *Yale Law Journal*, Vol. XXIV, No. 8 (June, 1915), 669–76.

Weinfeld, Abraham C. "What Did the Framers of the Federal Constitution Mean by 'Agreements or Compacts'?" *University of Chicago Law Review*, Vol. III, No. 3 (April, 1936), 453–64.

Weston, Melville F. "Political Questions," *Harvard Law Review*, Vol. XXXVIII, No. 3 (January, 1925), 296–333.

Wiener, Frederick B. "Courts-Martial and the Bill of Rights: The Original Practice," *Harvard Law Review*, Vol. LXXII, No. 1 (November, 1958), 1–49; No. 2 (December, 1958), 226–304.

————. "The Militia Clause of the Constitution," *Harvard Law Review*, Vol. LIV, No. 2 (December, 1940), 181–220.

Wigmore, John H. "Required Numbers of Witnesses," *Harvard Law Review*, Vol. XV, No. 2 (June, 1901), 83–108.

Willcox, Walter F. "Last Words on the Apportionment Problem," *Law and Contemporary Problems*, Vol. XVII, No. 2 (Spring, 1952), 290–301.

Williston, Samuel. "Does a Pardon Blot Out Guilt?" *Harvard Law Review*, Vol. XXVIII, No. 7 (May, 1915), 647–63.

Wright, Quincy. "Congress and the Treaty-making Power," *Proceedings of the American Society of International Law* (1952), 43–58.

————. "The United States and International Agreements," *American Journal of International Law*, Vol. XXXVIII, No. 3 (July, 1944), 341–55.

INDEX

494

The Constitution of the United States has been set in various sizes of Linotype Caslon Old Face, which is reproduced from a handset foundry type design used in the print shop of Benjamin Franklin, as well as in most other printing houses of his time. Besides being associated with the emergence of the Federal Union in American history, Caslon faces have long been recognized as some of the most readable types ever designed. This pleasant combination of historical suitability and functional legibility has resulted in what is hoped to be an ageless book page for all time.

UNIVERSITY OF OKLAHOMA PRESS

Norman